Culture and Related Corporate Realities

Text, cases, and readings on organizational entry, establishment, and change

The Irwin Series in Management and the Behavioral Sciences
L. L. Cummings and E. Kirby Warren; *Consulting Editors*

Culture and Related Corporate Realities

Text, cases, and readings on organizational entry, establishment, and change

Vijay Sathe

Associate Professor
Graduate School of Business Administration
Harvard University

1985

RICHARD D. IRWIN, INC.
Homewood, Illinois   60430

ISBN 0-256-03142-8

Library of Congress Catalog Card No. 84–62325

Printed in the United States of America

1 2 3 4 5 6 7 8 9 0 ML 2 1 0 9 8 7 6 5

Preface for teachers

It is now widely acknowledged that corporate culture has a subtle but pervasive influence on companies and their managers. Corporate culture has an important bearing on organizational performance and affects managerial ability to make needed organizational improvements. It is also difficult to deviate from or change corporate culture, when responsible managerial action calls for this. And corporate culture has a profound influence on new managers in terms of their recruitment, socialization, and contribution to the organization. Despite these and other reasons that have led to its recognition as an important topic, as yet there is no available organized body of knowledge, techniques, and teaching materials in this subject area. This book attempts to address this important pedagogical void.

Although the study of corporate culture is a relatively new area of inquiry, long-standing traditions of theoretical and empirical work in several academic disciplines (including cultural anthropology, sociology, social psychology, cognitive psychology, and organizational behavior) inform the study of culture within the corporate context. I have tried to synthesize this literature in order to provide the necessary research and theoretical underpinnings for the book. In addition, since this literature tends to be descriptive rather than normative, concepts and analytical techniques have been carefully selected and developed in order to make the subject "actionable."

Intended Market for the Book

This book is for MBAs and other graduate students interested in learning to work better with the prevailing corporate culture and related corporate realities. It is ideally suited for use in a full-length course on the subject for students who have already taken a course in organizational behavior. However, others may also be able to use it because three chapters in the book (3, 9, and 11) provide basic coverage of the essential organizational behavior topics.

The purpose of the introductory chapters (Part 1) is to lay the necessary conceptual groundwork. The remainder of the book on implications for action has a dual focus:

>*Focus A: Identifying and adjusting to a new corporate culture.* How to make the transition from a new manager to an established manager by effectively anticipating, entering, and contributing in a new corporate culture (Part 2 and the first chapter of Part 3).

>*Focus B: Operating within and changing a corporate culture.* How to effectively utilize and constructively deviate from and change a corporate culture when responsible managerial action calls for this (balance of Part 3 and Part 4).

Because of this dual focus, the book may also be adopted as a supplementary text in a variety of other courses:

1. *Comprehensive organizational behavior.* Focus A and/or Focus B could be incorporated into such a course. Focus A could be included toward the end of the course when it is the last OB course that students will take before graduating and commencing work. Focus B could be used to supplement coverage of implementation and change in organizations.

2. *"Micro" (individual and group) organizational behavior.* Part 2 of the book could be incorporated into such a course to focus on how the individual can better anticipate and enter a new organization. Part 3 could supplement material on group pressures and how to constructively manage them.

3. *"Macro" organizational behavior.* Part 4 of the book could be used to supplement material on organizational change and development.

4. *Career management.* Focus A could be incorporated to cover issues concerning recruiting, organizational assessment, entry, and establishment in a new organization. This approach would enable these topics to be covered in greater depth and with more practical guidance than I think is typically done in these courses.

5. *Organizational reality.* Any part of the book could be used as supplementary material in such a course to cover the action implications of culture and related corporate realities.

6. *Strategy implementation.* Focus B could be incorporated into such a course to help students appreciate the subtle but powerful way in which culture can facilitate or impede the implementation of strategy and what managers can do about it.

Trade-Offs in Coverage of the Subject Matter
There are both advantages and disadvantages in covering all these topics in one book. On the positive side, students learn to appreciate the

range of organizational issues affected by culture and how they may be better managed. I also hope that the availability of a single comprehensive casebook will facilitate the introduction of courses devoted to corporate culture at other institutions. On the negative side, the coverage of any one topic in the book is necessarily limited. Difficult trade-offs had to be made in order to limit the book to a manageable length. Two important ones are:

1. *Focus A over Focus B*. Although both are important and are covered in the book, I have devoted more space to the former because it is a neglected subject that is particularly important and relevant for MBAs and other students commencing work upon graduation.

2. *Text and Cases over Readings*. I have devoted more space to the former because, to my knowledge, text and case materials on the action implications of corporate culture are not available. Several additional readings would have been included if the book could have been longer. A synopsis of 20 recommended supplementary readings is included at the end of the book to provide a brief orientation for interested students.

An Alternate Sequence for Covering Subject Matter

An important decision had to be made concerning the positioning of Part 2 of the book (anticipating and entering a new corporate culture). This part provides concepts and techniques that: (1) help avoid irreconcilable culture-person misfits, which ultimately hurt managerial and organizational effectiveness, (2) help a new manager make a smoother entry into the company and become effective more quickly on the job, (3) have repetitive value in that the process of "anticipating and entering" continues throughout a career as a manager moves from one work unit to another within the same company or from one company to another, and (4) help managers in general, and human resource specialists in particular, do a better job of recruiting and socializing newcomers, which is a major organizational task.

From the standpoint of the most logical progression in the development of these and other course concepts and techniques, it would be better to proceed from Part 1 to Part 3, with Part 2 following Part 4:

Part 1—Understand culture and how it is related to other corporate realities.

Part 3—How to get established and operate effectively within the prevailing culture (without changing it).

Part 4—How to influence change in the prevailing corporate culture.

Part 2—How to anticipate and enter a new corporate culture, survive culture shock, and become effective as a newcomer.

This "layering" of subject matter has greater conceptual merit than the one used in the book, in which Part 2 precedes Parts 3 and 4, because it is useful to first understand the difficulties that even an established manager faces in attempting to constructively deviate from or change corporate culture (subjects covered in Parts 3 and 4) in order to more fully appreciate the special problems of the newcomer who does not yet completely understand the prevailing culture and the related corporate realities (the subject of Part 2).

However, I have not used this alternate organization for the book because of two interrelated pedagogical reasons. First, when the book is used in the last semester before students graduate, as it has been, Part 2 is positioned too late in the semester to be of help to students in deciphering company cultures during their interviewing and prior to accepting a job offer. The earlier positioning enables them to immediately put the concepts and ideas presented in Part 2 into practice in their concurrent recruiting, resulting in what many students refer to as "real-time learning."

A second pedagogical consideration is that Part 2 produces disconfirmation for students and is personally threatening to them ("you can get chewed up if you don't do a good job of anticipating and entering a new culture"). This creates excellent student motivation for learning early in the course. The advance positioning of Part 2 immediately brings home the significance of culture and helps students "hook into" the course and engage later parts of it with energy and sensitivity. With a later positioning, one not only foregoes this front-end motivating potential, but one also risks generating too high a level of student anxiety toward the end of the course, where it could interfere with attempts to achieve course closure.

Because of these considerations, my assessment is that the book is better organized as it currently is, with Part 2 ahead of Parts 3 and 4. However, it is possible to cover the material in the book according to the alternate sequence if the instructor chooses to do so.

A Note on the Case Materials

When I began developing these materials, I had hoped to include a larger proportion of audiovisuals, incorporating "tours" of the company facilities and visits with the cast of characters, both in interaction with each other and alone, "on camera." My assumption was that the imagery conveyed by these media would help bring culture and other corporate realities more effectively into the classroom. What I discovered, however, was that in many cases the relevant information was so sensitive that individuals and companies could not reasonably be expected to release it undisguised, let alone on camera. Thus, after considerable deliberation and some regret, one of the most important strategic choices I made was to opt for disguised cases having the necessary sensitive information, rather than undisguised cases and audiovisual supplements that would have precluded such information.

A major task, then, was to develop cases that not only contained the necessary sensitive information, but also made it possible for the reader to at least vicariously experience some of the textured richness that undisguised audiovisual materials might have conveyed. The case development strategy that emerged to address these requirements called for in-depth field work (with interviews typically exceeding 30 hours with each of the principal subjects) and special attention to (a) concrete detail ("what a movie camera might have captured") and (b) critical incidents. This level of detail was needed in order to ground the case in an action perspective and to capture the emotional tone and sense of drama that actually prevailed.

Can the richness of culture be captured in the few pages of a case? This is a matter of degree. Even the most detailed ethnographies may fall short of capturing culture as it is actually experienced by the "natives." I believe the cases have sufficient cultural richness in them for purposes of the book.

Acknowledgments

Over the past four years, a number of people have helped me in the development of this book and the course on which it is based. Foremost among them are the case subjects (most of whom must necessarily remain anonymous), the casewriters (whose names appear on the cases), the students who have taken this course (too numerous to mention individually), who provided intellectual stimulation with their criticisms and comments, the faculty and staff of the Division of Research at the Harvard Business School (Ray Corey, Joanne Segal, and Kathryn May), who provided financial and other critical support, and four colleagues (Jack Gabarro, John Kotter, Paul Lawrence, and Dick Vancil) who provided sustained encouragement and support for this venture.

Those who have provided detailed comments on an earlier draft of the text and other vital assistance in connection with the book and the course include Chris Argyris, Tony Athos, S. K. Bhattacharyya, Paul Dredge, Bob Duncan, Hilary Eaton, Jack Gabarro, Dave Giber, Rob Kaplan, Steve Kerr, John Kotter, Paul Lawrence, Clive Munro, Jeff Pfeffer, Paul Reynolds, Paul Robershotte, Elizabeth Sawyer, Ed Schein, Ron Tagiuri, Art Turner, Dick Vancil, and Michael Zur-Scerpio.

Comments and other important assistance were also received from Barrie Atkin, Jose Anzizu, By Barnes, Mike Beer, Tom Bonoma, Eliza Collins, Stew Dougherty, Bob Eccles, Tim Hall, Jane Hodgetts, Dan Isenberg, Rosabeth Kanter, Ed Lawler, Pat Light, Les Livingstone, Jay Lorsch, John Matthews, Keith Merron, Lisa Novachek, Andrew Pettigrew, Lou Pondy, Winn Price, Len Schlesinger, Jeff Sonnenfeld, Howard Stevenson, Phil Stone, Judy Uhl, Bill Ury, John Van Maanen, Dick Walton, and three anonymous reviewers for Little, Brown, and Company.

Joan Terrall edited an earlier draft of the text and all the cases, and the staffs of the word processing center at the Harvard Business School and Letter Perfect Office Services typed the many versions and revisions of these materials. My secretary, Dianne Pacl, provided invaluable coordination and support of these activities.

My wife, Shanu, and our young children, Jay and Sheila, showed more patience and offered more emotional support than anyone could ask. This book and the course on which it is based would not have materialized without this understanding and help.

Vijay Sathe

Contents

Effectiveness and Satisfaction. Summary Illustration: Organizational Dynamics. Model B—Individual Dynamics: Individual Behavior within Organizational Reality. Summary Illustration: Individual Dynamics.

PART 2   Anticipating and entering culture and related corporate realities   83

Chapter 4   Assessing one's fit with the organization   86
Understanding Individual-Organization Fit: *Culture Map: Culture Caricatures
for Studying Cultural Nonconformity. Understanding the Nature of the Individual's
Involvement in the Organization. Four Ways to Use the Culture Map. Other Individ-
ual-Organizational Fits.* Learning about Oneself: *Nature of Personal Beliefs and
Values. Gaining Self-Insight.* Learning about One's Organization: *Important
Questions to Think about (Organized by the Major Variables in Models A and B,
Figure 3–1).*
      APPENDIX 4–1   Organizational Assessment: A Summary of Important
                Questions to Think About, 106

Chapter 5   Understanding and coping with recruiting realities   109
Questions to Ask versus Questions to Keep in One's Head. Questions to Ask
Verbally versus Questions to Ask with One's Eyes. Subtle Traps: *Traps under
the Organization's Control. Traps under the Individual's Control.* Coping with the
Subtle Traps. Conclusion.

Chapter 6   Surviving and contributing as a newcomer   123
Understanding the Socialization Process: *Organizational Socialization Strategies.*
Learning the Ropes: *Learning from Available Information. Managing Interactions,
Incidents, and Shocks. Proactivity: Developing Information Sources and Networks.
Learning the Ropes: A Summary.* Contributing as a Newcomer: What Is the Real
Assignment? *Stated versus the Real Assignment. "Can You Give Me a Little History?"
The Phoney First Assignment. The "Impossible" First Assignment. Going against the
Grain of the Culture.* Contributing: A Summary. The Advantages of Newness.

Chapter 7   Settling in or moving out   137
Monitoring the Individual's Progress: *The Rites of Passage.* Reassessing One's
Fit with the Organization. Making the Initial Adjustment: *Signaling One's In-
tention to Remain.*

PART 3   Getting established and operating within culture and related corporate realities   251

Chapter 8   Developing credibility and gaining acceptance   253

Developing Credibility with Others in the Organization: *The Individual's Accomplishments. The Individual's Situation. The Individual's Relationships with Others. Understanding Working Relationships. Stages in the Development of New Working Relationships.* Gaining Acceptance in the Organization's Culture: *Gaining Acceptance via Culture Change. Gaining Acceptance via Changes in Self. Gaining Acceptance via Changed Perceptions. The Dynamics of Tokenism: A Special Case of Organizational Misperception. Organizational Misperception versus Prejudice.* Summary.

Chapter 9   Understanding organizational pressures and how culture affects them   271

Formal Pressures: *Formal Authority. Formal Rules and Procedures. Rewards and Sanctions.* Social Pressures: *The Nature of Social Expectations. Benefits of Compliance. Social Sanctions.* Political Pressures: *Sources of Power. Techniques of Influence. Political Coalitions.*

Chapter 10   Utilizing and constructively deviating from culture   280

Becoming Culturally Astute: *Cultural Awareness and Knowledge. Resistance as an Invitation to Understand Oneself. Resistance as an Invitation to Understand the Culture. Willingness to Work with Culture. Cultural Skills.* Going against the Grain of the Culture: *Why Is Counterculture Action Undertaken? Constructively Deviating from Culture.* Going against Other Beliefs and Values: *Dealing with Conflict.* Going against Those Personally Threatened: *Opponent's Agendas. Proponent's Options.*

Chapter 11   Changing organizational behavior patterns   364
Resistance to Change (R). Motivation to Change (M1): *Intrinsic Motivation.
Extrinsic Motivation.* Model for Change (M2): *Mundane Tools.* Method for
Change (M3): *Processes for Dealing with Resistance. Choosing Implementation Speed.
Orchestrating the Change.* Conclusion.

Chapter 12   Changing organizational culture   380
Ethics of Culture Change. How to Assess Resistance to Culture Change:
Change in Culture's Content. Resistance to Culture Change. How to Influence Cul-
ture Change: *Behavior. Justifications of Behavior. Cultural Communications. Rele-
vance of Part 2. Two Special Cases of Culture Change.* How to Know Whether or
Not Culture Change Is Occurring: *1. Is There Evidence of Intrinsically Motivated
Behavior? 2. Is There Evidence of Automatic-Pilot Behavior? 3. Is There Evidence of
Countermandated Behavior?* When to Attempt Culture Change: *When to Change
Culture's Content. When to Change Culture's Strength.* Alternatives to Major Cul-
ture Change.

Introduction

Although the importance of corporate culture is now widely acknowledged in both business and academic circles, the available literature leaves something to be desired. The popular writing explains why the subject is of concern to top managers and describes some of the actions they are taking in an effort to better manage company culture (see Readings 4–2 and 4–3 for recent examples). However, this literature does not emphasize the concerns of lower-level managers seeking to work more effectively within the prevailing culture. Neither does it emphasize the difficulties faced by new managers as they attempt to break into the company culture, try to cope with culture shock, and strive to contribute as newcomers before they can get established. This literature is also generally not well grounded in systematic theory and research. Furthermore, the scholarly work on the subject tends to be descriptive ("Isn't corporate culture an interesting and important phenomenon to study and better understand?") without a corresponding emphasis on prescription ("What should managers do to better work with corporate culture, given our current understanding of the subject?").

This book considers the implications of corporate culture not only for top managers but for lower-level managers and new managers as well. The book's title and subtitle are intended to clearly convey that the interest here is not in culture per se but rather in its implications for managerial action. Since culture cannot be considered in isolation in taking such action, related corporate realities are also examined in this book. The emphasis is on practical application, and the implications and recommendations are derived from systematic, theoretical, and empirical work.

The book is written from the particular, though not exclusive, perspective of MBAs and other managers who will be entering the organization in entry-level positions, and the issues are covered in the rough sequence in which these aspiring managers will experience them in commencing their careers. More seasoned managers should also find the concepts and analytical techniques that are presented useful in managing the issues of particular concern to them, in organizing their experience, and in helping newcomers do a better job of contributing to and advancing in the organization.

Before describing the specific aims of the book, it will be useful to clarify the basic terminology.

Basic Terms Defined

The terms *culture, company culture,* and *corporate culture* have become popular, but not everyone uses them in the same way. We will define these terms as follows:

Culture: The set of important assumptions (often unstated) that members of a community share in common.

Company culture: The culture of the corporation or the company as a whole.

Corporate culture: The culture of any corporate community. Thus, the company culture, or any company *sub*culture, will be referred to as a corporate culture.

Depending on the circumstances, one or more of these corporate cultures may have to be considered in taking managerial action. Except as needed, the discussion will be developed with reference to an organization and its culture without specifying a particular corporate culture.

As explained in Chapter 1, stronger cultures have a more profound influence on organizational life than weaker cultures do. We will not use the word *strong* as a qualifier every time the word culture is used, but it should be remembered that anything we say about culture always needs to be qualified by its strength.

Effectiveness of Managerial Action

It is perhaps useful to state explicitly what is meant by "effective" managerial action. From the standpoint of an individual manager, effective action is that which helps both that manager *and* the organization. Four effectiveness caricatures are shown in Figure I–1. It should be recognized that there are many definitions of effectiveness; the purpose of the figure is merely to highlight four particular patterns or "ideal types."

A manager whose actions over time tend to help himself or herself but not the organization may be described as *careerist*. This term is commonly used to refer to someone who is only looking out for his or her own

Figure I–1
Effectiveness Caricatures for Managerial Action

| | | Effect on the Organization | |
		Hurt	Helped
Effect on the Manager	**Helped**	Careerist action	Effective action
	Hurt	Ineffective action	Kamikaze action

advancement—if necessary, at the expense of the organization. The opposite pattern may be called *kamikaze*, because here the manager's actions over time tend to help the organization but at grave personal cost. *Ineffective* action benefits neither the manager nor the organization. In contrast, *effective* action carries both personal and organizational benefits. Indeed, one of the creative aspects of management is the search for effective courses of action. This search is likely to be more fruitful if the manager understands and anticipates the prevailing corporate culture and learns to work better with it.

It is important to judge the effectiveness of managerial action over a reasonably long period because particular actions may not immediately produce intended results. Also, a manager's situation at a particular time may make it difficult to achieve better results. An important case in point is the situation faced by a new lower-level manager who knows what needs to be done to help the organization but is reluctant to attempt it for fear of being rejected before having a chance to get established. Such managers may appear to be careerist in the short term, but if they are later able to successfully take the necessary actions that benefit the organization, they will be effective. On the other hand, a new manager is ineffective if, despite good intentions, he or she moves too quickly and fails as a result.

This example is not meant to suggest that a new manager must always wait to get established before proposing and undertaking important action that is counterculture or personally risky, for that is not necessarily the case, as will be seen. However, the example does emphasize the need to take a reasonably long-term perspective in judging the effectiveness of managerial action.

Purpose of the Book

At the most general level, the purpose of this book is to help students understand the implications of corporate culture for effective managerial action. The central message is that one's contribution to the organization as well as one's survival, success, and satisfaction in it can be enhanced by understanding, anticipating, and appropriately working with the prevailing corporate culture. More specifically, the book's aims are to develop the following:

A sensitivity to the subtle but pervasive influence of corporate culture.

A systematic understanding of how culture is related to other corporate realities, and the accompanying organizational and individual dynamics that must be considered in taking managerial action.

An appreciation of the potential for enhancing both individual and organizational effectiveness and satisfaction by appropriately managing culture, the related corporate realities, and the associated dynamics.

A grounding in the relevant concepts and analytical techniques needed to realize this potential for enhancing both individual and organizational performance.

Organization of the Book

In order to achieve these aims, the book is divided into four parts. The parts are presented according to the sequence in which most students will encounter culture and other corporate realities in the companies they recruit with and eventually join:

Part 1.   Understanding culture and related corporate realities.
Part 2.   Anticipating and entering a new corporate culture, surviving culture shock, and becoming effective as a newcomer.
Part 3.   Getting established and operating effectively within the prevailing culture (without changing it).
Part 4.   Influencing change in the prevailing corporate culture.

Brief Overview of the Book

Part 1 develops a way of thinking about culture and a vocabulary for describing it that can be used to analyze and address managerial problems. The basic groundwork is laid in Chapter 1. Culture is defined, and two of its major elements—content and strength—are discussed. Procedures for deciphering culture and identifying subcultures are also presented.

Chapter 2 explains why culture has such a profound influence on organizational life. The answer lies in culture's impact on several basic processes that are at the heart of organizations. Chapter 3 considers how culture and other corporate realities interact to influence performance. Two basic models are presented—one of organizational dynamics, the other of individual dynamics—for taking effective managerial action. These models also provide a conceptual framework for organizing and relating the material in the rest of the book.

Part 2 is concerned with the period leading up to the acceptance of a company's job offer and the first several months after joining the company. Chapter 4 considers assessment of the organization and oneself. It is emphasized that this assessment should begin before joining a new culture, but the learning involved continues after joining. However, it is important to conduct a good investigation, beforehand if possible, in order to avoid irreconcilable mismatches between oneself and the organization and also promote a more effective performance and greater satisfaction after joining the organization. The pressures and constraints of the recruitment process, which seriously influence this early assessment prior to accepting a company's offer, are addressed in Chapter 5.

No matter how good a job of assessment and selection is done, some culture shocks (and other kinds of reality shocks) are the rule rather than the exception after entering a new organization. Chapter 6 explains why these shocks are inevitable, how they hit the newcomer, and the implications for the initial work assignments the novice must engage in while learning the ropes. The concern in Chapter 7 is with monitoring one's progress in the new organization, reassessing one's fit with it, and making the initial adjustment in order to settle in or move out.

Surviving culture shock, contributing as a newcomer, and settling in do not ensure continued success, of course, and Part 3 considers the question of how to get established and operate effectively in a culture when changing it is either infeasible or inappropriate. Chapter 8 indicates that the keys to success are the ability to develop sufficient credibility and acceptance in the new organization's culture. To be effective at getting things done, one must also understand the organization's formal, social, and political pressures and how they are influenced by culture. This is the subject of Chapter 9. How to manage these pressures by appropriately utilizing the prevailing culture, constructively deviating from it when necessary, and engaging in other conflict when responsible managerial action calls for this is the subject of Chapter 10.

Up to this point in the book, culture is implicitly taken as a given. Culture is rather resistant to change and tends to perpetuate itself; but culture is not immutable, and Part 4 takes up the subject of culture change. Although they are interrelated, it is useful to distinguish behavior change from culture change. Accordingly, the subject of how organizational behavior patterns may be altered is dealt with in Chapter 11. Chapter 12 focuses on culture change.

How to Read the Book

Since it is for aspiring managers, the book is written in a straightforward manner with the practitioner's interest in mind. The detailed notes for each chapter at the end of the book are for scholars interested in the research and theoretical underpinnings of the book. Other readers are

requested to ignore these notes as well as the citations to them throughout the text. The cases provide detailed illustrations of the issues of
interest and an opportunity to apply the concepts and analytical techniques that are presented in concrete situations.

The readings included in the book complement the material in the
text. Those interested in additional information on the subject may wish
to obtain copies of the recommended supplementary readings for which
brief synopses are provided at the end of the book.

Each chapter in the text begins by highlighting key points to help
orient the reader to the material ahead. Two different groupings of
these chapters may be noted. First, eight of the chapters examine culture
together with related corporate realities that must be considered when
taking managerial action. The other four chapters deal primarily with
culture:

On Culture	On Culture and Related Corporate Realities
1	All others
2	
10	
12	

Second, after the necessary conceptual groundwork is laid in Part 1,
the remainder of the book on implications for action has a dual focus:

On Identifying and Adjusting to a New Corporate Culture	On Operating within and Changing Corporate Culture
4	9
5	10
6	11
7	12
8	

An understanding of these distinctions should help the reader to better anticipate the material that follows.

Part 1

Understanding culture and related corporate realities

It is now generally agreed that corporate culture has a powerful impact on managers and their organizations, but it is not equally clear why this is the case and what can be done about it.* In this first part of the book, an attempt is made to clarify the concept of culture and to show how a better understanding of it can provide important insights for dealing with various managerial situations.

Chapter 1 indicates the principal ways in which culture has been studied and illustrates why the particular view of culture adopted in this book appears to offer the greatest benefits for understanding and analyzing problems of managerial concern.

Chapter 2 elaborates on one of these benefits in some depth, for a better understanding of why culture has such a subtle but powerful influence on organizational life. Despite its pervasive impact, culture is not the *only* important factor affecting performance. In order to take effective managerial action, it is important to understand how culture and related corporate realities *interact* to influence organizational and individual performance. This is the subject of Chapter 3.

The ideas presented in these chapters are illustrated with examples from several sources. The case Cummins Engine Company: Jim Henderson and the Phantom Plant (Case 1–1 in the book), and two

---

* All footnotes are included at the end of the book. These notes are for scholars interested in the research and theoretical underpinnings of the book. Other readers are requested to ignore all these notes as well as the citations to them throughout the text.

companion videotapes,* are used to provide one comprehensive illustration.

---

* There are two videotapes accompanying the case Cummins Engine Company: Jim Henderson and the Phantom Plant (Case 1–1 in the book): (a) "Managerial Philosophy, Personal Style, and Corporate Culture" (Videotape 9–880–001, 28 minutes); (b) "The Phantom Plant" (Videotape 9–880–002, 14 minutes). Both videotapes are available from Case Services, Harvard Business School, Boston, Mass. 02163.

Chapter 1

What is culture?

Orientation   This chapter has to be read slowly to absorb it because several new concepts and terms necessary for understanding, analyzing, and working with culture are introduced. Those who wish to first better appreciate why culture has such a pervasive influence on organizational life should read Chapter 2 before reading this material.

There are many definitions of culture.[1] Early authors defined culture rather broadly to include knowledge, belief, art, law, morals, and customs. Two major schools of cultural anthropology have influenced our modern concept of culture.[2] The view of culture favored by the "adaptationists" is based on what is directly observable about the members of a community—that is, their patterns of behavior, speech, and use of material objects. The "ideational" school prefers to look at what is shared in the community members' *minds* in defining culture—that is, the beliefs, values, and other ideas people share in common. Consider this familiar situation:

> Over a period of years, employees of a small, highly successful company came to share many of the same assumptions concerning the virtues of informality, frequent contact, face-to-face communications, and minimal red tape. As the company grew, its complexity and size made it more and more difficult to operate in this way. The employees' inability to behave in a manner consistent with their shared beliefs and values became a source of heightened frustration and anxiety for them and had to be dealt with.

The cultural adaptationists would say that the culture of this company altered considerably because the employees' behavior changed. The ideational school would say that, since these people continued to share many of the same assumptions, this company's culture did not change much.

The example shows one reason the subject of culture is confusing—different people think of different slices of reality when they talk about culture. It is pointless to argue about which view is correct because, like other concepts, culture does not have some true and sacred meaning that is to be discovered. Each view has its place, depending on what one is interested in. Managers are concerned about how people behave as well as what they believe. These two aspects sometimes converge, but not always. In the case just described, the fact that the employees shared important beliefs and values that they could not live by is an essential element to be recognized and dealt with before the situation can be improved.

In general, problems of interest to managers are better understood and addressed if a distinction is made between patterns of belief and patterns of behavior and if *both* areas are attended to. To facilitate this, a three-level model of culture proposed by Edgar Schein will be adapted for use here:[3]

The *first level* of culture is composed of technology, art, audible and visible behavior patterns, and other aspects of culture that are easy to see but hard to interpret without an understanding of the other levels. This is the slice of cultural reality that the adaptationists have been most interested in. We will denote this level by the terms *organizational behavior patterns* and *behavior*.

The *second level* of culture reveals how people communicate, explain, rationalize, and justify what they say and do as a community—how they "make sense" of the first level of culture. We will denote this level with the terms *cultural communications* and *justifications of behavior,* or *justifications*. Both the adaptationists and the ideationalists have been interested in this level of culture.

The *third level* of culture goes deeper still and is the level in which the ideational school has been most interested. It consists of people's ideas and assumptions that govern their communications, justifications, and behavior. We will denote this level by the term *culture,* which we will define specifically as follows.

Culture Defined[4]

Culture is the set of important assumptions (often unstated) that members of a community share in common. Shared assumptions in the minds of people in an organization are not as obvious as their communications, justifications, and actual behavior patterns. Labeling these assumptions *culture* draws attention to an important organizational reality that is easily missed because it is unseen and maybe unheard. Defining culture in this way makes measurement more difficult, as we shall see. However, our aim is not to make the job of measurement easier but rather to develop and use a concept that has the potential to yield greater organizational insight and analytical power.

Limiting the concept to the assumptions shared by people in a community does not imply that the other two levels of culture are unimportant. Rather, the levels are interrelated but sufficiently distinct so that combining them is not analytically advantageous.[5] The specific analytical benefits of separating these levels of culture will become clear in subsequent chapters. However, the main advantages of this analytical approach are briefly noted below.

First, it becomes possible to see more clearly how people's basic assumptions influence their communications, justifications, and behavior when these levels are separated. Second, the important distinction between nonconformity in behavior and nonconformity in beliefs can be understood and accounted for in thinking about an individual's fit with the organization and action that bucks the system, subjects that are covered in Parts 2 and 3 of this book. In Part 4 we will see that behavior change does not necessarily produce belief change, and vice versa, in part because of the intervening level of cultural communications and justifications of behavior. These processes cannot be understood and managed if all three levels are included under the culture label. In short, there is much to be gained by using different terms for each level and examining all three levels.

The Meaning of Important and Shared Assumptions

In reference to the definition of culture, the important assumptions are those that are sufficiently central to the life of the community to be of major significance. From the variety of assumptions that the people in a community may hold, the cultural assumptions are those that are widely enough shared and highly enough placed relative to other assumptions in the community so as to have a major impact on it. There are two principal types of assumptions that members of a community hold in common:

Beliefs include basic assumptions about the world and how it actually works. They derive from personal experience and are reinforced by it but, since some of the physical and social world cannot be experienced or verified directly by any one person, individuals also rely to some degree on the judgment and expertise of others whom they trust or can identify with to help them decide what to believe or not believe (that money is the most powerful motivator, for example, or that most people follow the leader).

Values are basic assumptions about what ideals are desirable or worth striving for. They derive from personal experience and identification with those who have had an important influence on one's personal development since early childhood. They represent preferences for ultimate end states, such as striving for success or avoiding debt at all costs.[6]

It is important to note that these definitions do not refer to what people *say* are their beliefs and values (that is, those they espouse) but rather the beliefs and values they *actually hold, whether consciously or otherwise*.[7] A person may prefer not to admit internalized beliefs and values because of external pressure—peer pressure, for instance. A person may also be unaware of these internalized beliefs and values. Assumptions that continue to be reinforced positively by experience may be taken for granted to the extent of dropping out of consciousness. One may be unaware of such preconscious or unconscious beliefs and values until they are violated or challenged.[8] Further, even after one becomes aware of them, these beliefs and values as well as those consciously held are not easily given up or changed, as will be shown in Chapter 4.

To illustrate, an important professional assumption for a lawyer is client confidentiality. This value is taken for granted, and a lawyer may become conscious of it only if it is challenged or violated. For example, a client might question the lawyer about it, or a fellow lawyer might violate it, which would draw attention to this important value. Even after surfacing, this value is still potent. It is also hard to change, as are other beliefs and values that the individual actually holds, consciously or otherwise.

With this clarification, the meaning of *shared* in the definition of culture that we have adopted can be made more explicit.

Shared Assumptions: Internalized Beliefs and Values that Community Members Hold in Common   A member of a community (or employee of a company) can simply be aware of the community's beliefs and values without sharing them in a way that is personally significant. The response has more personal meaning if an individual complies with the set of values as a guide to appropriate behavior in the organization. The individual becomes fundamentally committed to the organization's beliefs and values when he or she internalizes them, that is, when the person comes to hold them as personal beliefs and values. In this case the corresponding behavior is *intrinsically rewarding* for the individual: He or she derives personal satisfaction from the content of the behavior itself because it is congruent with corresponding personal beliefs and values.[9] It is through the process of internalization by individual members of an organization that the assumptions become shared assumptions.

Such a conceptualization is analytically more useful than one that looks at mere awareness or compliance with the basic assumptions of others in the community because internalized beliefs and values tend to operate at a preconscious level, as we have seen. Employees may no longer be aware of how much their communications, justifications and behavior are influenced by these shared assumptions. Despite their profound influence on thought and action, internalized beliefs and values tend to have a subtle effect that is easily taken for granted. The proposed conceptualization alerts us to the irony of culture (and the reason it can be so treacherous).

Like the process of breathing, internalized beliefs and values have a powerful influence on organizational life that normally escapes the attention of those it most affects.

Internalized beliefs and values also have a more enduring influence on the life of the community than those that members are merely aware of or comply with. This is true because people do not easily give up internalized beliefs and values. Thus the effects of culture conceptualized in this way are not only more subtle and powerful, but more persistent as well.

Culture and Related Concepts

It is useful to distinguish this definition of culture from two related concepts. (Appendix 1–1 describes other concepts that are related to culture.) First, there is a considerable body of literature on the difference between attitudes and behavior and how the two are related. Attitudes indicate how people feel about particular objects or situations, as distinct from their actual behavior toward these objects or situations. Although this parallels the distinction between culture and behavior, culture defined in terms of internalized beliefs and values is analytically a more powerful concept than attitudes because, as explained in Chapter 4, such beliefs and values are a more central feature of an individual's personality than are his or her attitudes. Just a few basic beliefs and values determine a whole host of attitudes. Although attitudes affect behavior, internalized beliefs and values affect both attitudes and behavior.[10]

Second, although the concept of *norms* is related to the concept of culture as defined here, there is an important distinction. Norms are prescriptions for behavior that emerge in a particular social context. They are more tactical and procedural than are internalized beliefs and values. Norms are standards of expected behavior, speech, and "presentation of self" (e.g., be on time, disagree politely, dress conservatively). Basic beliefs and values, on the other hand, represent more fundamental assumptions and preferences for more ultimate end states (e.g., respect for individuality, freedom of expression). As in the case of attitudes, norms refer to more overt and surface characteristics of people in an organization than does their culture as defined here. To better understand this concept of culture consider two of its major elements—*content* and *strength*.

Content of Culture

The content of a culture influences the *direction* of behavior. Content is determined not by an aggregate of assumptions, but by how they interrelate and form particular patterns. A key feature of the pattern of a culture is the relative *ordering* of its basic assumptions, which indicates what policies and principles should prevail when conflicts arise between different sets of assumptions.

For example, two companies may each value cooperation and internal competition, but one company may emphasize cooperation more in the decision-making process and in its system of promotion and rewards, and internal competition may predominate in the other. The cultures of these two companies consequently have quite different content, even though some of their basic assumptions about cooperation and internal competition are the same. This difference in content leads to quite different communications, justifications, and behavior patterns in the two companies.

Factors Affecting Content of Culture

What accounts for differences in culture's content? The influence of the business environment in general, and the industry in particular, is one important determinant. For instance, companies in industries characterized by rapid technological change, such as computers and electronics companies, normally have cultures that embody the ethic of innovation to some degree. Those that don't might not survive. Nevertheless, while sharing some beliefs and values in common, the cultures of companies in the same industry can differ. Differences in the personal beliefs and values of company leaders, particularly strong leaders in the company's early history (often the company's founder), explain some of the differences in company culture. For example, William McKnight's philosophy lives on in the 3M culture; the culture at IBM was molded by Tom Watson, Jr.; and Irwin Miller had a major influence on the culture of Cummins Engine Company. Founders put their imprint on the culture by bringing in people who share certain beliefs and values with the founder, and these people will eventually share others as they identify increasingly with the founder and the enterprise.

As Edgar Schein explains in Reading 1–1 ("The Role of the Founder in Creating Organizational Culture"), the content of a culture ultimately derives from two principal sources: First, there is the pattern of assumptions that founders, leaders, and organizational employees bring with them when they join the organization (which in turn depends on their own experience in the culture of the national, regional, ethnic, religious, occupational, and professional communities from which these people come).[11] Second is the actual experience people in the organization have had in working out solutions for coping with the basic problems of adaptation to the external environment and internal integration. In short, the content of culture derives from a combination of prior assumptions and new learning experiences.

Several important implications follow from this understanding of culture's content. First, culture is subject to development and change because of the learning going on in the organization as it copes with its problems of external adaptation and internal integration. Second, because existing basic assumptions do not change readily, such change is normally incremental and evolutionary rather than radical and revolutionary. In other words, culture is fairly resistant to major change, especially in the short run.[12] Third, because its roots are in the cultures of the wider communities from which the people in the organization come, the content of an organization's culture is apt to be a variation on the themes of the host cultures.

Not all cultures produce equally powerful effects. The properties described below make a difference and collectively represent the second major element of culture—its strength.

Strength of Culture

The strength of a culture influences the *intensity* of behavior. The three specific features of culture that determine its strength are *thickness, extent of sharing,* and *clarity of ordering.* The number of important shared assumptions vary from one type of organization to another. Thick cultures have many; thin cultures have few. Cultures with many layers of important shared beliefs and values generally have a stronger influence on behavior. IBM, for example, has a thick culture made up of numerous shared beliefs and values, including respect for the individual, encouragement of constructive rebellion, and doing what is right. Thinner cultures have fewer shared assumptions and thus have a weaker influence on organizational life.

Second, some important assumptions are more widely shared than others. Few are completely shared in the sense that every member of the community has internalized them. Cultures with more widely shared beliefs and values have a more pervasive impact because more people are guided by them. At IBM most of the cultural assumptions are very widely shared.

Finally, in some cultures the shared beliefs and values are clearly ordered. Their relative importance and their relation to each other are fairly unambiguous. In less ordered cultures, relative priorities and interrelationships are not so clear. Cultures whose shared assumptions are clearly ordered have a more pronounced effect on behavior because members of the organization are sure of which values should prevail in cases of conflicting interests. For IBM people the values just mentioned clearly rank higher than other basic assumptions that are part of the IBM culture.

In sum, whereas its content determines in what direction a culture will influence organizational behavior, the intensity of its effect on behavior depends on a culture's strength. The stronger cultures are thicker, more widely shared, and more clearly ordered and consequently have a more profound influence on organizational behavior. Such cultures are also more resistant to change, as will be explained in Chapter 12. IBM's culture is strong because it has numerous widely shared and clearly ordered beliefs and values.

The term *culture* will hereafter imply a relatively strong culture. It is well to keep in mind, however, that what we say about culture must always be moderated by its strength. The stronger the culture, the more powerful its effects; the weaker the culture, the less pervasive and direct they are.

Factors Affecting Strength of Culture[13]

What makes some cultures stronger than others? Two important factors are the number of employees in the organization and their geographical dispersion. A smaller work force and more localized operations facilitate the growth of a stronger culture because it is easier for beliefs and values to develop and become widely shared. Yet larger organizations with worldwide operations, such as IBM, can also have strong cultures that derive from a continuity of strong leadership that consistently adheres to the same beliefs and values, as well as a relatively stable and longer-tenured work force. Under these conditions, a consistent set of enduring beliefs and values can take hold over time and become widely shared and clearly ordered.

Deciphering a Culture

Culture, conceptualized as internalized beliefs and values that members of a community share in common, cannot be easily measured or directly observed. Neither can one decipher a culture simply by relying on what people say about it.[14] Other evidence, *both historical and current,* must be taken into account to infer what the culture is. A systematic procedure for doing this is spelled out below. It must be pointed out, however, that reading a culture is an interpretive, subjective activity. There are no exact answers, and two observers may come up with somewhat different descriptions of the same culture. The validity of the diagnosis must be judged by the utility of insights it provides, not by its correctness as determined by some objective criteria. The author's reading is that the managers at Cummins Engine Company (Case 1–1 and the companion videotapes—see Introduction to Part 1) shared five important assumptions, ordered as follows:

Cummins Management Culture
1. Provide highly responsive and high-quality customer service.
2. Get things done well and quickly ("expediting").
3. Operate informally without systems.
4. Top management will tell us what to do if there is a problem.
5. See the company as part of the family.

How this culture was deciphered is now explained.

Inferring the Content of Culture

The framework presented in Figure 1–1 provides a systematic method to help make such inferences. Each important shared assumption listed in Figure 1–2 is inferred from one or more shared things, shared sayings, shared doings, and shared feelings. One may come up with a somewhat different list, but the point is to distill from these various cultural manifestations—that is, the cultural communications, justifications, and behavior—a much more concise set of important shared beliefs and values.

Figure 1–1
Framework for Deciphering Culture

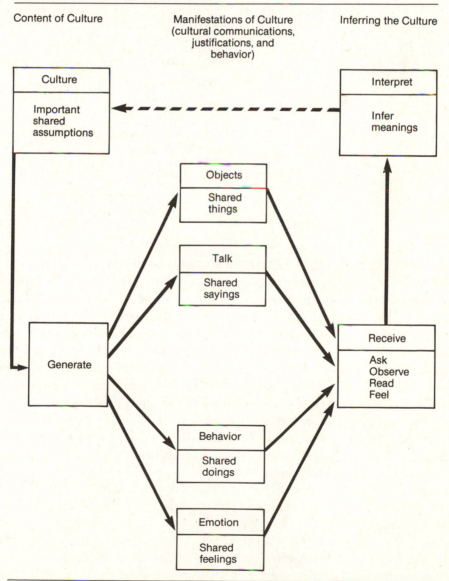

Figure 1–2
Inferring Important Shared Assumptions from Shared Things, Shared Sayings, Shared Doings, and Shared Feelings for Managers at Cummins Engine Company (Case 1–1)

Important Shared Assumptions

1. Provide highly responsive, high-quality customer service (SS1, SS2, SD4, SD5, SF3).
2. Get things done well and quickly ("expediting") (SD1, SD4, SD5, SF3).
3. Operate informally without systems (ST1, ST3, SS2, SD3, SD6).
4. Top management will tell us what to do if there is a problem (SS3, SD2, SF2).
5. See the company as part of the family (ST2, ST4, SD6, SF1).

Shared Things

ST1. Shirt sleeves.
ST2. One-company town.
ST3. Open offices.
ST4. No parking privileges.

Shared Sayings

SS1. Belief in travel, "get out there" to understand the customer.
SS2. "Systems won't work" to meet customer needs.
SS3. "Top management will tell us" what to do.

Shared Doings

SD1. Lots of meetings.
SD2. Close direction from the top.
SD3. Personal relationships and communications.
SD4. Rallying to a crisis to meet the needs of the customer.
SD5. Expediting behavior to achieve highly responsive service.
SD6. Close relationships with union.

Shared Feelings

SF1. The company is good to me.
SF2. We don't need to worry about what to do in a crisis.
SF3. We take pride in shipping faster to the customer than our competition does.

Both implicit and explicit forms of communication must be attended to when examining the manifestations of culture. The former include rituals, customs, ceremonies, stories, metaphors, special language, folklore, heroes, logos, decor, dress, and other symbolic forms of expression and communication.[15] Examples of the latter are announcements, pronouncements, memos, and other explicit forms of expression and communication. It is also important to reflect on cultural manifestations that are *missing*. This is admittedly a difficult task, since there are endless possibilities, but it is important to think about what is not seen, not said, not done, and not felt in the culture relative to what one expected to find or has noticed in comparable cultures. By so doing one increases the chances of discovering what is taboo in the culture. Missing at Cummins, for instance, were assigned parking spaces and closed offices for managers as commonly found in many other companies.

The most subjective and tricky part in the process of deciphering a culture is in "distilling" the content of culture from its many manifestations. To do it well, those attempting to read a culture must empathize with the people in question and try to understand them in their own terms, rather than in the observer's terms. With this frame of mind, three basic questions may be explored to decipher culture.

1.   *What Is the Background of the Founders and Others Who Followed Them?*
An understanding of the background and personality of the founders
and others who helped mold the culture offer important clues about the
content of culture (see Reading 1–1 for more on this). To illustrate,
Irwin Miller at Cummins strongly believed in community service and in
"rooting out bureaucratic behavior," which led to two important cultural
assumptions (number 5, the company is part of the family, and number
3, operate informally without systems). Also, most of the Cummins employees came from the local community, and many were from families
whose members previously or currently worked at the company, further
reinforcing the cultural belief that the company was part of the family.

2.   *How Did the Organization Respond to Crises or Other Critical Events, and
What Was the Learning from These Experiences?*   Since culture evolves and
is learned, focusing on stressful periods of an organization's history can
provide two types of important clues to help decipher culture. First, this
may reveal how particular assumptions came to be formed. For example,
the inventory crisis of 1974 at Cummins ultimately caused the belief in
operating informally without systems to get transformed into a new belief in using systems to do the routine work and in relying on informal
operation to expedite. Second, by focusing on stressful periods in history, particularly those that were traumatic for the organization, one also
has the opportunity to discover the *ordering* of the cultural assumptions.
Order is hard to decipher during normal periods because assumptions
may not ordinarily conflict with each other. However, during a stressful
period, the organization may be forced to choose between two important
assumptions.

For example, although Cummins did not like to lay people off, it did so
during periodic downturns. This suggests that the first four cultural
assumptions, which were not affected by these traumatic events, were
more important than an assumption that was violated to some extent—
number 5, the company is part of the family. Similarly, the 1974 inventory crisis brought assumptions 1 and 2 into conflict with assumptions 3
and 4 (Figure 1–2). Since the latter were questioned and were eventually
modified, but the former were not, assumptions 1 and 2 must be considered more central than assumptions 3 and 4.

The people at Cummins had so thoroughly bought into the values of
(1) highly responsive, high-quality customer service and (2) expediting
behavior that these ideals had become more than strategic objectives and
operational directives. They had become taken-for-granted shared assumptions that were a central part of the Cummins management culture.
These assumptions were never questioned by the managers at Cummins,
even during times of stress, such as the economic downturn and the
inventory crisis. Indeed, the purchasing managers went so far as to *ignore*
higher management directives and order extra parts because they believed customer service would otherwise be adversely affected.

3. Who Are Considered Deviant in the Culture? How Does the Organization Respond to Them?   In a sense, deviants represent and define a culture's boundaries. An understanding of who and what is considered deviant in a culture helps in deciphering it. For instance, Cummins hired lots of MBAs from among the brightest and the best in the early 1960s, many of whom didn't make it in the company. Those who survived were culturally compatible. Many of those who disappeared were deviants—people who believed in systems and procedures and those who believed their talent and professional education gave them special status in the company ("I am a hotshot MBA; I'll teach these guys how to do it right"). These people violated important cultural assumptions (expedite, operate informally without systems, the company is part of the family), which are revealed by trying to understand why these people were rejected by the culture.

A cultural assumption may be so consistently adhered to and taken for granted that almost no one ever violates it. Such an assumption may be particularly hard to discover. The centrality and power of such an assumption may only be revealed on those rare occasions when someone knowingly or inadvertently violates it, incurring the wrath and fury of the entire community.

For instance, a columnist for *The Wall Street Journal* recently admitted he was able to sell his information before it appeared in the paper because buyers believed his column influenced the stock price.[16] Presumably this was not punishable under the existing securities laws, but it did violate an important assumption shared by professional journalists: Never compromise the story for personal gain. This disclosure stunned and infuriated the reporting community. The columnist, who admitted feeling shame and guilt, was fired. An example of such an assumption in academia is intellectual integrity. A recent case in point is the disbelief and controversy surrounding the chairman of medicine of a prestigious school who has been accused of plagiarism.[17] Much can be learned about a culture by looking for such infrequent but critical incidents that deeply offend the people in the community.[18] There was no indication of such a critical incident at Cummins.

Investigator's Skill and Status
It is important to consider who is doing the investigation because this determines what is revealed. Some people are more skilled at reading culture than are others. Skill comes with practice; those who have been exposed to different cultures will have had greater opportunity to develop these skills because culture is more readily deciphered *in contrast* to other cultures one has experienced. The investigator's status relative to those whose culture is being read also affects what is revealed. Consider three important cases: established member, newcomer, and outsider. The established member has the benefit of experience in the culture and

the native's point of view. The irony is that this great asset is also a liability in that some of the cultural assumptions may be so taken for granted by the established member that he or she may find it difficult to surface them. Both newcomers and outsiders may be able to help identify these assumptions.

Newcomers are not deeply immersed in the culture and have the benefit of contrast, being able to compare it with the culture of the organization they are coming from (whether it is a business organization or a school—see Reading 2–2). They are therefore more likely to notice the cultural manifestations,[19] and *perhaps* the underlying assumptions, than are the established members who have come to take them for granted. The qualifier is important because the newcomer may not as yet have access to all the information (especially information considered sensitive and embarrassing by the established members), and the newcomer who has not yet understood the native point of view may also misinterpret the culture's content.

Outsiders are likely to be at an even greater disadvantage than the newcomer in terms of access to sensitive information and in understanding the native perspective, but they have the benefits of greater objectivity and contrast. Outsiders may find it difficult to decipher the cultural content from its surface manifestations, which they can readily notice, unless they can enlist the help of those who are inside the culture. Conversely, established members of a culture can ask for help from outsiders and assist them in deciphering their culture.

The process works best if the outsider teams up with one or more established members to *jointly* explore the culture.[20] The inquiry should proceed from observations that puzzle the outsider because the insider's assumptions are more easily surfaced by contrast to the outsider's initial assumptions. Within limits imposed by the difficulty of disclosing sensitive information, this process of joint discovery can also work for the newcomer who is able to team up with one or more established members, and conversely for established members who are able to solicit the help of newcomers in this way.

I am very familiar with the Cummins situation, but as an outsider. The culture was deciphered from information provided by company insiders, including Jim Henderson, the president of Cummins. However, I did not jointly explore the Cummins culture with these people. The description given might have been improved if such a process had been undertaken.

Estimating the Strength of Culture

In inferring the content of culture, it has already been determined how many important shared assumptions the company's culture has and how clearly they appear to be ordered. The *extent of sharing,* the third property that affects the strength of culture, remains to be assessed.

One clue is how extensive the cultural manifestations are from which the inferences are made—the *proportion* of people in the organization who demonstrate that they share the same physical attributes, words, practices, and feelings. In general, a higher proportion indicates the beliefs and values are more widely shared. Other clues may be obtained by examining the factors mentioned earlier that influence the strength of culture.

The Cummins management culture was relatively strong because there were several important assumptions that appeared to be widely shared and clearly ordered. History, leadership, organizational size, geographical dispersion, and the stability of the work force all had an impact. In its 60-year history, Cummins had only two generations of top management, and the first, highly influential generation (Irwin Miller and Don Tull) were still serving as chairman of the board and chairman of the executive committee, respectively, at the time of the case. Cummins was medium sized; most of its operations were close together; and turnover among managers was low.

Identifying Subcultures

For a belief or value to be considered a cultural assumption, it must be widely enough shared and highly enough placed relative to other beliefs and values in the community so that is has a major impact on the life of the community. It is not necessary for all people in a community to hold all the cultural assumptions, and some people may hold assumptions that contradict the important shared assumptions. As some anthropologists say in a somewhat exaggerated way to make their point, at some level all communities have all beliefs and values represented in them. For instance, even cultures in Communist countries have people who genuinely believe in the free enterprise system, just as there are individuals in the cultures of the free world who espouse the Communist ideology. If deviation from the main cultural pattern is shared by a sufficient number of people in the community, a subculture may form. There are three basic types: enhancing, orthogonal, and counterculture.[21]

An enhancing subculture has the same content but is stronger than the company culture. Management at the Cummins main engine plant, where the company originally began operations, seemed to have an enhancing subculture. An orthogonal subculture has content that is different from, but consistent with, the content of the company culture. For example, the research and development managers at Cummins seemed to have a subculture that supported the company management culture but had its own distinctive assumptions in connection with the design of a "technically superior engine." Finally, a counterculture has content that opposes the content of the company culture. The data processing managers at Cummins, for example, valued systems and procedures that ran against the company value of operating informally without systems. There was reportedly a conflict between the "old guard" and the "new guard," indicating the presence of a counterculture of newer, more professionally trained managers who also opposed this company management value.

The process of identifying such subcultures is necessarily subjective, as is the process of deciphering the content and strength of each once they are identified. An understanding of the factors that determine the content of culture (discussed earlier) provides some clues about where to look for such subcultures. Any definable set of people in the organization who come from the same national,[22] regional, ethnic, religious, professional, or occupational cultures, and who have had enough of a shared history in working out solutions to the problems of external adaptation and internal integration, may develop a distinctive subculture.

For example, managers in the main engine plant where Cummins originally started were all from the local community and had a long and rich history of shared experiences that led to the formation of the company management culture. The research and development managers at Cummins were all engineers and also had a shared history of working together to produce technically superior engines. Finally the newer professionally trained managers as well as the data processing managers at Cummins each were from the same professional and occupational backgrounds (MBAs in the case of the former, systems analysts and computer specialists in the case of the latter), and each group had shared experiences and had learned together from attempts to introduce systems into the company over several years.

Companies typically have one or more subcultures. For instance, there usually is a management culture, which may coincide more or less with the company culture. In the case of the functionally organized company, different functional cultures may coexist with the company culture (engineers who value perfection, manufacturing people who believe strongly in efficiency and cost control, salespeople concerned with quotas and volume, etc.). The company subcultures may in fact be stronger than the company culture. For example, a company may have a strong management culture but a relatively weak company culture. Or a multinational company may have strong cultures in its overseas offices and may have no company culture to speak of.

All the relevant cultures must be identified, deciphered, and taken into account in taking managerial action if the action is to be effective. Except as needed, the discussion in the remainder of the book will be developed for an organization and its culture without referring to a particular culture or subculture.

Appendix 1–1 / Some Concepts Related to Culture*

In addition to attitudes and norms as defined and used in the text, the following concepts are related to culture.

Climate[23]—The attitudes toward work in the community. Climate surveys report aggregated perceptions on how clearly employees understand goals and policies, the degree of personal responsibility they feel for their work, how well they believe they work together as a team, etc.

Identity[24]—The sense that members share about themselves and what they stand for as a community (assumption number 5 in Figure 1–2).

Ideology[25]—The dominant set of interrelated ideas that explains to members of a community how the important assumptions they share fit together and make sense. An ideology gives meaning to the content of a culture. At Cummins the ideology is:

> Expediting behavior is valued because it is critical to our competitive edge of highly responsive, high-quality customer service. Further, informal operations are encouraged because we believe these behaviors help bring about such service. Basically this is a family that pulls together, and top management, as head of the family, tells us what to do when times get tough.

Image[26]—The community's identity as understood by people in other communities or organizations.

---

* These definitions follow the work of several others; citations indicate these sources, which are included in the Notes for Chapter 1 at the end of the book.

Chapter 2

How culture influences organizational life

Orientation   This chapter describes the various ways in which culture influences organizational life. Two major points should be noted. First, culture's influence on behavior is not a one-way process; behavior influences culture as well. Second, culture influences not only what people do, but also how they communicate, feel, think, and justify their actions.

Culture is an asset that can also be a liability. It is an asset because culture eases and economizes communications, facilitates organizational decision making and control, and may generate higher levels of cooperation and commitment in the organization. The results is efficiency, in that these activities are accomplished with a lower expenditure of resources, such as time and money, than would otherwise be possible. The stronger the culture, the greater its efficiency.

Culture becomes a liability when important shared beliefs and values interfere with the needs of the business and of the company and the people who work for it. To the extent that the content of a company's culture leads its people to think and act in inappropriate ways, culture's efficiency will not help achieve effective results. This condition is usually a significant liability because it is hard to change culture's content.

To take a closer look at how culture influences organizational life, we will examine seven basic processes—cooperation, decision making, control, communication, commitment, perception, and justification of behavior—that lie at the heart of any organization. The first three correspond to the first level of cultural reality (behavior); the next four represent the second level (cultural communications and justifications of behavior) indicated in Chapter 1.

Cooperation

True cooperation cannot ultimately be legislated. Management can resort to carefully worded employment contracts, spell out detailed expectations, and devise clever, complicated incentive schemes to reward just the right behavior. However, even well-thought out formal procedures can never anticipate all contingencies. When something unforeseen occurs, the organization is at the mercy of the employee's willingness to act in the spirit of the law, which involves intent, goodwill, and mutual trust. The degree of true cooperation is influenced by the shared assumptions in this area. In some companies, a high value is placed on being a team player. In others, internal competition is valued more. Such differences in the relative importance of shared beliefs and values concerning group versus individual effort (which are differences in the content of the culture) significantly influence the degree of true cooperation in the company.[1] At Cummins the shared beliefs and values of informality and family spirit generated high levels of true cooperation.

Decision Making

Culture affects the decision-making process because shared beliefs and values give organizational members a consistent set of basic assumptions and preferences. This leads to a more efficient decision-making process, because there are fewer disagreements about which premises should prevail. This does not necessarily mean that there is less overall conflict in a stronger culture than in a weaker one. That would depend on what the shared beliefs and values are concerning the role of conflict in organizational life. Where constructive dissent is a shared value, there would be greater conflict than where this is not a shared value—other things being equal. All that is implied is that there are fewer areas of disagreement in a stronger culture because of the greater sharing of beliefs and values and that this condition is efficient.

As pointed out earlier, however, efficiency does not imply effectiveness. If the shared beliefs and values are not in keeping with the needs of business, the organization, and its members, dysfunctional consequences will result. At Cummins, for instance, the reliance on the people at the top in crisis situations ("top management will tell us what to do if there is a problem") was efficient but no longer effective in the complex, multiplant environment that Jim Henderson faced. This assumption had to be changed, and Henderson eventually succeeded in changing it.

Control

The essence of control is the ability to take action to achieve planned results. The basis for action is provided by three different control mechanisms, referred to as markets, bureaucracies, and clans.[2] All three mechanisms are employed in varying degrees in different organizations. Clan control derives from culture.

The market mechanism of control relies on price. If results fall short of goals, prices are adjusted in an attempt to accomplish the desired performance. Prices refer not only to those charged to customers for the organization's products and services, but also to those paid to suppliers and employees for the organization's inputs. The underlying assumption is that the revised prices and payments will stimulate the necessary changes.

The bureaucratic control mechanism relies on formal authority. The control process consists of adjusting rules and procedures and issuing directives. One underlying assumption is that managers at higher levels in the hierarchy know what rules, procedures, and directives will yield the hoped-for results. Another basic assumption is that within a certain "zone of indifference" employees will be willing to follow directives from superiors without questioning their premises.[3]

The clan mechanism of control relies on shared beliefs and values. In effect, shared beliefs and values constitute an organizational compass that members rely on to choose appropriate courses of action.[4] The clan mechanism of control assumes that organizational members are sufficiently committed, knowledgeable, and competent to decide what specific action is needed, given the general guidance provided by the compass of the culture.

The discussion on control may be summed up as follows: The three control mechanisms of market, bureaucracy, and clan are not mutually exclusive. A strong culture facilitates the control process by enhancing clan control, which relies on shared beliefs and values. Clan control is highly efficient, but again, efficiency and effectiveness should not be confused. At Cummins, for instance, there was heavy use of clan control. People responded to the rapid growth of the early 1970s, the unexpected surge in product demand in the first half of 1974, and the downturn that followed with "automatic pilot" responses. There was no reliance on special incentives to motivate people to put out the extra effort (no market control) and very little use of systems, procedures or directives (little bureaucratic control). However, the clan method of control had become inefficient because of growth and expansion. Jim Henderson was attempting to change the Cummins culture so that there would be more value placed on using systems to do the routine work without giving up the valued expediting behavior.

Culture affects not only how people act, but also how they communicate with each other, how they feel about the organization, how they perceive their situation, and how they justify their actions. These processes correspond to the second level of cultural reality (cultural communications and justifications of behavior) indicated in Chapter 1.

Communication

The major reasons people miscommunicate daily in organizational and everyday life include the technical problem of distortion between the point where a communication starts out and the point where it is received. A good example is the familiar parlor game in which a sentence that one person speaks at the start of a human chain comes out distorted at the other end. A second and more important hurdle in communication concerns difficulties in interpretation. Even two-person, face-to-face communication, where the technical problem is minimal, is fraught with the danger of each person misunderstanding the other's meaning.[5] More complex is the communication problem of one member of an organization trying to communicate with someone located in a different unit, or of the corporate senior executive trying to communicate with the entire work force.

Culture reduces these dangers of miscommunication in two ways. First, there is no need to communicate in matters for which shared assumptions already exist; certain things go without saying. Second, shared assumptions provide guidelines and cues to help interpret messages that are received. An example from a company with a strong culture will illustrate this:

> A disagreement had developed between the company's head of research and development and one of the company's general managers (GMs) concerning the resources to be committed to a development program called SURE. The corporate research head argued that 50 engineers (a crucial corporate resource for this company) should be added to the program immediately to protect the company's competitive position in the future. The GM agreed SURE was an important program but stated that he did not have the budget to obtain the additional engineers. Staying within budget was an important corporate guideline. The disagreement was escalated to the group vice president, the executive vice president, and ultimately to the executive committee of the board. After deliberating the issue, the executive committee affirmed the importance of SURE to the company and emphasized the need to ensure the program's success.
>
> The research head, a relative newcomer to the company, was puzzled by this directive. He believed it meant the GM had authorization to go ahead and hire the 50 additional engineers. However, the GM put only 10 new engineers on SURE. An established member of the company's strong culture, he interpreted the message as "Mr. GM, we think this program is very important to the corporation's competitiveness in the future, and we are holding you responsible for its success. We do not have the time, the knowledge or the inclination to get into a debate about body count. You make the trade-off between risking program slippage, for lack of adequate engineering talent, versus the risk of exceeding the budget. We may have to judge later how good we think your judgment was in this connection."

Notice that some things didn't have to be communicated to the GM, in this case the assumption that, in matters such as these, the executive committee would leave it up to the GM to work out such specifics as head count. For other questions—such as Is the program important enough to exceed the budget?—the GM relied on their common assumption that although the budget was to be taken extremely seriously, it was not inviolable. The company culture had clarified the relative importance of these two assumptions. Once the importance of SURE was affirmed by the executive committee, the GM knew that the budget could be exceeded by the amount essential for the program's success. Without the benefit of such shared assumptions, a much longer communique from the executive committee would have been required, which would have been a time-consuming and somewhat awkward process. The advantage of efficiency in a strong culture should not be underestimated; communications such as this are the lifeblood of organizations.

Culture's content affects the content of communication. In some organizations, the culture values open communications: "Bad news is bad, but withholding it is worse." Other cultures do not value open communication. In these cultures withholding of relevant information that has not been specifically requested, secrecy, and outright distortion may prevail.[6] The content of the Cummins culture valued informal and open communication and, since the culture was strong, this was highly efficient. For instance, the Cummins culture greatly facilitated the crucial task of expediting customer requests.

Commitment

A person feels committed to an organization when he or she identifies with it and experiences some emotional attachment to it. A variety of incentives—salary, prestige, and personal sense of worth—tie the individual to the organization. Strong cultures foster strong identification and feelings through multiple beliefs and values that the individual can share with others.

In making decisions and taking actions, committed employees automatically evaluate the impact of alternatives on the organization. Committed people will put out the extra effort needed to get the organization out of a bind. For instance, at Cummins the shared value of highly responsive customer service led the people to move mountains to meet the unexpected surge in product demand in the first half of 1974, without being given special incentives to do so. People had so thoroughly bought into the values of high-quality customer service and expediting behavior that these had become more than strategic objectives or operational directives. They were taken-for-granted assumptions for the people at Cummins.

Perception

Organizational reality is socially constructed. What an individual sees is conditioned by what others sharing the same experience say they are seeing.[7] Shared beliefs and values influence this process by providing members of the organization with shared interpretations of their experience. For example, a recent study found that the differences in the cultures of two comparable community hospitals led their managers to perceive an important cost-containment regulation very differently, and this led the two management teams to define the situation and respond to it in very different ways.[8] At Cummins the highest-ordered values of responsive customer service and expediting behavior led the people there to perceive the downturn and the inventory crisis very differently than did some of their competitors, whose inventories were reportedly reduced so drastically that customer responsiveness and service were adversely affected.

Justification of Behavior

Culture also helps people in an organization make sense of their actions by providing justifications for it.[9] The people at Cummins justified their behavior in terms of the value placed on informal operation without systems as well as the higher values of expediting and highly responsive, high-quality customer service. Such justifications provide powerful reinforcement for existing behavior and is a great asset when the behavior is well suited to the situation. When the behavior is ill-suited, the reinforcement becomes a liability, as it did at Cummins.[10]

The justification process provides an important means for changing culture itself. Since people use culture to justify behavior, managers can create culture change by first changing peoples' behavior (via incentives and other means).[11] This is what happened at Cummins. Jim Henderson first induced his managers to engage in the desired behavior (take more personal responsibility for the problem, use systems to do routine work), and this ultimately led people to change their beliefs in these areas.

For this process to work, however, steps must be taken to ensure that people cannot justify their new behavior while holding onto their existing beliefs and values. This requires special attention to how the behavior change is induced, as well as careful intervention in the cultural communication and justification process, as shall be seen in Part 4.

Summary

Culture has a pervasive influence on organizational life, but people working in an organization do not ordinarily recognize this because the basic assumptions and preferences guiding thought and action tend to operate at a preconscious level and remain outside their realm of aware-ness. Some of culture's *manifestations*—the shared words, actions, physical ambience, and emotional tone indicated in Figures 1–1 and 1–2—may be apparent, but the underlying beliefs and values are frequently un-stated and not always obvious. Their subtle quality is easily taken for granted. Like the fish who do not realize how much they depend on water, those who are most affected by culture overlook its basic impact on cooperation, decision making, control, communication, commitment, perception, and justification of behavior.

The strength of culture determines its efficiency. However, the con-tent of culture determines its effectiveness because content determines the direction in which culture influences behavior. If the content of the culture guides organizational thinking and action in ways that are out of keeping with the needs of business, the organization, and its employees, culture becomes ineffective, regardless of its efficiency.

Despite culture's crucial consequences, it is only part of the reality that affects organizational performance. The next chapter expands the dis-cussion to examine these interrelationships and their consequences.

Chapter 3

How culture and related corporate realities interact to influence performance

Orientation   Culture influences communications, justifications, and behavior, but it also affects other organizational realities. In order to take effective action, managers must examine how culture and these realities together influence organizational performance.

Two models are presented. Model A (organizational dynamics) should be familiar to those who have taken a course in organizational behavior; the role played by culture is highlighted here. Model B (individual dynamics) parallels Model A. Together these models provide a parsimonious way of thinking about culture in relation to other corporate realities at both the individual and the organization levels of analysis. They also offer a complete framework for action taking as well as providing a conceptual foundation for the book.

Model A in Figure 3–1 helps the manager understand the dynamics of an organization from the outside. Model B helps the manager think about the appropriateness of his or her actions from within the same organization portrayed in Model A.[1] Conceptually, both models are grounded in the contingency view of individual and organizational behavior. The essence of this perspective is that behavior appropriate for task accomplishment is contingent on the context, or situation.[2]

Both Models A and B assume that actual behavior may or may not match the required behavior for three major reasons. The individual or organization (1) may not *want* to behave as called for by the situation (motivation problem), (2) may not *understand* how to behave in order to be effective (knowledge problem), and (3) may not *be able* to behave appropriately (skill problem). The more closely actual behavior matches required behavior, the more effectively the individual or organization accomplishes its task.

Figure 3–1
Basic Conceptual Framework

Model A—Organizational Dynamics: Organization as the Unit of Analysis (Culture as a Part of Organizational Reality)

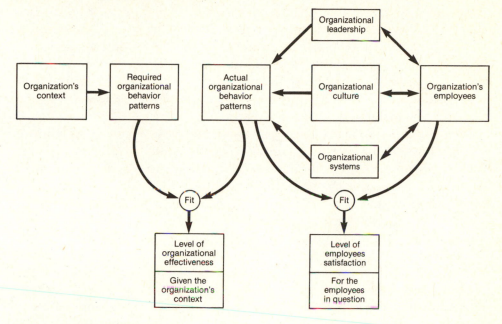

Model B—Individual Dynamics: Individual as the Unit of Analysis (Individual Behavior within Organizational Reality)

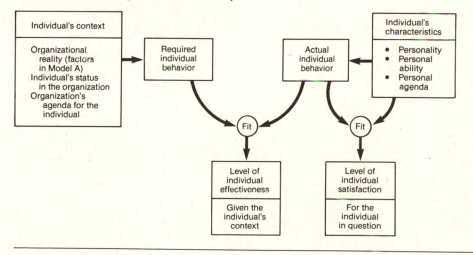

Another question of fit is whether the actual behavior is contrived or comes naturally to the individual or the employees in question. The more the actual behavior is attuned to the characteristics of the person or organization, the less stress and the more satisfaction is achieved.

One should not always strive to minimize stress and increase satisfaction. Some degree of discomfort and dissatisfaction may well be a spur to individual and organizational growth and development.[3] What the models point up is the need for managers to recognize the link between effectiveness and satisfaction in taking managerial action.

It should be noted that effectiveness and satisfaction are *relative* concepts. The level of effectiveness represents the degree of accomplishment compared with the best that can be hoped for, given the particular situation the individual or organization are in. The level of satisfaction reflects what is experienced by the individual or the employees in question. A different individual or other employees may experience a different level of satisfaction in the same situation.

Even an individual or an organization that is working at maximum effectiveness can try to further improve performance by making needed changes in their context. Although there are limits to how much and how fast the context can be changed, the individual and the organization must explore opportunities to increase absolute performance in this way. Individual or employee characteristics can also be changed, within limits and over time, so there is the potential to enhance the absolute level of individual and employee satisfaction in the organization as well.

Models A and B provide an overall perspective and framework for studying how managerial action is taken. Managers can step back from their situation from time to time and reflect on the implications of these models for actions they might take.[4] This discussion will focus on the major factors of each model and examine their interrelationships. The example of Cummins Engine Company will continue to be used from time to time for purposes of illustration. The major factors in Model A (Figure 3–1) are shown in greater detail in Figure 3–2.

Model A—Organizational Dynamics: Culture as a Part of Organizational Reality

The contingency perspective indicates that the organization's context determines appropriate behavior patterns for effective organizational activity. A description of how specific variables determine what organizational behavior is appropriate follows.

Contextual Factors and Required Organizational Behavior Patterns

Organizational Features

Geographical Spread The organization may be more or less geographically dispersed, which affects the required behavior patterns in two important ways. First, the more far-flung the operations, the more difficult it is to monitor and control them. Second, to the extent that geographical

Figure 3–2
Model A—Organizational Dynamics: Organization as the Unit of Analysis (Culture as a Part of Organizational Reality)

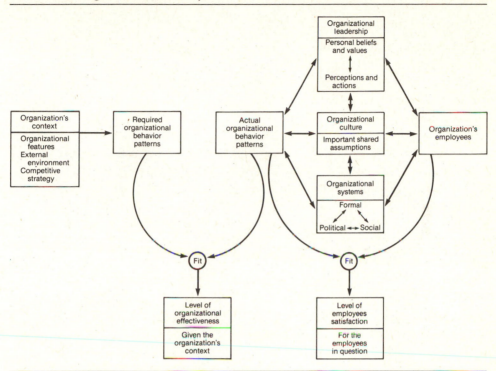

spread means operations in different countries and regions of the world, these difficulties are further complicated because of the underlying cultural differences.

Cummins had just ventured into multiple plants, and the difficulties of controlling dispersed operations were vividly illustrated by the inventory crisis. The information and control system was based largely on personal verification and personal knowledge and was insufficient to cope with dispersed operations. Personnel at the remote plants were not imbued with the culture prevailing at the main facilities, and this cultural heterogeneity increased the difficulties of achieving the necessary coordination and control. Changes in geographical spread created changes in task requirements, and consequently in required organizational behavior patterns.

Technology   The coordination problems that technology poses affect the required organizational behavior patterns.[5] Cummins used batch production technology, calling for intense organizational coordination around the needs of the customer. For a company utilizing a different technology, such as mass production or process control, the coordination problems for the organization would be different.

External Environment

Two fundamental dimensions of importance in relation to the external environment are environmental uncertainty and resource scarcity.

Environmental Uncertainty The external environment, composed of the technological, market, and economic environment, is characterized by more or less change, depending on the circumstances. The greater the uncertainty the external environment poses for the organization, the greater is the need to understand and manage it better—which calls for increased information processing. More flexible, "organic" organizational behavior patterns, characterized by greater emphasis on informal communications, lateral relations, and consultative decision making appear better suited to these conditions.[6]

Cummins faced a moderately uncertain external environment, tied principally to the overall economy. Therefore some organizational flexibility was appropriate, but greater reliance on formal systems, such as those for information and control, was both possible and beneficial.

Resource Scarcity External environments are also characterized to greater or lesser degrees by resource scarcity. The important resources an organization needs are financial, technological, market, and human (people in appropriate numbers with the necessary skills and predispositions). Scarce resources pose contingencies that the organization must either overcome or learn to cope with, which has implications for the required organizational behavior patterns.[7]

For Cummins the key scarcity concerned the financial resources. The company was highly leveraged, and the inventory buildup was threatening to push the debt-to-equity ratio even higher. Bankers were expressing concern about this, and the company was attempting to cope by using better formal control systems and making associated changes in required behavior patterns.

Competitive Strategy

Competitive strategy (the organization's formula for how it is going to compete with other companies and what its goals should be) has a major influence on the required organizational behavior patterns. Two organizations having similar organizational features and competing in the same external environment may have very different required behavior patterns because of differences in their competitive strategies.[8]

Cummins followed a competitive strategy focused on superb customer service, and this had an important bearing on the required organizational pattern of expediting behavior.

Actual Organizational Behavior Patterns

The actual behavior patterns of the organization depend on employee perceptions of what is required to be effective and employee ability and willingness to behave as called for by the situation. Such perceptions and behavior are affected by three important factors. One is organizational culture (Chapter 2). The other two are leadership and the organizational systems (formal, social, political, as shown in Model A, Figure 3–2).

Organizational Systems

The organization's formal systems—structure and systems for measurement, reward, selection—are referred to collectively as the organizational design. These formal systems influence actual behavior patterns (1) by conveying formal expectations about the behavior required of employees; (2) by influencing their selection, training, and development; and (3) by measuring and rewarding the expected behavior. Such systems are effective when they facilitate required behavior patterns and also meet the needs of the people involved—when there is consistency, or a good fit, between the organizational task, the design, and the people (Figure 3–3).[9]

How can formal systems be designed to improve effectiveness and satisfaction (Figure 3–2)? Analysis can begin at any point; it is an iterative process that should address the following questions:

1. What is the task (required behavior), given the context?
2. What design (formal system) is appropriate, given the task definition above?
3. What are the requirements for people (organizational employees), given the task and design considerations above?

If there are major inconsistencies, some combination of changes is needed to bring these three basic dimensions of task, design, and people back into alignment. The actual combination of changes made is dictated partly by constraints of the context and partly by the judgments and preferences of the organization's leadership.

Cummins operated with a job shop production process, and its strategy was to provide superb customer service, calling for custom work, which in turn demanded a high degree of responsiveness to the marketplace. Given these required behavior patterns, both the task and the design's reliance on few formal systems were consistent with the needs of a long-tenured, loyal work force. There was a good fit here among the task, the design, and the people.

Although this organizational alignment was generally appropriate for the context, several changes in the context were increasing task complex-

Figure 3–3
Formal Systems: Task, Design, People Fit

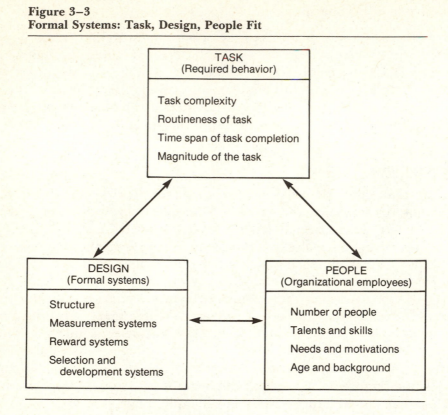

ity and beginning to call for a more formalized information and control system and more professional management. In other words, changes in the context were creating a disequilibrium in the organization; proposed changes in the task, the design, and the people had to be internally consistent to assure fit and eventually establish a new equilibrium.

The design of the organization or the formal system specifies who does what job and who reports to whom. In addition to formal relationships, people in organizations have social and political relationships, which also determine with whom they associate and interact and whom they influence and are influenced by. The social and political systems are functions of organizational interdependencies imposed by the task (who is dependent on whom, who interacts with whom) as well as the personalities, predispositions, and tastes of the people in the organization (who wants what, who likes whom). Thus the social and political systems are interdependent, and each in turn is linked to the formal system.[10] The way in which these systems operate and are affected by culture is explored in greater detail in Chapter 9.

The social system at Cummins was highly developed. A lot of informal networks permeated the company and extended to employees' families. The political system was not as obvious but could be deduced. For example, those individuals who were key links in the ad hoc networks that facilitated expediting and others who made unique contributions in terms of expediting probably exerted greater power and influence.

Organizational Leadership

The personal beliefs and values of company leaders and their perception and definition of the situation have an important influence on organizational behavior patterns. At Cummins chairman Irwin Miller's values about ethical, nonbureaucratic behavior influenced both the choice of key people (strong, operating types) and how they interacted with each other (informally). Similarly, Miller's perception and definition of the situation just before World War II ("We want to remain a small operation") sustained the company's informal systems. Indeed, it may well have been his strong belief in the virtue of informal organization that led him to perceive and define the situation in a way that sustained this belief.

This means not only that seeing is believing, but also that believing is seeing.[11] If the organization's leaders are not mindful of this phenomenon, their beliefs and values can lead them to perceive and define the situation as a self-fulfilling prophecy (not necessarily in tune with important environmental and corporate realities). This discrepancy may not be noticed until it is too late to recover lost ground.

The actions of leaders also play an important role in shaping organizational attention and behavior. For example, the increased emphasis that Jim Henderson placed on the Cummins' financial control system meant that more attention had to be paid to the financial numbers, which meant a change in behavior for the operating people. The weekly inventory meetings and the plant visits he initiated also helped to alter the behavior of the operating people in the company.

Interrelationships among Leadership, Systems, and Culture

Having seen the impact of leadership, systems, and culture on actual organizational behavior patterns, it is well to note that these three major organizational characteristics can also influence each other. Cutlure's influence on leadership is similar to its effects on others in the organization (Chapter 2), and culture's influence on organizational systems is described in Chapter 9. The question of how leadership and organizational systems can in turn affect culture is addressed in Part 4 on organizational change. The three major organizational characteristics—leadership, systems, and culture—also influence other major factors in Model A (Figure 3–2) and are in turn influenced by them, as illustrated below.

The need for more professional management led Cummins to seek and ultimately appoint professionally trained managers to leadership positions in the company in the mid-1960s, for example, Jim Henderson.

However, leadership in turn influenced the choice of formal systems. For instance, Jim Henderson was attempting to build a more professional organization that made greater use of information and control systems.

Another illustration from Cummins further indicates these interrelationships. The trend toward multiplant operations (change in one organizational feature) meant a more complex task of coordination and control (required behavior), which brought into question the important shared assumption concerning informal operations (culture). Changes were attempted in the information and control system (formal system), but these could not come about without accompanying changes in the social and political system.[12] For instance, increased reliance on information and control systems (formal system) to get the job done meant a loss of power (change in political system) for those with the ability to expedite. These changes also meant disruption of the many ad hoc social relationships (social system) built up around the need to expedite.

Let us now consider the major outcome variables in Model A (Figure 3–2).

Organizational Effectiveness and Satisfaction

The distinction between organizational effectiveness and satisfaction is an important one because the two may be somewhat at odds, and yet both must be achieved to some extent. If actual organizational behavior patterns do not serve the organization's interests, organizational effectiveness is impaired. Also, if these behavior patterns are basically inconsistent with the needs, values, and skills of the organizational members, dysfunctional consequences develop in the form of excessive stress, frustration, and turnover.[13]

A dilemma for short-term and long-term organizational effectiveness and satisfaction is that either or both of these may be improved in the short run but at the cost of long-term benefits, and vice versa. The well-known tactic of bolstering annual performance in a bad year by deferring maintenance and other discretionary expenditures, including those for human resource development, is one example. More generally, critics point out that American industry has been plagued with performance myopia in recent years, to the detriment of long-term competitiveness.[14]

In the case of Cummins, organizational effectiveness was relatively high because the actual behavior patterns of expediting and highly responsive customer service were close to what was required, given the context. Employees were generally satisfied, motivated, and shared the basic beliefs and values that guided these behavior patterns. Thus there was both organizational effectiveness and satisfaction. However, the practice of managing each downturn in the economy with a fire-fighting approach made it difficult to get managers to take more personal responsibility for solving such problems and to help prevent their recurrence by installing and using the formal systems needed in the longer term. It was against this backdrop that Jim Henderson was attempting to achieve short-term effectiveness (reduced and fully accounted inventory) in a way that also yielded the desired outcomes in the longer term (managers taking personal responsibility and making use of formal information and control systems). His handling of this inventory crisis will now be illustrated using the complete model of organizational dynamics shown in Figure 3–2.

Summary Illustration: Organizational Dynamics

The expediting behavior so valued by Cummins fit the company's strategy of highly responsive customer service and led to organizational effectiveness and satisfaction. This behavior was reinforced by the company's leadership, the company culture, the formal system (virtually nonexistent), the social system (lots of informal practices and friendships that helped expedite), and the political system (operating people were powerful).

The inventory crisis of 1974 illustrates how Jim Henderson's leadership in inventory meetings, unannounced visits, and team problem solving helped the company cope in a manner that went somewhat against the grain of the company culture. Two shared assumptions were important: Top management will tell us what to do if there is a problem, and operate informally without systems. These assumptions were called into question by Henderson's refusal to issue orders in the old way to fix the problem and by his reliance on the controller and the financial information system to highlight the inadequacy of the existing systems. Over the next four or five years these assumptions were modified: All managers should take personal responsibility for problem solving; and use systems to do the routine work, but operate informally to expedite.

In this case changes in the external environment (the downturn) and organizational features (growing size, multiplant operations) prompted Jim Henderson (leadership) to change the behavior of the operating people (behavior patterns), which eventually led to the revision of two important shared assumptions (culture).[15]

As this example indicates, a behavior change can lead to a culture change. Why this change occurred here but may not always occur is explained in Part 4. The dynamics portrayed above also indicate the manner in which cultural change usually takes place. It is typically a *gradual process* (over several years), whereby one or more important shared assumptions are revised or replaced by new ones. Dramatic shifts in important shared beliefs and values are the exception, as is also shown in Part 4.

Model B—Individual Dynamics: Individual Behavior within Organizational Reality

Model B in Figure 3–4 postulates that appropriate or required individual behavior is contingent on three major sets of factors: the organizational reality (the set of factors in Model A), the individual's status in the organization, and the organization's agenda for the individual.

Figure 3–4
Model B—Individual Dynamics: Individual Behavior within Organizational Reality

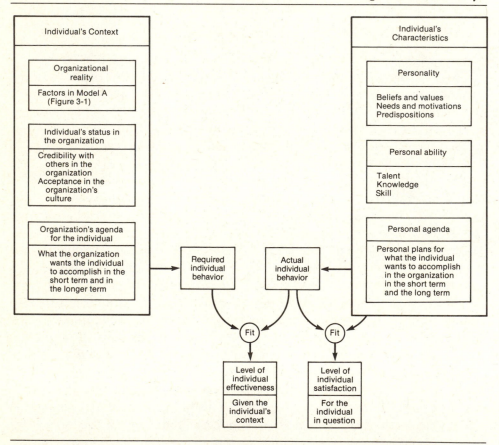

Identical jobs (e.g., plant controller) in two different organizational realities require different behavior in order to be effective. For example, an effective plant controller at Cummins at the time of the case had to rely on personal contacts and informal relationships to a far greater degree than did a peer in a company like ITT, wherein the culture placed greater value on formal controls and procedures.

Second, for two individuals with identical jobs in the same organizational reality, the behavior required to be effective will differ depending on the individual's status in the organization; that is, his or her credibility with others in the organization and acceptance in the organization's culture. For instance, an established plant controller at Cummins could count on a level of openness and support from operating people that would be unavailable to a new controller.

Finally, for identical jobs in the same organizational reality performed by individuals with the same organizational status, the required behavior will vary depending on the organization's agenda for each individual. Organizational agendas are the set of expectations that leaders of the organization have for the individual, including those concerning his or her ability to contribute to the corporation.[16] For example, an established plant controller at Cummins assigned to work with a financially astute plant manager would be expected to spend less time helping this manager with financial analysis than would an established controller teamed up with a plant manager who is not so financially able.

In the example just cited, the organization's agenda is straightforward. However, subconscious expectations could also be part of an organization's agenda for the individual, and these may become apparent only after the individual has failed to live up to them. These expectations go beyond the psychological contract, and involve such unspoken and unforeseen issues and questions as these: Can this individual be trusted? Is he or she committed to the organization? Does the individual show promise of contributing and thriving in this environment? If the person doesn't quite fit into our culture at present, is this likely in a reasonable period of time? If not, will there be sufficient contribution in the interim?[17]

At Cummins, for example, Irwin Miller and Don Tull paid Jim Henderson an unexpected visit during the depth of the inventory crisis in early 1975. They had never had such an unplanned, closed-door session with Henderson during his 10 years with the company. Miller and Tull urged Henderson either to take the old, hardline approach to controlling inventories or to "get a strong man to do it." It is possible that the two top executives were simply concerned about the worsening situation and wanted it fixed. It is also possible that there was another conscious or subconscious organizational agenda: to test whether or not Jim Henderson was presidential material. Did he have conviction about what he was doing, and would he stand up for his conviction?

It turned out that Jim Henderson asked for an opportunity to solve the problem in his own way, and Miller and Tull agreed to go along. Henderson eventually solved the problem in the way he wanted it solved and helped change the culture so the problem was less likely to recur. Henderson was also later promoted to become president of Cummins.

Did the organization's agenda in fact include the element of testing suggested here and, if so, was Henderson aware of it? One cannot be sure, but the point is that Henderson should have thought about this possibility, and he may have done so. A manager is more likely to take effective action if he or she has consciously thought about the organization's possible agendas. This awareness also increases the chances that a manager will respond appropriately in a critical incident, like the one that Jim Henderson faced, where there is little time for deliberation.

Required individual behavior is *ideal* behavior in the sense that it results in maximum individual effectiveness on the job. It may be recalled that level of effectiveness is judged relative to the best that can be hoped for, given the individual's context—the reality of the organization the individual is in, the individual's status in the organization, and the organization's agenda for the individual (Figure 3–4). As in the case of the organization, a person who is already working at maximum effectiveness can still try to improve performance by making needed changes in his or her own context. First, the person can try to gain further credibility and acceptance in the organization and benefit from the greater access to information, resources, and support that come with higher status. Second, a manager already working at maximum effectiveness has the opportunity to make additional gains in performance if he or she is successful in altering the organizational reality and/or the organization's agenda so that they become more conducive to such improvements. There are limits to how much and how fast one's context can be changed, but the possibility is worth exploring to see if the absolute level of performance can be increased.

For two different sets of reasons, the individual may not actually behave as required to be effective on the job. First, the person may be unaware of the required behavior because of miscommunication, misperception, or lack of understanding (knowledge problem). Second, the individual may be unable or unwilling to carry out the required behavior. Inability may be due to some personal predisposition or lack of necessary talent (personnel selection problem). However, even those with the necessary knowledge and aptitude may be ineffective because they do not know how to perform the required behavior (skill problem). Good personnel selection ensures the necessary aptitude; knowledge may be acquired through education; and skill comes with training and practice. Unwillingness to behave as required can indicate a conflict with personal beliefs, values, needs, and motivations or a conflict with the employee's personal agenda—what the person is trying to accomplish in the organization in a broader sense than that specified by the job.[18] Another possibility is that the individual may be conforming to cultural norms that differ from the required behavior.

The level of effectiveness on the job is determined by how well one's actual behavior fits the required behavior. A second kind of fit has to do with the individual's level of stress and satisfaction. To the extent that one's behavior is in tune with the personal characteristics of personality, ability, and agenda, the level of personal stress is minimal, and satisfaction is high (Figure 3–4). On the other hand, the poorer the fit, the lower the personal satisfaction.

A moderate amount of stress and dissatisfaction could spur the individual's personal growth and development, but the issue here is the amount of stress and dissatisfaction being experienced and its cause. Too much stress and dissatisfaction could be personally destructive; too little may be insufficient for unlocking present behavior patterns and allowing desired changes in the individual to take place.[19] The cause of stress is also important. Stress caused by the difficulty of learning new skills and competencies is qualitatively different from that caused by having to behave in a way that violates personal beliefs and values. There is a limit to how much one can act out of character and get away with it, not only because the personal stress may become unbearable, but also because others in the organization may perceive the individual to be a phoney. This could hurt one's credibility and acceptance in the organization and diminish performance.

Summary Illustration: Individual Dynamics

Model B in Figure 3–4 helps explain Jim Henderson's actions at Cummins during the inventory crisis. The key is his agenda. In the short run he wanted to overcome the inventory crisis. But he wanted to do it in a way that changed the company culture and thereby reduce the chances of such crises recurring in the future. His actual behavior did not fit the behavior prescribed by the prevailing culture, but it was aimed at influencing a change in the culture. Eventually, this would translate into a new kind of required behavior.

In the meantime, the discrepancy between required and actual behavior raised questions in the minds of Irwin Miller and Don Tull about the effectiveness of Henderson's actions in regard to the inventory crisis (as symbolized by their unexpected visit to his office).

The organization's agenda for Henderson is also relevant here. Miller and Tull were apparently grooming him for taking on the company presidency (which he eventually earned) and were also expecting him to solve the inventory crisis. Henderson's actions went against the grain of the prevailing company culture and created an interim loss of effectiveness because of the continuing and deepening inventory crisis. His actions were personally risky, but such is the nature of leadership and culture change.

Henderson's actual behavior during and after the inventory crisis appears to be in tune with what he is like as an individual. His behavior is also consistent with his personal agenda. Thus there is a good fit between his actual behavior and his personal characteristics, leading to personal satisfaction and probable absence of ulcers.

Henderson could have been more effective in the short run by "doing it the old way" as urged by Miller and Tull. However, this would have been out of character for Henderson; he had a more participative style than did Miller and Tull and wanted to make greater use of systems in managing his operations. Also, by solving the crisis in the old way, Henderson would have helped to reinforce and perpetuate the prevailing culture rather than helping to change it.

In sum, we understand from Model B that Henderson's actions hurt his individual effectiveness in the short term. His effectiveness increased, and he continued to be satisfied, as the organizational reality (culture) was appropriately modified. Model A shows that both organizational effectiveness and employee satisfaction at Cummins had decreased as a result of a change in the organization's context (more geographically dispersed operations, more professional managers who wanted to use systems). Henderson's actions helped increase organizational effectiveness and satisfaction by altering the culture and systems to promote organizational behavior that was more in line with what was required in the new context. Combining these results, Henderson's managerial actions over a period of four or five years (1974–79) must be judged effective, for he helped achieve both individual and organizational effectiveness as well as satisfaction.

This example illustrates how a manager can use the two models in conjunction with each other: Model A, which is a part of Model B, for understanding the organizational reality and influencing a change in it; Model B for managing within the existing organizational reality.

Chapter 4 shows how these models can be used to assess the organization and one's fit with it.

CASE 1–1 Cummins Engine Company: Jim Henderson and the Phantom Plant

Richard F. Vancil
Vijay Sathe

In November 1974, Jim Henderson, 40, executive vice president and chief operating officer of Cummins Engine Company, faced a difficult inventory situation. Although marketing was projecting continued high demand for the company's product—diesel engines—into the foreseeable future, Henderson's other sources, and his analysis of industry and economic trends, gave him little cause for optimism. Anticipating a sharp downturn in early 1975, he viewed the company's rising inventory levels, now approaching 80 days' supply, with growing concern. In addition, there was a major discrepancy between the materials management records and the financial accounting records on inventory levels. No one knew where the missing inven-

tory was physically located. As the discrepancy approached the inventory levels of a typical Cummins engine plant, it became dubbed "the phantom plant."

The ballooning inventories and the phantom plant were particularly alarming because recent new plant start-ups and acquisitions had already caused the debt-to-capital ratio to climb to nearly 50 percent, well above the historical Cummins average of about 35 percent. The added strain from inventories on working capital threatened to push the ratio above 50 percent for the first time in the company's history, and bankers were beginning to express concern about the company's leverage. Continued growth in sales would be difficult to sustain if inventories were not brought back in line.

Company History

Cummins Engine Company, incorporated in 1919, had its headquarters in Columbus, Indiana. From modest beginnings as a machining shop, the company had become a major industrial firm by 1974, with some 20,000 employees worldwide, net sales of $802 million, and aftertax profit of $24 million. The company's growth occurred in roughly three major phases: survival (1919–1933), takeoff (1934–1945), and postwar boom (1946–1969).

The company was founded by Clessie Cummins, with the financial backing of William G. Irwin, banker and industrialist. Cummins was Mr. Irwin's chauffeur and had earlier started building engines in the family garage. Operations began in a single 15,000-square-foot factory with less than 20 employees. From the start there were many technical difficulties, but Clessie Cummins was not easily discouraged. With his persistence and the continued financial support of Mr. Irwin, the company was able to sustain losses during its first 17 years while it learned how to make a successful truck diesel engine.

Several key developments marked the take-off period (1934–1945). In 1934 Mr. Irwin's nephew, J. Irwin Miller, recently graduated from Yale and Oxford, joined the company as general manager. Miller assumed full leadership of the company almost immediately and steered it through much of its period of rapid growth. Another key development was the establishment of a strong network of independent regional distribution and service centers to attend to the ongoing needs of customers. This network became the cornerstone of Cummins's competitive success in the following years.

The company became profitable for the first time in 1936. In 1937 Irwin Miller suggested that Cummins's workers organize to improve cooperation between management and labor, and in 1938 they chose to do so. The Cummins labor force opted for an independent local union, rather than joining the United Auto Workers, which had sought to organize them. This critical event set the stage for several decades of constructive relations between labor and management, in spite of occasional layoffs during slack periods.

In 1940 Mr. Irwin publicly stated that Cummins did not wish to grow, but rather would avoid the problems of a big engine works with peaks of production and periods of shutdown. At the time, the company employed between 700 and 800 people. The entry of the United States into the Second World War put an end to this slow-growth strategy. By 1945 the company had more than 1,700 employees. In 1947 Cummins Engine Company became publicly owned. Clessie Cummins sold most of his common shares and the Irwins made some of their holdings available to the public. Even then, the Irwin family continued to own about 75 percent of the company's common stock.

After the war, the company continued to experience remarkable sales growth, mainly from the production of diesel truck engines. The expansion was spurred by the conversion of an increasing number of truck fleets from gasoline to diesel engines—what came to be called the "dieselization of the U.S. trucking fleet." At the same time, opportunities opened up in overseas markets as a result of the use of many diesel trucks abroad during the war. Many of these vehicles remained overseas and required servicing and parts. Thus the Cummins dealer network was expanded. In 1956 an engine assembly plant was established in Scotland, the first of what was later to become a sizable group of plants, both wholly owned and joint ventures, in various parts of the world.

Cummins maintained its competitive posture during the postwar boom period by undertaking extensive cost-saving and efficiency campaigns and by continuing to emphasize engineering and design improvements based on engine performance feedback from users through the dealer and service network.

Evolution of Cummins's Leadership

The dominant figures in the early years were Clessie Cummins and Mr. Irwin. From his arrival on the scene in 1934, however, Irwin Miller was the central figure in the company. Miller grew up a small-town boy. He had contracted polio as a child, but recovered fully, growing to an imposing six feet, two inches tall. His education in the liberal arts and his family background made him a man of broad-ranging interests. He was a lover of the arts and an accomplished musician. Miller was active in community and national political affairs and was also a philanthropist and civic leader. Under his guidance, Cummins set aside 5 percent of its earnings for charitable causes.

Although Miller joined the company as a member of the Irwin family, he clearly intended to run the business. Despite his liberal arts background, he became well versed in the technical side of the business. Miller emphasized the importance of hiring competent people and of community involvement. He set a strong ethical tone for the organization and focused his attention on rooting out any "bureaucratic" behavior. Miller commanded the respect of all in the company. A hallmark of his leadership style was the ability to ask the tough but important questions.

As a strong, visionary leader, Miller found he worked best with a strong operating head, and he discovered an ideal one in Don Tull. When Tull became foreman in 1935, he began a lengthy management career that took him to the company's presidency in 1960. Tull was a contrast to Miller in many ways. With only a high school education, Tull was a self-taught businessman. Through years of intimate exposure, he became familiar with all the details of the company's operations. He also excelled in customer relations. The truck fleet owners and the people in the distributor network trusted Tull, and he represented them well in the company. Tull managed by staying on top of everything personally. He knew most employees by name, having interviewed almost everyone hired in the forties and fifties. He was close to the union and well known in Columbus and the surrounding communities. Where Miller was eclectic and visionary, Tull was practical and focused on the immediate. While Miller planned for the future, Tull managed in the present.

Together, Miller and Tull had a profound influence on the Cummins organization during a period spanning 30 years, from the late thirties to the late sixties. During this time the company was closely directed from the top. Emphasis was placed on finding managers who were strong individual performers and who stayed on top of all the details of their parts of the business. Because the company was largely under one roof, costly and cumbersome management systems were not required. Tull himself was constantly present on the plant floor, checking the work flow, quality control, employee morale, inventory levels, and shipment schedules. Since the company emphasized extraordinary service to its customers—particularly the original equipment manufacturers (OEMs)—which was an important competitive edge over other suppliers, a good manager in top management's eyes was one who could always find a way to expedite a special customer request.

During the periodic business cycle downturns which hit the truck manufacturing industry and its component suppliers especially hard, Tull did not hesitate to batten down the hatches. He would let part of the work force go, cut off all capital spending, and cancel orders to suppliers. Tull and the controller could be found on such occasions out on the receiving dock turning away deliveries. If a purchasing agent was reluctant to cancel an order for fear of jeopardizing relations with a supplier, Tull would do so himself.

In the mid-60s, as the company grew and the facilities expanded, Miller realized the need to build a management team. He began to turn top management responsibilities over to younger, more profes-

sionally trained managers. Henry Schacht was appointed vice president for finance, and Jim Henderson vice president for personnel and management development. Both had MBAs from the Harvard Business School. When Tull stepped up as chairman of the Executive Committee in 1969, Schacht became president and Henderson executive vice president for operations. Both were then 35 years old.

Schacht grew up in Pennsylvania and studied at Yale before going to Harvard. He was viewed within the organization as bright, self-confident, and able to grasp things quickly. His role soon emerged as that of planner, risk assessor, external deal maker, and company spokesman. He became heavily involved with OEMs and customers in the trucking industry. Prior to his assumption of the presidency, Schacht had held no line position within the Columbus operations.

By way of contrast, Henderson was a local Indiana boy who went to Princeton and joined the Navy before going for his MBA at Harvard. He was seen in the organization as equally bright and quick on his feet, but more people-oriented than Schacht. Henderson believed in organizational development and was interested in fostering the growth of the company's human resources. As such, he tended to give his subordinates greater responsibilities and accept the risk that some failures would occur in the process of enhancing their growth. Henderson's role emerged as head of operations for the engine business. He tended to spend a lot of time and attention on details, frequently visiting the shop floor. He would talk at length with workers on such visits. One notable feature of Henderson's job was that the two executives who had preceded him in it had been less than successful.

Schacht and Henderson were only two of a large number of young managers whom Miller attracted into the company in the sixties from various business schools and from other companies. Schacht and Henderson continued this policy of bringing trained managers into entry-level jobs, but the bulk of the senior operating management and staff positions were filled by older managers with proven track records. Exhibit 1 provides summary background information on 14 key managers in the company.

Evolution of Cummins's Strategy

The thrust of Cummins's early business strategy focused on the technical development of a working diesel engine and the discovery of the most promising market for its application—trucking. In a second stage the company added a marketing dimension. It built a dealer and service network through which it could communicate with engine users. This allowed Cummins to make engineering and design decisions that were responsive to user needs and to pursue a "pull" marketing strategy with the OEMs. Later, the company entered the international diesel engine market. It then diversi-

fied into allied industries. Anticipating a slackening in growth of engine sales to about 6 percent a year, the company undertook diversification into carefully selected high-growth, unrelated businesses in the late sixties.

The bulk of Cummins's sales and earnings remained in the engine business, however. The key to the company's success still lay in its ability to design a technically superior engine, with high performance and reliability, coupled with an aggressive, user-oriented parts distribution and service network, which created among truck buyers a demand for trucks with Cummins engines.

As the seventies rolled along, Cummins found that is had greatly underestimated the rate of growth of the North American diesel engine market, which continued to surge ahead at close to 15 percent per year. The company was overextended financially as it struggled to keep up with demand. It had to retrench from its diversification into unrelated businesses by selling all of them, in order to finance the continued growth of its engine manufacturing capacity and reduce the danger of a major loss in market share. Organizationally, the company was bursting at its seams. Plant capacity in Columbus was woefully inadequate to meet the rising demands of the engine business. Exhibit 2 shows the dramatic increase in sales, earnings, employment, engine shipments, and physical plant capacity through 1974.

The facilities expansion was first

Exhibit 1
Personal Data on Key Managers (as of December 31, 1974)

Name	Title and Position	Age	Education	Total	Current Job	Career Path in Company
				Years with Company		
J. Irwin Miller	Chairman of the Board of Directors	65	BA, Yale MA, Oxford	40	23	President, Executive VP, VP and General Manager
Richard B. Stoner	Vice Chairman of the Board of Directors	54	BS, Indiana Univ. JD, Harvard	27	5	Executive VP and Corporate General Manager, Executive VP Operations, VP Operations, VP Manufacturing, VP Personnel, Other Administrative and Executive positions
E. Don Tull	Board Member and Chairman of the Executive Committee	68	AMP, Harvard LLD, Franklin	38	15	President, Executive VP, VP Personnel, Works, Manager
Henry B. Schacht	President and Chief Executive Officer	40	BA, Yale MBA, Harvard	10	5	Group VP International and Subsidiaries, VP and Manager Central Area (International), VP Finance
James A. Henderson	Executive VP for Operations and Chief Operating Officer	40	AB, Princeton MBA, Harvard	10	4	VP Operations, VP Personnel, VP Management Development, Assistant to the Chairman
John T. Hackett	Executive VP for Finance and Chief Financial Officer	42	BS, Indiana Univ. MBA, Indiana Univ. PhD, Ohio State	9	4	VP Finance, Director Long-Range Planning
C. R. Boll	Executive Vice President	54	BS(EE), Purdue	28	7	Executive VP Corporate Marketing, Executive VP International, Executive VP Marketing, VP Sales, General Sales Manager, Manager Engine Sales, Asst. Regional Manager, Sales Engineer

Name	Title	Age	Education			Positions
W. D. Schwab	Vice President Research and Engineering	54	BS(ME), Rose PolyTech.	27	2	VP Product Development, Executive Director Product Development, Administrator Research Laboratory, Technical Specialist, Design Engineer
T. W. Head	Vice President Management Systems	48	BS(ME), Purdue	10	2	VP Program Management, VP Research and Engineering, VP Engineering, Executive Director Engineering, Director Product Improvement, Project Manager
P. W. Schutz	Vice President North American Automotive	44	BS(ME), Illinois Institute of Technology	9	3	VP Market Development, Executive Director Product Development, Director Technical Planning, Technical Advisor, Engineering Department
L. P. Brewer	Vice President of U.S. Manufacturing	43	BS(Ind. Eng.) Iowa State MBA (Business) Univ. of Detroit	4	3	VP Columbus Manufacturing
H. E. O'Shaughnessey	VP Parts, Advertising and Promotion	54	BA(Ec.) Wittenberg JD, Indiana Univ.	8	3	VP Parts, Sales-Special Products, VP Advertising and Field Sales
M. C. Dietrich	Executive VP and General Manager Industrial Group	52	BA(Ec.) Yale MBA, Harvard	12	3	VP Marketing, VP International Marketing, VP Corporate Development and Planning, VP Special Sales
T. A. Lyon	Vice President International	47	BS(EE), Univ. of Arkansas MBA, Chicago	10	1	VP and Managing Director UK/Europe, VP International Manufacturing, VP UK Manufacturing, Controller
W. P. Snyder	Vice President Columbus	39	AB (Soc.) Notre Dame	18	2	Plant Manager Columbus Engine Plane, VP and General Manager Atlas, Director of Production Control, Director of Customer Services, Assistant to the President, Manager Material Planning and Scheduling

Reproduction of original company document.

Exhibit 2
Selected Historical Data

	1960	1969	1973	1974
Financial Operating Data				
Sales (millions)	$136	$392	$637	$802
Net earnings (millions)	6	18	26	24
Percent of sales	4.4%	4.6%	4.1%	3.0%
Per share data				
Earnings		$2.87	$3.87	$3.31
Dividends		.71	.95	.98
Percent return on equity		14.7%	13.9%	10.8%
Physical Operating Data				
Employment				
United States		11,000	13,500	14,100
Overseas		3,000	6,000	6,200
Total	5,000	14,000	19,500	20,400
Number of engines shipped	20,000	89,000	115,000	126,000
Physical facilities				
Columbus				
No. plants/other	2/–	5/5		7/6
Square footage (000)	1,496	2,224		3,340
Other U.S.				
No. plants/other		3/–		6/2
Square footage (000)		683		3,160
Overseas				
No. plants/other	1/–	3/1		5/1
Square footage (000)	145	650		1,477
Market Share Data				
Cummins share of truck market				
Diesel trucks	61.1%	43.5%	37.9%	40.1%
All heavy duty trucks	27.4%	30.9%	30.3%	32.2%
Financial Position Data (millions)				
Cash and short-term investments				
less loans payable		$ 12.8	$ (9.3)	$ (35.3)
Working capital		87.5	149.1	178.0
Property, plant, and equipment (net)		104.6	203.1	253.0
Long-term debt		61.9	170.7	209.9
Shareholders' investment		130.8	200.2	241.4
Total capital		192.7	370.9	451.3
Percent long-term debt of total capital		32.1%	46.0%	46.5%

Source: Annual reports and company records.

undertaken on a crash basis in Columbus in 1970. Ground was broken for a second major manufacturing plant, and a separate parts distribution center was established. This was done under heavy time pressure, and involved difficult coordination tasks. Disruptions occurred as heavy machinery was moved and the production of particular engine or component series was transferred from one plant to another at short notice. The rationalization and development of formal management and control systems to support a multiplant operating mode had to wait until later. For example, inventory control for all three plants in Columbus continued to be carried out at the main engine plant.

It soon became clear that these facilities would prove inadequate. Instead of tapering off, truck demand hit record highs in 1973 and 1974—well above any trend line on the most optimistic predictions. Plans were therefore set in motion to expand production facilities once again. A plant in Charleston, South Carolina, was bought in 1972 and another in Jamestown, New York, in 1974. A separate facility to handle engines for the industrial markets was purchased in Seymour, Indiana.

Cummins entered 1974 pushing against the limits of its plant capacity. It was also straining under the growing difficulty its suppliers were having in delivering orders on time, and in the amounts needed. As a result, the prospect of a significant drop in market share again developed. Managers were pushing their people and machines to their limits and making heroic efforts to break production bottlenecks.

Corporate Culture

In spite of its dramatic growth, in many ways Cummins Engine Company still was a small-town company. It remained the largest employer in Columbus, and its history of close relations with an independent local union fostered a sense of special concern for local issues. There was a long tradition of keeping people on the payroll unless unusually difficult times came along. Many employees belonged to families with members who worked or had worked for the company. Most of the middle-aged and older employees and managers had grown up with the business. They had come on board in the thirties, forties, and fifties

when the organization was still small and relatively simple.

Cummins employees had experienced years of successful growth under the leadership of Miller and Tull. It was an informal management style where close supervision and attention to detail went hand in hand with the expectation that each manager and employee would show initiative in responding adequately to changing conditions, particularly with regard to customers' late requests. For years employees had been rewarded for expediting a critical piece of work without upsetting the smooth operation of the plant. Over time, ad hoc relationships and arrangements became customary practice. These informal networks of communication extended to customers and suppliers as well. Many of these relationships were often personal, with particular individuals becoming indispensable members of a chain without whom it was hard to get things done. A permanent sense of crisis management pervaded the operating side of the engine business much of the time. Several managers had attempted to introduce systems to provide a more orderly approach to production management. These efforts, however, never had the support of top management.

Organization

Managers found it difficult to discuss the company's organization in concrete terms. There was no ready-made chart to which one could turn. Rather, managers spoke of Leo Brewer's division or Marion Dietrich's group, personalizing the organization, yet acknowledging its divisions. Alternatively, they referred to specific plants or office locations. The organizational structure was fluid, with new arrangements coming about frequently.

It was with the emergence of the international markets and the early diversification moves of the sixties that Miller and Tull first clearly parceled out functional responsibility. Chart A in Exhibit 3 represents the basic outline of the organization around 1965. With the appearance of Jim Henderson as the operating manager for the engine business after 1969, certain pieces of the organization began to drift under his influence, but the process was gradual. Chart B in Exhibit 3 shows that research and engineering as well as marketing were still formally reporting di-

Exhibit 3
Organization in Early Years

A. Mid-60s

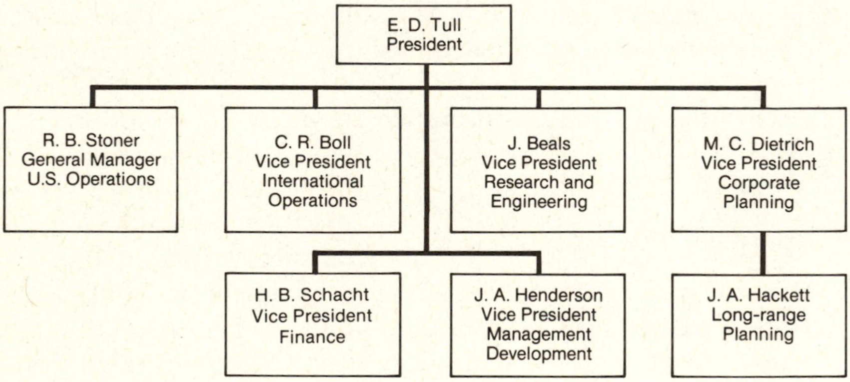

B. 1972

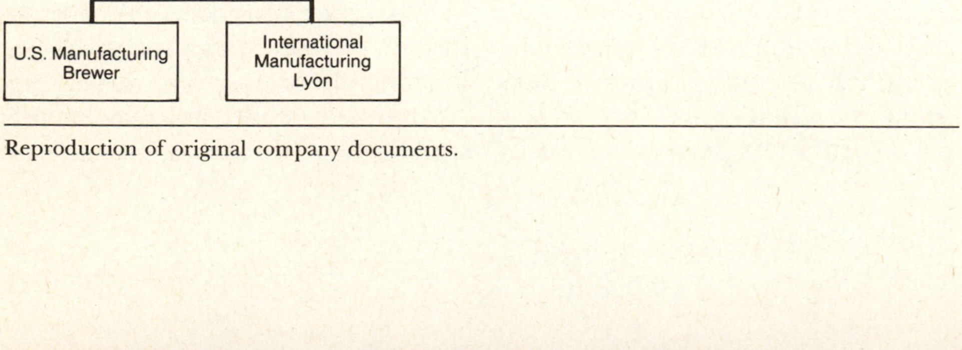

Reproduction of original company documents.

rectly to the president. By 1974 Henderson's formal authority over all aspects of the engine business was clearly recognized. The corporate controller did not report to him, however. (See Exhibit 4, which was drawn up for this case. It did not exist within the company.)

Operating Interdependence

The manufacture of components and assembly of engines took place in a web of interrelationships among many plants and distribution facilities throughout the world. Between and among plants flowed large quantities of bulky semiprocessed and finished goods. Exhibit 5 attempts to represent some of the complexity involved.

In order to comprehend the magnitude of the coordination problem, consider that on a typical day in 1974, 600 engines were completed at six different engine assembly plants, each typically comprising 600 to 700 distinct parts. Each of these was either manufactured at one of 11 machining plants or purchased from a supplier. To make matters more complicated, Cummins built eight different types of engines and encouraged users to request special design or assembly features.

Management Processes

Perhaps the most salient management process in 1974 was still the traditional exercise of the art of expediting. Since the mid-sixties, top management had been pushing to professionalize management and build a more rational and systematic set of organizational systems. The reality of 1974, however, was that demand was growing so fast that only the expert old hands who knew how to coax the last ounce of productivity out of the operating system could keep the production schedule from slipping. Given these circumstances, the principal feedback to top management on organizational performance came from the line organization. This was in the form of weekly and sometimes daily verbal or telex reports on the engine build rate and the engine ship rate and reports from marketing on demand projections for the coming months.

On the other side of the house, the financial staff captured the overall results of operations in terms of their impact on the company's financial position. This information was also made available to top management on a regular basis, but was not reported to all operating managers because it could not be adequately broken down according to their areas of responsibility. This dual flow of information sometimes provided contradictory data to top management, causing considerable consternation and a call for more consistent and reliable reports.

At the lower levels of the organization, the systems analysts and the data processing people were also dissatisfied. As the relationships among multiple organizational units became increasingly complex, they felt a need for more elaborate, accurate, and timely exchanges of relevant information. But they

Exhibit 4
1974 Organizational Plan

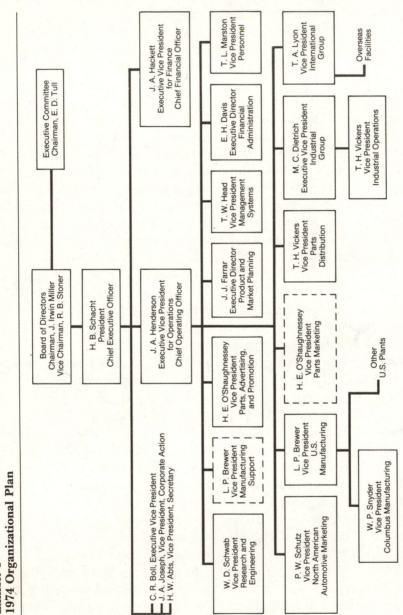

Exhibit 5
Partial Representation of Parts and Components Flow among Plants and Distribution Centers in 1974

Finished engines

Charleston
engine plant
engines
Components

Seymour plant
Turbo chargers
and components

Atlas plant
Crank shafts
and components

Components
and parts

Components
and parts

Jamestown plant
Components

Walesboro
component plant
Components

Fleetguard plant
Accessories

Components

Columbus parts
distribution
center

Columbus engine plant
Engines
Components

Finished
engines

Markets

Components
and parts

Cummins industrial
center
Final engine
assembly

Finished engines

Parts

Components
and parts

Finished engines

Components

Parts

Other parts distribution
centers:

New Jersey
Florida
United Kingdom
Germany
France
Australia
Singapore

Distributor
network

Plants abroad:

United Kingdom
Japan
Brazil
Mexico
India

Parts

Parts

Parts

Source: Information supplied by company officials.

were hard pressed to come up with an adequate design that could handle the various pieces under different people's control. Several task forces had been established for improving information generating, reporting, forecasting, and plan integration. However, they frequently found that the assumptions upon which they were working had become outdated by the time they were ready to present their recommendations. Also, upper level managers were frequently tied up in crisis management and were unavailable to participate.

In short, as the complexity of interrelationships among operating units increased as a result of continued rapid growth, the traditional coordination processes absorbed more and more time, leaving operating managers with little or no time to search for improved modes of coordination.

The Situation in the Fall of 1974

The October Meeting

Jim Henderson reviewed the inventory situation at the monthly sales and production planning meeting with his division managers and staff officers in October 1974. Sales forecasts for the next six months from the marketing departments were bullish. OEMs in the truck manufacturing industry continued to report record order levels with up to 11-month backlogs. These projections indicated that the build rates should be kept as high as possible.

Henderson took a more cautious view, based on personal contacts with industry executives and analyses of broader industry and economic trends. He reminded his colleagues that Cummins was in a strongly cyclical business. In the past, purchases of new trucks had dropped considerably during periods of recession, sometimes with reductions of up to 20 percent in sales. On such occasions, the company had had to run a very tight ship. Order backlogs were meaningless, as orders could be canceled. Henderson also had a nagging feeling that much of the

current backlog of orders facing the truck manufacturers reflected unusually heavy buying before new, controversial, and costly regulations concerning truck braking systems, which had recently been passed by Congress, went into effect in mid-1975.

With inventories exceeding projections, efforts were started at several levels of management to determine the causes. Pat Snyder, vice president for the U.S. Automotive Group, informed the group that the inventory problem was in part due to a buildup of work in process, because delays in the arrival of components made it difficult to complete engines. Growing numbers of "90 percent finished" engines were sitting around waiting for parts. Suppliers were stretched, and lead times for deliveries were getting very long. The purchasing people had been doing a great job selling suppliers on the advantages of giving Cummins preferential treatment as a stable and reliable customer, but difficulties were inevitable because of the surging demand for machined parts throughout the industry. "But if we can agree on a forecast for the next six months," Snyder assured the group, "our production people will move mountains to meet it. In the past year we have surprised even ourselves in exceeding what everyone thought was the limit of our production capacity at the Columbus engine plant."

The controller was less exuberant. He knew that the current severe inflation accounted for some of the rise in inventory value and that this aspect of the problem would continue to put pressure on working capital even if measures to reduce physical inventories were successful. (Cummins's materials costs rose 26 percent in 1974). It also bothered him that the materials management record-keeping system and the corporate accounting system had never been adequately integrated. His financial records suggested that the inventory problem was more severe than the production people realized. In his judgment, the company lacked sufficient control over its inventory to cope adequately with a sharp downturn in sales.

The October meeting closed with an agreement to trim back the sales forecast slightly, recognizing that the market might be softening. It was also agreed that the production control and materials management people in each plant would initiate steps to bring inventory levels back down from about 75 days' supply to a more manageable 60 days'.

The November Meeting

At the November 1974 meeting, marketing reported continued high levels of demand for the foreseeable future. Henderson, however, could see definite black clouds gathering on the horizon. Production managers indicated that engine shipments in October had dipped by about 5 percent under the build rate for the month (indicating engines awaiting parts), but that inventories would soon be brought into line because of the projected strength in the market

forecast for the upcoming six months. The Cummins controller, however, reported a further sharp rise in inventory levels, now approaching 80 days' supply.

After deciding to keep material ordering rates well below sales forecasts, Henderson felt it would be a good idea if weekly meetings were also held to monitor inventory trends. He hoped that the increased visibility this would give to the inventory problem would lead plant management to take a serious look at what it could do to tighten things up.

Weekly Inventory Meetings

Henderson began to meet weekly with his group heads, their plant managers, and the controller to monitor the inventory situation. The Columbus plant managers usually brought their materials people to these meetings. A pattern soon emerged. The more they talked about lowering inventories, the higher they went. The initial downward shifts in production schedules due to the trimming back of sales forecasts took three weeks to be reflected in revised detailed part specifications, on which the purchasing department based its orders. These in turn were followed by lead times of from six to eight weeks (six months for international suppliers). Furthermore, the purchasing agents in contact with suppliers were very reluctant to cut back or reschedule orders, because demand for parts and components throughout the industry remained at record highs. Poor relations with suppliers would mean the sure loss of their good-will, which was critical to maintain to secure deliveries. With the lower build rate out of synchronization with the arrival of supplies, inventories continued to edge up.

There was also disagreement between the materials management records and the financial records as to the rate of growth in inventories. According to the accounting records, engine inventories in Columbus alone were reaching $100 million, whereas the sum of the dollar values of the inventory records at the various Columbus plants was only $88 million. No one knew for sure where the remaining $12 million worth of inventory was physically located. It became a grim joke at the meetings to refer to this missing inventory as "the phantom plant." At one point, Henderson quipped that he would have to stop calling the weekly meetings, because every time they met the inventories went up, and nobody knew where. Finally, Henderson said he was appointing the controller as plant manager for the phantom plant.

It soon became clear to Henderson that the production and materials control departments were so caught up in translating production schedules into specific detailed part breakdowns for use by the purchasing department that little if any time was spent on the physical control of materials after their arrival at the plant. What control there was, was done from the office with computer printouts. At the time, Cummins had over 75,000 active part numbers. There was no prioritization of parts according to cost and volume that would allow particular attention to be paid to the small number of parts that accounted for the bulk of inventory value. The goals for inventory turns that existed at plant levels were not meaningful, and no plans existed to meet them.

READING 1–1 The Role of the Founder in Creating Organizational Culture

Edgar H. Schein

Minerva, the Roman goddess of wisdom, is said to have sprung full-blown from the forehead of Zeus. Similarly, an organization's culture begins life in the head of its founder—springing from the founder's ideas about truth, reality, and the way the world works.

How do the entrepreneur/ founders of organizations create organizational cultures? And how can such cultures be analyzed? These questions are central to this article. First I will examine what organizational culture is, how the founder creates and embeds cultural elements, why it is likely that first-generation companies develop distinctive cultures, and what the implications are in making the transition from founders or owning families to "professional" managers.

The level of confusion over the term *organizational culture* requires some definitions of terms at the outset. An organizational culture depends for its existence on a definable organization, in the sense of a number of people interacting with each other for the purpose of accomplishing some goal in their defined environment. An organization's founder simultaneously creates such a group and, by force or his or her personality, begins to shape the group's culture. But that new group's culture does not develop until it has overcome various crises of growth and survival and has worked out solutions for coping with its external problems of adaptation and its internal problems of creating a workable set of relationship rules.

Organizational culture, then, is the pattern of basic assumptions that a given group has invented, discovered, or developed in learning to cope with its problems of external adaptation and internal integration—a pattern of assumptions that has worked well enough to be considered valid and, therefore, to be taught to new members as the correct way to perceive, think, and feel in relation to those problems.

In terms of external survival problems, for example, I have heard these kinds of assumptions in first-generation companies:

The way to decide on what products we will build is to see whether we ourselves like the product; if *we* like it, our customers will like it.

The only way to build a successful business is to invest no more than 5 percent of your own money in it.

The customer is the key to our success, so we must be totally dedicated to total customer service.

In terms of problems of internal integration the following examples apply:

Ideas can come from anywhere in this organization, so we must maintain a climate of total openness.

The only way to manage a growing business is to supervise every detail on a daily basis.

The only way to manage a growing business is to hire good people, give them clear responsibility, tell them how they will be measured, and then leave them alone.

Several points should be noted about the definition and the examples. First, culture is not the overt behavior or visible artifacts one might observe on a visit to the company. It is not even the philosophy or value system that the founder may articulate or write down in various "charters." Rather, it is the assumptions that underlie the values and determine not only behavior patterns, but also such visible artifacts as architecture, office layout, dress codes, and so on. This distinction is important because founders bring many of these assumptions with them when the organization begins; their problem is how to articulate, teach, embed, and in other ways get their own assumptions across and working in the system.

Founders often start with a theory of how to succeed; they have a cultural paradigm in their heads, based on their experience in the culture in which they grew up. In the case of a founding *group,* the

theory and paradigm arise from the way that group reaches consensus on their assumptions about how to view things. Here, the evolution of the culture is a multistage process reflecting the several stages of group formation. The ultimate organizational culture will always reflect the complex interaction between (1) the assumptions and theories that founders bring to the group initially and (2) what the group learns subsequently from its own experiences.

What Is Organizational Culture about?

Any new group has the problem of developing shared assumptions about the nature of the world in which it exists, how to survive in it, and how to manage and integrate internal relationships so that it can operate effectively and make life livable and comfortable for its members. These external and internal problems can be categorized as shown in Figure 1.

The external and internal problems are always intertwined and acting simultaneously. A group cannot solve its external survival problem without being integrated to some degree to permit concerted action, and it cannot integrate itself without some successful task accomplishment vis-à-vis its survival problem or primary task.

The model of organizational culture that then emerges is one of shared solutions to problems which work well enough to begin to be taken for granted—to the point where they drop out of awareness,

Figure 1
External and Internal Problems

Problems of External Adaptation and Survival

1. Developing consensus on the *primary task, core mission, or manifest and latent functions of the group*—for example, strategy.
2. Consensus on *goals,* such goals being the concrete reflection of the core mission.
3. Developing consensus on the *means to be used* in accomplishing the goals—for example, division of labor, organization structure, reward system, and so forth.
4. Developing consensus on the *criteria to be used in measuring how well the group is doing against its goals and targets*—for example, information and control systems.
5. Developing consensus on *remedial or repair strategies* as needed when the group is not accomplishing its goals.

Problems of Internal Integration

1. *Common language and conceptual categories.* If members cannot communicate with and understand each other, a group is impossible by definition.
2. Consensus on *group boundaries and criteria for inclusion and exclusion.* One of the most important areas of culture is the shared consensus on who is in, who is out, and by what criteria one determines membership.
3. Consensus on *criteria for the allocation of power and status.* Every organization must work out its pecking order and its rules for how one gets, maintains, and loses power. This area of consensus is crucial in helping members manage their own feelings of aggression.
4. Consensus on *criteria for intimacy, friendship, and love.* Every organization must work out its rules of the game for peer relationships, for relationships between the sexes, and for the manner in which openness and intimacy are to be handled in the context of managing the organization's tasks.
5. Consensus on *criteria for allocation of rewards and punishments.* Every group must know what its heroic and sinful behaviors are; what gets rewarded with property, status, and power; and what gets punished through the withdrawal of rewards and, ultimately, excommunication.
6. Consensus on *ideology and "religion."* Every organization, like every society, faces unexplainable events that must be given meaning so that members can respond to them and avoid the anxiety of dealing with the unexplainable and uncontrollable.

become unconscious assumptions, and are taught to new members as a reality and as the correct way to view things. If one wants to identify the elements of a given culture, one can go down the list of issues and ask how the group views itself in relation to each of them: What does it see to be its core mission, its goals, the way to accomplish those goals, the measurement systems and procedures it uses, the way it remedies actions, its particular jargon and meaning system, the authority system, peer system, reward system, and ideology? One will find, when one does this, that there is in most cultures a deeper level of assumptions which ties together the various solutions to the various problems, and this deeper level deals with more ultimate questions. The real cultural essence, then, is what members of the organization assume about the issues shown in Figure 2.

In a fairly "mature" culture—that is, in a group that has a long and rich history—one will find that these assumptions are patterned and interrelated into a "cultural paradigm" that is the key to understanding how members of the group view the world. In an organization that is in the process of formation, the paradigm is more likely to be found in the founder's head, but it is important to try to decipher it in order to understand the biases or directions in which the founder "pushes" or "pulls" the organization.

Figure 2
Basic Underlying Assumptions Around Which Cultural Paradigms Form

1. *The organization's relationship to its environment.* Reflecting even more basic assumptions about the relationship of humanity to nature, one can assess whether the key members of the organization view the relationship as one of dominance, submission, harmonizing, finding an appropriate niche, and so on.

2. *The nature of reality and truth.* Here are the linguistic and behavioral rules that define what is real and what is not, what is a "fact," how truth is ultimately to be determined, and whether truth is "revealed" or "discovered"; basic concepts of time as linear or cyclical, monochronic or polychronic; basic concepts such as space as limited or infinite and property as communal or individual; and so forth.

3. *The nature of human nature.* What does it mean to be "human," and what attributes are considered intrinsic or ultimate? Is human nature good, evil, or neutral? Are human beings perfectible or not? Which is better, Theory X or Theory Y?

4. *The nature of human activity.* What is the "right" thing for human beings to do, on the basis of the above assumptions about reality, the environment, and human nature: to be active, passive, self-developmental, fatalistic, or what? What is work and what is play?

5. *The nature of human relationships.* What is considered to be the "right" way for people to relate to each other, to distribute power and love? Is life cooperative or competitive; individualistic, group collaborative, or communal; based on traditional lineal authority, law, or charisma; or what?

How Do Organizational Cultures Begin? The Role of the Founder

Groups and organizations do not form accidentally or spontaneously. They are usually created because someone takes a leadership role in seeing how the concerted action of a number of people could accomplish something that would be impossible through individual action alone. In the case of social movements or new religions, we have prophets, messiahs, and other kinds of charismatic leaders. Political groups or movements are started by leaders who sell new visions and new solutions. Firms are created by entrepreneurs who have a vision of how a concerted effort could create a new product or service in the marketplace. The process of culture formation in the organization begins with the founding of the group. How does this happen?

In any given firm the history will be somewhat different, but the essential steps are functionally equivalent:

1.   A single person (founder) has an idea for a new enterprise.

2.   A founding group is created on the basis of initial consensus that the idea is a good one: workable and worth running some risks for.

3.   The founding group begins to act in concert to create the organization by raising funds, obtaining patents, incorporating, and so forth.

4.   Others are brought into the group according to what the founder or founding group considers necessary, and the group begins to function, developing its own history.

In this process the founder will have a major impact on how the group solves its external survival and internal integration problems. Because the founder had the original idea, he or she will typically have biases on how to get the idea fulfilled—biases based on previous cultural experiences and personality traits. In my observation, entrepreneurs are very strong-minded about what to do and how to do it. Typically they already have strong assumptions about the nature of the world, the role their organization will play in that world, the nature of human nature, truth, relationships, time, and space.

Three Examples

Founder A, who built a large chain of supermarkets and department stores, was the dominant ideological force in the company until he died in his 70s. He assumed that his organization could be dominant in the market and that his primary mission was to supply his customers with a quality, reliable product. When A was operating only a corner store with his wife, he built customer relations through a credit policy that displayed trust in the customer, and he always took products back if the customer was not satisfied. Further, he assumed that stores had to be attractive and spotless and that the only way to ensure this was by close personal supervision. He would frequently show up at all his stores to check into small details. Since he assumed that only close supervision would teach subordinates the right skills, he expected all his store managers to be very visible and very much on top of their jobs.

A's theory about how to grow and win against his competition was to be innovative, so he encouraged his managers to try new approaches, to bring in consulting help, to engage in extensive training, and to feel free to experiment with new technologies. His view of truth and reality was to find it wherever one could and, therefore, to be open to one's environment and never take it for granted that one had all the answers. If new things worked, A encouraged their adoption.

Measuring results and fixing problems was, for A, an intensely personal matter. In addition to using traditional business measures, he went to the stores and, if he saw things not to his liking, immediately insisted that they be corrected. He trusted managers who operated on the basis of similar kinds of assumptions and clearly had favorites to whom he delegated more.

Authority in this organization remained very centralized; the ultimate source of power, the voting shares of stock, remained entirely in the family. A was interested in developing good managers throughout the organization, but he never assumed that sharing ownership through some kind of stock option plan would help in that process. In fact, he did not even share ownership with several key "lieutenants" who had been with the company through most of its life but were not in the family. They were well paid, but received no stock. As a result, peer relationships were officially defined as competitive. A liked managers to compete for slots and felt free to get rid of "losers."

A also introduced into the firm a

number of family members who received favored treatment in the form of good developmental jobs that would test them for ultimate management potential. As the firm diversified, family members were made division heads, even though they often had relatively little general management experience. Thus peer relationships were highly politicized. One had to know how to say in favor, how to deal with family members, and how to maintain trust with non-family peers in the highly competitive environment.

A wanted open communication and high trust levels, but his own assumptions about the role of the family, the effect of ownership, and the correct way to manage were, to some degree, in conflict with each other, leading many of the members of the organization to deal with the conflicting signals by banding together to form a kind of counter-culture within the founding culture. They were more loyal to each other than to the company.

Without going into further detail, I want to note several points about the "formation" of this organization and its emerging culture. By definition, something can become part of the culture only if it works. A's theory and assumptions about how things "should be" worked, since his company grew and prospered. He personally received a great deal of reinforcement for his own assumptions, which undoubtedly gave him increased confidence that he had a correct view of the world. Throughout his lifetime he steadfastly adhered to the principles with which he started and did everything in his power to get others to accept them as well. At the same time, however, A had to share concepts and assumptions with a great many other people. So as his company grew and learned from its own experience, A's assumptions gradually had to be modified, or A had to withdraw from certain areas of running the business. For example, in their diversification efforts, the management bought several production units that would permit backward integration in a number of areas—but, because they recognized that they knew little about running factories, they brought in fairly strong, autonomous managers and left them alone.

A also had to learn that his assumptions did not always lead to clear signals. He thought he was adequately rewarding his best young general managers, but could not see that for some of them the political climate, the absence of stock options, and the arbitrary rewarding of family members made their own career progress too uncertain. Consequently, some of his best people left the company—a phenomenon that left A perplexed but unwilling to change his own assumptions in this area. As the company matured, many of these conflicts remained, and many subcultures formed around groups of younger managers who were functionally or geographically insulated from the founder.

Founder B built a chain of financial service organizations using sophisticated financial analysis techniques in an urban area where insurance companies, mutual funds, and banks were only beginning to use these techniques. He was the conceptualizer and the salesman in putting together the ideas for these new organizations, but he put only a small percentage of the money up himself, working from a theory that if he could not convince investors that there was a market, then the idea was not sound. His initial assumption was that he did not know enough about the market to gamble with his own money—an assumption based on experience, according to a story he told about the one enterprise in which he had failed miserably. With this enterprise, he had trusted his own judgment on what customers would want, only to be proven totally wrong the hard way.

B did not want to invest himself heavily in his organizations, either financially or personally. Once he had put together a package, he tried to find people whom he trusted to administer it. These were usually people who, like himself, were fairly open in their approach to business and not too hung up on previous assumptions about how things should be done. One can infer that B's assumptions about concrete goals, the means to be used to achieve them, measurement criteria, and repair strategies were pragmatic: Have a clear concept of the mission; test it by selling it to investors; bring in good people who understand what the mission is; and then leave them alone to implement and run the organization, using only ultimate financial performance as a criterion.

B's assumptions about how to integrate a group were, in a sense, irrelevant, since he did not inject himself very much into any of his enterprises. To determine the cultures of those enterprises, one had to study the managers put into key positions by B—matters that varied dramatically from one enterprise to the next. This short example illustrates that there is nothing automatic about an entrepreneur's process of inserting personal vision or style into his or her organization. The process depends very much on whether and how much that person wants to impose himself or herself.

Founder C, like A, was a much more dominant personality with a clear idea of how things should be. He and four others founded a manufacturing concern several years ago, one based on the founder's product idea along with a strong intuition that the market was ready for such a product. In this case, the founding group got together because they shared a concept of the core mission, but they found after a few years that the different members held very different assumptions about how to build an organization. These differences were sufficient to split the group apart and leave C in control of the young, rapidly growing company.

C held strong assumptions about the nature of the world—how one discovers truth and solves problems—and they were reflected in his management style. He believed that good ideas could come from any source; in particular, he believed that he himself was not wise enough to know what was true and right, but that if he heard an intelligent group of people debate an idea and examine it from all sides, he could judge accurately whether it was sound or not. He also knew that he could solve problems best in a group where many ideas were batted around and where there was a high level of mutual confrontation around those ideas. Ideas came from individuals, but the testing of ideas had to be done in a group.

C also believed very strongly that even if he knew what the correct course of action was, unless the parties whose support was critical to implementation were completely sold on the idea, they would either misunderstand or unwittingly sabotage the idea. Therefore, on any important decision, C insisted on a wide debate, many group meetings, and selling the idea down and laterally in the organization; only when it appeared that everyone understood and was committed would he agree to going ahead. C felt so strongly about this that he often held up important decisions even when he personally was already convinced of the course of action to take. He said that he did not want to be out there leading all by himself if he could not count on support from the troops; he cited past cases in which, thinking he had group support, he made a decision and, when it failed, found his key subordinates claiming that he had been alone in the decision. These experiences, he said, taught him to ensure commitment before going ahead on anything, even if doing so was time-consuming and frustrating.

While C's assumptions about how to make decisions led to a very group-oriented organization, his theory about how to manage led to a strong individuation process. C was convinced that the only way to manage was to give clear and simple individual responsibility and then to measure the person strictly on those responsibilities. Groups could help make decisions and obtain commitment, but they could not under any circumstance be responsible or accountable. So once a decision was made, it had to be carried out by individuals; if the decision was complex, involving a reorganization of functions, C always insisted that the new organization had to be clear and simple enough to permit the assignment of individual accountabilities.

C believed completely in a proactive model of man and in man's capacity to master nature; hence he expected of his subordinates that they would always be on top of their jobs. If a budget had been negotiated for a year, and if after three months the subordinate recognized that he would overrun the budget, C insisted that the subordinate make a clear decision either to find a way to stay within the budget or to renegotiate a larger budget. It was not acceptable to allow the overrun to occur without informing others and renegotiating, and it was not acceptable to be ignorant of the likelihood that there would be an overrun. The correct way to behave was always to know what was happening, always to be responsible for what was happening, and always to feel free to renegotiate previous agreements if they no longer made sense. C believed completely in open communications and the ability of people to reach reasonable decisions and compromises if they confronted their problems, figured out what they wanted to do, were willing to marshal arguments for their solution, and scrupulously honored any commitments they made.

On the interpersonal level, C assumed "constructive intent" on the part of all members of the organization, a kind of rational loyalty to organizational goals and to shared commitments. This did not prevent people from competitively trying to get ahead—but playing politics, hiding information, blaming others, or failing to cooperate on agreed-upon plans were defined as sins. However, C's assumptions about the nature of truth and the need for every individual to keep thinking out what he or she thought was the correct thing to do in any given situation led to frequent interpersonal tension. In other words, the rule of honoring commitments and following through on consensually reached decisions was superseded by the rule of doing only what you believed sincerely to be the best thing to do in any given situation. Ideally, there would be time to challenge the original decision and renegotiate, but in practice time pressure was such that the subordinate, in doing what was believed to be best, often had to be insubordinate. Thus people in the organization frequently complained that decisions did not "stick," yet had to acknowledge that the reason they did not stick was that the assumption that one had to do the correct thing was even more important. Subordinates learned that insubordination was much less likely to be punished than doing something that the person knew to be wrong or stupid.

C clearly believed in the necessity of organization and hierarchy, but he did not trust the authority of position nearly so much as the authority of reason. Hence bosses were granted authority only to the extent that they could sell their decisions; as indicated above, insubordination was not only tolerated but actively rewarded if it led to better outcomes. One could infer from watching this organization that it thrived on intelligent, assertive, individualistic people—and, indeed, the hiring policies reflected this bias.

So, over the years, the organization C headed had a tendency to hire and keep the people who fit into the kind of management system I am describing. And those people who fit the founder's assumptions found themselves feeling increasingly like family members in that strong bonds of mutual support grew up among them, with C functioning symbolically as a kind of benign but demanding father figure. These familial feelings were very important, though quite implicit, because they gave subordinates a feeling of security that was needed to challenge each other and C when a course of action did not make sense.

The architecture and office layout in C's company reflected his assumptions about problem solving and human relationships. He insisted on open office landscaping; minimum status differentiation in terms of office size, location, and furnishings (in fact, people were free to decorate their offices any way they liked); open cafeterias instead of executive dining rooms; informal dress codes; first-come, first-serve systems for getting parking spaces; many conference rooms with attached kitchens to facilitate meetings and to keep people interacting with each other instead of going off for meals; and so forth.

In summary, C represents a case of an entrepreneur with a clear set of assumptions about how things should be, both in terms of the formal business arrangements and in terms of internal relationships in the organization—and these assumptions still reflect themselves clearly in the organization some years later.

Let us turn next to the question of how a strong founder goes about embedding his assumptions in the organization.

How Are Cultural Elements Embedded?

The basic process of embedding a cultural element—a given belief or assumption—is a "teaching" process, but not necessarily an explicit one. The basic model of culture formation, it will be remembered, is that someone must propose a solution to a problem the group faces. Only if the group shares the perception that the solution is working will that element be adopted, and only if it continues to work will it come to be taken for granted and taught to newcomers. It goes without saying, therefore, that only elements that solve group problems will survive, but the previous issue of "embedding" is how a founder or leader gets the group to do things in a certain way in the first place, so that the question of whether it will work can be settled. In other words, embedding a cultural element in this context means only that the founder/leader has ways of getting the group to try out certain responses. There is no guarantee that those responses will, in fact, succeed in solving the group's ultimate problem. How do founder/leaders do this? I will describe a number of mechanisms ranging from very explicit teaching to very implicit messages of which even the founder may be unaware. These mechanisms are shown in Figure 3.

As the above case examples tried to show, the initial thrust of the messages sent is very much a function of the personality of the founder; some founders deliberately choose to build an organization that reflects their own personal biases, while others create the basic organization but then turn it over to subordinates as soon as it has a life of its own. In both cases, the process of culture formation is complicated by the possibility that the founder is "conflicted," in the sense of having in his or her own personality several mutually contradictory assumptions.

Figure 3
How Is Culture Embedded and Transmitted?

Each of the mechanisms listed below is used by founders and key leaders to embed a value or assumption they hold, though the message may be very implicit in the sense that the leader is not aware of sending it. Leaders also may be conflicted, which leads to conflicting messages. A given mechanism may convey the message very explicitly, ambiguously, or totally implicitly. The mechanisms are listed below from more or less explicit to more or less implicit ones.

1. *Formal statements of organizational philosophy, charters, creeds, materials used for recruitment and selection, and socialization.*
2. *Design of physical spaces, facades, buildings.*
3. *Deliberate role modeling, teaching, and coaching by leaders.*
4. *Explicit reward and status system, promotion criteria.*
5. *Stories, legends, myths, and parables about key people and events.*
6. *What leaders pay attention to, measure, and control.*
7. *Leader reactions to critical incidents and organizational crises* (times when organizational survival is threatened, norms are unclear or are challenged, insubordination occurs, threatening or meaningless events occur, and so forth).
8. *How the organization is designed and structured.* (The design of work, who reports to whom, degree of decentralization, functional or other criteria for differentiation, and mechanisms used for integration carry implicit messages of what leaders assume and value.)
9. *Organizational systems and procedures.* (The types of information, control, and decision support systems in terms of categories of information, time cycles, who gets what information, and when and how performance appraisal and other review processes are conducted carry implicit messages of what leaders assume and value.)
10. *Criteria used for recruitment, selection, promotion, leveling off, retirement, and "excommunication" of people* (the implicit and possible unconscious criteria that leaders use to determine who "fits" and who doesn't "fit" membership roles and key slots in the organization).

The commonest case is probably that of the founder who states a philosophy of delegation but who retains tight control by feeling free to intervene, even in the smallest and most trivial decisions, as A did. Because the owner is granted the "right" to run his or her own company, subordinates will tolerate this kind of contradictory behavior, and the organization's culture will develop complex assumptions about how one runs the organization "in spite of" or "around" the founder. If the founder's conflicts are severe to the point of interfering with the running of the organization, buffering layers of management may be built in or, in the extreme, the board of directors may have to find a way to move the founder out altogether.

The mechanisms listed in Figure 3 are not equally potent in practice, but they can reinforce each other to make the total message more potent than individual components. In my observation the most important or potent messages are role modeling by leaders (item 3), what leaders pay attention to (item 6), and leader reactions to critical events (item 7). Only if we observe these leader actions can we begin to decipher how members of the organization "learned" the right and proper things to do, and what model of reality they were to adopt.

To give a few examples, A demonstrated his need to be involved in everything at a detailed level by frequent visits to stores and detailed inspections of what was going on in them. When he went on vacation, he called the office every single day at a set time and wanted to know in great detail what was going on. This behavior persisted into his period of semiretirement, when he would still call *daily* from his retirement home, where he spent three winter months.

A's loyalty to his family was quite evident: He ignored bad business results if a family member was responsible, yet punished a nonfamily member involved in such results. If the family member was seriously damaging the business, A put a competent manager in under him, but did not always give that manager credit for subsequent good results. If things continued to go badly, A would finally remove the family member, but always with elaborate rationalizations to protect the family image. If challenged on this kind of blind loyalty, A would assert that owners had certain rights that could not be challenged. Insubordination from a family member was tolerated and excused, but the same kind of insubordination from a nonfamily member was severely punished.

In complete contrast, B tried to find competent general managers and turn a business over to them as quickly as he could. He involved himself only if he absolutely had to in order to save the business, and he pulled out of businesses as soon as they were stable and successful. B separated his family life completely from his business and had no assumptions about the rights of a family in a business. He wanted a good financial return so that he could make his family economically secure, but he seemed not to want his family involved in the businesses.

C, like B, was not interested in building the business on behalf of the family; his preoccupation with making sound decisions overrode all other concerns. Hence C set out to find the right kinds of managers and then "trained" them through the manner in which he reacted to situations. If managers displayed ignorance or lack of control of an area for which they were responsible, C would get publicly angry at them and accuse them of incompetence. If managers overran a budget or had too much inventory and did not inform C when this was first noticed, they would be publicly chided, whatever the reason was for the condition. If the manager tried to defend the situation by noting that it developed because of actions in another part of the same company, actions which C and others had agreed to, C would point out strongly that the manager should have brought that issue up much earlier and forced a rethinking or renegotiation right away. Thus C made it clear through his reactions that poor ultimate results could be excused, but not being on top of one's situation could never be excused.

C taught subordinates his theory about building commitment to a decision by systematically refusing to go along with something until he felt the commitment was there and by punishing managers who acted impulsively or prematurely in areas where the support of others was critical. He thus set up a very complex situation for his subordinates by demanding on the one hand a strong individualistic orientation (embodied in official company creeds and public relations literature) and, on the other, strong rules of consensus and mutual commitment (embodied in organizational stories, the organization's design, and many of its systems and procedures).

The above examples highlighted the differences among the three founders to show the biases and unique features of the culture in their respective companies, but there were some common elements as well that need to be mentioned. All three founders assumed that the success of their business(es) hinged on meeting customer needs; their most severe outbursts at subordinates occurred when they learned that a customer had not been well treated. All of the official messages highlighted customer concern, and the reward and control systems focused heavily on such concerns. In the case of A, customer needs were even put ahead of the needs of the family; one way a family member could really get into trouble was to mess up a customer relationship.

All three founders, obsessed with product quality, had a hard time seeing how some of their own managerial demands could undermine quality by forcing compromises. This point is important because in all the official messages, commitment to customers and product quality were uniformly emphasized—making one assume that this value was a clear priority. It was only when one looked at the inner workings of A's and C's organizations that one could see that

other assumptions which they held created internal conflicts that were difficult to overcome—conflicts that introduced new cultural themes into the organizations.

In C's organization, for example, there was simultaneously a concern for customers and an arrogance toward customers. Many of the engineers involved in the original product designs had been successful in estimating what customers would really want—a success leading to their assumption that they understood customers well enough to continue to make product designs without having to pay too much attention to what sales and marketing were trying to tell them. C officially supported marketing as a concept, but his underlying assumption was similar to that of his engineers, that he really understood what his customers wanted; this led to a systematic ignoring of some inputs from sales and marketing.

As the company's operating environment changed, old assumptions about the company's role in that environment were no longer working. But neither C nor many of his original group had a paradigm that was clearly workable in the new situation, so a period of painful conflict and new learning arose. More and more customers and marketing people began to complain, yet some parts of the organization literally could not hear or deal with these complaints because of their belief in the superiority of their products and their own previous assumptions that they knew what customers wanted.

In summary, the mechanisms shown in Figure 3 represent *all* of the possible ways in which founder messages get communicated and embedded, but they vary in potency. Indeed, they may often be found to conflict with each other— either because the founder is internally conflicted or because the environment is forcing changes in the original paradigm that lead different parts of the organization to have different assumptions about how to view things. Such conflicts often result because new, strong managers who are not part of the founding group begin to impose their own assumptions and theories. Let us look next at how these people may differ and the implications of such differences.

Founder/Owners versus "Professional Managers"

Distinctive characteristics or "biases" introduced by the founder's assumptions are found in first-generation firms that are still heavily influenced by founders and in companies that continue to be run by family members. As noted above, such biases give the first-generation firm its distinctive character, and such biases are usually highly valued by first-generation employees because they are associated with the success of the enterprise. As the organization grows, as family members or nonfamily managers begin to introduce new assumptions, as environmental changes force new responses from the organization, the original assumptions begin to be strained.

Employees begin to express concern that some of their "key" values will be lost or that the characteristics that made the company an exciting place to work are gradually disappearing.

Clear distinctions begin to be drawn between the founding family and the "professional" managers who begin to be brought into key positions. Such "professional" managers are usually identified as nonfamily and as nonowners and, therefore, as less "invested" in the company. Often they have been specifically educated to be managers rather than experts in whatever is the company's particular product or market. They are perceived, by virtue of these facts, as being less loyal to the original values and assumptions that guided the company, and as being more concerned with short-run financial performance. They are typically welcomed for bringing in much-needed organizational and functional skills, but they are often mistrusted because they are not loyal to the founding assumptions.

Though these perceptions have strong stereotypic components, it's possible to see that much of the stereotype is firmly based in reality if one examines a number of first-generation and family-owned companies. Founders and owners do have distinctive characteristics that derive partly from their personalities and partly from their structural position as owners. It is important to understand these characteristics if one is to explain how strongly held many of the values and assumptions of first-generation or family-owned companies are. Figure 4 examines the "stereotype" by polarizing the founder/owner and "professional" manager along a number of motivational, analytical, interpersonal, and structural dimensions.

The main thrust of the differences noted is that the founder/owner is seen as being more self-oriented, more willing to take risks and pursue noneconomic objectives and, by virtue of being the founder/owner, more *able* to take risks and

Figure 4
How Do Founder/Owners Differ from "Professional Managers"?

Motivation and Emotional Orientation	
Entrepreneurs/founders/owners are . . .	**Professional managers are . . .**
Oriented toward creating, building.	Oriented toward consolidating, surviving, growing.
Achievement-oriented.	Power- and influence-oriented.
Self-oriented, worried about own image; need for "glory" high.	Organization-oriented, worried about company image.
Jealous of own prerogatives, need for autonomy high.	Interested in developing the organization and subordinates.
Loyal to own company, "local."	Loyal to profession of management, "cosmopolitan."
Willing and able to take moderate risks on own authority.	Able to take risks, but more cautious and in need of support.

Analytical Orientation	
Primarily intuitive, trusting of own intuitions.	Primarily analytical, more cautious about intuitions.
Long-range time horizon.	Short-range time horizon.
Holistic; able to see total picture, patterns.	Specific; able to see details and their consequences.

Interpersonal Orientation	
"Particularistic," in the sense of seeing individuals as individuals.	"Universalistic," in the sense of seeing individuals as members of categories like employees, customers, suppliers, and so on.
Personal, political, involved.	Impersonal, rational, uninvolved.
Centralist, autocratic.	Participative, delegation-oriented.
Family ties count.	Family ties are irrelevant.
Emotional, impatient, easily bored.	Unemotional, patient, persistent.

Structural/Positional Differences	
Have the privileges and risks of ownership.	Have minimal ownership, hence fewer privileges and risks.
Have secure position by virtue of ownership.	Have less secure position, must constantly prove themselves.
Are generally highly visible and get close attention.	Are often invisible and do not get much attention.
Have the support of family members in the business.	Function alone or with the support of nonfamily members.
Have the obligation of dealing with family members and deciding on the priorities family issues should have relative to company issues.	Do not have to worry about family issues at all, which are by definition irrelevant.
Have weak bosses, boards that are under their own control.	Have strong bosses, boards that are not under their own control.

to pursue such objectives. Founder/owners are more often intuitive and holistic in their thinking, and they are able to take a long-range point of view because they are building their own identities through their enterprises. They are often more particularistic in their orientation, a characteristic that results in the building of more of a community in the early organizational stages. That is, the initial founding group and the first generation of employees will know each other well and will operate more on personal acquaintance and trust than on formal principles, job descriptions, and rules.

The environment will often be more political than bureaucratic, and founder-value biases will be staunchly defended because they will form the basis for the group's initial identity. New members who don't fit this set of assumptions and values are likely to leave because they will be uncomfortable, or they will be ejected because their failure to confirm accepted patterns is seen as disruptive.

Founder/owners, by virtue of their position and personality, also tend to fulfill some *unique functions* in the early history of their organizations:

1. Containing and Absorbing Anxiety and Risk Because they are positionally more secure and personally more confident, owners more than managers absorb and contain the anxieties and risks that are inherent in creating, developing, and enlarging an organization. Thus in time of stress, owners play a special

role in reassuring the organization that it will survive. They are the stakeholders; hence they do have the ultimate risk.

2. Embedding Noneconomic Assumptions and Values Because of their willingness to absorb risk and their position as primary stakeholders, founder/owners are in a position to insist on doing things which may not be optimally efficient from a short-run point of view, but which reflect their own values and biases on how to build an effective organization and/or how to maximize the benefits to themselves and their families. Thus founder/owners often start with humanistic and social concerns that become reflected in organizational structure and process. Even when "participation," or "no layoffs," or other personnel practices such as putting marginally competent family members into key slots are "inefficient," owners can insist that this is the only way to run the business and make that decision stick in ways that professional managers cannot.

3. Stimulating Innovation Because of their personal orientation and their secure position, owners are uniquely willing and able to try new innovations that are risky, often with no more than an intuition that things will improve. Because managers must document, justify, and plan much more carefully, they have less freedom to innovate.

As the organization ages and the founder becomes less of a personal force, there is a trend away from this community feeling toward more of a rational, bureaucratic type of organization dominated by general managers who may care less about the original assumptions and values and who are not in a position to fulfill the unique functions mentioned above. This trend if often feared and lamented by first- and second-generation employees. If the founder introduces his or her own family into the organization, and if the family assumptions and values perpetuate those of the founder, the original community feeling may be successfully perpetuated. The original culture may then survive. But at some point there will be a complete transition to general management, and at that point it is not clear whether the founding assumptions survive, are metamorphosed into a new hybrid, or are displaced entirely by other assumptions more congruent with what general managers as an occupational group bring with them.

4. Originating Evolution through Hybridization   The founder is able to impose his or her assumptions on the first-generation employees, but these employees will, as they move up in the organization and become experienced managers, develop a range of new assumptions based on their own experience. These new assumptions will be congruent with some of the core assumptions of the original cultural paradigm, but will add new elements learned from experience. Some of these new elements or new assumptions will solve problems better than the original ones because external and

internal problems will have changed as the organization matured and grew. The founder often recognizes that these new assumptions are better solutions and will delegate increasing amounts of authority to those managers who are best "hybrids": those who maintain key old assumptions yet add relevant new ones.

The best example of such hybrid evolution comes from a company that was founded by a very free-wheeling, intuitive, pragmatic entrepreneur: "D" who, like C in the example above, believed strongly in individual creativity, a high degree of decentralization, high autonomy for each organizational unit, high internal competition for resources, and self-control mechanisms rather than tight, centralized organizational controls. As this company grew and prospered, coordinating so many autonomous units became increasingly difficult, and the frustration that resulted from internal competition made it increasingly expensive to maintain this form of organization.

Some managers in this company, notably those coming out of manufacturing, had always operated in a more disciplined, centralized manner—without, however, disagreeing with core assumptions about the need to maximize individual autonomy. But they had learned that in order to do certain kinds of manufacturing tasks, one had to impose some discipline and tight controls. As the price of autonomy and decentralization increased, D began to look increasingly to these manufacturing managers as potential occupants of key general management positions. Whether he was conscious of it or not, what he needed was senior general managers who still believed in the old system but who had, in addition, a new set of assumptions about how to run things that were more in line with what the organization now needed. Some of the first-generation managers were quite nervous at seeing what they considered to be their "hardnosed" colleagues groomed as heirs apparent. Yet they were relieved that these potential successors were part of the original group rather than complete outsiders.

From a theoretical standpoint, evolution through hybrids is probably the only model of culture change that can work, because the original culture is based so heavily on community assumptions and values. Outsiders coming into such a community with new assumptions are likely to find the culture too strong to budge, so they either give up in frustration or find themselves ejected by the organization as being too foreign in orientation. What makes this scenario especially likely is the fact that the *distinctive* parts of the founding culture are often based on biases that are not economically justifiable in the short run.

As noted earlier, founders are especially likely to introduce humanistic, social service, and other noneconomic assumptions into their paradigm of how an organization should look, and the general manager who is introduced from the outside often finds these as-sumptions to be the very thing that he or she wants to change in the attempt to "rationalize" the organization and make it more efficient. Indeed, that is often the reason the outsider is brought in. But if the current owners do not recognize the positive functions their culture plays, they run the risk of throwing out the baby with the bath water or, if the culture is strong, wasting their time because the outsider will not be able to change things anyway.

The ultimate dilemma for the first-generation organization with a strong founder-generated culture is how to make the transition to subsequent generations in such a manner that the organization remains adaptive to its changing external environment without destroying cultural elements that have given it its uniqueness and that have made life fulfilling in the internal environment. Such a transition cannot be made effectively if the succession problem is seen only in power or political terms. The thrust of this analysis is that the *culture* must be analyzed and understood and that the founder/owners must have sufficient insight into their own culture to make an intelligent transition process possible.

Acknowledgments and Selected Bibliography

The research on which this paper is based was partly sponsored by the Project on the Family Firm, Sloan School of Management, M.I.T., and by the Office of Naval Research, Organizational Effectiveness Research Programs, under Contract No. N00014–80–C–0905, NR 170–911.

The ideas explored here have been especially influenced by my colleague Richard Beckhard and by the various entrepreneurs with whom I have worked for many years in a consulting relationship. Their observations of themselves and their colleagues have proved to be an invaluable source of ideas and insights.

Earlier work along these lines has been incorporated into my book *Career Dynamics* (Addison-Wesley Publishing, 1978). Further explication of the ideas of an organizational culture can be found in Andrew M. Pettigrew's article "On Studying Organizational Cultures" (*Administrative Science Quarterly,* December 1979), Meryl Louis's article "A Cultural Perspective on Organizations" (*Human Systems Management,* 1981, 2, 246–258), and in H. Schwarz and S. M. Davis's "Matching Corporate Culture and Business Strategy" (*Organizational Dynamics,* Summer 1981).

The specific model of culture that I use was first published in my article "Does Japanese Management Style Have a Message for American Managers?" (*Sloan Management Review,* Fall 1981) and is currently being elaborated into a book on organizational culture.

Consider the following account from the entry experience of a new manager, Bob Drake:

The first unpleasant surprise for Bob came on his third day with the company when he heard two senior colleagues arguing "in public," cursing and shouting at each other. Within the next few weeks he realized this wasn't aberrant behavior in the company. He was also struck by the very long hours, the few group meetings, and the unusually high amount of rumor and gossip. Bob had previously worked for a company where more polite public behavior, shorter hours, more team play, and more openness prevailed. He was disturbed, but reasoned: "It's too bad they operate this way, but I can live with that without becoming a part of it."

The next shock was of higher voltage. After about two months with the company, Bob was called into his boss's office and told he was not being "tough enough." To "really contribute in this environment," he was told, he would have to "be more aggressive." Bob was upset, but tried to keep cool. For one who prided himself on his managerial competence, the last thing he felt he needed was "advice on management style."

Bob decided he would redouble his efforts "to show these people what I can contribute." A large part of Bob's job involved dealings with peers in another department, and he decided to communicate his willingness and ability to contribute by putting in hours with them and going out of his way to help them.

Part 2

Anticipating and entering culture and related corporate realities

What Bob experienced, however, was fierce internal competition, with such tactics as memo battles, information withholding, and "end running" apparently condoned; appeals to various parties were to no avail. At the six month's performance review Bob's boss told him that he had failed to learn from the feedback given earlier. This was open competition, he was told, and he was not measuring up. Bob got an unsatisfactory rating and was given the option to resign. He did.

Such entry experiences are certainly not unusual. This part of the book deals with what a new manager can do to better anticipate and manage them.

There are three major themes in these chapters. First, in order to avoid *irreconcilable* mismatches between the individual and the organization (which ultimately benefit neither party), careful attention must be paid to anticipating culture and other significant realities prior to making the decision to join a new organization. Second, *some* degree of misfit between the individual and the organization is almost inevitable and indeed may ultimately benefit both parties. Finally, the poorer the job done of anticipating culture and other corporate realities prior to entry, the greater the difficulties after entry.

The material in Part 2 may be linked directly to the conceptualization in Part 1 by noting that the new manager needs to learn about all the factors depicted in Models A and B in Figure 3–1. The process of learning the culture is part of the process of learning the corporate reality. Although this learning process continues for some time after joining a new organization, it must begin in earnest well before accepting a company's offer to avoid serious misfits.

Culture and other significant organizational realities cannot be *fully* anticipated. Changes, transfers, terminations, deaths, and reorganizations are difficult or impossible to predict. Information that is available to employees of a company is not openly shared with people on the outside. Many reasons for this will become clear as the discussion proceeds, but essentially, why should the organization bare itself to a relative stranger? Even an outsider who has accepted an offer to join the company cannot be trusted to handle confidential information until he or she is on the inside and has proven trustworthy.

Yet much can be learned about the organization before deciding to join it. This learning is also critical for someone without bargaining power who has only one job offer and believes the offer must be accepted. One can do a better job of anticipating the situation to be encountered and of getting up to speed more quickly in the new organization if one has conducted a better assessment prior to joining. Unfortunately, both the organization and the individual consciously and subconsciously tend in their own separate ways to make such learning difficult. The purpose of

Part 2 is to highlight these difficulties and offer suggestions for overcoming them.

Chapter 4 begins with a useful way of thinking about one's fit with the organization. The importance of self-awareness and how it may be enhanced is considered next. This is followed by a discussion of particular areas in which it is crucial to gain organizational awareness before joining. Chapter 5 is devoted to the pragmatic difficulties of the recruiting process that inhibit getting all the information on the organization that one would ideally want before accepting an offer. Specific suggestions are offered for helping a recruit deal with these difficulties.

The first weeks and months after entry are crucial, for this is when the individual and the organization get a more realistic picture of each other. One or more culture shocks and other reality shocks may be expected during this period. How to deal with these while getting the first assignment off the ground, or becoming operational, is the subject of Chapter 6. Chapter 7 deals with the initial adjustments that must be made—reassessing one's fit with the organization in light of one's initial experience and settling into the new organization or moving out.

The chapters in Part 2 are written from the standpoint of the new manager entering an organization. The case of Bob Drake just mentioned will be used from time to time for purposes of illustration. The concepts and techniques that are presented have repetitive value in that the process of "anticipating and entering" continues throughout a career as a manager moves from one work unit to another within the same company or from one company to another. These ideas and approaches can also be used by managers in general, and human resource specialists in particular, to do a better job of recruiting people, avoiding irreconcilable individual-organization misfits, and socializing newcomers, which are major organizational tasks.

Chapter 4

Assessing one's fit with the organization

Orientation   Appropriate job choice, and successful anticipation and entry into an organization require that a manager have a way of thinking about his or her fit with the organization and learn to assess it by gaining self-insight and organizational awareness. How to do this is the subject of this chapter.

Understanding Individual-Organization Fit

It is important to assess one's fit with the organization because this has major implications for one's effectiveness and satisfaction in the organization (Model B, Figure 3–4). A perfect fit with the organization is not generally possible, nor is it necessarily desirable. Misfits are common because both individuals and organizations differ in many obvious and subtle ways. Certain kinds and degrees of misfit can in fact help both parties because misfits can spur individual and organizational development if they are constructively managed.

One's fit with the organization can improve or worsen over time because both the individual and the organization can change. It is important to assess fit not only prior to and during entry into a new organization, but also on a periodic basis after one has become established in it.

An individual can be a misfit in an organization on three major dimensions: personal agenda, personality, and personal ability (see Model B, Figure 3–4). Bob Drake, for example, joined the company because his personal agenda was to become a line manager, and he understood the company would soon give him this opportunity. The company's agenda, however, was to utilize Bob's analytical talent in a staff capacity for longer than he had anticipated. Bob was also a misfit in that his talents, analytical skills, and technical competence were largely missing in this company.

But this is the kind of misfit that has the potential to benefit the organization and the individual if it is successfully managed. The company needed Bob's skills and contributions; unfortunately, Bob couldn't contribute because of the agenda mismatch and also due to a culture-personality misfit. Bob valued teamwork and a cooperative environment. The organization Bob joined believed in cutthroat internal competition. Bob's overall misfit with the organization was such that he was both unwilling and unable to behave in a manner required to be effective in his situation (Model B, Figure 3–4).

In order to avoid irreconcilable individual-organization misfits and to deal with others in a constructive manner, a manager needs to think about and consciously assess his or her fit with the organization. A conceptual scheme for studying culture-person fit is first presented.

Culture Map: Culture Caricatures for Studying Cultural Nonconformity

Nonconformists are people who don't believe and behave as prescribed by the culture. They are resisted for two principal reasons.[1] First, others in the organization see them as threats to the internal functioning of the organization. As explained in Chapter 2, culture facilitates basic organizational processes. Nonconformists throw a monkey wrench into the smooth functioning of these processes. They also call into question accepted ways of perceiving, thinking, and behaving, which is upsetting to others.[2]

Nonconformists are seen as a threat to the organization's external function as well. There is concern on the one hand about whether "proven" ways that have worked well in the past should be given up for untried and untested alternatives and concern on the other hand that new ideas and methods, if they do work, will change the prevailing world view and the established ways of doing things.

Nonconformity is a matter of degree. Depending on the circumstances, more or less may be tolerated by others in the organization. Nonconformity is also a matter of kind. There are different implications, depending on whether one is violating culturally prescribed behavior (cultural norms) or whether one is rejecting cultural beliefs and values (culture) or both.

The conceptual scheme in Figure 4–1 may be called a culture map. It is a useful tool for visualizing and analyzing varying degrees and kinds of cultural nonconformity. The scheme is based on the distinction between culture and behavior and derives from the fact that cultural beliefs, values, and norms are seldom completely shared—that is, not everyone believes and behaves as prescribed by the culture. The scheme can be viewed from either the individual's or the organization's perspective, and the following questions are asked. First, to what extent does the individual behave as prescribed by the culture (comply with the cultural norms)? The answer could range from *completely*, which indicates behavior con-

Figure 4–1
Culture Map: Culture Caricatures for Studying Cultural Nonconformity

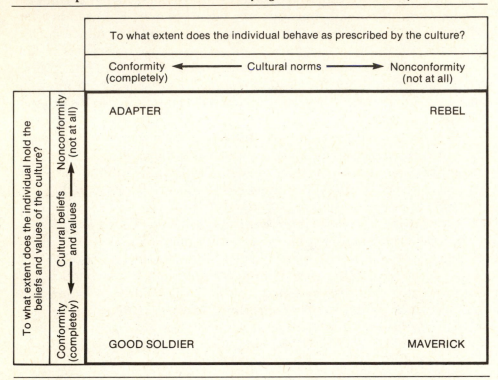

formity) to *not at all* (behavior nonconformity). Second, to what extent does the individual hold the beliefs and values of the culture (has internalized them)? The answer could similarly vary from *completely* (culture conformity) to *not at all* (culture nonconformity). The answers to these two questions place an individual somewhere on the culture map shown in Figure 4–1. The four corners of the map are labeled *good soldier, adapter, maverick,* and *rebel*. These culture caricatures are intended to be memory and discussion aids for use in analysis; one should not fall into the trap of stererotyping flesh-and-blood people with these terms.

Understanding the Nature of the Individual's Involvement in the Organization

An organization and an individual can accept each other and arrive at a workable accommodation. To do so, each side makes both tangible and intangible contributions and receives sufficient financial and nonfinancial incentives in return, which make it worthwhile for each side to continue to engage the other. These conditions provide a viable contract, not just in formal terms, but in social and psychological terms as well.[3] Such an accommodation can be reached in any location of the culture map (Figure 4–1), and this will now be illustrated for the culture caricature

Figure 4–2
Culture Caricatures: Understanding the Nature of an Individual's Involvement in the Organization

Individual's Location in the Culture Map (Figure 4–1)	Possible Reasons Others in the Organization Accept the Individual	Possible Reasons the Individual Remains in the Organization
Good Soldier	Others value individual's excellent fit with the culture.	Individual values his or her excellent fit with the culture.
Adapter	Individual is willing and able to do what he or she is told to do.	Individual works to make a living.
	Individual will go along with the others and conform to the cultural norms.	Individual values other organizational benefits.
Maverick	Individual violates cultural norms but contributes valued results.	Individual buys into the cultural values.
	Individual's norm violation is accepted because of past accomplishments or potential future contributions.	Individual values other organizational benefits, perhaps including the fact that he or she is allowed to do things differently or that he or she can get away with them.
Rebel	Individual is a complete nonconformist but is tolerated because of his or her critical contributions.	Individual cannot leave the organization because he or she is unable to contribute elsewhere (lack of comparable opportunities).
	Individual is tolerated because of his or her formal position in the organization.	Individual is a reformer—he or she wants to transform the organization to fit an ideal.

locations (see Figure 4–2). This discussion is not meant to be exhaustive. Some of the reasons a workable accommodation is possible in one location may also apply in the case of another.

One of the reasons individuals located in the *good soldier* position are accepted by others in the organization is because of their excellent fit with the culture. They both believe and behave as prescribed by the culture. The intrinsic value of having this ideal fit may be one of the reasons they stay in the organization.

One of the reasons individuals in the *adapter* location are accepted is because of their flexibility—the ability and willingness to go along with the cultural norms and do what one is told to do. A person in this location may be working simply to make a living and may have little concern about his or her belief and value misfit with the organization. The employee values the benefits (such as status and perks) that come with remaining in the organization.

Those in the *maverick* location may be accepted by others in the organization if they contribute results that are culturally valued. A maverick's violation of cultural norms may also be accepted because the person is seen as having earned this right based on past accomplishments or because the employee is perceived as capable of delivering valued results if allowed to deviate from the norms. A person may remain in the organization as a maverick because he or she cherishes the cultural values. The person's quarrel is with the current organizational practices that are seen as dysfunctional or inconsistent with the underlying values, and the maverick is willing and able to violate the norms to deliver culturally valued results. A maverick may stay because of other valued organizational benefits, including perhaps the recognition that comes from being allowed to do things differently or the satisfaction of doing what is right despite the odds.

Rebels are considered outsiders by others in the organization because they neither believe nor behave as prescribed by the culture. An individual in this position is tolerated if he or she delivers results that are vital to the organization, especially if these critical contributions cannot be obtained from others in the organization. A rebel may also be tolerated because others in the organization have no choice in the matter—formal, social, or political position may give the rebel enough clout to stay. An example would be a manager who is assigned to turn around a division and decides a fundamental transformation is needed, requiring changes in cultural beliefs, values, and norms. A manager may also remain in a rebel position without the agenda of a "reformer" because he or she lacks opportunities to make a contribution elsewhere. The manager may be stuck with the organization and vice versa.

Bob Drake was a cultural rebel. He didn't survive because although his potential contributions were needed, they were not seen as critical by the organization, nor did he have sufficient clout to flaunt the cultural beliefs, values, and norms. Bob was not trying to be a reformer, but what if he had been? Or what if Bob had wanted to make it in the organization despite the major misfit? What could Bob have done differently?

There are at least two choices, and each has its own difficulties. First, he could have tried to be more flexible by conforming to more cultural norms to become more of an adapter, or bending some of his personal beliefs and values to become more of a maverick, or doing some of both.[4] Although Bob might have found such conformity or personal metamorphosis painful, such a change might have permitted him to survive in the organization, make valued contributions, and later earn the right to become more of a nonconformist. Second, Bob might have concluded that the misfit was so great that it was irreconcilable and decided to leave sooner. Other options will be discussed later.

Bob's case is not unusual. The basic dilemma is commonly encountered because some degree of misfit is inevitable. Chapter 7 will provide some ideas and approaches for thinking about and resolving this dilemma.

Four Ways to Use the Culture Map

There are four interrelated ways in which the conceptual scheme in Figure 4–1 can be used:

1. To Better Understand One's Place in a Culture   Since a new manager's position in the culture has important implications for his or her survival and ability to contribute in the organization, the culture map can be used to think about such questions as:

- Where am I located on the map? Why?
- What are the implications for my survival and contribution in the organization? What is the nature of my involvement in this organization?
- If the current location is untenable, what are my alternatives?
- Where do I want to be on this map in the future?

2. To Determine the Positions of Other Organization Members on the Culture Map   Think about the distribution of others in the organization relative to the culture caricatures. For example, an organization with no mavericks or rebels is qualitatively different from one that accepts such nonconformity. In general, the greater the crowding of people near the good soldier corner, the more conformist is the organizational culture.

3. To Better Understand an Organization's Cultural Norms and Values   In trying to place oneself and others on the culture map, one is forced to think more consciously about its two dimensions—culture (beliefs/values) and norms. Used in this way, the map is a tool that consultants and others interested in organizational assessment can use for deciphering a culture and its norms.

4. To Think about What Kind of Culture One Wants to Have   Both organizational leaders and members can use the culture map to reflect on the kind of culture they desire. An organizational leader can place himself or herself at the good soldier location and ask: What are the beliefs, values, and norms I am trying to instill in this organization? How many people have bought into these beliefs and values? How many of them are complying with the norms? What should the distribution of people on the culture map look like?

An organizational member can ask: Is this the kind of culture I want to work in? Why? What can I do to change the distribution?

Other Individual-Organizational Fits

There are important implications to be derived from a better understanding of one's fit with a culture, but this is not the only kind of fit that a manager must think about in relation to his or her organization. As illustrated for Bob Drake, other dimensions are important as well. In order to be effective, a manager must also understand the individual and organizational dynamics that influence performance and satisfaction. For these reasons, a manager must be able to assess all the individual and organizational characteristics in Models A and B in Chapter 3 (Figures 3–2 and 3–4). Ideas and approaches for making this assessment are now presented. The importance of understanding oneself is taken up first. Questions for assessing one's organization are considered later.

Learning about Oneself

Bob Drake thought he understood himself well and was clear about what he wanted when he accepted the company's offer. However, he later concluded he was wrong about this.[5] He believed he had failed to anticipate his multiple misfits with the company and had ignored several early warning signs during the recruiting. Bob was also convinced he had been seduced by the company's extremely high salary offer and the tempting promise of line management, which he felt they had not kept. He also concluded that he had seduced himself by not thinking more clearly about what he really wanted in the job. The money and the opportunity had blinded him to other important personal values—professionalism and team play, for instance—that he had taken for granted. He considered these values much more carefully in his next job, where he has been very successful.

People often don't know their own beliefs and values as well as they think. The reason is rooted in the very nature of personal beliefs and values, which we will now try to better understand. This is also essential for a better understanding of culture, since beliefs and values are its principal elements. Following this discussion, two basic methods for gaining insight into one's beliefs and values will be presented: (1) questionnaires and tests and (2) self-examination using personal experience. A manager can use these concepts and techniques for better self-insight and better understanding of co-workers.

Individual characteristics other than beliefs and values (Model B, Figure 3–4) must also be assessed, and these will be considered in this discussion. However, a full treatment of self-assessment is beyond the scope of this book. The subject is worthy of a separate book, and at least one good source is available.[6]

Nature of Personal Beliefs and Values

By the time a person reaches adulthood he or she has come to accept numerous beliefs about what is true or not true about the physical and social world. The following classification scheme is useful for better understanding the nature of these personal beliefs:[7]

Sensory beliefs rest on faith in the credibility of one's own sensory experience. They are based on personal encounter with the object of the belief, experiences that may or may not be shared by others. At one extreme some of these beliefs are supported by unanimous agreement of others, such as, "I believe this is an annual report," and "I believe its cover is white." Such beliefs are so taken for granted that they are rarely, if ever, a subject for discussion or controversy. At the other extreme are sensory beliefs that may not be supported by anyone else; these are phobias, hallucinations, and various ego-enhancing and ego-deflating beliefs arising from intense personal experience. They take the general form: "I believe, but no one else could know, so it doesn't matter what others believe."

Authority beliefs, unlike sensory beliefs, rest on the authority of others one trusts. They do not have the same taken-for-granted quality as sensory beliefs because they rest not on what one personally experiences, but on what one is told by others. Many facets of physical and social reality have alternative interpretations or cannot be easily verified or experienced. To determine their own beliefs in these cases, persons rely on others they identify with and trust—for instance, "I believe the figures in the annual report are accurate."

Derived beliefs are based on other beliefs one holds. When dismantled by analysis, such beliefs are found to rest ultimately on one or more sensory or authority beliefs. "I believe smoking causes cancer" may be derived from one or more of the following types of belief chains:

1. The surgeon general says smoking causes cancer (sensory belief), and I believe the surgeon general is a trustworthy expert (authority belief); hence I believe smoking causes cancer (derived belief).
2. My aunt contracted cancer (authority belief); she had smoked for years (sensory belief); hence smoking causes cancer (derived belief).

Belief System This discussion illustrates that one's beliefs are not held independently. Some beliefs depend upon certain others, resulting in a more or less interconnected, organized collection of beliefs referred to as one's belief system. The more beliefs one has that rest on a particular belief, the more central that particular belief is in the belief system. The most central beliefs are most interconnected with other beliefs and consequently are most resistant to change. Conversely, if one central belief changes, this results in wider repercussions through the rest of the belief system than if a peripheral belief changes. Relating the classification of beliefs to this conceptualization, sensory and authority beliefs are more central than are derived beliefs, and the sensory beliefs at the heart of one's belief system are the most central of all.[8]

Belief systems may be described as more or less *linked* through various interconnections within the system of beliefs. Tightly linked belief systems are more resistant to change than are loosely linked systems. Individuals with personalities described as rigid have a more tightly linked belief system.

Beliefs can be interconnected without being strictly logical or rational. Faulty reasoning, flawed premises, or the personal need to enhance one's self-image may be responsible for some irrational interconnections to the extent necessary in defense of one's self-image and ego.[9] It is possible for a person simultaneously to hold two beliefs that are inconsistent or even contradictory. Pointing out such inconsistencies and contradictions may not produce a change in the individual's beliefs, depending on how important it is to the person to defend and maintain any irrational discrepancies. Indeed, such an attempt to change beliefs could trigger a process of rationalization and self-justification that might make the individual hold on to old beliefs more rigidly.[10]

How Beliefs Change   Beliefs ultimately rest on whom one trusts and faith in one's own personal experience. Beliefs do not change until one of these underlying factors has changed. Even then a change in beliefs and the extent to which it occurs depends on the individual's cognitive equipment and personality needs.

Values   Values also ultimately rest on one's direct personal experience or on the authority of others one trusts. Values represent what the individual believes is good, preferable, or desirable and thus constitute a special class of beliefs, called evaluative beliefs, representing a preference for certain end states (equality, self-fulfillment, or freedom) or certain modes of conduct (courage, honesty, friendship). Values are strongly shaped by those who have a particularly important influence on one's development from early childhood, beginning with family and school and continuing with teachers, friends, and others with whom one identifies.[11]

Values occupy a central place in one's belief system. They also determine one's attitudes or likes and dislikes about specific objects or ideas. Many different personal attitudes depend on far fewer personal values. Values also provide an individual with standards or criteria for taking action, for justifying one's own and others' actions, and for comparing self with others.[12] Because of their central importance, an understanding of one's values contributes significantly to an understanding of oneself.

Value System   An individual is often in a situation that brings certain values into conflict. For instance, the person may have to choose between behaving truthfully or compassionately. Over time, a person develops a set of rules that becomes his or her value system for making such choices as these. An important aspect of one's value system is the *ordering* of one's values according to relative importance.[13]

One's value system may not be entirely consistent from a strictly logical or rational standpoint, any more than beliefs are. Value inconsistencies may remain unresolved, without the individual's being aware of them, until a choice has to be made that brings out the inconsistencies. If it causes more pain and anxiety to recognize an inconsistency than the person is able or willing to endure, the inconsistency may be resolved by repressing it.[14]

Obstacles to Value Change   People are typically stubborn or intolerant when their values are challenged. Values occupy too central a position in one's belief system and are too important an aspect of one's personality to permit them to be readily changed. Attempts that others make to directly confront and change a person's values are rarely effective and are likely to provoke emotional reactions or hostility. The tendency to accept one's own values as right and to reject those that conflict with them as wrong leads to stereotyping people with very different values are misinformed or ignorant at best and stupid or evil at worst.

What can be done about this? Understanding the nature and importance of personal values and why they hold a central place in one's own and other's lives is an important first step. Becoming more consciously aware of one's own values and value system is the next step, to which we now turn.

Gaining Self-Insight

Self-Insight from Tests and Exercises   The relative *ordering* of values is what distinguishes one person's value system from another's. Two people may hold many of the same values, but when these values come into conflict, the individuals may prioritize them very differently. Bob Drake and his peers believed internal competition and cooperation were important for the effective functioning of a work group. However, Drake's peers considered internal competition far more important, and for Drake cooperation was much more important. Drake and his peers had very different value systems.

Several tests are available to rank a set of values and determine their relative importance to the individual. These tests differ in the choice of the particular set of values to be ranked.[15] One widely used test is based on a classification scheme developed by the German philosopher Eduard Spranger for the purpose of distinguishing between different individuals. Spranger's categories classify six ideal types, summarized as follows:[16]

1. The *theoretical* person is primarily interested in the discovery of truth and the systematic ordering of knowledge. The person's interests are empirical, critical, and rational. Scientists or philosophers are often of this type (but not exclusively so).
2. The *economic* person is primarily oriented toward what is useful. He or she is interested in the practical affairs of the business world; in the production, marketing, and consumption of goods; in the use of economic resources; and in the accumulation of tangible wealth.
3. The *aesthetic* person finds chief interest in the artistic aspects of life, without necessarily being a creative artist. The person values form and harmony and views experience in terms of grace and symmetry.

4. The essential value for the *social* person is love of people—the altruistic or philanthropic aspect of love. People are valued as ends, and the person tends to be kind, sympathetic, unselfish.
5. The *political* person is characteristically oriented toward power, not necessarily in politics, but in whatever area he or she functions.
6. The *religious* person seeks to relate to the universe in a meaningful way and has a mystical orientation.

Self-reported tests, including those used to assess personal values using such categories as these, have their limitations.[17] They should not be expected to yield definitive answers. Rather, they provide an opportunity for self-reflection and should be viewed as sensitizing aids in the quest for self-insight. Relating to the personal characteristics in Model B, Figure 3–4, tests are available for such other aspects of one's personality as needs, motives, and perdispositions, as well as for such aspects of ability as talents, skills, and competencies.[18]

Vocational counseling and assessment centers may also be consulted for additional insight into personality and personal ability. Vocational counseling provides systematic testing on a wide range of individual characteristics and the opportunity to analyze and interpret the results with professional staff assistance. Help is also available from psychologists specializing in vocational therapy and career development. Assessment centers, which are more focused and more comprehensive in their approach, offer an assessment of three basic dimensions: individual-job fit, individual potential, and individual development needs. Experienced assessors use a wide variety of exercises to arrive at their conclusions: in-basket exercises, management games, role-playing simulations, leaderless group discussions, and oral and written presentations. The use of multiple sources of information by multiple assessors who are professionally trained builds a person's confidence in the validity of the results, but these approaches do have limitations.[19]

Unlike personality and personal ability, an individual's personal agenda (personal plans for what the individual wants to accomplish in the organization in the short term and the long term) may vary depending on the organization and the job under consideration. The explicitness of personal agendas varies from person to person, and many individuals seem unable to discover their own agendas without the help of others. A small group technique stimulates such discovery.[20] Each person in the group writes down what he or she believes is a personal agenda. Next, each one is probed and queried by others in the group to better understand the individual's written agenda. This cross-examination can lead to a much better understanding of one's personal agenda because it forces one to make explicit what may have been implicit and subconscious.

Self-Insight from Personal Experience   Experience is a great teacher if one is willing to learn from it. Unfortunately, the human tendency to engage in self-justification and rationalization may make this learning difficult by thwarting accurate personal feedback and encouraging the individual to see things as he or she would prefer to see them rather than in perspective. For instance, when the going is bad, one tends to take comfort by rationalizing poor outcomes and attributing them to causes other than oneself. Consider the following case.

One new manager, Jerry Rowland, did a poor job of anticipating and entering a rather hostile culture, as he called it, and was fired three months after joining. He did not reflect on what really happened; nor did he learn from the experience. There were in fact several red flags Jerry hadn't attended to during recruitment and entry, but Jerry proceeded to convince himself and persuade others that the company he had joined was crazy: "Boy, you should have seen those guys—they were really weird." Jerry didn't learn much from his experience because he took no personal responsibility for his actions. He failed in two subsequent jobs but continued to look outward, and never inward, for his answers.

In contrast, Bob Drake took some personal responsibility for his failure and learned that his values were ordered differently than he had thought. Money and line management opportunity were less important; a cooperative and professional working environment were more important to him than he had realized. Bob's insight led him to take some steps to remedy his situation. He sold his high-priced home and moved into a more modestly priced one to reduce his dependence on his high income, and he looked for a company with which he would have a much better fit. He has done very well both for the new company and for himself.

People can also fail to learn from experience when things are going extremely well because they tend to take personal credit for positive outcomes. For example, the top management of one large, highly profitable company became afflicted over the years with the "golden touch" syndrome ("We can't go wrong. Anything we touch turns to gold"). They explained their enviable financial record largely in terms of the top-notch management talent they had, discounting the perhaps more important near-monopoly position their major product lines had enjoyed because of patent protection. These product lines had been developed by the *prior* management generation, who had since departed. When competition that had been waiting in the wings finally came, the company's fortunes plummetted. The "golden generation" *was* highly talented, but these managers had not been tested as a team and been proven effective. The golden position they had inherited had lulled them into complacency and self-indulgence.

In sharp contrast the managers of another company that enjoyed the same kind of market dominance and financial success were much more self-critical. When people inside and outside the company complimented them strenuously on their spectacular success, these managers tended to acknowledge they had a good team that worked hard but would include caveats: "Don't kid yourself, though. We are fortunate to have products and resources that our competition hasn't got. And we make our share of mistakes too, but we try to learn from them." Depending on the audience, one or more revealing war stories would follow to make the point that they were fallible and had to keep learning. These managers continued to stay on top, and the company has remained an industry leader.

The individual's *locus of control* is one aspect of personality that may account for some of these judgment errors.[21] Those who have an external locus of control believe they have very little control over what happens and view themselves as *pawns* on the chessboard of life, pushed around largely by the force of circumstance. In contrast, those referred to as *origins* have an internal locus of control and tend to view themselves as much more in command of their own destiny. Jerry Rowland, the manager who failed to learn from his mistakes, was a pawn. Pawns are less inclined to take undue personal credit when the going is good, but they are also less inclined to take personal responsibility for their difficulties. Thus pawns are more likely to commit an error when the going is not so good. In contrast, origins are more likely to err when the going is good. Bob Drake and the managers in the other two cases were origins.

What can be done to overcome these tendencies? First, one must recognize that they exist. Second, one should assess one's own tendency to be like a pawn or an origin, susceptible to one type of error or the other. When things are going well and one is congratulating oneself on results, the question to ask is: "What did I *really* contribute here?" When the going is not so good, one should ask, "To what extent am *I* a part of the problem?" Keeping oneself honest in this way helps maintain a frame of mind that increases one's chances of gaining insight from experience.

Much can also be learned from some disciplined reflection on past experience by thinking about such questions as these:

- In what previous jobs and working conditions have I been most productive? Happy?
- What are the three or four previous occasions when things really didn't go as well as I had expected? What did I learn from these events and from other critical incidents when I felt acute disappointment[22] or surprise?
- How have I responded to authority figures in the past?
- What kinds of people do I most like to work with? Least like to work with? Why?

The list can go on, but the point is that one's own experience contains a wealth of relevant information that can be activated to good use if one is prepared to engage it by discounting one's tendency to rationalize and self-justify.

Learning about One's Organization

Choosing one's organization wisely and effectively anticipating one's entry into it also requires insight into the organization. This section will cover questions that provoke constructive forethought about organizational realities one should be aware of before accepting an offer to join a new organization and in planning entry into it.

One should focus on important aspects of the organizational reality to be encountered and their impact on oneself. Models A and B in Figure 3–1 are a convenient summary of these factors, and can be used as a framework for analyzing organizations. What follows is *not* a comprehensive discussion of how relevant information on each of these factors may be obtained. Rather, these are questions to provoke constructive forethought about organizational culture and other realities and to focus on particular areas that are not readily revealed. These are important questions to think about and may be used as a checklist in the following ways:

- As a tickler list for periodic use to keep track of what one has learned, and what remains to be understood.
- As a device for sensitizing oneself to important questions in preparation for an upcoming visit to the prospective organization and/or interviews with its representatives.
- As a review mechanism after interviewing to think about what information one couldn't or didn't get and why.
- As a check on oneself, by asking whether one is subconsciously not exploring certain topics or questions because one doesn't *want* the information. Reasons might be fear of appearing pushy or premature or fear that the information will be unfavorable and therefore difficult to deal with.

These questions are not intended for use during the actual interviewing. Their use could cramp the applicant's style and become dysfunctional.

The list to be presented may seem too long, but insight comes from probing the same phenomenon in different ways rather than by looking for a correct answer with a few quick questions. For convenient reference, a list of the questions alone is repeated in Appendix 4–1 at the end of this chapter. The term *organization* in the following discussion refers to the corporation as a whole, a work unit, or any other relevant organizational unit. The questions to think about that are marked with an asterisk (*) are adapted from the work of Harry Levinson (see recommended supplementary reading Number 5).[23]

Important Questions to Think about (Organized by the Major Variables in Models A and B, Figure 3−1)

Organization's Employees

1. *How did the organization get to be the way it is?** This question gets at the history of the organization and the important forces that shaped it. Understanding the critical turning points in its development provides important insight into the current organization and its employees.

2. *What are the people here like to work with? Why?** An aspect of individuals in an organization that is important to consider is what they are like as human beings. The question probes for a general understanding of the personalities of the people in the organization.

Systems

3. *What are the spotlight measures of performance and the spotlight rewards and punishments?* Performance *visibility* and *visibility* of rewards and punishment are two particularly important aspects of the systems used to monitor and control organizational performance. The question attempts to tap these measurements and control dimensions by spotlighting the performance measures most keenly watched and the rewards commanding the greatest attention within the organization.[24]

4. *What is done to help a person along once he or she starts work in this organization?** The question seeks to understand the formal and informal systems used in the socialization, training, and development of newcomers. The coping mechanisms and the style of supervision may also be indicated. The *personal* experiences of someone in the organization, if they can be elicited, may reveal the feelings aroused during one's initial period of disorientation, strangeness, and helplessness in the organization.

5. *What does it take to do well in the organization? How are good people recognized?* This question attempts to understand what kind of person gets ahead in the organization and how this person is noticed by those higher up. In addition to the kind of performance that is important, the question may reveal particular background or personality characteristics that the organization considers desirable.[25] Is it a fast-track organization for MBAs? For engineers? For marketing people?

6. *How does one find out how one is performing in this organization?** The attempt here is to understand the performance and other feedback mechanisms used within the organization. The question also reveals the quality of superior-subordinate and peer relationships. Healthy relationships would be characterized by open and helpful feedback.

7. *What are the ways one finds out what is really going on in the organization?** The question probes for an understanding of how people communicate with one another in the organization and reveals the extent to which people trust each other. Heavy reliance on rumor indicates a gen-

erally low level of mutual trust. Conversely, if people are well informed and knowledgeable about what's going on in the organization, a higher level of trust is indicated.

8. *How does the organization make use of a person's experience and ideas?** The answer reveals the degree to which individuals participate in organizational decision making and the extent to which the individual's wisdom and creativity are respected.

9. *If the organization had to stop doing some of the things it now does, what would not be changed?** The question reveals the most critical organizational activities and functions. Those who make an important, hard-to-substitute contribution to the effective performance of these activities and functions are likely to be quite powerful within the organization. Deciphering the organization's power structure is tricky business because power is often exercised most effectively when its presence is not revealed.[26] Information on the power structure of an organization is therefore considered extremely sensitive and is difficult to get by questioning organizational members directly, particularly when outsiders or newcomers ask the questions. Such indirect questions as this one and the next three may help in unraveling the organization's power structure.

10. *Which outside groups does the organization pay attention to? Why? How?** Answers to the first two parts of the question reveal the extent and nature of the organization's various dependencies. These groups have significant actual or potential influence on the organization. Understanding how the organization manages these dependencies provides insight into the critical workings within the organization. Individuals or groups who play an important part in helping the organization manage its external dependencies are likely to be powerful within the organization, particularly if they cannot be easily replaced.[27]

11. *What must the organization do particularly well in order to succeed?* This question elicits an understanding of other critical organizational workings. Again, the individuals and groups performing these vital tasks are likely to be powerful inside the organization.

12. *How does one go about selling a new idea in this organization? Who are the key individuals and groups one has to persuade?* The attempt here is to understand how responsive the organization is to new ideas and to identify powerful individuals and important political camps.

13. *What are the important strategies and tactics for getting things done in the organization?* The question probes for an understanding of the informal workings of the organization, as well as the political games that facilitate or hinder one's ability to get things done within the organization.

Culture

The process of deciphering culture, including three general types of questions that may be explored to facilitate this, were covered in Chapter 1. Two additional points are made here. First, the typology of four ideologies or cultures developed by Roger Harrison and further elaborated by Charles Handy (see recommended supplementary readings number 1 and 2 at the back of the book) may be used to help decipher culture. Harrison defines these ideological types as follows:

a. *Power orientation*—the desire to dominate the environment and van-quish all opposition, organizational life being principally governed by the use of power and politics.
b. *Role orientation*—the desire to be as rational and orderly as possible, organizational life being governed principally by considerations of rights, privileges, legality and legitimacy.
c. *Task orientation*—the desire to get the job done and achieve results, organizational life being dictated mainly by what would facilitate task accomplishment.
d. *Person orientation*—the desire to serve the needs of the organization's members, organizational life being principally guided by consider-ations of what would best satisfy the members' needs.

Viewing these as four cultural types, Handy has associated each with a picture and has given each the name of a Greek god as a memory aid (see Figure 4–3). He has also attempted to categorize certain industries according to the typology and has tried to show what it is about these industries that leads them toward the type of culture indicated.

As Harrison and Handy have cautioned, this typology, like any other, is in danger of becoming an oversimplification if users try to pigeonhole actual organizations into one of the ideal types. The typology should be viewed as portraying general tendencies deriving from the influence of industry context on culture and, in this sense, may provide helpful ideas and clues for deciphering culture. The following specific questions may also be useful to think about in this connection.

14. What are the most important tacit assumptions that members of the orga-nization share about work, human nature, and human relationships? The at-tempt here is to understand the organization's most basic assumptions about the nature of truth and reality and about human nature (see Figure 2 in Reading 1–1).[28] An understanding of these basic premises helps reveal the important assumptions shared by people in the organiza-tion.

15. What does the organization stand for? What is its motto? The question seeks to get at the organization's highest value. The answer may also reveal the organization's ideology.

16. What does it take to be highly successful in this organization? What kind of person is most respected? What is considered heroic? These questions pro-vide an operational statement of what is most valued in the organization. If several members of the organization point to the same basic value, this may be one of the highest values in the organization.

Figure 4–3
Gods of Management*

God	Zeus	Apollo	Althena	Dionysus
Picture				
Culture	Club	Role	Task	Existential
Roger Harrison's terminology (HBR, 1972)†	Power	Role	Task	Person
Illustrative industries and types of firms	• Small • Entrepreneurial firms • Investment banks • Brokerage houses • Political groupings • Start-up situations	• Bureaucratic organizations • Insurance companies • Commercial banks	• Consulting firms • High technology firms	• Professional groups (doctors, lawyers, etc.) • Universities • Research and development departments

* Adapted from Charles Handy, *Gods of Management* (London: Souvenir Press, 1978).
† Roger Harrison, "Understanding Your Organization's Character," *Harvard Business Review*, May–June 1972, pp. 25–43.

17. What is viewed as serious punishment in this organization? What kinds of mistakes are not forgiven? This is the other side of the coin revealed by the previous question. It gets at values that are counterculture.

18. What company folklore, rituals, symbols, and ceremonies best reveal the essential character of the organization? This is an attempt to understand the important shared assumptions by examining the various cultural communications[29] and justifications—the second level of culture described in Chapter 1.

*19. Make believe this organization is a person. How would you describe this person?** This is another way to tap into the culture of the organization, by using the "character" metaphor. A pooling of the responses of several organizational members to this question may also reveal the organization's identity.

*20. What are the main rules that everyone has to follow in this organization?** The question is intended to tap organizational dos and don'ts (the organizational norms) in such areas as dress, lifestyle, areas to live in, places to be seen, whom to associate with, whom not to criticize in public, hours of work, what to say and do, how to deal with others.

Leadership

21.   *Who are the three or four key people in the leadership of the organization? How did they get to the top?* The answers should reveal the backgrounds and accomplishments of the key figures in the organizational leadership and perhaps their personalities, personal values, and personal agendas.

Organizational Effectiveness and Satisfaction

22.   *What is the one thing the organization doesn't do as well as it should?* By focusing attention on *one* important area, the general level of organizational effectiveness and satisfaction may first be grasped. The follow-up questions about other things the organization doesn't do as well as it should would indicate how effective the organization is and how satisfied the employees are.

23.   *Where is this organization headed?* The attempt here is to get some assessment of the likely long-term outcomes. Combined with the previous question, this should also give some clue about the extent to which short-term considerations affect the long-term outlook in terms of both organizational effectiveness and satisfaction.

24.   *What is the employee turnover in the organization relative to other comparable organizations?* Studies reveal that satisfaction is strongly linked to employee turnover.[30] Thus an examination of employee turnover, particularly in relation to other comparable organizations, is a good indicator of the level of organizational satisfaction.

Status of Individual in the Organization

25.   *What is the prospective boss like?* The boss's personality, style, and expectations have an important influence on a person's effectiveness and satisfaction.[31] Research on socialization of newcomers has shown that one's first boss in an organization has an especially strong impact, not only on short-term results, but on one's long-term effectiveness and satisfaction.[32] A prospective boss in the organization one contemplates joining and one's first job there thus merit special attention.

26.   *On which key groups or individuals, in addition to one's prospective boss, would one be most dependent to get the job done successfully?* These individuals could be prospective subordinates, peers, or any other group or individual. Managing these dependencies, which require the development of power and influence, is crucial to effective job performance.[33] One must know who they are, what their power bases and motivations are, and how and why the newcomer's effective performance will be critically dependent on their cooperation and assistance.

27.   *What are the biggest hurdles that have to be overcome to do the job well?* These hurdles could be technical, logistical, interpersonal, or political ("Who are the likely adversaries or saboteurs?"). The assessment here could consider *what* it will take and *how long* to overcome these hurdles

relative to the atmosphere of urgency and timing that one will have to deal with on the job.

28. *What important sources of support are potentially available for getting the job done?* Here the attempt is to understand the technical, logistical, interpersonal, and political factors that are potentially available to facilitate one's ability to get the job done. The assessment ("Who are the likely supporters and allies?") should cover what these sources are and how long it will take to tap them, relative to the atmosphere of urgency and timing on the job.

29. *Is there a possibility of becoming stereotyped in the organization? What is the status and progression of those who are similarly stereotyped?* The attempt here is to examine whether or not one's particular background characteristics (age, sex, ethnic heritage, educational background) are likely to lead to stereotyping.[34] If so, what will be the impact on one's status and ability to get things done? Some knowledge of the status and effectiveness of others with similar backgrounds who are already in the organization can provide valuable clues about what a newcomer may encounter in the organization.

One should be careful not to jump to conclusions on the basis of simple comparisons, particularly with only one or two other individuals. One's status, effectiveness, and progress in an organization are influenced by many factors; explaining these outcomes in terms of stereotyping alone could become a self-fulfilling prophecy.[35] On the other hand, stereotyping is often encountered, and its consequences may be significant. Pretending or hoping it doesn't exist is dangerous too. Balanced assessment requires astute observation and careful, objective reasoning from evidence.

30. *What are the prospects for the newcomer's acceptance into the culture?* Even when the individual is joining as a well-known expert or a senior manager, acceptance into the culture will take time. Fellow employees will judge a newcomer on the basis of *consistency* of words and actions. Initial perceptions are important, but people will not be fully convinced until the newcomer passes various tests. Only then may acceptance take place, as discussed more fully in Chapter 8.

Organization's Agenda for the Individual

It may prove difficult to decipher the organization's agenda for the individual. In addition to the organization's consciously held, explicitly communicated assumptions and expectations, one must probe for others that are not being communicated or negotiated. Subconscious expectations may not surface until they are violated, and this may be too late. The following questions may help discover the organization's agenda.

31. *Why does the organization want to hire the individual? What does it value about the individual?* This line of thinking is directed at the question of what it is that makes the recruit particularly attractive to the organiza-

tion—background, personality, training, talent, skills, and so on. Of greatest interest are assumptions and expectations that the organization will not or cannot communicate or negotiate.

32.   Where are the individuals now who previously held the job for which the individual is being recruited? Why did they move on? If there is a consistent pattern of movement of people who held the prospective job or similar jobs, this may give a clue to the organization's agenda for the individual. For example, if there is a consistent record of involuntary turnover in the prospective job or in similar positions, it is important to understand why these people didn't work out. Why were they considered recruiting mistakes? Why were these failures not anticipated during subsequent recruiting?

Other organizational agendas may be revealed by this kind of probing. The *bait-and-switch* technique lures the person into a position he or she finds attractive then switches him or her to a job more favorable for the organization. *Bait-and-keep* gets the individual into a job that is not very attractive by promising a switch to another job later on then attempts to keep the individual there by various means (for example, using salary raises or stock options as "golden handcuffs"). *Bait-and-eat* grasps the person the organization desperately needs, knowing he or she may not stay long but will contribute something badly needed.

Attempting to make sense of how others progressed who started out in a capacity similar to the potential recruit's can also reveal the organization's view of the prospective job and how easy or difficult it is to change jobs or functional areas within the organization.

We turn next to the realities of the recruiting process. What one would *like* to know and what one *can* know are two separate questions. The purpose of the following chapter is to point out certain subtle dangers that plague the recruitment process and to outline some strategies for overcoming them.

Appendix 4–1 / Organizational Assessment: A Summary of Important Questions to Think About

Organization's Employees
1.   How did the organization get to be the way it is?*
2.   What are the people here like to work with? Why?*

Systems
3.   What are the spotlight measures of performance and the spotlight rewards and punishments?

---

* These questions are adapted from Harry Levinson, *Organizational Diagnosis* (Cambridge, Mass.: Harvard University Press, 1972), Appendix A, pp. 519–38.

4. What is done to help a person along once he or she starts work in this organization?*
5. What does it take to do well in the organization? How are good people recognized?
6. How does one find out how one is performing in this organization?*
7. What are the ways one finds out what is really going on in the organization?*
8. How does the organization make use of a person's experience and ideas?*
9. If the organization had to stop doing some of the things it now does, what would not be changed?*
10. Which outside groups does the organization pay attention to?* Why? How?
11. What must the organization do particularly well in order to succeed?
12. How does one go about selling a new idea in this organization? Who are the key individuals and groups one has to persuade?
13. What are the important strategies and tactics for getting things done in the organization?

Culture
14. What are the most important tacit assumptions that members of the organization share about work, human nature, and human relationships?
15. What does the organization stand for? What is its motto?
16. What does it take to be highly successful in this organization? What kind of person is most respected? What is considered heroic?
17. What is considered serious punishment in this organization? What kinds of mistakes are not forgiven?
18. What company folklore, rituals, symbols, and ceremonies best reveal the essential character of the organization?
19. Make believe this organization is a person. How would you describe this person?*
20. What are the main rules that everyone has to follow in this organization?*

Leadership
21. Who are the three or four key people in the leadership of the organization? How did they get to the top?

Organizational Effectiveness and Satisfaction
22. What is the one thing the organization doesn't do as well as it should?

23.   Where is this organization headed?
24.   What is the employee turnover in the organization relative to other comparable organizations?

Status of Individual in the Organization
25.   What is the prospective boss like?
26.   On which key groups or individuals, in addition to one's prospective boss, would one be most dependent to get the job done successfully?
27.   What are the biggest hurdles that have to be overcome to do the job well?
28.   What important sources of support are potentially available for getting the job done well?
29.   Is there a possibility of becoming stereotyped in the organization? What is the status of those who are similarly stereotyped?
30.   What are the prospects for the newcomer's acceptance into the culture?

Organization's Agenda for the Individual
31.   Why does the organization want to hire the individual? What does it value about the individual?
32.   Where are the individuals now who previously held the job for which the individual is being recruited? Why did they move on? Is "bait and switch," "bait and keep," or "bait and eat" the organization's agenda?

Chapter 5

Understanding and coping with recruiting realities

Orientation To avoid an irreconcilable misfit with the organization and to increase the chances of becoming effective more quickly after entering it, one needs to better assess oneself and the organization prior to joining. Unfortunately, several difficulties in the recruiting process can undermine this effort.

This chapter will look into the importance of careful interviewing and probing during the actual recruiting. We will see that all one would *like* to know about a company prior to joining must be tempered by what one *can* know, given the realities of recruiting. Several subtle traps that plague the recruiting process will be described. Suggestions for coping with these difficulties and subtle dangers will be made.

Learning about culture and other organizational realities begins with one's initial encounter with the organization, intensifies during one's first few weeks after joining, and continues thereafter. With some forethought, careful probing, and reasoned assessment, however, it is possible to learn a good deal about the organizational reality prior to accepting a company's offer.

Questions to Ask versus Questions to Keep in One's Head

As a guide to making information-gathering plans during recruiting, on should ask: In light of my circumstances and preferences, what questions are absolutely essential to answer before making the decision to join? These key questions become a starting point in the quest for relevant information; other questions can be answered later on, even after starting the new job.

Another important point to consider when collecting information is what data would be relatively easy to get and also valuable to have. Knowing this could help prioritize the questions. In general, it makes sense to get a preliminary reading on the organization by asking some valuable questions on which valid data are readily available before venturing into other important but more sensitive issues.

Questions to Ask Verbally versus Questions to Ask with One's Eyes

Many questions that would be important and relevant to a candidate for a job are directed at matters that company employees cannot discuss openly—questions concerning the organization's agenda, taboos, secrets, personalities, and politics. Further, the difficulty in asking questions verbally is that either the subjects might be considered taboo or the manner of asking them might seem too direct, confronting, oblique, vague, or wordy in the context of the culture. This important trap is less commonly mentioned than the well-known analogous issue of personal grooming, dress, and presentation. One can ameliorate these inherent difficulties by asking many questions *with the eyes*—by reading and observing such details as these:[1]

• Use of space (office location, office space, where people live, etc.)
• Use of time (actual working hours, punctuality, tempo, etc.)
• Use of things (dress, opulent versus Spartan furnishings, symbols, logos, etc.)
• Use of language (often repeated words and phrases, jargon, etc.)
• Use of body language (expressions, gestures that affect the importance of what is said.)

Asking questions with the eyes includes noticing and reflecting on the significance of people, places, and things *not* seen as well as those read about and observed:

• Why were certain people not included on the interview list? (Why were prospective peers not included?)
• Why were certain places not shown (such as one's prospective office location or office space)?
• Why was certain information not revealed? (Turnover was indicated, but actual names of people who left or transferred out were never revealed.)

If one begins by carefully observing and confines the verbal questions to those that are relatively nonthreatening, later verbal questioning can make use of the knowledge gleaned from observation. This approach can be extremely useful in helping the recruit deal with an important dilemma: The significance of the words used by the people in a culture may not become apparent until the culture's language code is broken, but it is hard to decode without some understanding of the culture.

Bob Drake, for instance, realized he had not really understood the underlying significance of several phrases used by company executives recruiting him: "We play to win." "This is a rough place, but a fun place." "You will have to fight here to get your points across." Given his background as a former star college basketball player, Bob thought that *team* play and a winning *team* were being alluded to. Apparently what was being communicated, however, was the importance of *internal individual* competition.

Unfortunately, such clues to an organization's culture may be obvious only in retrospect after entry, when one has gained additional exposure and insight into the culture. Nonetheless, a recruit's chances of unraveling a culture's language code increase if he or she has a preliminary reading on the culture and probes judiciously to try to understand the underlying *meaning* of the words and phrases that people in the culture use.

Bob Drake might have reflected on why no peers had been included on the interview schedule the company had prepared for his visit. He was also aware that turnover at his level had been high. When he asked about this, he was told that "only strong managers survive here, weak ones don't cut it." No names of the "weak ones" were offered. Bob might have tried diplomatically to get the names of one or two of those who couldn't cut it to find out why. A company may be reluctant to divulge such information (especially the names of those who may be critical of the organization), but discovery of such reluctance is itself an important piece of information. There is a real danger that the recruit may get biased information from a malcontent who is no longer in the organization. However, much can be learned from those who have left the organization if one proceeds with an understanding of these difficulties.

Even without being able to contact one of those who had left, Bob Drake might have reflected on why turnover was so high relative to the company's industry and tried to find out what people in the culture meant by "strong" managers versus those who were "weak" and unable to "cut it." He might also have thought about, and *perhaps* asked: "Whom are you playing *against*?" "Why is it a *rough* place?" "What do you mean by having to *fight* to get your point across?"

Having some notion of the culture of the organization and its language may help one to avoid questions that are viewed as counterculture or asking the questions in the wrong way. One must also consider *who* is the best person to question about a particular point—a prospective boss, peers, subordinates, or a knowledgeable outsider (e.g., customer or competitor). A good early understanding, however approximate and incomplete, can be valuable in making such a determination.

In deciding *what* questions to ask, *when* and *how* to ask them, and *whom* to ask, one must think about his or her bargaining position vis-á-vis the organization in general and the interviewer in particular. An applicant in a relatively strong bargaining position may be more comfortable asking sensitive questions than someone in a weaker position would be. People with more interpersonal competence and good interviewing skills may be able to ask questions that others should avoid asking. With these caveats in mind, these four types of questions can be used to probe sensitive areas where one does not seem to be getting satisfactory answers:

1. *Nonsense questions.* These questions evoke an apple-pie-and-motherhood answer. An example is "What is the future here for a person like me?" Nonsense questions are good for filling time and leave the door open for respondents to answer as frankly and specifically as they feel free to do. Being open ended, these questions could also lead into more important areas, depending on the willingness of the respondent to be helpful and the ability of the listener to understand the underlying meaning.

2. *Sensing questions.* These take a position based on one's sense of the situation and invite the respondent either to agree or disagree—for instance, a question that begins, "From my day here, my sense is that. . . ." These questions let the respondent know that the questioner has some opinion on the subject, albeit incomplete and tentative, making a nonsense answer a bit more difficult.

3. *Paradoxing questions.* These are more provocative versions of the sensing questions. Here one dramatizes some knowledge of the situation, inviting the respondent to tone it down to reality: "Everything appears *perfect* around here . . . ," to which the answer might be, "That's great to hear, but let me tell you something. . . ."

4. *"Illegitimizing" questions.* These questions show the greatest confidence in one's knowledge of the situation, making a nonsense answer difficult—for instance, "All companies I know experience some turnover of newcomers for a variety of reasons. How many recent hires have turned over here?" Implicit in this example is the presumption that one aspect of organizational reality is a tendency for newcomers to turn over, which the respondent must either accept or challenge.

The preceding types of questions and the discussion on what, when, how, and whom to ask can be helpful, but one must ultimately trust one's judgment and feelings about what is appropriate.

Subtle Traps

Next to consider are the subtle dangers that arise from *interactions* between the individual and the organization. The organization directly controls some of these dangers, but the individual has primary responsibility for preventing others. Ultimately, it is beneficial to both sides to be aware of these potentially dangerous traps because the probability of individual survival, satisfaction, and task effectiveness depend on realistic recruitment.[2]

Traps under the Organization's Control

Organizational Oversell Since a company is understandably trying to attract the best qualified candidates, there are strong incentives to oversell the organization by accentuating its positive features and deemphasizing the negatives.[3] The "golden future" syndrome is one way of steering the interview, by playing up hoped-for future benefits and downplaying current realities. This overselling can be hyped up to the point that the applicant will seem more valuable to the organization than he or she really is.

Organizational Seduction A more subtle but powerful organizational technique of influencing recruits is seduction.[4] Whereas applicants are generally aware of the games of overselling just mentioned and attempt to discount for them, they are less conscious of organizational seduction, which persuades the individual to accept a position without being informed of negative factors that could have prevented him or her from joining.

For instance, an applicant might join an organization whose cultural values are incompatible with the individual's personal values. This does occur because inconsistent or even contradictory values sometimes go unnoticed. The discrepancies may not come to light until these values come into open conflict. By then the individual who has already signed up with the company may be locked in golden handcuffs. The choice then is among (1) rejecting the organization's values, thereby alienating the individual from the organization, (2) reordering personal values, or (3) repressing the value conflict if it cannot be resolved.

The technique of organizational seduction involves three steps:

1. Make the individual an extremely tempting offer, say 50 percent above the highest offer he or she is considering.
2. Bathe the individual in flattery, with statements like "We look only at the best, and you are the best among the best."
3. Give the individual the appearance of free choice: "We are in no rush. Take as long as you want to make a decision." This is a shrewd step, because volition is essential to the commitment process.[5]

What is so wrong about this process? Can an organization be faulted for wanting a strong candidate or for making a high offer and allowing plenty of time for a decision?

If the flattery represents the facts of the case as honestly perceived by a company's representatives, nothing may be wrong about this process— *except* insofar as important information concerning the organization's real values and agenda for the individual is consciously withheld because such disclosure might cause the individual to refuse the offer. (If the organization did disclose its real intentions and other relevant information, the three steps outlined above would be a model for gaining the genuine commitment of the individual.)

Bob Drake believed he had been seduced by the company. He may have been right, since their real agenda for Bob appeared to be to use his analytical talent in a staff capacity longer than he had been led to believe. They had recruited him with an offer of a very high salary, lots of flattery, and all the time he needed to make a decision. Since Bob knew the offer was extremely attractive and had noted the excessive flattery, he might have asked himself: It's good to hear this, but am I really that great? Why does this company think so? Why does this organization want me so badly? What is the organization's agenda, especially in the short term? Are bait-and-switch, bait-and-keep, or bait-and-eat likely possibilities? Is their agenda consistent with my own? Will I be required to operate in a way that violates any of my basic personal values?

Organizational seduction may also be involved when a manager is being recruited for a new job or a special assignment within the same company. A senior manager, Thom Sailer, recruited John Hastings, a middle manager from another part of the company, with an offer John couldn't refuse. John was given a chance to be Thom's special assistant for a year or two as a stepping stone to line management. John was away at an advanced management program at the time and felt flattered that Thom, who was highly regarded in the company, had taken the trouble to visit him to make the offer in person. Thom needed help in implementing systems in his group and told John he could make an important contribution to the company. Thom made passing reference to John's first assignment, which was to be a live case study of a "human behavior" problem. John accepted. He learned only later that the case study was an intense interpersonal conflict that Thom was having with a powerful peer. The offer had led John into what he perceived as an assignment he couldn't succeed at—mediating a conflict between two powerful superiors. Assignment seduction may have been involved because the case study was clearly Thom's highest priority in recruiting John, but either consciously or subconsciously, Thom withheld the critical details from John at the time.

If the organizational seduction techniques of tempting offer, flattery, and plenty of time to decide are apparent, a manager must probe further to determine what the other party's real agenda might be.

Homosocial Reproduction[6]   People have a tendency to hire and select others in their own image. The candidates chosen are perceived to be "my kind of person" or "our type." Comparisons are made more or less consciously on the basis of such surface similarities as age, sex, ethnic background, social class, education, and training.[7] The prevalence of these surface similarities in a prospective organization indicates a strong possibility that homosocial reproduction is responsible.

This tendency exists because uncertainty and the necessity for coping with it has important implications for managers and their subordinates. One such implication is the need for mutual trust; this need drives people to seek recruits who seem to resemble themselves and to avoid others they perceive as different. The greater the uncertainty, the stronger is the tendency for those who need to trust each other to fall back on surface similarities and attempt to form a homogeneous group.[8]

Homosocial reproduction constitutes a subtle danger because the perception of similarity usually includes assumptions and expectations about the individual's personality, ability, and likely performance that may not be at all valid. Possible discrepancies may not become apparent immediately. When they do surface, surprise and disillusionment can lead to keen disappointment or other dysfunctional consequences for both employee and employer.

It is wise to ask, "Why does the organization want me?" Company representatives may consciously or unconsciously reveal that surface similarities are factors when they say why they think the individual would fit in. Such remarks as these were made by those who recruited Bob Drake: "We need people like you." "You are our kind of person." "People who look like you do well in our organization." Bob might have taken these as clues to probe further for the underlying meaning of the phrases "like you" and "our kind." What was being alluded to was Bob's athletic, strong physical presence, which apparently led the recruiters to impute to Bob certain values he did not share—extreme aggressiveness and cutthroat competitiveness. If surface characteristics alone are implied in speaking of a good fit, the individual can anticipate and perhaps clarify what the implicit assumptions and expectations are.

"Four-Minute Decision"   Similar to the tendency to make snap judgments is the propensity to jump to conclusions on the basis of preliminary information.[9] Research indicates that the conventional wisdom about the importance of initial impressions appears to be well founded. Information obtained early has a more significant impact on a recruiting interviewer than does information obtained later in the interview. This finding has been referred to as the primacy effect. One early study found that interviewers on the average reached a conclusion about job candidates after only *4 minutes* during a 15-minute interview—approximately 25 percent of the time available.[10] This tendency for the real interview to be over shortly after it begins should be noted (and discounted for) by both parties.

Interviewer's Agenda   The individual should keep the personal agenda of the interviewer, as well as the organization's agenda, in mind. It would be useful to ask: "Why is this person on my interview schedule? What is the person's stake in this process and his or her personal agenda?"

A recruiter who has a long list of candidates to be interviewed may be looking primarily for reasons to reject candidates. If the recruiter's own performance evaluation by the company is based on a batting average on retention of those hired (the percentage of those the recruiter has recommended who eventually remain with the organization), the recruiter may prefer to play it safe and produce a short list of sure stayers. On the other hand, if the recruiter's batting average is based on an ability to attract certain kinds of people, such as MBAs or engineers, in a tight hiring market rather than on their record of retention, the recruiter may be more inclined to use enticement or seduction techniques.

Finally, the recruiter may simply be interviewing to add bodies to the denominator of the fraction called the selection ratio, which is the number hired divided by the number interviewed. A low ratio indicates that many people were screened in selecting the chosen few; this is sometimes used to prove the thoroughness of a company's selection procedures. The point is that the individual should be cognizant of this kind of motivation underlying the interviewer's agenda, rather than that measurement systems are prone to this type of misuse.[11]

Traps under the Individual's Control

Self-Seduction   The individual is prone to overselling, just as the organization is, and for the same basic reasons.[12] A danger analagous to the organization seducing the individual is the parallel possibility of self-seduction by the candidate.

Again, seduction is distinguished from overselling by the critical test of whether the individual is aware of what is happening. Self-seduction is involved when candidates lull themselves into making things appear in a favorable light, rather than as they really are. Four common patterns or syndromes of self-seduction are described below.

1.   *Offer-collection syndrome.* Some people attempt to get a great many offers in order to look as good as possible to themselves and others. If asked to explain what they are up to, such a person might say: "I will collect a lot of offers by aggressively selling myself. Having plenty of good options will allow me to pick one that is the best overall fit. In addition, the increased bargaining power will put me in a better position to negotiate my terms." The subtle danger here is failing to recognize that: (a) overselling leads to unrealistic expectations on the part of the organization that are difficult to renegotiate later; (b) the time spent collecting offers could be spent trying to gain a deeper understanding of the companies one is really interested in, thus permitting a better assessment of fit and a smoother entry; and (c) the purpose of collecting offers may be ego enhancement rather than having a wider choice or better bargaining power and fit.

2. *Lack of focus.* "I don't know what I want, but if I look around long enough, sooner or later I'll find something I really like." There is nothing wrong with lack of focus if the reasons for it are genuine. Self-seduction is involved, however, if the lack of focus is merely an excuse to avoid the critical thinking and the careful picking and choosing necessary for a more focused search.

3. *Pressure from one's reference group.* Perceived pressure from those to whom one compares oneself and one's peers in particular may have to do with what types of industries and organizations are considered desirable and why. The candidate may be responding to the expectations of peers who believe that the higher the starting salaries, the better; or the less time it takes to complete the recruitment process, the better. Such pressures could lead to a poor individual-organization fit by inducing candidates to look at industries or companies that would be incompatible with their personal characteristics, to emphasize salary at the cost of other substantive considerations, and to make a shorter, more superficial job search. Not recognizing these pressures for what they are is another type of self-seduction.

4. *Self-delusion.* When the search gets discouraging, applicants are more likely to delude themselves into believing that available alternatives are better than they are. During a period of slow offers, they are less likely to keep an open mind and a critical attitude about the available options; they tend not to probe too deeply for the real meaning of what people in the prospective organization are saying. Another tendency is not to explore certain topics because of not wanting to face up to the information that might come to light.

By playing make-believe, self-seduction promotes inadequate testing in important areas, discourages critical examination of the available information, and leads to suspension of good judgment. These responses may be temporarily soothing, but the brute force of reality will sooner or later have its impact.

The Implicit Favorite   A study of applicants engaged in the recruiting process revealed that they tended to follow this self-seductive sequence:[13]

- At some (unspecified) point in the search process, the individual intuitively selects an implicitly favored job offer.
- A straw man offer is then picked for comparison with the implicit favorite, and the choice is progressively narrowed to these two alternatives.
- Additional information continues to be gathered to make a wise decision, but the game is in fact over. The individual has already selected the implicit favorite and is simply trying to build a case to reject the straw man.

There are two subtle dangers in making choices this way. First, there is the danger of cloaking the decision in a misleading aura of rationality;

the rationale is retrospective and justifies a choice made intuitively and perhaps prematurely. Second, although it is natural to look for assurance that one has made the right decision (research confirms that one goes through a period of doubt *after* making a decision), an extended period spent in justifying it is not time well spent.[14]

To deal with this problem, one must acknowledge an implicit favorite as soon as one's pattern of choosing suggests that it has appeared. One should then explicitly test the implicit favorite against the straw man *and other alternatives* to see if it still holds up. With the following frame of mind, one is likely to make a more carefully reasoned decision, either for or against the implicit favorite: "I like the implicit favorite so much, I need to find out exactly why I like it by comparing it to other prospects and crystallizing its pleasing attributes."

External Justifications   The decision to join an organization may be made on a rational basis, but a recruit who doesn't feel real commitment to the decision may continue to question the soundness of the choice even after joining the organization. This doubt could hurt individual and organizational effectiveness, as well as the individual's satisfaction and even survival.[15]

It is possible to be rational without real commitment because one must feel that he or she chose the organization and job primarily for their *intrinsic* value in order to be committed to them. If they fit well with one's personality, ability, and agenda, the commitment develops. If the person explains a choice on the basis of extrinsic factors ("The money was the determining factor," or "I had no other offers"), this external justification hurts real commitment.

The danger in not being sensitive to this general tendency is that the individual may not feel intrinsic commitment simply because external justifications are available.

Coping with the Subtle Traps

Many of the dangers mentioned exist simply because they are subtle. Consciousness raising by learning how these processes operate is one way to innoculate oneself against them. Many of the processes are also dangerous because they block critical reasoning and impede rational choice.

One can guard against them by imposing some ground rules for recruiting that will help give objectivity and reason a fighting chance against impulsiveness and emotion. A number of questions can help a recruit examine the situation objectively, along with specific techniques for achieving rational choices.

Following is a list of questions to ask oneself from time to time during the recruiting process:

1. What is my personal agenda? Does it make sense, given the organization's agenda?
2. What do I *dislike* most about the preferred organization and job?
3. What am I trying to *avoid* finding out? Is there useful information that I need and can get but am afraid of having to deal with?
4. Am I confusing hopes with expectations?
5. What options do I have if it turns out the organization or the job is a poor fit for me? Can I leave the organization or move elsewhere within it?
6. Am I testing my assumptions and expectations with relevant people inside the organization, with knowledgeable outsiders, and with those who know me well?
7. Am I confusing the question of the organization and the job I like with the question of where I would be effective?
8. When surprising or ambiguous bits of information crop up, do I rationalize them according to my hopes and desires, or do I further probe them in the spirit of discovery?
9. Do I trust my feelings to guide my inquiry and to complement my analysis, instead of either shutting them out or letting them dominate my thinking?
10. Do I take time to mull over difficult choices, or do I jump to quick conclusions?

Irving Janis and his co-workers have developed techniques to help people make better choices.[16] *The balance sheet* procedure is designed to facilitate consideration of all relevant positives and negatives from four angles: tangible gains and losses for self, tangible gains and losses for others, self-approval or disapproval, and approval or disapproval of others. A second technique, *outcome psychodrama,* is a kind of role-playing exercise conducted under the guidance of a counselor. The counselor asks the individual to assume that some time has passed since a choice has been made and to speculate aloud on what has happened in that period. The individual is asked to repeat and expand upon the scenario until all the potential risks and benefits have been flushed out.

In essence, these techniques acknowledge that many of the dangers inherent in the choice process operate at a preconscious level. Balance sheet preparation and scenario writing force these issues into the open and enable them to be dealt with more effectively.

Another consciousness-raising technique is to keep a "recruiting diary" to record surprising, confusing, or critical bits and pieces of information from one's dealings with a prospective company. Good gauges of when to record something are intuition and instincts. If something doesn't feel right, it should be recorded rather than discarded. Any one of the recorded items may not mean very much, but together they could reveal a pattern that provides important insights into the organization or oneself.

A trusted friend may also help by serving as a counselor and devil's advocate during the recruiting process, since sympathetic cross-examination can also lead to a more conscious and reasoned process of job choice.

Conclusion

The message of this chapter is *not* that individual-organization fit should be every recruit's first job-selection criterion, but rather that it is a very important factor affecting both individual and organizational effectiveness and satisfaction that is often ignored or misread. An attempt should be made to consider this issue explicitly during recruiting. The degree of importance to be given to it in making a job decision depends on how flexible the individual is in terms of personal beliefs, values, and behavior. Those who have the capacity and willingness to be more adaptive can afford to place less emphasis on the question of fit.

How much time and effort should be put into researching culture and other corporate realities? First, some aspects may be difficult or impossible to anticipate accurately, regardless of how much time and effort are put in. Even those who have researched and prepared for corporate entry find surprises. For instance, interviews of several alumni of the course on which this book is based indicated three months after their entry that they had failed to adequately anticipate one or more of the following aspects of the organization:

- Specific processes involved to get things done.
- How the organization pushes people to work harder.
- Words the people in the organization use and their true meaning.
- Who the jerks versus the high-status people in the organization are.
- Personalities within a seemingly faceless culture (see the culture map, Figure 4–1).
- Informal channels used.
- How the organization reacts to stress and crisis.
- Subcultures in the organization.
- Outside versus inside perception of the organization (image versus identify, see Appendix 1–1).
- Pace—faster or slower than anticipated.
- Minute-by-minute action.
- Culture at higher levels.

Second, one's actual fit with the organization is *not completely* determined by how much time and effort one puts into recruiting. At least two other factors, which the individual does not control in the short run, are important. (See Figure 5–1). One is bargaining power. Those who have more bargaining power are likely to receive more offers and to feel confident in probing deeper into those organizations to discover culture and other corporate realities, thus increasing the chances of achieving a

Figure 5–1
How the Quality of Recruiting and Other Factors Influence the Potential for Individual-Organizational Misfit

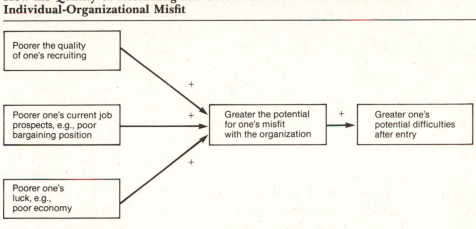

Implications for the Recruit:

1. Since factors other than recruiting influence fit, and since culture and related corporate realities cannot be fully anticipated, try to avoid being either paranoid or cavalier during recruiting.
2. Try to avoid irreconcilable misfits, and anticipate others to the extent possible.
3. The greater the anticipated misfit, the greater the potential difficulties after entry, and hence the greater the need to remain alert and flexible during entry (Chapter 6).

better fit. Marketability can be increased over the long haul (by enhancing one's base of knowledge, skills, and competence, for example), but it cannot be changed in the short term. Chance events can also play a role. For instance, a person in the job market when the economy is bad may find few job openings available. Even one who has done a good job of anticipating fit with the organization may discover later that the reality has changed because of circumstances or events that could not have been anticipated—for instance, changes in key organizational personnel caused by turnover or death that could not possibly have been foreseen by the recruit.

Given these difficulties, two considerations should be kept in mind in deciding how much time and effort to put into recruiting. First, the less the time and effort put in, the greater the potential for individual-organizational misfit. Also, the less one has tried to anticipate this misfit, the greater the difficulties to be expected after entry. Second, since factors other than the care of recruiting also affect fit with the organization, and since culture and related corporate realities cannot be *fully* anticipated, it makes little sense to be obsessive about one's recruiting. If all one does is to try to anticipate a better tomorrow, there is no time to live well today. It pays to avoid being either paranoid or cavalier in one's recruiting efforts and to keep one's antennae, awareness, and flexibility high in preparing to enter a new organization.

Bob Drake erred in the direction of being cavalier. He had five very good job offers, and two of them seemed to be a much better fit for him.

Unfortunately, Bob didn't adequately anticipate and consider the question of fit. Instead, he conducted a lengthy but superficial job search and apparently succumbed to organizational seduction, homosocial reproduction, self-seduction (offer-collection syndrome, lack of focus, peer pressure), and implicit favorite. Neither the company nor Bob gained very much as a result, with one important exception: Bob did learn from his traumatic experience and took steps to do a better job of assessing and entering the next organization he joined, where he has done very well. However, both Bob and the company paid dearly for his lesson.

In sum, the chances of better anticipating a prospective organization and of achieving a better fit with it are increased by following the guidelines presented here. To that extent, the breaking-in process is made less difficult. Yet, no matter how good the apparent fit with the organization, a note of caution bears repeating: It is best to anticipate that culture (and other important organizational realities) cannot be *fully* anticipated. The first few weeks and months after entry are a period when surprises, trials, and tribulations are bound to occur.

Chapter 6

Surviving and contributing as a newcomer

Orientation   Research studies in a wide range of organizational settings have reached the one basic conclusion that an individual's early organizational experiences strongly influence his or her later contribution and advancement in the organization.[1] This being the case, one's first few weeks and months in a new job deserve to be managed particularly well. Unfortunately, a variety of factors conspire to make this a particularly stressful and difficult period for the newcomer.[2] This chapter and the next will examine these factors and their underlying dynamics and provide a basis for understanding and managing this crucial early period. The period is characterized by the "liability of newness," to borrow a phrase from the entrepreneurship literature that refers to a similarly treacherous period faced by new businesses.

The first few weeks and months after entry are a difficult and vulnerable period for the newcomer. First, the new employee feels overwhelmed by unfamiliar faces, names, titles, work roles, and locations. Many day-to-day matters of organizational living that are normally taken for granted suddenly become problematic. Questions come up about how to use time, where to go, what to do, what to wear, and how to behave, as well as one's relationships, friendships, competence, and expectations about the work to be done and one's future in the organization. This disruption of a daily rhythm of activities and everyday order can be disconcerting to the most well-informed and well-prepared newcomer.

Second, the new employee is at a disadvantage relative to established people in the organization because the newcomer has not figured out how to negotiate the culture and the other significant organizational realities. Obviously, the better the person anticipates these realities prior to entry, the smaller the handicap. However, since these realities cannot be fully anticipated, the newcomer must determine just how much of a disadvantage he or she has relative to established employees and how soon the handicap can be neutralized.

Finally, established people in the organization will have a wait-and-see attitude until the newcomer proves worthy in the new situation. Some in the organization will want to see the newcomer succeed and will offer help, but they may also have unrealistic expectations of him or her. Others may feel threatened by the newcomer and consciously or subconsciously try to precipitate the person's failure. If the newcomer commits too many errors early on, it may be difficult to recover lost ground.

Given these difficulties, a newcomer's feelings at entry are somewhat akin to the stage fright experienced by actors and actresses new to the stage, apprehension about performing up to their own and others' expectations in the glare or organizational publicity.[3] What can the newcomer do to better manage the liability of newness? First, it helps to try to understand the organization's socialization process. Second, the newcomer must continue to learn the ropes of the culture and the other important realities (see Figure 3–1). The questions to think about (Appendix 4–1, Chapter 4) that one did not or could not get answered prior to entry (Chapter 5) can be reviewed as guides. Third, one must make the effort to become *operational,* which means contributing to the organization by getting the job done and producing valued results. Remaining sensitive to the organization's agenda is vital to this effort, for the real job assignment may be different from the formal job assignment.

These entry tasks are interrelated and must be dealt with simultaneously, but we will cover them sequentially.

Understanding the Socialization Process

Organizational socialization[4] is the process by which people in the organization teach the newcomer the organization's culture[5] as well as the appropriate behaviors and skills required to be effective in the organization. Socialization takes place in three more-or-less distinct phases.[6] The first, called prearrival or anticipatory socialization, begins prior to the individual's joining the organization, when the individual acquires some understanding of the relevant behaviors, skills, and cultural assumptions in anticipation of joining up. The previous chapter dealt with this phase. The next socialization phase is breaking-in or encounter. This phase covers the first few weeks and months following the newcomer's actual entry into the organization. This period in which the individual and the organization get a more realistic picture of each other is the subject of this chapter. Finally, in the settling-in or mutual acceptance phase, the individual and the organization succeed or fail to reach an accommodation with each other. The next chapter considers this phase.

Organizational Socialization Strategies

In Reading 2–1 John Van Maanen describes and analyzes seven organizational socialization strategies. The characteristics and implications of these strategies are summarized in Figure 6–1 for purposes of review and convenient reference after reading the article.

It is important for the newcomer to recognize these and other socialization strategies being used by the organization because an understanding of how they condition the learning environment can help the newcomer in learning the ropes and becoming operational.

Figure 6–1
Socialization Strategy Dimensions: Their Characteristics and Implications* (This Summary Is for Purposes of Review after Completing Reading 2–1.)

Socialization Strategy Dimension	Characteristics	Implications
1. Formal (versus Informal)	"Newcomer status" emphasized and made explicit. Socialization occurs in a setting separate from the work setting.	First round of socialization, stressing general skills and attitudes (versus second round, emphasizing situational application within the context of work setting). Newcomer feels personal anxiety and stress because his or her newness and the need to learn is highlighted by different location and title, e.g., "trainee" (versus the personal anxiety and stress from having to negotiate and learn in an unstructured environment).
2. Individual (versus Collective)	Newcomers socialized individually (versus bunched together at the outset and "processed" through an identical set of experiences).	Newcomer's learning strongly influenced by the knowledge of the organization's "socialization agents" and his or her relationships with them (versus learning strongly influenced by the collective experience of others in the same boat being concurrently processed). Newcomer less able to deviate from the organizational culture or resist organizational influence (versus greater ability to do so because the batch being processed develops its own subculture).
3. Sequential (versus Nonsequential)	Newcomers pass through a series of discrete, identifiable transition stages during the socialization process, e.g., job-rotation training (versus absence of such stages, i.e., the entire process in one transition stage only).	Newcomer has opportunity to learn from a variety of socialization agents who may not know each other, who may be separated spatially, and who may have different perspectives and knowledge of the organizational reality (versus no such opportunity).

Figure 6–1 *(concluded)*

Socialization Strategy Dimension	Characteristics	Implications
4. Fixed (versus Variable)	Newcomer has a clear understanding of how much time it normally takes to pass through one or more transition stages in the socialization process (versus no such precise knowledge of the "transition timetable").	Newcomer has a basis for judging his or her rate of learning and progress against what the organization considers normal (versus no such clearcut basis, in which case newcomer must look for other clues and make this assessment in a more ambiguous environment).
5. Tournament (versus Contest)	The socialization process sharply separates the winners from the losers, and the tournament rule is: "When you win, you win only the right to go onto the next round; when you lose you lose forever" (versus no such sharp distinction; a newcomer who "fails" can try again to advance to the next round).	Newcomers experience anxiety and insecurity, and extreme pressure to perform (versus less anxiety, insecurity, and pressure to perform). Fosters competition among newcomers (versus collaboration). Leads individuals to adopt "safe strategies," given the risk of failure (versus promotes risk taking and perseverance because one setback does not mean a permanent loss).
6. Serial (versus Disjunctive)	Newcomer has access to predecessors with similar background (e.g., sex, age, ethnicity, education, training, etc.), in whose footsteps he or she can follow (versus no such access to similar others who have already been through the socialization process).	Newcomer can learn from prior experience of similar others (versus no such opportunity). Allows continuity, but risks stagnation and loss of innovation (vs. allows inventiveness and originality, but risks unnecessary complication and confusion).
7. Investiture (versus Divestiture)	The socialization process affirms and celebrates the newcomers background (versus putting down the background characteristics the newcomer possesses).	Newcomer experiences the socialization process as a positive experience (versus as an ordeal). Organization utilizes the incoming characteristics of the newcomer without attempting to change them (versus "unfreezing" the newcomer and attempting to influence a major change in one or more of his or her entering characteristics).

* Based on John Van Maanan, "People Processing: Strategies of Organizational Socialization," *Organizational Dynamics,* Summer 1978, pp. 19–36 (Reading 2–1 in this book).

Learning the Ropes

The process of learning the culture and other important organizational realities begins prior to entry but typically continues for 6 to 10 months afterward.[7] Not all learning takes place at the same speed. Technical jargon and special terminology used in the organization is usually tackled first. Without it, a newcomer cannot understand enough of what is being communicated to determine what information is important.[8]

Next comes an understanding of the essentials of the business and the technical aspects of the company and job. Knowledge of the culture and the social and political system is perhaps the most difficult to acquire and comes last. Unfortunately, these corporate realities are the hardest to learn and are also perhaps the most critical differential to early success.[9] It pays the newcomer to try to formulate some understanding of these realities as quickly as possible and to reassess them periodically.

Learning from Available Information

Learning takes place as follows. Everyday conversations and observations provide raw material that the newcomer uses to learn the ropes. The rate at which this occurs depends on the individual's capacity for absorbing routine information and making sense of it. Rapid learning requires that the newcomer avoid the temptation to jump to quick conclusions in making inferences from this information. The newcomer should test interpretations of daily events and occurrences with established members of the organization or knowledgeable others. If discrepancies show up, these must be explored further to understand their underlying significance.

From time to time, the newcomer will experience a critical incident. Examples are an interaction with a boss or peer that could become a turning point in the relationship and a dramatic episode, such as the discovery that someone has intentionally withheld important information. Such critical incidents and episodes serve to crystallize or dramatically alter the newcomer's accumulated experience. They must be managed well to ensure the newcomer's success.

From time to time the newcomer may also experience a culture shock or other reality shock.[10] An example is the rude awakening or painful revelation that occurs whenever the newcomer confronts a major discrepancy between his or her expectations and hopes of the culture or other organizational realities and what the organization is really like. The stronger the culture and the more control the organization exerts over its employees, the more intense the culture shocks and other reality shocks are likely to be.[11] Also, the greater the misfit and the less effort the newcomer has made to anticipate entry, the more intense the shocks will probably be. These shocks signal that the newcomer has not yet understood the organizational realities, and they are best viewed as traumatic but opportune invitations to discover the realities.

Because of their importance to the newcomer, these routine interactions, critical incidents, and reality shocks must be carefully managed. The following guidelines are presented.

Managing Interactions, Incidents, and Shocks

First, it is well to review the organization's and one's own agenda from time to time. This review helps create a frame of mind that allows one to better respond to various situations as they arise. Interactions, incidents, and shocks usually occur spontaneously, with little time for thinking or reflecting. Being sensitive to one's own and others' agendas increases the likelihood that the reflexes and reactions will respond to the needs of the moment.

Second, one must recognize that the organization's tolerance for error in the management of these interactions, incidents, and shocks will vary depending on what the culture specifies in this regard, but tolerance usually increases as one becomes established in the organization. The dilemma is that effective management of these situations is a precondition for becoming established. The way out of this dilemma is to recognize the crucial importance of *early* encounters, especially with those who appear to have some preconceived negative stereotypes about the individual—such as, overambitious, overconfident, brash, theoretical, idealistic, naive, immature.

Where the individual has a negative credit rating in the eyes of the organization, it is generally wise not to take dogmatic positions early on. One may not yet understand enough about the culture and other significant realities to see the potential difficulties or to see that other approaches are possible. Taking firm or rigid positions before one has developed credibility may also be self-defeating in a symbolic way if it reinforces negative stereotypes.

When the organization has more positive stereotypes about the individual or has bestowed a more favorable credit rating, there is more latitude for error during the period of orientation and exploration. It generally pays to use this grace period ("honeymoon") to learn the culture and other organizational realities rather than to take strong positions before getting one's bearings.

Perhaps most important, one's perspective is conditioned by the culture of the school or other organization one is *coming from,* and one may be only partially aware of this. In Reading 2–2 John Van Maanen describes how different business schools forge different student cultures and the implications of these different frames of reference for the graduates and the companies hiring them. Whether one is a new graduate or an experienced manager, it pays to enter a new organization with an awareness of this prior cultural conditioning, together with a willingness to discover the point of view shared by others in the new organization. Especially for those entering the organization in entry-level positions and having low incoming credit ratings, it helps to approach early encounters with others in a spirit of give and take, with an inquisitive rather than an evaluative attitude, while looking and listening for the underlying *meanings.*

Bob Drake, for instance, reacted to the shocks he experienced with disappointment and anger but with increased determination to overcome the obstacles he had encountered. Had Bob viewed the resistance he encountered as a clue to *understanding* the organization and its culture (rather than seeing resistance simply as something to be overcome), he might have learned the underlying significance. The culture of the business school Bob had graduated from and the culture of the company he had worked for prior to that were ordered very differently from his new company culture. Cooperation prevailed over internal competition where he had studied and worked previously; in his new company it was the other way around. Had he grasped this in the beginning, he might have been able to take appropriate action.

Proactivity: Developing Information Sources and Networks

It is no mean trick for the newcomer to get access to sensitive organizational information. It takes time, perhaps several months to a year or more depending on the size and complexity of the situation, to know who the key people are, their quirks, the subtleties of the business, the nuances of the industry, and other idiosyncrasies germane to the situation. Having this knowledge gives experienced employees an enormous advantage, no matter how bright and capable the inexperienced newcomer may be. Under what conditions will knowledgeable insiders share this advantage?

The first condition would be a culture that encourages such disclosure. A second would be demonstration by the newcomer of the ability to use sensitive information with discretion. A third would be the newcomer's possession of something else to offer in trade. Thus, the speed and effectiveness with which the newcomer can proactively develop valid information sources depends not only on what the culture prescribes, but also on his or her resourcefulness.

The organization Bob Drake joined was very secretive. Bob's boss was reclusive, and peers gave Bob little or no help. As his frustration with the organization mounted, Bob began to voice some of his concerns to the few people in the organization he felt were being open with him. He later learned that one of these "friends" had communicated Bob's frustrations to others in the organization, including Bob's boss' boss. Had he understood his company's culture, Bob might have talked less and listened more in order to survive and contribute in the organization.

Learning the Ropes: A Summary

The process of learning the ropes of the culture and other significant realities may be facilitated by following these general guidelines:

1. Consult Figure 3–1 from time to time to review what has been learned, and what remains to be understood. The questions to think about (Appendix 4–1, Chapter 4) that were not adequately answered prior to entry (Chapter 5) should be used to guide this learning process.

2.   Recognize how the socialization strategies in use affect one's susceptibility to organizational influence (see Figure 6–1). Research suggests that the informal socialization practices have a more profound influence on the newcomer than do the formal ones, perhaps because their spontaneity makes them less suspect.[12]

3.   Try to figure out the agendas of others in the organization, especially the agendas of one's boss, his or her boss, and their idiosyncrasies and "hot buttons."

4.   View routine interactions, critical incidents, and reality shocks as invitations to learning, which is facilitated by maintaining a spirit of inquiry and by testing one's private interpretations of these events against those shared by established employees. Probe any discrepancies further to learn their underlying significance. Ask oneself: Did my standing with others in the organization improve or diminish as a result of how I managed this episode? (Did I gain or lose points with others on this one?)

5.   Proactively develop information sources and an information network by remaining sensitive to its nature and importance. It may be difficult to know who is providing valid information and with whom it is safe to be open. It may take from several months to more than a year to develop the necessary trust levels with others in the organization and to accumulate sufficient experience to know if there are any phonies or spies in the organization who cannot be trusted.

Contributing as a Newcomer: What Is the Real Assignment?

It takes some time for the individual to learn the culture and other significant realities of the organization. In the meantime, the newcomer is expected to start functioning, become operational, and get the first assignment done. This is one of the reasons the period just after entry is treacherous; indeed, it is a major factor in the liability of newness. Getting the job done under these circumstances is a little bit like shooting at a target in the dark (because one doesn't adequately understand the culture) while being shoved and pushed from time to time (by culture shocks and other reality shocks).

The first assignment can be particularly difficult for the newcomer because it has unusual symbolic and substantive import. Getting off to a good start contributes immeasurably to creating a favorable first impression. Doing a job well often leads to liking the job more, and both tend to enhance self-esteem.[13] This self-esteem increases the likelihood of success on the second assignment; and as the cycle repeats itself, a success syndrome develops.[14]

The following guidelines can help the newcomer better manage the crucial first assignment and subsequent early assignments, despite the liability of newness.

Stated versus the Real Assignment

The newcomer may begin by asking what the *real* assignment is. Too often, newcomers charge ahead to get the job done without stopping to consider whether the assignment as presented to them is the real assignment. Any discrepancy between the real and the stated assignments can be discovered through such questions as these:

1. What is the organization's agenda? (Figure 3–1, and Questions 31 and 32 in Chapter 4).

2. If the newcomer has possibly been seduced, are bait-and-switch, bait-and-keep, or bait-and-eat techniques a part of the real assignment? (Chapter 5).

3. What will be stressed when superiors judge how well the assignment has been completed? Most organizations look not just at achievement of results but also at *how* the results were achieved. Thus the real assignment often includes both ends and means. In the case of newcomers, the question explicitly or implicitly asked by those already established in the organization is: Does this individual operate in a manner that gives us confidence in him or her?

"Can You Give Me a Little History?"

Much can be learned by asking for a little background on the assignment before accepting it. Unfortunately, the newcomer either doesn't think of asking the question or doesn't consider it sufficiently important. Most people in most organizations consider such a question perfectly reasonable. Subsequent probing, if it is done judiciously, can uncover potentially valuable background material. Questions such as the following may be asked:

- Who was the last person to work on this assignment (or a similar assignment)?
- What happened in that case? Why?
- What has experience taught us about the obstacles and roadblocks that may be encountered in such assignments, and how might they be overcome?
- Who are likely to be opposed to this assignment? Who are likely to support it? Why?

The list could be expanded, but the main thing to recognize is that most assignments have a technical, political, social, and cultural history that is ignored only at one's peril. It is foolish to proceed without attempting to learn these lessons.

The Phoney First Assignment

Those newcomers who begin as trainees sometimes find their early assignments to be meaningless practice sessions or Mickey Mouse exercises. Newcomers who begin their jobs without going through any formal in-house training program may have similar reactions to their first assignment as phoney or meaningless chores with little substance. Many companies recognize that this kind of introduction to a new job can demotivate newcomers, particularly those with high potential, and they try to avoid lengthy full-time training programs or unchallenging early assignments.[15] In organizations that do not avoid this demoralizing initiation, what can the newcomer do to manage the situation better?

First, the newcomer must recognize that it is unreasonable to expect the organization to trust anyone who is still largely unproven with large doses of responsibility and challenge at the outset. As credibility is earned over time, more challenging and responsible work will come with it. Second, the level of challenge in the first assignment does not necessarily reflect the level of confidence the organization actually has in the newcomer, for purely circumstantial reasons. It may just happen that there is not enough challenging work to assign to the newcomer at the time he or she arrives. Or assignments may have been created to fill time for a talented person whom the organization needs for more serious challenges ahead.

Finally, having understood why an initial assignment is not challenging, the newcomer can view this slack as an opportunity to *create* meaningful assignments. If it is done with sensitivity, this use of energy can help the organization and demonstrate the newcomer's ability to take initiative. One can also use elbow room in the first assignment as an opportunity to learn the culture and other realities of organizational life.

The "Impossible" First Assignment

Some newcomers may find their first assignments to be overly simple or phoney, and others may be confronted with assignments that carry too much responsibility and challenge. Such an impossible mission may mean that managers in the company grossly overestimate the newcomer's capacity and ability and underestimate his or her liability of newness. The commissioning agent, typically the boss, may feel threatened by the newcomer and consciously or subconsciously want the newcomer to fail. This failure can then be treated as evidence that "the new kid on the block is not that great after all." Sometimes an impossible task is assigned to chasten the newcomer. Edgar Schein provides a classic example:

> [A]n engineering manager . . . gave every new college graduate who entered his group the task of analyzing a special circuit which violated some textbook assumptions and therefore looked as though it could not work, yet which had been sold for years. When the new employee would announce that the circuit could not work, he was told that it did and was asked to figure out why. He typically could not explain it, which left him thoroughly depressed and chastened about the value of his college education. The manager felt that only at this point was the new employee "ready" to learn something and to tackle some of the "real" problems on which the company was working.[16]

Such "upending experiences," as Schein calls them, are designed to "unfreeze" the newcomer by dramatically violating his or her basic assumptions about self or organization and to predispose the employee to learn the new skills, behaviors, and attitudes required on the new job.

A newcomer who recognizes such assignments for what they are has a perspective on them, and that makes it easier to develop a strategy for dealing with them. Unrealistic assessments and expectations on the part of the company may be reduced by individuals who communicate more valid information about themselves. This will usually be in their self-interest in the longer term because it increases the chances of starting out well and letting the success syndrome take hold.

If the people responsible for the assignment are feeling threatened by the newcomer, the situation is more tricky. Any effort to build credibility to deal with the perceived threat usually takes some time. In the meantime, it may be necessary to find a way to avoid playing the game. Renegotiating the assignment, refusing it, or transferring to a different work unit and boss in the company are three alternatives, but each has obvious difficulties.

For instance, one new assistant product manager thought her boss was expecting too much of her too soon in order to "break her," rather than to break her in. She believed that both her talent and his sexist attitude were causing him to feel threatened by her. After attempting to work with and around him for a while, this manager decided to transfer to a different unit in the company. In the new unit, she flourished, contributed, and eventually rose far above her first boss, who might well have blocked her had she remained under him.

Going against the Grain of the Culture

The newcomer must consider two basic questions in deciding whether to go against the grain of the prevailing culture in initial assignments: What are the chances that I will be able to do so effectively? Am I willing and able to bear the associated personal risks?

Attempts to go against the grain of the culture may be stalled by open or underground resistance. Employees on whom the newcomer depends to get the job done may openly refuse to cooperate. More often and much more frustrating, fellow employees may agree to help and appear to be cooperative but see that nothing substantive gets done. A newcomer who lacks sufficient trust and clout to ensure the cooperation or compliance of relevant others may have little choice but to defer such action to a later date when this can be accomplished. Where appropriate action does not require the cooperation of others, the new manager may be able to personally deviate from the culture if he or she can bear the associated risks.

There are two basic approaches for such deviation. One is to first conform and contribute valued results and then to use this credit to go against the grain of the culture. Another option is to deviate immediately but produce valued results quickly enough so that the personal risk is manageable.

The question of how to constructively deviate from culture is taken up in Chapter 10, and the subject of culture change is covered in Chapter 12.

Contributing: A Summary

Three general guidelines will help the newcomer embark on the crucial first assignment and subsequent early assignments. First, and perhaps most important, the newcomer must begin with the right attitude. As Edgar Schein concluded from his study of a panel of MIT Sloan School alumni:

> I got the impression that those few graduates who accepted the human organization, with all its foibles, as a reality soon learned to apply their analytical abilities and high intelligence to getting their jobs done within it, but that those who resisted this reality at an emotional level used up their energy in denial and complaint rather than in problem solving. The "selling," and "compromising," and "politicking" necessary to get their ideas accepted were seen as "selling out" to some lower value system. The same person who would view a complex technical problem as a great challenge found the human problem illegitimate and unworthy of his efforts. The unlearning of this attitude may be one of the key processes in becoming an effective supervisor and manager. At the time I interviewed the alumni, most of them were still in a state of shock and had not begun to reexamine or unlearn this attitude, however.[17]

These findings are not peculiar to the particular sample studied. Other graduates appear to be susceptible to the same danger.[18]

A second guideline for the newcomer is to recognize the critical importance of one's first boss and to try to decipher and keep his or her agenda in mind. The substantive and symbolic significance of one's first encounters and first assignments in the organization should also be recognized and appropriately dealt with. It is important to start interacting with people before becoming fully aware of the culture, but it seldom pays to plunge in to do the job *as stated*. It is more sensible to find out what the real assignment is, what is really valued, and especially to know if it is a phoney or impossible assignment. Having grasped this to some extent, the newcomer can strike a more appropriate balance between responding to the verbalized demands of others and crusading on one's own.

Finally, the newcomer must recognize his or her place in the organization—little or no credibility with others and low acceptance in the organization's culture (Model B, Figure 3–4). This suggests what one's required behavior should be in the context of the organization's agenda, and it highlights the importance of improving one's status in the organization by developing credibility and acceptance in the organization, which is the subject of Chapter 8.

The Advantages of Newness

Seeing the liability of newness should not blind one to its advantages. These can be utilized to the benefit of both the organization and the newcomer.

One advantage is the *honeymoon*. Its duration varies with the newcomer's incoming credit rating (the more favorable the rating, the longer the honeymoon) and the organization's socialization strategy (investiture strategies come with a longer grace period than do harsher strategies—see Reading 2–1). The newcomer can put the available honeymoon period to good use not only to learn the ropes, but also to deviate from the cultural norms if constructive action calls for this. A newcomer's norm violation is more likely to be tolerated because others figure he or she doesn't know better. However, this advantage is a short-lived one. It can backfire if the newcomer appears not to have learned the culture long after the period it normally takes to do so.

Another advantage is *low equity*. Since the newcomer's stake in the organization is low relative to that of the established member, the newcomer may be willing to take more personal risk in the interest of organization and self. If things don't work out, the newcomer can leave with a smaller loss of investment.[19] For instance, Mark Wyman, MBA, began his managerial career as a foreman of a work group that was performing well below what Mark thought the group could put out if certain changes in work methods were made. Mark's boss wasn't enthusiastic; other supervisors told him that higher-ups didn't like needless experimentation and wouldn't tolerate mistakes. Mark, who had prior production experience, decided to proceed with the changes after getting his boss' acquiescence ("Go ahead, but it's your idea"). Mark was confident of his approach and believed that the immediate improvements in results he expected would speak for themselves. He also believed he had less to lose than his reticent peers who had been with the company much longer, were set in their ways, and appeared unwilling to rock the boat.

A third asset the newcomer has is *objectivity*. Since he or she doesn't have an organizational ax to grind and is not vested in the organization's past decisions, the newcomer could be valuable as an unbiased source of information and opinion. The newcomer can also utilize the asset of objectivity by not taking sides early on. Being more likely to be *perceived as unbiased* owing to the newness, the newcomer has a chance to better understand different points of view in the organization. Objectivity permits dispassionate action as well, which is one reason why turnaround managers assigned to rescue ailing organizations often come from the outside.

In addition to seeing the organization in better perspective, the newcomer has an opportunity to bring a *fresh perspective* to the organization. If utilized effectively by the newcomer and the organization, this newcomer asset can help the people in the organization better understand themselves and their culture (see the section on "Status and Skill of the Investigator" in Chapter 1) and can provide the organization with new ideas and insights.

Finally, the newcomer brings *new skills and values* that could benefit both the organization and the newcomer if utilized well. Such misfits can enhance both individual and organizational development. Unfortunately, as in the case of Bob Drake, too often both the newcomer and the organization conduct their affairs in a manner that makes this contribution difficult. The lessons of this chapter and the two previous ones make it possible to successfully utilize the newcomer to the mutual benefit of the individual and the organization.

The next chapter considers some important initial assessments and adjustments the newcomer must make that determine whether he or she settles in or moves out of the organization.

Chapter 7

Settling in or moving out

Orientation   The previous two chapters dealt with the prearrival and break-ing-in phases of the socialization process. This chapter will explain how the third phase, settling-in, can be managed. First, the individual must monitor how he or she is doing in the new organization. Second, one must reassess one's fit with the organization. Third, one must determine whether one is willing and able to make the necessary initial adjustment in order to settle in and begin the process of becoming an established member of the organiza-tion.

Monitoring the Individual's Progress

While learning the ropes, discovering the organization's agenda, and becoming operational, new employees should also reflect on how well they are doing in the new organization by asking these questions: How well am I doing compared with the expectations and aspirations of: (1) Myself? (2) Those most like myself (my peers)? and (3) Those in positions that I aspire to in the organization (typically superiors)?[1]

Since it is hard for a newcomer to make these judgments without the perspectives of others in the organization, some companies assign a coach to see that the newcomer is properly instructed, advised, and groomed.[2] A good coach can make an enormous difference in the quality of the newcomer's entry experience and can guide the newcomer through the metamorphosis that eventually must take place before he or she becomes an established and productive organizational member.[3] In companies that don't assign a coach, it behooves the newcomer to try to recruit one.

A common procedure that can communicate the organization's view of how the newcomer is coming along is the performance appraisal. The problem lies in not knowing what discount factor to apply in interpreting the significance of the evaluation: Is the supervisor telling it like it is? Is this person able to? Does every newcomer get the same song and dance? Essentially, the questions center on the organization's use of the performance appraisal to provide newcomers with accurate feedback on how they are coming along and the capability of its officials to do this constructively.

One of the things the newcomer can do to increase the chances of getting useful feedback on how he or she is doing is to communicate to superiors *early on* that one would like some "informal feedback" *prior to* the six-month or annual review commonly used. Those with a short first assignment—for example, a first project in a consulting firm—could request such feedback at the end of this task. Those with longer first assignments could request feedback at the end of the first month or the first three months.

There is a danger that one may be perceived as overly anxious or pushy because of this request. The degree of danger depends on what the cultural assumptions and norms about appraisal and feedback are, so it is important *how* this request is made. It helps to frame the issue and ask for assistance in a way that makes sense in light of the prevailing culture. For example, one might say, "I don't know about others, but I find such feedback to be extremely useful in helping me to quickly get up to speed." The appropriateness of such a request and its timing also depend on the position of the new manager. Those in entry-level positions may be able to make such a request. This may be infeasible for those in higher positions because it takes longer to judge how well one is doing in these jobs. It may also be unwise to make such a request if one is expected to be self-assured and able to make such judgments on one's own.

In addition to the boss and the coach, the newcomer can talk to fellow newcomers, peers, and others in the organization at large to acquire various perspectives on important experiences. While remaining sensitive to the question of whom to trust and alert to who the organizational phonies might be, it is generally unwise to draw conclusions silently. Without the benefit of others' impressions and judgments, it is hard to know how much to discount for the biases of the particular boss or work group where one happens to be first assigned.

The individual should also remain alert to events that symbolize his or her progress and acceptance in the organization. Edgar Schein has described these explicit and implicit organizational signals that the newcomer must learn to read, and the section that follows is based on his work.[4]

The Rites of Passage

The salary increase is one index of how the organization perceives the newcomer—not the absolute amount or the percentage increase so much as the percentage increase relative to others in a similar bracket. The significance of the raise must be deciphered in light of prevailing competitive and economic conditions. A person's boss, coach, or peers may be able to provide the organizational perspective needed to understand what each raise means.

An important signal for the newcomer is what kind of *second* assignment (and subsequent ones) he or she is given. The first assignment, whether phoney or challenging, was made with limited information and some preconceived notions about the new recruit. The second and later assignments, however, are made with the knowledge of what that person has actually accomplished in the organization. The change in degree of responsibility from the first to the second and subsequent assignments is the significant index. As in deciphering the implication of salary increases, however, the newcomer should have a clear perspective on the situation and hear what others have to say before drawing these conclusions. For instance, the organization may have liked the newcomer's initial contribution but have no important assignments available at the moment.

An initiation rite is another important signal. Examples are a party, hazing, invitation to join a club, visits to important insiders' homes, assignment of a private office or secretary, use of a company automobile, stock options and other perks, and appointment to prestigious committees in the organization. These rituals and symbols represent overt investment on the organization's part and frequently help to alter the emotional tone of a person's relationship with the organization.

Finally, the sharing of organizational secrets is an important signal. Privileged information may include unreported, private, and possibly embarrassing aspects of the organization's history and current functioning:

- Specific technologies, marketing techniques, or production methods, which must not be revealed to competitors.
- Political situations, informal procedures that have to be followed to get work done, and key people to watch out for.
- What really happened around key historical events that the employees may have been aware of but may never have fully understood, such as why a certain product or program was "really" discontinued, or what "really" happened to the person who retired unexpectedly.

The organization is making itself vulnerable to the individual by revealing such secrets as these, since the individual can use the information to embarrass or hurt the organization. As such, sharing them is an especially important symbol of acceptance. There are many layers of secrets in organizations. The deeper and more sensitive layers are revealed as the individual gets established in the organization by developing credibility and gaining acceptance (Chapter 8).

Reassessing One's Fit with the Organization

As individuals accumulate experience in the new organization, they get a better feel for their fit with it. However, such recognition builds slowly and may be hard to accept. The tendency to ignore or repress the growing evidence of a poor fit may go on for too long, until a critical event, dramatic episode, or reality shock finally crystallizes it. Bob Drake, for example, didn't really grasp the extent of the misfit until his first formal appraisal, when he was given the option to resign. The newcomer can benefit by periodically reviewing the assessment made prior to entry to see if it has changed significantly in light of one's deepening understanding of the organization or self (Chapter 4). The objective should be to determine the kinds and degrees of misfits between oneself and the organization and the implications for both parties in the short term as well as in the longer term. The newcomer may encounter two common dilemmas. One is that the fit looks better for the longer term than for the short term. For instance, an MBA brought into an organization as part of an effort to bring a more analytical orientation to a company may remain a misfit unless the company culture eventually changes to become more analytically oriented. In assessing such a misfit, one needs to consider what is reasonable and legitimate from the standpoints of both the individual and the organization, since each has to adjust to the other to some extent.

A related situation is that one's fit looks bleak in the work group but looks bright in the organization at large. For instance, one may perceive a major misfit with the culture of one's work group but a good fit with the company culture or other subcultures in the company. One may have to consider (1) withdrawing immediately from the work group and relocating elsewhere in the company and, if so, how to withdraw diplomatically; (2) withdrawing from the work group later, after building bridges to other parts of the organization; (3) remaining and either waiting out the problem or attempting to influence changes in the work group to make it a more attractive place to continue working.

Making the Initial Adjustment

If fundamental and irreconcilable misfits between the individual and the organization are apparent, it may be best for the individual to leave. Biting the bullet may be less costly than an eventual withdrawal, for both parties.

However, unless the newcomer is willing to reexamine and perhaps comply with or internalize some new beliefs and values and engage in the required behavior, neither the newcomer nor the organization is likely to gain very much. The newcomer will probably either leave or be asked to leave if the misfit leads to poor performance. The next organization may or may not fit the individual better. The inherent difficulties that created such misfits in the first place remain. Discovering this can create disappointment, disillusionment, a loss of idealism, and even progressive cynicism.[5]

To accept the reality of organizational life at both an intellectual and an emotional level, one needs to reconcile expectations constructively with experience.[6] Such constructive reconciliation requires that the individual learn to accept some personal metamorphosis as inevitable and even desirable after entering a new organization and to seek the kind of change that facilitates growth and development. The key is to strike a balance between compromising important aspects of self and being inflexible.

One should think about both the *degrees* and *kinds* of misfits in assessing progress and prospects in the organization. Is there a misfit on several dimensions of personality, personal ability, and personal agenda, or on just one or two dimensions? Further, is the kind of misfit healthy for the individual and the organization? If the misfit is the kind that comes from having the capabilities and skills that the organization needs now and in the future, as in the case of Bob Drake's technical competence and analytical skill, it is a more healthy mismatch than if the organization needs the individual's skills for a short period of time only. Conversely, when the newcomer possesses the basic knowledge and skills needed for the job but lacks some skills required for professional development (supervisory skills needed on the shop floor, for example), the misfit is healthier than misfits without such potential.

Culture-person misfits may be conveniently visualized and analyzed using the culture map (Figure 4–1). The following questions should be asked. Which culture caricature (good soldier, adapter, maverick, or rebel) best represents my position on the map? Why? Is this where I want to be? Is this position tenable in light of my newness and lack of credibility in the organization? Is the organization looking for a maverick or a rebel to shake things up? Does the organization need a system shaker?

One approach to dealing with culture-person misfits is for the individual to accept only the most central organizational beliefs and values. Such "creative individualism" may ultimately be in the best interest of both the individual and the organization.[7] Initially at least, one is only required to comply with the cultural norms; that is, become more of an adapter on the culture map. Internalization of the corresponding beliefs and values (buying into them) may come later after the individual has had time to develop more personal relationships[8] in the organization and ponder such questions as these: Why am I resisting the organization's beliefs and values? Are they fundamentally incompatible with my own? Or is it because they imply new behaviors and skills that I am afraid I will not be able to learn?

For the new manager who decides to leave, the process of leave taking deserves some attention.[9] How one departs from an organization affects one's reputation, and the quality of that reputation is based partly on one's impact on the people left behind.

Those who intend to remain must be sure of *signaling* this intention appropriately to others in the organization. Edgar Schein has provided a good discussion of how to do this, as summarized in the following section.[10]

Signaling One's Intention to Remain

In many organizations, the intention to remain or leave is not discussed openly. A person who decides to leave customarily finesses the situation by keeping his or her intentions secret until just prior to departure. In these organizations, the committed individual must find some indirect means of communicating to the organization his or her intention to remain. Of course, when the prevailing culture encourages open dialogue on this question, a person can make the intention known directly.

One way of communicating the intention to remain is by demonstrating motivation and commitment as displayed by high energy, long working hours, willingness to do extras, and enthusiasm for the work. Since these are some of the indicators the organization uses to gauge the individual's intention to remain, employees may be misunderstood if they fail to signal their intentions in this way, even though they are involved in their work, like the organization, and want to remain.

The individual can also communicate an intention to remain by tolerating various kinds of constraints, delays, or undesirable work as temporary conditions. If the organization has promised challenging work, salary increases and promotions on a schedule that it is not delivering, this could be interpreted as meaning that the organization is rejecting the individual. However, if a person has reason to believe that this is not true, a willingness to accommodate the inconvenience and put up with the apparent abrogation of the implicit contract is a good symbolic way of communicating commitment to the organization. However, this behavior can lead to misunderstanding and game playing unless both sides are careful to read each other's actual situation and intentions.

If the individual intends to remain with the organization and communicates this effectively and if the organization reciprocates, the first workable accommodation has been reached. However, it must be remembered that the importance of monitoring progress, reassessing individual-organization misfits, and making adjustments continue as the individual proceeds with the process of getting established in the organization.

CASE 2–1
Mike Miller (A)

C. Paul Dredge
Vijay Sathe

Early on the morning of Friday, February 23, 1979, Mike Miller sat at his desk in his basement office contemplating his appointment later in the morning with Wynn Mason, senior vice president of operations for the Frontier Finance Corporation. Their meeting was to be an evaluation of Mike's performance during his six months as national small business operations manager, which Mike considered a rather high-level responsibility for a new MBA, even one from Harvard Business School. Frontier had wooed and won Mike with an impressive and gracious recruiting tour, young and dynamic executives and, most of all, a big starting salary with a bonus on top. But now Mike wondered if he had made a mistake and was considering resigning from his executive position after only seven months with the company.

With revenues approaching half a billion dollars, Frontier Finance Corporation made a substantial profit making loans that other lending institutions wouldn't touch because of their high risk. Frontier's founders had devised some fine-tuned statistical procedures which provided a more accurate assessment of a potential customer's creditworthiness than the standard methods used by most firms. Frontier had a top-notch legal staff to press its claims, which it did not hesitate to do, and a collection department known in the industry as "Frontier's badgers," noted for their persistence and success in making collections. The company's location in northeastern New Jersey had been a key element in building a good business in personal, small business, and venture capital loans.

Background

Mike Miller came from what he considered to be an unusual background for a Harvard MBA. His father was a machine tool and die maker with an entrepreneur's instincts. Mike traced his determination to avoid failure to the failures of his father's four businesses, two of which had ended in bankruptcy. "It does something to a kid to come home and find somebody picking up your furniture," he recalled.

Because he had always dreamed of being a paratrooper like his dad, Mike decided to become a Green Beret officer in the Army. His appointment to the West Point Academy led to a general engineering degree and a commission upon graduation in 1967. In 1968 Mike married Jennifer.

Early Work Experience

Mike's military service was successful and yet not particularly satisfying to him. As Captain Mike Miller, he established and administered a leadership school for his division and taught booby-trap warfare to junior enlisted personnel. Mike also designed and supervised the building of a 600-person jungle training facility. However, Mike noticed that his upward mobility in the Army was related almost solely to his time in rank—less able contemporaries received promotions at the same pace he did.

In 1973 Mike ended his military career and went to work for Pointer. There he was assigned to supervise the design of one of the first computerized cost-estimating systems to be developed by the heavy construction industry. In two years the system was completed and working well. Mike's next assignment as a construction estimator led him to face a new stage in his career. He knew that to become a really good estimator would take about 15 years—too long, he felt, to stay at one job, especially with his rather late career start. Also, his personal ethic of "a fair day's work, fair day's pay" was strained in a firm where it was necessary to maintain employment of a large work force between major projects—he estimated that only about 40% of his time was spent in doing necessary work.

Mike enjoyed coordinating and having command. He had held relatively high levels of responsibility in his military career and liked the feel of being in charge. He began to think about how to find a way to be trained as a manager. At age 30 Mike felt he should aim at a fast track and a high starting salary, both of which would be possible if he could graduate from a top-ranked business school. Mike was accepted by both Harvard and Stanford. He chose the former because to him Harvard "more strongly suggested prestige, success, connections, and money."

Harvard Business School

"When I began at Harvard in September 1976, I was happy to learn that the median starting salary for an MBA there was $20,000—it helped me cope with the thought of $18,000 in loans to pay for the degree" (the eventual figure was $24,000). Mike finished the first year with all satisfactory grades.

In his second year, Mike chose a curriculum that closely fit his career aspirations. Mike hoped for an initial staff position in a company where he would later have ample advancement opportunity in line management. He had decided against consulting, despite the high salaries, because of the excessive travel involved. He also knew that some consumer products—liquor in particular—would be hard for him to represent. Two of the faculty counseled Mike to go into an industrial firm as a more appropriate environment than consumer goods to utilize his experience in engineering and heavy equipment.

Rather than sign up for a string of interviews, Mike went to hear recruiters from the companies that he thought might be good possibilities. He was cautious and selective.

Starting in November, he researched prospective firms every Friday afternoon in the career resources library. He looked at videotapes, read company-supplied literature, and made methodical lists. It was at the library that Mike ran into Ted Wilson and learned about Frontier. Ted, a first-year section classmate, spoke of how he had enjoyed the challenges of his summer with Frontier—the special treatment, the lack of pressure, the parties every two weeks at executives' homes. Ted said that he had in fact mentioned Mike's name to his employers because "you're the kind of guy they're looking for." Mike thought, "A finance company? That's the last place for me," but after he looked at the available information on Frontier, he thought about the high pay, the fast promotions, and the location of the company near Jennifer's parents. Before Thanksgiving, he wrote to Frontier to ask for an appointment on their closed interview schedule. Mike also sent his resume to Defense Systems Inc., National Aerospace, International Electronics, and Pointer.

Frontier

In late January 1978, both the chairman and the president of Frontier Finance Corporation arrived at Harvard to speak and interview students. Mike was impressed that the company was so eager to recruit Harvard graduates that the top brass came. On the evening of Frontier's presentation, Mike and several other students were sitting at a table visiting and eating pizza with Rick Wesley, the president. At one point in the conversation, Wesley pointed to Mike and said: "We need people who look like him." Mike's six-foot, athletic build and clean-cut appearance were augmented on that occasion by a three-piece, herringbone grey suit, a white shirt, scarlet tie with small white dots, and wing-tip shoes. Wesley himself was young, congenial, and not one to stand on ceremony—he did a lot of talking with big bites of pizza in his mouth. To Mike, he appeared to be a vibrant, unpretentious, direct individual, much like himself. The chairman, Chuck Ferris, was also young and energetic, but seemed more slick—a fast-talking, aggressive recruiter.

On the following day, Mike had a cordial but intense interview with Frank Collins, vice president of Business Loan Marketing (Exhibit 1). Collins asked the usual questions about aspirations and abilities; Mike felt that the interview had gone extremely well. One week later, Wynn Mason, senior vice president of operations, called to arrange a February visit for Mike and Jennifer to Frontier headquarters in Montclair, New Jersey.

Mike's initial letter to Frontier had been designed to sell himself aggressively: "Based on my broad experience in the military and in business, and my successes in all my endeavors, I should be ideal for you." He had written "what one says to convey the picture of an HBS graduate who would break his or her back to do the job." In

Exhibit 1
Frontier Finance Corporation: Partial Organization Chart, February 1978

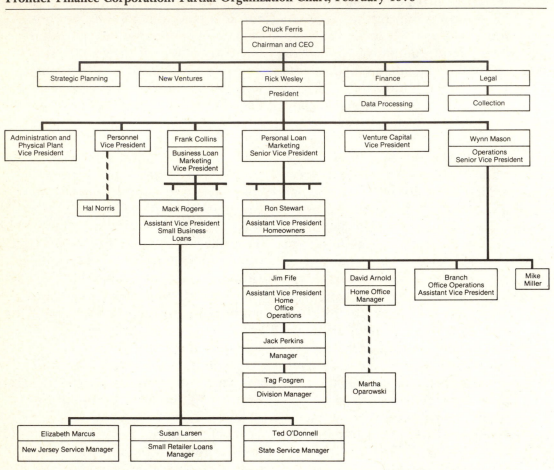

their visit to Harvard, the Frontier managers had stressed that they were looking for "extremely aggressive" people, ready to work in a "combat" environment. It was rhetoric to warm the heart of an ex-Green Beret officer.

In early February, Mike and Jennifer flew to Montclair at company expense to interview Frontier. Jim Fife, assistant vice president of home office operations, met them at the airport in the evening and drove them to a fancy hotel where they had dinner with Fife, his wife, and Mr. and Mrs. Tag Fosgren. Fosgren, a former golf professional, was a second-level supervisor in Fife's department (Exhibit 1). Both Fosgren and Fife were pleasant company and very interested in Mike. The next morning the Fosgrens picked up Mike and Jennifer and drove them out to a modern, opulent company headquarters building. Typed interview schedules were waiting for both of them. Mike had interviews scheduled all day; Jennifer was to go with someone in personnel to look at real estate. Everything had been planned immaculately.

Susan Larsen from Small Business Loan Marketing showed them around and continued to make sure Mike got to where he was supposed to be throughout the day. Susan, who had been with the company only three months, appeared cheerful and obviously happy with her job. Mack Rogers, assistant vice president to whom Susan reported, took Mike and Jennifer to lunch. Rogers was one of the first MBAs from a prestigious business school that Frontier had hired and had been rapidly promoted. Neither Mike nor Jennifer particularly liked him; he seemed to be a brash, rather insensitive man of about Mike's age. Mike met with all the vice presidents, the president, and the chairman of the board that day (see Exhibit 1).

The interview that most intrigued Mike was with Wynn Mason, the senior vice president of operations, who was to become Mike's first boss. Mason sat Mike down in a big chair opposite a couch in his office, curled himself up on the corner of the couch with his hands under his chin, and fired off a series of questions at Mike. Mason's manner was charming and friendly, but he seemed to be sitting on a barely concealed mine of aggressiveness, tension, and nervous energy. When Mike answered his questions candidly, Mason would respond with, "I agree with that 100 percent." Mike found himself saying things he wouldn't ordinarily have said, criticizing practices of past employers and of-

fering his own off-the-cuff suggestions. Mason obviously liked this and seemed pleased with him; this made Mike feel important, but he still felt the interview was rather strange.

At one point during the day, Mike and his escort, Susan Larsen, met Tag Fosgren in the elevator. Having heard the news from Fife, Mike congratulated Fosgren on his promotion from supervisor to division manager. Fosgren appeared subdued and somewhat embarrassed in his acknowledgement; Larsen seemed stunned and was silent. Mike later learned that the two had been vying for promotion; Mike had inadvertently leaked the news before Susan or anyone else had heard it.

The people Mike met that day were friendly and eager to please an outsider. They would gesture at the posh decorations of the office suites and ask with obvious pride: "Well, what do you think of the place?" Beyond the well-appointed architectural and decorative style, Mike noticed that most of the women in the office were young and very attractive—in fact, he had never seen so many beautiful women in one place. Another thing that Mike noticed was the efficiency of the personnel department. They sat him down, asked for the appropriate receipts, and within 15 minutes gave him a check for the total amount of his expenses, including the anticipated cab fares for his return to Boston.

Mike took the opportunity to ask a few more questions about the company. The man who gave Mike the check described Frontier as dynamic and aggressive. "I hope you don't mind fighting to get your point across," he said. By the end of the afternoon, Mike was feeling very positive about the company. What he had seen served to confirm what the articles that Wynn Mason had sent him indicated about Frontier: a fast-growing dynamic company whose earnings, according to annual reports and a *Fortune* magazine article, had grown at an annual compound rate of 30 percent for the past 10 years. This was the kind of place Mike wanted to start out in—and several other Harvard MBAs already had.

Ron Stewart, a golf player like Fosgren and many others, was one of them and had been promoted recently to assistant vice president. Stewart and Fosgren and their wives took Mike and Jennifer to dinner that night along with an MBA from Columbia University and his wife, who were also there for an interview. Given the opportunity to ask candid questions, Mike sought to confirm his impressions of the company. Everyone was enthusiastic about Frontier except Stewart's wife, Marge. After downing a good bit of Chivas Regal, she began to say what seemed to Mike to be pretty outrageous things about the company. "Frontier pays big salaries, but they're cheap. Ron is never home, he works all day Saturday. Frontier is pretty on the outside, rotten on the inside." Ron kept giving his wife dirty looks; embarrassed, Mike and Jennifer helped change the subject. That night Jennifer expressed

some reservations: "If Marge is right, then all the others are hiding the truth." But Mike and Jennifer both concluded that listening to an inebriated malcontent run off at the mouth was hardly a way to make judgments about a company that seemed so impressive.

The day after Mike and Jennifer returned to Boston, Chuck Ferris, Frontier's chairman of the board, called. "Wynn Mason said you were the best he has ever interviewed. We see you as a manager, not an analyst, and we pay for potential. It's safe to say that you can expect an offer from us."

A week later on February 20, 1978, Wynn Mason called Mike at home in the evening: "This may not be exactly what you were expecting (Mike's heart fell to his toes as he held his breath). We are prepared to offer you $30,000 annual salary and a $5,000 bonus at the end of the first year, assuming you're still with us—and of course you will be. Your job will be personal loans operations manager." Mike allowed a wide smile: "I really appreciate your offer." Mason made further encouraging remarks and told Mike he could take as long as he needed to make a decision. As he hung up, Mike raised his fist in the air, jumped up, and yelled: "Yahoo! I'm in!" He was particularly gratified to have this early offer in his pocket before evaluating the other companies on his interview schedule.

In the ensuing weeks, several very solicitous letters followed, always including current news about Frontier which had just been published in a journal or magazine, whether favorable or unfavorable to the company (Exhibit 2).

Other Offers

Mike had developed a set of criteria to guide his deliberations about where to seek employment. First was money, because of his huge debt and because he felt he had grown up "without anything." Second, Mike felt that any company he considered should provide opportunities for fast advancement and therefore not be so loaded with young managerial talent that the competition would put him at an unnecessary disadvantage. Third, he wanted a place that would be reasonably close to Jennifer's parents, who were becoming real parents to him also. Finally, he wanted to work for a company that wanted *him*, for what he was. In that regard, Mike found Frontier's offer particularly satisfying because they had recruited other Harvard MBAs aggressively and had said he was the best they had interviewed.

In early March 1978, Mike visited the headquarters of Defense Systems, Inc. in Minneapolis. Defense Systems was interested in Mike's military and engineering background and thought he could make a contribution in their planning area. Although the manager of product planning told Mike, "We could use someone *like you*," Mike had the impression that Defense Systems had no clear idea of what to do with him. When the planning manager asked him

about salary, Mike mentioned he would not consider any offer below $24,000, and the response was, "That's a lot of money for a guy coming right out of school." (The median starting salary for the class that graduated in June of 1977 was $22,000.) On March 7, Mike received a form letter from Defense Systems, with an offer for $24,000—there was a short description of some possible positions Mike would fill if he accepted the offer, but no personal reference whatsoever. Mike turned down this offer on March 10.

One of Mike's previous neighbors who was a manager for National Aerospace had mentioned to Mike that the company was looking for planners. Mike followed up a campus interview with a visit to its headquarters in Dallas on March 14. There he was interviewed by two of the vice presidents, both older men, and had lunch in the plant with a group of executives which included a nephew of the founder. National Aerospace appeared to be a well-run company with a strong industry position. All but one of the eight people at lunch were over 50; there was obviously a great deal of room for career advancement here, Mike reasoned. National wanted Mike to join its strategic planning staff—a group of 23 people, of whom 16 were over 60 years of age. They treated Mike with respect as a professional and seemed interested in the idea of training him for the job. The company was full of experienced managers who were as pleased with Mike's MBA as he was

Exhibit 2
Letters from Frontier Prior to Accepting Their Offer

FRONTIER FINANCE

Mr. Michael G. Miller   March 10, 1978
18 Pleasant Street
Cambridge, MA 02139

Mike,
   Attached is a copy of our annual report. 1977 will not be our
best year, but this may be the best report we have ever written. I'd
appreciate any comments you have on it.
   I have also included a copy of our quarterly earnings release,
which shows revenues down 5.8%. Nevertheless, we continue to strive for
and believe that 1978 will be a good year.
   I hope everything is going well for you and your charming wife
Jennifer.
   Have you set a date for your next visit to Montclair? If you
need help, I am only a phone call away.
                                        Warm professional greetings,

                                                  Wynn

                                        Wynn Mason

WM/pcv

FRONTIER FINANCE

Office of the Chairman   March 10, 1978
of the Board & Chief Executive

Mr. Michael G. Miller
18 Pleasant Street
Cambridge, MA 02139

Mike,
   Just a note to express my personal delight on learning that
Wynn had made you an offer.
   There's no question in my mind that you have the energy,
aggressiveness, and business savvy to immediately impact at Frontier.
Unquestionably, you also have the training and talent to make major long
term contributions.
   If there is anything I can do to help you or your charming wife
learn more about Montclair or the job, just pick up the phone and call
me collect. I look forward to having you come work with us to help make
our growth "dreams" become realities.
                                        Warm professional greetings,

                                                  Chuck

                                        Chuck Ferris

with their apparent business savvy and self-confidence. The Frontier offer had some competition now, Mike thought with satisfaction.

On March 21, Mike interviewed at the Spokane, Washington, computer division of International Electronics Corporation. Mike was met at the airport by Pete Fisher, Harvard MBA 1977, who was a marketing engineer. Mike interviewed Pete, Pete's boss, and one of Pete's peers in the management structure. Later in the day Mike spent 40 minutes with the general manager of the Spokane division. Mike noticed that what he had heard about the International management style—"management by walking around"—seemed actually to be the case. It appeared to be informal, consensual, and considerate of individual differences and needs.

Shortly after his last interview that day, Mike was taken to see George Ryan, one of the personnel officers, a "woodsman" type with a beard and a Pendleton shirt (not unusual attire at the plant, even for management). Ryan handed him a written offer for a job in product planning, a $24,000 starting salary with $4,000 bonus to be paid after six months of good performance. He said that while the salaries weren't the best in the industry, the company's progressive personnel policies, congenial working atmosphere, and the comfortable family communities chosen by the company were worth some extra money to most people. Ryan also mentioned that the consensus of those who had interviewed Mike

that day was: "Let's make the offer right now. Mike's personality will make him an excellent addition here."

On the flight back, Mike thought about the group of really nice people he had met, the way they seemed to enjoy being together, and the fact that International was a growth company. He also thought about the cluster of the company's 300 Harvard MBAs struggling to move up in an ever narrowing management pyramid leading to the top. But most of all, he kept saying to himself, $24,000, $24,000, $24,000!

On March 24, Mike received a letter from his previous employer, Pointer, stating that there was no suitable opening for him at the management level but that he would be welcome to return to his former job as estimator. Mike wrote them back immediately to terminate his leave of absence. With a self-imposed deadline of the first week in April for making a decision, Mike waited for some word from National Aerospace and contemplated the offers from Frontier and International Electronics.

Decision

On April 6, Mike wrote the International plant in Spokane to turn down their offer. Despairing of ever hearing from National and puzzled by their lack of response after such an enthusiastic reception, Mike called his contact, the vice president of planning, several times and left messages. Hearing nothing, Mike decided they were just not interested in him. In any case, he felt they would have a hard time matching the offer from Frontier. Mike also thought about the personal advantages of the Montclair/Newark/New York area—neither National Aerospace nor International Electronics were located near his or Jennifer's family.

On Friday, April 8, six weeks after receiving their offer, Mike wrote to Wynn Mason at Frontier to accept. In a sense, Mike was glad to be freed from the difficulty of making the decision. That weekend was the most relaxed and happy he had enjoyed in a long time.

Monday brought a surprise which was an additional boost to Mike's ego, but at the same time it was somewhat unsettling. Mike's contact at National Aerospace called to make an offer, apologizing profusely for the delay. He said he had drafted the offer and left for China three weeks earlier, but his secretary's husband had suffered a heart attack the same day, and she had left the company abruptly. No one had looked at his office mail and messages. Mike was a bit flustered but turned down the offer, explaining that he had already accepted another job. Mike's contact at National expressed his disappointment and mentioned that, if for any reason things didn't work out in the new position, Mike would still be welcome at National Aerospace. Later that week, International Electronics called to express similar sentiments.

Mike had visited four companies and had received four offers. He had made his decision and, despite the last-minute development at National, felt good about his choice. When people asked Mike about his job he would mention the position with Frontier rather casually without going into details. In June 1978, Mike graduated from HBS with second-year honors.

On the Job

Because of family obligations and various other matters which had been put off until school was over, Mike and Jennifer did not arrive in New Jersey until the 23rd of July. They had followed the advice of people they met at Frontier and bought a large, beautiful house in one of the "right" communities— Essex Falls. Most of the managers at Frontier lived there, or in Green Hills or Roseland. The house needed some work—particularly a paint job on the inside—and was much bigger than the couple needed, but it seemed to suit Mike's new identity as a young, aggressive manager associated with a dynamic company.

Mike began working at Frontier on Tuesday, August 1, 1978. Wynn Mason was out of town, but Mike was introduced to all the vice presidents and other key managers he had not met, especially those in the operations department, and was shown all around the company. Mike spent the balance of the first day reading company literature at his desk, just outside Wynn Mason's office on the first floor (Exhibit 3, location 1).

The next day Mike had a chat with Mason about his new responsibilities in operations. Mason said that the position originally intended for Mike as personal loan operations manager was not yet available but that there were several special projects he could work on in the meantime that would help Mike familiarize himself with the company and the way it did business. The first project had to

Exhibit 3
Office Locations

First floor plan, Frontier Finance Corporation

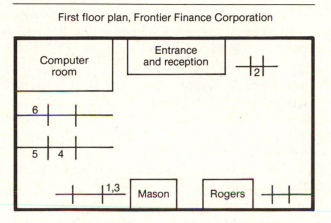

Basement plan, Frontier Finance Corporation

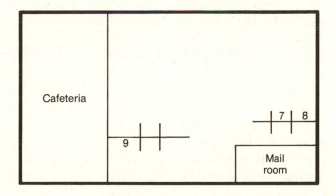

1.   August 1—August 10
2.   August 10—August 31
3.   September 1—September 15
4.   September 16—October 4
5.   October 5—October 31
6.   November 1—November 24
7.   November 25—January 2
8.   January 3—February 5
9.   February 6—March 13

do with reducing the number of errors that the clerical people were making. Mike felt some disappointment at this change in assignment, but decided to say nothing and to see how things developed.

On this second day of work at Frontier, Mike was surprised to see David Arnold, one of the managers, yelling at an associate in the hall between their offices. Mike was a bit troubled by such unprofessional conduct and made a mental note to look out for Arnold in the future.

During the first week, Mike attended an orientation workshop for new employees every afternoon. Officers of the company came each day and gave presentations on their areas. Mike soon sensed that the sessions were meant to be an opportunity for new employees to meet each other and to be mutually impressed by the quality of their associates. Most of the presentations contained a stab or two at the relative stupidity of other companies in the loan business, their problems with bad management, and their outdated policy positions on risky loans. These sessions also demonstrated that the underlying principle at Frontier was that money was the most powerful motivator and the most important corporate goal. While revenue and profit growth were important corporate objectives, the most sacred goal was profitability. Frontier's return on equity was among the highest in the industry, and management sought to retain this level, sacrificing growth if necessary.

The loan marketing area was run as a revenue center, with managers' performance evaluated on the basis of their ability to generate revenue. The operations area, of which Mike was a part, was evaluated as a cost center, with the emphasis on keeping costs to an absolute minimum. Mike's project on clerical error was part of this cost-cutting strategy. On August 10, Mike was moved to an office at the far corner of the first floor, where he continued his project (Exhibit 3, location 2). He was learning quite a bit about the company from the interviews that were part of his assignment; in the process he found out that the project he was working on had been *routinely* assigned to newly hired MBAs.

During his third week, Mike joined a big crowd at lunch in the basement cafeteria. The occasion was a send-off for Bert Morgan, an employee who was quitting to go back to school. At one point in the festivities, one of Morgan's friends pretended to be a new arrival interviewing the departing employee for advice: "What does it take to be successful at Frontier?" Morgan was asked. His reply was: "First of all, you have to play golf; second, you have to have an MBA; third, you have to wear a three-piece suit and wing-tip shoes; fourth, you have to work on Saturdays, and if you want brownie points, on Sundays too." Everyone present laughed.

Mike had already noticed that although the official Frontier working day was from 8 to 5, managers were invariably at their desks before 7 in the morning and rarely left before 7 in the evening. He had also noticed on Saturday shopping runs that the Frontier parking lot was usually well filled on Saturday mornings. From observation, Mike had the impression that the long hours were not always productively spent by Frontier employees, including the managers who stayed so late. Mike had worked intensively on his previous jobs but usually left the office at what he considered a reasonable time of the evening. In view of the prevailing practice, Mike felt it necessary to mention to Wynn Mason that with the immediate demands of painting and getting settled into his new home, he would have to leave the office at 5 during the first few weeks. Mason indicated he was willing to put up with that for a limited time, but said he hoped Mike wasn't another "Mr. 40," the nickname of a company manager who had the well-known habit of working 8 to 5 only. Wynn clearly expected Mike to fit eventually into the live-with-the-job pattern of the other managers. It became obvious that to get ahead at Frontier he would have to work long on weekdays and on weekends, too.

One day during his third week at Frontier Mike was standing in the hallway with Susan Larsen when Mack Rogers, the assistant vice president she reported to (Rogers had taken Mike and Jennifer to lunch during their interiew visit in February) came up to Susan, put his arm around her, and made a kissing gesture. "When are we going to go on another business trip together?" he asked. Larsen excused herself and Rogers walked away laughing. Mike was appalled. Susan Larsen later told Mike that she and Mack Rogers had gone to Texas on a business trip, and Rogers had suggested that they sleep in the same room and save the company the cost of a second room. She had refused.

Troubled by such behavior, Mike mentioned the incident to Jack Perkins, a long-time management employee in operations who had become a good source of information for Mike. Perkins told Mike that Rogers wasn't the only male manager interested in extramarital liaisons with female employees. Perkins mentioned that the chairman and chief executive officer, Chuck Ferris, often invited attractive young company women to his office, where he would arrange a game of golf, or some other sport, followed by dinner and a night together. Of the men in the upper levels of the company, Perkins said that to his knowledge only Rick Wesley, the president, was "not cheating." Mike himself noticed that the conversation of the men in the company was often what he considered base and crude, loaded with sexual innuendo. Mike's personal ideals and his desire always to be a gentleman were deeply offended by such conduct.

Before long, Mike realized that the David Arnold yelling incident which he had witnessed on his second day at work was not exceptional at Frontier. In mid-September, Mike was sitting in his office, now back across from Mason in the place where he had started (Exhibit 3, location 3), when he heard some distant but clearly angry shouting. He stepped around the corner and heard, much more clearly, an argument between Ferris, the CEO, and Wesley, the president. They were shouting at each other at the top of their voices in the hallway about the level of cash reserves on hand for new loans. "If you would just get your head out of your ass, you could see that we need more than that!" shouted Ferris. Wesley retorted loudly in equally vulgar language. Mike couldn't believe his ears.

Mike learned that other kinds of openness were customary at Frontier. Susan Larsen had once gone to her boss's boss, Frank Collins, the marketing vice president, and complained to him about a problem she was having in dealing with Mack Rogers on an assignment Rogers had given her. The next day Rogers called her into his office, where he read her a transcript of her conversation with Collins and chastised her for not dealing with him directly. Mike sensed from this and other incidents that the company paid strict attention to the chain of command and that going around the boss was less acceptable at Frontier than in other companies.

As time went by, Mike learned from his friend Perkins, and also from a 25-year veteran of the company named Martha Oparowski, that there was considerable resentment in the company about the MBAs' salaries. They were clearly on the fast track, but people with long experience and knowledge of the company's operations were often indignant at having to teach the young MBAs the ropes while they were paid only one half to two thirds as much. Mike observed the difference in how the two kinds of employees dressed at the office. MBAs and other fast trackers always wore three-piece suits to work, always wore wing-tip shoes (even the ambitious female managers wore high-heeled wing-tips), and once in the office never kept their coats on. Perkins himself, a division manager, regularly came in without a coat, wearing a short-sleeved shirt with the top button undone and a tie loosely knotted around his neck. By dressing like that he identified himself as what he called a "steady Eddie" type of person who would always be in that fairly responsible job in the company but never get promoted. Perkins often complained about his job; he had looked at other places, but his salary was much higher than he could get anywhere else with his B.A. in education.

It seemed that Frontier kept the people it wanted with golden handcuffs, whatever their level in the hierarchy. The ambitious ones were kept happy with large bonuses, impressive titles, offices close to their bosses, and golf and other sports privileges. Martha Oparowski told Mike hat those on the fast track were worked hard, and then they either quit in frustration or were weeded out after a couple of years. Only the most aggressive made it up to the company's higher echelons. She showed him an organization chart that had come out a year earlier; fully a third of the employees on the chart at the division supervisor level and above were no longer with the company.

Mike's cubicle was relocated again in September, down the hall and out of sight and earshot of Mason's office (Exhibit 3, location 4). Mike wasn't surprised he was being moved around so much because whole departments and their complete equipment seemed to be regularly relocated to different parts of the building. New Jersey Telephone had a man assigned to Frontier full time, just to keep up with the changes. Most of the office space was divided into cubicles or stations by movable partitions. Only vice presidents and top executives had private offices. The small fourth floor was an exception to the crowding and lack of privacy. Ferris, Wesley, and a few senior staff executives had the only offices there; they were large and opulently furnished.

A New Assignment

On September 27, about two months after joining Frontier, Wynn Mason called Mike into his office and told him he was being assigned to a newly created line management position. Mike was to be the national small business operations manager. Unlike the clerical error project and others Mike had been working on, this job had definite lines of authority and criteria for evaluation. In his new position, Mike was to take charge of all small business loan processing for the

entire company, including the operations outside New Jersey—in Georgia, Texas, Arizona, and Illinois. For his first six months, Mike would be evaluated on the basis of four criteria: implementation and testing of a new computer system for small retailer loans (10 percent), accounts servicing (20 percent), organization (30 percent), and cost containment (40 percent). He was to report directly to Wynn Mason and work closely with Mack Rogers, who had supervised the organization that Mike was being assigned to take over (see Exhibits 4 and 5).

During this initial meeting about the new assignment, Mike asked Wynn Mason about the seeming inconsistencies in the organizational structure, and, in particular, why business loans were serviced by operations, while personal loans were serviced by the loan marketing departments themselves. Mason's reply was: "Do you want this job or don't you?" In that same meeting Mason indicated he felt there was "too much fat" in the small business service staff and that he planned to fire 8 of the 98 employees on Mack Rogers' service team for small business loans now that they would be under his (Mason's) control. Mason also said he planned to demote Susan Larsen from a manager to supervisor—a change of more than title, since she would have far fewer employees reporting to her (Exhibits 4 and 5). Mason told Mike he would not announce Mike's new assignment to the operations department for another day, since he wanted first to

Exhibit 4
Partial Organization as of September 27, 1978 (Prior to the Reorganization)

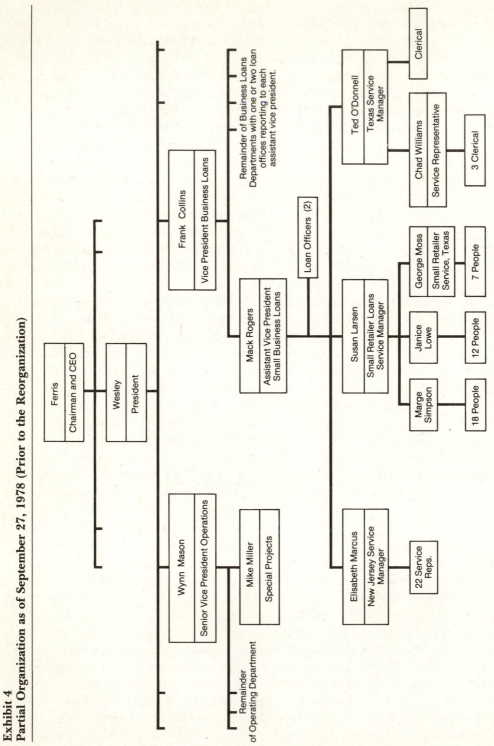

Exhibit 5
Partial Organization as of October 16, 1978 (After the Reorganization)

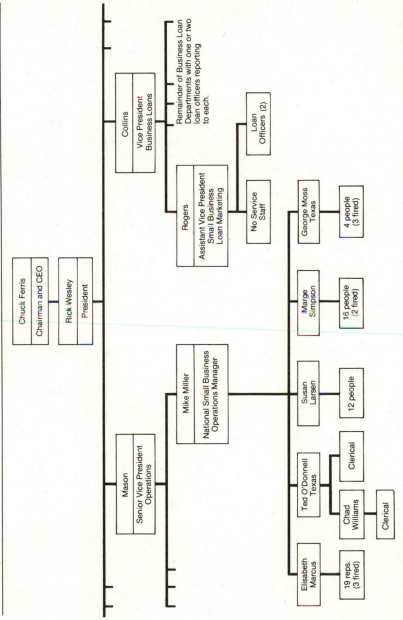

inform the affected employees located in the field.

Later the same day, September 27, Susan Larsen, Janice Lowe, and Marge Simpson, all processing managers in the organization that Mike was about to take over, came to Mike's office to congratulate him. People in nearby cubicles were surprised to hear the news. Given Mason's instructions, Mike felt very awkward about the congratulations and went in to talk with Mason about what to do with his visitors. Mason angrily told Mike to go back and emphatically deny that he had been given the position. When Mike did so, the three seemed completely befuddled. One of them commented, "Well, this is just another example of the Frontier way—great communications!"

Later Mike learned that the company's executive committee had informed all vice presidents about Mike's new job the same day Mason talked to Mike about it. Frank Collins, vice president of Business Loan Marketing, had immediately communicated the appointment to the affected supervisors—and Larsen, Lowe, and Simpson had come to congratulate Mike right away. When they told Frank Collins that Mike had denied he had the position, Collins was "all bent out of shape" by the implication that he didn't know what he was talking about. On October 4, Mike was moved into a new cubicle on the first floor, this time some distance from Mason, to begin his responsibilities as an operations manager (Exhibit 3, location 5).

Though they seemed to continue performing well professionally, Susan Larsen and Elisabeth Marcus made no bones about their disappointment at not getting the job that Mike now held. Marcus, the accounts service supervisor for New Jersey, and a Frontier veteran, was apparently very upset that Mike got the job. She told Mike that he was her 19th boss in nine years and that she was getting tired of training her bosses. Mike later discovered that Marcus became agitated whenever he tried to reorganize her area or make any moves to alter things in the group he was managing. Mike sensed that Susan Larsen was holding back information he needed; she seemed willing enough to help him learn the ins and outs of small retailer operations, but Mike felt that she was not telling him all she knew.

The Texas Incident

One afternoon in October, Wynn Mason called Mike into his office and told him that the cost of running the operation in Texas had to be reduced. There were three managerial personnel in Texas—both before and after the recent reorganization of small business loan servicing—George Moss, Ted O'Donnell, and Chad Williams (see Exhibits 4 and 5). All were located in Dallas, where they managed Frontier's business in Texas and adjacent states.

Mason had decided that Chad Williams should be transferred to Houston to provide local coverage and save on travel expenses incurred in serving the Houston market from the office in Dallas. Mike knew that it couldn't be done—Williams's wife was six months pregnant, and they had just closed on a house in Dallas—and told Mason as much. Mike pointed out to Mason that the move would end up costing the company more money than Williams's travel expenses would come to. Mike suggested the alternative of enticing Williams to relocate by giving him a cost-of-living adjustment, paying his moving expenses, and making good on whatever he might lose by selling his house so soon after buying it. That would not be as expensive in the long run as hiring someone else to work in Houston, Mike argued, because salaries in Houston were higher than in Dallas. An additional benefit was that there would be no loss of momentum in loan servicing from the extra cost of training a new employee. Mason disagreed. If Williams couldn't be moved to Houston without incurring additional cost to the company, Mason suggested Williams be fired.

Despite Mike's protests, Mason held firm on his decision. The discussion then turned to the problem of how much notice Williams should be given. Mike said that if Williams had to be fired, he would give him two weeks' notice, as provided for in Frontier's personnel policy. Mason snapped at that: "Don't do any such thing—I don't want him to be looking for a job while we're paying him; I want him to work up to the last day he's here. Tell him on a Friday afternoon

that that is his last day." Mike then argued that they should at least give Williams severance pay. Mason refused: "All those personnel policies are just guidelines." This shocked and angered Mike. He showed Mason the company regulations and insisted that the severance pay decision was Mike's to make. Williams got severance pay, but he didn't get advance notice he was being let go.

After this incident, Mike felt he more clearly understood top management's attitude toward employees. It was discouraging that company officers, and particularly his boss, cared little about the conditions that the people in the company were working under. "Cutting costs at all costs" was apparently all that concerned Frontier management.

At a company talent show one evening soon afterwards, one of the skits portrayed Rick Wesley, the company president, skulking around the building on Saturdays taking roll. Another was a kind of basketball game in which the score reflected the number of divorces chalked up to the players on each team, divorces that were clearly a direct result of how hard the players fought for the team. That day, Mike's desk had been moved to the far end of the building; he felt somewhat relieved to be even further away from Wynn Mason (Exhibit 3, location 6).

Colleagues

Mike found that of the five people he felt he had to count on most in order to get his job done (Mason, Rogers, Larsen, Marcus, and Simpson), only one could be relied on to assist him without conflict. Marge Simpson knew the small retail loan processing operation well; she had written the computer algorithms being tested and was an energetic and forceful supervisor. Though Marge was helpful, Mike did not find her very intelligent, and he doubted that she would ever get ahead in the company. After working at his job for a couple months, he even came to feel that he might actually be better off without her. But for the time being, Mike relied on her as a kind of go-between, someone to educate him and keep him informed on the retail loan program that Mack Rogers was continually modifying. Marge also took on the bulk of the computer system analysis project that was part of Mike's new assignment.

The other two women who worked for Mike, Larsen and Marcus, were reasonably good employees, but Mike did not feel he could trust either of them. At annual salaries of $17,000 and $18,000, respectively, they shared the common attitude of Frontier employees toward MBAs: that at more than $30,000 per year, MBAs, even those new to the organization, should be able to "walk on water." Mason's management by decree, his increasing abrasiveness with Mike, and Mike's inability to earn his confidence, were all a growing source of frustration in Mike's dealings with his boss. Mason was the least well educated of all the company officers. Despite

his 16 years with the company, Mason was known to feel threatened because he did not have an MBA.

But Mike's biggest problem was Mack Rogers. When Mike took on the assignment as national small business operations manager, he was unaware of the long history of competition and animosity between Mason and Rogers. As Mike soon discovered, Mason and Rogers had been locked in an organizational battle for over a year. The dispute had centered on who should control the processing and servicing of the small business loans, the job Mike was eventually assigned to. As the most rapidly growing market segment, Rogers had wanted to retain control of small business loan servicing (i.e., renegotiating loan provisions and other matters requiring personalized service) after the loan had been made by the loan officers reporting to Rogers. Since this was a new area for the company, Rogers had been able to build up his own service staff—something no other assistant vice president in the business loan area had done. As a manager with profit responsibility for small business loans, Rogers felt that the servicing of these loans ought to be under his jurisdiction. "Operations ought to be concerned only with the handling of payments and other paperwork on the computer," Rogers had argued.

Mason had felt otherwise, and he had ultimately prevailed. He had persuaded Rick Wesley, the company president, that it was in Frontier's best interest to have the servicing of small business loans handled by his operations unit even though these loans had never been serviced by the operations personnel. The service organization that Rogers had built up for the small business segment was thus transferred to Mason, who then assigned Mike to supervise it. Rogers was left with a staff of only two loan officers (see Exhibit 5).

Rogers's anger at losing his empire was no trivial matter. During Mike's first month with the company he had seen Rogers make a scene in the computer room. Rogers had picked up a computer program that he had written and torn it to shreds, yelling obscenities as he did so. One of the computer operators had evidently been having difficulty following the program instructions and was asking for clarification—the shreds of the program were flung in the operator's face as Rogers stomped off. Mike had observed that Rogers was a hothead, but he only lost his temper at the little people who would not affect his advancement. With his superiors, he was a master at managing impressions and power plays. With his peers he was a subtle adversary, as he demonstrated repeatedly in his dealings with Mike.

Because he was the marketing manager for small business loans, Rogers made the decisions as to how these loans would be structured, serviced, and processed. Mike was responsible for carrying out his decisions by managing their servicing and processing. Within a month after Mike took the new assignment, Rogers prepared a

memo telling Mike to update the processing of small business loans to conform to a new policy he had developed on delinquent payments. A copy of the memo was sent to Mason two days later, but Mike didn't receive the memo until two days after that. Before then Rogers had gone to Mason to complain that several days had passed but nothing had been done by "your new MBA manager." Another memo from Rogers requested Mike's action on an issue by November 14; it had apparently been dictated on the 17th but backdated the 11th, arriving at Mike's desk on the 18th. A copy went to Mason, who also got a copy of another memo dictated and delivered to both Mike and Mason on the 20th. In the second memo, Rogers told Mike that he had failed to do what Rogers had requested, that he had not cooperated with Rogers, and that Mike had neglected his responsibilities and not performed the job he was being paid to do.

Mike approached Mason a couple of times to indicate that several memos had been backdated, but Mason didn't seem to believe him. Mike also went directly to Rogers and complained, but met with cold indifference. Mike felt stumped. On November 24, Mike and all his home office employees were moved to a new operations area in the basement of the office building (Exhibit 3, location 7).

As evidenced by the memo wars, Mason and Rogers continued to play a rough game of kick ball, often with Mike Miller as the ball. Rogers would come down to see Mike and tell him to do things one way. Mason would tell Mike to disregard what Rogers was saying because Mason was running the show. Mike needed Roger's help and Mason's help and got neither. Mike began to feel that he was in the wrong place at Frontier or that Frontier was perhaps the wrong place altogether for him.

One person who persuaded Mike to stay on was David Arnold, the manager who had been yelling in the hall on Mike's second day at Frontier. It turned out that Arnold was one of the more mild mannered of the Frontier managers, and one of the very few who had brought experience from another finance company with him to the job. The degree to which Mike became really thoroughly versed in the workings of the operations department was to a great extent the result of Arnold's assistance, for Arnold was a manager of long standing in home office operations. David Arnold shared some of Mike's negative reactions about the company but had no alternative employment options that would pay him anywhere near his salary at Frontier.

Arnold told Mike many stories about Frontier managers who had been fired for having two declining quarters in a row; of managers who had failed to predict difficulties in their portfolios and then been fired when problems showed up on the quarterly reports. Arnold also spoke of the success of some of the loan marketing managers: people who had come up with ingenious ways to cut the risk of default, people who designed new loan pack-

ages, people who had made loans to high-risk but eventually very profitable ventures. On hearing these stories, Mike wished he had insisted on the position in personal loan operations that he had been promised when hired. Arnold also mentioned that the woman who took that job, starting the first of November, was doing especially well for a non-MBA who had been promoted from within the company. Mike wondered how she might have done as the pawn sitting between the two jousting knights, Mason and Rogers.

On February 6, Mike's group was moved next to the basement cafeteria (Exhibit 3, location 9). Mike commented to Hal Norris, a friend in personnel, about the endless moving of people, furniture, and equipment at Frontier and the incessant screaming and yelling. Mike had met Norris in November when they had discussed the possible hiring of a new loan service representative for the Arizona office. Norris was an older man, a fatherly type of person whom Mike found easy to talk to. They had chatted over lunch several times about Mike's growing frustrations with his job, and especially the doubts he had about whether he could get the job done in the company. Norris asked lots of questions and showed the kind of sympathy that made Mike feel comfortable sharing confidences with him.

The next day Mike had a chance to visit with his friend, Jack Perkins. Mike told Jack of his feeling about his latest move and mentioned having a conversation about it with Norris. "Hal Norris from personnel?" Jack asked. Mike nodded yes. Jack slapped himself on the head and said: "Norris is an informer for top management at Frontier." Known as the father confessor, Norris saw to it that the confessions he heard made their way quickly to the ears at the top. In his 10 years at Frontier, Norris had been moved strategically through all the departments so that he could find out how they worked and get acquainted with many of the key personnel. Norris not only befriended new managers, Perkins said, but also called on his long-time acquaintances for performance evaluations.

By mid-February, Ted O'Donnell in Dallas had finally been able to find a new supervisor to take the place of Chad Williams, at $3,000 more than they had been paying Chad. The morale of the Texas employees which had plummeted because of Williams's unexpected firing, was slowly beginning to recover. Mike had been able to decrease costs in the Texas operations by 40 percent, and in New Jersey by 30 percent. The computer evaluation project which Marge Simpson had conducted for Mike had also been completed. Despite the many problems, Mike felt that he had established a reasonable performance record considering the circumstances. He still was not sure what Mason thought about his performance. Mike had promised himself that he would remain at Frontier for at least the first six months, and wondered what he should do now that he had.

On Friday, February 23, 1979, Mike walked briskly into Mason's office at 10, ready for his first six-month performance evaluation at Fronter. He hoped he would handle it well.

CASE 2–2
Eric Weiss (A)

Jay A. Conger
Vijay Sathe

Eric Weiss had been working a little over two months in the Miami branch of Superior Foods when he received a letter from the corporate personnel director, Barry Walls. The letter said Walls had "something important to discuss" and asked Eric to be available at 10:30 A.M. on Friday, September 9, 1977. Eric marked the date on his calendar and stopped to reflect on the problems he had encountered since his job started. To begin with, there was confusion over who was responsible for his training program. Corporate kept in touch by phone but provided no direction. The local branch manager, Anatol France, was too busy to take time to map out Eric's responsibilities; in fact, he felt that was corporate's job. And when Eric had come up with projects on his own initiative, France had not been supportive.

This case was prepared by Jay A. Conger (under the direction of Vijay Sathe).

Being new to Miami only seemed to aggravate Eric's situation. Local attitudes here seemed so different from those in his native Boston.

Eric thought back to the opportunities he had anticipated at Superior. He had been attracted by the idea of becoming a branch manager in only two years after graduation, with responsibility for his own operations and a bonus tied to profits. That expectation was fading as his frustrations grew. Still Eric felt that the letter from Walls was a hopeful sign of change; it seemed that corporate would intercede at last and clear things up.

Superior Foods Inc.

With revenues now exceeding $500 million, Superior Foods Inc. had enjoyed rapid growth in the dairy products industry. Through local distribution branches, it provided a full range of dairy and other food products to supermarkets, restaurants, and institutions throughout the United States. From humble beginnings as a regional dairy producer and distributor in the Midwest, the company had moved toward rapid expansion in the early 1970s by acquiring additional dairy operations, building an extensive network of company-owned distributors, and broadening the product line to include juices, meat products, and bakery goods. These new products accounted for 30 percent of Superior's product line, while the remaining 70 percent was in dairy products.

The company operated on a de-centralized basis with branches serving as profit centers. Corporate provided support functions and products to the 26 branches. Revenues from branches ranged widely, from a high of $50 million at the San Francisco branch to $5 or $6 million in smaller units. In addition to the dairy lines, the company owned several food-processing plants which produced juices, packaged meats, and other Superior-branded products.

Competition within the industry was strong but localized. A majority of the firms were smaller regional operators with independent owners. Of the few "nationals," Superior was among the largest. A firm's success was determined largely by competitive product quality, prompt delivery service, an extensive product line, and the personal selling efforts of local managers. Superior was known for its quality and full-line service at competitive prices.

At the branch level, however, selling skills and delivery service varied. Since both were critical to strong customer relationships, corporate was highly dependent upon the branches for the company's overall success. It was company policy to keep in close contact with them. Local managers knew they could call on Jay Kunz, the president of Superior, at any time, and Jay would personally give them assistance with any problems. The branches' autonomy extended to being allowed to supplement the Superior line with local products on an as-needed basis.

As Superior grew, its lack of professional management skills at the local branches began to present serious difficulties. Many of the local operators had come up from the ranks, starting as dairy sales and delivery persons. These so-called old timers lacked the sophisticated management skills needed to keep the growing operations profitable, and corporate was struggling with ways to solve this problem. Superior was exploring the possibility of infusing the company with MBAs: After a two-year training program, they would be candidates for the position of branch manager. It was too early to tell how effective this program would be.

Background

Eric Weiss, 25, had a B.A. in finance and accounting from the University of Chicago. He worked for a management consulting firm for two years prior to joining Harvard Business School in the fall of 1975. He was ambitious for financial success and intrigued with the possibilities of entrepreneurial ventures. He was full of new ideas. During his first summer at HBS, Eric began a new venture, the *Campus News*. During his second year, he was a consultant to Atlantic Engineering, where he worked on an inventory control problem. He also operated a resume-production service.

The Job Search

During the summer between his first and second years, Eric had fallen in love with a young woman named Ruth. But by January the tumultuous romance had ended abruptly. When Eric began interviewing in February, he seemed to be unable to concentrate. He was anxious to find a job and finish school.

Eric was looking for a position in brand management or branch management with certain criteria of independence: wide discretion, rewards tied to results, and opportunities to be creative in a job that was both lucrative and fun.

On February 2, 1977, Eric had his first interview, with a consumer products company. Two weeks later, he was invited to visit corporate headquarters. He enjoyed the people he met and found product management appealing, but to his disappointment, no offer came through.

Two weeks later, Eric interviewed with a large manufacturer of fasteners. He was excited by the company's innovative character and felt that he had made a favorable impression. However, when he visited the company's headquarters again in April, he got the impression either that the company hadn't formalized its position or had simply decided that Eric would not be a good fit. As he had expected, no offer was made.

On February 15, Eric interviewed with the community development division of a large corporation. He liked its entrepreneurial character, and the location, California, seemed like an ideal place to live. Eric was invited for further interviews and was made an offer as a financial analyst. But his real interests were in line management, and he hesitated to accept a staff position. He had until April 15 to decide.

On February 16, Eric met with Frank Smallwood, manager of labor relations for Superior Foods. Smallwood mentioned that they were looking for MBAs who were not afraid to get their hands dirty and who were interested in managing one of their branches after two years of training. The idea appealed to Eric. When the personnel director, Donald Thomas, a Harvard MBA, called to give him the names of two new MBAs at Superior who might give him their impressions of the company, Eric got in touch with them.

This led to a long conversation a few days later with John Drayton, who had graduated from HBS in 1975 and started in one of Superior's branches. John described the environment at Superior as lacking in "professional management." He said he was as much a tutor to his own boss as he was a subordinate. He pointed out that the success of Eric's training program would depend largely upon which branch he was in and stressed the importance of carefully considering his fit with the local branch manager. In general, John felt positive about the company and his potential for contributing to its success.

Pat Donahue, a Wharton MBA, was less enthusiastic. Eric's conversation with him did not flow as openly as the discussion with John, but Eric thought this might be partly because Pat was not from HBS.

Some time later, Frank Smallwood invited Eric to visit Superior's offices in Milwaukee. Eric made the trip on March 30. Smallwood explained to him that Superior was trying to upgrade the quality of its branch managers through an MBA training program. Eric would be in that pilot project if he was accepted. Smallwood emphasized that most branch managers had come up from the ranks and, despite their good selling skills, often lacked managerial skills. By bringing in people like Eric, Superior hoped to ensure itself of a supply of good branch managers. These MBAs would have to spend two years in the field riding around in delivery trucks, making sales calls, and generally getting their hands dirty. Smallwood mentioned that John Drayton, the Harvard MBA, was doing very well in his local branch. He thought Eric would be a good fit too.

After the interview, Smallwood introduced Eric to Barry Walls, a human relations consultant to Superior, who would be coordinating the MBA training program. Unfortunately, Walls was on his way to a meeting and had only a few minutes to chat. He appeared to Eric to be an even tempered man with a cautious style, who wanted to convey the impression of being a nice guy.

Eric was then introduced to Jay Kunz, the president of Superior. Kunz was an imposing man in his 40s, the son of Superior's founder. He had a down-to-earth manner, was well tailored, and wore a gold tie pin and cuff links studded with emeralds. Eric thought to himself, "This man knows he's successful." As they talked, Eric found Kunz to be a warm, impressive man. His knowledge of the business and apparently sincere interest in his people appealed to Eric. Kunz spoke of the firm's need to grow and the necessity of upgrading the quality of branch management. He asked Eric's opinion of the industry and how he thought MBAs could play a useful role. Eric felt the interview had gone well, and Kunz closed with "I hope I've been of help to you."

As he left Kunz's office, Eric sensed that Superior was the place for him. The new MBA training program with its emphasis on working in the field appealed to him. Riding around in delivery trucks might even be fun for a while. He figured the work would be hard for the first two years and probably tedious at times. But after that he would have his own branch and be his own boss. As he flew home that night, Eric fantasized: He would transform this mom-and-pop company into a 20th-century corporation.

On his return, Eric read through Superior's annual report for information on the company's profitability, size, and philosophy. The report showed sales at $520 million with moderate profitability. Growth had been consistent, and Superior was clearly a dominant member of its industry. His classmates' reactions were mixed. Some thought the dairy food industry would be dull. Others were im-

pressed that within two years Eric could have his own branch with a bonus tied to branch profitability.

On the morning of April 4, Barry Walls called to offer Eric a place in the MBA training program at Superior. Eric was ecstatic to hear that Walls would be custom tailoring the program to suit him and that San Francisco appeared to be the likely branch. He also said that Eric had until April 15 to make his decision. Walls indicated he would be acting as full-time director of personnel, since Thomas had just been made vice president of manufacturing.

Eric thanked Walls and requested a letter outlining the offer. Walls said that letters were not usually mailed out until after an offer had been accepted. Eric was surprised but requested that a letter be sent nonetheless. Several days went by with no letter from Walls. Eric called Walls and was told that the written offer was on its way. Again, after several days had passed, Eric called again, and was told the letter had been mailed. When he finally received the letter, Eric skimmed to the bottom line where he read, "Once again, Rich, welcome to Superior Foods, Inc."

The San Francisco Fiasco

On April 14, Eric called Walls to accept the offer. He initially reached Walls's secretary, Gladys, who apologized profusely for typing the "clerical error" in his offer letter. Shortly afterwards, Eric received a call from Walls to tell him that arrangements had been made for Eric to visit the San Francisco branch. It was the company's largest, with revenues exceeding $50 million.

Eric flew to the West Coast 10 days later to meet Al Weiner, manager of the San Francisco branch. Walls had told Eric that senior management at Superior thought Weiner was doing wonderful things. Weiner had an MBA from Darden, and was a slender, athletic-looking man in his early 30s. People in the office addressed him as "Mr. Weiner."

Weiner began the interview with some suprising questions. He asked Eric what he would be doing for the company and what the management training program was all about. Eric soon realized that Weiner didn't know much about the program or why Eric had been hired. Eric was amazed by this lack of communication with the corporate office. He wondered whether Weiner saw him as a possible threat.

Toward the end of the interview, Weiner mentioned that he wasn't sure that Superior would be making Eric an offer but that they would be in touch. Eric was astonished that Weiner was unaware that Superior had already made the offer.

As Eric was about to leave, Weiner said he would like to ask a personal question. Eric gestured that he didn't mind. "Do you come from a wealthy family?" Weiner asked. Stunned, Eric replied that he did not and thanked Weiner for his time.

The visit had lasted two hours. During this time, Eric had met only two other individuals, each for about 10 minutes and simply to exchange pleasantries. Eric knew how unsatisfactory the interview had been and wondered what Weiner and Walls would do. Despite the poor start, Eric thought San Francisco would be a good place to get some training. It seemed well organized, and Eric liked the prospect of living in California. He believed he could handle Weiner's toughness and learn something from him, but he was upset that corporate had handled communications with the branch so poorly in connection with his training program.

On the way home, Eric stopped over in Milwaukee for a prearranged meeting with Walls to debrief the branch visit. At breakfast, Walls commented that while "things looked O.K. in San Francisco," it might be advisable for Eric to visit the Denver branch also. Eric told him that he preferred San Francisco, but Walls said it would be worthwhile to have a point of comparison. Denver might turn out a better fit, and Marv Eakman, the Denver branch manager, needed professional help. Eric realized then that the result of his San Francisco interview was even worse than he had imagined.

Off to Denver

By the end of the following week, on May 6, Eric arrived in Denver. Marv Eakman met him and drove him out to the office in a large silver Cadillac. Marv appeared to be a real salesman—all smiles and back-slapping. He was in his 60s, perhaps, with grey hair and thick glasses. He talked non-stop. Eric thought he could "train" Marv, and that Marvin would be more human to work with than Weiner. Two years of paying dues in Marv's branch might not be so bad.

At the office, Marv spoke of himself as a self-made man who began by selling milk off the back of a truck. He seemed tireless in his descriptions of life in those days. Gradually, Marv shifted to asking Eric what he would like to do in the Denver office. After the San Francisco incident, Eric knew he had to make a good impression on Marv. Eric decided to project a Harvard MBA image—confident, bright, and articulate. Eric spoke of his skills in the use of traffic algorithms, inventory control, and data processing. But he could see that Marv was becoming uncomfortable. At one point, Marv interrupted and tried to change the subject. The interview ended half an hour later, and Eric was left wondering whether he might have been more cautious in articulating his professional skills.

Walls's manner was abrupt when Eric called on his return to Boston. He wanted to know what Eric had said to Marv. Eric said he had talked about restructuring the organization and using more sophisticated control and scheduling systems. Eric had evidently scared Marv, Walls said, so Denver was not a "good fit," Walls continued, but there were other options: Mi-ami, Detroit, or Pittsburgh. Miami, in particular, would be a real challenge because it was a turnaround situation.

Eric felt shaken as he hung up. Now, for the first time, he began to wonder whether Superior was the right company for him. However, another round of interviews seemed more than he could face, and he also had financial and time pressures to contend with.

Eric was scheduled to go to Europe for two weeks' vacation before beginning work at Superior. He wasn't sure which branch he would be assigned to on his return. There were too many loose ends. Before he left, Eric dropped off a resume to Sony Industries in response to their advertisement for MBAs.

The Miami Visit

After his return from Europe on Sunday, May 29, Eric called Walls and was told that arrangements had been made for him to visit Miami. Walls would be going too.

As agreed, Eric met Walls at the Eastern Airlines ticket counter at the Miami airport on Monday, June 13. On their way out to the Miami branch, Eric decided to accept Wall's advice—that Eric should simply tell Anatol France, the branch manager, that he was good at problem solving. Eric felt uneasy about this coached setup, but was determined to settle the question of where he would work and what he would be doing.

Walls explained that France was new to the Miami branch and was overseeing it as a temporary assignment. France had been very successful at the Farmland Corporation, and Superior management hoped he would be able to revitalize the ailing Miami branch. He retained his position as a regional vice president overseeing two other Superior branches in the South (see Exhibit 1). The Miami branch had been in serious trouble with high overhead costs and level sales at $9 million.

would be doing at the Miami branch.

Walls had been visiting with France in the meantime but excused himself when the other two arrived at France's office. Eric and France sat down to talk. France was a large man, about 6 feet, 6 inches tall, and weighing perhaps 200 pounds. Eric learned that he was an ex-pro basketball player and, indeed, he radiated the go-like-hell

Exhibit 1
Organization Chart

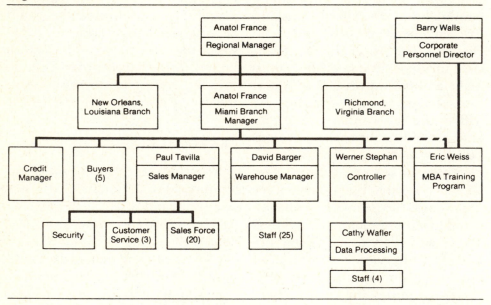

Before Eric met with France, he was escorted around the facilities by Paul Tavilla, the sales manager. Tavilla, a short, balding, middle-aged man, appeared jovial and placed his arm around Eric's shoulder as he showed him the facilities. Despite the show of friendliness, Eric sensed an underlying uneasiness as Tavilla asked Eric what he

attitude of a professional athlete. France described the problems of the branch and said he needed professional help. He asked Eric how he thought he could help, and Eric spoke briefly about his skills at problem solving.

The interview went well. As they drove away, Walls turned to Eric and said, "I don't know what you did, but Anatol liked you. So you're going to Miami." Eric could only feel a sense of relief.

Miami Operations

Two weeks later, on June 27, Eric began work at the Miami branch. Reporting to the branch manager was a controller, a sales manager, a full-time sales force of 20, a warehouse crew of 25, 5 food buyers, and a small office staff (Exhibit 1). The branch serviced approximately 1,500 accounts, all within one day's drive from the warehouse. The sales area had been broken down into territories, each with its own salesperson. Accounts varied widely and included supermarkets, restaurants, and institutions. Competition was fairly strong, with the largest firm being a local dairy operation with $20 million in sales.

Sometime later, Eric learned that the Miami branch had a history of management problems and that it was still plagued with excessive overhead costs. Superior had acquired the branch in 1973 from a local distributor. Sales at the time were $15 million and had since dropped to their present level of $9 million. The original owner had stayed on after the acquisition, but conflicts had led to his dismissal. New management had been unable to improve a deteriorating sales position. Corporate reasoned that the original owner had developed important account relationships which no longer existed and, in desperation, asked the original

owner to rejoin the firm. Conflicts arose again, however, and he was asked to leave the branch a second time. Since his departure, there had been significant turnover in branch management. Among the office staff, there was apparently a standing joke about who would be "fired next Friday." This lack of management continuity had led to continued tension between corporate headquarters and local managers. Overhead costs grew as sales dipped to 50 percent of their earlier levels. Only two thirds of the branch's warehouse space was currently being utilized (see Exhibit 2). Transportation costs remained as high as they had been when sales were double the current level because the distance of the delivery routes, which accounted for most of the costs, had not appreciably changed.

The First Project

On his first day at work, June 27, Eric met with the staff to talk about what they did and about the company in general. His first task was to reorganize the warehouse inventory by systematically numbering pallet locations. A deadline was set for the second week of July.

Because the first project was taking longer than expected, Eric decided to do extra work on the fourth of July. He was riding a pallet jack in the warehouse freezers when he heard the phone ring in an outside office. As he turned the jack toward the exit, the front forks plunged to the wall. Eric swung the

Exhibit 2
Office Layout

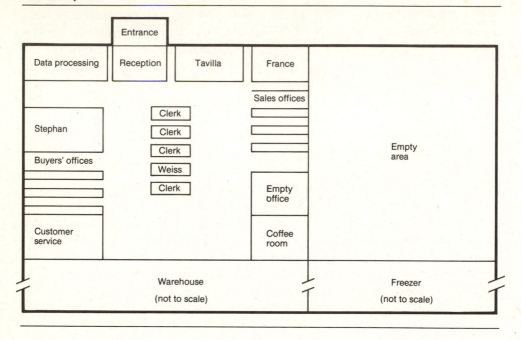

jack out and saw that the rear of the jack was now headed for the wall. He kicked out his foot to push off the freezer wall and suddenly found his foot pinned between the fork and the wall. Eric had to spend that afternoon in a hospital.

Getting to Know the Office

In addition to the pallet numbering project, Eric's first month was taken up with devising more efficient truck schedules, supervising the physical inventory, and making sales and delivery calls. The novelty and variety of his work pleased him, but Eric felt frustrated by the noise and activity around his office, which was located in the main office area. It was difficult to concentrate on projects with people constantly coming and going and often talking loudly. When Eric asked France if he could use an adjacent empty office, he was told that it was reserved for corporate headquarters personnel who frequently visited the branch.

By the end of the first month, Eric had become acquainted with the key personnel in Miami. While he liked most of the staff, he found their "Southern" pace much slower than his own. France, his immediate supervisor, was more difficult to deal with than Eric had anticipated. It seemed that France often masked his true feelings and was uncommunicative. His responses to Eric's questions sounded expedient rather than helpful, and discussions of Eric's role in the branch apparently made him ill at ease. Eric knew France was under pressure to turn the branch around and that France had more on his mind than corporate's plans for an MBA training program. He suspected that France's underlying message to Eric was "You know more about your training program than I do—talk to corporate." Eric had seen how France manipulated others, and this worried him because he was dependent on France not only for his performance evaluation, but also for determining when he was ready to become a branch manager.

Tavilla, the sales manager, was also a problem, as Eric had sensed he would be from the very beginning. Behind his friendly facade, Tavilla was resentful, Eric thought, that he would be a branch manager in only two years, when Tavilla had spent most of his long career seeking that goal. Eric suspected that Tavilla knew Eric was earning $26,000 compared to his $27,000. Tavilla apparently thought that Eric's presence in Miami was a step toward a takeover of the Miami operations. Eric had overheard several telephone and other conversations Tavilla had with corporate, and a friend of Eric's, Sylvia in Customer Service, had confirmed that Tavilla had close ties to headquarters.

Tavilla had been the branch sales manager during a long period of considerable management turnover. Tavilla alone symbolized continuity in the Miami operations. Eric learned that Tavilla and France were seemingly close and that Tavilla expected to replace France once the major problems at the branch had been brought un-

der control. Their relationship, however, seemed to go in cycles. They would have run-ins occasionally, and Eric suspected that Tavilla often tried to pressure corporate to get France off his back. At the moment, Tavilla had no title. He had recently hired John Barkman as sales manager and was evidently preparing to become branch manager himself.

Eric's relationship with David Barger, the warehouse manager, was more congenial. David was in his 50s, tall and soft spoken—a real Southerner, who called everyone Mr. or Miss. He apparently was not close to France and preferred to be left alone to run the warehouse. Anything Mr. France approved, David would agree to do. Eric often went to the back of the warehouse where David's office was, to chat.

Eric was just becoming friendly with Werner Stephan, the branch controller, who had arrived a week ahead of Eric. A small man in his 30s, Werner spoke rapidly and was often referred to as the "efficient Northerner." He wanted everyone to be productive. As manager of the accounting department, Werner was continually in contact with Eric through work on data processing projects. Eric suspected that Werner had little influence with France. Werner had upset the office staff several times over such matters as proper completion of time cards; staff members had complained to France about Werner's "Northern efficiency." One day, Eric saw France ask Werner to fire a buyer on his behalf; he suspected France was trying to use Werner as his hatchet man.

Werner supervised Cathy Wafler, the data processing manager. Cathy seemed to be in her late 30s. She was very conscientious, but she became quite a source of irritation for Eric. Except for himself, Cathy was the only person who understood data processing, and Eric saw this made her relatively powerful within the branch. She appeared to be on close terms with Tavilla and France. Eric did not believe Wafler had the necessary skills for the branch. Her lack of technical ability often caused delays, and she seemed to resist every change in the computer programs that Eric was working on. A new routing system that he had attempted to institute required additional data to be listed on the warehouse computer documents. Cathy objected that that would take months to do, but Eric knew the project would take between 10 and 50 hours of programming time. In an attempt to get around Cathy's resistance, Eric went directly to France and said that the new routing system was ready to go. When he mentioned Cathy's objection that it would take several months to complete the new system, France suggested that Werner, Cathy, and Eric make a decision. Werner, who was Cathy's superior, ultimately agreed to assign the project to Cathy, but not on a priority basis. Werner knew little about programming, and Eric interpreted this as a political move by Werner to protect his relationship with Cathy and France.

Superior's group controller for the Southeast, John Sewell, was frequently called in to assist the Miami branch in improving its control and reporting functions. Eric discovered that he had much in common with John. They both shared accounting and finance backgrounds, and both enjoyed discussions as professionals. John was a friendly, outgoing man in his 30s. He told Eric about the conflict between France and Tavilla and his own disagreements with them over corporate reporting responsibilities. John was frustrated at having to spend 80 percent of his time in Miami when other branches needed his attention. In one of their discussions, John confided that he was planning to leave Superior because of his troubles with the Miami branch.

The Desk Incident

About a month after his arrival in Miami, Eric walked into the office at 9 o'clock one morning and found his desk missing. He remembered that the office was to be redecorated the previous night. Several people joined Eric in the search for his desk. About 15 minutes later, the desk was discovered in one corner of the warehouse (Exhibit 2). Eric was upset to see that the drawers were opened and certain project files were missing. He was beginning to lose his patience with Miami. The place was too noisy, he was always being interrupted, everything was poorly organized, and now his files were gone.

Suddenly, one of the staff appeared with the missing files and said Tavilla had found them. Eric headed for France's office, but France was not in. Eric then went to Tavilla and told him he felt the office was too distracting, and he would do better working at home that day. Eric asked Tavilla to tell France that he could be reached at home. Eric knew he was being rebellious. He also knew he needed to get out of the office. Later he phoned France's office and left a message to return the call, but France never called back.

The next morning Eric entered France's office and apologized: "I'm sorry I took off yesterday. Things were pretty crazy here. With all the distractions, I thought I could get more work done at home." France responded that noise and interruptions were common in the business and that Eric had better get used to them if this was the career he had in mind. France then declared: "Maybe you'd be better off in a corporate environment, an ivory tower looking out to the future." Later that day, a staff member told Eric he had overheard France and Tavilla expressing their anger at Eric's abrupt departure the previous day.

After that, Eric's contact with France diminished significantly. Eric continued to approach France to ask if he had heard anything from corporate about his training program, but France would simply reply he thought corporate was supposed to be in direct contact with Eric.

The Inventory Episode

The Miami branch accounted for its physical inventory at the end of July for corporate reporting purposes. Eric knew how inventory counts were done and volunteered to supervise this task, which he felt would be seen as a plus on his record. On July 28, Eric started the project off, dividing staff members into two-person teams, each with a counter and a checker. Available to help were France, Tavilla, Stephan, the warehouse staff, and salespeople. Because of their knowledge of the product line, the salespeople traditionally had helped with the physical inventory count.

Once the task began at 8 A.M., every aisle was to be counted by the counter and double-checked by the checker. But as the counting progressed, they kept disappearing. Apparently, the salespeople hated the task and attempted to do as little as possible and to leave as soon as they could. They went to their offices or ended up on the phone with a customer. Then France and Tavilla vanished. Everyone apparently assumed that Eric was supervising the effort and left him to worry about how the task would be completed.

Eric became more and more frustrated and apathetic. With everyone disappearing, entire sections were skipped over. When the results were compiled at 3 P.M. and compared with the perpetual inventory records, an enormous discrepancy showed up. The perpetual inventory record was far in excess of the actual count. Eric realized the afternoon's effort was meaningless and watched helplessly as France and Tavilla expressed amazement at the gap. They insisted Eric, as supervisor, was responsible for it.

Eric protested he had had no support, but France appeared unimpressed. They resumed the task later that afternoon. By 8 P.M. Eric felt the project was not accomplishing anything. He walked over to France, who was helping count the inventory, said good night, and left for home.

By the next morning, the inventory was still unresolved, and Stephan had been assigned to the project. France said nothing to Eric, but Tavilla smiled and made a joke about the affair. Eric knew that he would have to do something dramatic to restore his relationship with France.

Wall's Visit

Over the next several weeks in August, Eric felt France was distancing himself even further from him. Eric was still working on the original projects and had little reason to approach France, which made things seem more bearable.

On Monday, September 5, a letter arrived from Walls indicating that he would be visiting the branch on Friday, September 9, and would like to meet with Eric to discuss an important matter. Eric speculated that Walls was probably coming to discuss his training program. Over the months, he had received an occasional call from Walls, asking how things were going. Eric had always said that things were going well; he had said his only regret was that France had little time to spend with him. It would be nice to see Walls, Eric thought, and to talk perhaps more openly about some of the problems Eric was facing. Later that day, Eric received a message that Walls was postponing his visit till after the weekend and would be arriving Monday, September 12. There had been a death in Walls's family.

CASE 2–3
Jennifer Bent (A)

Robert Mueller, Jr.
Vijay Sathe

Jennifer Bent smiled to herself when the secretary to the personnel director for Wendell Records, Inc. told her that her boss, Carl Sides, was at lunch. Jennifer was a second-year student at Harvard Business School, and for the past six weeks she had avoided giving the company a response to a job offer made on April 20, 1980. She

This case was prepared by Robert Mueller, Jr. (under the direction of Vijay Sathe).

was glad her tactical maneuvers, such as calling at lunch or after 5, had worked, but she knew that time was running out, and a choice soon had to be made. The financial offers before her were Wendell's low of $32,500, Compusound's high of $50,000, and an as yet untendered offer from the Heslop House Recording Company. The choice was not as simple as it seemed.

Nineteen-eighty was not a good year to be looking for a new job, particularly in classical music recording, the slowest growth area of the industry. Nevertheless, Jennifer's life had always revolved around music, and her ambition was to head a classical recording company. Wendell was a 60-year-old, family-held firm with an elitist reputation and an incomparable list of musicians and orchestras on contract. The disadvantages were the low salary offered her and an uneasy recruiting experience, which included some sexual harassment. Compusound offered a high salary but, as its name implied, it had little to do with classical music. Heslop House, an old company, was pushing ahead with new recording and video technologies, but it could not make an offer for another month. Jennifer was left staving off Wendell while she waited for better offers.

Background

Jennifer grew up in a family of professional musicians. Her mother was a clarinetist who had played with the Cleveland Symphony for most of her career, and her father taught music appreciation classes at the college level. Internationally famous musicians, composers, conductors, and impresarios often visited her family, and the house would be filled with music, foreign accents, laughter, and conversations ranging from international politics to musical gossip. It was a heady environment for Jennifer to grow up in, and one which she wanted to maintain in her adult life.

Jennifer studied violin and piano as a child and went to Oberlin College on the assumption that she, too, would pursue a career as an orchestral musician. When she graduated in 1974, Jennifer was still planning on a performing career, but opportunities to play with a prestigious symphony were scarce. In order to pay the bills and also hedge her long-term bet, Jennifer accepted a job as secretary to the production manager of the Hamilton Record Company in Philadelphia.

After 18 months at Hamilton, Jennifer decided the position was a dead end. She moved to San Francisco for a junior production position with DLA Records, where she had the opportunity to produce a string quartet recording. But she found that at DLA she had to contend with an assumption that women were not as smart or creative as men and that they gave way under pressure.

In the summer of 1977, Jennifer answered an ad for a California sales representative with the New York-based Symphony Records,

Inc. Women were just beginning to get into record sales, and Jennifer felt it would help round out her experience in the record industry. She was hired, and she enjoyed her one year with Symphony. There seemed to be little, if any, discrimination. She was well liked and appreciated the company's emphasis on merit. It convinced Jennifer that she wanted to stay in the recording industry, though it changed her strategy for getting to the top. Most record executives came from the creative, talent-development side of the industry, but a growing number of "business types" were moving up to the top, and Jennifer decided her chances would be better if her expertise were more business related. On February 14, 1978, the last day on which third-period applications were allowed, Jennifer applied to the Harvard Business School. On March 27, she was accepted.

Harvard Business School

When Jennifer called her parents with the news that she had been accepted at Harvard Business School, her father was surprised and disappointed that she had so definitely chosen to forego a career as a violinist. He doubted that business school would be a valuable education. It took some persuasion for Jennifer to convince her father that she had not totally abandoned the world of fine arts and culture for mammon. Jennifer found HBS difficult but felt on balance that she had received a "terrific education" at Harvard.

Prestige Records

Jennifer worked at Prestige Records, a subsidiary of Wendell, during the summer between her first and second years. Prestige, which produced the Great Masters series, had been acquired by Wendell 10 years earlier, in 1969. The Great Masters series repackaged the most familiar movements of already recorded symphonies. At their most sophisticated, these recordings would appear as "Bach's Greatest Hits"; at their lowest level they would be a mix of compositions that had later become pop tunes. Since the recordings were reprints of older, more mediocre productions, the major task for Prestige was marketing and selling the anthologies, rather than recording them.

Though Prestige and Wendell were both located in Philadelphia, their plants were physically separated. The financial link between the two was valuable to Wendell, which took care, however, not to tarnish its elitist image by too close an association with Prestige. During her summer with Prestige, Jennifer worked on marketing the Great Masters series and was able to enlarge both the product line and the promotional budget. Joan Redmon, the president of Prestige who hired Jennifer, had come just a month before Jennifer's arrival, after 15 years at Wendell. Before the summer ended, Joan left to accept a far more lucrative offer elsewhere. She was replaced by a man, also from Wendell, with whom Jennifer had little rapport.

Jennifer learned a lot about Wendell while she worked for its subsidiary. An old, privately held firm, it was evidently conservative, secretive, elitist, and profitable. Most people in the company did not know what its gross sales were, and those few who did would not talk about it. Its trappings were somber, in good taste, but frugal. Simple offices were arranged in orderly rows, as were the secretaries' desks. Whenever Jennifer visited the parent offices, the environment seemed efficient to the point of resembling a well-oiled machine. People worked intently at their desks with little informal communication. Even the coffee machine did not seem to serve as a gathering point. Wendell considered itself thoroughly bureaucratized— no one was considered indispensable. This imposing conservative image correlated with the elitist image of the company and its famous musicians.

Record Industry

By 1979, the recording industry was facing a number of market stresses. The growth years of the 60s and 70s were coming to a halt with the end of the baby boom and technological changes in related industries. The number of buyers at the youth end of the market had flattened out, and video games began to compete for their limited money spent on entertainment. Records began to seem like an archaic technology that would be replaced eventually by cassettes, discs, and digital record players. At the same time, recording artists from rock groups to orchestras began to demand higher royalties. The low state of the economy made it impossible for record companies to increase their margin with higher prices. Some record companies responded to this challenge by restructuring themselves; the classical recording industry's general response was to hide.

Recruitment

Having had a successful summer with Prestige, Jennifer planned to make use of her connection to reach the parent company, Wendell Records. As vice president of the HBS Communications Club, she organized a recruiting reception for recording companies on February 2, 1980. All the companies she invited declined except for Wendell, which sent five representatives. At the end of the reception, they asked Jennifer to join them for dinner at the Ritz-Carlton.

The dinner was a breath of fresh air for Jennifer. The Wendell group consisted of Carl Sides, personnel director; Maryanne Robinson, Classical Music Division marketing analyst; Eben Jones, strategic planning director, HBS '76; Cliff Stubbs, Classical Music division vice president; and Jack Lawton, producer (Exhibit 2). The conversation ran from politics to music to industry anecdotes. Everyone was familiar with the music and musicians Jennifer had grown up with. The food was delicious, the banter funny, and the interaction collegial. Jennifer felt she had come home.

The only disconcerting note of the evening was that several times when Jennifer made a remark, the chubby, jovial Carl Sides would pat or stroke her head in a fatherly way. This minor distraction was lost in an evening of eating and drinking, heightened by Eben's thoughtfulness in surprising Jennifer with a birthday cake and candle. Jennifer left a little after midnight, but the other revelers stayed.

The next day, Jennifer called Maryanne in Philadelphia. The summer before, she had considered the tall, elegant Maryanne a potential mentor, although she knew her only slightly. They had a lighthearted conversation, with Maryanne noting "they are all hung over today." Jennifer expressed her enthusiasm by saying, "I had thought Wendell was a bunch of stiffs, but you seem to get along so well!" Maryanne replied that the dinner wasn't exactly representative, but said that yes, they did get along in the office.

Jennifer also mentioned Carl's behavior and said she hoped Maryanne didn't think his having patted and stroked her head was odd. Maryanne said that she didn't even notice. Relieved, Jennifer went on to ask Maryanne if she could arrange to have Jennifer's interview with Eben Jones rather than Carl when the Wendell staff returned on February 8. Jennifer knew that Eben had two jobs to offer and was closer to the action than Carl. Maryanne agreed to do whatever she could.

Interviewing

The day after Jennifer talked to Maryanne, Eben called to set up an interview for February 8 at 3:30 P.M. Jennifer agreed to he time, but Eben called again on the seventh and asked if Jennifer would rather meet over dinner. Jennifer, remembering that Wendell provided sumptuous dinners, agreed.

As Jennifer walked to Harvard Square to meet Eben on the eighth, she had trouble picturing what he looked like. But Eben picked Jennifer out, and she remembered him more clearly from the week before as tall, thin, and self-assured. The two went to a nearby bar where they joined Carl Sides and his assistant. Over drinks, it became obvious that Eben was trying to arrange things so that the personnel people would not join them for dinner.

When Eben and Jennifer had separated from Carl and his assistant, Eben's behavior toward Jennifer seemed to her to change markedly. He was trying to entertain her in a way that seemed highly flirtatious. When Jennifer tried to turn the subject to the two jobs he had open, he said, "You don't want to talk about jobs, do you?" to which she responded, "Yes, I do." Eben continued to keep Jennifer on the spot by jesting: "Are you always so serious?"

Jennifer tried to shift the conversation toward work, but she felt blocked. She was seriously interested in the jobs he had available, and as the strategic planning director at Wendell, he was certainly in a position of power. Jennifer felt she did not want to create a scene, but she definitely wanted to discourage his amorous advances. Every effort she made to redirect the conversation only changed his tactics. Eben talked about his successes at Harvard Business School; how he had consulted to Wendell and then been brought on board; about his recent divorce; and about his significant talents as a song writer. He told Jennifer that he was the president's golden boy in the classical music division. He felt he could do pretty much as he pleased.

Jennifer persisted in her efforts to change the subject, but Eben was not one to give up easily. He told her that he was a descendant of the Pilgrims on the Mayflower and suggested that he was a good bet. He told her over and over how attractive she was and how much they were alike. He pressed his assumed intimacy by saying he felt that he already knew her and seemed diverted by everything she said.

Jennifer, by now seething inwardly about the direction of the conversation, decided to end the dinner. Eben said he could still make the 9:00 P.M. shuttle to New York. When she got back to her apartment, Jennifer slammed the door in frustration and launched into a tirade. She could not believe that anyone could be so presumptuous on a job interview. He had never even asked if she were seeing someone else.

After she had calmed down, Jennifer called Maryanne in Philadelphia and told her what had happened. She rhetorically asked, "What is it about the men at Wendell, can't they control themselves?" Maryanne laughed supportively, and Jennifer asked if Maryanne could keep Eben away from her. Maryanne volunteered to arrange discreetly to be Jennifer's contact.

Mea Culpa

The next morning, February 9, Eben Jones called at 9:00 A.M. to say, "I would like to apologize for last night. I didn't behave very professionally, and I'm sorry I came on. I hope you will forgive me." When Jennifer responded directly, saying "I didn't appreciate what you did. I want a job, not to be hustled," she felt she was being tough. She wanted the message to sink in. He apologized again and hung up. Jennifer resolved not to bear a grudge against Eben. Maryanne called back the same day to say that she, rather than Eben, would be her conact at Wendell, and Jennifer was pleased with that solution.

About a week later, Jennifer received a letter from Eben Jones, dated the ninth. In it Eben reaffirmed his romantic interest in Jennifer. He acknowledged her rebuff, but left his phone numbers and hoped that she would call him. The letter, offensively erotic, suggested that they get together sometime at Eben's family's summer house on Martha's Vineyard. It was clear to Jennifer that the apology was not sincere and that Eben would continue to be a major problem for her.

Jennifer spent the day trying to analyze the situation she faced and develop possible scenarios and strategies. If she wrote or called Eben and told him even more forcefully that she was not interested, it would mean a direct confrontation with an authoritative insider at Wendell. If she called Maryanne again, she ran the risk of seeming to be the kind of person who attracted problems. Jennifer decided not to respond at all for the time being, and to deal with the issue when and if she were hired.

Disheartening Signals

When Jennifer had last talked to Maryanne on the ninth of February, Maryanne had said they would call in a week to arrange to fly Jennifer down to Philadelphia for a visit at Wendell. In the three weeks following this conversation, Jennifer heard nothing. Then, on February 28, Eben called once more. He told Jennifer that the "head of the classical division asked me what I thought of you. I wouldn't tell him not to hire you, but I wouldn't tell him *to* hire you either. I did tell him that I thought you would be great for the company." All Jennifer could find to say to this cryptic message was, "Oh." When Jennifer hung up, the depth of the problem struck her. The thought that this man was playing games with her job search was alarming, especially because Wendell was a record company that she was actively consider-

ing. All of a sudden, her musical background, recording experience, summer at Prestige, Harvard MBA, and the reception she had received at Wendell seemed like useless assets against an antagonistic and powerful insider.

Now that her future in classical recording looked so much less promising than it had three weeks earlier, Jennifer began a more aggressive job search. She started by writing letters to the presidents of several dozen record companies around the country. The initial response from most of them was that there were no MBA jobs. In fact, record companies could see little use for MBAs. Record company executives, especially in the classical end of the industry, were selected for their track record at talent development, rather than their managerial expertise. This point was brought home to Jennifer when she had an interview with the president of EMC Records in early March.

The president of this prestigious and profitable record company had responded immediately to Jennifer's letter and invited her to New York for an interview. This led Jennifer to believe that there might be some record companies that knew what to do with MBAs. When she arrived at EMC headquarters, its style seemed to match its successful reputation—low-slung, white, Italian designer furniture; sumptuous carpets; and beveled mirrors on the wall. As Jennifer was ushered into a corner office overlooking midtown Manhattan, she felt a renewed sense of confidence. The president shook Jennifer's hand, waved her toward a chair, and, propping his feet on the desk, barked, "So, you're from Harvard. What makes you think you're so swell?" After an hour of sparring, Jennifer felt she had won several word duels but not a job.

Other interviews in New York were less dramatic, but not much more fruitful. At Ely Records, Jennifer had an informal chat with the only Harvard MBA in the company, who told her that Ely felt threatened by MBAs. He said she was overqualified for the only available job, which was in sales, with a starting salary of $22,000.

She heard that a job in direct-mail marketing of classical records had just opened up at Heslop House. A quickly arranged interview with the direct-mail manager was satisfactory, but this manager felt she could not hire the first person through the door. Jennifer also interviewed with Compusound, a new company that specialized in converting records to state-of-the-art technologies. This interview went well, and Compusound seemed interested in Jennifer's knowledge of the industry as well as her training in marketing.

Gradually, Jennifer realized that there *were* jobs in the industry, but that it would take time to find them or to allow companies to create them for her. It was now the seventh of April, and the silence from Wendell had extended to six weeks. Though she had called Carl Sides periodically, she decided to call him again the next day to see if she could arrange for her official interview in Philadelphia.

When Jennifer talked to Carl the next morning, he apologized for the long delay in setting up a formal interview. Jennifer was going to be in Philadelphia on April 15, and she asked if that would be a convenient date for her to visit. Carl said it would be fine; he arranged for Jennifer to spend half the day at Wendell.

Philadelphia Visit

At 9:30 A.M. on April 15, Jennifer passed through the heavy glass doors on the 13th floor of the Wendell Building and was greeted by the receptionist. The offices of Wendell Records had changed little from what Jennifer remembered them to be the summer before. Maryanne Robinson came out and led Jennifer through the dense maze of cubicles to her own small office. Jennifer thought how easy it would be to get lost here. The place looked seedier than she had remembered it.

Jennifer talked to Maryanne for half an hour, and though the conversation was friendly, Maryanne did not seem as open and warm as she had been in the past. She answered Jennifer's questions about the long delay in arranging the interview in a tone that seemed to Jennifer somewhat distant and cagey. When Jennifer said that she thought things would be fine with Eben, Maryanne simply said, "Good." Gone was the laughter and the inside joking that Jennifer remembered from their earlier conversations.

Jennifer also met with Cliff Stubbs, the vice president for talent development for the Classical Records Division. Cliff spent most of the time describing what was done in the company and who did it. He was not so clear when it came to describing the job Jennifer was being considered for. When she asked him to describe the assistant marketing analyst position, currently vacant under Maryanne, Cliff said only, "You would have to figure it out as you went along." He did note that the position demanded strong quantitative skills, as it involved analyzing sales data. Though these expectations did not tap Jennifer's strengths, she felt that if Maryanne, an ex-English teacher, could handle the position, then she herself could deal with it. Jennifer was frustrated that Cliff did not take the time to introduce her to other staff in the marketing department. She understood there were four or five people in the group, though she could not be sure (see Exhibits 1 and 2). Through it all, Cliff did not appear to be terribly outgoing, but that was how Jennifer recollected him from the reception at Harvard in February. She concluded her morning with an interview with Carl Sides, who seemed as jovial and encouraging as always.

Five days later, on April 20, Jennifer received the long-awaited call from Wendell. It was Carl Sides calling to say that they wanted to hire her to work for Maryanne as an assistant marketing analyst in the classical division. Carl added that "you should work through me, because I am dealing with everything now." The offer was for $30,000, and the company would be flexible about when Jennifer wanted to start. Jennifer was pleased to get the offer, though it seemed low to her, and she thought it odd that Maryanne had not called with the news. She called

Exhibit 1
Wendell Records, Inc.

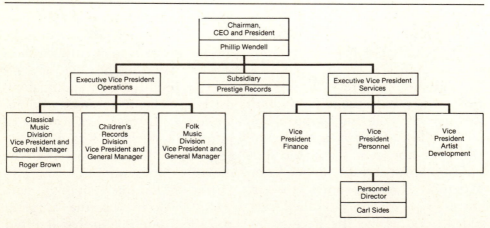

Exhibit 2
Classical Music Division

Organization chart for the Classical Music Division:

- Vice President and General Manager — Roger Brown
  - Vice President Marketing Services
  - Vice President Finance
  - Vice President Production
  - Vice President Sales
  - Vice President International Licensing
  - Vice President Talent Development — Cliff Stubbs
    - Head of Marketing — Belinda Brenner
      - Marketing Analyst — Maryanne Robinson
        - Assistant Marketing Analyst
        - Assistant Marketing Analyst — Jennifer Bent
          - Marketing Assistant
  - Director Strategic Planning — Eben Jones

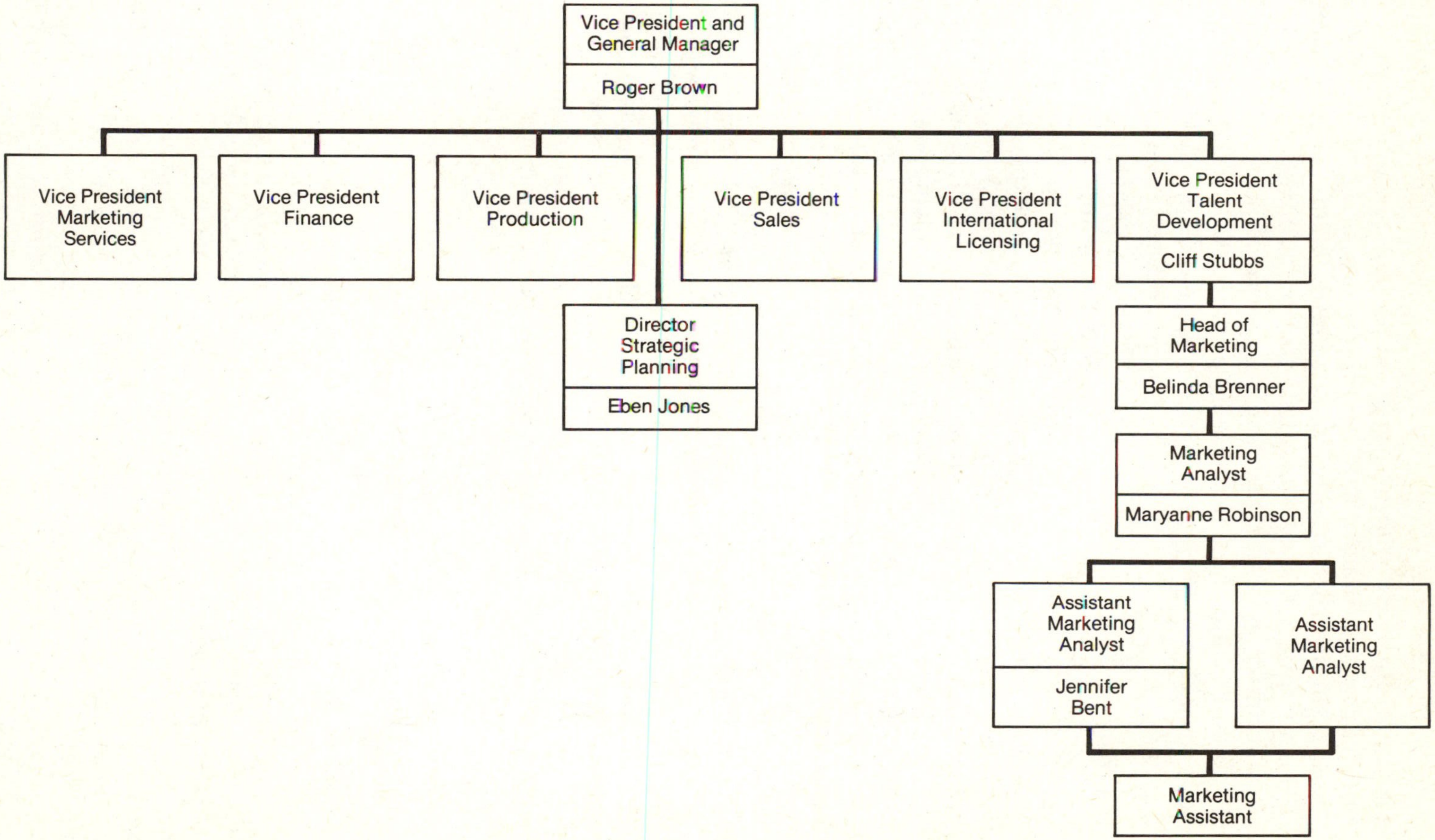

Maryanne the next morning to thank her. Maryanne sounded pleasant but not particularly cordial, and the conversation was brief. Jennifer told her that she would take some time to decide about the offer.

Haggling

Jennifer did not call Wendell again until three weeks later, on May 10, when she learned that a classmate of hers had been offered a job at the Wendell subsidiary, Prestige Records, where Jennifer had worked the summer before. While Jennifer was happy for her friend, she was not pleased that this less experienced woman had an offer of $32,500!

Jennifer immediately called Carl and asked, "Why is Carolyn being offered more than I am?" Carl sighed and said, "I thought you'd find out. Prestige is not as constrained by hierarchy as we are; they can be freer with their salaries over there. Here at Wendell you must be slotted in. We have salary compression, Prestige does not. The extra $2,500 would put you too close to the next level." After this elaboration, Carl said, "I'm only telling you all this because I like you, and I think you are a Wendell type. I'll see what I can do, but you'll have to trust me." Jennifer said that was fine, but that she wanted another couple of weeks to think about it.

Other Offers

Heslop House continued to be interested in Jennifer, though they said they needed more time to make an offer. The other offer Jennifer had received was her "safety," Amalgamated Goods, a large consumer marketing company. It was for $33,000.

Compusound called in late April and offered Jennifer a job at $35,000. Stretching the truth by $5,001, Jennifer responded that that was her lowest offer, and she would be unlikely to accept at that level. Eleanor Watson, the woman who ran the division where Jennifer was applying, was the daughter of the owner of a major recording studio and a graduate of HBS. Eleanor invited Jennifer back to New York at the end of May to discuss the matter.

On May 20, Jennifer returned to New York for a final interview at Compusound. Eleanor asked Jennifer about the possibility of coproducing video discs with a record company. Compusound wanted such an arrangement in order to have access to prestige artists under contract elsewhere. The payoff for the record company would be the opportunity to test market its product in conjunction with a new technology. Eleanor showed Jennifer a list of 20 possible recording companies that Compusound had considered approaching and asked Jennifer her opinion. Jennifer ran down the list and checked the three firms that she thought might be open to the venture.

Eleanor, who seemed impressed with Jennifer's confidence, pressed the issue further by asking, "Why have you left out Prestige? We had heard that they do outside coproductions." Jennifer replied that they had in the past, but now only with the son of the former owner of Prestige. Jennifer, with Eleanor listening in, then called her contact at Prestige to ask about coproductions. The contact responded to the query by saying in a conspiratorial tone that the only coproductions they did were with the former owner's son. Eleanor put down the phone and added $10,000 to her original offer. Over the next week, the offer grew to $50,000, including bonuses.

The Options

By early June, the choices still did not seem clear-cut to Jennifer. Amalgamated Goods was the only option that did not really interest her. Wendell was the kind of company Jennifer most wanted—the business of producing classical recordings by the world's most accomplished musicians. But though Carl promised to do better, the official offer still stood at $30,000. The largely unresolved situation with Eben was another obstacle. In his powerful position, he might easily embarrass her or otherwise make life difficult at Wendell. On the other hand, at Wendell there was the chance to work for a woman whom she greatly admired and who might take on a mentoring role. Maryanne knew the business and seemed a sophisticated, good-humored kindred spirit.

Compusound, at the other extreme, had lots of money to offer, but little else. Jennifer could not get too excited about pushing rerecorded video discs. However, many of her close friends pointed to the

new technologies as the wave of the future in audio media and said places like Wendell were like over-romanticized dinosaurs and would soon be extinct. Her friends' counsel was to go for the money.

There remained the hope of an offer from Heslop House, which was as elite as Wendell, but seemed to be more forward looking and aggressive. If she had a comparable offer from Heslop, the choice over Wendell would be easy. But at this point Jennifer felt that she could not put off Wendell any longer; it had been almost six weeks since they had made their offer, and she did not want to lose that.

Decision

On the afternoon of June 2, 1980, Jennifer called Carl Sides, personnel director at Wendell Records, Inc. to accept the offer. Her only proviso, she said, was that they improve their offer by $2,500 to $32,500. Carl, who agreed to her condition, seemed genuinely elated that Jennifer had decided to accept. He said, "I'm very happy about this; we really wanted you, and you'll make a great addition." He again told Jennifer that he would be able to work something out about the salary and added, "By the way, don't talk to Maryanne Robinson about this." Jennifer, caught off guard, said, "Why?" Carl merely repeated what he had said, and the two hung up.

Closing the Deal

A week later, on June 9, Jennifer went to Philadelphia to look for a place to live and to meet with Carl. She found Carl to be his usual amiable self. They talked for about 40 minutes, mainly about logistics. Jennifer told him that she wanted to take six weeks off for a vacation before starting, which Carl agreed to. He, in turn, told her that he had had to go all the way to Phillip Wendell to increase Jennifer's salary to $32,500, as he had promised he would try to do.

At the end of the conversation, Carl remarked, "Oh, by the way, you won't be working for Maryanne. You will report directly to Cliff Stubbs." Jennifer was stunned by this and asked Carl to explain it more fully. But Carl offered little by way of explanation, and Jennifer concluded by saying, "I'll have to think about it."

Maryanne had been a good friend and a buffer through her difficulties with Eben, and Jennifer had looked forward to the possibility of gaining a strong woman as a mentor. While Jennifer did not have anything against Cliff, she did not know him very well. He had always seemed rather aloof. She returned to Boston, feeling ruffled by this latest unexpected turn.

Second Thoughts

For the next couple of days, Jennifer reconsidered the situation. She had gained $2,500, lost a mentor, and still had the unresolved Eben problem. She felt she had been partially deceived by Carl when he made her the offer because he must have known she would be reporting to Cliff. She knew little of Cliff, but what she had seen was not terribly inspiring. On the other hand Wendell was undeniably a respected name in the classical music industry. With the movers coming on June 14 and her personal life in turmoil, Jennifer decided to keep the job at Wendell. It would be a great place to have been, and she could always move on if she had to.

Jennifer got settled in Philadelphia over the next two weeks, and then left for what she felt was a well-deserved vacation in Europe on July 4. Returning on August 5, Jennifer felt rested and renewed in her excitement about starting her new job. She began work on Monday, August 9, and started in as an assistant marketing analyst for Cliff Stubbs.

CASE 2–4
Kirk Stone (A)

Robert Mueller, Jr.
Vijay Sathe

In late January 1979, Kirk Stone answered the intercom in his office at C'est Bien, a Los Angeles company that manufactured fashion jeans. Bob Goetze, the in-house data processor, was on the line. "Did you hear what happened in Dallas?" he asked. "Bersin and Oppenheim have been fired." Kirk was shocked by the news. Peter Bersin and Jeff Oppenheim were the deputy managers of C'est Bien's newest division, Children's Clothing, which had opened only six months earlier and was running well ahead of projected sales for July through January. Kirk's surprise was compounded by pain at the prospect of losing his closest allies in the company. Kirk had joined C'est Bien in July 1978 as assistant to the president, several weeks before the Children's Clothing kickoff, and he had shared the pleasure of Peter's and Jeff's success from its first week.

When he and Bob finished talking, Kirk counted back the number of top people who had left or been fired from this lean family business during his brief tenure. Bill Avery, the general manager for Children's Clothing, quit in August; Linda Lyon and Sherry Cohen, project coordinators, quit in October; and only the week before a clothes designer, a presidential assistant, and a data processor had all been summarily fired. This list did not include the two MBAs who had preceded Kirk in his position for the two years prior to his joining the firm. It was hard for Kirk to believe that he could have been so wrong about a job that he had accepted with great excitement and anticipation only eight months earlier.

Personal Background

Kirk Stone, 28, was born and raised in Taos, New Mexico, and had gone on to receive his bachelor's degree from the University of New Mexico in 1972. After he graduated from the University of Oregon Law School in 1975 and passed the New Mexico bar exam, he returned to Albuquerque to settle into a career as house counsel for a bank. Kirk dealt mostly with commercial loans, and he became the resident expert in the technical rules of the Uniform Commercial Code.

After one year, Kirk became bored with the limited scope of his position. When he tried to expand the range of his responsibilities, the bank resisted, and Kirk began to think about moving on. He had been married two years by 1976 and had a six-month-old baby. As Kirk thought about his future, he considered three career options: (1) go into private law practice with two friends; (2) expand the part-time real estate business he ran on

This case was prepared by Robert Mueller, Jr. (under the direction of Vijay Sathe).

weekends; or (3) go to a business school. Because learning was important to him, and because he wanted to see more of the East, he decided that Harvard Business School would offer the best opportunities.

Kirk entered HBS in 1976 and quickly settled into the fast-paced demands of the business-school environment, a clear contrast to the slower, less competitive pace of New Mexican life. The demanding program heightened the sense of achievement Kirk felt when he was successful in his courses. In the winter of 1978, armed with a law degree, bank experience, and a prospective Harvard MBA, Kirk began his search for a job.

Recruiting

Kirk was quite certain of the kind of position and environment he was looking for; he was not interested in prestige jobs and money in and of themselves. Kirk's family was important to him, and he did not want to work 80-hour weeks. He wanted a job in a small company or division that would be challenging, build upon his past experience, and offer room to grow. The ideal environment he was looking for would be multifunctional, rewarding, and consistent with his values. Kirk decided to look at consulting firms mainly out of curiosity and at commercial banks as a fall-back option.

Kirk started his interviewing with three prestigious national consulting firms in February: O'Donnell, Inc., Blaire Associates, and Claflin Beale. While all three firms seemed to find Kirk's background interesting, his legal training was not particularly useful in their line of work. Negotiations were therefore broken off after the first interview.

Two consulting firms which ostensibly presented a closer fit were the Washington-based Hadden House and the Boston-based Environmental Resource Planners. In early March, Hadden House let Kirk know that they were looking for a person who had banking and antitrust experience. To Kirk, it seemed that the job was a perfect fit, though it later became clear that his antitrust experience was not specific enough. At Environmental Resource Planners, he had two interviews in which he felt he and the interviewers got along very well. He liked the people and the assignments the firm undertook, but, again, his legal background was not essential to their line of work. A final consulting firm was Adams and Bucknell, which had an opening in strategic planning. Kirk had an interview with the current occupant of the position, an MBA from Stanford, who was about to move up in the organization. When Kirk expressed interest in the position, the interviewer said it would be available, but he advised Kirk against it because he himself had felt bored and unchallenged in the job. By early March, Kirk had eliminated all consulting firms from further consideration.

In the middle of that month, Kirk found an intriguing job description in the Career Development Office. The position was assistant to the president of the Los Angeles-based fashion jeans manufacturer C'est Bien. The description went on to say that the company was in the process of expanding its clothing line and needed a strong generalist to aid the president in this activity. More specifically, C'est Bien was looking for an MBA with strong interpersonal skills, a facility with numbers, and negotiating skills. The cover letter also noted that Robert Fong, Jr., the president's son, was employed by C'est Bien. No salary was specified, but competitive offers were promised. Kirk decided to send them his resume.

Kirk spent the month of March at several large commercial banks. Both the New York-located Newcomps Bank and the West Coast Bank of San Francisco expressed interest in hiring him. But real estate lending no longer appealed to Kirk, and he was not interested in living in New York City. He kept these banks on hold while he flew to New Mexico with his family in late March to look at job opportunities there. Jobs were available in Albuquerque, but the firms Kirk looked at did not feel that they could afford him. When they returned home on a Sunday in early April, Kirk was not worried about getting a good job. He had several offers, but he had not yet been able to track down the position that seemed to meet his needs closely.

The next day Kirk got a call from Robert Fong, Jr., who had graduated from a well-known western business school two years ear-

lier. Robert talked extensively with Kirk about the position and about Kirk's background. Robert explained that C'est Bien was a family-run business with only 10 executives in the corporate office. The job was being offered because as the firm had grown, his father, Robert Fong, Sr., had come to need professional help on a regular basis.* He wanted to be able to delegate a large number of corporate projects to a generalist with a strong business and legal background. Kirk expressed interest in continuing the discussion, but he was curious about why two previous MBAs had turned over in the same position within a two-year period. Robert explained that one man, a Harvard MBA, "had not been able to cut it," while the other, a Stanford MBA, had learned enough in a brief period to go into business for himself. Kirk was satisfied with this explanation and agreed to fly to Dallas on Friday to meet with Fong, who was visiting that city in connection with the soon-to-be-opened Children's Wear Division. Robert said he would also be present.

Dallas Interview

On the Friday in April that Kirk flew to Dallas, he was met by Linda Lyon, a salesperson for the new Children's Wear Division. She had started at C'est Bien three years earlier as a secretary and had quickly moved up. Besides her sales responsibilities,

---

* Henceforth, Robert Fong, Sr., will be referred to as Fong, and Robert Fong, Jr., as Robert.

she was providing general coordination while the Dallas site was being made ready for the opening.

Linda took Kirk to the new plant for a tour. As they moved through the new building, Kirk asked her what it was like to work for this company. Linda answered: "C'est Bien work is rough, interesting, exciting, and very busy." She went on to say that she really enjoyed it and that "the people were great to work with." The tour ended half an hour later when Linda delivered Kirk to an office where he was to meet with Fong.

As Kirk came through the door of the austere, 12×10 foot office, he saw Fong behind a small desk poring over some papers. Fong rose and said, "This will be the general manager's office." As they shook hands, Kirk saw that Fong was a good-looking man about 5 feet, 5 inches, dressed in a very stylish and obviously expensive suit. When the two were seated, Fong took out Kirk's resume and scanned it. He then said, "I guess you have talked with my son, Robert?" Kirk nodded that he had and began by sketching the content of that conversation for Fong. Fong said, "Let me tell you about myself; we run a lean organization here, and I make more money than the chairman of Exxon. I have a lot of things going on here and I need help; if you come to work here, you can start right near the top and learn from a master of this business." When Kirk asked about chances for advancement, Fong said that he was not yet 55 years old but that he was thinking of early

semiretirement. He added, "I want to move out and leave this business to my son and professionals like you. I also want to start a charitable foundation and give away some of the money I have made." Kirk thought, "This is what I went to the B-school for, to have an opportunity like this." Kirk was also impressed that Fong's interest seemed to go beyond simply making money. Since Fong had expressed an interest in Kirk's legal training, Kirk asked Fong how he felt about litigation. Fong said he thought only lawyers benefited from lawsuits. When Kirk said that he had not practiced in California and would not want to be considered the corporation lawyer, Fong said that was fine with him.

The interview ended with an offer of $30,000 for Kirk and provision for a $4,000 raise every six months. (The median starting salary for the class of 1978 was $24,000). The two men shook hands and Fong personally escorted Kirk through the offices and the production floor of what he considered to be the most modern clothing plant in the country. Kirk left Dallas elated that he had found a job on the West Coast that would be interesting and provide a good fit with his personal values, for Fong had said he liked to hire family men. Kirk postponed giving Fong his decision until he had spoken with his wife, but he was pretty sure of his answer.

When Kirk got back to Cambridge, he told his wife with great excitement about the job opportunity that had opened up. The family could move closer to New Mexico, and Kirk would have a chance to work at a strategic level for a dynamic young company. Five days after the interview, Kirk called Fong, on April 12, to accept the offer. Later, after all arrangements were final, Kirk asked if he could come to L.A. to see the headquarters and "kick the tires." Fong said such a trip would not be necessary, but looked forward to seeing Kirk on July 3.

Beginnings

On Monday, July 3, Kirk entered the small brick-front headquarters of C'est Bien in L.A. to start his new job. The receptionist welcomed him and showed him to his new office, explaining that Mr. and Mrs. Fong were returning from Europe later in the morning and that Robert was in Dallas. Kirk was acclimating himself to his new surroundings when, at 11 o'clock, the intercom buzzed and Fong summoned Kirk to his adjoining office. Fong's office was large, dominated at one end by a large marble-top desk, and at the other by several pieces of exquisite Eastern sculpture.

Kirk sat down and Fong asked, "Are you ready to get down to work here?" Fong then handed Kirk several things from his desk which included information on the closing of a loan to cover a portion of C'est Bien's expansion plans and a request from Fong to hire an accounting consultant. He wanted Kirk to review the loan agreement and hire the consultant to analyze current accounting procedures at C'est Bien. When Kirk asked if there was a specific consultant Fong would like to use, Fong said it was a simple job and any competent accountant would be all right. Kirk left Fong's office feeling glad that he would so quickly be able to earn his pay at C'est Bien.

Kirk's banking and legal background were extremely useful in reviewing the loan agreement. He was able to find weaknesses in the contract and put his suggestions for revision in the form of a memo to Fong. Kirk felt that his recommendations would lower both Fong's risk and the cost of the financial arrangement. For the accounting job, he made a series of calls to gather information on the services provided as well as fees. Most firms charged on either a flat-fee or time-and-expenses basis, so Kirk analyzed which payment method would be most beneficial to C'est Bien. In the end, he accepted a flat bid of $10,000 to perform the accounting review, which was done in the two-week period while Fong was traveling.

On July 18, Fong called Kirk into his office again. He was standing behind his desk holding Kirk's memos and looking extremely agitated. "What is this?" he demanded, shaking the memos at Kirk. Kirk attempted to explain that they described the final phases of the work Fong had assigned; but he was interrupted by Fong who shouted, "Yeah, but this is not the way I remember telling you do to it!" He paused and then said, "What can I expect, you're ignorant about this industry. Don't you know that you never hire a consultant on a flat fee? It's just a chance to steal from me." Fong then picked up the phone, called the accounting consultant, and spoke angrily as Kirk listened, "You got my ignorant employee, and that's why you got a flat fee on this—I won't pay it, I want you to charge me on a time-and-expense basis instead." With that he hung up the phone and glared at Kirk. Fong went on to say that Kirk's loan-closing recommendations also showed ignorance of the industry.

Kirk, who was stunned by this tirade, said that he had signed a contract with the consulting firm and that the company was obligated to pay the fee. He felt that his name was on the line. Fong said, "Don't let that be a problem," but Kirk continued to feel that it was, if for no other reason than that he was being forced to go back on his word. Kirk returned to his office and slumped into his chair as he tried to figure out what had just happened. When the bill came in several days later, it was for $15,000.

The week after this explosive episode with Fong, Kirk got a phone call from John Kim, an old law school friend. Kim, who was Korean, was calling Kirk to see how he was doing and to find out who his employer was. When Kirk told him, Kim exclaimed, "You are working for a Korean?" To this Kirk simply said "Yeah," and Kim continued, "Don't you remember when I worked for a Korean family business where a son was being groomed to take over? I thought you would learn from my experience." Kirk now began to wonder about his choice.

Robert Fong, Sr.

Kirk learned that Fong had emigrated from Korea to the United States in 1952, when he was 24 years old. He had left Korea with only $60 in cash and had enrolled at the University of California, Berkeley, on the basis of a scholarship that he had received from a foundation. He spent two years at Berkeley before transferring to the Fashion Institute of Technology (FIT) in New York. At FIT, Fong developed technical design skills to apply to his already strong creative talents. After graduating, he spent 10 years working as a designer for a variety of clothing manufacturers and fashion houses before moving to Los Angeles to start his own fashion design business.

Calclothes, a small clothing manufacturer, hired Fong to design a pair of fashion jeans in 1970. The firm was old, and its sales had been declining for six years. Just as the company was about to go into production with Fong's design, it went bankrupt. Seeing an opportunity to move into the production end of the business, Fong got a loan to buy Calclothes and move his newly named C'est Bien jeans into production. In the eight years since then, C'est Bien, Inc. had grown to annual sales of $150 million with two thirds of the revenue generated by C'est Bien jeans. The corporate offices in L.A. housed Fong,

Exhibit 1
C'est Bien Offices

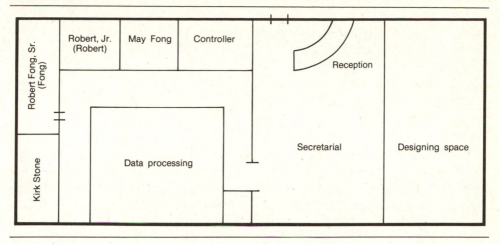

his wife May (who worked as the bookkeeper), their son Robert, the designers, data processing people, the controller, and clerical help— 30 employees in all (see Exhibit 1).

Calclothes Division

During the next few weeks, Kirk undertook a review of the Calclothes division, which was made up of those clothing lines that predated Fong's purchase of the company. Kirk completed an informal market analysis and a projected cash flow. The simple truth seemed to be that the line was not selling and that the company was expending a great deal of energy trying merely to keep it afloat. The future of the company was moving rapidly in the direction of a young fashion market, and it did not seem wise to Kirk to hold onto the old line.

Armed with a written summary of his findings, Kirk asked Robert to join him in his office. They re-viewed Kirk's report together and agreed that either the market or the concept behind the line was wrong, for it was not moving. Robert agreed that dropping the line would make the most sense. But when Kirk suggested that they pass this on as a recommendation to Robert's father, Robert pulled himself erect and said, "Oh, no, Dad is very attached to this line; and besides it is important to maintain it as a security measure. What if the bottom falls out of the fashion jeans business?" Robert made it obvious that he was not interested in pressing the issue and returned to his office.

Kirk decided that the issue was important enough to pursue but that the odds would be against him if he were to see Fong alone. Fong's wife, May, who was the bookkeeper, had an office diagonally across from Kirk's. Kirk's impression was that May would be willing to listen, and he knew she had Fong's ear. This might be a way to get his point across. He walked into her office to broach the subject of dropping the Calclothes line.

Kirk prefaced his remarks by suggesting that his role in the organization would sometimes demand that he play devil's advocate. She enthusiastically agreed, adding that such a role would be far more useful in the long run. She, too, could see that Calclothes was not worth the energy being put into it. With none of her son's reluctance, she took Kirk's report and promised to escalate the discussion to Fong.

Kirk noted several instances during the following week when Fong, Robert, and May met in May's office. Though it was not obvious what they were saying, the whole office staff could hear that they were arguing. They sounded exactly like family fights, but Kirk knew they were discussing Calclothes. Inasmuch as Kirk and Robert were the only professional managers in the company, Kirk felt it was unfortunate that he was not participating in these "discussions."

About a week after Kirk had met with Robert and then with May, a meeting was called in Fong's office. Present were Kirk, Fong, Robert, May, and several designers. Fong, seated behind his marble-top desk, said that he had been thinking a long time about the future of Calclothes. His considered opinion was that the line was draining too much cash and that it should be dropped. He said he would set this process in motion immediately. There was a brief discussion, and everyone returned to their respective offices. As Kirk returned to

his, he reflected that it was possible for him to get things done here, as long as he was willing to play by Fong's rules and expect no credit for his ideas.

Dallas and the Children's Division

One Thursday in late July, Fong told Kirk to meet with the management staff in Dallas the following Monday to help them review their advertising plans and contractual agreements. This staff included Bill Avery, general manager; and Peter Bersin, Jeff Oppenheim, and Jack Brower, deputy managers. Fong had deliberately given all four men general responsibilities, with the specifics to be worked out among themselves. Robert had also taken on the task of overseeing the division's startup activities for corporate and was usually in Dallas.

Fong told Kirk to leave the next day, but Kirk said it was not necessary to spend the weekend in Dallas for a Monday meeting. Fong insisted that Kirk would not be there early enough if he left Monday, but Kirk did not agree. After Fong strode off, Kirk had the secretary make arrangements for an early Monday morning flight.

Kirk was met at the Dallas airport by a limousine, sent by Robert, and driven to the new plant in a suburb for an early afternoon meeting with the management group. After a brief discussion, Robert turned to Kirk and asked, "Do you play bridge?" Kirk said that he did, so Robert, Bersin, Oppenheim, Brower, and Kirk spent the rest of the afternoon discussing business over cards. The bridge game had become the afterhours norm for this group, even though it meant that the Dallas staff had to keep playing until 10 or 11 at night, spent less time with their families as a result, and had to make up missed work the next morning. Robert was the instigator of the bridge games, and although the others apparently disliked him, they played.

All three of the young deputy managers had been wooed from fashion houses in New York to take on this project, while the older one, Bill Avery, had long experience as an executive with a retail clothing chain. In conversations with Kirk over the next several days, Bersin, Oppenheim, and Brower said they felt that Fong had made a point of not assigning task areas for them, expecting that they would fight it out. There were no job descriptions when they were hired. Oppenheim felt that Fong managed deliberately by ambiguity, letting each of them prove how tenacious they could be in fighting for Fong's approval. He believed that it was Fong's way of testing and measuring them. Kirk had thought that this must be Fong's version of survival of the fittest.

Partly because they got along so well together, the three had refused to fight for Fong's recognition. They had separated their job responsibilities into different areas: Bersin would handle marketing, Oppenheim sales, and Brower production. They also said it was impossible to deal with corporate

because of the Fongs. Avery claimed that every time he would make a decision, Robert (whom the group called the "snake") would overrule it. An example of such overruling was the parking liability problem. People from nearby offices were using a future C'est Bien building lot next to the Dallas plant as a parking area. Avery asked Kirk if this exposed the company to liability. Kirk said it did and advised putting up warning signs, but Robert tore them down, claiming that they had not been authorized by his father. Robert asserted that it was the construction company's liability, but Kirk knew it was also the Fongs's. Whenever the Dallas managers called Fong in L.A. for advice, he would merely say, "Work it out yourselves." As a result, the Dallas group felt there there was nothing they could be sure of.

One day during the late summer, Kirk heard from Jack Brower that the general manager, Bill Avery, had quit in disgust and taken another job in New York. He, Brower, was the new general manager, but he did not have authority to act as one because Robert kept overruling him. Orders for the new Children's line were running ahead of expectations, and clothes would be in the stores in time for the back-to-school retail season. Fong had hired Richard Keeler Associates of Dallas to put together the children's wear ad campaign, and Brower was encouraged by its success. The account was Keeler's largest, and he earned his fee by charging a commission on all ads. Public media events, such as press conferences or promotions, were not charged.

Fong, Robert, and Kirk

After he had been on the job several months, Kirk felt that Robert had the toughest role of all. Nothing Robert did was good enough for Fong. When the builder of the Dallas plant used Fong's concrete forms to build another company's plant, Fong blamed Robert. When Robert defended himself saying that he was a businessman, not an architect, Fong castigated him, saying, "I have to be everywhere; I can't trust you. Why did I pay for your expensive education anyway?"

When Robert visited Los Angeles from his banishment in Dallas, his mother would buy him new suits and expect him to dine with her and Fong every night. It appeared to be a no-win situation for Robert; initiative was seen as stupidity, and inactivity worse. The only viable path seemed to be one of blind subservience to his father.

Kirk, who was not bound by the same ties, wanted only to be near the action and do as good a job as possible. To make sure that his good work was seen he made sure in these early months that he stayed in the office until after Fong had left. Not only Fong but also Robert took note of Kirk's arrival and departure times. Kirk developed a close relationship with the Dallas group in this period. Their ages and lifestyles were similar, and they seemed to have a similar

commitment to excellence. They would call Kirk for advice, and he would share his legal and operations knowledge with them. Kirk also got involved in an informal way with the advertising campaign that the division was developing with the Dallas ad firm. At this point Kirk felt he was as much of an insider as was reasonable to expect, but Brower warned him that Robert was getting jealous of Kirk's position.

Fall of 1978

During the entire fall, sales for children's clothes continued to be strong, and from September on, the division was in the black. Despite this success, other important personnel decided to leave C'est Bien. In October both Linda Lyon and Sherry Cohen quit. Linda had been actively involved in the successful sales campaign and had come a long way from her secretarial position three years earlier. When Kirk asked her why she was leaving, she said only, "I've had it with him. It's too bad, but I can't take it anymore. I was supposed to be in Dallas for two weeks—it has become six months, and now my whole personal life in L.A. is wrecked. Fong has absolutely no respect for my needs." Kirk was sorry to see her go.

Kirk's main reason for being in Dallas during November was to "keep an eye on the lawyers" who were closing a long-term loan for Fong. This task dragged on until the week before Thanksgiving, when Fong came down from L.A.

On Wednesday morning before Thanksgiving, in a meeting at a Dallas coffee shop, the parties to the loan celebrated its execution. After a brief conversation, Kirk got up from the table and said he had a 2 o'clock plane to catch. Fong looked at his watch and said that he was not leaving until 8 o'clock, and asked Kirk how he could leave when the C'est Bien controller had not deposited the check. Kirk, feeling that he did not have to stay to watch a check deposited, said that he planned to spend Thanksgiving with his family, not bankers. When Fong persisted, Kirk held firm until Fong walked out of the room.

January 1979

Christmas came and went with record sales throughout the C'est Bien line. It was then that Kirk was shocked to hear from Bob Goetze that Bersin and Oppenheim had been fired. He put through a call to Bersin at the Dallas plant, then to his home, to express his sympathy and to find out more about why he had been fired. Bersin said that in December, "Fong promised each of us a $10,000 bonus by the end of January. Then when he saw that sales were off for the first weeks of January, and advertising was over budget, he panicked." Kirk and Bersin discussed the fact that everyone knew that January was a slow month for the whole industry, but Fong had done so much bragging in the industry that a sales drop had apparently hurt his ego. When Kirk asked how it happened,

Bersin said, "'The snake' (Robert) called us in together and just fired us—no explanations; I think he liked doing it!" Bersin also said that when Robert had found out that Bersin's moving expenses had not yet been paid, he was actually pleased.

Bersin asked Kirk if he had any legal right to either the promised bonus or the moving expenses for which he had receipts. Kirk said that the bonus issue would be difficult to challenge in court, but added "you could make a damn good case that he was obligated to pay moving expenses. You were an agent on Fong's behalf. The moving was for Fong's, not your, benefit." Bersin then said that when he had called Fong, Fong had offered to pay the expense if Bersin would voluntarily quit. Kirk paused, and then said that the conversation was putting him in an awkward position. He was offering legal advice that would be used against his employer. Despite the dilemma, Kirk pointed out to Bersin that the only reason Fong would make such an offer would be so that he would not have to pay unemployment. After a longer personal discussion, Kirk and Bersin hung up, promising to keep in touch.

In the ensuing weeks, the firing of Bersin and Oppenheim was never mentioned at the L.A. office. When Kirk asked Fong if he should call Bersin about a marketing question, Fong looked at Kirk with a curious expression on his face and said, "He's no longer with us." Kirk then said, "Oh, that's interesting!" No discussion followed.

Richard Keeler Associates

Throughout the kickoff of the children's clothes line at C'est Bien, the ad campaign had been developed and produced by Richard Keeler, a respected member of the Dallas business community. Although Keeler had never worked for Fong before, he knew Fong through relatives and through some business associates who were connected with banks and other institutions that had financed Fong's various ventures. Keeler had taken on the job enthusiastically and had relished Fong's style of discussing everything in controlled public forums, such as press conferences. Keeler was able to arrange public events like fashion shows and five-mile runs to benefit local charities that inevitably brought a great deal of media coverage. The fashion show, which featured children's wear, was also picked up by several network news shows. At these functions, Fong was able to get center-stage attention and to talk about how proud he was to be an adopted son of the Dallas community. The campaign had been a success, and the proof was in the August through December sales.

When Fong was in Dallas in late January, he had seen the monthly advertising invoice, which showed that Fong had already paid Keeler $600,000 and that the accrued bill was over $1 million. Fong was irate, as the *total* advertising budget was only $150,000. The advertising overrun coincided with the January downturn, and Fong had immediately accused Bersin of "throwing away his money" and of "taking kickbacks from Keeler." It was afterward that both Bersin and Oppenheim were fired.

Fong told Kirk that he would not pay Keeler the $400,000 that Keeler claimed he still owed. Fong said that a budget that size had never been authorized and that if Keeler did not like it, he could sue him. Which is exactly what Keeler proceeded to do, for he did not have the cash to pay his own creditors for this, his largest account. Without the owed money, Keeler said he would be forced out of business.

As Kirk thought back over the advertising campaign, the suggestion that these expenditures had been embezzled seemed ridiculous. Although he had no proof of Bersin's innocence, there seemed to be a lot of circumstantial evidence on his side. First of all, the industry standard was at least $1.25 million in advertising for an ongoing line this big. And in startup cases, it was inevitably higher. Second, Fong got monthly invoices from Keeler, and the $150,000 mark had been passed as early as in September. Finally, Robert participated in the Dallas advertising decisions on a very regular basis. Kirk could recall being present at several meetings with Robert, Keeler, and the C'est Bien advertising in Dallas at which Robert would initially complain about the proposed advertising expenditures ("Oh, no, we wouldn't approve an amount this big") and then okay it anyway ("Well, all right, let's do it").

To Kirk, the facts just did not

add up. But, knowing Fong, it was conceivable that he had not kept track of the invoices. And knowing Robert's relationship with Fong, Kirk thought it was also possible Robert had not kept Fong fully informed of the advertising expense overruns. Nevertheless, there was little doubt that Fong was both morally and legally obligated to pay Keeler his total bill of $1 million. Whether or not Fong had been aware of these expenditures, Robert as his agent had certainly authorized them, although he now claimed he had not.

Lawsuits

As a result of Keeler's suit, Fong decided to countersue for the difference between the $150,000 he said he had authorized and the $600,000 he had paid. Kirk knew that Fong's money could keep a legal process going long enough to drive Keeler out of business. Even if Keeler survived and eventually won his case in court, Fong would have the use of a substantial amount of Keeler's money for several years. This would yield Fong an attractive net interest because the market rate Fong would earn on the money would be considerably greater than the legal rate Fong would eventually have to pay Keeler. This delay-the-payment-whenever-you-can tactic reminded Kirk of the first assignment Fong had given him. Fong simply ignored the accounting consultant's $15,000 bill and the subsequent reminders for several months. Finally, Kirk arranged to have the

bill paid on his own authorization limit, without asking for Fong's approval.

Fong told Kirk to "take care" of Keeler because he refused even to talk to him again. If Keeler called, only Kirk was to answer. Kirk had become fond of Keeler in the months he had worked with him. He respected him as a man of honor and disliked the prospect of having to represent Fong's interest against Keeler. He felt he was being forced into the position of lying on behalf of his boss. It was painful to him now to make arrangements to go to Dallas, not only because of his mission, but also because his closest allies in the company were gone. It seemed to Kirk that the job had placed him in an intolerable position.

CASE 2–5
Lisa Benton (A)

Jane Lynn Hodgetts
Vijay Sathe

Early one afternoon in mid-October 1978, Lisa Benton, 27, sat at her desk looking around at the thin partitions of her cubicle and thought back over the past four months that she had been working in the Home Care Division of Houseworld. Lisa was bored with

This case was prepared by Jane Lynn Hodgetts (under the direction of Vijay Sathe).

Copyright © 1982 by the President and Fellows of Harvard College
Harvard Business School case 9–483–044.

her job and lack of responsibility and especially frustrated in her relationships with her boss, Deborah Linton, and the associate product manager, Ron Scoville. From her first day at work, when Deborah had informed her that she didn't like Harvard MBAs, Lisa had struggled unsuccessfully to please her boss. The stormy relationship that had developed with Ron Scoville only compounded her problems. On one occasion, Ron got Lisa into trouble with Deborah, and recently he had yelled at her for being a cocky MBA when she expressed her opinion. Lisa was concerned about all these events, and especially about her less-than-promising performance review, and wondered about her future with the company.

Background

Lisa Benton was married to a resident at the Cook County Hospital in Chicago. As part of a dual-career marriage, Lisa had coordinated the location of her business school with her husband's internship in Boston. Lisa's husband had encouraged her to apply to HBS and supported her during her two years at Harvard.

Lisa finished her first year with all satisfactory grades. Between the first and second years at HBS, she worked as assistant to the president of Right-Away Stores, a premier chain of convenience food stores in Chicago. Lisa enjoyed the job and was proud of the new nonmerchandising services—film, car rental, and roller skating—that she

had successfully introduced into many of the stores. Her most significant accomplishment that summer was coming up with the idea of roller skate rentals, a project she had supervised from start to finish. Before distributing the skates to the stores, Lisa organized a company roller-skating cookout to kick off the new roller-skate rental program. The party turned out to be a great morale booster for Right-Away employees, and Lisa's efforts earned her a lot of points with the president. She was especially pleased with herself for performing outstandingly in an organization where she was the first woman manager. In the roll-up-your-sleeves environment, Lisa had been able to relate well to employees at all levels and won people over who initially had been wary of a woman MBA manager. Her summer with Right-Away Stores culminated in an attractive offer for a full-time position after graduation, as well as consulting work during her second year at HBS.

Job Choice

While Lisa tolerated being separated from her husband for a couple of months while working at Right-Away, she was unwilling to continue this on a regular basis and had to juggle locations for a permanent job with her husband's residency. Chicago was mutually agreed upon, and Lisa had to choose between working as director of marketing at Right-Away or as assistant product manager at Houseworld. Scott Kingston, the president of Right-Away and a Harvard MBA, had made Lisa a very enticing offer. It was $8,000 more than the job at Houseworld. He also promised to make her a vice president in four or five years and to provide her with a company car.

Although Lisa felt flattered by the offer, her limited experience made her apprehensive about taking a position with so much marketing responsibility. Learning by the seat of her pants was a prospect she found a bit frightening. Lisa knew that Scott Kingston believed in her abilities, but she would be reporting directly to the vice president of operations and wasn't at all sure how he felt about her. While the offer sounded glamorous, Right-Away was anything but a glamorous company. Corporate headquarters were located in a rather ugly old building in an old warehouse section of Chicago. And while Lisa enjoyed receiving a lot of attention as the first woman manager, she also missed having other women managers around.

In contrast, the assistant product manager position at Houseworld appealed to Lisa because she would receive classical marketing training in a structured environment with one of the industry leaders. Lisa was also attracted to the educated and outgoing marketing professionals, both men and women, whom she met on her interviews and was excited by the idea of working in the company's cosmopolitan office building in downtown Chicago.

Lisa turned down the job at Right-Away in early April 1978,

eight months after she had been invited to return and just after she had accepted the Houseworld offer. Even though Lisa had stopped consulting for Right-Away in January 1978 and had told Scott Kingston that she intended interviewing other companies, he was still infuriated when Lisa rejected his offer. He said he had invested so much time and money in her because he believed she, in particular, not just any MBA, could fit well into his tightly knit organization. The summer experience, as well as the months of consulting, were all part of his plan to draw her gradually into his company. He said he was set back a year because of her decision. Lisa reminded Scott that she had told him she would be looking at other companies and said she felt that at Houseworld she would get the extra marketing training she needed at this point in her career. She said she wanted to keep in touch with Scott and hoped that he would keep her in mind in the future. Scott wished Lisa good luck but said she was making a big mistake.

Houseworld

Before actually interviewing with Houseworld, Lisa had tried to learn as much as possible about the company. She read the relevant material in the Career Resource Center and also spoke with Neal Simpson, a product manager at Houseworld to whom she had been referred by a friend at HBS. From these sources she gathered that Houseworld, an established consumer products company specializing in home care goods, enjoyed the largest market share in many of its product groups. While it was regarded as a conservative company, Lisa knew its reputation for providing excellent marketing training had attracted MBAs from the top-tier business schools. Houseworld consisted of three decentralized divisions: Home Care, Paper, and Laundry. Home Care, considered to be the rising star of the company and the grooming ground for top management talent, was the division that was recruiting at HBS. Neal Simpson spoke highly of the president of Home Care. Neal described him as an aggressive innovator who had great plans for turning the division into the dominant factor at Houseworld. Neal mentioned that Home Care was a secure division but that morale in the marketing area was low at present because there had been very few promotions in the past couple of years. Neal said that he liked the marketing staff, however, and that they were a decent group of people.

When Lisa was called back to visit Home Care, she was interviewed by several product managers and was really impressed with Richard Clark, a group product manager (Exhibit 1). Richard asked Lisa questions about how she could apply her experience and knowledge to product management. Lisa also talked more informally at lunch and dinner with some of the assistant and associate product managers. Gary Carter, a Wharton MBA, told Lisa that the

product management staff were a supportive bunch who worked hard but liked to have fun. The hours which most marketing people kept, from 8 to 5:30, seemed very reasonable to Lisa. She planned to lead a balanced life. Gary informed her that most of the marketing staff were married, particularly at the product management level and higher, although there were several divorcees and singles. Gary made Lisa feel really good when he said: "You're the kind of person the company wants. You're so enthusiastic."

At lunch the next day with some of her prospective peers, Lisa asked what her role would be as a new assistant product manager. They told her she would assume responsibility quickly and become a product manager within two to three years. Lisa knew from researching the other top consumer package companies that the route to product management usually took from three to four years, and she was attracted by Home Care's faster career path. In the first year she could expect to become immersed in the day-to-day brand business. She would be given different assignments and be integrated into the product management team. She learned that Houseworld used an MBO evaluation process (conducted once a year in January or February, using very specific objectives) and that promotion occurred from within. It was the product manager's responsibility to groom his or her associates to be "promotable." Helene Brenner, an assistant product

Exhibit 1
Home Care Division

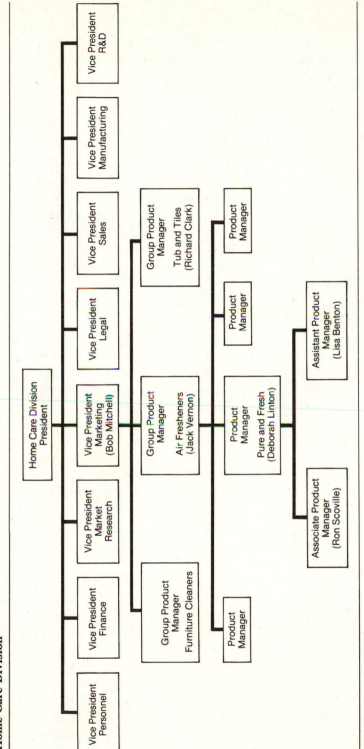

manager, explained that product managers generally moved every year and a half to two years, and associates and assistant product managers moved every year to a year and a half. This practice, which was typically followed in the leading brand management companies, allowed product managers to acquire experience in different stages of the product life cycle. Helene also commented that this sometimes made it difficult to develop close working relationships.

Lisa was offered the job of assistant product manager in the Home Care Division and was invited to return to the company for a second visit. She was informed that she wouldn't know until the first day of work who her boss was or what product she had been assigned to. This was standard operating procedure for Home Care, and also for several other consumer package companies where Lisa's HBS peers were planning to work. Lisa felt somewhat nervous about this because working relationships had always been important to her, but it was reassuring to know that she had liked all of the people she had met at Houseworld. They seemed warm and down to earth, and Lisa thought she would be able to get along with most of them. On her second visit to Home Care, she had a pleasant dinner with Carol Patlin, an enthusiastic assistant product manager. When Lisa asked about dressing for work, Carol replied that she usually wore conservative business suits like the grey one she was wearing to dinner. On April 7, 1978, Lisa accepted the job at Home Care.

Initiation

Lisa arrived at 8:30 A.M. on June 15 for her first day of work. Her carefully coordinated outfit consisted of a navy blue suit, a white blouse, a designer scarf, and navy pumps. She wanted to look conservative and sophisticated. The personnel officer brought Lisa to her new boss's office on the 20th floor. She was Deborah Linton, a woman that Lisa had not met during the interview process.

Lisa was immediately struck by Deborah's chic appearance. Probably in her early 30s, she was perfectly made up, wore a stylish tailored dress, and had a fastidious hairdo with curls neatly held in place by little combs. She seemed the epitome of what a confident and successful businesswoman should look like; next to her, Lisa felt stiff and conservative. Deborah said in a pleasant voice that she wasn't expecting Lisa for another week and that her office wasn't set up yet. She called in Ron Scoville, her associate product manager, a six-foot-tall, broad-shouldered man who also appeared to be in his early 30s and wore dark-tinted glasses. Deborah asked Ron to help Lisa get settled.

The cubicles for the assistant and associate product managers were situated in the middle of a skyscraper floor. Five-and-a-half-foot dividers separating the small, rectangular offices had given it the nickname "Hamster Haven" (Exhibit 2). The walls of the cubicles were decorated with product advertisements and storyboards; photographs and personal paraphernalia were noticeably absent. While gathering supplies for her new office, Lisa noticed Richard Clark, the group product manager who had impressed her during the recruiting process. She was disappointed that he barely remembered her and didn't stop to welcome her aboard.

Later that morning, Deborah invited Lisa into her office to get acquainted. She sat back in her chair with her hands neatly folded on the desk and began, "I've seen your resume and know something about your experience. I think you'll find your position an interesting one." Deborah began to explain the demands of the job and at one point declared in a quiet but firm tone: "MBAs act like they know a lot more than they do. The only way to learn is on the job, and your formal education won't help you. I've known some Harvard MBAs, and I

Exhibit 2
Marketing Floor

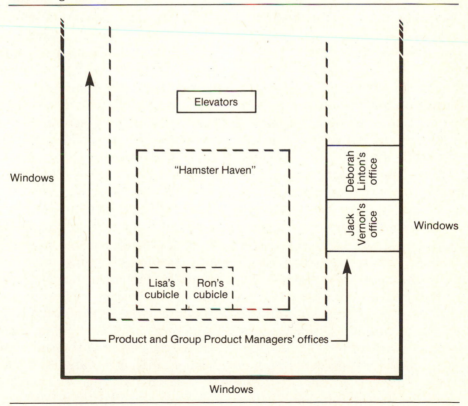

don't like them." Deborah mentioned that she didn't have an MBA, had worked her way up without one, and warned Lisa that she would have to prove herself like anyone else. Deborah revealed that she had been with the company for seven years and was one of Houseworld's first woman product managers. Lisa leaned forward uncomfortably in her chair. Rather than act defensively, she responded:

It makes sense to me that in this job, like most jobs, you have to learn from the bottom up. I also agree with you that some MBAs are arrogant, but I am willing to work hard and prove myself. At Right-Away Stores I rolled up my sleeves and did all sorts of tasks, from getting the shelves ready for the roller skates to financial planning.

Lisa hoped this would convey the impression that she was a down-to-earth person with no pretensions.

Deborah explained that this was an extremely busy time in the product management cycle and that she wouldn't have much time for Lisa in the first few weeks but that she should definitely feel free to come by her office if she had any questions. Lisa's job would be to help with the brand review and assist Ron Scoville. She told Lisa to get to know her way around and that, in a couple of weeks, they would sit down and work out objectives. Deborah stated that Lisa was to report to her and not to Ron, and spoke in vague terms about a bad experience in the Home Care

Division where an associate product manager had supervised an assistant product manager.

Around noon, Ron came to Deborah's office to take Lisa out to lunch. Deborah promised to take her out when she had time. Lisa felt let down by her new boss's cool and disinterested reception. Ron escorted her across the street to a small crowded restaurant. He opened the door and pulled her chair out for her, and Lisa suddenly felt conscious of the fact that she was a woman. Ron, with his baggy brown pin-striped suit, scruffy-looking shoes, and oily unkempt hair, appeared quite different from the well-dressed, carefully groomed men she had noticed on the marketing floor. Ron mentioned that he wasn't impressed with MBAs, especially those from Harvard, but that if Lisa relied on him, she would learn a lot. Ron had moved from operations into marketing and didn't have an MBA. Lisa felt Ron was acting like an overbearing big brother. At one point he looked at her intensely and asserted: "I'm a corporate misfit, so don't develop a style like mine. But I'm smarter and more competent than most people at Home Care. My problem is style, not substance." Lisa inquired: "What is your style, Ron?" He replied that he had an aggressive, no-nonsense style with absolutely no patience for politics. He said with disdain that some of the successful product managers and associates focused on pleasing other people and were into playing politics.

Ron promised to teach Lisa all

the ropes of product management. He pontificated:

> Lisa, bear in mind that for the first six months you're in a learning mode. Even though you'll have to dig in and learn the brand business, you won't be expected to be a brand wizard or decision maker until several months from now.

Ron gave Lisa the impression that Home Care was a highly structured environment with a lot of rules that he expected her to follow, even though he seemed to feel that he was above them. He told her she shouldn't be late for meetings, and not to rely on the train, the means of transportation she said she was planning on, because sometimes she would need to stay late.

After the lunch, which lasted two hours, Lisa returned to her new office and started reading through the product literature on Pure and Fresh, the solid air freshener brand which Deborah had assigned her that morning. Carol Patlin, the assistant product manager Lisa had dined with during recruiting, stopped by her cubicle and gave Lisa a warm, enthusiastic welcome. Lisa felt slightly disconcerted by Carol's unspoken response of a grimace when Lisa told her she was working on the Pure and Fresh brand with Ron and Deborah. Dismissing her worry for the moment, Lisa suggested they get together for lunch sometime soon. Around four o'clock, Lisa asked Ron what she could do to help on the brand review. He handed her a big stack of reports to copy, and Lisa com-

pleted the task around 7 P.M. Most of the other product management staff had left around 5:30.

Driving home, Lisa felt ambivalent about her rather odd first day at Houseworld. On the one hand, she was excited about working in a glamorous environment where people seemed intelligent and sophisticated. But she was disappointed in her brand assignment. Pure and Fresh seemed like such an unnecessary consumer product; she would be slightly embarrassed to talk about it with her HBS friends. She would have preferred a furniture cleaning product because she loved fine furniture and cared about its maintenance. Still, she was glad that the work promoting a successful new brand would be exciting and that top management would be likely to pay close attention to its progress.

Lisa felt unsettled and hurt by Deborah's cool welcome. At the same time, Lisa was impressed with her confident manner and hoped she could become more like this well-dressed, soft-spoken quintessential business woman. Ron's overbearing and condescending manner was intimidating, and Lisa knew it was going to be difficult to get along with him. However, her first impressions had been wrong before, and she wanted to give Ron a chance. Ron was not to supervise her, Deborah had said, but Lisa was to work closely with him, and Deborah herself was going to be too busy for Lisa. Ron certainly acted like a supervisor, and it was much easier to ask him questions in the next cubicle than walk all the

way across the floor to Deborah's
office. (See Exhibit 2.)

First Two Months

On Lisa's second day of work,
she settled into her cubicle and
read some more company and
product literature. Around 10:00
A.M. she walked over to Deborah's
office to find out if there was anything she could do. Ron was sitting
very close to Deborah discussing
some aspect of the brand review.
Lisa thought they seemed somewhat intimate, and she felt like an
intruder. Deborah suggested that
Lisa keep reading and getting to
know her way around the company
and that she would sit down with
her and tell her about Pure and
Fresh's history in a little while.
Later, Deborah spent about an
hour with Lisa. Lisa learned that
Deborah had been in her present
job about eight months, since November 1977, and that Lisa would
be the first assistant product manager assigned to the brand.

At noon time, Helene Brenner,
an assistant product manager Lisa
had met during the interviewing,
invited Lisa to join her and some
other product management staff
for lunch in the company cafeteria.
Helene mentioned that everyone
in the company ate there and that
Lisa could get a complete dinner
for less than $1.50. While anyone
could eat anywhere, marketing
people usually sat together in
groups of four or five at the long
tables. Lisa noticed that the marketing people she was with were
much more conservative and formal in their dress than other people in the cafeteria. In Lisa's group
of five, everyone was from a different brand. They were all very
friendly and asked Lisa questions
about her background and personal life—they seemed more interested in her than Ron and Deborah had been.

Lisa listened to a discussion
about MBAs in product management and learned that prior to
1978, new assistant product managers were selected from a mix of
MBA and non-MBA candidates.
The recruiting practices had been
changed under the direction of the
vice president of marketing, Bob
Mitchell, a Harvard MBA (see Exhibit 1). The emphasis now was on
recruiting MBAs from top-notch
schools for entry marketing positions. With this change, the
makeup of the 40 product managers, associates, and assistants in
the Home Care Division was becoming increasingly dominated
by people holding MBAs. Lisa
thought this helped explain Ron
and Deborah's apparent resentment of her. The two associate
product managers at Lisa's table
complained about the lack of upward mobility in Home Care beyond their level. Mark Wheeler, an
associate product manager in the
tub and tile group, told Lisa that if
anyone ever asked her what her
goals were, she should reply that
she wanted to get ahead at Houseworld. He warned her never to say:
"I'm at Houseworld to get some
good marketing training."

Early in the morning of her
fourth day at Houseworld, Lisa jot-

ted down some questions she had about Pure and Fresh, such as, What kind of trade deals were offered, and How should one read SAMI (share of market) reports? At 9:15 Lisa walked over to Deborah's office hoping to get some answers to her questions. Since Deborah's desk faced the window, Lisa could only see the back of Deborah's head as she prepared to enter her office. Lisa tapped on the door and inquired, "Do you mind if I ask you a few questions?" When Deborah realized that it was Lisa, she quickly covered up what she was writing, and replied curtly, "I'm doing something right now, why don't you come back later?" Lisa thought her boss looked as if she was not quite awake, and once again Lisa felt she was intruding. It disappointed Lisa that Deborah didn't want to make any time for her.

Lisa trudged back to the other side of the floor and asked Ron Scoville her questions. Ron leaned back in his chair and, in an all-knowing manner, gave Lisa his answers. He ended by saying: "Don't worry about asking me questions. You're in a learning mode as an assistant and can't be expected to know that much." Lisa didn't enjoy Ron's condescending attitude, but she appreciated his taking the time to answer and began turning regularly to Ron when she needed to know something.

Lisa's formal orientation to Houseworld began during her second week, and it was to last for a month. Two days a week she met with department heads of the staff groups from finance, market research, R&D, legal, and manufacturing and was oriented to the different functions in the company. Lisa was advised that she should learn about the chemistry of the air freshener, as well as about the design, package, financial, and legal aspects of the product. She was uncertain where to get the information, since the few assignments she was given did not use any chemistry knowledge base.

One job that Ron asked Lisa to do was to take artwork approval forms for Pure and Fresh promotional coupons to all the departments for sign-off. Lisa walked around and waited until the secretaries were able to get their bosses to sign these forms. She felt like a gopher; it seemed strange to be meeting with department heads for orientation and waiting on their secretaries for minor administrative details. Lisa assumed this boring task was just another part of being an assistant. She hesitated to ask for more responsibility for fear of coming across as an aggressive MBA.

In her third week, Lisa started to accompany Ron and Deborah in meetings with the different staff groups and the ad agency. She usually deferred to Ron and Deborah and refrained from saying: "Well, I think we should. . . ." Lisa remembered what Ron referred to as her "learning mode," and thought it best to be quiet and act like a learner. At first she didn't feel that she had a point of view and was somewhat overwhelmed by the background knowledge that she needed to acquire for Pure and Fresh. Deborah's presentations at these meetings impressed Lisa as articulate and very persuasive. Ron and Deborah rarely asked Lisa for her opinion and made no apparent effort to treat her as one of the brand team. Lisa felt like a third wheel.

One day, when she had been at Houseworld for about a month, Lisa went out after work for drinks with Helene Brenner, the assistant product manager she had become friends with. Helene was in her late 20s, had an MBA from Columbia, and had been at Home Care for about nine months. Helene described a presentation that she had done for her group product manager that day:

> I think I really impressed Richard Clark with all my charts and slides. You know, Lisa, when you do presentations around here, you've got to be buttoned up and completely prepared with all the facts and figures. Presentations are one of the main ways to get visibility with your group product manager and higher.

When Lisa asked, "When did you give your first presentation?" Helene replied, "About three months after joining Houseworld." Lisa felt it was too early for her to be concerned about presentations, but she asked what else was important to becoming successful in marketing in Home Care. Helene thought the people who were succeeding were enthusiastic, but not pushy loud mouths, and were ambitious, creative, and analytical. Helene cautioned Lisa about working long hours:

> Don't stay at the office after 6. You don't get brownie points around here for working late. I heard about an assistant product manager who didn't get promoted because he was really disorganized and was always at the office until at least 7.

After discussing some other company practices and talking about their personal lives, Lisa thanked Helene and suggested that they go out for drinks more often.

In Lisa's fifth week Deborah asked her to analyze some Nielsen consumer sales data and to write a memo on her findings. Lisa knew memos were important at Houseworld and that writing good ones was a key to receiving top-management visibility. Deborah had Lisa revise her memo four times before she passed it up to the group product manager, Jack Vernon. The memo was well received, and Jack personally commended Lisa on her work with a scrawl at the top of the memo saying, "Nice job." Lisa derived little sense of accomplishment, however, because she wasn't allowed to make recommendations or take any action beyond the analysis. Instead, Ron and Deborah used the analysis to develop plans for Pure and Fresh. Lisa felt that memo writing was just an exercise, almost busy work. She knew that Ron and Deborah were planning brand promotions and were involved in the creative development of new television ads, all of which looked much more exciting than her assignments. From what she had been told in the recruiting process, and given her responsibilities and accomplishments at Right-Away, Lisa expected to be more involved in the day-to-day business of the brand, such as working on pricing issues and ironing out problems that developed in the sampling program. After developing action plans every day for two years at HBS, she was frustrated with just performing analyses of the data.

On the train going home several days later, Lisa spoke with Gary Carter, one of the associate product managers she had first met, and a person that she chatted with regularly on the train. Gary's brand group also had a new assistant who had just come on board, and Lisa was curious as to what the person was working on. "Oh, she's helping us plan a promotion for next year, and working on pricing recommendations. Why do you ask?" Lisa described the assignments that she had been given, such as the Nielsen analysis, and revealed to Gary that she felt frustrated and underutilized. Gary agreed that Lisa's abilities were not being fully taken advantage of, but had no explanation for her situation. Lisa was discouraged and wondered if she was doing something wrong or if she had gotten stuck with a lousy management team. She was reluctant to mention to Gary, or her other peers, the difficulties she was having with her boss and associate manager because of her belief that loyalty to one's superiors was essential in the corporate world.

Lisa thought that she was getting along well with her peers, the secretary, the other staff groups, and Jack Vernon, the group product manager. Her peers frequently invited her to go to lunch and for drinks after work. Lisa often chatted with Virginia Mason, Pure and Fresh's secretary, and had no problems in getting her work typed by Virginia on time. When Lisa needed people from the staff groups (under the VPs listed in Exhibit 1), such as the market research analyst, to provide her with information on customer complaint letters or the financial analyst to give her cost data, she always got their cooperation. Lisa made a point of being friendly to the staff people. She was confident that Jack Vernon liked her, based on his commendations on her memos and from chats the two had had about Harvard. Jack had a Harvard chair and a Harvard picture in his office and was impressed that Lisa had attended HBS.

But Lisa found it increasingly difficult to cope with Ron's condescending manner and Deborah's detachment. Ron was constantly calling over the divider: "Lisa, can you run these numbers for me?" and "Lisa, when will the approvals be all signed?" With his abrasive management style, Ron often had trouble getting others to do his bidding and frequently ended up doing tasks, such as financial analysis and sales forecasting, by himself.

Lisa had been at Houseworld for approximately six weeks, and Deborah still hadn't sat down with Lisa and given her objectives as she had promised Lisa on the first day, nor had she taken Lisa out to lunch. Since half of an assistant's time was spent with the brand team, and the first year with Homeworld was supposed to be critical for later success, Lisa began to have some doubts about her future with the company. They were intensified by some incidents that occurred in her third and fourth months.

The Typing Incident

One afternoon in mid-August, Lisa was trying to complete a memo on a project comparing Pure and Fresh sales by units with sales by ounces. She noticed that the headings on one of her charts, which had been typed by Virginia, were not lined up properly. Since error-free reports were expected in Home Care, she decided this must be corrected. Virginia was on vacation, and Lisa knew the other secretaries were extremely pressed for time while the brand review was being formalized, so she sat down at a typewriter for about five minutes and redid the copy herself. She had only just returned to her office on the other side of the floor when Jack Vernon, the group product manager, strode in. It was unusual for Jack to come by Lisa's cubicle. She was surprised and disturbed by his insistence that she come to his office immediately. Once inside his office, Jack quickly shut the door, which he usually kept open. He then leaned back in his Harvard chair, and, with his arms bent behind his head, began in a kind but firm voice:

I don't know what you were doing, but I never want to see you at a typewriter in this company again. We have secretaries to do that kind of work, and there is no reason why you, particularly a woman, should be seen typing. It destroys your credibility not only with the people you work with, but also in the secretaries' eyes.

Lisa responded with annoyance in her voice:

You really misinterpreted the situation. I was only typing for a few minutes and thought it would be much quicker to fix the heading on one of my charts myself than to wait until one of the other secretaries had some time to make the correction. We really don't have adequate secretarial coverage with Virginia on vacation.

Jack repeated what he had just said, and Lisa told him she appreciated his concern, and that it wouldn't happen again. Nevertheless, Lisa felt angry. She regarded her work as part of a team effort and thought Jack's criticism was ridiculous—it was such a tiny incident. But Lisa recognized that Jack had a point and that he was looking out for her interests.

Later in the afternoon, Deborah asked Lisa about the incident with Jack. Deborah's office was right next to Jack's; she had seen Lisa go into his office and watched the door shut. Deborah, who had often spoken with disdain about Jack, became furious. "He had no right to tell you that," she said when she heard Lisa's story. "First of all, he should have told me and let me talk to you, and secondly, that whole typing issue itself is ridiculous." Lisa wasn't sure whether she agreed with Deborah on that. She only knew that her boss was fuming because Jack had gone over her head and approached Lisa directly.

Several days later, Deborah mentioned to Lisa that she had spoken with Jack about the incident. She seemed to support Lisa's behavior and commented: "There are times and places when we have to do things like typing." While Lisa still wasn't sure what she should do in future situations, she concluded that since Jack was the high man on the totem pole, she would follow his instructions.

The Xeroxing Episode

On the morning of August 25, a week after the typing incident, Lisa was in the midst of some work on a coupon test market booklet. The booklet would include coupons from other manufacturers and be mailed to 600,000 homes in three test cities. Redemption rates of the coupons would be measured to see if they were good promotional vehicles. Lisa's job was to help design the Pure and Fresh coupons and to work out the details with the company that produced the booklets. Deborah and Ron were putting the final touches on the marketing plan and were rushing to meet their own deadlines.

From the next cubicle, Lisa heard Ron calling her to come to his office. She was losing patience with Ron's patronizing style and snapped, "I'll be there in a minute." Five minutes later, she walked into his office.

Ron wanted Lisa to do some xeroxing for him while he made some last minute corrections on the marketing plan. Aside from her misgivings about clerical tasks since the episode with Jack Vernon, Lisa was upset that Deborah and Ron had left her out of the preparation of the marketing plan. She told Ron she could do the xeroxing *with* him in a while, but she was occupied with her own project for the moment. Ron insisted on Lisa's doing the xeroxing immediately. Lisa, tired of Ron's servant-girl treatment, retorted: "Ron, why don't you plan your time better and do your own xeroxing?" He sneered, "Oh, I see, you're too good for xeroxing." Lisa grabbed up the papers and left to begin the chore.

When Lisa returned from lunch, a note was on her desk summoning her to Deborah's office. Lisa could see that the chic businesswoman had fire in her eyes: "I understand you're too good for xeroxing." With pursed lips, Lisa glared at Deborah. It was the first time that Lisa felt real animosity toward her, and she angrily proclaimed:

That is patently false. Half of the material is already on Ron's desk, and I'm going to finish the rest this afternoon. I was upset because he treated me like some servant girl, and I was getting tired of his patronizing attitude. I have never felt too good for this kind of work. In fact, when I was at Right-Away last summer, I counted inventory in the stores and dusted the shelves. I . . .

Deborah cut her off and screamed:

This is a *team* effort. Everyone is overworked. You'll just have to *contribute*. Xeroxing is a part of your job, even if you *are* a Harvard MBA.

Lisa felt there was no point in arguing with her. Turning on her heel, she snapped, "I'm going to do the rest of the xeroxing right now."

Lisa was furious and frustrated. It was the first time in her entire working history that a boss had actually yelled at her. Instead of acting as a buffer between Ron and Lisa, Deborah blamed Lisa and didn't really seem interested in Lisa's side of the story. Lisa marched into Ron's office, looked him in the eye, and said:

You had a lot of gall going to Deborah, when I've been doing a lot of tasks for you. I don't mind xeroxing, and I've never felt too good for xeroxing, but I expect you to ask me for favors without being so condescending.

Ron apologized: "I'm sorry this happened. I had no idea that I came across so brusquely, or that you would be so sensitive. I'll try to work on my behavior next time."

Lisa felt that her position was untenable. If she performed clerical tasks, she would be criticized by people like Jack Vernon. But if she didn't go along with Ron's requests, she'd be chewed out for not being a team player. She wondered how she could manage these difficult relationships.

On the train ride home that evening, she mentioned the incident to Gary Carter. Gary was surprised; Lisa had rarely talked about Ron because she knew that Gary got along with him. Now she asked Gary for advice on how to deal with Ron. Gary suggested that Lisa should stand up to him and not take his crap. Lisa felt that was easier said than done; she thought if she followed Gary's advice, she would get flack from Deborah. While Lisa was beginning to feel freer to talk with trusted friends about Ron, it still seemed important to be loyal to her boss, and she played down Deborah's role in the xeroxing incident.

Five days later, on August 30, 1978, Jack Vernon, the group product manager, unexpectedly called Lisa into his office. He shut the door ceremoniously and asked in a concerned voice: "Lisa, are you happy here?" The question came out of the blue, and Lisa guessed that her unhappiness probably showed in her demeanor, since she usually was enthusiastic. She replied: "Yeah, I'm okay. I have my ups and downs like everyone else." Jack wasn't satisfied and probed: "Well, you don't seem happy. Are you sure there isn't something that you want to talk about, like how things are going with Ron and Deborah?" Jack seemed genuinely concerned, but Lisa felt she should be cautious. "I'm having some problems with Ron, but Deborah's been really good about helping me." Jack agreed that Ron's style was difficult to deal with, and Lisa thanked him for his interest.

After her meeting with Jack, Lisa thought she had been smart politically, by expressing loyalty to her boss and making her look good in her superior's eyes. However, she still had no clue as to how to manage her relationships with Ron and Deborah more effectively.

Performance Evaluation

Two weeks later, on September 10, Lisa went out for drinks with her friend Carol Patlin. Carol had been with the company for four years and had moved over from finance into marketing. She had been an assistant product manager for a year and a half and knew a lot about company practices and office rumors. Carol asked Lisa if she had had a performance review yet. Lisa inquired: "Should I have?" Carol explained that it was customary to have a review after one's first three months with the company and suggested that Lisa ask Deborah to give her some feedback about Lisa's performance.

On September 15, three months after Lisa had joined Houseworld, she decided to ask Deborah for a performance review. Nervously, Lisa said: "I've been here for three months and understand it's customary to have a review after that time period. I want to know if I'm meeting your expectations and how to work on plans for my development." In a flat voice, Deborah

responded: "If you really want one, I'll sit down with you in a few days and give you a performance review." Again, Lisa seemed to be imposing on Deborah's time.

A week later, Deborah took Lisa out to lunch for the first time. Seated in a quiet little booth in an unappealing hotel restaurant, Lisa felt uncomfortable. Her boss didn't waste any time on ordering drinks or small talk, but drew a small folded piece of paper out of her maroon leather designer handbag. She told Lisa that she had jotted down some notes about her performance and that she wanted to keep the discussion informal.

Deborah began by listing Lisa's strengths. She commended her on her ability to get along with the staff groups and with the marketing department, for learning how the company's system worked and about the staff interrelationships, and for her written communication skills. Overall, she said that Lisa was doing a nice job but that there were several areas in which she needed to improve. Very matter of factly, sitting back with her hands folded in her lap, she reviewed Lisa's weaknesses: not taking initiative in mapping out projects for herself, lack of assertiveness in making her opinions known, and being too quiet in meetings with Ron and the staff groups. She also mentioned that Lisa lacked confidence, but she thought she was intelligent. Deborah's feedback was primarily on style, and not on specific incidents, so Lisa asked her to cite some examples of behavior that needed improvement. Deborah replied: "When we are in meetings with the ad agency, you rarely contribute your opinions. You always qualify your recommendations with, 'I'm not really familiar with. . . .' "

Lisa listened and nodded and tried not to get defensive, but on the inside she felt disappointed and misunderstood. She explained that she had just been trying to act like a learner. Lisa hesitated to say negative things about Ron, since she knew that Deborah had a close relationship with him. Several weeks before, over drinks, Carol had told her about a rumor that Deborah and Ron had had an affair. Lisa didn't know if it was true, but when she was with them there seemed to be a dimension to their relationship that went beyond business. Lisa, therefore, diplomatically related to Deborah that Ron often acted a bit patronizing with her and that it was difficult to be forceful and assertive around him since he was so overbearing. While Deborah agreed that Ron's management style left a lot to be desired, she believed that Lisa should be able to get along with him. She pointed out that she never had any problems with Ron, herself, and couldn't understand Lisa's difficulties. Lisa politely agreed to work on the areas identified by her boss and asked if she, in turn, would define some responsibilities for her that would be separate from Ron's job. Deborah agreed.

After the luncheon, Lisa was very upset that her superior had failed to recognize some of her major strengths: analytical skills, intellectual capacity, and organizational abilities. She was disturbed by Deborah's feedback about being unassertive and lacking in initiative. Lisa believed that Deborah's criticisms accurately described her behavior at Houseworld, but they were incongruent with Lisa's image of herself as aggressive and opinionated. On the one hand, Lisa felt that Deborah hadn't given her the opportunity to demonstrate her real personality, but on the other hand, Lisa blamed herself for not being true to her own character.

Lisa also felt that she had struggled with conflicting messages from the very beginning: She was warned not to act like an arrogant MBA, and she was faulted for not being assertive and aggressive enough. She had tried to apply the lessons about managing one's boss that she had learned in her course on Power and Influence at HBS, and wondered if she had failed in some major respect. Since the manager's opinion was key to promotions at Houseworld, she had serious doubts about whether she would succeed in the company. Lisa decided to act more like herself and present her opinions, but was doubtful about what kinds of projects she could initiate.

Another Run-in with Ron

While Deborah seemed to make a token attempt to provide Lisa with projects separate from Ron, more often than not she found herself working on projects with him. Lisa tried using humor to get along with Ron and was beginning to state her opinions and make firm suggestions at ad agency meetings, as Deborah had advised. Once again, however, she discovered that following a superior's orders conflicted with the reality of dealing with Ron.

It was the afternoon of October 2, 1978, 10 days after the performance appraisal, and Lisa had just spent hours on an analysis of Pure and Fresh pricing. She stepped into Ron's office to show him her analysis and recommendations. He seemed impressed, and Lisa thought to herself that he finally was beginning to believe she had some brains. Pleased with herself, she returned to her desk to complete the profit calculations. Ron strolled in five minutes later and asked her how she arrived at her profit figure for the small size of Pure and Fresh, vehemently disagreeing with Lisa's conclusions. Lisa stuck to her guns and showed Ron her algebra. An escalating argument ensued. Frustrated with Ron's overbearing manner, she asserted: "That's ridiculous." The six-foot-tall, hulking man towered over her desk and yelled in a voice audible across the floor:

> You arrogant MBAs are all alike. You think you know everything. You're so cocky. When you've been around for a while, you'll see that your analysis isn't suitable.

Deciding not to come down to his level by yelling back, Lisa retorted that she was trying to express her point of view. Fuming on the inside, she finally pronounced: "Oh, for-

get it and just get out of here." Ron huffed out of her office.

Lisa was furious and stunned, yet felt embarrassed and humiliated. She fought back the tears that welled up in her eyes and thought: "I hate it here. I want to leave. I don't need to put up with this." One of the other associates, Ann Hutchings, a woman that Lisa was not particularly fond of, saw Lisa's distraught face and suggested that the two of them go to the conference room to talk. Ann sensed that Lisa had a lot to get off her chest. Lisa, who until now had volunteered very little about her problems with Ron and Deborah, spilled out her frustrations:

> I'm so sick of trying to get along with that creep. He is so condescending and makes me feel so small. I've tried to talk back to him, but it hasn't worked.

Ann agreed that Ron was a creep and revealed that many of the other product management people had the same negative opinion. She advised Lisa to ignore him and just get through her time with Ron. Ann indicated that with his abrasive management style and iconoclastic behavior, he wouldn't be at Houseworld for long. Ann asked Lisa if Deborah had helped Ron and Lisa with their problems in getting along. Lisa replied, "She's told us to work things out ourselves. I'm pretty annoyed with her; I think she has just been copping out." When their talk was over, Lisa borrowed some makeup from Ann, pulled herself together, and returned to her desk.

Lisa thought that was the end of the episode, but later that afternoon, Deborah called her to her office. Word had gotten around about the incident with Ron; Deborah told Lisa that several people, including Ann's product manager, had complained about Ron's destructive behavior and his condescending treatment of Lisa. Deborah said once more that she couldn't understand Lisa's problems with Ron and inquired why she hadn't discussed them with her. Lisa replied that she believed they were close friends and she didn't think Deborah was receptive to criticisms about Ron. Deborah said: "Ron is one of my best friends. I know others don't like him, but I think he is misunderstood and that he has a heart of gold." Deborah promised again that she would try to assign them discrete projects but insisted that they try to get along with each other. Lisa agreed to work things out, knowing that Deborah would do nothing to make the relationship any better.

Lisa then went into Ron's office and suggested that they talk after work over drinks. She realized that getting along with him was essential to her success with the brand. While Ron's style was abhorrent, Lisa felt he was open to feedback. And strangely enough, there had been occasions when he had come across as a decent, even warm, human being. It almost seemed that he was basically a nice guy who just could not curb his strong temper, irritating mannerisms, and intimidating style. Over drinks at the top of the John Hancock building, Ron apologized for hurting Lisa's feelings and talked about his frustration with the organization and the fact that he hadn't been promoted yet. They agreed to try to cooperate.

Soul Searching

While Ron and Lisa managed to avoid confrontation, Lisa still felt overshadowed. Ron still dominated meetings, talking loudly and abrasively, while Lisa faded into the background. After the yelling incident with Ron, five or six of the other associates and assistants in Hamster Haven rallied to Lisa's support. She was repeatedly invited to lunch by peers she didn't know well. The general advice she received was to "hang in there." She was reminded that Pure and Fresh was only a temporary assignment, thanks to Houseworld's policy of rotating marketing staff. They all agreed that Ron couldn't get along with anyone. Lisa's peers viewed Deborah as an excellent performer with a great track record of brand successes but a poor trainer and manager of subordinates. During one of Lisa's unsolicited luncheons, an assistant product manager who had worked for Deborah the previous year told her that Deborah had done a terrible job of training him. He said he was now working double time trying to catch up on things he should have learned in his first position. This new information was disconcerting to Lisa.

Lisa appreciated the camaraderie and support from her peers, but her concerns about her future with Houseworld were not alleviated. She was still bored and wanted some responsibility and thought that her talents and training were not being fully utilized. Lisa was especially troubled by Deborah's lack of interest in her development, even after Lisa had gone on several field visits with her boss. During these day-and-a-half trips, Deborah seemed as detached and businesslike as ever, and quite inaccessible. It was clear that her mind was preoccupied with other matters.

Lisa was worried about how her slow start at Houseworld would affect her prospects of promotion. She considered talking to Jack Vernon, the group product manager, who seemed to like and respect her, to ask for a switch to another brand, but as far as Lisa knew no assistant product manager had ever done this at Houseworld. She was reluctant to alienate not only her superiors but possibly her peers as well by making such an unusual request. She was also aware of how Deborah hated to have anyone go over her head and thought if she ever discovered that Lisa had, she could make life even more difficult for her.

Lisa was tempted to call her boss from her summer job, Scott Kingston, the president of Right-Away Stores, to inform him that she had made a mistake in turning down his attractive offer. At Right-Away, Lisa had been a star and had no trouble managing her superiors. Although Scott had been angry with Lisa for rejecting his offer, Lisa thought she could call him if she was absolutely serious about

leaving Houseworld because her former marketing assistant at Right-Away had said recently that Scott still spoke highly of Lisa's contributions to the organization.

READING 2–1 People Processing: Strategies of Organizational Socialization

John Van Maanen

Van Maanen identifies seven dimensions or strategies of socialization, together with their often fateful consequences for the individual and for the organization. And he makes clear that socialization is too important to be left to chance or inertia.

Socialization shapes the person—a defensible hyperbole. Organizational socialization or "people processing" refers to the manner in which the experiences of people learning the ropes of a new organizational position, status, or role are structured for them by others within the organization. In short, I will argue here that people acquire the social knowledge and skills necessary to assume a particular job in an organization differently not only because people are different, but, more critically, because the techniques or strategies of people processing differ. And, like the variations of a sculptor's mold, certain forms of organizational socialization produce remarkably different results.

Socialization strategies are perhaps most obvious when a person first joins an organization or when an individual is promoted or demoted. They are probably least obvious when an experienced member of the organization undergoes a simple change of assignment, shift, or job location. Nevertheless, certain people-processing devices can be shown to characterize every transition an individual makes across organizational boundaries. Moreover, management may choose such devices explicitly or consciously. For example, management might require all recruits or newcomers to a particular position to attend a training or orientation program of some kind. Or management may select people-processing devices implicitly or unconsciously. These strategies may simply represent taken-for-granted precedents established in the dim past of an organization's history. The precedent could perhaps be the proverbial trial-and-error method of socialization by which a person learns how to perform a new task on his own, without direct guidance.

Regardless of the method of choice, however, any given socialization device represents an identi-

fiable set of events that will make certain behavioral and attitudinal consequences more likely than others. It is possible, therefore, to identify the various people-processing methods and evaluate them in terms of their social consequences.

Background

Three primary assumptions underlie this analysis. First, and perhaps of most importance, is the notion that people in a state of transition are more or less in an anxiety-producing situation. They are motivated to reduce this anxiety by learning the functional and social requirements of their new role as quickly as possible.

Second, the learning that takes place does not occur in a social vacuum strictly on the basis of the official and available versions of the job requirements. Any person crossing organizational boundaries is looking for clues on how to proceed. Thus colleagues, superiors, subordinates, clients, and other work associates can and most often do support, guide, hinder, confuse, or push the individual who is learning a new role. Indeed, they can help him interpret (or misinterpret) the events he experiences so that he can take appropriate (or inappropriate) action in his altered situation. Ultimately, they will provide him with a sense of accomplishment and competence or failure and incompetence.

Third, the stability and productivity of any organization depend in large measure on the way newcomers to various organizational positions come to carry out their tasks. When positions pass from generation to generation of incumbents smoothly, the continuity of the organization's mission is maintained, the predictability of the organization's performance is left intact, and, in the short run at least, the survival of the organization is assured.

A concern for the ways in which individuals adjust to novel circumstances directs attention not only to the cognitive learning that accompanies any transition, but also to the manner in which the person copes emotionally with the new situation. As sociologist Erving Goffman rightly suggests, new situations require individuals to reassess and perhaps alter both their instrumental goals (the goals they wish to achieve through their involvement in the organization) and their expressive style (the symbolic appearances they maintain before others in the organization).

In some cases, a shift into a new work situation may result in a dramatically altered organizational identity for the person. This often happens, for example, when a factory worker becomes a foreman or a staff analyst becomes a line manager. Other times, the shift may cause only minor and insignificant changes in a person's organizational identity; for instance, when an administrator is shifted to a new location or a craftsman is rotated to a new department. Yet any of these shifts is likely to result in what might be called a "reality shock" for the person being shifted. When people undergo a transition, regardless of the information they already possess about their new role, their *a priori* understandings of that role are bound to change in either a subtle or a dramatic fashion. Becoming a member of an organization will upset the everyday order of even the most well-informed newcomer. Matters concerning such aspects of life as friendships, time, purpose, demeanor, competence, and the expectations the person holds of the immediate and distant future are suddenly made problematic. The newcomer's most pressing task is to build a set of guidelines and interpretations to explain and make meaningful the myriad of activities observed as going on in the organization.

To come to know an organizational situation and act within it implies that a person has developed some beliefs, principles, and understandings, or, in shorthand notation, a *perspective* for interpreting the experiences he or she has had as a participant in a given sphere of the work world. This perspective provides the rules by which to manage the unique and recurring strains of organizational life. It provides the person with an ordered view of the organization that runs ahead and directs experience, orders and shapes personal relationships in the work setting, and provides the ground rules to manage the ordinary day-to-day affairs.

Strategies of People Processing

Certain situational variables associated with any organization transition can be made visible and shown to be tied directly to the perspective constructed by individuals in transit. The focus here is not on perspectives *per se,* however, but rather on the properties peculiar to any given people-processing situation. These properties are essentially process variables akin to, but more specific than, such generic processes as education, training, apprenticeship, and indoctrination. Furthermore, these properties can be viewed as organizational strategies that distinctly pattern the learning experiences of a newcomer to a particular organizational role.

The people-processing strategies examined below are associated to some degree with all situations that involve a person moving from one organizational position to another. Although much of the evidence comes from studies concerned with the way someone first becomes a member of an organization, the techniques used to manage this passage are at least potentially available for use during any transition a person undergoes during the course of a career. Thus the term "strategy" is used to describe each examined aspect of a transition process because the degree to which a particular people-processing technique is used by an organization is not in any sense a natural condition or prerequisite for socialization. Indeed, by definition, some socialization will always take place when a person moves into and remains with a new organizational role. However, the form that it takes is a matter of organizational choice. And, whether this choice of strategies is made by design or by accident, it is at least theoretically subject to rapid and complete change at the direction of the management.

This is an important point. It suggests that we can be far more self-consious about employing certain people-processing techniques than we have been. In fact, a major purpose of this article is to heighten and cultivate a broader awareness of what it is we do to people under the guise of "breaking them in." Presumably, if we have a greater appreciation for the sometimes unintended consequences of a particular strategy, we can alter the strategy to benefit both the individual and the organization.

Seven dimensions on which the major strategies of people processing can be located will be discussed. Each strategy will be presented alongside its counterpart or opposing strategy. In other words, each strategy as applied can be thought of as existing somewhere between the two poles of a single dimension. Critically, across dimensions, the strategies are not mutually exclusive. In practice, they are typically combined in sundry and often inventive ways. Thus, although each tactic is discussed in relative isolation, the reader should be aware that the effects of the various socialization strategies upon individuals are cumulative—but not necessarily compatible (in terms of outcome) with one another.

I do not claim that these strategies are exhaustive or that they are presented in any order of relevance to a particular organization or occupation. These are essentially empirical questions that can only be answered by further research. I do claim and attempt to show that these strategies are recognizable, powerful, in widespread use, and of enormous consequence to the people throughout an organization. And, since organizations can accomplish little more than what the people within them accomplish, these people-processing strategies are of undeniable importance when it comes to examining such matters as organizational performance, structure, and, ultimately, survival.

Formal (Informal) Socialization Strategies

The formality of a socialization process refers to the degree to which the setting in which it takes place is segregated from the ongoing work context and to the degree to which an individual's newcomer role is emphasized and made explicit. The more formal the process, the more the recruit's role is both segregated and specified. The recruit is differentiated strictly from other organizational members. In an informal atmosphere, there is no sharp differentiation, and much of the recruit's learning necessarily takes place within the social and task-related networks that surround his or her position. Thus informal socialization procedures are analytically similar to the familiar trial-and-error techniques by which one learns, it is said, through experience.

Generally, the more formal the process, the more stress there is influencing the newcomer's attitudes and values. The more concerned the organization is with the recruit's absorption of the appropriate demeanor and stance, the more the recruit is likely to begin to think and feel like a U.S. Marine, an IBM executive, or a Catholic priest. In other words, formal processes work on preparing a person to occupy a particular *status* in the organization. Informal processes, on the other hand, prepare a person to perform a specific *role* in an organization. And, in general, the more the recruit is separated from the day-to-day reality of the organization, the less he or she will be able to carry over, generalize, and apply any abilities or skills learned in one socialization setting to the new position.

From this standpoint, formal socialization processes are often only the "first round" of socialization. The informal second round occurs when the newcomer is placed in his designated organizational slot and must learn informally the actual practices in his department. Whereas the first wave stresses general skills and attitudes, the second wave emphasizes specified actions, situational applications of rules, and the idiosyncratic nuances necessary to perform the role in the work setting. However, when the gap separating the two kinds of learning is large, disillusionment with the first wave may set in, causing the individual to disregard virtually everything he has learned in the formal round of socialization.

Even when formal socialization is

deliberately set up to provide what are thought to be practical and particular skills, it may be still experienced as problematic by those who pass through the process. In effect, the choice of a formal strategy forces all newcomers to endure, absorb, and perhaps become proficient wth *all* the skills and materials presented to them, since they cannot know what is or is not relevant to the job for which they are being prepared. For example, in police training academies, recruits are taught fingerprinting, ballistics, and crime-scene investigation, skills that are, at best, of peripheral interest and of no use to a street patrolman. One result is that when recruits graduate and move to the mean streets of the city, a general disenchantment with the relevance of all their training typically sets in.

Even in the prestigious professional schools of medicine and law, the relevance of much training comes to be doubted by practitioners and students alike. Such disenchantment is apparently so pervasive that some observers have suggested that the formal processes that typify professional schools produce graduates who have already internalized standards for their everyday work performances that are "self-validating" and are apparently lodged well beyond the influence of others both within and outside the professional intellectual community that surrounds the occupation.

Formal strategies appear also to produce stress for people in the form of a period of personal stigmatization. This stigmatization can be brought about by identifying garb (such as the peculiar uniform worn by police recruits); a special and usually somewhat demeaning title (such as "rookie," "trainee," or "junior"); or an insular position (such as an assignment to a classroom instead of an office or job). A person undergoing formal socialization is likely to feel isolated, cut off, and prohibited from assuming everyday social relationships with his more experienced "betters."

Informal socialization processes, wherein a recruit must negotiate for himself within a far less structured situation, can also induce personal anxiety. Indeed, the person may have trouble discovering clues as to the exact dimensions of his or her assigned organizational role. Under most circumstances, laissez-faire socialization increases the influence of the immediate work group on the new employee. There is no guarantee, though, that the direction provided by the informal approach will push the recruit in the right direction so far as those in authority are concerned. Classical examples are the so-called goldbricking and quota-restriction tactics invented by employees in production situations to thwart managerial directives. Such practices are passed on informally but quite effectively to newcomers against the desires of management.

Left to his own devices, a recruit will select his socialization agents. The success of the socialization process is then determined largely on the basis of whatever mutual regard is developed between the agent and the newcomer, the relevant knowledge possessed by an agent, and, of course, the agent's ability to transfer such knowledge. In most Ph.D. programs, for example, students must pick their own advisors from among the faculty. The advisors then act a philosophers, friends, and guides for the students. And among professors— as among organization executives—it is felt that the student who pushes the hardest by demanding more time, asking more questions, and so forth, learns the most. Consequently, the recruit's freedom of choice in the more informal setting has a price. He or she must force others to teach him.

Individual (Collective) Socialization Strategies

The degree to which individuals are socialized singly or collectively is perhaps the most critical of the process variables. The difference is analogous to the batch versus unit modes of production. In the batch or mass-production case, recruits are bunched together at the outset and processed through an identical set of experiences, with relatively similar outcomes.

When a group goes through a socialization program together, it almost always develops an "in the same boat" collective consciousness. Individual changes in perspective are built on an understanding of the problems faced by all members of the group. Apparently as the group shares problems, various members experiment with possible solutions and report back. In the course of discussions that follow, the members arrive at a collective and more or less consensual definition of their situation.

At the same time, the consensual character of the solutions worked out by the group allows the members to deviate more from the standards set by the agents than the individual mode of socialization does. Therefore, collective processes provide a potential base for recruit resistance. In such cases, the congruence between managerial objectives and those adopted by the group is always problematic—the recruit group is more likely than the individual to redefine or ignore agent demands.

Classic illustrations of the dilemma raised by the use of the collective strategy can be found in both educational and work environments. In educational settings, the faculty may beseech a student to study hard while the student's peers exhort him to relax and have a good time. In many work settings, supervisors attempt to ensure that each employee works up to his level of competence while the worker's peers try to impress on him that he must not do too much. To the degree that the newcomer is backed into the corner and cannot satisfy both demands at the same time, he will follow the dicta of those with whom he spends most of his time and who are most important to him.

The strength of group understandings depends, of course, on the degree to which all members actually share the same fate. In highly competitive settings, group members know that their own success is increased through the failure of others. Hence, the social support networks necessary to maintain cohesion in the group may break down. Consensual understandings will develop, but they will buttress individual modes of adjustment. Junior faculty members in publication-minded universities, for instance, follow group standards, although such standards nearly always stress individual scholarship.

Critically, collective socialization processes can also promote and intensify agent demands. Army recruits socialize each other in ways the army itself could never do; nor, for that matter, would it be allowed to do. Graduate students are often said to learn more from one another than from the faculty. And, while agents may have the power to define the nature of the collective problem, recruits often have more resources available to them to define the solution—time, experience, motivation, expertise, and patience (or the lack thereof).

Individual strategies also induce personal changes. But the views adopted by people processed individually are likely to be far less homogeneous than the views of those processed collectively. Nor are the views adopted by the isolated newcomer necessarily those that are the most beneficial to him in his transitional position, since he has access only to the perspectives of his socialization agents, and they may not fully apprehend or appreciate his immediate problems.

Certainly, the newcomer may choose not to accept the advice of his agents, although to reject it ex-

plicitly may well lose him his job. Furthermore, the rich, contextual perspectives that are available when individuals interact with their peers will not develop under individual strategies. In psychoanalysis, for example, the vocabulary of motives a recruit-patient develops to interpret his situation is quite personal and specific compared with the vocabulary that develops in group therapy. Of course, individual analyses can result in deep changes, but they are lonely changes and depend solely on the mutual regard and warmth that exist between agent and recruit.

Apprenticeship modes of work socialization bear some similarity to therapist-patient relationships. If the responsibility for transforming an individual to a given status within the organization is delegated to one person, an intense, value-oriented process is likely to follow. This practice is common whenever a role incumbent is viewed by others in the organization as being the only member capable of shaping the recruit. It is quite common in upper levels of both public and private organizations. Because one organizational member has the sole responsibility, he or she often becomes a role model. The recruit emulates that person's thoughts and actions.

Succession to the chief executive officer level in many firms is marked by the extensive use of the individual socialization strategy. Outcomes in these one-on-one efforts depend on the affective relationships that may or may not develop between the apprentice and his master. In cases of high affect, the process works well and the new member internalizes the values of the particular role he is eventually to play quickly and fully. However, when there are few affective bonds, the socialization process may break down and the transition may not take place.

Overall, individual socialization is expensive in terms of both time and money. Failures are not recycled or rescued easily. Nor are individual strategies particularly suitable for the demands of large organizations, which process many people every year. Hence, with growing bureaucratic structures, the use of mass socialization techniques has increased. Indeed, collective tactics, because of their ease, efficiency, and predictability, have tended to replace the traditional socialization mode of apprenticeship.

Sequential (Nonsequential) Socialization Strategies

Sequential socialization refers to transitional processes marked by a series of discrete and identifiable stages through which an individual must pass in order to achieve a defined role and status within the organization. Many banks groom a person for a particular managerial position by first rotating him or her across the various jobs that will comprise the range of managerial responsibility. Similarly, police recruits in most departments must pass successively through such stages as academy classroom instruction, physical conditioning,

firearm training, and on-the-street pupilage.

Nonsequential processes are accomplished in one transitional stage. A factory worker may become a shop supervisor without benefit of an intermediary training program. A department head in a municipal government may become a city manager without serving first as an assistant city manager. Presumably, any organizational position may be analyzed to discover whether intermediate stages of preparation may be required of people taking over that position.

When examining sequential strategies, it is crucial to note the degree to which each stage builds on the preceding stage. For example, the courses in most technical training programs are arranged in what is thought to be a progression from simple to complex material. On the other hand, some sequential processes seem to follow no internal logic. Management training is often disjointed, with the curriculum jumping from topic to topic with little or no integration across stages. In such cases, a person tends to learn the material he likes best in the sequence. If, on the other hand, the flow of topics or courses is harmonious and connected functionally in some fashion, the various minor mental alterations a person must make at each sequential stage will act cumulatively so that, at the end, the person may find himself considerably different from the way he was when he started.

Relatedly, if several agents handle different portions of the social-ization process, the degree to which the aims of the agents are common is very important to the eventual outcome. For example, in some officers' training schools of peacetime military organizations, the agents responsible for physical and weapons training have very different attitudes toward their jobs and toward the recruits from the agents in charge of classroom instruction. Officer trainees quickly spot such conflicts when they exist and sometimes exploit them, playing agents off against one another. Such conflicts often lead to a more relaxed atmosphere for the recruits, one in which they enjoy watching their instructors pay more attention to each other than they do to the training pro-gram. An almost identical situation can be found in many police train-ing programs.

In the sequential arrangement, agents may not know each other, may be separated spatially, and may have thoroughly different im-ages of their respective tasks. Uni-versity-trained scientists, for exam-ple, apparently have considerable difficulty moving from an aca-demic to an industrial setting to practice their trade. The pattern disconcerts many scientists as they discover that their scholarly train-ing emphasized a far different set of skills and interests from those re-quired in the corporate environ-ment. It is often claimed that to be-come a "good" industrial scientist, you must learn the painful lesson that being able to sell an idea is as

important as having it in the first place.

Consider, too, the range of views about a particular job an organiza-tional newcomer may receive from the personnel department, the training division, and colleagues on the job, all of whom have a hand (and a stake) in the recruit's transi-tion. From this standpoint, empa-thy must certainly be extended to the so-called juvenile delinquent who receives "guidance" from the police, probation officers, judges, social workers, psychiatrists, and correction officers. Such a se-quence may actually teach a person to be whatever his immediate situa-tion demands.

Besides the confusion that comes from the contradictory demands that are sometimes made on peo-ple, there is also likely to be misin-formation passed along by each agent in a sequential process as to how simple the next stage will be. Thus the recruit may be told that if he just buckles down and applies himself in stage A, stages B, C, D, and E will be easy. Agents usually mask, wittingly or unwittingly, the true nature of the stage to follow. Their reasoning is that if a person feels his future is bright, reward-ing, and assured, he will be most cooperative at the stage he is in, not wishing to jeopardize the future he thinks awaits him.

When attempts are consistently made to make each subsequent step appear simple, the individual's best source of information on the sequential process is another per-son who has gone through it. If the recruit can find organizational members who have been through the process, he can use them to help him obtain a more reality-oriented perspective. But some organizations go out of their way to isolate recruits from veteran members. Certain profit-making trade schools go to great lengths to be sure their paying clientele do not learn of the limited job opportunities in the "glamorous and high-paying" worlds of radio and TV broadcasting, commercial art, or heavy equipment operation. Door-to-door sales trainees are continually assured that their success is guaranteed; the handy-dandy, one-of-a-kind product they are preparing to merchandise will "sell itself." When recruits are officially allowed the privilege of interacting with more experienced organizational members, those controlling the process invariably select a veteran member who will present a sanitized or laundered image of the future.

The degree to which an individual is required to keep to a schedule as he goes through the entire sequence is another important aspect of the sequential socialization strategy. A recruit may feel that he is being pressured or pushed into certain positions or stages before he is ready. This position is similar to that of the business executive who does not want a promotion but feels that if he turns it down, he will be damaging his career. A professor may feel that he cannot turn down the chairmanship of his department without rupturing the respectful relationships with his faculty members that he now enjoys.

On the other hand, if the person does not slip, falter, fail, or seriously discredit himself in any fashion, sequential socialization over his full career may provide him with what has been called a "permanent sense of the unobtained." Thus the executive who, at 30, aims toward being the head of his department by the time he is 40, will then be attempting to make division head by 50, and so on. The consumer sequence that stresses accumulation of material goods has much the same character as the artistic sequence that stresses the achievement of the perfect work. Sequential socialization of this sort has a rather disquieting Sisyphus-like nature as the person seeks perpetually to reach the unreachable.

Fixed (Variable) Socialization Strategies

Organizational socialization processes differ in terms of the information and certainty an individual has regarding his transition timetable. Fixed socialization processes provide a recruit with a precise knowledge of the time it will take him to complete a given step. The time of transition is standardized. Consider the probationary systems used on most civil service jobs. The employees know in advance just how long they will be on probation. Educational systems provide another good illustration of fixed processes. Schools begin and end at the same time for all pupils. Students move through the system roughly one step at a time. Fixed processes provide rigid conceptions of "normal" progress; those who are not on schedule are considered "deviant."

Variable socialization processes do not give those being processed any advance notice of their transition timetable. What may be true for one is not true for another. The recruit has to search out clues to his future. Prisoners who serve indeterminate sentences, such as the legendary and properly infamous "1 to 10," must dope out timetable norms from the scarce materials available to them. Apprenticeship programs often specify only the minimum number of years a person must remain an apprentice and leave open the precise time a person can expect to be advanced to journeyman.

Since the rate of passage across any organizational boundary is a matter of concern to most participants, transition timetables may be developed on the basis of the most fragmentary and flimsiest information. Rumors and innuendos about who is going where and when characterize the variable strategy of socialization. However, if a recruit has a direct access to others who are presently in or have been through a similar situation, a sort of "sentimental order" will probably emerge as to when certain passages can or should be expected to take place. And whether or not these expectations are accurate, the individual will measure his progress against them.

The vertically oriented business career is a good example of both

variable socialization and the "sentimental order" that seems to characterize such processes. Take the promotional systems in most large organizations. These systems are usually designed to reward individual initiative and performance on current assignments and are therefore considered, at least by upper management, to be highly variable processes. But, for those deeply concerned with their own (and others') progress in the organization, the variable process is almost inevitably corrupted, because would-be executives push very hard to uncover the signs of a coming promotion (or demotion). These people listen closely to stories concerning the time it takes to advance in the organization, observe as closely as possible the experiences of others, and develop an age consciousness delineating the range of appropriate ages for given positions. The process is judgmental and requires a good deal of time and effort. However, in some very stable organizations, such as government agencies, the expected rate of advancement can be evaluated quite precisely and correctly. Thus the process becomes, for all practical purposes, a fixed one.

In some cases, what is designed as a fixed socialization process more closely approximates a variable process for the individual described by the cliché "always a bridesmaid, never a bride." The transition timetable is clear enough but, for various reasons, the person cannot or does not wish to complete the journey. Colleges and universities have their "professional students" who never seem to graduate. Training programs have trainees who continually miss the boat and remain trainees indefinitely. Fixed processes differ, therefore, with regard to both the frequency and the rate of the so-called role failure—the number of recruits who for one reason or another are not able to complete the process.

Some organizations even go so far as to provide a special membership category for certain types of role failures. Some police agencies, for example, give recruits unable to meet agent demands long-term assignments as city jailers or traffic controllers. Such assignments serve as a signal to the recruit and to others in the organization that the individual has left the normal career path.

To the extent that these organizational "Siberias" exist and can be identified by those in the fixed setting, chronic sidetracking from which there is rarely a return is a distinct possibility. On the other hand, sidetracking is quite subtle and problematic to the recruit operating in a variable socialization track. Many people who work in the upper and lower levels of management in large organizations are unable to judge where they are going and when they might get there because of further rise in the organization depends in part on such uncertain factors as the state of the economy and the turnover rates above them. Consequently, variable processes can create anxiety and frustration for people who are unable to construct reasonably valid timetables to judge the appropriateness of their movement or lack of movement in the organization.

It is clear that to those in authority within the organization, time is an important resource that can be used to control others. Variable socialization processes give an administrator a powerful tool for influencing individual behavior. But the administration also risks creating an organizational situation marked by confusion and uncertainty among those concerned with their movement in the system. Fixed processes provide temporal reference points that allow people both to observe passages ceremonially and to hold together relationships forged during the socialization experiences. Variable processes, by contrast, tend to divide and drive apart people who might show much loyalty and cohesion if the process were fixed.

Tournament (Contest) Socialization Strategies

The practice of separating selected clusters of recruits into different socialization programs or tracks on the basis of presumed differences in ability, ambition, or background represents the essence of tournament socialization processes. Such tracking is often done at the earliest possible date in a person's organizational career. Furthermore, the shifting of people between tracks in a tournament process occurs mainly in one direction: downward. These people are then eliminated from further consideration within the track they have left. The rule for the tournament socialization strategy, according to Yale University sociologist James Rosenbaum, is simple: "When you win, you win only the right to go on to the next round; when you lose, you lose forever."

Contest socialization processes, on the other hand, avoid a sharp distinction between superiors and inferiors of the same rank. The channels of movement through the various socialization programs are kept open and depend on the observed abilities and stated interests of all. In perhaps 75 percent of American public high schools, school administrators and teachers have made student tracking decisions by the ninth grade (and even before). Thus only students on a college-bound track are allowed to take certain courses. But some schools practice a contest mode. They give their students great freedom to choose their classes and allow for considerable mobility in all directions within the system.

Although little empirical research has been done along these lines, there are strong reasons to believe that some version of the tournament process exists in virtually all large organizations. Often someone who is passed over for a management job once is forever disqualified from that position. And accounts from the women's movement strongly suggest that women in most organizations are on very different tracks from men and have been eliminated from the tournament even before they began. A similar situation can be said

to exist for most minority-group members.

Even the so-called "high-potential employee" has something to worry about in the tournament process. Often the training for the "high potentials" is not the same as that for the other employees. The "high potential" track will differ considerably from the track afforded the average or typical recruit. But tournament strategy dictates that even among the "high potentials" once you are dropped from the fast track you can't get back on it.

As you move through higher and higher levels in the organization, the tournament strategy becomes even more pervasive. Perhaps this is inevitable. The point here is simply that the tournament socialization process (particularly if an extreme version is used across all levels in an organization) has widespread consequences.

One consequence is that when tournament processes are used, the accomplishments of an employee are more likely to be explained by the tracking system of that organization than by the particular characteristics of the person. Thus the person who fails in organization X might well have succeeded in organization Y. Also, those who fall out of the tournament at any stage can expect only custodial socialization in the future. They are expected to behave only in ways appropriate to their plateaued position, are treated coolly, and are discouraged from making further efforts. The organization, in other words, has completed its work on them. As can be seen, tournament socialization, more than the contest mode, can shape and guide ambition in a powerful way.

Consider, too, that in tournament processes, where a single failure has permanent consequences, those passing through tend to adopt the safest strategies of passage. Low risk taking, short cycles of effort, and ever-changing spheres of interest based primarily on what those above them deem most desirable at any given time are the norm. It follows that those who remain in the tournament for any length of time are socialized to be insecure, obsequious to authority, and differentiated, both socially and psychologically, from one another. On the other hand, those who do not remain in the tournament tend to move in the other direction, becoming fatalistic, homogeneous, and, to varying degrees, alienated from the organization.

The attractiveness and prevalence of tournament socialization strategies in work organizations appear to rest on two major arguments. One is that such processes promote the most efficient allocation of resources. Organizational resources, its proponents say, should be allocated only to those most likely to profit from them. The other, closely related argument, is based primarily on the faith that an accurate and reliable judgment of an individual's potential can be made early in one's career. They believe that the principles of selection and personnel psychology (which are uncertain at best) can be used to separate the deserving from the undeserving members of the organization. Various tracks are then legitimized by testing and classifying people so that each test and the resulting classification represent another level in the tournament process. The American Telephone & Telegraph Co. is perhaps the foremost proponent and user of this socialization process. Each transition from one hierarchical level to another is accompanied by the rigorous evaluation of the ever-declining cadre still in the tournament.

Contest socialization, on the other hand, implies that preset norms for transition do not exist in any other form than that of demonstrated performance. Regardless of age, sex, race, or other background factors, each person starts out equal to all other participants. As in educational systems, this appears to be the stated policy of most American corporations. However, those who have looked closely at these organizations conclude that this Horatio Alger ideal is rarely even approximated in practice.

There is some evidence (primarily from studies conducted in public schools) that contest socialization processes, where they do exist, encourage the development of such characteristics as enterprise, perseverance, initiative, and a craftlike dedication to a job well done. We also have the occasionally impressive results of the workplace experiments that are designed to create autonomous work groups, open and competitive bidding for organizational jobs, and the phasing out of the predictive types of psychological tests used to locate people in the "proper" career track (sometimes in secrecy). Instead of tests, a few organizations have moved toward simply providing people with more reliable career information and voluntary career counseling so that people can make more knowledgeable choices about where to go in the organization.

In summary, tournament socialization seems far more likely than contest socialization to drive a wedge between the people being processed. In tournament situations, each person is out for himself and rarely will a group come together to act in unison either for or against the organization. Contest strategies, as the label implies, appear to produce a more cooperative and participative spirit among people in an organization. Perhaps because one setback does not entail a permanent loss, people can afford to help one another over various hurdles and a more fraternal atmosphere can be maintained.

Serial (Disjunctive) Socialization Strategies

The serial socialization process, whereby experienced members groom newcomers about to assume similar roles in the organization, is perhaps the best guarantee that an organization will not change over long periods of time. In the police world, the serial feature of recruit socialization is virtually a taken-for-

granted device and accounts in large measure for the remarkable stability of patrolman behavior patterns from generation to generation of patrolmen. Innovation in serial modes is unlikely, but continuity and a sense of history will be maintained—even in the face of a turbulent and changing environment.

If a newcomer does not have predecessors available in whose footsteps he can follow, the socialization pattern may be labeled disjunctive. Whereas the serial process risks stagnation and contamination, the disjunctive process risks complication and confusion. The recruit who is left to his own devices may rely on definitions for his task that are gleaned from inappropriate others.

But the disjunctive pattern also gives a recruit the chance to be inventive and original. Without an old guard about to hamper the development of a fresh perspective, the conformity and lockstep pressures created by the serial mode are absent. Most entrepreneurs and those people who fill newly created positions in an organization automatically fall into a disjunctive process of socialization. In both cases, few, if any, people with similar experiences are around to coach the newcomer on the basis of the lessons they have learned.

Similarly, what may be a serial process to most people may be disjunctive to others. Consider a black lawyer entering a previously all-white firm or the navy's recent attempts to train women to become jet pilots. These "deviant" newcomers do not have access to people who have shared their set of unique problems. Such situations make passage considerably more difficult, especially if the person is going it alone, as is most often the case.

Sometimes what appears to be serial is actually disjunctive. Newcomers may be prepared inadequately for spots in one department by agents from another department. This is often true when the personnel department handles all aspects of training. Only later, after the newcomers have access to others who have been through the same process, do they discover the worthlessness and banality of their training. Agent familiarity with the target position is a very crucial factor in the serial strategy.

Occasionally, what could be called "gapping" presents a serious problem in serial strategies. Gapping refers to the historical or social distance between recruit and agent. For example, a newcomer to an organization has the greatest opportunity to learn about his future from those with whom he works. But the experiences passed on to him—no doubt with the best of intentions—by those with whom he works may be quite removed from his own circumstance.

Typically, recruits in the first class will set the tone for the classes to follow. This is not to say that those following will be carbon copies, but simply that it is easier to learn from people who have been through similar experiences than it is to devise solutions from scratch.

So long as there are people available in the socialization setting the recruits consider to be "like them," these people will be pressed into service as guides, passing on the consensual solutions to the typical problems faced by the newcomer. Mental patients, for example, often report that they were only able to survive and gain their release because other, more experienced, patients "set them wise" as to what the psychiatric staff deemed appropriate behavior indicating improvement.

From this perspective, serial modes of socialization provide newcomers with built-in guidelines to organize and make sense of their organizational situation. Just as children in stable societies are able to gain a sure sense of the future by seeing in their parents and grandparents an image of themselves grown older, employees in organizations can gain a sense of the future by seeing in their more experienced elders an image of themselves further along. The danger exists, of course, that the recruit won't like that image, and will leave the organization rather than face what seems to be an agonizing future. In industrial settings, where worker morale is low and turnover is high, the serial pattern of initiating newcomers into the organization maintains and perhaps amplifies an already poor situation.

The analytic distinction between serial and disjunctive socialization processes is sometimes brought into sharp focus when an organization cleans house, sweeping old members out and bringing new members to replace them. In extreme cases, an entire organization can be thrown into a disjunctive mode of socialization, causing the organization to lose all resemblance to its former self. For example, in colleges with a large turnover of faculty, long-term students exert a lot of control. Organizations such as prisons and mental hospitals, where inmates stay longer than the staff, are often literally run by the inmates.

Investiture (Divestiture) Socialization Strategies

The last major strategy to be discussed concerns the degree to which a socialization process is set up either to confirm or to dismantle the incoming identity of a newcomer. Investiture processes ratify and establish the viability and usefulness of the characteristics the person already possesses. Presumably, recruits to most high-level managerial jobs are selected on the basis of what they bring to the job. The organization does not wish to change these recruits. Rather, it wants to take advantage of their abilities.

Divestiture processes, on the other hand, deny and strip away certain entering characteristics of a recruit. Many occupational and organizational communities almost require a recruit to sever old friendships, undergo extensive harassment from experienced members, and engage for long periods of time in what can only be called "dirty work" (that is, low-status, low-pay, low-skill, and low-in-

terest tasks). During such periods, the recruit gradually acquires the formal and informal credentials of full and accepted membership.

Ordained ministers, professional athletes, master craftsmen, college professors, and career military personnel must often suffer considerable mortification and humiliation to pay the dues necessary before they are considered equal and respected participants in their particular professions. As a result, closeness develops among the people in that occupation and a distinct sense of solidarity and mutual concern can be found. Pervasive and somewhat closed social worlds are formed by such diverse groups as policemen, airline employees, railroad workers, nurses, symphony musicians, and funeral directors.

Investiture processes say to a newcomer, "We like you as you are; don't change." Entrance is made as smooth and troublefree as possible. Members of the organization go to great lengths to ensure that the recruit's needs are met. Demands on the person are balanced to avoid being unreasonable. There is almost an explicit "honeymoon" period. At times, even positions on the bottom rung of the organizational ladder are filled with a flurry of concern for employee desires. Orientation programs, career counseling, relocation assistance, even a visit to the president's office with the perfunctory handshake and good wishes, systematically suggest to newcomers that they are as valuable as they are.

Ordinarily, the degree to which a setting represents an ordeal to a recruit indicates the degree to which divestiture processes are operative. Rehabilitation institutions, such as mental hospitals and prisons, are commonly thought to be prototypical in this regard. But even in these institutions, initiation processes will have different meanings to different newcomers. Some "rehabilitation" settings, for example, offer a new inmate a readymade home away from home that more or less complements his entering self-image. Thus, for some people, becoming a member of, say, the thief subculture in a prison acts more as an investiture than a divestiture socialization process. In such cases, one's preinstitutional identity is sustained with apparent ease. Prison is simply an annoying interval in the person's otherwise orderly career. The analyst must examine socialization settings closely before assuming powerful divestiture processes to be acting homogeneously on all who enter.

Yet the fact remains that many organizations consciously promote initiation ordeals designed primarily to make the recruit whatever the organization deems appropriate. In the more extreme cases, recruits are isolated from former associates, must abstain from certain types of behavior, must publicly degrade themselves and others through various kinds of mutual criticism, and must follow a rigid set of sanctionable rules and regulations.

This process, when voluntarily undergone, serves, of course, to commit and bind people to the organization. In such cases, the sacrifice and surrender on the part of the newcomers is usually premised upon a sort of institutional awe the recruits bring with them into the organization. Such awe serves to sustain their motivation throughout the divestiture process. Within this society, there are many familiar illustrations: the Marine Corps, fraternal groups, religious cults, elite law schools, self-realization groups, drug rehabilitation programs, professional athletic teams, and so on. All these organizations require a recruit to pass through a series of robust tests in order to gain privileged access to the organization.

In general, the endurance of the divestiture process itself promotes a strong fellowship among those who have followed the same path to membership. For example, college teaching, professional crime, dentistry, and the priesthood all require a person to travel a somewhat painful and lengthy road. The trip provides the newcomer with a set of colleagues who have been down the same path and symbolizes to others on the scene that the newcomer is committed fully to the organization. For those who complete the ordeal, the gap separating recruits from members narrows appreciably while the gap separating members from nonmembers grows.

Clearly, divestiture rather than investiture strategies are more likely to produce similar results among recruits. And, it should be kept in mind, the ordeal aspects of a divestiture process represent an identity-bestowing, as well as an identity-destroying, process. Coercion is not necessarily an assault on the person. It can also be a device for stimulating personal changes that are evaluated positively by the individual. What has always been problematic with coercion is the possibility for perversion in its use.

Summary and Conclusions

I have attempted to provide a partial framework for analyzing some of the more pervasive strategies used by organizations to control and direct the behavior of their members. For instance, the tightness or looseness of day-to-day supervision could also be depicted as a socialization strategy. So, too, could the degree of demographic and attitudinal homogeneity or heterogeneity displayed by the incoming recruits, since it could affect the probability that a single perspective will come to dominate the group of newcomers. What I have tried to do here, however, is describe those processes that are most often both ignored by organizational researchers and taken for granted by organizational decision makers.

It is true that someone undergoing a transition is not *tabula rasa,* waiting patiently for the organization to do its work. Many people play very active roles in their own socialization. Each strategy discussed here contains only the possibility, and not the actuality, of effect. For example, those undergoing collective socialization may withdraw from the situation, ab-

staining from the group life that surrounds other recruits. Or a person may undergo a brutal divestiture process with a calculated indifference and stoic nonchalance. A few exceptions are probably the rule in even the most tyrannical of settings.

However, the preponderance of evidence suggests that the seven strategies discussed here play a very powerful role in influencing any individual's conception of his work role. By teasing out the situational processes variables that, by and large, define an organization passage, it becomes apparent that for most people a given set of experiences in an organization will lead to fairly predictable ends.

If we are interested in strategies that promote a relatively high degree of similarity in the thoughts and actions of recruits and their agents, a combination of the formal, serial, and divestiture strategies would probably be most effective. If dissimilarity is desired, informal, disjunctive, and investiture strategies would be preferable. To produce a relatively passive group of hardworking but undifferentiated recruits, the combination of formal, collective, sequential, tournament, and divestiture strategies should be used. Other combinations could be used to manufacture other sorts of recruits with, I suspect, few exceptions.

At any rate, the single point I wish to emphasize is that much of the control over individual behavior in organizations is a direct result of the manner in which people are processed. By directing focused and detailed attention to the breakpoints or transitions in a person's work career, much can be gained in terms of understanding how organizations shape the performances and ambitions of their members. And, most critically, the strategies by which these transitions are managed are clearly subject to both empirical study and practical change.

Increased awareness and interest in the strategies of people processing may be a matter of some urgency. The trend in modern organizations is apparently to decrease control through such traditional means as direct supervision and the immediate application of rewards and punishments and increase control by such indirect means as recruitment, selection, professionalization, increased training, and career path manipulation. To these more or less remote control mechanisms, we might well add the seven strategies described in this paper.

Certain features of organizations promote behavioral styles among subordinates, peers, and superiors. Since many of the strategies for breaking in employees are taken for granted (particularly for employees beyond the raw recruit level), they are rarely discussed or considered to be matters of choice in the circles in which managerial decisions are reached. Furthermore, those strategies that are discussed are often kept as they are simply because their effects are not widely understood.

People-processing strategies are also frequently justified by the traditional illogic of "that's the way I had to do it, so that's the way my successors will have to do it." Yet, as I have attempted to show, socialization processes are not products of some fixed, evolutionary pattern. They are products of both decisions and nondecisions—and they can be changed. Unfortunately, many of the strategies discussed here seem to be institutionalized out of inertia rather than thoughtful action. This is hardly the most rational practice to be followed by managers with a professed concern for the effective utilization of resources—both material and human.

Selected Bibliography

For a much fuller consideration of just how these socialization strategies are linked to one another and how they can be used to help predict the behavioral responses of people in organizational settings, see John Van Maanen and Edgar H. Schein's "Toward a Theory of Organizational Socialization," in Barry Staw's (ed.) *Research in Organizational Behavior* (JAI Press, 1978). Some of the ideas developed in this paper are also to be found in John Van Maanen's "Breaking-In: Socialization to Work," a chapter in Robert Dubin's *Handbook of Work, Organization, and Society* (Skokie, Ill.: Rand McNally, 1976). An examination of the contrast between the content variables of organizational socialization and the process variables treated here can be found in several of the selections in the recent book edited by Van Maanen, *Organizational Careers: Some New Perspectives* (New York: John Wiley & Sons, 1977).

The view of the individual presented in this paper places greater emphasis on the social situations and institutions in which a person resides than it does upon the inner personality. This view suggests that man is social to the core not just to the skin and it is presented best by Erving Goffman in his classic works, *The Presentation of Self in Everyday Life* (Garden City, N.Y.: Doubleday Publishing, 1959) and *Asylums* (Anchor, 1961). Goffman has recently published a difficult but ultimately rewarding book, *Frame Analysis* (Cambridge, Mass.: Harvard University Press, 1974), that summarizes and ties together much of his sometimes obscure earlier writings.

Some of the better treatments of the sociology of human behavior in organizational settings of direct relevance to managers include Everett C. Hughes's *Men and Their Work* (Free Press, 1958), Melville Dalton's *Men Who Manage* (New York: John Wiley & Sons, 1959), and, most recently Rosabeth Kanter's *Men and Women of the Corporation* (New York: Basic Books, 1977). A somewhat broader but nonetheless still pertinent examination of the issues addressed in this paper can be found in Orville Brim and Stanton Wheeler's *Socialization after Childhood* (New York: John Wiley & Sons, 1964) and Blanch Greer's (ed.) *Learning to*

Work (Beverly Hills, Calif.: Sage Publications, 1972). And for a most practical effort at weaving many of these sociological ideas into the psychological fabric that presently informs much of our thinking about behavior in organizations, see Edgar H. Schein's suggestive treatment of *Career Dynamics* (Reading, Mass.: Addison-Wesley Publishing, 1978).

READING 2–2 Business School Cultures and Corporate America

John Van Maanen

A hot topic these days among observers of the business scene concerns the fairly fuzzy notion of 'corporate culture.' Successful companies, we are told, can be distinguished from their less successful competitors not only on the basis of their rounded bottom-line figures, but also on the basis of their richer, stronger, and presumably more industry-appropriate company cultures. Thus, for example, IBM is supposedly a well-mannered, classy operation that values managers who are exceptionally responsive to long-term customers;

Careers and the MBA, 13th ed., 1984 Bob Adams, Inc.

DEC claims to resemble a chaotic beehive of would-be entrepreneurs each beating on the other in a family way; J.C. Penney is legendary for its dedicated, lifetime employee whose measure of performance is based more on loyalty and adherence to corporate codes of conduct than on formal measures of marketplace performance in the departmental trenches.

Culture is used as a shorthand code for a lengthy list of 'shared understandings' seemingly held by the managers (if not all members) of a particular organization. These understandings are expressed by the language they use, aims they follow, accomplishments they honor, standards they heed, mistakes they abhor, rituals they perform, styles they initiate, and so on. People are the carriers of a particular corporate culture, in particular, highly touted and highly paid people, who are not born but recruited into the organizational tribe. And, perhaps most important, those who are recruited bring with them a culture which, in many cases, is a culture learned (if not loved) in business school.

I think business students are currently overimpressed with company socialization and the culture thought to be distinctive to corporate indoctrination programs. Managers may indeed come to sing each morning of harmony, strength, and profit at Dear Old Acme Inc., but, unlike their Japanese counterparts (where many of the corporate culture truths and myths arise), an increasing number of American managers already possess deeply held perspectives on business and business technique before they fully embrace corporate life.

Too little attention is being directed to managerial socialization provided by business schools. These institutions are increasingly creating and transmitting the knowledge and skills on which management practice is based and, by implication, are increasingly influencing the way managerial work is organized and carried out in the country. Critical literature has begun to accumulate, but what is rarely recognized in this literature is the great variety of managerial education currently available. Of note are those carefully screened, relatively insulated, residential management programs located in the elite universities of the land where contrasting student cultures are forged which may well be carried by graduates of these programs through long and successful managerial careers.

The culture lived in and absorbed by would-be managers in business school provides students with what I call a 'culture of orientation.' Moreover, it is a culture that is sought, bought, and put to immediate use in many of the most well regarded business enterprises of this society. This essay is about such cultures of orientation. The specific focus is on two prestigious schools that graduate yearly cadres of MBA's, eager and presumably well prepared to enter the primal soup of corporate life. The examples of choice are rather near and dear to my heart: MIT's Sloan

School of Management (where I currently teach) and, upriver, Harvard's School of Business Administration, more commonly, The *B-School*.

Management Education at MIT and Harvard

The two business schools discussed here are presented publicly as quality institutions which transform high-potential but essentially raw recruits into astute observers of the business scene. What is learned in graduate schools of business, within and beyond the classroom, is related to the way various learning tasks are organized for students by the faculty and administration. Both settings are intentionally designed to change people; to make them smarter, wiser, more skilled, knowledgeable, and the like. Of course, more is accomplished than the simple transmission of knowledge and technique. This 'more' often includes the transmission of values, preferences and distastes for certain activities, standards of evaluation, new friends and associates, the refinement of social skills, and so forth.

Graduate students seeking the Harvard MBA do so in splendid isolation. The business school campus is across the river from the main campus and is literally a self-contained educational plant with its own bookstore, libraries, pub, administrative offices, recreational facilities, and living quarters to house the majority of the student body. The school operates on its own quite distinctive class schedule

and academic calendar, which neither begins nor ends a term in harmony with other schools at Harvard, or elsewhere. It is altogether possible, if not probable, that a student in the business school will complete a two-year course of instruction without meeting another Harvard student outside those already enrolled in the B-School.

The students at Harvard are organized by section. Each entrant is assigned membership in one relatively large section, consisting of 70 or so students, in which he/she must take, in lockstep, the same classes, in the same order, at the same time, with the same fellow students. Identical academic tasks face all members of a given section so that whatever educational problems a student encounters are problems at least nominally shared by every member of that section. As a result of both good sense and gentle but persistent faculty urging, the vast majority of students at the B-School form within-section study groups as a way of handling what is almost universally regarded as a very heavy work load. In the second year, when only one course is required and the remainder of a student's course load is filled by electives, section ties often persist.

Downriver, MIT's Sloan School organizes its educational mission in far different ways. There is no sectioning of entering students at MIT, although the 150 or so student class size might allow for a few sections of the Harvard variety. Beyond the modest snack bar and student lounging areas, there are no special business school facilities or dormitories. The buildings which house the Sloan School also house MIT's economics and political science departments. Few courses are restricted solely to Sloan School students. In fact, about 25 percent of the enrollment in most courses taken by Sloan master's students consists of non-Sloan students.

One rarely sees nameplates in MIT classrooms, and classroom participation is either an insignificant or nonexistent portion of a student's grade in all but a few classes. As might be expected, attendance norms at Sloan are far more variable than at Harvard, where one's absence is sure to be detected quickly by one's section mates, if not the faculty. There are also differences in the time students are required to spend in class. Although the number of classes required for graduation are roughly the same, Harvard students are expected to spend about thirty percent more time in class than those at MIT.

As is the case at Harvard, almost all entering students at MIT graduate on schedule. But at MIT the routes taken to graduation are more varied than at Harvard. For example, MIT requires from each student a Master's Thesis and a declared area of concentration. Harvard does not. The task structure at MIT results in a rather personalized educational experience, and among students there is relatively little recognition of common problems and virtually no recognition of what might be common solutions to the dilemmas posed.

On the basis of these sketches of organizational and structural dissimilarities, some tentative cultural descriptions can be offered. Although both institutions are preparing students for managerial careers, the orientations their graduates take with them are noticeably distinct.

At Harvard there appears to be a uniformity of impact regarding life at the B-School. Students seem to collectively love and hate various aspects of the curriculum. There is also something of a 'siege mentality' that characterizes the early experiences of students in the school. Many students are at least initially convinced that the faculty is highly organized and 'out to get them'; an us-versus-them spirit results. This spirit strengthens section ties since section members are all more or less in the same boat. Collective solutions to common problems are the result, and information-sharing norms are highlighted, even when such norms are openly discouraged by faculty members.

Considerable effort goes into 'pegging production' by controlling both the rate busters who could make other section members look bad, as well as rate shirkers who might draw unwanted faculty attention to the entire section. Study group norms develop in a similar manner to help members control those ever-ready workaholics, who would keep the study group grinding away around the clock, those after-class commandos who would suck up to a professor at the expense of those not so sucking, or those equally deviant gleaners or leeches in the study group who would absorb group efforts without reciprocation or contribution.

The competition at Harvard may be peaceable on the surface and savage underneath, but it is a form of competition kept in check by the simple fact that students are convinced that if they each are to do well in the program, they need one another. Student groups are typically formed not on similarities, but on principles of mutual disinterest, such that most study groups represent a planned and clever mixture of individual skills, each applicable to different domains of the curriculum. In this manner, the organization of the B-School produces a fairly dense, encompassing, collegial culture wherein the student collective exercises considerable influence over its members and, some would say, over the faculty as well.

Relative isolation and independence characterize occupational initiation at MIT. Competition tends to be self-directed. Guilt, as compared to shame, is a controlling sentiment at MIT, serving to animate and usually motivate individual students. In contrast to Harvard, students at Sloan have relatively few opportunities to perform within particular classes and must invent standards for comparison since the instructional programs of fellow students vary. The comparable measures of performance available, written work and grades, are easily kept private.

Friendships at Sloan appear to be based more upon common interests outside the classroom than problems or interests shared within the program. In general, students seem relatively more compliant to the faculty's authority at MIT than at Harvard. The Sloan faculty has been able, however unintentionally, to divide and more or less conquer the student body. Compared to Harvard, students at MIT are seldom bothered at the same time by any particular aspect of their graduate programs, and even if they were, there would be no organization in place (other than that explicitly condoned by the school) through which insurgency might be effected. By sectioning students Harvard also empowers them.

Getting along with one's classmates is situationally defined at Sloan because the various student groupings are temporary, shifting, and subject specific. By and large, MIT students would never act collectively to bring the public foibles of a classmate to a halt, despite their disgust with what is going on.

The Sloan program brings about an overall adjustment of students that strengthens the individualistic and differentiated responses of the student body. Collective solutions to common problems are rare, and the students who learn best are those who do so on their own. What is valued at MIT is individual performance in those courses thought to be tough and demanding. Performance champions in these courses emerge with reputations and ascribed characteristics that are respected but not necessarily envied by the cohort group.

Insulated by heavy schedules and suffering from common woes, students moving into either Harvard or MIT adapt to their respective tasks and organizations in ways that go beyond personal explanations. There are different cultures here, the result of the systematic organization of the student's life and education. Independent of coursework, personal background, areas of concentration, or those well-honed technical skills developed in both schools, MIT and Harvard graduates will seldom bring similar interests, abilities, and learning preferences to the corporate worlds they join.

Recruiters sharply contrast the graduates of the two programs. Harvard students have an edge over Sloan students, in the eyes of recruiters, in terms of their perceived interpersonal skills, aggressiveness, and candidacy for general management, but the edge is reversed when analytic competence and managerial techniques are considered.

Placement statistics bear out these differences. When faced with postgraduation decisions, Harvard graduates are more likely to find Fortune 500 companies attractive, especially those which emphasize managerial teamwork as the key to career advancement. MIT graduates are responsive to firms that claimed to link rewards to individual performance. Staff positions, technical consultant roles, small firms, risk-seeking, high-potential-growth companies are those likely to attract higher percentages of MIT than Harvard graduates. In 1982 small firms gathered up 40 percent of MIT's graduates, compared to 11 percent of Harvard's graduates. For large firms the figures are reversed with 67 percent of Harvard's class choosing to work for big corporations, compared to 48 percent of MIT's class. In terms of functional breakdowns, the picture is less clear, but still in the expected direction, since more Harvard graduates report taking general or project management positions than MIT graduates (47 to 34 percent, respectively).

It appears that the academic culture nurtured at MIT favors the growth of managerial specialists, interested, at least at the outset of their respective corporate careers, in planting their own rather fully developed technical skills within managerial fields. In contrast, Harvard graduates come to appreciate not only their fellow graduates, as do MIT graduates, but also what is seen by them as the roundedness and generality of their managerial education. That neither the individual or collective orientation is derived solely from the coursework or educational materials to which students are exposed at MIT or Harvard is the central point of this discussion. Both orientations stem largely from each institution's very distinct culture-building and culture-maintaining organization of student life.

Some Implications

On the basis of this quick look at MIT and Harvard, we should not be surprised when we read in the popular press of senior corporate officials who complain loudly that subordinate managers seem more loyal to their business school ways than they are to the ways of their employing organizations and, more pointedly perhaps, to them. Indeed, business schools seem able to generate among their graduates some rather fixed but contrasting ideas about how business is to be conducted. Moreover, these ideas may be remarkably stable across time and careers. It may well be that the two years students spend in graduate school is the longest and most intensive *in situ* socialization period they ever experience.

Newly initiated managers are unlikely to immediately begin dismissing whatever perspectives they may have picked up during their arduous and costly professional education. Learning to live within corporate confines hardly remakes the ex-MIT or ex-Harvard student. If anything, it may heighten the relevance of these sought-after identities. While corporate socialization will continue to influence people, this new orientation may not represent much of an ordeal for recruits since many of them will find confirming positions in industry that will essentially attest to the appropriateness, good sense, and overriding value of their graduate training.

A consequence of the cultural learning taking place in business schools is the mobilization of a selection bias within and across organizations. A Pogo-like aphorism is apparent: "We have met the recruits and they are us." Harvard graduates will prefer their own kind as will MIT grads. Sources of diversity within organizations are frequently driven out, not by the work of clever social control agents, but by the reproductive work of cooperating recruits sharing similar cultures of orientation. This may well be one reason for the much-lamented absence of managerial innovation in many firms.

What corporate cultures can do is help shape the kinds of obligations and commitments people have toward one another. When action is required, those sharing a particular culture know what to expect from each other—even if they have never met. From this perspective, culture is a problem-solving device, and it is serviceable whether one is learning to write cases, analyze financial statements, and impress one's peers and superiors or choosing between work as a corporate manager for IBM or Wang.

To close on this theme, I offer this anecdote. A very shrewd answer was provided this fall by a student of mine whom I'd asked to describe the culture of the Sloan School. Without hesitation, she replied, "Oh, that's easy. It's all the things we aren't tested on." Precious little as this may be, it is not a bad answer. In the context of the preceding description, we would predict that whatever these things are, they will be dragged from school elsewhere. The question to be asked is how such a culture of orientation will aid or hinder this intrepid adventurer in any or all the organizations she moves into after leaving MIT. This is not a question to which an answer can readily be assumed.

Part 2 dealt with one's first few weeks and months in an organization, culminating in the newcomer reaching the first workable accommodation with the organization, or leaving it. If the initial adjustment is successful, the process of getting established in the new organization continues for several years as one discovers additional layers and deeper meanings of the culture and becomes more or less committed to it.

The extent to which the individual is willing and able to develop credibility and acceptance in the organization's culture have an important bearing on his or her establishment in the organization (Figure 3–4). Chapter 8 explains how such credibility and acceptance may be developed.

In order to take effective action, it is also important to better understand the organization's formal, social, and political pressures and how they are influenced by culture. This is the subject of Chapter 9. In Chapter 10, attention turns to how one can utilize the prevailing culture, constructively deviate from it, and manage other conflict when responsible action calls for this.

Part 3

Getting established and operating within culture and related corporate realities

Chapter 8

Developing credibility and gaining acceptance

Orientation This chapter could have been included in Part 2 because the process of developing credibility and gaining acceptance begins with one's first encounter with the organization. It is positioned here because the process continues for several years after the newcomer has made the initial adjustment and settled in.

In order to be effective, a newcomer must improve his or her status in the organization from a relatively unknown and unproven outsider to a trusted, influential, and valued insider. The concept of status is here used to denote the importance, weight, and following one commands in the organization.[1] One's status in an organization reflects how much one is valued by others as a member of their community.

So defined, status is an important sensitizing concept. It suggests, first, the difficulty of executing an action successfully if it is opposed by persons with higher status. It also indicates the need for sufficient status before actions that run against the grain of the culture can be carried out effectively. The definition also reminds us that one needs considerable status to attempt to influence change in the prevailing culture.

Status is a function of one's credibility with others in the organization and one's acceptance in the culture.[2] Although they go hand in hand, credibility and acceptance are distinct characteristics. Briefly, credibility gives some assurance that the individual has the ability and intention to deliver valued results; acceptance implies that the individual is perceived as part of the community. High status is achieved with a high level of either credibility or acceptance and at least a moderate level of the other.

For instance, Al Hirsch, an individualistic and highly creative manager, had high credibility with upper management. They perceived that he had both the ability and the intention to deliver valued results. However, some saw him as a maverick, and others saw him as a rebel (Figure 4–1). This low acceptance in the upper-management culture was blocking his promotion. They trusted his technical judgment and business acumen, and thus saw him as highly credible, but they were unsure of his loyalty to the firm—an important upper-management-shared value.

With this framework in mind, let us take a closer look at how the individual's credibility and acceptance in an organization's culture develop.

Developing Credibility with Others in the Organization

As Figure 8–1 indicates, an individual's credibility is the perception of others in the organization of his or her ability and intention to deliver valued results. Such perceptions by established persons in the organization are based on (1) the individual's accomplishments, (2) the individual's situation, and (3) the individual's relationships with others in the organization.

The Individual's Accomplishments

One can gain credibility with others in the organization by contributing *valued* results. Credibility does not come from delivering results that the

Figure 8–1
Factors Related to Individual's Credibility with Others in the Organization

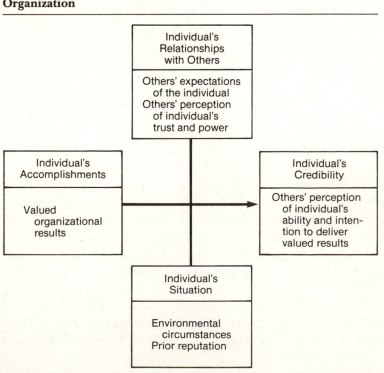

individual personally values or those one thinks the organization should value, or even those that others say are valued. It comes from results that are actually valued. What is really valued depends on what the organization's culture is.

Sometimes a manager is brought in to accomplish results that are important but may not be valued in the organization's culture. Such was the case with the managers brought in to install information and control systems at Cummins Engine Company in the 1960s. Had these managers succeeded, they would have gained credibility with those who had brought them in to make these contributions. However, these managers would not have increased their credibility with others in the organization until the culture changed to place more value on the role of systems at Cummins.

If the culture changes over a period of years so that the same results are perceived as less valuable, the individual's credibility with others in the organization will decrease. For instance, one entrepreneurial general manager, Don Starr, was a natural in a highly entrepreneurial company that valued and rewarded his contributions. Unexpected changes at the top, following an airplane crash in which the CEO and his heir apparent were killed, brought to the helm a team of managers with a different set of values. The company's culture gradually drifted away from being entrepreneurial and became much more political. Don Starr recognized the wind was shifting but didn't realize how much credibility he had lost as a consequence until one day, eight years after the change at the top, a manager who was known to be relatively weak was promoted ahead of him.

Valued results are important, but they are not the only determinant of an individual's credibility with others in the organization. Two other factors are also important.

The Individual's Situation

Perceptions by established persons in the organization are not based directly on valued results because the interdependency and uncertainty of organizational life frequently make it difficult to know just what the individual's contribution was. People in the organization rely on their own understanding of the situation, including the individual's prior reputation, in making this determination. In the extreme, either positive or negative results can be attributed to a favorable or an unfavorable situation, with the individual getting little personal credit or blame, as the case may be.

The Individual's Relationships with Others

The attributions that established persons in the organization make also depend on the quality of the individual's relationships with them. With better relationships, the attributions are likely to be more favorable.

Good relationships also affect achievement of the actual results because one relies on others to get things done in an organization.

There are thus two reasons why developing effective working relationships is an integral part of the process of developing credibility with others in the organization: (1) The quality of these relationships has an important impact on results, and (2) they affect the way others in the organization attribute the results and the extent to which the individual gets credit for them.

Figure 8–1 makes clear why newcomers have little or no credibility. First, newcomers have had little time to develop effective working relationships with others in the organization. Second, they have had little opportunity to contribute valued results. Third, whatever reputations they have at the outset are based on background, expertise, and prior accomplishments in other contexts, which employees in the new organization tend to discount. Established members usually adopt a wait-and-see attitude until they have an opportunity to work with new individuals and see firsthand what they can accomplish in *their* organization.

Not much can be done to improve the individual's situation (Figure 8–1) in the short run; it will improve if the person's reputation in the organization is enhanced over time. But newcomers can concentrate on contributing valued results to gain credibility. They can also try to get others to contribute to the accomplishment of these results, and can try to influence how the results are attributed, by building effective working relationships with others.

Understanding Working Relationships

What are the important relationships? Obviously, those with one's immediate subordinates and bosses are important, but relationships with other superiors, indirect subordinates, relevant peers, and others with whom one must work to get the job done also need attention. John Gabarro has provided a way of thinking about these relationships that is useful to this discussion.[3] Three particularly important and interrelated factors in working relationships are mutual expectations, trust, and power.[4]

Expectations   Each party in a working relationship has expectations about the other and self in these areas:
- *Performance*—what goals to strive for and how they should be achieved, including priorities and standards to be adopted.
- *Roles*—what part each person should play to get the job done, including questions of responsibility and accountability.
- *Trust*—how open and supportive each person should be and how conflict should be resolved.
- *Influence*—to what extent each person should attempt to affect the behavior and thinking of the other.

In attempting to discover the other party's expectations, one should think about what the other's *agenda* might be. (See Chapter 4). What does the other person really want from the relationship? What are his or her real concerns and motives? In figuring out the answers to such questions, one should bear in mind the other's known predilections and reputation, as well as his or her organizational context. Does the person have a history of poor working relationships? What happened to those the person worked with and why? Does he or she have set ideas about certain kinds of issues or people (dislikes MBAs, hates finance)? What kinds of personal and organizational pressures does the other individual feel? If the other person works in a different organizational subculture, what are the implications?

Trust   Trust reflects the degree of openness in a relationship. Others trust a person to the extent that they feel assured that the person will not take malevolent or arbitrary action. Their trust is demonstrated by how frankly they increase their own vulnerability[5] and is based on how they perceive one's character and competence.[6] Included in their perceptions of character are:

- *Integrity*—how the others perceive one's basic honesty.
- *Motives*—how others perceive one's intentions.
- *Consistency*—the sense others have of how reliable and predictable one's behavior is.
- *Openness*—the sense that one is leveling with the other in discussing problems.
- *Discretion*—the assurance that one will not violate confidences or carelessly divulge sensitive information.

Their perceptions of competence include:

- *Specific competence*—one's competence in the specialized knowledge and skill required to do the job.
- *Interpersonal competence*—one's competence at working with people to get the job done.
- *Business sense*—one's general competence to manage in a business environment.

As the above list indicates, trust is multidimensional, and each party assesses the other on a variety of bases: "Her integrity is not in question, but I don't trust her business judgment." "His motives are beyond reproach, but his handling of people leaves a lot to be desired." Thus the key question is in what areas and to what extent one is trusted by the other.

Power   Power is one person's capacity to affect the behavior and thinking of another. Influence is the process of using power to affect the behavior and thinking of the other. As with trust, power is a characteristic of a relationship rather than an attribute of an individual. Power also has several bases, which may be grouped into two major categories: positional bases of power associated with one's formal authority in the organization and personal bases of power, which derive from one's personality, ability, resourcefulness, and other personal assets.[7]

The positional bases of power that are linked to formal authority include these:

- Power to structure another's tasks or formal organizational relationships.
- Power to reward and punish the other person.
- Power to allocate or control resources valued by the other person.
- Power to direct the other person.

The personal bases of power (personal power) include:

- Ability to create perception of common goals.
- Charismatic appeal in the eyes of the other person.
- Creating a sense of obligation in the other person.
- Building a reputation as an expert in the eyes of the other person.
- Fostering the other's conscious or subconscious identification with oneself.
- Affecting another's perception of dependence on oneself for resources and help.
- Ability to persuade the other person.
- Possession of personal information and resources valued by the other person.
- Ability to reduce the uncertainty felt by the other person.

Thus the bases of power, like the bases of trust, are differentiated. One may have the power to exert influence over another in some areas but not in others, just as one may be trusted in some respects but not others. This differentiation is an important feature of both power and trust, but for the sake of convenience we will refer to these terms in the aggregate.

Developing high credibility requires a high level of either power or trust accompanied by at least a moderate level of the other.[8] Trust provides some confidence in the individual's intentions; power indicates the capacity to do what is intended. However, power and trust are not by themselves enough to determine credibility because other factors (Figure 8–1) and the attributions mentioned at the beginning of this section also come into play. The next section takes a closer look at how trust and power develop in new working relationships.

Stages in the Development of New Working Relationships

The process of forming relationships as described here was developed by John Gabarro and is based on his detailed clinical study of superior-subordinate relationships.[9] The process occurs in four basic stages: learning, exploration, testing, and stabilization. The characteristics, major tasks, issues, and questions that must be addressed at each stage are summarized in Figure 8–2.

Gabarro is careful to point out that it is unclear whether or not this basic development process applies directly to other types of working relationships, but it seems to hold for *superior-subordinate* relationships regardless of differences in the leadership and interpersonal styles of the individuals. The four stages of the process do not have distinct beginnings and endings, but they do occur in sequence. The duration of each phase is unpredictable; the estimates in Figure 8–2 are merely rough and suggestive. The critical thing to notice is that, although there is a great deal of variation, it usually takes between *12 and 18 months* to develop an effective working relationship. If one feels one has developed a good relationship in three or four months, for instance, it may pay to try to determine what stage the relationship is really in (Figure 8–2).

In building relationships, both parties work out an interpersonal contract—a tacit but agreed-upon set of mutual expectations concerning performance, roles, trust, and power. The effectiveness of the working relationships and the interpersonal contract depends on *how* the two parties progress through the stages of the process. Effective and satisfying relationships and contracts evolve when both parties clarify their expectations early on, explore their specific expectations in detail, surface and negotiate their differences, and test and work through the bases and limits of trust and power before the relationship stabilizes. If the relationship and the contract reach a stabilization point too early, the exploration and testing have been too superficial, and the relationship subsequently becomes destabilized while the interpersonal contract unravels.

In the testing phase, one must recognize that persons in the organization will be testing the newcomer for both *capacity* and *willingness* to perform various kinds of work, but the two should not be confused. In some areas, the organization may be testing for both capacity *and* willingness, but in other areas it may be a test of one or the other. "*Can* the newcomer play our game?" is a different question from "Does he or she *want to* play it?" Depending on the circumstances, superiors and peers in the organization may be most concerned about just one of these questions.

Much of the learning, exploration, testing, and negotiation involved in developing these new working relationships and interpersonal contracts takes place during routine interactions in the course of a typical work day. Critical incidents (such as the discovery that one party has intentionally withheld important information) sometimes serve either to crystallize or dramatically alter the accumulated experience. In general, the relationship development process is similar to the learning process described in Chapter 6—gradual, with a few sharp discontinuities.[10] Credibility is

Figure 8–2
Stages in the Development of New Working Relationships: Characteristics, Tasks, and Issues*

Stage	Characteristics	Major Tasks	Issues and Questions
I. Orientation: Impression formation	Brief period, perhaps lasting the first several days. Mutual sizing up beginning with first impressions and continuing with more extended and less stereotyped interactions. Trust is impressionistic and undifferentiated. Personal influence not yet developed.	Deal with the question of the other's motives. Exchange an initial set of expectations at a general level concerning objectives, roles, and needs. Develop initial understanding of how both parties will work together in the future.	How competent, reliable, and open is the other person? What are the other's concerns, motives, and intentions? How open and forthright to be with the other person?
II. Exploration: Beyond impressions	Longer period than Stage I, perhaps lasting the first several weeks. General and tentative expectations of Stage I become more specific and concrete. Rapid learning to search out the other's important assumptions and expectations and to communicate one's own. Both parties begin to assert their personal identities, styles, and values. Leads to confirmation or rejection of initial impressions.	Explore in more detailed and concrete terms other's expectations about goals, roles, and priorities. Surface and clarify differences in expectations. Explore and identify questions and sources concerning trust in terms of motives, competence, consistency and openness. Explore and identify questions and sources concerning influence in terms of positional and personal attributes.	How much can the other person be trusted in terms of integrity, motives, competence, judgment, and consistency of action? How safe is it to be open with the other person in terms of problems or differences of opinion? What is the other person's credibility and decisiveness?
III. Testing: Testing and defining the interpersonal contract	A long period, perhaps six months to a year in duration, but could be longer. Minimal expectations, areas in which trust exists, and limits of each person's influence on the other are tactily and overtly tested. As a result, limits of the evolving interpersonal contract are defined for better or for worse.	Test the mutuality of expectations and the bases and limits of trust and influence. Work through and negotiate basic unresolved differences. Assess the degree to which mutual accommodation is possible, and whether the costs of achieving it are acceptable. Define stabilized set of expectations concerning each other's role and the bases for trust and influence in the relationship.	To what extent is the situation (e.g., environment, structure, culture) rather than the other person the cause of the difficulties in the relationship being experienced? How long should the testing continue? How to know when enough is enough? How to ensure adequate testing to avoid a superficial and unsatisfactory relationship, without pressing too hard and risking unnecessary or unproductive confrontation?

Figure 8–2   *(concluded)*

Stage	Characteristics	Major Tasks	Issues and Questions
IV. Stabilization	Interpersonal contract becomes defined. Little further effort goes into learning about or testing each other. Aspects of the relationship—such as expectations, trust, and influence—undergo little additional changes. Major event or change needed to destabilize the relationship.	If events or episodes lead to negative feelings (e.g., conflict over a decision, slight or oversight), take steps to repair the damage. Ensure that the relationship continues to be productive, adaptive, and satisfying as the needs of the situation and the parties changes. If a major episode (e.g., one party's actions violate the level of trust built up) or a significant environmental change destabilizes the relationship, rework the earlier stages of the relationship-building process from the point of regression.	Is the interpersonal contract appropriate, given changes in the individuals or the situation? How to keep the interpersonal contract viable in the face of major individual and situational changes?

* Based on John J. Gabarro, "Socialization at the Top—How CEO's and Subordinates Evolve Interpersonal Contracts," *Organizational Dynamics,* Winter 1979, pp. 3–23.

gained in inches but lost in yards. Big points can be lost if too many interactions and incidents are poorly handled early on, a position from which it may be difficult to recover.[11]

Given their importance to the reality-learning and relationship-building process, these routine interactions and critical incidents must be carefully managed, as described in Chapter 6.

The effective working relationships and credibility that the individual has developed is one important way in which an individual can increase his or her status in the organization. The other important means is described below.

Gaining Acceptance in the Organization's Culture

Acceptance in the organization's culture is the extent to which others perceive one believes and behaves as prescribed by the culture. In terms of the culture map (Figure 4–1, which is also shown in Figure 8–3), one's acceptance may be graphically portrayed by one's distance from the good soldier location; the closer one is to this corner, the greater is one's acceptance in the culture. Bob Drake, whose case was used for illustration in Part 2, had very low acceptance because he was located very far

Figure 8–3
Acceptance in the Organization's Culture: Location of Person on the Culture Map
(Figure 4–1) and Its Implications

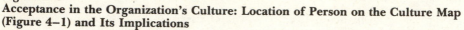

Explanatory Notes:

Person	Located How Far from the Good Soldier Corner?		Acceptance in the Organization's Culture	Comments
Bob Drake	0–D:	Very far	Very low	To survive and contribute in this location, Drake needed high credibility—which he did not have. He was fired.
Don Starr				
In 1970	0–S1:	Close	High	Starr's acceptance (and credibility) diminished over time as the culture shifted away from his entrepreneurial values.
By 1978	0–S2:	Far	Low	
Heidi West				
In 1976	0–W1:	Moderately far	Moderately low	West's acceptance increased over time as she was stereotyped less, as the culture shifted toward one of her values, and as one of her values became modified.
By 1982	0–W2:	Moderately near	Moderately high	

from the good soldier corner. To survive and contribute in this location, Bob needed high credibility—which he did not have as an entry-level new manager. He was fired. Don Starr, the manager who lost credibility as the culture shifted away from his entrepreneurial values, lost acceptance over time as well because he became more of a rebel. This happened not because he changed, but because the "ground" moved from under him to become much more political ("cronysim"). Heidi West suffered from being misperceived when she joined the organization as the lone woman manager. She was stereotyped as "not tough enough." Over time, her acceptance in the organization's culture increased as her stereotyping by others diminished. In terms of an important cultural value, she was now seen as "compassionate but tough." The culture also shifted toward one of Heidi's personal values, "professionalism;" and one of Heidi's values was modified by the culture, from "analyze thoroughly" to "analyze but use intuition as well." These changes further contributed to her increased acceptance in the culture.

Two points should be noted. First, the lower one's acceptance in the culture, the more credibility one needs to survive and contribute in the organization. Since entry-level new managers, like Bob Drake, generally begin with low credibility, it is very difficult for them to get off the ground too far from the good soldier location—that is, with too great a misfit in the organization's culture. Second, as is true for credibility, one's acceptance can change over time, so it must be continuously monitored.

There are three ways to increase acceptance in the organization's culture: (1) changing the organization's culture toward one's personal beliefs and values, (2) changing one's assumptions to conform more with the culture, and (3) managing how one is perceived.

Gaining Acceptance via Culture Change

One having sufficient status in the organization can gain acceptance in the culture by changing it to better fit personal beliefs and values. An example would be a culture turnaround manager, whose high status is typically derived from a formal position in the organization. Those with lower status may also be able to nudge the culture in their direction if there are sufficient numbers of them to influence this change over time.

Culture can also change in one's favor without one's initiative in the matter, as it did in the case of Heidi West. She had been brought in by new leadership that was trying to make the culture more professional, and they eventually succeeded. Thus two important questions to ask in monitoring acceptance in the culture are: "Is the culture shifting? If so, will I gain or lose acceptance as a result?"

Gaining Acceptance via Changes in Self

For a variety of reasons mentioned in Chapter 4, an individual is likely to resist major changes in his or her basic beliefs and values. Radical conversion is rather rare and normally occurs only as a result of some traumatic personal experience.[12] Social and organizational experiences that are capable of changing an individual's less central beliefs and values usually take place only in personal relationships that the individual values.[13] Mentors play an important role in such conversion. It takes time for the individual to develop these kinds of relationships in the organization.

Heidi West, for example, gradually came to change one of her values ("analyze thoroughly") due to a close, professional relationship she developed with Rolf Montogomery, a senior manager she greatly admired. Rolf was not against good analysis, but he was intuitive as well and believed in betting on people and opportunities, "betting on your gut" as he called it, which sometimes required quick action with little or no analysis. As Heidi came to identify with Rolf and saw his methods work, her value became modified ("analyze but use intuition as well").

Gaining Acceptance via Changed Perceptions

As in the case of credibility, acceptance is in the eyes of the beholder. One's acceptance can either benefit or be hurt by others' misperceptions. Two possibilities exist: (1) Others misperceive the individual because he or she is acting out of character, and (2) others misperceive the individual even though he or she is acting in character.

Distorted perceptions may not last forever, but they do have a significant impact while they last.

Acting Out of Character   One of the options a newcomer in Bob Drake's position (low acceptance and low credibility) has is to "put on the airs" of a good soldier. This can be done by trying to "look like" others in the organization by dressing, talking, and acting as they do. If one happens to come from the same national, ethnic, religious, professional, or occupational cultures, this can further contribute to one's attempts to be seen as one of them. All this may work for a while because one of the ways in which people judge others is reasoning by analogy to self.[14] ("Those who look like me and have the same background as I have are perhaps like me in other respects as well.")

Several questions must be raised. First, is it ethical to manage others' perceptions in this way? The answer depends on the areas in which one has tried to influence the organization's perceptions and the lengths to which one has gone to do so. Conformity in dress and grooming is one thing; telling outright lies to persuade others one possesses skills and competencies that one does not really have is quite another thing. Second, how long can this last? The more people act out of character, the more stressful it is for them, and the sooner others will see through the facade. Third, what happens when the true self is revealed? Again, the more one has misled the organization in important areas, the greater the loss not only of acceptance in the culture, but of credibility as well (because whatever trust may have been built up is destroyed).

In general, conformity in surface manifestations (dress, grooming, use of language) raises fewer ethical questions, is relatively painless for most individuals, can be sustained for longer, and causes little loss of acceptance and credibility if one's true preferences in these areas are later revealed. Whatever acceptance one may gain in this way may be worthwhile, especially for the newcomer who needs some time to more fully discover the culture and his or her true fit with it. If there is a basic misfit, acting out of character is generally not a viable long-term strategy for gaining acceptance in the culture.

Organizational Misperceptions   In addition to analogy to self, people make inferences about others by analogy to their previous experience (what was my experience with those persons this individual most reminds me of?) and by such basic perceptual cues as colors, forms, and speeds one regards as good or bad.[15] Such perceptions can be in error.

An example is Al Hirsch, the individualistic and highly creative manager mentioned earlier. He had high credibility but lost a lot of acceptance points in the company culture because it frowned on the high-priced European cars he drove. Other managers in the company all drove modestly priced American cars. They recognized Al's contributions but resented his flamboyant driving habits. When I asked these people, whom I have known for several years, why this was relevant ("Isn't it *results* that count around here?"), I learned that the flashy cars gave Al a certain unfavorable image in their eyes ("Of course results count, that is why he is well paid, but . . . he thinks too much for himself"). Those who worked closely with Al didn't think he was a snob. But the cars threw off signals that were misperceived by those who didn't have personal contact with Al or with his close associates.

Did it matter? Yes, because it hurt Al's acceptance in the company culture. These people were less open and helpful to Al *and to the organization that reported to him*. When I tested my findings with Al, he agreed that it was a problem. However, he said he was not going to "prostitute himself" for what he perceived as "their problem." In contrast, another maverick manager, Roderick Smallwod, consciously dressed, groomed, spoke, and drove to conform to the culture in these areas because, in his words, "Those things are not important—I use my credit where it *counts* to get results." Roderick had violated corporate policy and superiors' directives on occasion to complete licencing deals and introduce new products that had become winners in the company.

These illustrations help make three points. First, people in the culture with whom one does not have either direct or indirect contact can misinterpret signals they perceive from surface manifestations, which may be all they have to go by. Second, whether or not one chooses to manage these perceptions, one should be aware of the potential loss of acceptance and try explicitly to evaluate the implications for one's status and effectiveness in the organization. Third, those who stand out in a culture because of their sex, race, age, or other distinguishing social characteristics cannot do much about sending all kinds of signals that may be misperceived by others, as shown in the following case.

The Dynamics of Tokenism: A Special Case of Organizational Misperception

This section is based on the work of Rosabeth Moss Kanter.[16] The discussion will be relatively detailed because tokenism is a special case of organizational misperception that has important consequences for the organization and has a major impact on those directly affected by it.

These experiences apply to any people who are numerically rare in a particular group—the few black among whites, the few whites among a group of blacks, the few males among many females, the only woman among a group of men, the MBA among non-MBAs, the foreigner among the natives, the blind person among the sighted, the young person in a group of older persons, and so on. The dynamics of tokenism are set in motion *not* by social characteristics per se but because of certain perceptual tendencies that arise simply because of the way in which the few in a group tend to be seen in relation to the many.

To illustrate, consider the case of a woman manager in an organization where all other managers are men. First, she may be overlooked, but if she is noticed she will get more attention than her average peer. Second, her presence makes the men more conscious of the social characteristic they share—being male—than they otherwise would be. Third, her presence may lead to invalid generalizations about all women and, conversely, stereotypes about women may be applied to her. Stereotyping is more difficult to do with the male managers because more examples of their type are available in the group. Their variety permits individuation and makes oversimplified generalizations about male managers less likely.

These three perceptual tendencies, which Kanter has labeled *visibility*, *contrast* and *stereotyping*, drive the dynamics of tokenism and lead to particular token responses or syndromes.[17] The basic forces at work and the types of response to them are the same regardless of what specific social characteristic is involved, but the way in which these dynamics and token responses are manifested depends on the particular social characteristic and the situation. To illustrate, let us continue with the case of the lone woman manager.

Visibility   Once noticed, she will get proportionately more attention than the typical male manager. Kanter describes three options she has for managing this perceptual tendency.

1.   *Fear of visibility:* She can become socially invisible by avoiding public events and occasions that demand any kind of performance in the

glare of publicity. She can quietly play background roles that keep the male managers in the forefront.

2. *Excessive trading on visibility:* She can take advantage of her visibility to get attention; but if this is perceived as overdone, she may alienate her peers. To maintain her visibility, she can attempt to discredit or exclude other women from joining the group, thus reinforcing the dynamics of tokenism and retaining her advantage.

3. *Walking a fine line between excessive trading on visibility and fear of visibility:* To create this delicate balance, she must be sensitive to the cultural and political forces at work. Public performance must be carefully orchestrated to minimize resentment and retaliation by peers and others. She must be able to survive organizational scrutiny and perform in the glare of publicity.

Contrast   Her presence makes the male managers more self-conscious of their social type (men), making it more difficult for her to become accepted into their culture. Kanter discusses three choices she has to deal with this perceptual tendency.

1. *Accept isolation:* She can become more an audience than a participant in the group's performance. This results in friendly but distant relations with the men, rather than gaining her acceptance in their culture.

2. *Join the dominants:* She can try to become an insider by showing that she believes and behaves like men. *If* this requires turning against her social category ("I am not like other women"), she must pay the psychic toll involved in doing this.

3. *Seek a creative synthesis:*[18] She can seek a course between isolation and insider by attempting a creative synthesis, accepting and acknowledging both the good and the bad in both male and female cultures. This creates more stress for her while the synthesis is being worked out but exacts a lighter psychic toll in the long run.

Stereotyping   Ironically, she is given visibility but denied individuality. Kanter mentions four caricatured roles into which she may be cast:

1. *Mother:* She may be stereotyped into the traditional nurturing-maternal role—giving care, feeding, and supporting the men.

2. *Seductress:* She may be cast as a sex object, introducing an element of sexual competition and jealousy among the men.

3. *Pet:* She may be taken along as a symbol or mascot. Competent performance by her may be played down with the look-what-she-can-do-and-she-is-only-a-woman attitude.

4. *Iron Maiden:* She may be cast as a tough woman, be feared, and face abandonment.

Kanter outlines two options she has for dealing with such stereotyping:

1. *Accept the stereotype:* This saves her the time and awkwardness involved in trying to correct the mistaken impression. But this limits her

range of expression, and makes it difficult for her to demonstrate her competence and true potential. It also perpetuates the dynamics of tokenism.

2.   *Fight the stereotype:* She can bend over backwards not to exhibit any characteristics that reinforce the stereotype. She must steer a course between protection and abandonment by the men.

Whatever coping strategy is adopted, there is psychological stress for the individual in the token position. On the other hand, the opportunity is also there for improving one's competence and self-esteem by mastering these difficult situations. One general approach is to go at it alone and bear the psychological cost. Another is to try to succeed and reduce that cost by forming an alliance with one or more others in a similar, or sympathetic, position.

Organizational Misperception versus Prejudice

Misperceptions often occur not out of prejudice or malice but because of perceptual errors of the kind described. Many misperceptions are rooted in the fact that there are limits to how much information people can absorb and comprehend in a given period of time. Stereotyping, for instance, is a way of reducing information overload by simplifying one's world view. To the extent that the stereotype is grounded in experience and is accurate, this is an adaptive shorthand way of dealing with the world. To the extent that it is inaccurate, it is maladaptive and potentially dangerous.[19]

People who have strong, deep-seated beliefs about a particular sex, race, age group, and so on, are unlikely to change their beliefs quickly (Chapter 4).[20] Indeed, their perceptions are likely to be controlled by their beliefs so as to reinforce their prejudice (Chapter 2).

Those who are not prejudiced are more likely to change their perceptions of an individual with the passage of time, as more information is absorbed and comprehended. Initial inferences drawn from the signals thrown off by the individual's surface characteristics (dress, grooming, language) and social characteristics (sex, race, age) are likely to be modified as these people experience how consistent the individual's behavior and actions are over time, how well he or she passes various tests of commitment and loyalty, and what those who are trusted in the organization believe and say about the individual. In short, first impressions are strong and hard to change, but others won't misperceive forever.

The implications of this are that one should not jump too quickly to assume that others are prejudiced when one feels one is being misperceived. It behooves the person to try to manage the signals being thrown off to the extent that he or she is willing and able to do so, to permit sufficient time to pass, and to allow opportunities for direct and indirect contacts to develop. In the case of Heidi West (Figure 8–3), it took a year or two for people to realize that their stereotype of her ("not tough enough") was in error. Her acceptance in their culture increased as a result.

On the other hand, one may encounter prejudice. It is foolish to pretend it's absent when there is a consistent stream of interactions and episodes to suggest the opposite. If prejudice is widely shared in the culture, one's only choices may be to grin and bear or leave, unless one has sufficient status and willingness to try to effect culture change.

It should be noted that the opportunity to personally interact with others is often the key to breaking down their misperceptions. As direct dealings with others increase, their perceptual errors about one are likely to be washed out. This is why it is possible to be perceived accurately in one's work group but to be misperceived in the wider organization, as Al Hirsch was. It is also the reason problems of misperception, and the opportunities to rectify them, continue throughout a career as one is transferred or promoted and brought into contact with people one has never interacted with before. Heidi West, for instance, has performed well and has advanced to become the lone woman in the top management of her divison. Because of management turnover and a fresh crew from the outside, she is now reliving some of the stereotyping she experienced when she first joined the company.

Summary

This chapter has pointed out how an individual can improve his or her status in the organization by developing credibility with others in the organization and gaining acceptance in their culture. Credibility requires that the individual be perceived as having the ability and intention to deliver valued results. In addition to the competence, skill, and effort needed to make these valued contributions, this requires the development of effective working relationships (characterized by the development of trust and power) that affect both the accomplishment of valued results and whether or not the individual gets due credit for them. Acceptance in the organization's culture comes from the perception by others that one believes and behaves according to the culture. Organizational misperceptions, such as those caused by the dynamics of tokenism, are a reality that must be dealt with in the process.

As the case of Heidi West illustrates, the process of developing credibility and gaining acceptance does not end once a person becomes established in the work group he or she initially joins in a company. It continues as one is transferred or promoted or leaves and joins another company during the course of a career. The enhanced reputation that comes from doing a good job gives the person an increasing incoming advantage (Figure 8–1) in each successive job, but to some extent credibility and acceptance must be reearned in every job, especially where new work associates are involved.

This is one way in which an individual can enhance his or her ability to take effective action. Another is to better understand the organizational pressures at work, to utilize culture well, and to constructively deviate from it when responsible action calls for this. The next two chapters cover these topics.

Chapter 9

Understanding organizational pressures and how culture affects them

Orientation This material could have been included within Chapter 3 because it elaborates on how culture affects the formal, social, and political pressures created by the organization's systems (see Model A, Figure 3–2). It is positioned here because an understanding of these pressures is helpful preparation for the subject to the next chapter.

Those who have taken a course in organizational behavior should be familiar with these pressures, which will be briefly reviewed here to describe how they are affected by culture.

Formal Pressures

An individual who joins an organization agrees to follow rules, procedures, and task-relevant directives in return for inducements, such as compensation and advancement. Failure to do so could bring sanctions. Managers can rely on these devices to bring formal pressure to bear.

Formal Authority

Formal authority is ordained power. It comes with the position. Exercising formal authority is so taken for granted that the ways in which it influences behavior are often overlooked.

The exercise of authority may be viewed as the acceptance of the superior's premises by the subordinate. The *zone of indifference* is the area within which the subordinate will accept these premises without conscious questioning or critical review.[1] The zone of indifference is affected by several factors, including the superior's formal position relative to the subordinate, the subordinate's confidence in the superior, and the degree to which the subordinate values the inducements the organization provides. The stronger these conditions are, the larger the zone of difference. Culture affects the zone of indifference because important shared assumptions extend to the exercise of authority and whether the superior's premises are accepted without criticism or challenge.[2] In one company, a rather widely shared assumption is that "insubordination is tolerated if the facts of the case indicate it was justified." The zone of indifference for the subordinate here is narrower than in a culture that always frowns on insubordination.

A special form of formal authority is vested in managers in staff positions, such as accounting, law, personnel, and public relations. Called staff or functional authority, it permits the staff to issue instruction and directives in their areas of technical expertise to managers in line positions.[3] Again, culture can influence how this kind of authority is exercised. In some organizations, the shared assumption is that the staff should be actively involved with the line in making business decisions. In others, the shared assumption calls for staff members to monitor and review the work of the line but to maintain their independence from the line. In some cases both these assumptions prevail; in others there are no important shared ideas about the authority of staff over line.[4] The essential point is that the manner in which authority is exercised will depend on what the shared assumptions are on this issue.

Formal Rules and Procedures

Organizations with lots of formal rules and procedures are often described as bureaucratic, rigid, or mechanistic. Those with fewer rules and procedures are labeled nonbureaucratic, flexible, or organic. Although this is a common and analytically useful distinction, it fails to capture the important feature that these rules can sometimes be bent.[5] Cultures vary in their shared assumptions on which rules may be bent, how far, and under what conditions and on which rules may *never* be bent.

For example, in one company where superb customer service is a central value, employees understand that certain rules designed to keep service costs down may be bent to serve a valued customer. It is also clearly understood that illegal or unethical conduct in the service of even the most valued customer is never acceptable. The important implicit assumption concerning customer service is: "Use every *honorable* means to provide valued customers the desired level of service."

A particular set of rules of special interest here concerns conflict resolution. To encourage constructive disagreement and reasonable resolution, some organizations have rules and procedures for airing out and working through their conflicts and differences. Two examples are formal contention systems, wherein those who disagree with proposed actions can file nonconcurrences, and such formal structures as a matrix organization designed to reveal and resolve conflict. Whatever the formal rules and procedures, however, the way they will in fact be used is influenced by the culture, specifically the important shared assumptions about airing and resolving conflicts.

Rewards and Sanctions

In an objective sense, the rewards and sanctions in most business organizations appear to be much the same—pay, bonus, fringe benefits, promotion, "attaboys," and so on. But the way rewards and sanction are applied and their significance to members of the organization can only be understood in the context of the prevailing culture. The "spotlight measures" used to watch closely certain aspects of performance and the "spotlight rewards" that are considered the outstanding form of recognition vary considerably from one organization to another. In one company, consistent financial performance is watched closely, and outstanding achievement is recognized by exposure to top management over a period of several weeks (including three weeks with the top brass in a company-sponsored vacation with spouses). In another company, the general managers' results are measured by how their business has grown over a number of years and is rewarded with relatively slow promotions but an extremely attractive financial compensation package totaling twice the industry average.

The meaning of mistakes and whether and how those responsible for them are penalized also varies from one organization to another. One company has a fairly clear shared assumption that distinguishes between pardonable mistakes (resulting from action taken in good faith following approved procedures) and unpardonable mistakes (resulting from clearly disapproved conduct). Punishment ranges from none in the case of the former to dismissal in the case of the latter. In another company an important shared assumption runs contrary to conventional beliefs; the assumption stresses the importance of distinguishing between bad decisions and bad luck in assessing failure and apportioning responsibility for it.[6] Bad decisions are sanctioned, bad luck is not. A third company's culture rejects the notion of bad luck. The shared assumption that "we don't believe in luck" is accompanied by a strong and widely shared belief in holding someone accountable for a failure, which company cynics refer to as "management by gotcha!"

In summary, this section has reviewed three major formal mechanisms for bringing pressure to bear on the individual—formal authority, formal rules and procedures, and formal rewards and sanctions. The discussion and the examples given emphasize that the way these mechanisms operate, and their significance, cannot be understood without reference to the prevailing culture. We now turn to a consideration of the social pressures that one must work with in taking action.

Social Pressures

Whatever initially drew an individual into a formal organization (remuneration and advancement in return for contributing to organizational objectives), once the person is there, social considerations become an important factor in determining what he or she is able to do.[7]

The Nature of Social Expectations

Formal expectations, in the form of directives, rules, and procedures, derive from the organization's need for tasks to be accomplished. What about social expectations?

Both the group history and the current preferences of members help determine specific social expectations concerning such issues as social interactions, relationships, rights, and obligations. One set of expectations that is fundamental to all social organizations is born of the quest for group survival. These concern the protection of the group from internal disintegration and outside interference.[8] The individual must do nothing to threaten internal group solidarity; and the individual must help the social organization maintain a united front in its dealings with other groups. Organization culture affects social expectations such as these.

Benefits of Compliance

Compliance with social expectations yields two major benefits—information and support.[9] The individual seeks information in order to know the world and be able to get along in it. In the uncertainty of organizational life, one relies on others in the same boat to arrive at a definition of the situation and decide what to believe or not believe. Those who fail to comply with social expectations may be cut off from access to valuable information that could be difficult to get otherwise. This information also gives a frame of reference for judging one's situation, performance, and progress.[10] These judgments are made by comparison with others in similar situations. Being deprived of access to information that the social organization can provide impairs the ability to make necessary comparisons and judgments.[11]

Although the intensity of affiliation needs varies relative to other basic needs, such as achievement and power, all individuals have some need for recognition, acceptance, and being liked by others.[12] Common observation suggests (and research confirms)[13] that people like others who seem to have attitudes similar to their own and who behave as they do. Knowing this, people who want others to like them try to demonstrate, in words and actions, the kinds of attitude and behavior they share in common.[14] This is one reason one notices similarity in dress styles, color preferences, and speech patterns of employees in many organizations. Thus the need to be liked is another basic human need that is satisfied when the individual conforms to social expectations. Noncompliance not only entails loss of these valued social rewards but invites direct application of various social punishments.

Social Sanctions

Social sanctions come into force in three rather distinct phases of increasing intensity. First, peers and others try to persuade deviants to change their ways. During this phase deviants get an unusual amount of overt and covert attention. Social pressure is brought to bear with such tactics as satire, gossip, nicknames, sarcasm, kidding, and ridicule directed at nonconformists.[15]

If these attempts fail, the group moves to isolate the deviant. Steps are taken to cut off communication links and reduce the person's impact on the group. Interactions with the deviant become less frequent and the interpersonal relationships become more formal, cool, and distant. Deviants who cannot be sufficiently isolated and whose actions threaten to weaken the group may be ostracized, "amputated" psychologically, and if possible physically removed from the group.

Despite their potency, social pressures only work if the individual really values membership in the group. If a person does not look to a particular group for information and support, social rewards and sanctions have only marginal influences. Although social sanctions may be unpleasant or even painful, they may not deflect people who consider themselves as merely nominal members of the group.

Such situations do occur within the corporate context; a person is frequently involved in action affecting a social group that he or she belongs to only marginally or is not directly associated with, such as a different work unit or division. In such situations, the affected group may be unable to bring social pressure to bear on the person. Under these and other conditions, political pressure may be applied instead.

Political Pressures

The concepts of power, influence, and politics are interrelated, and sometimes the terms are used in a pejorative sense.

> *Power* is a measure of a person's potential to get others to do what he or she wants them to do, as well as to avoid being forced by others to do what he or she does not want to do.[16]

> *Influence* refers to the process of using power to alter others' behavior, attitudes, or feelings.

> *Organizational politics* involve those activities taken within organizations to acquire and develop power and use influence to obtain one's preferred outcomes.[17]

Political pressure thus denotes the use of power and influence to obtain preferred outcomes. Such pressures may be applied by an individual or by a political coalition of individuals acting in concert.

As used here, the concepts of power, influence, and politics have neither favorable nor unfavorable connotations. Power can be misused, in
which case the bad image that power, influence, and politics sometimes
get is deserved. One example is the use of political pressure in self-
serving ways that ignore, or actually impede, organizational effectiveness—the "careerist" mode of operation. (Figure I–1). However, power,
influence, and politics are essential for accomplishing individual and
organizational objectives. Without power, a person is likely to be ineffective as well as vulnerable to exploitation.[18]

To assume that either good or evil is inevitable with the use of power is
to take a naive or cynical view of reality.[19] A better understanding of how
power, influence, and politics operate can prevent their misuse and enhance their benefits. We will first take a closer look at sources of power
within the organizational context and then examine specific ways in
which power is used to influence others. Finally, we will explore methods
by which political pressure is applied, including the effects of culture on
power, influence, and political activity.

Sources of Power

As discussed in Chapter 8, power derives from two principal sources—
one's position in the organization and oneself. Whether the bases are
positional or personal, three facets of power are important. First, power
refers to the *capacity* to get others to do one's bidding. The *exercise* of this
potential is denoted by the dynamic concepts of influence and politics.
Second, power is an attribute of an individual or entity *in relation to* some
other individual or entity. Such phrases as "He is a powerful manager"
and "The finance people have a lot of power" mean something only
when the implicit question is either clearly stated or obvious. The question is: With respect to whom?

Finally, as the list of power bases indicates, power is largely in the eyes
of the beholder. Power over another person depends on the extent to
which the person *believes* one has the capacity to get him or her to do
one's bidding. Since beliefs are not simply based on facts and objective
considerations alone, those seeking to develop and maintain power are
necessarily concerned with how others perceive them and how to manage
these impressions. Such perceptions are also colored by the shared assumptions about which positions and persons in the organization have
relative power. This is how culture affects the role of power in organizations.

Techniques of Influence

Each power base has its advantages and drawbacks, and one or more
may be used to exert influence. John Kotter has provided a convenient
summary (Figure 9–1).[20]

Figure 9–1 Methods of Influence*

Face-to-Face Methods	What They Can Influence	Advantages	Drawbacks
Exercise obligation-based power.	Behavior within zone that the other perceives as legitimate in light of the obligation.	Quick. Requires no outlay of tangible resources.	If the request is outside the acceptable zone, it will fail; if it is too far outside, others might see it as illegitimate.
Exercise power based on perceived expertise.	Attitudes and behavior within the zone of perceived expertise.	Quick. Requires no outlay of tangible resources.	If the request is outside the acceptable zone, it will fail; if it is too far outside, others might see it as illegitimate.
Exercise power based on identification with a manager.	Attitudes and behavior that are not in conflict with the ideals that underlie the identification.	Quick. Requires no expenditure of limited resources.	Restricted to influence attempts that are not in conflict with the ideals that underlie the identification.
Exercise power based on perceived dependence.	Wide range of behavior that can be monitored.	Quick. Can often succeed when other methods fail.	Repeated influence attempts encourage the other to gain power over the influencer.
Coercively exercise power based on perceived dependence.	Wide range of behavior that can be easily monitored.	Quick. Can often succeed when other methods fail.	Invites retaliation. Very risky.
Use persuasion.	Very wide range of attitudes and behavior.	Can produce internalized motivation that does not require monitoring. Requires no power or outlay of scarce material.	Can be very time-consuming. Requires other person to listen.
Combine these methods.	Depends on the exact combination.	Can be more potent and less risky than using a single method.	More costly than using a single method.

Indirect Methods	What They Can Influence	Advantages	Drawbacks
Manipulate the other's environment by using any or all of the face-to-face methods.	Wide range of behavior and attitudes.	Can succeed when face-to-face methods fail.	Can be time-consuming. Is complex to implement. Is very risky, especially if used frequently.
Change the forces that continuously act on the individual: Formal organizational arrangements. Informal social arrangements. Technology. Resources available. Statement of organizational goals.	Wide range of behavior and attitudes on a continuous basis.	Has continuous influence, not just a one-shot effect. Can have a very powerful impact.	Often requires a considerable power outlay to achieve.

* From John P. Kotter, "Power, Dependence, and Effective Management," *Harvard Business Review*, July–August 1977, p. 133.

The way in which power is used is conditioned by the prevailing culture. We saw this for two of the positional bases of power in an earlier section of this chapter on formal pressures: The use of the power to reward and punish and of the power to direct others depends on the important assumptions concerning inducements and sanctions and the zone of indifference. The exercise of other bases of power is affected in much the same way. Thus culture determines which bases may be used legitimately and the ways in which power may legitimately be exercised.

The exercise of legitimated power is accepted as a matter of course, without conscious consideration or evaluation. A concept that is legitimate in one social setting may be illegitimate in another. The cultures of some companies value positional power over power based on expertise; in other cases the emphasis is reversed. Many bureaucratic organizations are examples of the former. Many professional organizations illustrate the latter. Since its exercise is accepted uncritically, use of legitimated power does not invite retaliation or resentment. This is why culture has important consequences for power and its use in organizations.

Those who try to wield power rely on three major approaches. One approach is to offer rationalizations and justifications to make the use of power seem legitimate. The method of persuasion in Figure 9–1 is one example. A second approach in using nonlegitimated power is to exert influence covertly. The first indirect method of influence in Figure 9–1, manipulation of the other's environment, is one example. Another is cue control, whereby knowledge of the likes and dislikes of others is used to trigger behavior in a desired direction.[21] Finally, nonlegitimated power may be used overtly, either subtly through warnings, recommendations, and suggestions or through less subtle techniques, such as bargaining and negotiation.[22]

If these methods fail, a manager may resort to threats and coercion. However, the adoption of such harsh techniques is risky. Immediate retaliation is likely when the other side has roughly equal power (or more). When this is not the case, use of illegitimate power may bring immediate compliance, but the cost may be the unleashing of covert countermeasures, such as sabotage and eventual retaliation.[23] Overt threats and coercive measures are only used as a last resort to influence others in organizations.[24] They are inherently unstable in the long run and use up more power than the other influence methods do. Individuals and groups attempting to exercise power prefer not to get to the point of actually having to use power overtly, especially in such extreme forms.

Political Coalitions

Political pressure may be applied either by an individual acting alone or by a political coalition of individuals acting in concert. Coalitions are formed either because common interests and objectives bring a group together around specific issues or because an individual seeks political support by lobbying and persuading other influential people to join a particular cause or support a certain position.

The political coalition is an important mechanism in that it can exert greater pressure than can the typical individual acting alone. As the old adage goes, strength lies in numbers. The composition of political coalitions may vary from issue to issue. When the same individuals join forces on a wide range of issues, they may be referred to as a *clique*. When a clique operates behind the scenes and relies mainly on covert techniques, it may be called a *cabal*. Cliques are more enduring than coalitions, and cabals tend to exert political pressure more surreptitiously. Coalitions, cliques, and cabals must frequently be dealt with in taking managerial action.

Having understood the nature of the formal, social, and political pressures and how they are affected by the assumptions people share, in the next chapter we will consider how one can utilize culture, and deviate from it and manage other conflict when responsible action calls for this.

Chapter 10

Utilizing and constructively deviating from culture

Orientation In order to take responsible and effective action, a manager must work with the prevailing culture to the extent possible and work against it to the extent necessary. This chapter begins with the importance of becoming culturally astute in order to utilize culture well in taking managerial action. Why one may have to personally deviate from culture and how to do so constructively are considered next. The chapter closes with a discussion of other types of conflict a manager must engage in to take responsible action.

Becoming Culturally Astute

To utilize culture well, a manager must become culturally astute by learning to do the following: (1) remain aware of what the culture is and know what to do to utilize it well and (2) be willing and able to do so.

Cultural Awareness and Knowledge

An important consequence of becoming an established manager is that one begins to take culture and other corporate realities more and more for granted. This is economical because it conserves one's limited energy and attention, but it also means that one may be blindsided by culture. One reason this happens is that one may assume that the same culture is present at a higher level in the organization, or in a different part of the organization, when it is not. Another is that one may assume that the culture is what it was earlier, when in fact it may have shifted, as in the case of Don Starr in Chapter 8 (Figure 8–3).

One way to avoid being blindsided by culture or other corporate realities is to reflect on them from time to time. The framework in Chapter 3

(Models A and B, Figure 3–1) is one mechanism that can be useful in this effort. Another way to remain alert to one's organizational reality is to view organizational resistance as an *agent for better understanding* oneself and the organization.

Resistance as an Invitation to Understand Oneself

Resistance from others may be due to aspects of oneself that one does not see very well. For instance, Jerry Rowland, the manager mentioned in Chapter 4, failed to learn about himself from the job turnover he had experienced and also didn't reflect on the resistance he encountered on the job. One of Jerry's bosses, Rob Zorn, exhibited a passive attitude when Jerry came to Rob for advice on what new projects to initiate. Jerry thought his boss felt threatened and was therefore passively resisting him. He didn't realize that Rob had been irritated by Jerry's repeated queries because he had expected Jerry, who had sold himself as a "little entrepreneur," to take more personal risk and initiative and to operate solo. Part of the problem was that Jerry needed more direction and less flexibility than his self-image would permit him to admit. He might have gained this insight had he reflected on the *pattern of resistance* he encountered—not just from his boss but from others he dealt with.

Resistance as an Invitation to Understand the Culture

Before fighting resistance, one should ask why these seemingly reasonable people are doing seemingly unreasonable things. Perhaps the people in question are not being very reasonable. It is also possible that the object of the resistance doesn't understand the others' perspective and culture well enough. Bob Drake might better have understood his company culture had he queried in this way.

There are several benefits to be gained by viewing organizational resistance as an agent for better understanding oneself and one's organization. First, one may gain new perspective on one's current fit with the organization. For instance, Bob Drake might have discovered his irreconcilable misfit with the culture much sooner than he did and benefited by either adapting or leaving earlier. One might also discover that one has a different location on the culture map than one assumed. For instance, Don Starr was operating on the premise that he was still basically a good soldier in an entrepreneurial culture, when in fact he had become more of a rebel in a political culture (Figure 8–3).

A better understanding of self and organization can permit one to act more effectively. For instance, Don Starr needed to operate differently as a rebel in a political culture than as a good soldier in an entrepreneurial culture. For one thing, he needed more credibility than before to retain the same level of personal effectiveness in the organization (Chapter 8). One may also discover that others are located differently on the culture map than one thought. The reasons a rebel is resisting organizational actions are likely to be different than why a good soldier is doing so. In the case of the former, value conflicts are more likely to be part of the resistance than in the case of the latter. A better picture of others' positions on the culture map permits a better understanding of the nature of their involvement in the organization (see Figure 4–2 in Chapter 4), which opens up possibilities for dealing with them more constructively.

Willingness to Work with Culture

Remaining aware of culture and knowing what it takes to utilize it well are not sufficient to become culturally astute. One must also be willing to operate in a manner that yields the available benefits. Al Hirsch was a creative and individualistic manager who was losing acceptance points in his company culture in part due to his flashy driving habits ("He thinks too much of himself"). Al was aware of the problem and knew what had to be done to try to remedy it, but he was unwilling to do so ("I am not going to prostitute myself").

Willingness to do what it takes depends on the situation and what one is seeking from it. For Al Hirsch the required "surrender" of personal material preferences was more than he was willing to pay for additional acceptance. For Roderick Smallwood, the contrasting case mentioned in Chapter 8, the price of conformity in what he considered to be "those trivial matters" was a bargain for the added acceptance he felt he derived as a result. He preferred to cash in this acceptance where he believed it was more important—in violating company policy and directives to do what he considered the responsible thing to do.

Cultural Skills

Awareness and knowledge of culture and a willingness to work with it may not go far enough if one doesn't have the necessary skills needed to take full advantage of the knowledge. Skill development comes with practice; three areas are particularly important.

Appropriate Use of Cultural Language and Symbols   If used with imagination, language and symbols can be subtle but powerful tools to activate culture to facilitate the actions one is taking. Conversely, cultural insensitivity in choice of words and symbols can create needless dissention and resistance. The key to using language and symbols effectively is to discover the meanings people attach to particular words, objects, or signs in their culture.[1]

At Cummins Engine Company (Case 1–1), Jim Henderson's use of the phrase "phantom plant" was an imaginative way to draw the attention of his operating people to the inventory problem. Also, his appointment of the controller as plant manager of the phantom plant was a nice, subtle way to try to get the line people to view this staff executive as one of their own and to help legitimize the controller's involvement in this operating problem in a culture that gave the operating people considerable status in the company.

In contrast, at Citibank in the early 70s, John Reed labeled his operating group a "factory" and proceeded to apply production management techniques to cope with the rising tide of paper.[2] Although the *concept* made sense in light of the situation, its implementation ran into difficulties for a number of reasons, including resistance from the middle managers. Although the word *factory* clearly and powerfully communicated the intended change, it offended the self-concept of these managers who had grown up as bankers (notwithstanding that it was in the back office that they grew up). A different word or phrase that paid more homage to the heritage of these people and also communicated the new concept would have created less resentment and done less violence to their self-esteem and self-image. One such phrase that was eventually adopted for the new back office at Citibank was "services management group." It honored their past (excellent *service* was provided by the old back office) while signaling the need for a new order (the old back office was not *managed* well).

Careful use of language is important because research has confirmed that certain words and phrases can arouse people's emotions, depending on what beliefs and values have become associated with them.[3] Although they can tap people's feelings and throw off appropriate or inappropriate signals, words and phrases by themselves will not make a difference in the long run; they will be viewed as mere gimmicks if they are not accompanied by an attitude of understanding and genuine empathy for the people in question.

Imaginative use of imagery and associated empathy may not have made all the difference in how the middle manager responded to and accepted the change at Citibank, but it could have helped a bit. This is one of the creative aspects of management. It is also the case that such attention to bits and pieces and their orchestration often makes the difference between success and failure in implementation.

Argumentation Skills   Closely related to the use of words and symbols is the skill in arguing for the proposed course of action in ways that honor rather than discredit cultural values. Those who are skillful in arguing that their position is in keeping with higher cultural values are likely to gain advantage. Those who can represent themselves as the cultural standard-bearers similarly stand to benefit.

Consultant Roles   In Reading 3–1 ("Consultants' Roles"), Fritz Steele describes several roles that the consultant can play to help the client organization. The roles of "barbarian," "advocate," and "ritual pig" are particularly relevant for this discussion. A manager can also contribute to organizational effectiveness by learning to play these roles and others as appropriate. The basic question to ask is: How can I as a manager better utilize the culture and interact with others so that both they and I can do more for the organization?

The manager may find it difficult to perform certain roles that are needed in the organization. Either internal or external consultants can provide the necessary help.

In sum, a manager becomes culturally astute by remaining aware of the culture, by knowing what to do to take full advantage of it, and by being willing and able to utilize culture well. Yet, at times a manager must deviate from the culture in order to take effective action.

Going against the Grain of the Culture

Why Is Counterculture Action Undertaken?

A manager may simply be unaware of the cultural beliefs and values and thus unwittingly go against them. Newcomers are particularly apt to do this. However, since cultural beliefs and values are seldom *completely* shared in the sense that every person in the organization holds them, even an established manager may espouse some actions that are counterculture.

A manager may go against the grain of the culture because it is the right action to take in a specific case or because certain beliefs and values that serve the organization well in general may be inappropriate for temporary periods, such as in a crisis. In other cases, a manager may believe that a cultural transformation is called for without being able to effect it. In this situation, the manager may decide that the best that can be done is to personally deviate from the prevailing culture in as constructive a way as possible.

There may also be personal agendas or deeper psychological reasons, like rebelliousness, that lead a manager to either consciously or subconsciously try to buck the culture. To the extent that these moves are not in the organization's best interests, they constitute irresponsible and destructive action. Whether a manager is unaware that an action is counterculture or consciously pursues it, the manager is likely to run up against resistance in the form of pressures to conform.

Managers who anticipate resistance to counterculture action must either (1) withdraw from the course of action and conform to the culture, (2) attempt to deviate constructively from the culture without trying to change it, or (3) attempt to change the cultural assumptions that are involved. The third option is taken up in Part 4. The second option is considered here.

Constructively Deviating from Culture

Culture has a powerful influence on behavior, but it is not a strait-jacket. Nevertheless, a manager who goes against the grain of culture (see Figures 4–1, 4–2, and 8–3) must be sensitive to resulting pressures and not only willing but able to overcome them. In general, the less acceptance one has in the organization's culture and the further the action digresses from the good soldier corner, the more the managerial status, determination, and marshaling of personal and organizational resources needed to survive and be effective. The following situation was encountered by one division general manager, Doug Mills:

> Doug had innovative ideas for growing his business, but they went against the grain of his company's risk-averse culture. Doug was frustrated and demotivated, believing that both he and the company were losing out. Doug was not in a position to change the company culture and saw it as getting in his way. He had bought into most of the company's basic beliefs and values—business professionalism, social responsibility, and respect for the individual—but he did not agree with risk aversion. Since Doug was a near conformist in terms of cultural norms, this placed him somewhere between good soldier and adapter in Figure 8–3. What he had to do, if he wanted to implement the courage of his convictions, was to "go east" on the culture map.

To the extent that one is culturally astute, one may be able to rely on this asset to deviate constructively. One could try to use cultural symbols to evoke appropriate images and argue for one's case by appealing to the highest cultural values that support one's course of action. Where the culture is such that there are limited opportunities for doing this, as was true in Doug Mills's case, one can still rely on the three basic strategies of self-insurance, culture insurance, and counterculture clout.

Self-Insurance   Using self-insurance means going against culture on the basis of one's credibility and acceptance in the culture. The more deviance the proposed action requires, the more one cashes in on these credits to successfully carry it out.[4] Further, the greater one's distance from the good soldier corner of the culture map (Figure 8–3), the greater the credit drain. In other words, good soldiers lose less points when they deviate than do others.[5] An example from the national political scene is President Nixon's China initiative. Nixon was seen as a good soldier in the American culture on the value of anticommunism. A president less conspicuously anticommunist might have lost more points in taking this initiative than Nixon did.

Effective use of the self-insurance strategy over time requires that at least some of the moves against the grain of the culture replenish the pile of "chits" from which the manager draws each time he or she deviates. The manager who can do this successfully over a period of time can acquire the reputation of a nonconformist "who gets away with murder around here"—an image that can enhance the individual's ability to continue to deviate from culture. Here is how Roderick Smallwood, whose case was mentioned in Chapter 8, did this:

> Over the years, Smallwood had gone out on a limb to stake his business reputation on ideas and products that others had described as "crazy." Several of these had eventually turned out to be stars in the corporate constellation. As his reputation grew and spread in the industry (he became the "industry godfather"), he continued to go against the grain of the prevailing culture when he felt his business convictions, based on in-depth industry knowledge, justified this. A certain amount of such nonconformity gradually became expected of Smallwood, and even after once engaging in insubordination, his internal credibility and ability to buck culture remained intact.

Al Hirsch, the other maverick manager described in Chapter 8, was also using up his credit when he violated cultural norms and assumptions to do what he felt was in the organization's best interest and was replacing his drained credit with chits he earned when some of these actions delivered valued results. However, Hirsch was using up more credit than Smallwood for similar actions because he was located farther from the good soldier corner than Smallwood was. Hirsch's reluctance to conform in matters of personal style (for example, the flashy cars that the culture frowned on) made him a *visible maverick* or a *visible rebel*. In contrast, Smallwood's willingness to conform in matters of personal style, which he felt was a small price to pay, made him a *closet maverick* or a *closet rebel*. Only those close to the scene of his "crime" knew what he was doing. Many of these people understood Smallwood's reasons and intentions, even if they disagreed with him. Hirsch's nonconformity extended to areas that were highly visible to the wider organization; most of these people didn't know Hirsch well and misperceived his signals ("he thinks too much of himself"). In a sense, Hirsch's personal value system was draining more of his organizational credit than was Smallwood's because Hirsch valued individuality in matters of personal style more than Smallwood did.

Both Hirsch and Smallwood were *noble mavericks* or *noble rebels;* their intentions were honorable. They should be distinguished from those whose actions have more to do with deep-seated personal or psychological reasons, such as egomania, rather than with what is in the best interests of the organization. The *arsonist* turns to destroy the fabric of the culture for such personal reasons.

Culture Insurance   The culture insurance strategy calls for the support of others with high status, particularly those close to the good soldier corner of Figure 8–3, thus spreading the risk of nonconformity among the culture's "old faithful." For example, consider Jim Henderson's actions at Cummins (illustrated in Part 1). Henderson not only relied on his high status in the organization, but also on the support of at least two higher-status individuals close to the good soldier corner—Irwin Miller, chairman, and Don Tull, chairman of the executive committee—both of whom had in fact molded the existing culture. Their willingness to let Henderson go against the grain of the culture gave him the breathing room he needed to work through the inventory crisis in the spirit of the new culture he was trying to get in place.

Counterculture Clout   A manager can also deviate from culture with the support of people with lower status in the organization, provided there are sufficient numbers of them. In the typical case of this strategy, the leader of an organizational subunit creates a counterculture whose following provides the clout needed to deviate from the company culture.

   The case of John Z. DeLorean at General Motors, as analyzed by Joanne Martin and Caren Siehl, is one example.[6] According to these authors, four core values at GM during DeLorean's tenure were: respect for authority, fitting in, loyalty, and teamwork. DeLorean was able to create a counterculture by articulating opposing values, translating them into concrete policy, and facilitating their implementation by personally role modeling the counterculture behavior.

   Ruth Leeds has analyzed the process by which a nonconformist leader of an organizational subunit, who is usually charismatic, uses the following he or she has built up to create an organizational counterculture to buck the culture of the parent organization.[7] Leeds also describes how the organization attempts to tame such a counterculture and its leader. The typical sequence in which this process unfolds is as follows:

1.   The subunit leader has a flair for originality, which permits him or her to create a new ideology and symbols that weld the subunit into a counterculture. The leader is also assisted by lieutenants who add to its missionary zeal. The symbols of unorthodoxy give visibility to the counterculture and help in recruiting others who share similar values and tendencies.

2.   The counterculture and its leader publicly challenge the norms and values of the parent culture and their applicability to specific situations in the hope of changing them without destroying the parent organization. Typically, the appeal is to the organization's highest values.

3.   Because of their visibility, commitment, and zeal, the counterculture is perceived as a threat by other organizational subunits, who feel overshadowed and inadequate in their energy and dedication.

4.   Once a counterculture emerges, mild checks are no longer adequate to control the nonconformity. If the leader is fired, lieutenants and other followers could become a problem by staying and carrying on the mission overtly or covertly or by leaving and depriving the orga-

nization of their high level of energy, enthusiasm, and potential contribution.

5. Since condemnation, avoidance, or expulsion are unlikely to be effective, top leadership attempts to tame the counterculture by trying to absorb its protest, which typically involves three phases:

Phase 1. The counterculture is usually opposed by the leader's immediate superiors in the middle hierarchy, who do not understand the significance of the counterculture's protest and attempt to suppress it by closing links between the leader and the top hierarchy and reducing the resources available to the counterculture.

Phase 2. The counterculture and its leader respond by trying to find other communication routes to the top. Direct contact with the top leadership or contact through an intermediary outside the middle hierarchy may be sought. The first round of protest absorption is completed when the top leadership recognizes the counterculture and gives it at least some elbow room to pursue the innovations it advocates.

Phase 3. Several more rounds of obstruction by the middle hierarchy and unorthodox communication with the top by the counterculture and its leader occur. Gradually, the counterculture is granted increasing resources, autonomy, and legitimacy. In exchange, the leader and the counterculture agree to certain stabilizers, such as rules subject to approval by the top, and to a defined arena to which the counterculture's unorthodoxy will be limited.

The process described by Ruth Leeds is more likely to emerge when the organization is having serious performance difficulties or facing a crucial external challenge or when the top leadership is going through personnel changes and a weakening of its formal authority. At other times the counterculture and its leader may not emerge, and if they do, they may not survive. For example, it is well known that DeLorean did not last at GM. Thus use of counterculture clout does not appear to be a viable strategy in all situations, perhaps because of the implied coercion as discussed in the previous chapter under political pressures.

Going against Other Beliefs and Values

The major difference between going against the grain of a culture and going against other beliefs and values is in the number of organizational members who are likely to be in the opposing camp. Going against the grain of the culture challenges important beliefs and values shared by a large proportion of the organizational community. Going against other beliefs and values is likely to offend fewer people. And since opponents may not be of one mind, there are more opportunities to form various coalitions and alliances to help take the necessary action.

Viewed as a contest to determine whose world views will prevail and to what extent, such conflict is an inevitable part or organizational life. The extent to which the conflict surfaces and can be dealt with constructively depends on what the culture prescribes to deal with these differences. Where the culture encourages constructive conflict, it will be more apparent.[8] Where the culture looks down upon conflict, it may become latent or driven underground, which makes it more subtle and difficult to locate. In this case the opposition's arguments may be reformulated or rephrased in ways that are more acceptable in light of the prevailing culture, or the conflict may go unverbalized but be expressed through lack of cooperation or even sabotage. These situations are obviously more difficult to deal with.

Dealing with Conflict

The emotional issues in conflict, including rivalry, threat, and personal agendas raise a distinctive kind of resistance. Substantive issues in conflict are more task related, having to do with basic differences in assumptions and preferences concerning what the organization should do, how it should do it, who should be held responsible for what, and how the credits and debits (the "attaboys" and the blame) should be apportioned.

One common variety of task-related conflict occurs between different functional subcultures within the company culture. For instance, the jobs to be performed by sales, research, and the production functions are sufficiently distinct so that they are typically staffed with people having different backgrounds and predispositions, and these differences are further reinforced daily because the tasks demand different orientations toward goals, time frames for getting things done, and interpersonal requirements.[9] Another common variety of conflict is that found between offices in different counties and between these offices and the headquarters of multinational or multiregional organizations. Here the differences in national or regional cultures may have a lot to do with why these people believe and behave differently on common issues.

To constructively deal with such conflict requires first understanding the underlying reasons for the manifest differences. The importance of viewing resistance as an agent of understanding is relevant here. With the benefit of such insight, one may be able to reduce dysfunctional outcomes by conceptualizing and trying to resolve the conflict in win/win terms rather than in win/lose terms to the extent possible.

However, basic situational differences do lead to basic differences in how conflicts become weighted toward win/win versus win/lose elements. In win/win situations, collaboration and problem solving may be more feasible. In win/lose situations, competition is the usual technique employed in conflict resolution.[10]

When competition is indicated, relative organizatinal status largely determines the outcomes. Unfortunately, status factors also often weigh heavily when collaboration and problem solving are called for. However, such tendencies may be more readily overcome in a culture that values confrontation, with formal and informal mechanisms to facilitate airing of differences and their resolution.

Leadership also plays a role in how such conflicts get resolved. For instance, Jim Henderson at Cummins experienced a conflict between the old guard (most of whom were used to direction from the top and operating informally without systems) and the new guard (most of whom were in favor of the changes Henderson was advocating). Rather than taking sides and polarizing the conflict, Henderson engaged both groups in joint problem solving. Instead of conceptualizing the problem as us (new guard) versus them (old guard), Henderson viewed it as a problem of understanding and education. He wanted to retain the pluses of the old guard culture and keep them coming with him. He succeeded by recognizing that there would be people on *both sides* who would see the inherent worth of what he was advocating and eventually change but that some on *both sides* wouldn't. That is what happened.

Two recommended supplementary readings for which brief synopses are included at the end of the book, one by James Ware (number 12) and the other by Richard Walton (number 13), contain additional information on bargaining and conflict resolution strategies.

Going against Those Personally Threatened

Resistance to managerial action may develop, even without any basic underlying differences in beliefs and values or substantive issues, if the action is perceived as a threat by one or more organizational members. For example, changes in prevailing formal procedures and systems, alterations in social relationships, and disturbances to the power structure imply new skills, new behaviors, new relationships, and new statuses that some individuals may interpret as a loss for themselves. In general, any action that seeks to alter the current functioning of the formal, social, or political system has the potential of being interpreted as a threat.

It is important to distinguish this type of conflict from the two previous ones because the real reasons for the resistance cannot be discussed. In most organizations, feeling threatened or inadequate is not a legitimate reason to oppose action. Thus the countervailing arguments may be couched in rational terms without acknowledging the emotion and perceived threat involved. Or the resistance may go underground and surface as opposition in some other form. In general, the culture of the organization influences whether and how such resistance is voiced and applied.

Since it is hard on one's ego to acknowledge a sense of threat or loss as a reason for resistance, especially when it is not considered legitimate in most cultures, the tendency is to emphasize, inflate, or even create substantive issues in order to displace or mask the emotional ones. Thus the resistance may be couched in the logic of saying the change is inconsistent with the culture's way of doing things (posing the issue as being counterculture) or by noting the reasonable differences of opinion regarding issues of substantive importance to the organization (posing it as a conflict over substantive rather than emotional issues).

Frequently, resistance based on emotion and personal threat takes the form of covert activities and tactics. Their exact nature and form depend on the prevailing culture, the relative status of the opposing parties, and their sense of ethics and personal values. The covert methods used are limited only by the ingenuity and integrity of those involved. Here we will illustrate some of the personal agendas and the corresponding strategies and tactics that may be more or less covertly applied and discuss some of the options available for dealing with them.

Opponent's Agendas

When opponents feel threatened, one or more agendas may consciously or subconsciously emerge to deal with the proponent. For each agenda, several strategies may be used, and various tactics are available to implement each strategy.

Agenda 1: Wear Down the Proponent The strategy of flooding the proponent with too much information may be implemented by the tactic of sending "pertinent" information extracted from thick reports and documents, which would take time and energy for the proponent to locate, analyze, and address.

A second strategy is to argue that the proponent has provided too little information to make a convincing case. An aggravating tactic is to pester the proponent with requests for additional details and clarifications that are peripheral to the salient issues.

A third strategy available to wear down the proponent is to deflect him or her from the proposed course of action by raising other "more important" (but less threatening) issues that need to be dealt with first. One tactic is to cite a previous study or to commission a new one in order to point out other issues that need more immediate attention. Another tactic is to get a committee (of one's supporters) to look into the question of where best to deploy the "scarce resources and time available." Where the opponent is in a superior position, he or she may simply load up the proponent with additional and allegedly more pressing assignments to deflect time and energy away from the proposed course of action.

Finally, the opponent may be able to wear down the proponent by demeaning him or her. The tactics available are not acknowledging the proponent's past or current contributions, or worse, taking credit for the proponent's accomplishments and ideas. An opponent in a superior position may also demean the proponent by giving him or her assignments and amenities that deny or inadequately recognize the proponent's contributions to the organization.

Agenda 2: Destabilize the Proponent   The second basic agenda that may characterize the opposition's response to perceived threat is to undermine and pull the rug from under the proponent. One strategy is to discredit the proponent. A tactic employed is to make the proponent look bad in the eyes of other organizational members, particularly those with higher status. For example, one peer who felt threatened by the proposals of an up-and-coming rival began to send him copious memos (with copies to significant others, including their common boss), backdated or delayed in such a way as to make it appear that the proponent was taking longer to act and respond than in fact he was. (For other tactics, see the section "Blaming or Attacking Others" in the recommended supplementary reading 10, "Organizational Politics" by Allen et al.)

Another destabilizing strategy is to lure the proponent into a situation where he or she is likely to come out looking bad. A tactic is to give an unsuspecting proponent a once-in-a-lifetime opportunity, such as passing on a prestigious client or customer who is in fact a can of worms or offering visibility in making the leadoff or concluding presentation before a group that the opponent knows will shoot down the presentation and the proponent.

Agenda 3: Eliminate the Proponent   A third and final agenda is the conscious or subconscious desire on the part of the opponents to eliminate the proponent from the organization. One strategy for doing this is indirect intimidation. Tactics include attempts to nullify, isolate, and eventually ostracize the proponent. A second strategy is direct intimidation. One tactic is defamation by spreading rumors and gossip to show the proponent is unworthy of the organization. Where the opponents can arrange it, another direct intimidation tactic is to seek the proponent's expulsion from the organization. (For more strategies and tactics aimed at neutralizing or eliminating the proponent, see recommended supplementary reading 11, "Intimidation Rituals" by Rory O'Day.)

Proponent's Options

The proponent has at least three basic options available to deal with the opposition's agendas. As in the case of other conflict, it helps to understand the underlying reasons for the threat perceived by others and to try and conceptualize the problem and move to resolve it in as constructive a manner as possible.

Option 1: Reason and Appeal   One option is to attempt a reasoned resolution by acknowledging and addressing the issues of real concern, the personal threat and emotion involved. One strategy available is to win the opposition over. It frequently takes time to do this, and the persuasion, to be effective, may have to rely on both overt and covert tactics.

Another strategy is to seek intervention of a relatively neutral third party with higher status. One manager got his boss two levels up to mediate a conflict with a peer in another department who also reported indirectly to the same boss. More formal third-party intervention may rely on a professional mediator, from either within or outside the organization. For third-party intervention to work, however, the opponents must be of relatively equal status, and the culture must allow open confrontation of differences. (See recommended supplementary reading 13, *Interpersonal Peacemaking* by Richard Walton).

The win-the-opposition-over and formal and informal intervention strategies are best suited to situations when opponents are few. When the opposition is more numerous and the perceived threat more widespread, the strategy of incrementalism may be used. Here the main idea is to proceed a step at a time, allowing consensus to build for one's position and to let meaning and significance of the actions appear only after they have been implemented. (See recommended supplementary reading 15, "Managing Strategic Change" by James Brian Quinn.) To the extent that this strategy relies on consciously withholding real intentions and objectives, it raises difficult ethical questions. Do ends justify the means? Is it correct to use covert methods in dealing with an opposition that itself relies on covert techniques?

Option 2: Avoidance   A second basic option in dealing with the opposition is avoiding it. One strategy is to withdraw from the opponent's turf. A manager who was being intimidated by a seasoned organizational shark decided to seek transfer to another division of the company to avoid this adversary who was trying to eliminate him. The argument for this tactic of survival is captured by the old saying, "He who fights and runs away lives to fight another day." The opportunity for doing what needs to be done is delayed to when it *can* be done.

Pragmatically, this strategy may lower the status and image of the withdrawing manager in the eyes of the opponent and others. It also raises ethical questions: If the opponent is harming the organization (by blocking this proponent's useful contribution and perhaps others), is it proper to leave such an opponent unchecked? Apart from the loss of organizational effectiveness, is it ethical to leave the opponent free to prey on unsuspecting others? Both the pragmatic and the ethical difficulties indicate the importance of *how* one withdraws from the opponent's turf. The pragmatic difficulty may be addressed if the proponent can withdraw without loss of face, perhaps even making it appear that the move is unrelated to the opponent's resistance. The ethical question may be dealt with more or less satisfactorily if the proponent succeeds in alerting those left behind to the opponent's ways.

A second avoidance strategy is to ignore the opposition. If the proponent has considerable status, he or she may be able to see the proposed action through despite resistance. One problem with this is that the wear and tear on the proponent may eventually neutralize his or her continued effectiveness as a manager. For instance, if the opponents have been attempting to eliminate the proponent with rumour and gossip, they could eventually hurt the proponent's credibility or acceptance. And this diminished status could make it more difficult to avoid the opposition by ignoring it in the future.

A third avoidance strategy is to give in. Unless the proponent has been persuaded that the opponent's resistance was in fact responsible behavior, the ethical questions this strategy raises are even more troublesome than avoidance by withdrawal. To use an extreme religious metaphor, here one has joined the devil.

Option 3: Fight the Opposition   This option calls for the use of force in overcoming the opposition. One strategy is to openly confront the opponent; this is the approach taken by the manager who was being sent backdated and delayed memos from a threatened rival. The strategy didn't work because the rival had more status in a culture where open confrontation was taboo. The rival appealed to the common boss on the basis of his "long and honorable record at the company," denied any wrongdoing, and asked for an apology from the proponent. In effect, the proponent played into the hands of the opponent and further undermined his own position. For this strategy to work, one must prepare to wage a fight on the basis of solid, unrefutable evidence; even then it may only work if the culture accepts open confrontation.

A second strategy to fight the opposition is to use the same arsenal employed by the opponent. The pragmatic question here is whether or not it will work. This depends on the proponent's relative support and skills. A proponent who is new to the games of sabotage played by the opposition may not be so effective with tools that the opposition has practiced with for some time. The ethical questions are: Do the ends justify the means? Can one condone the strategy on the basis that the other party is doing the same thing?

A third strategy is to build alliances. The key here is the aggregate status of one's supporters versus the opposition's. This strategy frequently works, and it may get results without incurring pragmatic and ethical difficulties. The major drawback of this approach is the amount of time it generally takes to build alliances and coalitions. This difficulty diminishes when a coalition stabilizes around several issues and actions, forming a clique.

The use of force is an inherently unstable alternative in the long run, as the previous chapter indicated. It breeds resentment, escalates tension higher on the conflict spiral, and could eventually bring retaliation. However, if reason and appeal is not a viable option in light of the culture and the actors, the choice for the proponent is either to avoid or to fight the opposition. Each raises its own questions concerning effectiveness and ethics. Recommended supplementary reading 17, "Organizational Statesmanship and Dirty Politics: Ethical Guidelines for the Organizational Politician" by Velasquez et al., provides a framework for thinking about the kinds of ethical issues discussed in this section).

CASE 3–1
Neill Hance (A)

Mark Rhodes
Vijay Sathe

Neill Hance had learned in law school that you can't argue with judges; you have to "win 'em over." Since then he had found that in many situations, "winning 'em over" often worked better than direct confrontation, especially in dealing with authority figures. In his first two years at the National Bank of California (NBOC) Neill had succeeded in making teammates of his rivals, and believers of his bosses.

But now, in May 1980, Neill felt stymied. A reorganization at NBOC's San Diego branch had brought in a whole new cast of characters, including many from NBOC's Mexican branches, where business was apparently done in an entirely different fashion than Neill was accustomed to. Recently, he had had difficulty in getting an important deal approved by Ken-

This case was prepared by Mark Rhodes (under the direction of Vijay Sathe).

Copyright © 1983 by the President and Fellows of Harvard College

Harvard Business School case 9–483–086.

neth Morrow, NBOC's vice president in charge of credit. It was impossible for Neill to get the approval of other vice presidents without going through Morrow, but Morrow was unyielding. For the first time since law school, Neill was having trouble falling asleep at night. He had failed to get help from the new management team in San Diego and had been disappointed in his effort to enlist the help of a mentor. To make matters worse, Morrow seemed to have been angered by Neill's efforts to win him over.

Background

Neill had always wanted to be an entrepreneur and had been successful at several small ventures in high school and college. However, his father, who had failed in a series of entrepreneurial attempts, strongly advised Neill against it and encouraged him instead to take up "a solid profession like law."

Neill hated law school. He felt the professors were intimidating and the pressure was relentless, partly because he had to stay in the top 20 percent of his class to keep his scholarship. But, despite these negative feelings, Neill did well in law school. He made it to *Law Review* and won appearances at moot court. Though he did not regret the experience, by his third year of law school Neill was convinced that the tedium of a law practice was not for him. He was convinced that he would only be happy as an entrepreneur, and an MBA would be more useful to him than his law degree. He applied to HBS and was accepted in the class of 1978.

Neill had definite ideas about HBS before his arrival, since a good friend from college, Sam Sturges, was in the program. On visits with Sam, Neill would hear HBS students make such remarks as, "Stay out of the stock market; I'm a Harvard MBA and even I can't beat the market," which Neill considered to be rather cocky. Neill also heard stories about courses in which successful behavior strategies were discussed. Neill was concerned about such manipulation and felt that if people were simply honest and sincere, no "strategy of behavior" was necessary. He determined that his only strategy would be to win people over sincerely as friends. With humor, humility, and sincerity, he believed he could get along with anyone, no matter how intimidating the first impression might be.

After he came to HBS, Neill found that, while some students kept the stereotype alive, there was much more variation than he expected in his classmates' personalities. He found most of them to be fascinating people. Neill enjoyed his first year, did well academically, and was particularly gratified by

feedback such as, "You really made that group work," and "I couldn't stand the tension without you around."

Summer Job

Neill restricted his summer interviews to banking firms. He decided that if he was going to be an entrepreneur, a few years of banking experience would work to his advantage in later ventures and possibly provide him with useful contacts. Neill had enjoyed his finance class and found that he liked looking at a firm's numbers and drawing conclusions. He believed that a job such as a corporate loan officer would provide a variety of short, interpersonal tasks, as opposed to the drudgery of reading legal briefs. And, if he were to decide against an entrepreneurial lifestyle, he thought that a career in banking would offer a secure financial future.

As he began his job search, however, Neill found that entrepreneurial experience was not considered an asset in banking. Several interviewers looked at his resume and said, "Oh, you're an entrepreneur, you won't be happy with us." Finally, one of his interviews with a representative from NBOC promised a more favorable opening. NBOC was a California-based bank with a consumer business as well as a corporate business in the western United States and several international markets. A follow-up interview was arranged for Neill with a woman named Linda Smargon. Before he left for San Francisco,

Neill learned from the NBOC personnel department that Linda's project was in finance.

When he met her, Neill found Linda to be very friendly. She picked up his resume and, instead of the standard response, said, "Wow, you're an entrepreneur! NBOC loves entrepreneurs." Neill talked mostly about his interest in finance and thought the interview went very well. A few days later, Linda's secretary called to say that Linda had tried to reach him to tell him that he did not get the job.

Neill was disappointed and, after some soul-searching, decided to call Linda. He said he understood that the decision had been made, but that he had wanted the job very much and hoped she could give him some feedback to help him with future interviews. Linda replied that she liked Neill and would be glad to help. She explained that there had been two primary problems: first, that the project concerned marketing, but Neill had stressed finance, and second, that Neill didn't seem aggressive enough.

Neill thanked Linda for her candor and told her that he knew the job had been given to someone else but that he wished to make a few comments for the record. First, personnel had indicated that the job was in finance, which was why he had focused on that topic. Neill then talked about the project with enthusiasm, giving her a few of the ideas he had been thinking about since the interview. Finally, Neill told Linda that he was in fact a very goal-oriented person, and gave a few examples. Linda agreed to recirculate Neill's resume in the hope that a job would become available and, a few days later, called to say that she and another manager had created a job for Neill. He would work half the summer for each of them. Neill accepted.

Neill worked on two projects that summer at NBOC. First, he designed a direct mail "promo" for selling a credit card to mortgage customers. Second, he analyzed the feasibility of opening some new automatic teller machines in San Francisco. Both projects were well received, and Linda assured Neill that he could count on good recommendations.

Toward the end of the summer, Neill began thinking about his second-year job search. He decided that he wanted to live in Southern California. Neill knew that NBOC had a branch in San Diego and made contact with that office through the husband of a woman he had worked with during the summer. (From the marketing-finance mixup earlier, Neill had learned not to go through NBOC's personnel department.) An interview was arranged for Neill during the last week of the summer with Dan Darley, the head of the San Diego office, and Allan Crick, who was in charge of lending to medium-sized regional companies (see Exhibit 1).

At his interview in late August of 1977, Darley seemed to Neill to be rather cold and detached. He answered questions abruptly and with some impatience. Neill learned that Darley was a non-MBA career

Exhibit 1
NBOC Organization on Neill's Entry, December 1978

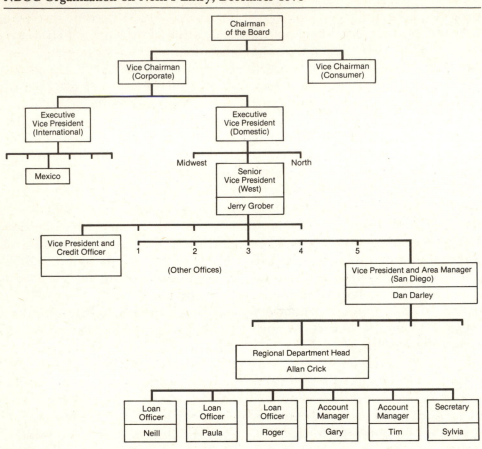

banker with 20 years at NBOC. Despite his reservations about Darley, Neill felt he himself had made a good impression and the interview had progressed smoothly.

Neill's next meeting was with Allan Crick and one of his subordinates, Nick Zorn. Over lunch, Allan and Nick discussed banking and the economy; during the course of the conversation they not only disagreed but argued in a way that Neill considered rather odd for a subordinate and his boss. Since neither seemed embarrassed

by the argument, he assumed this must be the normal tone of their relationship.

Neill had a private session with Nick Zorn after lunch. Nick appeared more friendly then and was anxious to answer any questions. When Neill asked how it was to work for Allan, Nick hesitated, as if choosing his words carefully. "Allan's O.K.—fair, and a straight shooter . . . not the world's best manager, but then again, you never find exactly what you want in a boss."

Just before Neill returned to HBS in September, he had a final appointment with Jerry Grober (Dan Darley's boss) in San Francisco. At the outset, Grober's offhand and chatty style suggested that the decision to hire Neill had already been made in San Diego and that, unless he drooled all over himself, Grober would approve him for the job. One half hour into the interview, Grober said that NBOC would like to make Neill an offer but wanted to know how long he needed to answer. September was early to make a decision, Neill told him, and he wanted to look around a bit. Grober asked Neill to give him a call when he would be able to give NBOC an answer fairly quickly. Grober encouraged Neill to look around but hinted that it would be unethical to use an NBOC offer as a lever with other banks.

In the next two and a half months, Neill did not find a position that interested him with any major bank in Southern California. In mid-November 1977, he called Darley and asked if NBOC could offer him a salary of $25,000, which Neill implied was the going rate and his own minimum. (The median salary for the HBS graduating class in June 1977 was $22,000.) Darley said that it would be tough but he would see what he could do. A week later, a letter came from Darley offering Neill $24,000: Neill would be hired as a loan officer (LO), and the job would begin with a five-month training program in San Francisco.

Such an arrangement was unusual at NBOC; most newcomers were hired as trainees and promoted to LO after completing the training program. At Darley's request, Neill called personnel and was told that he would receive a rent subsidy of $500 per month while he was in San Francisco. Adding the $2,500 rent subsidy to his salary, Neill decided that $26,500, and being able to live in San Diego, were enough incentive for him. He accepted the job in early December 1977.

Neill was relieved that he would be spared the uncertainty that most of his peers had to endure during the spring interview season. Yet, as the months went by and his friends began to relate their job-hunting experiences, Neill began to feel left out of the action.

Neill called Allan Crick in late March 1978 to arrange for his San Francisco rent subsidy. Allan didn't believe there was such a subsidy, but Neill explained that personnel had promised it, and he had counted on it as part of NBOC's offer. Allan said, unsympathetically, that he didn't think Neill should receive a subsidy, but he agreed rather grudgingly to look into the matter.

Neill was very disturbed by Allan's attitude and its financial implications. He felt he had wasted the spring interview season and now, as a result, he had no options aside from NBOC. On March 28, 1978, Neill sent Allan what he hoped was a tactful but firm letter, saying that even if a mistake had been made by personnel, he thought it was good policy to honor the offer of employment that Neill had accepted. Neill had made up his mind to look for another job if NBOC refused.

Allan called Neill on April 5, 1978, to say there would be some subsidy, but the exact formula had not been determined. He added that he himself disagreed with the decision. Again, Neill felt irritated when he hung up. As long as NBOC would indeed provide a subsidy, why did Allan not portray himself as the hero by taking responsibility for it or try to generate some positive feeling instead of creating resentment? Nevertheless, Neill decided to stick with NBOC since they were apparently going to come through on their commitment.

Neill moved to San Francisco after his graduation in June 1978 and began his training program. He was in considerable debt after five years of graduate school and was anxious to get going. After some delay, Allan wrote to Neill that NBOC would pay all rent over $400. Neill's rent in San Francisco turned out to be $650, so he ended up receiving half the subsidy he had anticipated.

Training Program

NBOC's training program usually spanned nine months, but since Allan was short-handed, he arranged for Neill to be exempted from the last four months on the basis of his MBA credentials. Neill's work at NBOC the previous summer had been very task ori-

ented and it was only at the training program that he began to learn what the organization was really like. NBOC seemed to have a reputation for hiring good people. Management appeared to emphasize rewards tied to performance, in contrast to other large banks that tended to follow strict promotion and salary increase schedules. Historically, young executives had risen quickly to the top of the company. All in all, NBOC was known for its aggressiveness, innovation, and people orientation.

NBOC had opened city offices, such as the San Diego office, only within the last five years. Prior to this change, young recruits like Neill had been placed at central headquarters. Neill could see that, with the new regional setup, his only link to headquarters would be through his bosses. Thus, he concluded, his dealings with superiors would be especially important.

Allan Crick happened to be in San Francisco during the first week of Neill's training program, and dropped by to see Neill. He made a point of introducing Neill to people in various departments and arranged for each of them to take Neill to lunch over the summer. Neill had not had much contact with Allan since the subsidy incident and was surprised at Allan's apparent warmth and enthusiasm. When they parted, Allan asked Neill to check out a bottling company that Allan was dealing with in connection with a loan.

Neill considered Allan's request as his first real assignment. He spent several hours in NBOC's library, drafted what he thought was an insightful competitive analysis of the company, and sent it to Allan within a week. Neill also met with each of the people Allan had introduced and, at the end of July, wrote Allan a letter including a humorous review of the restaurants he had sampled in the course of these meetings. Neill never heard from Allan. Neill did ask Allan somewhat later whether the competitive analysis had helped. Allan answered, "Oh yeah, well, I really only needed a couple of sentences."

Forebodings

On September 3, 1978, Neill noticed Paula Lynch's name on a list of participants for a September 13 seminar. He had not met Paula in San Diego, but he knew that she was one of the LOs with whom he would be working. Neill called Paula and made a date for lunch during her stay in San Francisco.

Neill met Paula at a nearby restaurant where it was quiet enough to talk. Paula, a young woman in her mid-20s, seemed to be a very open, honest person, but there was an element of subtle probing in some of her questions. Neill sensed that whatever impression he made would be relayed to the San Diego office. Paula asked Neill if he had worked "really long hours" at school and whether he had time for outside interests, evidently checking to see if he was going to be a rate-busting workaholic. Neill admitted to having worked hard in school and said that doing well at

his job was important to him but added that the reason he had taken a bank job was that he hoped to catch up on some of his outside interests. Paula then asked if Neill thought an MBA made him better equipped to be a banker. Neill knew that Paula did not have an MBA, and her opinion on that score was obvious. She seemed reassured when Neill replied that he felt the perceived value of an MBA was greater than the real value. Paula shared with Neill her resentment about doing the same work as MBAs but at a lower salary.

Toward the end of the meal, a pensive smile crossed Paula's face as if she were undecided about saying something. Neill gestured encouragingly, and Paula said, "Can I tell you something off the record? You're not nearly as much of an asshole as we figured you'd be. In fact, you're kind of a nice guy." Neill allowed Paula to pay for lunch since she said she could put it on her expense account.

With Paula's remarks in mind, Neill decided to get together with Cathy Clay. Paula had mentioned that Cathy, who did not have an MBA either, had transferred recently to San Francisco from the San Deigo office. Cathy had left the training program prior to Neill's arrival and had spent only five months in San Diego before returning to San Francisco. Given her abbreviated stay, Neill suspected that Cathy had had problems in San Diego.

Neill found out what department Cathy was in and asked her to lunch. Cathy agreed to meet for breakfast instead. Neill learned from Cathy that she had requested a transfer because her fiancé lived in San Francisco. Relieved by this news, Neill told Cathy that he hoped she could better acquaint him with the San Diego office when they met.

Over breakfast the next week, Cathy seemed determined to steer the conversation toward other topics than the San Diego office. As time went on, however, Cathy began to open up. As rapport developed Cathy began to indicate that she had not been happy at San Diego. She thought Allan was a "male chauvinist" and didn't manage women well. Cathy told Neill that she had never felt accepted in the San Diego office. She described an unpleasant run-in she had had with Allan's secretary, Sylvia, who, Cathy said, had pried into her personal affairs and told her boss about them.

As they were about to leave at the end of their breakfast, Cathy said to Neill:

Look, I'm going to tell you something, but if you ever repeat it I'll swear I never said it. Those people are all scared to death of you down there and are just waiting to prove you aren't the hotshot Allan has been telling everyone you are. And the one you really better watch out for is Sylvia. She's Allan's little spy; everything anybody says she repeats to him, and she feels he's her special property. She knows he's looking to you for something special, and she has a Gatling gun pointed at the door for the day you walk in.

Several days later, in late November 1978, Neill flew to San Diego to commence work. Neill took the elevator to the third floor of NBOC's office building and, as the elevator doors opened, he couldn't help wondering if he should duck.

First Week: Disarming the Cannons

Neill was greeted by an empty office. Allan and the other LOs were out on calls. A secretary showed Neill to his office, and on the way, Neill met Sylvia, a tall woman who appeared to be in her mid-20s. Throughout the day, Sylvia glared at Neill when he passed by and gave him curt answers whenever he asked a question. At one point, Neill overheard Sylvia and another secretary discussing a movie. "*The Graduate*?" Neill offered, trying to join in. "No—*Casablanca*," Sylvia fired back disdainfully, as if Neill had defiled their conversation.

Over the first week, Neill made a point of being quiet and shy. He asked questions humbly and was careful not to challenge the reasoning behind any procedures or make any suggestions. He tried to be as helpful as he could and refrained from his usual bantering humor. When he went downstairs to the first floor coffee machine, he always asked if anybody wanted anything.

Sylvia remained a stone wall throughout Neill's first week. Neill continued to go out of his way to show her respect, apologizing when he intruded upon her time. Later, on Friday afternoon, Neill ran into Sylvia in the hall. "Well," he said, "I survived a week, do you think I've a chance of lasting?" Sylvia smiled, and Neill believed he had started to win her over.

Neill began as an LO in Allan Crick's group (see Exhibit 1). It consisted of Paula Lynch and Roger Smallwood, both LOs, and Gary Dorf and Tim Sutherland, who were account managers. (Most LOs were promoted to account manager within their first few years with the bank.) There were two secretaries: Sylvia, who reported only to Allan, and Tamara Brown, who assisted the rest of the group. Neill quickly developed a rapport with the other LOs.

Neill tried to balance humility and sensitivity to his peers with integrity and professionalism in his approach to the job. For instance, determined to do well, Neill began working late hours. But so as not to appear as a rate buster, Neill started coming in to work about half a hour later than the rest of the staff. His office mates started joking that Neill was the "second shift." With his late arrivals as justification for staying late in the evenings, Neill felt he could work into the night without stepping on anyone's toes.

Neill did not see much of Dan Darley (Exhibit 1), but one day in early January 1979, Darley walked into Neill's office and said, "Take off your shirt, son." "Why?" Neill replied, feeling off balance and a bit intimidated. "I want to see if there's an S on your chest." Darley

was beaming and said that Neill's record from the training program had arrived and that in 20 years he had never seen such an evaluation. Neill had been awarded excellents in all of the 40 categories assessed.

Neill felt elated that he had gained the acceptance of his co-workers and that his superiors were impressed by his performance. He had begun making solo visits to customers, too, and found he enjoyed working in the field. Everything seemed to be going right for him.

Digging In

As the weeks passed, Neill became more thoroughly acquainted with the nature of his job. Being an LO, Neill explained to his friends, was akin to being a professional schizophrenic because he alternately wore a marketing hat and a weeding-out hat. He spent much of his time on calls looking for new business, but it was also his job to evaluate the risk of a potential NBOC loan. Neill's performance would be judged on his ability to meet loan volume, loan profit, and new business development objectives.

The San Diego office dealt primarily with domestic corporate loans. Neill's particular area included Santa Barbara and Whittier, California. The marketing aspect of Neill's job involved calling on companies with which NBOC had no current business, and also maintaining existing accounts. Neill spent about a week each month out of town, "selling" not only credit, but various services as well. One such service was the Cal-Link, a computer terminal hookup to NBOC's central facility. This made it possible for customers to keep continual track of their bank balances and have access to other information relevant to their accounts. The credit aspect of Neill's job involved the evaluation of present and prospective customers. Each LO at NBOC conducted a quarterly review of each client company judged to be in a higher credit risk category. Accounts with a lower credit risk were reviewed annually.

One of Neill's accounts scheduled to be evaluated was the Jefferson account. Al Jefferson, the president of a $50 million construction company that had borrowed $3.5 million from NBOC, was interested in buying out an electrical subcontractor for $8 million. Jefferson hoped that the addition of this company would give him vertical integration and increase his profitability. Neill ran an analysis on the subcontracting company and learned that the bargain price was due to its position of near bankruptcy. Neill convinced Al that borrowing money to buy a company with a poor performance record was a great risk, both for himself and for the bank. It was essential that Neill handle situations of this kind in such a way that the client would feel he had been helped rather than rejected and would not feel discouraged from applying for loans for other projects.

Credit approval, as Neill learned, presented delicate situations not only between client and LO, but within the bank hierarchy. Every loan required three bank officers' signatures. One could go up, down, or laterally in the bank hierarchy to acquire them, which could lead to interpersonal tension, especially if a lower-ranking person were asked to cosign a questionable deal by someone who could affect that cosigner's career. Loans under $1 million required at least one vice president's signature. Loans of $1 million to $10 million required two. For loans over $10 million, one of those two vice presidents had to be the credit officer on the senior vice president's (Jerry Grober's) staff (Exhibit 1). While the senior vice president and the area managers reporting to this position were responsible for profitability, the credit officer's job was to ensure that loans made in his or her region were acceptable credit risks from the bank's standpoint.

The First Raise

On June 8, 1979, when he had been one year at NBOC and just over six months in the San Diego branch, Neill was sitting in his office with Paula and Tim when Dan Darley walked in. In his gruff, unsmiling way, Darley wrote $3,000 on a piece of paper and handed it to Neill. "Your raise," he said. Neill was embarrassed that Darley had done this in front of his peers. It had been an unspoken rule among the LOs never to discuss salary. The raise seemed like a lot, but Neill grabbed his calculator and immediately figured out that it was only a 12.5 percent raise. By the bank's standards this was a good raise, but it was less than some of Neill's classmates in other industries were getting. "You know, this isn't much at all when you figure out the percentage," Neill told Darley. "It's a hell of a lot more than you were making at Harvard," retorted Darley.

Neill was embarrassed that the conversation had taken this sharp turn and that it had occurred in front of his peers. He thought about the situation all evening and decided that he had the advantage. He had a good education, a solid performance record, and headhunters had been calling him. Neill felt he could afford to insist on what he believed was fair compensation for his work. On the other hand, Neill knew that Darley had to stay inside a budget. He also sensed that Darley expected Neill to be grateful for what seemed to the 20-year career banker to be an enormous raise. Neill felt he should impress his viewpoint upon Darley, but he did not want to back Darley into a corner. Neill had recently read some of Clavell's novels about Eastern culture, and he wanted to present the situation in such a way that Darley, whom he saw as an old-style, strong-minded, benevolent dictator, could save face.

Darley stopped by Neill's office the next day and said that Neill had seemed dissatisfied the day before and asked if he wanted to talk about it. Neill explained his perspective—that in joining the bank

at the age of 30, he felt that he must either work very hard and be good at it and be rewarded, or, if he was not good at it, he must find something else that he could do very well. He could not settle for being mediocre at this point in his career. Neill agreed that a 12.5 percent raise was good by bank standards, where the mean was around 8 percent, but he knew that other firms who competed with NBOC for MBAs gave higher raises. Neill's final point was that if Darley was merely indicating that Neill could expect another 12.5 percent raise after another year, this would fall short of personal goals, and they should perhaps reevaluate how well their goals meshed. However, Neill told Darley, the situation would be different if Darley had recommended this raise three months earlier on the basis of much less evidence of Neill's ability; or if in six months, after the minimum time for promotion to account manager, Neill could expect a promotion and a larger raise. In that case, he would have an incentive and would do everything he could to earn it.

At the close of their lengthy conversation, Neill believed that he had given Darley a way out. He thought that he had left Darley feeling that he was not being challenged but that Neill had understood his position and even appreciated the raise he had received—in the proper context. Darley concluded by saying that he could make no promises, but if Neill continued to do well promotions and raises would follow.

The Second Raise and Promotion

About six months later, in December 1979, Allan informed Neill that he would be receiving a 17 percent raise with a promotion. Neill's high spirits were tempered by knowing that Paula, who was out of the office at the time, would be upset that he had been promoted ahead of her. He was also afraid that Allan would not handle the situation tactfully when Paula returned—Allan had a knack for saying the wrong thing at the wrong time.

Neill caught Paula at her office when she came in. "Paula," he said, "I don't know if you know, and I feel uncomfortable, but I thought I should tell you that I got promoted today." Paula looked startled and shocked. "I can't believe he's done this to me," she said, meaning Allan. Nevertheless, she thanked Neill for telling her, and encouraged him to go out and celebrate.

Later that day, Neill was surprised to overhear Paula's raised voice in Allan's office. He had not expected her to react against Allan in this way. Outside, Sylvia seemed to be tittering gleefully.

Enter: A New Team

In February of 1980, two months after Neill's big raise, and over a year after coming to San Diego, Darley was transferred out. Julio Cruz, who had been running NBOC's Mexico City branch, was named the new San Diego area manager. Along with Cruz came Bob Hernandez, an account manager, and Robin Cross, an LO, from the Mexico City branch (see Exhibit 2). At about the same time, Allan Crick announced that he would soon be transferring out as

Exhibit 2
Old/New Organization of West Division

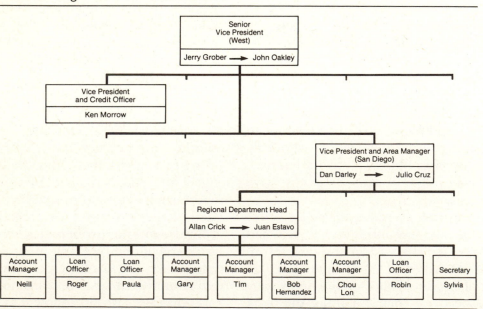

well and that he would be replaced by Juan Estavo, another Mexican, who had not worked with Cruz. The Mexico City operation was much larger than the one in San Diego, and Neill heard that Cruz had been reluctant to take the new position. His job in Mexico was said to have given him considerable local prestige, including such amenities as a chauffeured limousine. The rumor was that upper management had convinced Cruz to take a job with less responsibility so that he could prove himself in a domestic branch en route to the upper echelons of the bank.

No one in San Diego was particularly glad when Cruz was chosen to take over. Rumors spread that in Mexico City Cruz had applied tremendous pressure on LOs to meet their budgets. Neill was aware that this kind of pressure could lead some managers to compromise their credit integrity in order to generate loan volume. Bob Hernandez told Neill that the atmosphere in Mexico City was very competitive; people fought over customers. Although Neill sensed that Cruz believed in internal competition more so than did his predecessor, Darley, Neill also had the strong suspicion that Bob Hernandez was greatly exaggerating Cruz's style and philosophy in this regard in order to intimidate his new associates. Bob Hernandez apparently both thrived on such competition and was the principal promoter of it.

The San Diego office, on the other hand, had developed a cooperative atmosphere in which prospects were freely traded, based on personal contacts or geographical preference. Neill had enjoyed this team spirit and the feeling of the whole office working toward overall goals and felt proud of his own efforts in helping to promote such an atmosphere. For instance, in his discussion with Darley about his raise, Neill had tried to remain sensitive to Darley's position while advocating his own. Neill's office had become the most popular meeting place for LOs; he had even rearranged his furniture to facilitate relaxed conversation rather than confrontation.

In his first few days at the San Diego office, Bob Hernandez managed to alienate all the women in the office. He ordered secretaries around and immediately antagonized Paula with a comment he made while he was giving her a ride home. "Cruz is quite a ladies' man," Bob had told Paula, "all you have to do to get ahead with him is wear short dresses." Paula could not conceal her anger the next day as she related the story to Neill. She had said nothing to Bob—his comment had stunned her.

On March 21, 1980, about a month after the new team had arrived, Gary, Neill, and several others were sitting in Neill's office around 5 P.M. when Paula came in. Paula was upset, but not as much as when she had related the story of Bob's crude comment. Paula told those present that Cruz had agreed to attend an important meeting with a client that she had scheduled for that morning and then had backed out at the last minute, saying he had to catch up on some paper work. Paula had been embarrassed to tell her client, who had explicitly asked to meet with Cruz.

Paula's experience gave Neill some cause for concern about a meeting he himself had scheduled with Cedar Box Company, which Cruz had also agreed to attend. After some reflection, Neill decided to talk to Cruz ahead of time. Neill wanted to be careful with his comments, since he had not had the time or opportunity to build the kind of rapport with Cruz that he had developed with Allan Crick.

Neill dropped by Cruz's office the next morning. He mentioned that the president of Cedar Box would be attending their meeting and stressed the importance of the account. "Please understand that I don't want to question you, but I'd hate for something to happen like your meeting with Paula," Neill said. "Don't worry," Cruz replied, adding, "I'd never do that to you." Neill said there was no need to explain, but Cruz insisted on telling Neill about an incident in which Paula had indicated to Cruz that she did not trust him. "So, my attitude is to hell with her," Cruz concluded. "Why should I go out of my way for her? But don't you worry." Cruz did attend Neill's meeting.

On April 11, 1980, Cruz sent out a memo indicating that the NBOC office would be divided into two teams. Neill, Roger, and Paula were to work with one team leader, Tim. Chou Lon, a Thai who had recently transferred to San Diego, would lead the other team, which included Gary, Robin, and Bob Hernandez (see Exhibit 3). Cruz's memo stated that Tim's team would handle larger accounts, while Chou's team would handle smaller accounts. There was a certain logic to this reorganization, Neill felt, since Chou, Bob, and Gary had experience in dealing with smaller accounts, but the pre-Cruz staff members (Paula, Roger,

Exhibit 3
Cruz's Reorganization—Two "Teams"

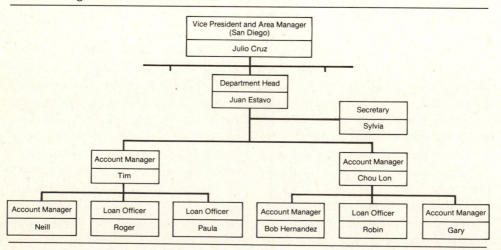

Gary, Tim, and Neill) were unhappy that they had not been consulted about the change. Gary was particularly upset because, although there was no loss of status in being assigned smaller accounts, he didn't relish the prospect of working exclusively with the three newcomers. Increasingly, the five old-timers gathered in Neill's office in the evenings to vent frustrations before departing for the day. These late conversations usually centered on Bob Hernandez. Bob had spread the word that the teams were intended to be competitive regardless of what Cruz said. He seemed to enjoy the idea of everyone's being subjected to the same pressures he was used to.

Cruz had inherited an optimistic loan volume and loan profitability budget, and as time passed his focus shifted increasingly toward "making budget." There was also a minor shuffling of accounts between the two teams. Still, the evening powwows in Neill's office continued as the old group, especially Gary and Paula, remained concerned over what could happen. Despite these grumblings, Neill did all he could to make Chou and Bob feel at home, offering to answer questions about their new surroundings and accompanying them on calls to show how the San Diego office sold itself to new customers. Bob seemed suspicious of his offers, as if he did not trust Neill's motives.

In early May 1980, Bob Hernandez asked Neill to join him on a call to a Los Angeles subsidiary of a San Diego-based company. Neill's own schedule was quite hectic, but he agreed to go and arranged some calls of his own in L.A. on the day before their meeting. He was to meet Bob for lunch on Wednesday. Just before Neill's departure for L.A., Bob called to say that Chou, his team leader, wanted to go along on the call. A three-on-one meeting would be rather overwhelming for the potential client, so Neill and Bob agreed that Neill should join them only if more than one person was coming from the client company. Bob said he would know for sure on Tuesday and would leave a message at Neill's hotel if he was not needed. Neill could then catch a late plane home to San Diego rather than wait. If there was no message, Neill was to meet Bob and Chou at Bob's hotel for lunch on Wednesday.

There was no message, but when Neill arrived at Bob's hotel, he learned that Bob and Chou had already left. Bob had forgotten to leave the message, and Neill had wasted an afternoon. Neill caught a 3 P.M. flight, frustrated at Bob's actions. He was anxious also because he was hoping to arrive in time to make a call to Ken Morrow, with whom Neill had recently run into some difficulties.

Ken Morrow

Throughout the early months of 1980, Neill had put in a lot of time on a deal between NBOC and six other banks and Jones Bros., a regional distributor for heavy construction equipment. Neill spent more time preparing a memo on the deal than he had on any project since his Dixon project during the training program. (Neill had recently been informed that his Dixon memo was to be used as a model in future training programs). Neill believed that he had covered all potential problems on the Jones deal and that his decision to go ahead was a sound one.

Since the loan amount was in excess of $10 million, Neill needed the signature of Ken Morrow as credit officer, along with that of one other VP. John Oakley, who had replaced Jerry Grober as SVP a year earlier, (Exhibit 2) had indicated that he would sign if Morrow did. Neill had developed a good rapport with Oakley; Neill and Oakley had been placed in the same foursome in NBOC's annual golf tournament that spring, and Neill, who was not a very good golf player, lost all 12 of his complimentary "NBOC" golf balls by the 12th hole. On the 13th green, Oakley noticed that Neill was putting with a range ball and teased Neill about that the rest of the afternoon. After returning home, Neill took the dirtiest, most cutup golf ball he could find and sent it to Oakley's office in San Francisco along with a humorous letter.

Neill's few encounters with Morrow had been much less friendly. Morrow, 40, seemed to put on an intimidating manner and turn to vicious personal attacks when challenged. In an early phase of the Jones deal, Neill had sat in on a conference call in which Morrow had chastised Allan Crick for his poor judgment on the deal, and

Morrow had even accused Allan of lying about the details of the loan. Neill knew Allan felt intimidated by Morrow, and he also knew that Cruz had not been on the job long enough to reasonably expect him to get involved in the details of such a deal, or to confront a credit officer of the bank on it. In fact, Cruz had not really moved in yet, and was in and out as he shuttled between San Diego and Mexico City trying to complete his transition.

After six or seven frustrating phone conversations with Morrow over a six-week period, Neill was feeling discouraged. Morrow had returned a memo about the deal that Neill had sent him with various questions that Neill thought were "nit picky." When Neill wrote a second memo addressing Morrow's questions, Morrow sat on the deal for a solid month. By April 1980, the six other banks were ready to sign a contract, and Neill felt he was on the spot.

For the first time since law school, Neill's "winning over" philosophy seemed to be ineffective. Morrow apparently disliked Juan Estavo, and Cruz, new to the region, was too unfamiliar with the situation to get involved. Neill finally decided to turn to Oakley, whom he viewed as a sort of mentor, in the hope that Oakley might intercede. The two had planned to make some calls together in San Francisco, and Neill used the trip as an opportunity to sound out Oakley for assistance. Oakley listened patiently as Neill eased into his story and seemed quite sympathetic but backed away when Neill suggested that Oakley talk with Morrow. "Well, that's something you'll have to work out with Morrow yourself," Oakley said.

Neill checked around and learned that previously Morrow had been assigned to clean up the bank's bad loans in Mexico City. This was before Cruz's tenure there, and the two men had never dealt with each other before Cruz arrived in San Diego. It was said that Morrow had had a bad experience with heavy construction equipment distributors in Mexico. Several of the bad loans had involved these distributors, and Morrow was said to have developed a distaste for the business. With the benefit of this information, Neill could appreciate why Morrow had seemed so cautious and nit-picky and why he wanted much tighter loan covenants than Neill thought were necessary. In this case Neill and Crick both knew the regional distributor, Jones Bros., and had confidence in the business and its owner. Morrow didn't.

On further investigation, Neill learned that Morrow had headed up an exciting new venture at bank headquarters after successfully completing his Mexico assignment. However, for strategic reasons having nothing to do with the performance of Morrow or his team, headquarters had disbanded this venture. Morrow, reportedly unhappy with this decision, was then appointed to his present position. As credit officer for the western region, it was his job to insure that large loans made by the San Diego branch and the other five branches in the region were acceptable credit risks. His performance was measured on the basis of the volume of delinquent loans rather than on profitability. The Jones Bros. deal was among the 10 largest loans that Morrow was examining at the time.

Moving Forward

After considering all the angles, Neill concluded that the Jones Bros. deal was extremely attractive for NBOC and would go a long way toward helping him meet his own loan volume, loan profit, and new business objectives for the year. He wondered how he could make Morrow feel more comfortable about the deal, given his prior experience with this kind of business in Mexico. Neill had been buying time with the other banks in the consortium who were eager to conclude the deal, but he knew that their patience and his time were running out. The lead bank (NBOC was the second largest lender in the bank consortium) had set Monday, May 13, 9 A.M., as the time for signing the deal with Jones Bros. in San Diego, and Neill had promised to come through on his end by then.

Neill decided to take a different approach with Morrow. He would show more understanding of Morrow's position in light of his experience and try to address his concerns in a diplomatic way. On Wednesday, May 8, 1980, the day Bob Hernandez had stood Neill up, Neill finally decided he was ready to call Morrow. He had rehearsed the phone call over and over on his flight from L.A., and he got back to his office by 4:45 P.M. just in time to make the call.

When he got Morrow on the phone, Neill got right down to business. He had never succeeded in getting Morrow to engage in small talk. "If this is really not a good deal," Neill began, "I don't want to do it. I respect your experience, and I'd like to learn from you." Morrow screamed into the phone, "You don't want to learn from me. You're just a young smart ass who thinks he knows everything. I'm gonna tell everyone in this goddamn bank about you!" With that, he hung up, and Neill, shocked, was left wondering how to proceed.

Neill spent a sleepless night trying to figure out what to do and came in to work early the next morning. He knew he had to act quickly and decisively to save the Jones Bros. deal, as well as his own professional reputation and credibility. As he was deliberating his options, Bob Hernandez stuck his head into Neill's office:

Bob: "You are in *early* this morning!"

Neill: "What happened yesterday?"

Bob: "Oh, I forgot to leave you a message. But you didn't miss much."

With that, Bob walked off and, for the first time in his dealings with Bob, Neill felt really angry. Neill couldn't believe that Bob had not only stood him up the previous day, but also that he had cared to give Neill neither an explanation nor an apology. Neill knew something had to be done, not only because Bob Hernandez was seriously disrupting the colleagial, cooperative, and effective peer relationships that Neill had enjoyed and helped foster at the San Diego branch, but also because Neill felt Bob had taken undue advantage of Neill's hospitality and willingness to help.

CASE 3–2
Jody McVay (A)

Jay A. Conger
Vijay Sathe

Jody McVay wondered if the talk she had just had with her boss would get her product the sales support it needed. Delight children's toothbrushes was a new product, and during a recent test market it had been given little attention—in certain locations it had not even reached the store shelves. At the root of her problem, Jody felt, were the recent merger of her division with another one and the arrival of a new corporate president. It was after these changes that division support for her product had apparently waned.

In her frustration, Jody had decided to hire two high school stu-

This case was prepared by Jay A. Conger (under the direction of Vijay Sathe).

dents to stock her product and then asked her boss to appeal to the division vice president for support. She hoped that these moves would counter the salespeople's failure to market her product.

BIFS

BIFS of West Germany manufactured and marketed a range of consumer goods throughout the world, principally personal care and detergent/soap products. The company's success was due principally to its technical expertise, which had made it a leader in introducing modern processing methods for detergents and innovations in personal care products. Its research facilities were known to be among the best in the world. The company's technical emphasis, however, led to a product rather than a market orientation. New products would often be evaluated solely by R&D, without the benefit of market research. Senior managers seemed to share an ingrained belief that competitive products had to be technically distinctive, whether or not consumers actually perceived the difference.

Within the United States, BIFS operated through the BIFS company, a New York subsidiary, whose product line included shampoos, soaps, detergents, and personal care and baby products. The BIFS company had enjoyed considerable success until the end of the 1970s, when the detergents and soaps industry ran into difficulties. Thirty percent of the firm's sales were in this industry and were seriously weakened by high supply prices, greater competition, and a lack of successful new products. In addition, BIFS's personal care business had stagnated despite its large market share, and its major products (shampoos, shaving creams, and toothpastes) were declining in a highly competitive market. Its baby products had also declined in share despite growing markets. Other product lines remained essentially stable.

In recent years, the firm's marketing strategy had been to follow the leader, as exemplified by the company's entry into the baby diaper market with a product that imitated a major U.S. brand. For the most part, BIFS had not had a successful new product in the United States since 1965.

Background

Jody McVay was 29 and married. She received her MBA from the Harvard Business School in 1979 and a B.A. from Michigan in social psychology in 1976. Prior to HBS, she had spent two and a half years working for an advertising agency. Those who worked with Jody described her as outgoing, enthusiastic, bright, and energetic. Jody's philosophy of life was to go out and strive. It was important for her to be excited by her work.

Jody's decision to join BIFS was based largely on one summer's experience with the firm, between her first and second years at HBS, when she had worked as a "rover" on several projects for the Soaps Division. Her supervisor, Frank

Hummel, a 1978 Harvard MBA, had convinced her that BIFS was going through a major upheaval and thus offered enormous opportunities for young MBAs. And the division's vice president, Al Johnson, had told her, "We need your skills. Too many of our staff are from sales. With your MBA, you'll stand out."

First Four Months

Jody began working at BIFS on July 9, 1979. She had been assigned to the Soaps Division as an assistant product manager on a soap line called Purity (Exhibit 1). Her initial responsibilities included budget preparation, sales forecasts, administration of consumer promotion, and postpromotion analyses. Since the division operated with a matrix structure, Jody had to compete with managers of other products and groups for the time and attention of the operations and support staff. Frank Hummel was her first boss, and she felt inspired by his determination to introduce more sophisticated marketing concepts into the division's operations.

By mid-August, about a month after joining BIFS, Jody realized that the Soaps Division was very much of a "guy's team." Jody was the only woman among a professional staff of 16. She learned from her secretary that three women had left over the past 12 months. A marketing trainee and an assistant product manager had been fired for incompetence, and a product manager, an HBS graduate, had left the division for better opportu-

nities. Jody observed that divisional camaraderie was based on sports and dirty jokes. It seemed that any new staff member who didn't participate would be isolated.

Jody was determined to break the ice, so at the division's annual softball outing in late August, she volunteered to play shortstop. She had played softball for years with her husband, Bill, and felt confident of playing well. When the game was over, several of the division managers remarked how impressed they were with her prowess. The next morning, a group of product managers stopped by her office to tell her some of their newest jokes and gossip.

By early September, Jody had sensed that BIFS had a country club outlook. There seemed to be a strong resistance to experimentation, and emphasis was mostly on harvesting existing products to ensure short-term profitability. Jody suspected that the company had no overall strategy for new products, and few innovative products had been introduced during the last decade.

In many ways, Jody saw that the company was a reflection of its president, Jack Rapport. She heard from staff that he and most of top management had been with BIFS for 20 to 30 years. She assumed that an old-boy network was probably a powerful force in the company. In several staff meetings she had seen Rapport and had been struck by how awkward and unimpressive his management style was. He seemed to be chronically unprepared at meetings and had diffi-

Exhibit 1
BIFS—Soaps Division
(November 1979–February 1980)

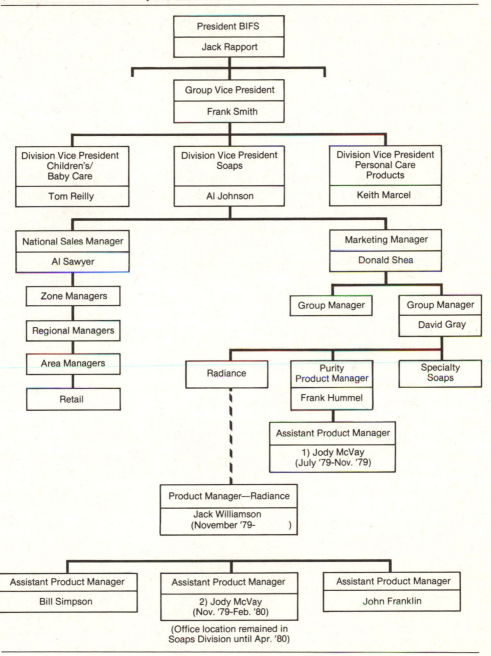

culty in communicating with others. Frank Hummel had mentiond that Rapport was oriented toward harvesting rather than building brand strength, and also that he was under increasing pressure from Germany to bring in high quarterly profits.

Jody observed that consensus was valued in her division and in the whole organization and that conflict was frowned upon. It seemed important for everybody to get along with everybody. Jody once complained about her secretary's poor performance to a senior manager, whose response was that she could clear up the problem by approaching her secretary on a personal basis.

Jody learned from Frank Hummel that most of the staff as well as top management had come up from the sales ranks. Sales experience was highly valued, almost a prerequisite for promotions to upper management. This was in sharp contrast to what Jody knew about BIFS's competitors, where professional marketers with little or no sales experience were the dominant force.

Jody also noticed how much time and energy people put into the execution of their presentations, rather than the analysis. Graphics, layout, and salesmanship seemed more important than the depth or the content of the presentation. This was a major source of aggravation for Frank Hummel, who considered analysis all important. She could understand why Frank was so aggressive in his attempts to bring a consumer-marketing emphasis into a division dominated by a tradition of salesmanship. Frank confided to Jody on many occasions that he and others of his bent, including herself, were the wave of the future—they would usher in professional marketing at BIFS.

Jody allied herself with Frank during her first three months. They would confer in each other's offices throughout the day and often have lunch together. Jody felt they really understood each other, but as time went on Jody realized that Frank was a lone voice in the department. While she identified with him because of his HBS background and similar interests, she began to feel that it would be politically unwise to align herself too closely with Frank. She feared guilt by association. She had never seen Frank win praise or recognition from division management, and she noticed that many members of management didn't socialize with Frank. She began to suspect that his push to bring analytical marketing techniques into a very traditional sales-oriented organization had more or less ostracized him. She concluded that if she too was associated with Frank and his ideas, she too would probably be on the outer circle. Jody was struck, however, by how little she had really comprehended Frank Hummel's status in the organization when she had worked for him the previous summer.

At the end of October, four months after Jody joined BIFS, Frank told her he was to be transferred to another division to work on a new product. He said that he needed experience on other brands, but Jody guessed that the transfer was actually a well-executed move by division management to get rid of Frank because he had generated too much friction. Jody decided she had to fit in to be successful, and it was important not to start out in an adversary role.

The Shift to Williamson

With Frank's transfer in November, Jody was assigned to Jack Williamson, the product manager for Radiance soap products (see Exhibit 1). Working for Williamson turned out to be a nightmare. He would come back from lunches tipsy from too many drinks, and he often told crude jokes to women staff. Jody had heard rumors that Williamson accepted graft from suppliers and had a history of poor management decisions. These stories were confirmed indirectly at a Christmas party that a supplier gave for the assistant product managers, where each person was given a bottle of champagne. When Jody requested one for Williamson, the supplier snapped, "Hell, we've done enough for him already. You have no idea of the things we've given him." In her own work with Williamson, Jody had seen that he had little analytical skill. She suspected that political connections were his lifeline in the division.

Williamson shifted Jody to more administrative work and moved her and another assistant product manager into a 9-by-12-foot office which opened onto the secretarial pool and its clamoring typewriters.

When Jody said the noise from the secretarial pool made it difficult to concentrate, Williamson responded, "Well, this will make you strive harder for a better office." Jody resented the remark. In her first week with Williamson, Jody finished negotiations which she had begun under Frank on a joint advertising promotion with Norton Fineproducts. Frank had approved her status as the company representative to the negotiations, but Williamson decided he would attend instead. Jody was disappointed, but decided at least to summarize her efforts to date and present them to Williamson. When he saw her summaries, Williamson chuckled, "You didn't have to have this typed up. I just wanted something scratched out on a sheet of paper." All Jody's work seemed to have amounted to nothing. Her presence and educational background were apparently too threatening for Williamson and made him reluctant to let her have any exposure.

A case in point were the advertising copy meetings, held about once a week, which played a central role in brand management. These meetings could not be scheduled in advance, but rather were held on an impromptu basis by the product manager, Williamson. Williamson had already stopped inviting Jody to these meetings and assigned her to do only clerical and administrative work instead.

One day in the company cafeteria, Jody joined a staff group for lunch. Except for one man who was working in the Baby Care Division, all of them were friends. Jody complained that Williamson hadn't allowed her in on staff meetings or in discussions on brand evaluations and promotions. The next day Jody was called into Williamson's office. "I hear you've been complaining about not being treated well," Williamson remarked dryly. Jody's mouth dropped. She surmised that the man from Baby Care had "squealed." She also realized how Williamson would interpret her behavior: "Here's the MBA who doesn't want to do grunt work, who's above everybody else." Frustrated, Jody simply said that she would like to take on more responsibility.

Jody's various attempts to get more involved in brand management were met by indifference and lack of support from Williamson. Fed up, Jody decided she had to risk going around her boss to higher ups if there was to be any hope of changing her situation. She figured she could always leave BIFS if she had to and find another job. After all, she had been with the company only a few months ("I have no equity here yet"), and she felt she was still very "marketable." Jody approached Peter Pollock, her original contact in the personnel office, who referred her to David Gray, Williamson's boss (Exhibit 1). Gray agreed that Jody needed greater involvement, and said that he would talk to Williamson about it. The following week Williamson invited Jody to the marketing meetings.

But her troubles with Williamson were not over. The next week,

Jody had some difficulty with a young assistant account executive from the division's advertising agency. The woman was being unreasonable and uncooperative, until Jody had to state flatly, "Look, I want you to do this because I want it done. I don't want to hear the B.S.!" The young woman complained to her boss at the agency, who called Williamson, who called Jody into his office and said "I hear there's a problem at the agency. Well, it's a well-known fact that women in business don't get along with each other." Jody retorted, "Not true, I get along with. . . ." and went on to list women in her department. Averse to further discussion, Williamson simply said, "Try to get along with her better in the future." It was clear that he did not want to hear Jody's side in the matter, but simply assumed that she was the guilty party.

By the end of November, Jody watched the division's morale slump as quarterly sales slipped significantly below forecast. Several secretaries suggested a morale party was in order. The division's managers liked the idea and arranged for an outing on a Friday. Jody learned from Williamson that she was expected to attend. She was amused that anyone would coerce her to attend a morale party. The idea of a morale party seemed typical of the division's approach to problems: Their solutions were always social. Rather than dealing with the underlying reasons for slackening sales, a party was called to raise everybody's spirits.

At the party, Jody had to listen to

the usual round of dirty jokes and comments like, "Women could never run this country." She realized the men were trying to bait her, not in a friendly way but deliberately to agitate her. A group manager came up from behind and kissed her on the neck. Jody gave no reaction. When he approached a second time, she turned and said in a soft but firm voice, "Don't ever do that again." "Why?" asked the group manager, with a wink and a smile. Jody allowed a moment to pass and then, looking the manager straight in the eye, said coldly: "Because we don't share that intimacy." As he left to join Williamson and his boss, Donald Shea, (Exhibit 1), Jody overheard him say, "You wouldn't believe what Jody just said." The men laughed, but Jody was not bothered again.

Jody felt that the way the division treated assistant product managers left a lot to be desired. In the first week of December, she and four others were asked to drive down to an eastern regional sales meeting in Philadelphia and return the same day, whereas the division's several hundred salesmen were given overnight hotel accommodations.

Certain obvious inequities among the assistant product managers were fostered by her boss, Williamson. A new assistant, John Franklin, had been promoted from the sales force and was assigned in November to work with Jody and Bill Simpson (Williamson's other assistant product manager). During the budgeting process in De-

cember, John had taken four days to prepare certain budget figures which Jody herself had previously accomplished in one day. Yet Jody realized that Williamson saw John as a fellow salesman. At the end of December, when Jody learned that Williamson had given John a high rating for his first month in the division, Jody was reminded that relationships were more important in the division than performance.

Also at the end of December, Franklin told Jody that the group manager, David Gray, had recommended Williamson for a promotion to group product manager. Jody was surprised. She concluded that Williamson's strength as a showman had appealed to senior division management and that the execution of a presentation counted more than the analysis. She also knew that Williamson was "in tight" with Shea, the division marketing manager. Jody often saw them at parties together and had heard that they spent Friday nights together at the local bar. Williamson was forever mentioning to Jody how Shea would like to see things done.

In the second week of January, six months into her job at BIFS, Jody returned to personnel to inquire if openings were available elsewhere in the company. She was frustrated by the division's atmosphere and her boss's behavior. She had heard that the New Products Division was headed by a very energetic and analytical manager who surrounded himself with bright young people. On learning that nothing was available at the time, Jody turned her search outside the firm and set up several interviews with major competitors for late January. Even before her first interview, however, she received a call from Terry Donaleshen, manager of New Products, who asked if she was interested in an assistant product manager position. He said he had heard from the company's advertising agency that Jody had a sharp mind and that she would probably fit in well at New Products.

In late January 1980, Jody had an interview with Terry. Terry needed help in applying more sophisticated analytical techniques to New Products strategies and thought her training at HBS would be helpful. He felt that if she worked hard, she could be promoted quickly. She would begin initially as an assistant product manager; her first assignment would be a consumer perception study of the personal care markets. The assignment and Terry's personality both appealed to Jody. A week later, she called Terry and accepted the position. Then she informed Williamson that it had been difficult to utilize her skills in the division and that she had decided to accept a position in New Products where she could be involved in more analytical projects. Williamson agreed that the other job would be a better fit and offered whatever help he could to ease the transition.

The New Products Division

In early February 1980, Jody assumed her new position as assistant product manager in Corporate New Products. She reported directly to Terry Donaleshen (Exhibit 2). Because of limited space in the New Products Division, she was to retain her office in the Soaps Division until April.

Jody began her initial assignment on a consumer perceptions study of BIFS's personal care line and competitor brands. She proposed that several current and planned products be redirected. Terry arranged for her to present her findings to a joint German parent—U.S. corporate meeting on market strategies for personal care products. She realized that Terry had created a tremendous opportunity for her. Jody noticed that the director of research and development of the German parent company chaired the meeting. During her presentation, she was also aware that interest was not focused on the consumer perceptions she had uncovered, but on the technical features of the products. The meeting confirmed Jody's observation that the parent company's orientation was toward technical expertise rather than marketing.

After completing the personal care project in early March, Terry asked Jody to conduct a detergents market study. During the project, she recommended to Terry that the company use the database "*Profit Impact of Marketing Strategies*" (PIMS) as an interim step to look at company markets. Terry agreed, and within a month, BIFS had subscribed to PIMS.

The final project recommendations of the detergents study were

Exhibit 2
BIFS—New Products Division
(February 1980–May 1981)

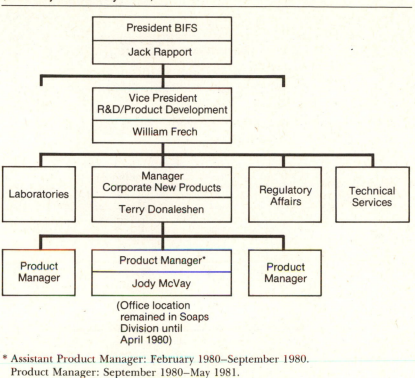

(Office location
remained in Soaps
Division until
April 1980)

* Assistant Product Manager: February 1980–September 1980.
  Product Manager: September 1980–May 1981.

presented to the corporate vice presidents, the company president, and German staff representatives of the international detergents operations. Jody saw this as another significant opportunity that Terry had arranged for her. Normally, Terry would have made the presentation himself. Instead, he gave her exposure to key company executives, several of whom later told her how well prepared and well executed her presentation had been. Jody realized how important Terry was becoming to her contribution and success in the company.

Jody came to respect Terry enormously and liked his soft-spoken and unassuming manner. She learned that Terry had been a Green Beret in Vietnam and carried with him a Green Beret's keen sense of competitiveness. To Jody, he always seemed ready to prove his worth, yet he never lost his cool. Jody respected that. She sensed that Terry was a success story at BIFS. She knew that he had joined the company only 10 years earlier, and already was the head of the New Products Division. She also knew that he had not come from the sales ranks, which was unusual for a senior manager at BIFS.

The "Soft-Tees" Offer

In September 1980, after eight months in New Products, Jody was promoted to product manager.

Terry told her he felt she had made several valuable contributions to the division, especially in her detergents study. Now Jody felt that she was on the fast track. None of her friends either inside BIFS or in other companies had attained a product manager's position in such a short period.

The very next week, Jody had a call from Glen Rowinski, the group marketing manager for baby care products, offering her a brand manager's position on the Soft-tees brand of baby diapers (Exhibit 3). Rowinski had seen her presentations and thought she would do well on the Soft-tees line. Soft-tees was a major brand, and Jody realized that if she aspired to higher

Exhibit 3
BIFS—Children's/Baby Care
(May 1981–August 1981)

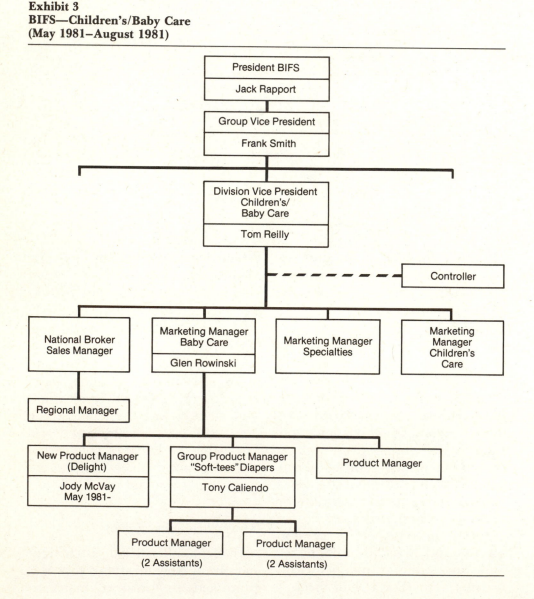

positions in the company, it was important to work as a product manager on such a high-volume established brand. Jody thought it would be an opportunity to prove to corporate that she could run her own brand. But she also enjoyed her work at New Products and valued her relationship with Terry. She approached Terry about the offer and asked for his opinion. He felt that she was right in her assumption that serving on a major brand was an important career step and felt the offer was a good one. Jody then scheduled an interview with Glen Rowinski, and also with Tony Caliendo, the Soft-tees group product manager.

From her interviews, Jody sensed that she would enjoy working with Rowinski. He seemed to have strong interpersonal skills and liked new ideas. Caliendo, on the other hand, reminded her of life back in the Soaps Division. He was too much of a salesman, and Jody disliked the way he eyed her physically. She felt uncomfortable about Caliendo. When Terry warned that Caliendo would be a poor teacher, and she would end up feeling frustrated under him, Jody concluded that this was just not the spot for her. She told Terry she would decline the offer.

Jody called Rowinski and told him that she didn't want to move yet out of New Products where she had a lot going for her. She mentioned, however, that she would be interested in future opportunities to work with Rowinski. She knew that at some point in the near future it would be important to move into a mainline business, and concluded from her interview that the Children's/Baby Care Division and Rowinski would be a good place to work, provided Rowinski was her boss.

During these interviews, Jody had noticed that the Children's/Baby Care Division was predominantly female (with the exception of top division management). Two of the division's three product managers were women. This contrasted sharply with the Soaps Division, where all the product managers were men. From her discussions with Rowinski, she also gathered that the division was marketing oriented, with a broker sales force, unlike the Soaps Division, which had its own internal sales organization.

Taking on Delight

Jody continued to work on various projects at New Products. She designed marketing plans for a toothpaste product and for a line of after-shave products. In March of 1981, Terry assigned her the test marketing plan for a new children's toothbrush line called Delight. Terry indicated that it was an important project and told her how pleased he was with the job she had done for him. Terry also suggested that Jody use the experience as a way of discovering more about the Children's/Baby Care Division to see if it fit her career needs and personality. He also explained that he was in line for a promotion, which would take him out of New Products, and that before he left he wanted to see that she was placed in a division she liked and on a brand that would be beneficial to her career.

Through the first three weeks of March, Jody worked with Rowinski's staff on the new Delight line. She was invited to present her initial plan to the division's weekly marketing meeting on March 24. Rowinski said to arrive promptly at 8 A.M., since his boss and the division's vice president, Tom Reilly, insisted on punctuality. Jody had already learned from Rowinski that Reilly was an ex-Marine who ran the division as if it were his platoon.

Jody arrived for the meeting at 7:55 A.M. Rowinski introduced her to Reilly, and Jody sensed a certain coldness in Reilly's hello. Before the meeting began, she asked Rowinski about Reilly's cold edge. He explained that Reilly and Terry Donaleshen had been archrivals for many years and that Reilly traditionally treated members of Donaleshen's staff coolly.

At 8 A.M. one staff member had yet to arrive for the meeting. Reilly swung the one empty chair to the center of the circle of staff members and began the meeting. When the individual arrived, Reilly had him sit throughout the meeting in the middle of the room, surrounded by the circle of staff members.

As Jody made her presentation, Reilly kept asking her one question after another. She sensed that he was attempting to find one that she would stumble over. After what seemed to be 20 or more questions,

Reilly stopped. Jody guessed that he was satisfied with her answers. After the meeting, he told her he had liked her presentation and its defense. Jody believed she had passed Reilly's test. Rowinski confirmed this and confided that Reilly's rite of passage was nicknamed Twenty Questions by the division staff.

Later Jody had a talk with Terry Donaleshen about his relationship with Reilly and mentioned the cold reception she had received. Terry explained that he had worked for Reilly six years earlier in the Children's/Baby Care Division and that they had had several clashes. Terry said Reilly valued loyalty highly and was slow to admit his own mistakes. Terry felt that in Reilly's eyes his own confronting style was tantamount to a breach of loyalty. Terry thought he was also too analytical for Reilly. Terry had finally left the division, and Rowinski had been chosen to fill his position.

About three weeks later, on April 10, 1981, Jody received a call from Rowinski. He offered her the brand manager's position on Delight, the product she had been working on. He explained that the division was ready to invest the resources necessary to launch the new product. The potential, he explained, was enormous. This would be Jody's chance to build a market from scratch, and the idea appealed to her. She also liked Rowinski, and he was to be her boss (Exhibit 3). In addition, she met with the group vice president, Frank Smith, who explained how impressed he had been with her

New Products presentations. "I want to get more people like you in my divisions instead of the sales types who run the place," he said. Jody sensed that he was personally behind the product and her career.

Building a market for a new product seemed to be an attractive challenge. She discussed the offer with Terry who cautioned her that her best career path would be on a major established brand and not a new and relatively untested product like Delight. But Jody believed Delight had enormous potential, and as product manager she sensed that she might ultimately be responsible for creating a multimillion dollar market. She decided to accept the offer.

On May 19, 1981, almost two years after her arrival at BIFS, Jody joined the Children's/Baby Care Division as the product manager for Delight. When she took over the brand, she was told that there was no division marketing plan. Her responsibilities were to sell the project to senior management and to design and implement a marketing plan. With a targeted final product introduction deadline of November 1981 just over six months away, Jody began work on the market plan and a proposed test market scheduled for July.

In June, Jody learned from Rowinski that Reilly was leaving for a new position in corporate marketing. Rowinski told Jody in confidence that the move was tantamount to a demotion, and surmised that Reilly had not been a success as division vice president.

The Shake-up

On July 2, 1981, Rowinski informed Jody that corporate had announced plans to merge the Children's/Baby Care Division and the Soaps Division. The broker sales force was to be disbanded, and Children's/Baby Care was to share the Soaps Division's sales force. Also, the group vice president, Smith, was to switch positions with Keith Marcel, head of Personal Care Products. Marcel was known to be a reasonably good manager, but he had a more financial and bottom-line orientation than Smith, who was perceived as a strategist. To Jody, the change was disturbing, since she had seen Smith as a possible mentor. Rowinski suspected that the change would mean trouble for the Children's/Baby Care Division. Behind it, Rowinski speculated, was corporate's belief that the Soaps sales force was underutilized and that reorganizing would be an opportunity to economize during a period of slackening sales.

Jody felt that the transition would lead to a great deal of conflict. To her, Children's/Baby Care was marketing oriented, whereas Soaps emphasized sales. Children's was more innovative, while Soaps was conservative. Jody was worried that the Children's division would have to accommodate to Soaps, since they would be using Soaps' sales force.

She was also concerned about the kind of support she would get for her product. She knew that Marcel had serious reservations about Delight. Terry had said that in corporate new project review meetings Marcel had consistently expressed skepticism about the new children's toothbrush. In her first meeting with Marcel, he had mentioned his involvement in a similar project in the 1950s which had proved unsuccessful.

Rowinski recalled some of the history of the Soaps Division for Jody. The tone of the division had been set by John Hoffman, who had been division general manager until 1977, when he retired. Rowinski recalled that he was a "charmer." He said Hoffman prided himself on being able to bring the division in consistently below budget on salary and market research expenses. Hoffman was a salesman at heart, Rowinski felt.

The next general manager, Rowinski said, was Al Johnson, who was an old buddy of Jack Rapport, the president. Johnson had come from another consumer products company, and was viewed by many as inept—"everything he put his hands on became unprofitable." Rowinski said the national sales manager, Al Sawyer, and his zone managers ran the division. He said the division's marketing manager, Donald Shea, was not a strong manager, as Jody herself recalled from her earlier experience in Soaps. Shea was the chief circulator of dirty jokes within the division. Whenever Jody appeared, he would always remark to one of the men: "Tell that joke again, Jody is one of the guys." Both he and his secretary were married, but Jody had heard that he was having an

affair with his secretary. Jody guessed that Shea's refusal to argue with the sales force had given Sawyer and his staff a dominant influence in the division.

After the merger in early August 1981, Jody thought morale among the Children's/Baby Care staff began to slip. Children's/Baby Care had previously been a more profitable unit than Soaps, but now it was merely an appendage. The split between the two groups was evident to Jody at the company's annual softball game, when the entire crossfunctional staff of the merged divisions joined up with the Soaps team. In the day-to-day operations, she found that Children's sales were being given a low priority by the Soaps sales force. Sales began sliding downward.

At the end of August, Jody accompanied Al Sawyer, the national sales manager, on a trip to San Francisco (Exhibit 4). One evening, Sawyer invited her to join him and several salesmen on a visit to the striptease area of San Francisco. Jody guessed that it was a test to see if she was "one of the boys" or not. She agreed, noticing a look of surprise on Sawyer's face. From that time on, Jody discovered that her access to the salesmen and sales managers had become much easier, and she found herself receiving invitations to lunch from people who previously had made little contact with her.

Change at the Top

In early September 1981, corporate announced that Rapport, the

Exhibit 4
Soaps/Children's Care Division
(August 1981–Present)

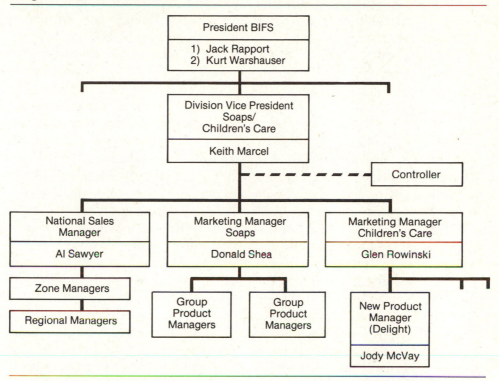

president, was to be promoted. A new president, Kurt Warshauser, was to take over. Jody read in press releases that Warshauser had been commissioned by the German parent to begin to rebuild the firm and to find a successor for himself in two years, after which he was to move on to German headquarters. Articles mentioned that he was highly regarded for his analytical skills, for asking the right questions, and for hiring the right people to execute his plans. His goals were to invest in businesses that held significant potential and drop those that were unprofitable or could not benefit from substantial advertising commitments. His approach was to strengthen and build the major brands and then move out to line extensions. He was interested in products for which customers were willing to pay a premium, rather than generic types. He believed that all major products had to be kept continually under review—reflecting the German view that technical expertise was critical. He was also known as a strong believer in retaining competing brands: "I think it is good that our people compete against each other, especially if their products are doing well."

Jody knew that several senior managers under Rapport had already left the company. She suspected that Warshauser would begin firing many of the old-line managers, which would affect support on her new line, Delight. She also guessed that Delight was too much of an unknown to appeal to Warshauser.

The Test Market

With Warshauser's arrival, Jody's test market of Delight had been postponed to September. She launched the first trials on September 15. These were to run for six months. On September 22, she visited the field to see how the test market was progressing and discovered then that her product had not even made it to the shelf in many places. Dismayed, she phoned the local sales office for an explanation. She was told that a cut in the sales force had prevented them from working on new products. She phoned Sawyer at the corporate headquarters and asked why her product wasn't out. Sawyer told Jody that she just wasn't a top priority. Her product was at the "bottom of the totem pole." Undaunted, she called a local high school and hired two high school students to distribute her product. That same week, Jody received a call from the ad agency explaining that by accident one of her newspaper ads had not run in two of her test markets. It was a big ad with coupons. Jody felt she was in trouble, but she knew that the other more established brands in Children's Care were also having their share of sales force problems.

Jody phoned a friend who attended corporate staff meetings and told her about Delight's problems. Her friend's response was not encouraging: "Well, you know, we don't hear much about Delight. There are no questions asked about it or anything." Jody then called a regional sales manager who had been supportive in the test marketing. He responded, "It doesn't seem to be a topic of discussion out here. When Marcel's out in the field, he never mentions it. He's so concerned about soap sales that he doesn't have time for anything else." Jody then went to Rowinski and presented her case: "I'm concerned that the lack of communications to sales has led them to put Delight on a low priority. They're not really behind it and neither is corporate. I think Marcel is projecting that Delight is not important. He ignores it at monthly meetings, and by not asking questions, he's jeopardizing the test market." At first, Rowinski was defensive, arguing that Marcel didn't really feel that way: "He hasn't just written it off." But Jody retorted, "O.K., if that's the case, we have to do some things that will communicate that to the sales force—otherwise it's a self-fulfilling prophecy of failure." Rowinski then agreed to talk to Marcel about it, and Jody wondered what she could do to give Delight the exposure and attention it deserved. Jody also thought about the changing situation at BIFS and what it meant for her future prospects in the company.

CASE 3–3
Dan Stewart (A)

Mark Rhodes
Vijay Sathe

The strange news of the reorganization of the Commercial Division in the Pharmaceuticals Group of the Pharma Corporation had dominated Dan Stewart's thoughts all week. The previous Monday, September 18, 1974, John Fielding, general manager of the division, had broken the news to him. The most startling aspect of the change for Stewart was that Scott Williams, who had been his subordinate only a week earlier, was his newly appointed boss (Exhibits 4 and 5). Stewart's emotional reactions ran the gamut from futility to rage, but he knew he must think carefully and act prudently if he was to survive in the corporation. It was the most difficult situation he had ever been in.

Stewart and Fielding had only recently reprimanded Williams for what they considered extremely poor performance. On September 4, after a disastrous presentation at the annual budget reviews, Williams had literally cried in apology to Fielding and his staff. Stewart, in turn, had apologized to Fielding for his subordinate's poor showing. They had agreed to place Williams

on "warning." Thus it was ironic that two weeks later Fielding broke the news to Stewart that he, Stewart, was to report directly to Williams. Stewart was even more stunned to learn that it was Stewart's mentor and friend, Jim Reilly, group vice president of the Pharmaceuticals Group (Exhibit 4), who had made the final decision on the reorganization.

At his office early on Monday, September 25, Stewart had nothing scheduled before his meeting with Al Bartley, executive vice president in charge of the Pharmaceuticals Group (Exhibits 4 and 5). Bartley had heard that Stewart was upset by the reorganization and had asked to meet with him. In the week since the news had broken, Stewart had had doubts for the first time in his career about his future with Pharma. As Stewart's peers and subordinates passed by his office that morning to express their empathy, Stewart felt grateful for all their support during his ordeal.

Company Background

Headquartered in Chicago, Pharma was a multibillion dollar corporation serving the pharmaceutical and related markets worldwide. From modest beginnings at the turn of the century, the company had grown steadily under the management of three generations of the founding Lyons family. James Lyons III, grandson of the founder, who was CEO from 1945 to 1964, oversaw the company's

This case was prepared by Mark Rhodes (under the direction of Vijay Sathe).

transition to public ownership. He relied extensively on acquisitions and believed strongly in letting the acquired entrepreneurial managers run their own show. Pharma prospered, and Jim Lyons was remembered as an astute businessman and deal maker in his choice of companies and individuals.

After Jim Lyons' retirement in 1964, the company's fortunes began to slide. His successor was a long-time Pharma executive, but a weak leader, and failed to maintain the company's momentum. Company morale began to slip. Employees came in late and left early; managers took three-hour lunch breaks and "vacationed on the job." A favorite pasttime among company managers was the game of poker, with drinks, that became a tradition on board the executive jet during business trips.

Richard Steele

In 1970, Pharma's board looked outside the company and recruited Richard Steele as chief executive officer in an effort to reverse the company's deteriorating financial and market position. Steele came from Cedar Mills, a huge textile corporation with a national reputation for well-managed operations. He had been passed over for the presidency there reportedly because of his management style, which was "too brash and insensitive for the team spirit philosophy" at Cedar Mills.

On taking over, Steele embarked on an ambitious set of programs to professionalize Pharma manage-

ment. He immediately instituted three important management tools: formal strategic planning by business units, management by objectives (MBO), and long- and short-term management incentives tied "mathematically" to MBO. Steel's commitment to these programs became well known throughout Pharma, as did his high personal standards of business conduct. One classic story was told of his first business trip with company senior management on the executive jet. After take-off, cards were being dealt and liquor served when someone asked Steele what he was going to drink. "Iced tea with honey," Steele replied. He proceeded to open his briefcase and added, in a no-nonsense tone of voice, "This is a business trip, gentlemen. Let's get to work." Speechless, the executives sheepishly set aside their drinks as the steward, who had had the good sense to find out in advance what Steele drank on such trips, brought out Steele's tall glass of iced tea with honey.

Although he earned their respect for his commitment, integrity, and energy, Steele did not endear himself to those who interacted with him. At six-foot-eight and 240 pounds, Steele had an imposing physical presence and a style that intimidated many. Stories circulated around Pharma about the way Steele handled contacts with his managers. When he was ready for an appointment, Steele would press a button to turn on a light outside his office door. When the person entered, Steele would turn around in his chair and without any greeting plunge into a discussion of their business. Many an executive had been cut off in midsentence as Steele whirled his chair around and broke off the meeting.

Dan Stewart's Background

Dan Stewart joined Pharma Corporation in 1963 after a four-year stint in the Navy. Stewart had graduated with an engineering degree from Columbia University in 1959. In 1974 he was 37 years old, married, with three children.

Stewart joined Pharma as a technical service representative, but his interests were more in sales and marketing. After about a year, he was put on temporary assignment to assist Jim Reilly, who was then director of New Products in the Plastic Materials Division (Exhibit 1). Reilly did not have any staff, but depended on borrowed personnel for special assignments, such as market testing a potential product or researching its profit potential.

Exhibit 1
Pharma Corporation—Partial Organization, Circa 1965

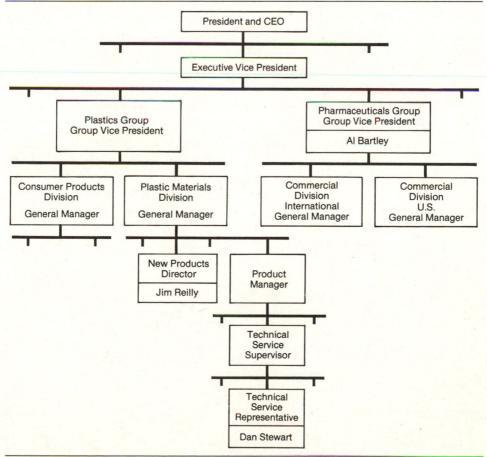

Stewart's task was to look into the market potential for a recently developed product. It was on this six-month assignment that Stewart first learned of Reilly's reputation as a man of driving ambition and cutthroat tactics.

Six years later, in 1970, Reilly asked Stewart to take a job as director of marketing in the domestic Commercial Division of the company's Pharmaceuticals Group. Reilly was then the division's general manager, while Stewart was working as a new products director in the Plastic Materials Division (Exhibit 2). Reilly said that a move to a director of marketing position would give Stewart broader responsibilities and would be an excellent career move. Reilly stressed that the job came with a private office, a contrast to the cubicle characteristic of Pharma middle-level management.

Stewart was not sure that he could get along with a boss who stressed such peripherals as office space and was noted for his impersonal style of management. Stewart had heard that Reilly would send terse demands in letters to employees, when others at his level would typically call in similar circumstances. Moreover, Reilly had told Stewart about the way he had taken charge as a new general manager. Almost immediately he had fired several staff members primarily for the psychological effect of keeping the remaining members of his organization on their toes. Despite his reservations, Stewart took the job because it offered a significant challenge, new learning experiences, and a good deal of contact with people (Exhibit 2).

Jim Reilly

Reilly prided himself on his intimidating tactics and would occa-

Exhibit 2
Pharma Corporation—Partial Organization, June 1970

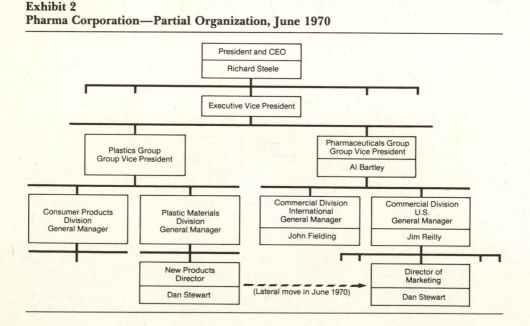

sionally tell Stewart about the various ways he had run rampant over people. He once humiliated Walter Brown, a man nearing retirement, by criticizing him sarcastically in front of his peers. Brown had "taken away" a product from under Reilly's jurisdiction earlier in his career, and it was believed that Reilly had never forgiven him. Yet, Stewart felt he himself received fair treatment in the sense that Reilly's demands were also pushing Stewart to higher achievement. Possibly Reilly needed a more sensitive person like Stewart around to repair the damage he inflicted on others. Reilly seemed to understand Stewart's role. When Stewart had first joined his division, one staff member had complained to Reilly, after a series of misunderstandings, that Stewart was not a good team player. Reilly called Stewart in to inform him of the misunderstanding. "I don't take it seriously," Reilly said. "In fact, I brought you in because you are the kind of team player I need." Over the years, Stewart developed a sense of loyalty to Reilly, and Reilly seemed to keep Stewart's best interests in mind. Regardless of Reilly's style, Stewart considered him the brightest and most articulate manager he had worked with.

Stewart attributed Reilly's rapid rise in Pharma to his ability to sell himself as much as to real accomplishment. Reilly had an uncanny ability to rewrite history. No matter how badly things were going, he was always able to make his superiors believe things would be a lot worse but for Reilly's heroic efforts. In 1972, for instance, Reilly got significant mileage with his superiors from the success of a campaign to change pharmacists' buying habits. Stewart knew that this "tremendous effort" was actually the result of an important external event rather than Reilly's efforts. This situation started with a decision to replace Pentac, a drug with an expiring patent, with Duratab, a superior product whose patent was protected until 1987. Before marketing efforts got underway to change pharmacists' buying habits, an important ingredient used in these products was restricted by the company, which used an internal quota system to cover supply shortages. Both Duratab and Pentac were exempted from this internal allocation, but Reilly called all the key customers and informed them that, since Pentac was on an internal quota system, he would appreciate their switching to Duratab instead. The tactic worked, and Duratab caught on easily. Without revealing these details to top managment, Reilly was able to attribute Duratab's success to his "tremendous marketing effort."

Reilly was a master of the art of impression management. The language he chose was both evocative and provocative. Among his pithy observations on management were: "The only time financial incentives work is the first time you try them," and "In playing the budget approval game with your superiors, underachieve to the point just short of getting fired." Convinced this was an inborn managerial tendency, Reilly squeezed his own subordinates' budgets to the utmost. He insisted that budgets prepared for his approval conform to a format he had personally developed, called RAMS (Reilly's Accounting Magic System). A variant of zero-base budgeting, the procedure forced careful scrutiny of discretionary expenditures. By squeezing subordinates' budgets, Reilly was able to propose his own budgets with a comfortable slack built in. Yet, when Richard Steele, Pharma's president and CEO, asked Reilly if his budget was "stretchy enough," Reilly responded with, "You know I would never play the budget game with you. My budgets are always stretched to a 50% probability of failure." Reilly was well aware of Steele's strong belief in "50–50" budgets.

Steele was so impressed by a business plan Reilly had prepared for his division in one early assignment that he gave Reilly a promotion. Steele referred to the business plan as "Jim's Gem," because he felt it was a unique contribution Jim Reilly had made to the corporation. The plan was followed by five years of declining profits at the division, but this did not hinder Reilly. With his rapid rise in Pharma, Reilly was never at a job long enough to become clearly associated with the consequences of his actions.

In full view of visitors to Reilly's plush office hung a 4-by-4-foot framed organization chart of Pharma Corporation. On it were marked, in bold red, the 13 positions Reilly had held in his 14 years with the company. The blue connecting lines densely crisscrossed the chart, to convey dramatically the breadth of Reilly's experience in his steep ascent up the Pharma ladder. From his current position on this chart radiated several green arrows, with question mark signs at their tips. When anyone, especially the CEO, asked Reilly what his career plans and aspirations were, he would point to the chart, smile confidently, and state flatly: "I want to be president of Pharma."

Scott Williams

In early 1972, Scott Williams was director of field sales on a peer level with Stewart, who was then director of marketing in the U.S. Commercial Division of Pharmaceuticals (see Exhibit 3.) Stewart's work brought him into close contact with Williams. The two held meetings to coordinate the efforts of Williams's sales staff with Stewart's marketing strategies for various products. Stewart knew Williams as a glib, self-assured person who had risen from the position of a pharmaceutical drug detail salesman on the basis of his flamboyance. He thought Williams "talked a good ballgame" but didn't find much substance behind the banter. Williams liked to fall back on clichés (such as "We've got to get back to basic blocking and tackling") in business discussions and enjoyed holding forth at meetings with his jokes. Stewart was surprised in March 1973 when he learned that Reilly had selected Williams to head European Operations in a proposed reorganization that would merge the U.S. and international commercial operations.

Stewart did not want to seem

Exhibit 3
Pharma Corporation—Partial Organization, 1972

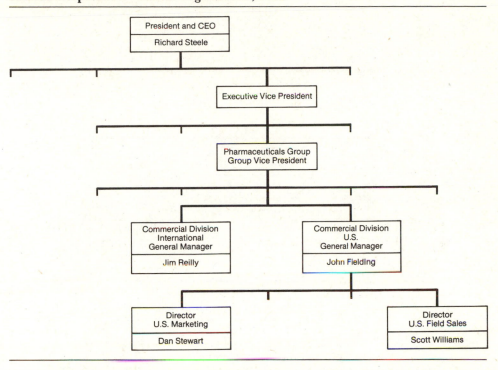

pushy, but he felt that Reilly, of all people, might show some empathy where matters of self-advancement were concerned. He scheduled a meeting and asked him directly whether the European job would not have been a good opportunity for him. Reilly had smiled and said that he didn't think the job would be a good learning experience. Six months later, in September 1973, Stewart was appointed head of worldwide operations with several regional supervisors, including Scott Williams, reporting directly to him. Stewart reported to John Fielding, who reported, in turn, to Reilly (see Exhibit 4).

In this newly created position, Stewart was responsible for worldwide sales, as well as for marketing outside the United States. Stewart was responsible for about 200 employees in the United States and as many overseas. In his first year, Stewart made two- to three-week visits to each of the world regions to assess people, needs, and strategies, in the hope of defining the appropriate leverage for moving products in each geographical market.

John Fielding

Stewart respected John Fielding for his friendliness, his dedication to his job, and the way he kept things organized. You could go to Fielding with a problem, and he would have a folder of relevant materials within reach in his drawer. It seemed to Stewart that Fielding's major weakness was ex-

Exhibit 4
Pharma Corporation—Prior to the Reorganization of September 1974

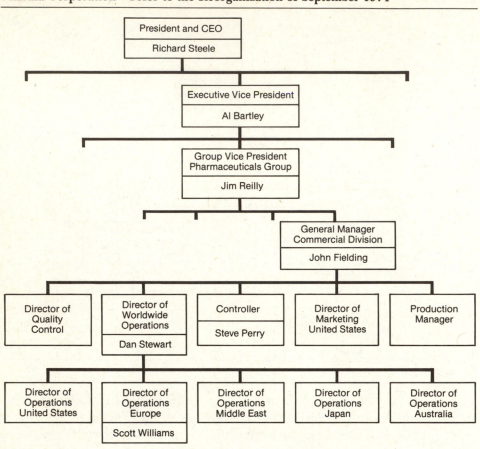

cessive attention to detail. Whereas Reilly operated on a conceptual level and made decisions almost impulsively, Fielding would respond to an idea with "Let me study it," when it was really time for action. Stewart, like Reilly, found errors of omission more frustrating than errors of commission, and thus was put off to see Fielding's pile of pending issues grow while he researched matters. Stewart referred to this phenomenon as paralysis by analysis. Subordinates never seemed to know the status of their ideas because Field-

ing played his cards close to the vest. Stewart gave his own subordinates immediate feedback in order not to frustrate them in this way. For these reasons, Stewart did not feel he could learn much from Fielding and never exerted himself to develop that relationship.

Al Bartley

With 24 years at Pharma, Al Bartley, 56, was regarded as an extremely powerful executive with a strong, intimidating personality. Bartley had long aspired to the company presidency and saw himself as second in command behind Steele. Bartley would say: "If Steele is hit by a truck, I am there to step in." Bartley had spawned and nurtured the early careers of both Reilly and Fielding and referred to them as his sons. Reilly was widely regarded as the favorite son and Fielding, once Reilly's rival, had long since conceded the race. In fact, Fielding viewed Reilly as a sort of mentor.

Bartley was both feared and respected in the organization. It was said that when Reilly once got bleeding ulcers from overwork and tension early in his career, Bartley had told him: "Good, Jim. Welcome to the club." Also in the Bartley folklore was the account of how Bartley intimidated Vic Thomas, who had his own reputation as an intimidator. Bartley assigned Thomas an office adjacent to his own, then, when Thomas was on a field trip, had the wall between their offices broken down. Bartley moved into more than half of Thomas's office, reportedly to "put Thomas in his place." Thomas was bewildered and humiliated when he had to adjust to cramped quarters.

Stewart knew Bartley had a low opinion of Scott Williams and considered him "a joker." At one sales meeting, Williams had just finished his usual round of obscene jokes to warm up the audience when Bartley, who was the keynote speaker, got up and began his speech with obvious disapproval: "I have not heard such bullshit in a long time. . . ."

The Pharmaceuticals Group under Bartley was by far the largest and most profitable group in Pharma. The Commercial Division (Exhibits 4 and 5) was one of three equally large and profitable segments of the Pharmaceuticals Group. The performance of the Pharmaceuticals Group in general, and the Commercial Division in particular, was critically dependent on long-term relationships with important customers. The management of these relationships was thus a vital part of ensuring the success of the business.

The Trip to Munich

In March of 1974, about six months into his new job, Stewart had planned a trip to Munich to meet with Scott Williams as director of European Operations and to evaluate the business situation firsthand. Stewart had wanted to assert himself as a leader, and thus was not pleased to learn that Fielding wished to come along. However, Stewart felt Fielding's personal warmth would make traveling more pleasant, and his eye for detail would help in evaluating the business, especially since he had held Williams's job a few years earlier and was familiar with the operations in Europe.

During their stay in Munich, it became obvious to Stewart and Fielding that Williams did not have a good handle on his business. Williams had been in the job a full year, but in their meetings he kept deferring to his subordinate, Luke White, for answers to such ques-

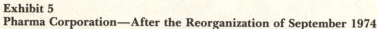

Exhibit 5
Pharma Corporation—After the Reorganization of September 1974

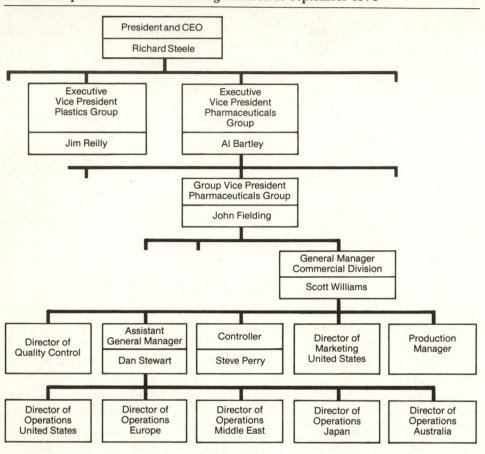

Important Notes:
1. Pharma is a multibillion corporation serving the pharmaceutical and related markets.
2. The Pharmaceuticals group is by far the largest and most profitable part of Pharma.
3. The Commercial Division is one of the three equally large and profitable segments of the Pharmaceuticals group.

tions as the status of several important customers. It seemed that Williams did not know the answers. Fielding knew Luke from his days in Munich and respected his work. Fielding confided his disappointment to Stewart and said, "It's obvious that Luke is doing all the work around here."

Fielding and Stewart also noticed during this trip that Williams resented having to report to Stewart. He felt he should be reporting directly to Reilly. Williams pointed out that, of the four operating companies in Europe (one for each of Pharma's major product groups), he was the only director who did not report directly to a group vice president. Stewart was surprised that Williams was so candid, especially with Fielding present, but he concluded that Williams was a personal friend of

Reilly's, and therefore probably felt quite secure in the organization.

Still before the Storm

About four months later, in late July 1974, Reilly dropped by Stewart's office to ask how Williams was doing. Stewart replied, "He still seems to be learning the business." Reilly appeared to be probing for negatives, but Stewart was reluctant to go into details on the spur of the moment. Stewart's style was to accentuate an individual's positive aspects and mention negative signs only if he or she had been unable to correct them. However, from the expression of concern on Reilly's face as he left the office, Stewart knew something was afoot. He wondered whether he should have said more about Williams, but he expected that Reilly would get the word on Williams from his boss, Fielding, who shared his own doubts about Williams's ability. Consequently, Stewart did not pursue the matter further; budget presentations were coming up, and he was extremely busy preparing for these meetings.

Budget Presentations

Williams arrived in Chicago on August 28, 1974, a week before the annual budget presentations were to begin. Stewart sensed that Williams needed help with his budget and asked Steve Perry, the division controller, to help him with the numbers. Perry ended up spending a great deal of time on Williams's budget, including several

lengthy phone conversations with Luke White in Munich. Stewart was apprehensive about Williams's presentation, but he knew that Williams was a good talker and figured he would make it through the meeting.

Unfortunately, Williams was not in good form. At 10:30 A.M., on Monday, September 4, Williams opened the meeting with an apology to the members of Fielding's staff who had helped him put his presentation together (see Exhibit 4). Williams was literally in tears as he pledged to become a good team player. The meeting dragged through the lunch hour as Fielding and his staff tried to sort through Williams's assumptions and analysis, pushing back a carefully planned agenda for the remainder of the day. Williams had little comprehension of his market and failed to answer questions concerning important customers. Mercifully, Fielding adjourned the meeting at 1 P.M. Stewart had no time to meet with Williams that day, but arranged to see him after lunch the next day at 1 P.M.

Stewart met with Fielding first thing the next morning. Fielding was not surprised by Williams's presentation, given their recent visit to Munich. He and Stewart agreed that Williams should be reprimanded for his performance and placed on "warning." Pharma had no standard procedure for this, so nothing was recorded on paper, but Stewart and Fielding agreed to communicate to Williams that his work was unsatisfactory and that they expected to see improvement. Stewart was to look for a lateral move for Williams, so that Luke White could take over European operations. Their meeting lasted 15 minutes. Stewart relayed these points to Williams at 1 P.M., and Williams took Stewart's warning with uncharacteristic humility.

Japan

Stewart had scheduled a two-week trip to Japan beginning on Friday, September 8, after the budget presentations were concluded. The day before his departure, Stewart ran into Reilly at a regional sales meeting. Reilly told Stewart that he did not think Stewart ought to go to Japan just then. Reilly was uncharacteristically vague about his reasons for saying so, but Stewart could not see any reason for postponing the trip. He decided to proceed to check out operations in Japan, the only region he had yet to visit. Meetings with several major customers had been scheduled months in advance, and Stewart thought it would be a mistake to postpone these meetings at such short notice without a very good reason.

Stewart's trip to Japan was productive. On Friday, September 15, he returned to his hotel room after a long day of meetings to find a message that Reilly's secretary, Linda, had called. Stewart called back and was told that Reilly had asked Stewart to return to Chicago immediately. Linda would not say what was going on, though he sensed that she seemed to know. Stewart guessed that it was some-

thing big, probably a major reorganization. He flew out of Tokyo the next morning.

Throughout the 36-hour trip home, Stewart mulled over the possibilities. If Reilly moved up again, other positions would open up. Was Stewart himself being moved up again so soon? The situation that would soon confront Stewart was the last thing he expected. His curiosity insatiable. Stewart called around upon his return home Sunday morning, September 17. The consensus was that some reorganization was imminent, but no one knew any details.

An old friend had heard a funny rumor that Pharma's President and CEO, Richard Steele, had visited with Williams in early July 1974 and had been "very impressed." As a result, Williams was to be brought in to take over as general manager of the commercial division. Stewart and his friend had a good laugh over that unlikely prospect.

The Bombshell

On Monday, September 18, Stewart entered Fielding's office at 11 A.M. Fielding told Stewart that Williams was to take over the division and that Stewart, along with his peers, would report to Williams. Stewart was to be named assistant general manager, but would retain most of his present responsibilities and subordinates (Exhibit 5). Stewart was stunned by the news. Stewart's anger built up as Fielding explained that Stewart's grade level would be raised. Uncharacteristically, Stewart began to shout until he heard himself screaming. He reminded Fielding of the action they had taken jointly only two weeks earlier, placing Williams on warning. In rage, Stewart rambled on about Williams's failures over the past year, though he knew Fielding was well aware of them.

Fielding offered his sympathy, but he seemed to see the situation as a promotion for Stewart. As it turned out, Fielding himself was being promoted to group vice president, replacing Reilly, who was moving up as executive vice president of the Plastics Group (Exhibit 5). Stewart walked out of the office, shaken.

About an hour later, Williams, who was staying at a local motel, called Stewart. Williams's tone was conciliatory as he spoke briefly about how they would "work well together as a team." Stewart thanked Williams for the call, and took the rest of the day off.

The next day, Stewart met with Reilly and bared his soul.

Stewart: How could you let this happen?

Reilly: This happens all the time. I have passed several capable people by.

Stewart: But this is different. Williams was my subordinate. Give me an example of a subordinate who was suddenly made the superior's boss.

Reilly: I guess I can't give you an example. Such things happen.

Stewart: To an *incompetent* subordinate? Williams was on warn-

ing for unsatisfactory performance.

Reilly: This the first time I am hearing of this.

The one-and-a-half-hour emotional meeting ended with Reilly sympathetic about Stewart's position but unwilling to make any changes. Stewart knew that Reilly would never admit to having made such a mistake, nor would he question his superiors if they had committed this error. Reilly, Stewart knew, both expected and gave military loyalty in dealings with his people. Nevertheless, Stewart felt better after speaking his mind to Reilly.

Stewart came into work around noon the next couple of days and spent several sleepless nights trying to figure out the various scenarios that would help explain the Williams appointment. (A schematic of the key players involved and their interrelationships is shown in Exhibit 6.) Stewart's interactions with Williams in the week following the announcement were tense at best. At times the situation seemed unbearable.

On Monday, September 25, one week after the bad news had been broken, Stewart was contemplating his 11 A.M. meeting with Al Bartley, executive vice president in charge of the Pharmaceuticals Group, who had asked Stewart to meet with him. At 10:50 A.M., just as he was about to depart, Stewart was jolted by a "red signal" call from Reilly on the special line to those with whom Reilly often dealt directly. The buzzing ring and flashing red light

Exhibit 6
Key Players and Their Interrelationships

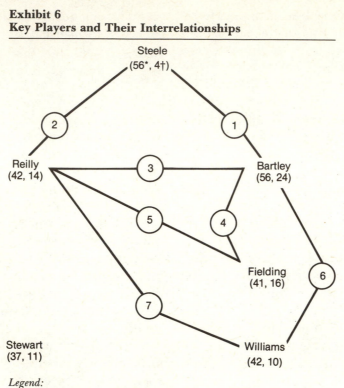

Legend:
   * Age in 1974.
   † Years with Pharma in 1974.

Brief Description of Relationships:
   1.   Relationship is not well understood by Stewart, but it is known that Bartley aspires to become president of Pharma.
   2.   Reilly's recent ascendency is widely attributed to Steele's high opinion of Reilly. Reilly sees Steele as his new mentor.
   3, 4, and 5.   Both Reilly and Fielding are Bartley's protégés, and Bartley refers to them as his "sons," with Reilly generally acknowledged as the "favorite son." Fielding, once Reilly's rival, has conceded the race to Reilly and now sees Reilly as a mentor.
   6.   Bartley has a very low opinion of Williams and considers him "a joke."
   7.   Reilly and Williams are social friends.

demanded immediate attention. Reilly advised Stewart that he should be careful not to lose his temper with Bartley or to go into much detail with him. There was tension in Reilly's voice. Bartley had been Reilly's boss and mentor until the reorganization, but they were at peer level now. Stewart was somewhat surprised that Reilly was so concerned about Bartley's reactions.

As Stewart walked across the Pharma campus toward the corporate offices in Building 701, he still did not know what he should tell Bartley. He was anxious to clear the air by telling him the whole story, but he also knew that his loyalty to Reilly was being tested.

CASE 3–4 Diagnostic Imaging Division— McKenzie-Higgins, Inc.: Context Note*

Chin B. Ho
Vijay Sathe

A pharmaceuticals and consumer products company founded in 1920, McKenzie-Higgins, Inc., stumbled along for years without significant growth or profits. Under the leadership of Will McLeod, however, the company dedicated itself to quality and was able gradually to promote an expanding product line that responded to the needs of the marketplace. Several major developmental programs resulted in an explosion of new technologies and a whole new look for the soon fast-growing company.

As McKenzie-Higgins continued to grow, managers were delegated more responsibility to encourage them to exercise more initiative. New management rules that McLeod outlined became the cornerstone of the company's philosophy and organization. McLeod set out to spur on enthusiastic managers with boundless interest in new uses for applied research in order to find new markets. Initiative and autonomy would be rewarded as long as they conformed to McKenzie-Higgins' general pattern of operation.

This philosophy gave rise to a "corporate entrepreneur" tradition. It was okay to "bootleg" projects and to bend the rules, as long as personal integrity and business ethics were not in question. The mistakes managers might make were not considered as serious in the long run as the mistakes top executives might commit if they stifled initiative. McLeod believed that a top management which was always second guessing lower-level managers would inevitably suppress the entrepreneurial spirit.

Not all initiatives were successful, and some ventures would prove unworkable, but McKenzie-Higgins' managers were given wide latitude and reasonable timetables to convert their ideas into profitable businesses. This acceptance of risk and willingness to try—and sometimes fail—became a hallmark of the company; as McLeod would say, "We will always have some of our units in sick bay." Managers trying to turn around ailing businesses received support and encouragement with the reassurance that even if "the patient" didn't make it, *they* would survive. The unsuccessful risk taker could always return to his or her old job, take another shot at becoming general manager of a division through more bootlegging and rule bending, or opt for some other assignment.

Over the years, the company had been able to continue achieving its goal of generating approximately 20 percent of sales from new products introduced in the previous four years. In 1970, McKenzie-Higgins was a multibillion dollar corporation organized into three principal product groups, encompassing 12 major operating divisions (Exhibit 1).

Strategy and Outlook

For years, McKenzie-Higgins' strategy had been to find new markets. The company's growth for the most part had been internally generated, but acquisitions also played a modest role. Management recognized that not everything could be invented internally; sometimes an acquisition was the obvious answer, either to get into a growth market or to fill out an existing product line.

Explaining McKenzie-Higgins' Success

Observers pointed to two company characteristics in explaining the company's success: corporate entrepreneurship and promotion from within. The former gave each division the freedom to pursue its own objectives within the framework of established corporate

Exhibit 1
McKenzie-Higgins Corporate Organization in 1970

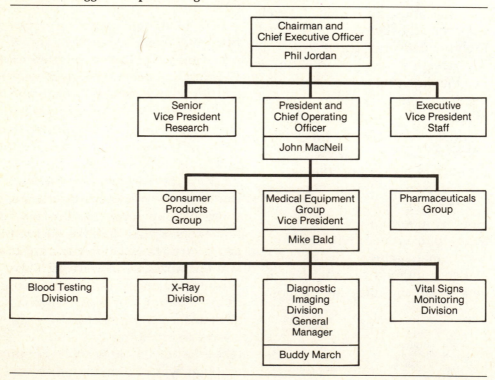

guidelines. Specifically, a division general manager was held accountable for three operating targets: a 20–25 percent return on sales; a 20–25 percent return on stockholders' equity; and real (uninflated) growth in sales of 10–15 percent per year. How the manager met these targets was more or less up to him or her. Moreover, it was clear that the division general manager had full responsibility for the overall growth and health of the division.

Promotion from within demonstrated the firm's long-ingrained habit of self-sufficiency in managerial talent. The company was reluctant to go outside for executive help. Most managers were hired right after college; they were usually engineering graduates from midwestern universities. This personnel practice resulted in low turnover and produced a corps of long-service managers deeply imbued with faith in the company's philosophy. Most of those who reported to the division general manager and above proudly wore their 25th anniversary gold watches. The aspiring corporate entrepreneur knew that the penalty for a product failure would only be lost time. After all, McKenzie-Higgins' growth had been based on its willingness to experiment, on its ability to accept its failures and, more important, to learn from them.

The Medical Equipment Group

The Medical Equipment Group (MEG), consisted of four divisions: blood-testing equipment, X-ray equipment, vital signs monitoring systems, and diagnostic imaging equipment (Exhibit 1). Production, sales, marketing, and research functions were assigned to the division, as they were also in the company's other groups.

Diagnostic Imaging Division

The Diagnostic Imaging Division (DID) under MEG served the scanning and imaging segment of the medical equipment market. Over the years, DID had grown rapidly with the success of a number of products generated internally as well as from acquisitions and joint ventures. In 1970, DID revenues were about $120 million, and although the division was highly profitable and an industry leader, these profitability levels were considered only marginally acceptable by McKenzie-Higgins standards. In addition to its nuclear and computerized tomography product lines, DID also had the Video Image Processing (VIP) Project under its wing.

S. M. "Buddy" March

S. M. ("Buddy") March, who was 50 years old in 1970, was general manager of Microscan when it was acquired in 1960 by Phil Jordan, current chairman and CEO, while he was group vice president of MEG. Earlier in his career at Microscan, Buddy March had developed the first commercially viable fluorescent screen for observing the results of an X-ray examination. In so doing, he spurred the

Exhibit 2
DID Division Organization in 1970

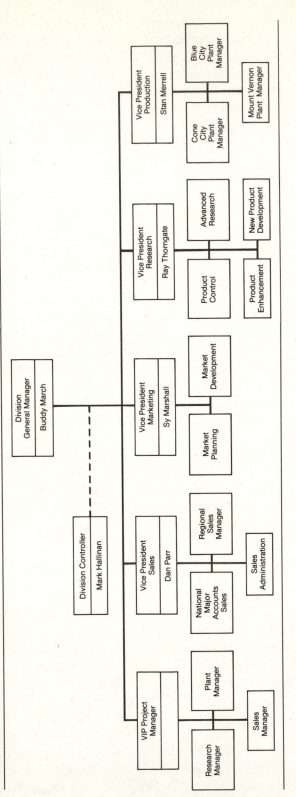

expansion of the X-ray market to include independent physicians as well as large public hospitals. Buddy had also developed an early prototype of a nuclear scanner while still at Microscan. Many of his innovations were patented.

Buddy had continued to foster innovations after he came to McKenzie-Higgins. He perfected the nuclear scanner and screen he had designed at Microscan. Under his leadership, DID developed the first nuclear camera, which used radioactive chemicals to detect abnormalities in tissues, particularly tumors. This innovation helped McKenzie-Higgins penetrate the market for nuclear scanning and imaging, then the largest area of non-X-ray diagnostics.

As the pioneer of nuclear diagnostics, Buddy assisted in developing the Federal Drug Administration's list of acceptable radioactive elements for use with nuclear cameras as well as the equipment's specifications and safety requirements. Because of his reputation as an innovator in this field, he came to be known as the "industry guru." Observers believed that this in-depth industry knowledge and reputation gave Buddy, DID, and McKenzie-Higgins a definite competitive edge over major industry rivals with shorter-tenure general managers (who had correspondingly less industry experience).

Within McKenzie-Higgins, Buddy was noted for his flamboyant ways. He drove a Lincoln Continental to work, whereas the other senior managers all drove more modestly priced American cars. In his business approach Buddy was known for his willingness to go out on a limb for any product that he strongly believed in. Buddy had stuck his neck out for many risky ventures; the Tanaka contract, the Unicare-McKenzie-Higgins joint venture, and the VIP Project were examples of Buddy's bold strokes as a corporate entrepreneur. (The DID organization under Buddy is shown in Exhibit 2.)

CASE 3–5 Buddy March (A): The Tanaka Contract*

Chin B. Ho
Vijay Sathe

Buddy March was chagrined by the conduct of Mike Bald, his boss, and one-time peer, who was eight years younger than he, but for almost two and a half years had been group vice president of McKenzie-Higgins' Medical Equipment Group (MEG). It was Friday afternoon, August 17, 1970. Bald had sent Buddy yet another memo from his 10th-floor office about the

* See Case 3–4, Diagnostic Imaging Division (9–482–079), for background information.

This case was prepared by Chin B. Ho (under the direction of Vijay Sathe).

Tanaka contract. In it he expressed mounting concern about the possible write-off from the program and wanted Buddy to terminate McKenzie-Higgins' dealings with the Tanaka Diagnostic Company of Tokyo.

Buddy was set for a Monday morning meeting with Tanaka executives in San Francisco. As general manager of MEG's Diagnostic Imaging Division (DID), Buddy March had personally engineered the two-part Tanaka contract; he believed that the current setback was only temporary, and more imagined than real. Part one, signed in July of 1969 at Tanaka's head office in Tokyo, had been a one-year agreement, enabling McKenzie-Higgins to distribute exclusively 260 units of the CT–260, a computer tomography scanner. The scanner passed X-ray beams

through the patient's body to detect subtle tissue abnormalities that were previously undetectable with conventional X-ray techniques. The contract allowed McKenzie-Higgins to distribute the CT–260 worldwide, except in the Far East and Australia. With part two, signed six months later in San Francisco, Buddy had secured an exclusive six-year license to manufacture and market the CT–260 under the McKenzie-Higgins brand name.

By August 1970, McKenzie-Higgins' total out-of-pocket cost on the Tanaka program was about $4 million (Exhibit 1). If successful, the program would generate a healthy 23.7 percent return on sales for the first year and close to 30 percent ROS thereafter (Exhibit 2). Buddy felt confident that, given time, demand for the CT–260 would spi-

Exhibit 1
DID's Total Out-of-Pocket Cost on Tanaka
CT–260 Program as of August 17, 1970 ($000)

Up-front payment (65 units)	$2,280
Selling and administrative expenses	1,200
Initial payment on license agreement (part two)	500
DID's total out-of-pocket cost	$3,980

Exhibit 2
Projected Income Statement

I. On First 260 Units	($000)		
Sales (260 × $70,000/unit)	$18,200		(100.0%)
Less Cost of Goods Sold	9,118	(−)	(50.1)
Less Selling and Administrative Expenses	4,768	(−)	(26.2)
Pretax Profit	$ 4,314		(23.7%)
II. Thereafter per Unit	$000 per Unit		
Sales	$ 70.0		(100.0%)
Less Cost of Goods Sold	33.6	(−)	(48.0)
Less Selling and Administrative Expenses	16.2	(−)	(23.1)
Pretax Profit	$ 20.2		(28.9%)

349

ral. Several studies conducted by DID had confirmed Buddy's intuitive expectation of a growth market, and Buddy was convinced the program would ultimately succeed. As the Tanaka "corporate entrepreneur," Buddy knew his reputation and credibility were on the line. He pondered how best to proceed before meeting his Japanese friends the following Monday.

Sticking His Neck out

Less than two years before, in October 1968, Buddy had spotted an early prototype of the CT–260 at a trade show in the Far East. Convinced of the scanner's commercialization potential, Buddy asked DID's vice president of research, Ray Thorngate, to come out to see the scanner. The CT–260 reduced the scan time from two minutes to 20 seconds, which greatly improved image clarity by reducing the blurring effects of involuntary body motion. Realizing that DID researchers could not develop a comparable scanner, Thorngate concurred with Buddy on a proposal to negotiate with Tanaka.

Every member of DID's management team, including Buddy himself, believed that ideally a product like the CT–260 should be developed internally. But Buddy and his top management team knew that McKenzie-Higgins did not possess this rapid-scanning technology and that the investments required for its development could only be justified if several McKenzie-Higgins divisions saw its value. Even then, it

would take at least three to five years to develop a marketable product. Several competitors had recently introduced scanners with faster scan time and better image clarity, thereby threatening McKenzie-Higgins' current products with obsolescence. Buddy, who had directed DID's research efforts to build up a lucrative business in nuclear cameras, felt the urgency of acquiring Tanaka's technology to ensure McKenzie-Higgins' position in the nuclear scanner marketplace. With Thorngate's backing, Buddy was able to sell his idea to his management team. The vice president of production, Stan Merrell, had argued against part one of the contract, which omitted manufacturing rights, but even he had deferred to Buddy.

Buddy knew that Tanaka had been outwitted by a large Japanese company on similar licensing agreements and would perceive manufacturing rights as a bread-and-butter issue. Buddy thought it was more important than anything else for him to develop mutual trust to seal a workable deal with Tanaka. Buddy also recognized the risks involved. The Tanaka contract would mean significant upfront outlays as well as massive marketing efforts to promote a relatively unknown product. But because the CT–260 filled a critical void in DID's product line, Buddy decided to stick his neck out.

When Buddy, Thorngate, and the corporate negotiator, Eric Jensen, first met in early 1969 to decide on a bargaining strategy, Buddy suggested a give-and-take approach. With the support of DID's vice president of research, Ray Thorngate, Buddy proposed that the company be satisfied with a provisional contract granting exclusive marketing rights. Manufacturing rights could be sought and secured at a later date, after Tanaka had become comfortable in dealing with McKenzie-Higgins. Jensen, a seasoned negotiator, had not been convinced. He would be responsible for legal details of the contract and had favored a tough approach of "asking for everything and then gradually backing down." Buddy and Thorngate expressed reservations, but they acceded to Jensen in order not to upset the 10th-floor executive suite on the eve of the initial Tanaka negotiations.

The Arigato Magic

Buddy had visited Japan on several occasions. He had studied the Japanese management system and had spent a good deal of time entertaining Japanese business leaders. Buddy even acquired a rudimentary understanding of the Japanese language and became familiar with Japanese body language. By the time of the Tanaka contract, Buddy was well versed with the Japanese and their business methods.

Shionoya Shuichi, Tanaka's owner-president, had previously dealt with another McKenzie-Higgins division, which had offended him by sending a junior executive to represent the company in business negotiations. A shrewd businessman, Shionoya decided to give McKenzie-Higgins one more chance and, when Buddy first contacted him, informed Buddy that he would be interested in exploring a business deal with DID. In Tokyo, Buddy was greeted by Yamamoto Mitsuo, Tanaka's executive vice president and chief operating officer, who escorted Buddy to meet with Shionoya. Charmed by Buddy's ability to converse in broken Japanese (his "arigato" magic), Shionoya agreed to further negotiations with McKenzie-Higgins.

In July 1969, after several meetings with Shionoya, Buddy flew to Japan for the negotiations. It had been agreed that Thorngate and Jensen would join him a few days later. Shionoya had invited "my friend March-san," as he had come to call Buddy during the months of their acquaintance, to his home for the weekend prior to the negotiations. At Shionoya's suburban home on the east side of Tokyo, Buddy was surprised to see a huge March-san portrait in the family living room. Although visibly embarrassed, Buddy realized that he had been accepted as an honored guest of Shionoya-san. There followed a lot of entertaining. Buddy and Shionoya visited teahouses for drinks and dinner. No actual business was discussed during the weekend; the two merely spent time nurturing their maturing friendship.

Successful Negotiation

Buddy was aware that difficulties in many Japanese-American joint ventures were caused partly by the language barrier, but mainly by a lack of understanding on each side of how the other did business and negotiated. For example, to the Japanese, a good personal relationship was more important than a tightly written contract. It was also imperative that no party suffer a loss of face in the negotiations. Determined to avoid any difficulties, Buddy worked hard at building a strong rapport with his Tanaka counterparts.

When Thorngate and Jensen arrived several days later as planned, Shionoya invited them, with Buddy, to a resort in the foothills of Fujiyama. Three other Tanaka executives also went along: Yamamoto, attorney Akiba Hiroshi (who also acted as the group's interpreter), and manufacturing vice president Ikeda Joōkuno. The purpose of this "Camp Fuji" meeting was to have an informal get-together to thrash out contested issues without a loss of face. Both sides agreed to test trial balloons on each other's final offer. In between, there was a lot of bantering, eating, and entertaining. Mutual acceptance was evident from the very beginning; the Tanaka executives and the Americans took to each other like ducks to water.

Camp Fuji made the final negotiations smoother. The concluding formal bargaining session began three days later at Tanaka's head office at 8 A.M. While the two attorneys, Jensen and Akiba, haggled away, the others watched. Whenever things got out of hand, they stepped in and reestablished an amicable and conciliatory tone. Akiba held firm to Tanaka's position on not allowing anyone else to manufacture the CT–260. The haggling continued until, at 4:30 P.M., Buddy pulled Jensen aside and forcefully told him that it was time to sign the contract. After some further discussion, Jensen relented and announced that McKenzie-Higgins would accept Tanaka's latest offer. The company would sign a one-year agreement committing the company to purchase 260 units of the CT–260 within 12 months of shipment of the first unit. McKenzie-Higgins was to have exclusive distribution throughout the world, except in the Far East and Australia.

Back from the Tokyo trip, Buddy called a meeting of his top management team to explain the Tanaka contract. The vice president of production, Stan Merrell, showed some concern but once again deferred to Buddy. As usual, division controller Mark Hallinan was suspicious of the sales forecast provided by the flamboyant VP of sales, Dan Parr, and indicated concern that the program might lose quite a lot of money initially. But all in all, no one showed strong resistance, and the program was given the go-ahead. As general manager in the McKenzie-Higgins system, Buddy was authorized to make the agreement, provided it was approved by the corporate lawyers who had to ensure that McKenzie-Higgins' technology was not being given away inappropriately in crosslicensing, that the interest of the other divisions were protected, and that antitrust matters were examined. This approval had been obtained.

Problems in the Field

The first CT–260 was shipped from Japan and sold in the United States in late October 1969. Two months later, in December 1969, Buddy and his team met with the Tanaka executives in San Francisco to negotiate part two of the contract. As Buddy had anticipated, the evolving trust between the two sides made the deliberations much smoother than they had been during the initial contract negotiations. Buddy obtained an exclusive six-year license DID had been seeking to manufacture and market the CT–260 (except in the Far East and Australia) under the McKenzie-Higgins brand name.

Then, in late March 1970, three months after part two of the contract had been signed, DID began to receive letters and phone calls from irate customers who complained that, at $70,000 per unit, they had expected better performance. Expressing concern that the CT–260's image quality had diminished significantly, DID customers wanted their units retested and, if necessary, replaced at no additional cost. To protect McKenzie-Higgins' business reputation, Buddy wrote off all 30 of the malfunctioning units and shipped them back to Japan for further testing and redesign. Buddy also sent three of his best engineers for the project over to Japan to help his Tanaka colleagues.

Buddy's Boss, Mike Bald

By August 1970, several problems with the CT–260 had been rectified with design changes, but DID was still awaiting a modification breakthrough on an important component, the screen refractor. Buddy's boss, MEG group vice president Mike Bald, was becoming increasingly anxious about the Tanaka program and the potential write-off if it failed. He had expressed his mounting concern about the program in numerous memos, which Buddy referred to as "snowflakes from the 10th floor." Buddy had heard that Bald had also ridiculed the Tanaka program in informal exchanges with others, such as over lunch, referring to it as a "rotten scanner" and "Buddy's bad bargain."

Bald's constant sniping, on this program and others over the past two and a half years had intensified Buddy's irritation because it reopened old wounds. Bald had been Buddy's colleague as general manager of McKenzie-Higgins' X-Ray Division for eight years. In March 1968, President Jordan had appointed Bald as MEG vice president, with Buddy reporting to Bald. Buddy felt deeply hurt because he had thought the job was rightfully his. Buddy had then seriously considered leaving McKenzie-Higgins to start his own company, but his wife had talked him out of it. And Buddy, who wanted to be "a big frog in the industry pond and make the pond grow," felt he could do more with the resources he commanded at McKenzie-Higgins than he could as an independent entrepreneur. Still, he had never totally accepted the younger Bald as his boss. In turn, Buddy felt Bald had never learned how to work properly with him, and the two remained awkward rivals.

Bald, who was 42 in 1970, had joined McKenzie-Higgins in 1950 right out of college. He had come up through the production function and had made his mark in the X-Ray Division when, as VP of production, he was credited with having achieved major cost reductions and manufacturing improvements. These contributions had helped propel Phil Jordan, who was then division general manager of the X-Ray Division, to group vice president of MEG in 1960, and Bald had moved up to replace Jordan. Eight years later, in early 1968, Bald was promoted to group vice president of MEG when Jordan became president of McKenzie-Higgins.

Buddy believed Jordan's loyalty to Bald, who had helped his career, had a lot to do with Bald's appointment as group vice president of MEG. The X-Ray Division had performed below the McKenzie-Higgins operating targets during Bald's tenure as general manager, and Buddy attributed this to Bald's inadequate understanding of the technology and failure to provide the necessary leadership. Buddy viewed Bald as a "personable man, extremely honest, and with a lot of smarts." He also thought Bald was a good politician and one who evoked considerable sympathy and

admiration in McKenzie-Higgins because of having overcome a bout with polio and the handicap of an artificial leg. However, it seemed to Buddy that Bald was "in over his head" as group vice president of MEG, and he wished that Bald had been allowed to advance in the production area instead.

Bald showed signs of being paranoid about the Japanese. Apparently he had been "burned" in earlier business dealings with a Japanese company, by what he considered an ingeniously worded agreement. This called for technology exchange and carried a license to manufacture the Japanese company's products under the McKenzie-Higgins name, but it did *not* offer McKenzie-Higgins exclusive distribution in the United States. Bald felt cheated because he believed the Japanese company was competing in the United States with its latest technology products and sharing only the older generation of technology with McKenzie-Higgins. Bald had boasted about his great deal before the debacle had unfolded and had never admitted subsequently to having negotiated a poor contract. But ever since, he sought to portray the Japanese as untrustworthy and had strongly opposed any dealings with "those people."

Buddy felt much more secure with the Japanese. He believed that the CT–260 product would have clear advantages over the competition once the screen refractors were perfected, and he continued to trust the Tanaka executives to deliver on their contractual obligations. Indeed, Buddy felt Tanaka had acted in good faith by not holding McKenzie-Higgins to the original timetable, which called for the sale of 200 units to DID by August 1970. Only 30 units in all had been shipped, and all had been returned to Japan for design modifications and further testing. Consequently, Buddy felt that his boss was putting unnecessary pressure on him. He also thought Bald was jealous of his, Buddy's, emerging success in his business dealings with the Japanese.

Buddy's Options

On Friday afternoon, August 17, 1970, Buddy had three main options: (1) try to cancel the Tanaka contract, (2) renegotiate better terms, and (3) maintain the present status of the contract. Bald favored the first option which, in Buddy's opinion, hardly made any economic sense. Cancelling the Tanaka contract would merely limit McKenzie-Higgins' losses to $4 million. Buddy also believed that the second option was silly since they had already secured an exclusive, irrevocable license to manufacture and market the CT–260. Renegotiation would be seen as bad faith in the eyes of the Tanaka people.

Buddy concluded that maintaining the present status of the Tanaka contract made the most sense. He could informally pressure his Japanese friends to appreciate his situation and to speed up the development of a new screen refractor. Buddy believed Shionoya and his colleagues would respond to a soft-sell approach rather than to arm twisting.

Ignoring Bald

Buddy decided to meet with the Tanaka team on Monday in San Francisco as planned. In ignoring Bald, Buddy felt he could count on President Phil Jordan for support. Jordan had brought Buddy into the company when he had acquired Microscan, and Buddy did not sense that his special relationship with Jordan had changed as a result of Bald's recent promotion. Also, as a division general manager, Buddy knew that he could exercise his judgment with a fair amount of autonomy. As one McKenzie-Higgins executive put it, "Insubordination is tolerated here if it is within reasonable bounds and results indicate it was justified." Confident that he would be right and willing to pay the penalty if he was wrong, Buddy decided to ignore Bald's copious memos. He felt certain that his business hunch would turn out to be accurate; excuses could always be found for ignoring memos.

READING 3–1 Consulting for Organizational Change

Fritz Steele

Consultants' Roles

When a person is functioning as a consultant, what kinds of things is he likely to be doing? One way of briefly describing these activities is to think metaphorically about the various roles a consultant might play in a client system, that is, traditional roles which would be descriptive of his behavior within or his function for the client system. The following are role metaphors that have helped me see more clearly what it was that I was actually providing when I was functioning as a consultant.

Teacher   At times, my main function has been simply to teach behavioral science theories or practical applications to clients. I use didactic processes, such as seminars, and experiential processes, such as short laboratory training sessions; but in either case I am defined as the teacher, and clients are the students.

Student   As well as being the teacher, there are situations where

my most effective role is as a learner or student. As I will discuss in the chapter on learning from consulting, this is a useful role because it both aids future consultation and models a learning role that I hope to transfer to the client: I hope to make him more curious about human behavior and more of a student of how things happen in groups and organizations. My best vehicle for demonstrating that is to be visibly engaged in that role myself.

Detective   I am often engaged in a kind of detection process, trying to discover evidence and fit it together in ways that will help me and the clients develop accurate pictures of the system, its problems, and its strengths. Because of its emotional potency, I chose this role to describe in detail in the chapter "Consultants and Detectives."

Barbarian   One of the reasons why human systems are not always self-correcting (i.e., able to readjust when they slide into ways of working that are not optimal) is that stable norms develop about what a "good" or "civilized" person ought to be like if he is to be a member of the system. Some of these norms facilitate productivity, growth, and enjoyment in the system; and others merely provide predictability or security, often at the cost of productivity or growth. As a consultant, one of my most important roles is to be a violator of comfortable but limiting norms: to be a barbarian who does not behave so politely as the rest of the members in the system. For instance, most groups develop taboos about openly discussing such issues as salaries or inadequate performance. As a barbarian, I often raise these issues, particularly if they are central to the group's problems. Not only does it help the group to deal with the issue (which is otherwise out of bounds and incapable of being influenced), but it provides a reflection to the group of their own self-created boundaries. I try to facilitate a process where they reexamine those boundaries and push back the ones that are blocking them excessively. Technical consultants serve as barbarians by questioning accepted ways of thinking about a problem area and not accepting the conventional wisdom which everyone inside the system thinks of as proper and right.

Clock   There have been projects where my most important role seemed to be that of a timer or clock for the client system to watch. When there was a regular schedule of visits that I would make to a system, I felt a bit like one of the little figures that come out of Bavarian clocks as the hour is struck. My presence (or the thought of it coming soon) served as a spur to clients to be thinking and experimenting so that they would have something to show me for the time in between my visits.

Monitor   Related to my role of clock is the role of monitor, where my function basically is to observe

the client in action and to provide an independent view of how I see him operating according to standards which we mutually agree are relevant to his problems and aspirations. I serve as a monitoring system set up and calibrated according to some model of effective task behavior.

Talisman   Another function of my presence in a system actually has little to do with what information I provide in my observations. In my role as taisman it is the *fact* of my presence that is important. This fact provides a sense of security and legitimacy which allows the client to feel comfortable enough to experiment in areas where he might not act without support.

Advocate   Another role I often play is that of an advocate of the values or principles of relations between the organization and the individual. There are certain fundamental qualities which I feel this relationship must have in order to be decent, nonexploitive, personally satisfying, and productive for both; and as an outsider I am often in a better position than members of the system to advocate these values openly. Of course, if I become too consistently at odds with those principles valued by the clients, I shall lose my access to the system (by withdrawing myself or by being fired).

Ritual Pig   Finally, there have been instances where, in retrospect, my function with a client system was to be a ritual pig.* By this I mean that I served as an outside threat which needed to be killed off (fired, challenged, resisted) in order for the system to develop enough sense of solidarity and po-tency to be able to begin some difficult self-change. I used to think that when my help was rejected, and a project ended in the early stages, that this meant no change would occur in the client system. Sometimes this is the case, but I have also seen instances where this event was the spur which drove the clients to begin to examine themselves in earnest. Hence my feeling of having been the ritual pig.

---

* I say in retrospect, because it is very difficult to recognize this role while in the middle of playing it out. It is hard for me to discriminate at the time whether we are going through a sacrificial ritual, or whether my rejection will be the end of the process with the client really preferring the status quo.

Orientation There are two major themes in this part of the book. First, culture change may or may not accompany behavior change, and vice versa. Second, to be effective, managers must conceive and implement organizational change using approaches and methods that flow from this understanding.

Parts 2 and 3 of the book dealt with how a manager can better anticipate, enter, get established, and operate within the prevailing culture and related corporate realities, without really changing them. Attention now turns to the question of how these organizational realities may be altered when responsible managerial action calls for this.

A basic conceptual framework was shown in Chapter 3. Model A of that framework, which was held in the background in Parts 2 and 3, will now be brought center stage (see Figure 3–1 in Chapter 3). Also, relating Model A to the three levels of culture introduced in Chapter 1, attention will focus specifically on how changes in the first level of culture (actual organizational behavior patterns or behavior) and the third level of culture (internalized beliefs and values shared by people in the organization—our definition of culture) affect each other and are mediated by the second level (cultural communications and justifications of behavior).

It will be seen that changes in behavior can lead to changes in culture, and vice versa. However, this is not inevitable or automatic, in

Part 4

Influencing change in culture and related corporate realities

part because of the role played by cultural communications and justifications of behavior. Depending on the situation, it may take from several months to several years before changes in one get reflected in changes in the other. Accordingly, it pays to distinguish between behavior change and culture change for analytical purposes and to examine both simultaneously.

There are three change possibilities (Figure IV–1). First, there can be some culture change without any behavior change (vertical movement up the left side of the figure). Individuals may change one or more beliefs and values but be unable to change their corresponding behavior. An example

from everyday life is people who believe smoking is bad for them but are unable to kick the habit. In the organizational context, a work group may have bought into new beliefs and values in an education or training program (such as the values of valid information, free and informed choice, and internal commitment to the choice) but find it difficult to adopt the necessary behaviors.[1] Or one or more basic assumptions shared by people in an organization may be altered as a result of major changes in the environment, calling for new skills and behaviors that the people have not yet been able to acquire and perform. Examples are companies affected by deregulation (changing

Figure IV–1
Change Possibilities: Relating Behavior Change and Culture Change

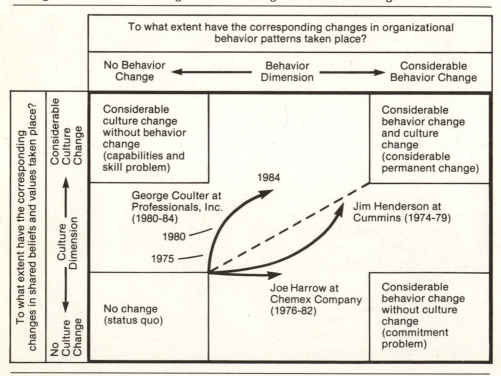

the assumption about the importance of competition) or international competition (changing the assumption about the importance of quality, in the U.S. automobile industry for example). In such cases, sufficient numbers of people may have "bought into" a new belief or value so as to alter an important shared assumption, without yet being able to change their corresponding behavior.[2] A case in point, which will be used for purposes of illustration in this part of the book, is the experience of George Coulter, managing partner of a fairly large accounting firm (about 300 partners) that we will refer to as Professionals, Inc:

Major changes in government regulation and industry structure since the mid-70s had increased competitive activity and made it increasingly clear that accounting firms would have to operate very differently in order to survive and succeed in the 80s. When George, who had risen rapidly through the ranks, took over in 1980 at the age of 45, a majority of the firm's partnership had given him the mandate to make changes that would enable the firm to not only cope with the new external reality but in fact take advantage of it.

Three important areas in which a majority of the firm's partnership had changed their basic assumptions over the previous several years were as follows (listed in decreasing order of the proportion of the membership who had "bought into" the new belief and values): (1) "Technical excellence is the key to establish-

ing and maintaining our audit clients" had changed to "Technical superiority *and* selling skills are critical in the audit business." (2) "Our management consulting practice is important but is secondary to, and can operate relatively independent of, the audit side of our house" had changed to "We must have more collaboration between the two, so that we can better leverage our management consulting practice off our audit client base." And (3) "Each local office can operate relatively autonomously as long as it is doing well" had changed to "All our offices must collaborate more to achieve better utilization of our resources and deeper penetration into selected industry segments."

After four years of George Coulter's leadership, an even greater proportion of the partnership had bought into the new assumptions, but the percentage of people who had been able to behave in accordance with these assumptions was still relatively small—in other words, changes in culture were leading changes in behavior.

In this case and others like it, the basic problem for the people involved is to acquire the necessary capabilities and skills in their relevant organizational context—that is, on-the-job rather than such off-the-job learning as in training laboratories or in management seminars (see Figure IV–1).[3]

In other cases, one or more individuals or groups within the organization may become convinced that the organization must change, but others in the organization may not have bought into the need for change. If those who feel the need for organizational change have sufficient status (typically the leadership does), they may be able to induce compliance from others in the organization because of their direct influence on them and also through the use of organizational systems to monitor and enforce the desired behavior change (see Model A, Figure 3–1). Depending on their position, change initiators may be unable to rely on formal systems but may still be able to exert some influence via the social and political system. Others, including those in leadership positions, may be able to issue directives and rely on changes in the formal systems as well (structures, measurements, controls, incentives, etc.) to try to induce the desired change. A case of this vintage that will be used for illustrative purposes in this part of the book concerns Joe Harrow, who was brought in from the outside to turn around a chemical company, call it Chemex:

When Joe took over Chemex at the age of 57 in 1976, he embarked to transform the company's middle and upper managers (some 1000 of them) in three basic ways: (1) from a manufacturing "mind set" to a market orientation, (2) from a seat-of-the-pants management to a more analytical approach, and (3) from relatively short-term, opportunistic thinking to longer-term, strategic thinking. To help effect these changes, Joe introduced several new analytical tools (such as PIMS, Profit Impact of Marketing Strategies), procedures (such as MBO, Management by Objectives), and structures (such as reorganization of the company by SBUs, Strategic Business Units). Further, to try to make these changes as rapidly as possible, Joe relied on external consultants, heavy use of incentives, and top-down implementation. Joe was personally committed to making these changes by utilizing the existing talent, rather than by mass firings and hirings of people at these levels. Some people did leave, and a few were brought in at senior levels from the outside, but in the main Joe Harrow succeeded in retaining most of the managers he had inherited.

When he decided to step aside six years later, in 1982, to make way for a rising star he had carefully groomed for his position, Joe could take satisfaction in the orderly succession and other improvements he had carefully orchestrated at Chemex. One of his disappointments, however, was that most managers were not attributing the company's improved performance and stronger financial condition to the analytical tools, techniques, and systems he had introduced ("Joe's alphabets," as they came to be called internally). Although the managers were using this new methodology, many of them didn't really seem to be committed to it. They attributed the company's success instead to several company acquisitions and divestitures, as well as to careful asset management, for which the rising star got most of the credit.

The basic problem in this case, and others like it, is lack of commitment (Figure IV–1). People go along because they feel they would lose valued rewards by not complying or because they like the incentives they get by conforming, rather than because they really believe in or value what they are being asked to do.

Finally, there can be both behavior change and culture change. This is permanent change in the sense that people genuinely believe and value their new way of doing things. Such change is likely to be more permanent because it is mutually reinforcing and thus self-sustaining—the behavior is intrinsically rewarding because people really believe in it and value it, and this in turn reinforces the behavior. The case of Jim Henderson at Cummins, which was used for illustration in Part 1, will be further discussed in this part of the book as an example of such a change (Figure IV–1). Over a period of about five years, behavioral changes were followed by changes in two shared assumptions held by the 200 or so middle and upper managers at Cummins. First, the assumption "Top management will tell us what to do when there is a problem" was replaced by the assumption "All managers should take personal responsibility for solving problems." Second, the important shared assumption "Operate informally without systems" was modified to "Use systems to do the routine work, operate informally to expedite." Why behavior change led to culture change, in this case, resulting in permanent change, but may not always do so (as in the case of Joe Harrow) will be explained.

In sum, permanent change may not be achieved for a considerable period of time, either because the people involved cannot learn the required capabilities and skills (no behavior change) and/or because the people in the organization are not really committed to the change (no culture change). In this part of the book, guidelines are presented to help managers decide how critical each of these changes is in light of their particular situation. Concepts and techniques that enable managers to create these changes are discussed. We begin by looking at behavior change in Chapter 11. Culture change is the subject of Chapter 12.

Chapter 11

Changing organizational behavior patterns

Orientation   Some of the topics dealt with in this chapter are well covered in the available management literature. These topics will be only briefly reviewed here. The recommended supplementary readings at the end of the book (numbers 18, 19, and 20) as well as the sources cited in the notes for this chapter may be consulted by those seeking additional information.

As depicted in Model A of Figure 3–1, a change in organizational behavior patterns with no change in organizational culture is possible because of the impact of leadership and the influence of systems in the organization. In order to see how this occurs, we need to understand organizational resistance to change and the way in which it is ovecome. The following formulation, adapted from the representation proposed by Michael Beer,[1] is a useful shorthand means for keeping track of what is needed to overcome the human tendency to resist change:

$$\underset{\text{(Resistance)}}{R} \quad < \quad \underset{\text{(Motivation)}}{M1} \quad \times \quad \underset{\text{(Model)}}{M2} \quad \times \quad \underset{\text{(Method)}}{M3}$$

This formulation does not denote a strict arithmetical operation, but implies that resistance to change is overcome when people feel a sufficient incentive to change (they are motivated), when they know what new behavior is expected of them (the new model is clear), and when the change process is appropriate to the needs of the situation (the method used is suited to prevailing conditions). The multiplicative relationship implies that unless all three facilitators are present to some degree, resistance will be very difficult to overcome.

Resistance to Change (R)

In order to anticipate resistance, one must understand the relevant prior history. Without an awareness of what changes were tried before, why they worked or didn't work, how people attributed the success or failure of prior attempts, and what they learned from it, a manager is unlikely to anticipate the resistance the proposed changes will encounter (see recommended supplementary reading number 18, "Change Masters and the Intricate Architecture of Corporate Culture Change," by Rosabeth Moss Kanter, for more on this). Further, resistance cannot be fully anticipated. When it is encountered, it is important to view resistance as an invitation to better understand oneself and the organization, as discussed in the previous chapter.

This is not to suggest that managers should ease up or stop the change process when resistance is encountered. Since meaningful change frequently involves pain before there can be much gain, resistance usually signals that the change process is on track. However, this is an assumption that must be tested. Trying to understand the underlying reasons for the resistance may reveal unanticipated problems with one's approach or offer additional insight into the organization and its workings. Some of the substantive and emotional reasons for people's resistance were discussed in Chapter 10. Let us now further examine the particular reasons why people resist having to behave in new ways.

People don't like to make the investment needed to develop new professional skills if the personal benefit does not seem worth the time, effort, and energy it takes to learn them. The more unattractive the required personal investment is, the greater the likely resistance. At Cummins, for instance, some people resisted the change because it required them to use new information and control systems (such as materials requisition planning) which they didn't understand or value and felt uncomfortable with. Some people may simply feel unable to learn the new skills required, regardless of the question of investment. Such people are also likely to resist the new behavior because they feel incapable of changing.

Second, new behavior may be resisted simply because habits are hard to break. This statement may be easily accepted on the basis of everyday experience, but recent research provides new insight into why this is so.[2] Essentially, it is because much day-to-day behavior occurs with minimal information processing and is guided by well-learned general scripts made up of a coherent sequence of expected events by the individual.[3] Each individual carries in his or her head perhaps several hundred such scripts, one for each predictable sequence of required behaviors. They serve a valuable function by freeing the mind of the need to process information consciously and act on it, a time-consuming activity that the mind seeks to conserve. Such "mindless behavior" cannot apply to new activity until it is repeated often enough that the new script becomes part of the person's repertoire. Until then, the individual must think about what behavior to adopt, which the mind prefers not to have to do. Surprising as it may seem, we prefer behavior that no longer requires thoughtful deliberation and resist that which does.

When behavior changes take place within the organizational context, they may require development of new working relationships and neglect established ones. Any disruption in the prevailing social system is apt to be resisted by those who experience this loss of existing social relationships and the need to build new ones.[4] At Cummins, for instance, the people valued informal relationships as much for their task value ("expediting") as for their social value ("company is part of the family"). The changes may also have implications for the prevailing political system.[5] For instance, new behavior may imply new types of expertise, which is one base of personal power (Chapter 8). Similarly, the new working relationships may alter the various dependency relationships and thus alter relative power. Individuals or groups who expect to lose power as a result of the required new behaviors are also quite likely to resist them. At Cummins, those skilled in the art of expediting stood to lose the most power as a result of the proposed changes because their contributions would become less valuable once the systems took over part of the critical day-to-day work they did so well.

This is one reason changes in *organizational* behavior patterns involve more than a mere aggregation of individual changes.[6] Questions concerning social and political resistance must also be considered. At Professionals, Inc., for instance, the proposed changes meant less power for the audit function (the traditional powerhouse in accounting firms) and more power for the management consulting function (traditionally the "poor cousin" in these firms). The changes also required greater collaboration between these two functions, which was difficult because each function typically had a poor image and relationship with the other. (Auditors: "We don't trust most of those guys—they can screw up our client relationships." Management consultants: "The auditors don't understand the nature of our work—project oriented—and feel threatened by our generalist competence.") The changes also implied less autonomy and power for the local offices, since the partner-in-charge of the local office was traditionally the "king of the hill." They implied more clout for the headquarters, which the local offices generally resented, saying, "The people at corporate have forgotten what it takes to make the cash register ring."

Thus managers have to pay careful attention not only to helping individuals learn the new skills and behaviors, but also to the overall process of orchestrating and implementing change so as to overcome such social and political resistance. These topics will be considered later in this chapter.

Motivation to Change (M1)

Energy needed to overcome resistance to change comes from two principal sources—intrinsic and extrinsic motivation.

Intrinsic Motivation

Intrinsic motivation is present when people want to learn and adopt the new behavior because they genuinely believe in or value the need for change. At Professionals, Inc. people internalized the new beliefs and values because of clear and irrefutable evidence from the environment over a period of several years, which convinced them of the need for change. For instance, they had witnessed the loss of several major audit clients, who had been "theirs" for a number of years, to more aggressive competitors. Each successive shock was accompanied by the same evidence and inference: "We lost another key audit client because we are not selling ourselves as aggressively as the others." The evidence finally led to a change in an important shared assumption—from "Technical excellence is key to our audit business" to "Technical superiority *and* selling skills are critical." This transformed assumption was reinforced and became gradually more widely shared and taken for granted as its validity was demonstrated in the marketplace. The few audit partners who were doing exceptionally well were those who combined technical mastery with excellent selling skills.

This illustration highlights two important features of the process by which environmental threats, crises, and other major events can help produce intrinsic motivation. First, there must be undeniable evidence that the survival and success of the people in the organization are at stake if the changes are not made. It usually takes several major events that lead to the same conclusion before people will be convinced of the need for a basic change. Thus, although a particular crisis may be the proverbial straw that breaks the camel's back, serving to crystallize and legitimize a new assumption, it must be recognized that the forces leading to such change typically will have been building for some time.[7] For instance, the crisis at Chrysler may have helped give visibility and legitimacy to important new assumptions, such as the importance of quality. However, several preceding years of losing market share to the imports were attributed in part to the better quality of the imported cars. This trend had gradually convinced people about the importance of quality. Similarly, George Coulter's election to managing partner at age 45 was an important event symbolizing and legitimizing the fact that the partnership had bought into the new assumptions that George had lived and risen by, but the forces leading up to this event that had helped set the stage for it had been building for several years prior to this event.

The second important feature to note is that intrinsic motivation builds as the new assumptions are tested and found to be valid; that is, as it is seen that they work. Such intrinsic motivation builds further as people get good at the new way of doing things and become skillful at it. As indicated in Chapter 6, doing a job well leads to liking the job more, and this leads to enhanced self-esteem and intrinsic motivation to continue to engage in the new behavior.[8] In orchestrating change, therefore, it is important to build-in feedback loops and other mechanisms that make early success visible to the organization so that people can derive positive reinforcement and intrinsic motivation from it.

To be effective, managers must anticipate environmental trends and get the people in the organization to perceive their significance before things get so bad that the importance of the need for change is self-evident. It helps to get at least some people to try the new way of doing things and become skillful at it early in this process in order to allow sufficient time for their success to spread in the organization and thus build further intrinsic motivation for the change.

It is not clear how effective Jim Henderson at Cummins was in this regard. He says on the videotape accompanying the written case that there was no strategy of waiting around for a crisis to come so he could implement the desired changes: "The crisis simply came before we had a chance to fix the problem." However, he admits the crisis did help in implementing the change. Some people may fault Henderson for not anticipating the inventory crisis and moving to remedy the problem before it became a major headache. Considering the fact that his two predecessors had failed in part because they had moved too quickly to implement such changes, I would argue that Henderson was smart to wait for an opportunity like the one provided by the crisis, if indeed he waited, either consciously or otherwise (his comments on the videotape notwithstanding). There was also little time to move earlier due to the rapid expansion of the early 1970s.

In any case, the crisis at Cummins, and the events preceeding it, did not provide the kind of irrefutable and undeniable evidence that the events at Professionals, Inc. provided. After all, Cummins was ahead of the competition and had successfully weathered downturns before. Henderson must be given high marks for getting his managers to see the inherent worth of the changes he was proposing. His unannounced plant visits and the weekly inventory meetings, wherein he got his managers to see the significance of the environmental data and engaged them in problem solving helped generate intrinsic motivation in his managers.

Joe Harrow's problem in this connection was similar to Jim Henderson's because the Chemex managers didn't believe that the new methodology Joe was championing would help improve the company's performance. The connection between the methods and the company's results was hard to establish and validate, and people remained largely unconvinced of the efficacy of "Joe's alphabets" after complying with his methods for six years. Joe was up against a difficult challenge in this area, but there is no evidence that he did much to try to overcome it.

Extrinsic Motivation

Behavior change can be induced without intrinsic motivation if individuals are provided sufficient extrinsic motivation. In this case individuals adopt the new behavior not because they are convinced of the need for it, but rather because they feel they must comply. The two principal mechanisms that can be used to induce compliance in an organization are leadership and systems (Model A, Figure 3–1).

Common examples of extrinsic motivators available to the organization's leadership are rewards and punishment, both tangible and symbolic.[9] For instance, leaders interested in creating change can provide explicit recognition or such symbolic incentives as appropriate use of time, space, and other implicit forms that communicate approval or disapproval. In the case of Chemex, Joe Harrow would make frequent use of "attaboys" in well-chosen forums and settings. For example, he used them in board meetings to reward such desired behavior as use of portfolio-planning methodology in management presentations. Other symbolic incentives took the form of allowing more visibility, time, and proximity for those who appeared to be demonstrating their allegiance to the new methodology, while denying these rewards to those who appeared to be slow to change.

Rewards and punishments can be administered through the formal systems in rather obvious ways by granting or withholding various monetary or nonmonetary incentives. Less obvious are the problems that can result when the rewards and punishments administered through the formal systems are not synchronized with the explicit or symbolic incentives administered by the leaders of the change effort. Joe Harrow did an excellent job in this respect by maintaining a high degree of consistency between the two to gain maximum effect.

The case of Jim Henderson at Cummins is notable for its sparse use of extrinsic motivators to induce the new behavior. No bonuses, incentives, or other extrinsic rewards and punishments were apparently used to effect the change. The only exceptions were the slight coercion implied in Henderson's *un*announced plant visits, but he used them to draw attention to the problem rather than to issue orders. There was also some peer pressure in the weekly inventory meetings. But all in all, this is very meager use of extrinsic motivators when compared with the case of Joe Harrow, and this has important implications for culture change as will be seen in the next chapter. Essentially, and perhaps somewhat counterintuitively, the heavier the use of extrinsic motivators in relation to the intrinsic ones to induce the desired new behavior, the more difficult it is to achieve a corresponding culture change.

Model for Change (M2)

Even if people are sufficiently motivated to change their behavior, they will not be able to change unless they know what the appropriate new behavior is. When the change agents are in leadership positions (the typical case), expectations can be communicated directly and also through the various formal systems. People will be confused and ineffective if they perceive the signals from the formal systems to be at odds with what the leadership is saying or if the leadership's words and deeds are inherently inconsistent.

Expectations are communicated through the formal systems by such means as organization charts and job descriptions. Various measurement systems, such as budgets, control reports, and business and individual performance evaluation systems, are also important. In all these cases, people tend to "read" important expectations by noticing what the monitors of these systems actually inspect.

Thomas J. Peters has provided an excellent discussion of the symbolic and other "mundane tools" that leaders can use to communicate their expectations credibly to the organization (see recommended supplementary reading 19). These are summarized briefly below:[10]

Mundane Tools

Manipulation of Symbols

- *Calendar behavior*—the activities on which the leader actually spends his or her time.
- *Reports*—what the leader actually looks at and spends time on.
- *Agenda*—what issues on the leader's agenda get "air time."
- *Physical settings*—where the leader spends his or her time (for instance, in the field or at headquarters).
- *Public statements*—what is emphasized and ignored in making these statements.
- *Staff organization*—How much does the leader emphasize the role of staff versus line? Does he or she allow staff to probe the line?

Patterns of Activity

- *Positive reinforcement*—praise desired behavior; allow the "bad" to be displaced by the "good" rather than trying to legislate the bad out of existence.
- *Frequency and consistency of behavior*—a pattern of frequent and consistent small successes has a powerful effect on expectations and behavior.

Settings for Interaction

- *Role modeling*—by your *actions* shall your intentions be judged.
- *Location of groups*—moving the location of a group or a meeting to a new venue to communicate what is important.

- *Attendance*—who is invited and excluded from meetings.
- *Presentation format*—what comes first versus last; what is emphasized.
- *Questioning approaches*—what items, issues, and aspects are probed; what is deemphasized in the questioning of subordinates.

In the case of Jim Henderson, the new "model"—take more personal responsibility, use systems more—wasn't communicated very explicitly. It emerged out of the process of problem solving he employed to dig the organization out of the crisis. Once again, the appropriateness of this can be argued both ways. Some would say Henderson should have communicated the model more clearly and sooner to facilitate the change. Others, including myself, think that even if he had a clear conception of his change agenda and model, communicating this too clearly and too quickly could have driven the people's defenses and resistance up before they had a chance to feel a sense of ownership and a chance to become comfortable with it. Thus, there is a fine line between embarking with a too clearly defined model too early in the change game and waiting too long to introduce, acknowledge, and legitimize a new model.

In the case of George Coulter at Professionals, the new model had emerged in people's minds over a number of years, and George's election as managing partner crystallized and legitimized it in the firm. Other "star partners" also provided new role models. The case of Joe Harrow provides a sharp contrast to Jim Henderson's case. Harrow had a very clear new model, and he masterfully communicated it to his managers using many of the mundane tools just described (both the model and the tools were proposed by the external consultants he had retained). In a sense, Joe tried to shove his alphabets down the organization's throat. His managers chewed on them, but in the end they didn't swallow them.

Method for Change (M3)

Even if people understand what the appropriate new behavior is and are motivated to adopt it, they may not be able to do so because it may take time and help to learn the new skills and behavior. The approaches used to implement change should take this feature into account. Other factors that the change process must also address are the location of relevant information, the nature of the social and political resistance to be dealt with, and the orchestration of the change—that is, the sequencing of various elements in the change process so as to create the best results.

Processes for Dealing with Resistance

John Kotter and Leonard Schlesinger have identified several approaches for dealing with resistance to change and have provided a convenient summary of the advantages and drawbacks of each (Figure

Figure 11–1
Approaches for Dealing with Resistance to Change*

Approach	Commonly Used in Situations	Advantages	Drawbacks
Education and communication	Where there is a lack of information or inaccurate information and analysis.	Once persuaded, people will often help with the implementation of change.	Can be very time-consuming if lots of people are involved.
Participation and involvement	Where the initiators do not have all the information they need to design the change and where others have considerable power to resist.	People who participate will be committed to implementing change.	Can be very time-consuming if participators design an inappropriate change.
Facilitation and support	Where people are resisting because of adjustment problems.	No other approach works as well with adjustment problems.	Can be time-consuming, and still fail.
Negotiation and agreement	Where someone or some group will clearly lose out in a change and where that group has considerable power to resist.	Sometimes it is a relatively easy way to avoid major resistance.	Can be too expensive in many cases if it alerts others to negotiate for compliance.
Manipulation and co-optation	Where other tactics will not work or are too expensive.	It can be a relatively quick and inexpensive solution to resistance problems.	Can lead to future problems if people feel manipulated.
Explicit and implicit coercion	Where speed is essential and the change initiators possess considerable power.	It is speedy and can overcome any kind of resistance.	Can be risky if it leaves people mad at the initiators.

* From John P. Kotter and Leonard A. Schlesinger, "Choosing Strategies for Change," *Harvard Business Review,* March–April 1979, p. 111.

11–1; see recommended supplementary reading 20). We will use their categories here to organize and discuss various issues concerning the process of dealing with resistance to change. Depending on the nature of the anticipated resistance, one or more of these processes could be employed:

Education and Communication Help people understand the need for change and its underlying rationale. The weekly inventory meetings as well as Henderson's plant visits at Cummins provided occasions for such education and communication. In addition, planned rotation of people, such as between line and staff positions and between headquarters and field locations, can help build understanding of other points of view in the organization, which can facilitate organizational responsiveness and reduce resistance to change when it is needed.

Participation and Involvement   Listen to those affected by the change and incorporate their advice. The weekly inventory meetings at Cummins provided a forum for Henderson to get such input from his managers.

Facilitation and Support   Offer training in new skills, give people time off after a demanding period, and provide empathy and emotional support. Many change efforts fail because this approach is underutilized or ignored. It is of critical importance where the major blockage to change is a skill problem (see Figure IV–1). Also, it is worth repeating that the trick in successful change is often the ability to get people to try the new behavior, on an experimental or trial basis if necessary. One way to facilitate this is at first to leave the old machines and other supports that people have come to identify with and rely on but to introduce the new machines and methods needed to perform the new behavior in parallel with the old, thus giving people some emotional support and a perception of choice: "We can always rely on or go back to the old way if this doesn't work." This can facilitate experimentation and ultimately helps to build commitment. When management at Inland Steel first switched to computer control for their rolling mills in the late 1960s, they did so smoothly by allowing a period of a year and a half for "dual control." The computers had been slowly phased in, but the old manual system was retained as a backup.

Resistance typically breaks down as people gain confidence and comfort with a new approach. And if people become skillful and highly competent at it, the new behavior can enhance self-esteem and generate intrinsic motivation to continue the new behavior and make it self-sustaining. Upon taking over as managing partner at Professionals in 1980, George Coulter began a set of ambitious training programs for all the firm's partners to help them acquire the new skills they needed. At the time of this writing, this approach has yielded some positive results but has not as yet reached the self-sustaining stage for most of the partners.

Negotiation and Agreement   Bargain and reach an acceptable agreement with active or potential resisters. It may pay to give in on some points where resistance is greatest, in order to get people to give the change a chance in other areas where their resistance is less. In cases where there is no skill problem, but the people are not motivated to engage in the new behavior, managers can sometimes get people to act out their resistance by agreeing too strenuously with resisters: "We know this is extremely difficult and will take some time." The employees might respond by showing management that it is not that difficult and can be done more quickly than management thought. By *acknowledging* resistance, managers of change can sometimes help to break it.

Figure 11–2
Summary of Three Illustrative Cases: George Coulter, Joe Harrow, and Jim Henderson (See Figure IV–1)

Case (See Figure IV–1)	Resistance (R)	Motivation (M1)	Model (M2)	Method (M3)			Outcomes
				Approaches Used	Attempted Speed	Orchestration	
George Coulter (300 partners) 1980–1984	High (skill problem)	Largely intrinsic, some extrinsic	Auditors must sell more. Auditors and management consultants must cooperate. Local offices must have less autonomy.	Education and communication. Participation and involvement. Facilitation and support.	Moderately fast	All at once	Limited behavior change in four years. Partners have "bought into" the model (M2) (culture change). Change is gaining momentum and may take hold.

Joe Harrow (1,000 managers) 1976–1982	High (skill and commitment problem)	Mostly extrinsic	Strategic thinking. Analytical thinking. Marketing orientation.	Explicit and implicit coercion.	Extremely fast	All at once	Limited to moderate behavior change in six years. Managers didn't "buy into" the model (M2). Changes didn't persist after Harrow departed.
Jim Henderson (200 managers) 1974–1979	High (skill and commitment problem)	Mostly intrinsic	Take personal responsibility. Use systems.	Education and communication. Participation and involvement.	Moderately slow	Focus on taking personal responsibility first, on systems later	Moderate behavior change in five years. Managers "bought into" the new model (M2) (culture change). Inventory crisis took several months to resolve.

Manipulation and Co-optation   Covertly use information and structure events to manipulate others; co-opt one or more resisters by giving them a key role in the execution of the change.

Explicit and Implicit Coercion   Force people to accept changes by use of implicit or explicit threats. Examples are promotion possibilities, actually firing people, and transferring people.

Choosing Implementation Speed

Kotter and Schlesinger have outlined four key situational factors whose assessment helps guide the choice of implementation speed:[11]

1. *Amount of anticipated resistance.* The greater the resistance anticipated from all possible sources, the slower the change process must be to deal with it. However, where there is a potential for sabotage, moving slowly may actually increase resistance as the people in question raise their defenses and take steps to ensure the failure of the proposed changes.[12]
2. *Power of those initiating the change versus those resisting it.* The lower the relative power of the change initiators vis-á-vis the resisters, the slower the change process must be to deal with it.
3. *Location of relevant data.* The greater the dispersion of relevant data and the dependence on others for it, the slower the change process must proceed in order to get the needed data.
4. *The short-run stakes.* The lower the short-run stakes (if there is no crisis situation), the slower the change process can proceed.

These criteria frequently conflict, so managers engaged in change need to balance these considerations in making the final determination. In the case of Cummins, for instance, the anticipated resistance was great, arguing for a slower implementation speed. The change was being resisted by established long-time insiders with a lot of political power in the organization, again calling for a slower speed. The relevant data was highly dispersed in the various plant locations, which also meant that a slower implementation would be effective. However, because the inventory crisis created high short-term stakes for the company and personally for Henderson, a faster implementation was called for. On balance, Henderson's relatively slow implementation seemed well suited to his situation and helped him eventually obtain the changes he was seeking.

Resistance was also high at Chemex for Joe Harrow. In addition, five times as many managers were involved (200 at Cummins versus 1,000 at Chemex). The managers at Chemex had high relative power; they had been around a long time and had political clout, whereas Joe was new to the job and an outsider. The relevant data was dispersed, largely in the hands and minds of the managers who were to use them more analytically and strategically. Also, Joe perceived the short-term stakes to be high for the company. In contrast to Jim Henderson, Joe Harrow tried to move fast—perhaps much faster than his situation allowed him to. He accomplished relatively less extensive and less permanent change than did Henderson.

Orchestrating the Change

Where should the change process begin? In what sequence should the various approaches for dealing with resistance (Figure 11–1) be used? Should all aspects of the model be explored and emphasized simultaneously or not? In what way should the motivators be used? Artful attention to such questions as these can greatly aid the change process and increase the chances of its success.

In general, it pays to begin in areas where there is the greatest agreement for change and at places in the organization where the resistance to change is likely to be the least. This increases the chances of obtaining early success that can then be used to energize, legitimize, and sustain the later steps in the change process. For the same reasons, it helps to first emphasize those aspects of the model and use those approaches to overcoming resistance that are likely to yield the quickest, safest, and surest results. This allows more time to plan the more difficult steps and for energy to build for dealing with them.

Both George Coulter and Joe Harrow emphasized all aspects of the new model simultaneously. In contrast, Jim Henderson first emphasized that his managers should take greater personal responsibility for solving problems, such as the inventory crisis. There was some latent agreement emerging on this point among the managers at Cummins, and Henderson helped to crystallize and legitimize this. Once the change was reinforced by success (the managers did solve the inventory crisis after taking more responsibility for it), it set the stage for their taking some responsibility for another problem that had been around for some time—the need to introduce and use systems, which they proceeded to do. These and other differences in the changes undertaken in the three cases that have been illustrated in this chapter, and the associated outcomes, are summarized in Figure 11–2.

Conclusion

Resistance to changes in organizational behavior patterns can be overcome if people are intrinsically or extrinsically motivated to change their behavior, if they understand what the appropriate new behavior is, and if the method used to implement change is well suited to the situation. These are some important questions that those embarking on change should ask:

1. What is the extent and nature of the anticipated resistance? What are the underlying reasons for the resistance, for instance, to what extent

is the resistance due to skill problems, commitment problems, technical difficulties, social disruption, loss of political power, perceived
personal threat, etc.?

2. What mix of intrinsic and extrinsic motivation is appropriate in light
    of the desired changes? Is such motivation possible to generate? In
    general, the greater the reliance on extrinsic motivators relative to
    intrinsic motivators to produce the new behavior, the more difficult it
    will be to achieve a corresponding culture change (the subject of the
    next chapter).

3. How clearly and how soon should the new model of behavior be
    introduced to the organization? In general, moving too quickly and
    too clearly with a new model that people don't feel any ownership for
    makes it more difficult to legitimize it and to get people to "buy into"
    it, thus making culture change more difficult.

4. What method is most appropriate in light of the anticipated resis-
    tance, given the available motivation and the required model? Specifi-
    cally:

    a. What mix of approaches for dealing with resistance (Figure
        11–1) are most appropriate?

    b. What speed of implementation is best suited to the situation?

    c. How should the change be orchestrated?

Since these questions are interrelated, and since the choices concerning the three Ms (motivation, model, and method) can themselves alter
the nature and extent of the resistance to be expected, the following
iterative procedure is useful in conceiving and planning change:

Step 1. Make the three Ms that one has tentatively decided on as
         explicit as possible.

Step 2. Anticipate the resistance and the outcomes likely to result
         from the planned use of the three Ms.

Step 3. If the anticipated resistance and likely outcomes are accept-
         able, proceed with the implementation. If they are not, recompute
         the three Ms, and repeat the three steps.

My experience has been that managers of change err in two directions.
First, during planning, too much time is spent on thinking about and
refining the model for change (M2), and too little on finding ways to
ensure sufficient motivation for change (M1), especially intrinsic motivation. Also, not enough time is devoted to the mundane, perhaps boring,
but always important task of deciding the appropriate methods for
change (M3). It generally pays to conserve the time and energy spent on
fine-tuning the model into elegance and to redeploy this attention instead to the feeding and care of the other two Ms. Second, change efforts
fail because of a failure of will during implementation. When people
begin to feel the pain of the change and complain loudly, there is a

tendency to ease up or to even stop the change process. By viewing resistance as an invitation to learning, as already discussed, one may better understand the real reasons for people's complaints. If they are due to the inevitable pain that accompanies meaningful change, the implications are clear: The change is on track, don't give up now!

As mentioned, culture change does not necessarily accompany changes in behavior patterns. How to influence culture change, and related topics, are considered in the next chapter.

Chapter 12

Changing organizational culture

Orientation The methods and techniques described in the previous chapter must be used more restrictively if behavior change is to be accompanied by a corresponding culture change. Other matters to be discussed in this chapter must also be attended to in order to create culture change.

Let us begin by asking an important question that managers engaged in culture change will sooner or later confront: Do managers have any business trying to change people's beliefs and values?

Ethics of Culture Change

The following points may be made in addressing this issue. First, questions about changing people's beliefs and values are laden with emotion because they connote "brainwashing." Especially in the United States, born of the quest for religious and political freedom, any hint of this raises eyebrows as well as adrenalin levels. Second, such questions are personally threatening because a lot is at stake for the individual. One's beliefs and values are not a random assembly; changes in one or more of them require changes in related others. Such reorganization is painful and frequently resisted because the learning of new skills and behaviors is implied.

Finally, it is important to note that we are talking here about organization-related beliefs and values, not such private beliefs and values as religious or political ones. The problem is that the two sets are interrelated. Changes in one set most likely affect the other; more theoretical and empirical work is needed to better understand the interrelationship between people's organization-related beliefs and values and their private ones.

Despite these reservations, most people I have talked to have argued that, just as it is in the nature of the manager's job to influence organizational behavior in a responsible and professional manner, so it is his or her job to conscientiously shape organizational beliefs and values as appropriate.[1] To do so, managers need to have ways of thinking about and addressing the following questions: How can resistance to culture change be assessed? How can a manager influence the desired culture change? How can one be sure that the attempted culture change is in fact occurring? When should culture change be attempted? What are the alternatives to major culture change? Each of these questions will be taken up in sequence in this chapter.

How to Assess Resistance to Culture Change

Culture change may involve more or less of a change in (1) the content and/or (2) the strength of the existing organizational culture.

Change in Culture's Content

Culture's content depends on what the shared assumptions are and how they are ordered, and it determines in what *direction* culture influences behavior, as explained in Chapter 1. A change in culture's content is produced in one or more of the following four ways:

Existing Beliefs and Values Are Reordered   For instance, the content of the culture of an organization in which internal competition prevails over cooperation would be transformed if these two values were reordered so that cooperation prevailed over internal competition.

Existing Beliefs and Values are Modified   This is what happened in the case of Cummins Engine Company and Jim Henderson as illustrated in Chapter 3. Two important shared assumptions (Figure 1–2 in Chapter 1) were altered. "Operate informally without systems" was modified to "Use systems to do routine work, operate informally to expedite." And "Top management will tell us what to do if there is a problem" was transformed to "All managers should take personal responsibility for problem solving." Existing beliefs and values were similarly modified in the cases of George Coulter at Professionals; this is also what Joe Harrow was attempting at Chemex (see Figure IV–1 and the column under Model (M2) in Figure 11–2).

Existing Beliefs and Values Are Removed   For instance, the content of the Cummins management culture would be changed if shared assumption number 5—"The Company is part of the family"—were no longer sufficiently central to the Cummins managers to be considered of major significance. This could have happened if the value had no longer been ordered high enough in the minds of a sufficiently large number of these managers at Cummins.

Nonexisting Beliefs and Values Are Added   This is the opposite of the situation just mentioned. To illustrate, many managers at Cummins valued close working relationships with the union (Figure 1–2), but this was not an important shared assumption. It would have become a cultural value if it had been placed higher relative to other values by a greater number of Cummins managers.

Relating to concepts discussed earlier in this book, two important features of a change in cultural content as defined here should be noted. First, we are not talking about changes in people's attitudes, which more readily accompany changes in people's behavior, but rather the changes in their more central beliefs and values (see Chapters 1 and 4). Second, changes in organizational behavior patterns may be accompanied by changes in some beliefs and values for a certain number of people in the organization. Such changes will not be viewed as cultural changes unless the beliefs and values in question are widely enough shared and highly enough placed relative to other beliefs and values in the organization. In short, culture change refers to a rather central and widespread change in organizational beliefs and values, and generally takes a long time to accomplish.

Incremental versus Radical Change in Culture's Content   The more radical the proposed change in culture's content, the greater its resistance to change.[2] A greater change in culture's content is involved to the extent that:

1. The change involves a *greater number* of important shared assumptions.
2. The change involves *more central* (highly ordered) shared assumptions.
3. The change involves a movement toward *more alien* (less intrinsically appealing) shared assumptions.

Alien versus Intrinsically Appealing Beliefs and Values   Three interrelated considerations help determine the intrinsic appeal of the beliefs and values in question. First, beliefs and values that are shared at some level by members of an organization are more intrinsically appealing than those that are not. At Cummins (Figure 1–2 in Chapter 1), the value of a close working relationship with the union was not shared widely enough, nor was it placed high enough in the company management's ordering of beliefs and values, to be considered a cultural value. However, this value was more intrinsically appealing for the people at Cummins than an "antiunion" value because many of the company's managers valued the role of the union and desired close relationships with it.

Second, beliefs and values that were once part of the organization's culture but have since atrophied and are no longer important shared assumptions are usually more intrinsically appealing than are beliefs and values that were never part of the organization's culture. At Cummins, for example, the assumption that "small is beautiful" was part of the company's heritage, but this value had atrophied after the expansion of the war years and was not part of the company's tradition by the time of the case.[3] This dormant value could have been more easily adopted by the people at Cummins than the value "bigger is better," for instance, which was never part of the company's culture.

Third, beliefs and values that are supported by the cultures of the national, regional, ethnic, religious, occupational, and professional communities to which the people in the organization belong are more intrinsically appealing than beliefs and values that do not find such support in the cultures of the relevant wider communities. For example, "service to the community" was an important value in the local community in which Cummins was headquartered. Accordingly, beliefs and values consistent with the notion of corporate social responsibility were more intrinsically appealing to the Cummins managers than beliefs and values that ran counter to this notion.

Resistance to Culture Change

A radical change in culture's content is more difficult to accomplish than is an incremental change. Further, for a given degree of change in culture's content, cultural resistance will be greater in a strong culture than in a weak culture because the former involves change for a larger number of organizational members than does the latter. Thus the degree of cultural resistance may be economically represented as follows:

Resistance to culture change	=	Magnitude of the change in the content of the culture, i.e., radical versus incremental change in the culture's content	×	Strength of the prevailing culture, i.e., strong versus weak culture

The culture change at Cummins modified two of the five important shared assumptions, but they were not reordered (Figure 1–2 in Chapter 1). Number 3, "Operate informally without systems," underwent a moderate change to "Use systems to do routine work, operate informally to expedite." Number 4, "Top management will tell us what to do if there is a problem," was substantially altered to "All managers should take personal responsibility for problem solving." Overall, the magnitude of the change in the content of the culture was more than incremental but less than radical. However, because Cummins had a relatively strong culture, the overall resistance was considerable, and these cultural changes took four to five years to accomplish.

Joe Harrow was attempting not only to modify three central assumptions of the strong management culture at Chemex, but also to reorder them. The prevailing culture was ordered as follows: (1) manufacturing orientation, (2) seat-of-the-pants decision making, and (3) short-term opportunistic thinking. Harrow was attempting to modify each assumption and reorder them as follows: (1) long-term strategic thinking, (2) analytical approach to decision making, and (3) marketing orientation. This represented a radical transformation in the Chemex management culture. Further, because the culture was strong, the overall resistance was so great that little or no culture change was accomplished six years after it was embarked upon. In general, the greater the cultural resistance, the more difficult and time-consuming the culture change will be. Also, the greater the number of people involved, the longer and more problematic the change will be. For example, even if the cultural resistance at Chemex had only been as great as in the case of Cummins, the former would have been more difficult because it involved 1,000 managers versus 200 or so at Cummins.

How to Influence Culture Change

As indicated in the Introduction to Part 4, changes in culture can either precede or follow changes in behavior. The former occurs when there is persistent and undeniable evidence that one or more new assumptions have greater merit and validity than existing ones, as in the case of George Coulter at Professionals (Figure IV–1). The major problem that the people in the organization typically face in such cases is the acquisition of new knowledge, competence, and skill that they need to behave in accordance with their new assumptions.

When the assumptions involved cannot be so convincingly invalidated and replaced by others that are supported by clear and compelling evidence, culture change is unlikely to precede behavior change. This is what happened in the cases of both Jim Henderson and Joe Harrow. The new assumptions they were advocating made sense to some people in the organization, but many others remained unconvinced for a period of time because it was difficult to establish and validate the "superiority" of the new assumptions. After all, Cummins had weathered previous downturns, had got along without systems for all of its history, and was continuing to do well relative to the competition.

In the case of Chemex, the managers believed their performance problems had nothing to do with the prevailing management culture, which they took pride in for its values of efficiency, street savvy, and entrepreneurship. Rather, most of the Chemex managers believed their current problems were due to several poor acquisitions and slip-shod cost control and asset management, for which they blamed the previous CEO whom Joe Harrow replaced. They viewed "Joe's alphabets" as needless bureaucratization that invited analysis by paralysis and was out of character with the company's identity—"This is first, and foremost, a *manufacturing* company." These managers believed Joe was advocating his alphabets not so much for business reasons as for personal reasons having to do with his background and personal agenda: "Joe was groomed in this methodology in a different industry where it may be more relevant." "These systems are really intended to take control away from us."

In cases such as these, changes in culture may lag changes in behavior by a considerable period of time (as in the case of Jim Henderson) and may never occur (as in the case of Joe Harrow). To understand what can be done about this, those interested in producing culture change must understand the processes that give culture a momentum of its own, creating in culture a tendency to perpetuate itself (Figure 12–1). Change

Figure 12–1
How Culture Tends to Perpetuate Itself

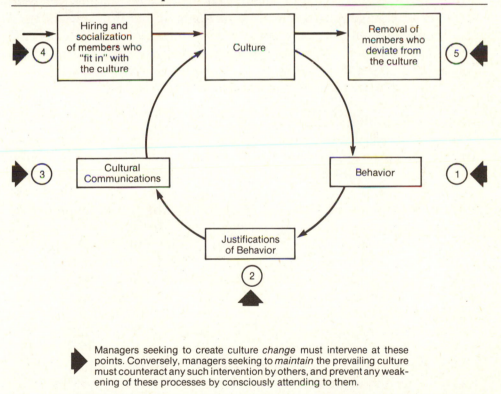

Managers seeking to create culture *change* must intervene at these points. Conversely, managers seeking to *maintain* the prevailing culture must counteract any such intervention by others, and prevent any weakening of these processes by consciously attending to them.

agents need to intervene in one or more of these processes as appropriate to effect the desired culture change. Conversely, those seeking to *maintain* the prevailing culture must resist active intervention in these processes by others and continually attend to them to ensure that the cultural momentum does not slow down and lead to *cultural drift*.

There are two basic approaches for effecting a desired culture change: (*a*) getting people in the organization to buy into a new pattern of beliefs and values (processes 1, 2, and 3 shown in Figure 12–1) and (*b*) adding and socializing people into the organization and removing people from the organization as appropriate (processes 4 and 5 in Figure 12–1). Let us consider each of these processes in turn.

Behavior

Behavior corresponds to the first level of culture as described in Chapter 1. The process by which culture influences behavior was described in Chapter 2, and it is consistent with the conventional wisdom—that is, that beliefs and values influence behavior (process 1, Figure 12–1). However, the opposite is also true. A considerable body of social science literature indicates that, *under certain conditions to be discussed shortly,* one of the most effective ways of changing people's beliefs and values is to first change their corresponding behavior.[4] The general techniques for creating behavior change were discussed in Chapter 11, but they must be used more restrictively if culture change is to be produced. Essentially, the motivation to change behavior must be based on *intrinsic* motivation rather than relying exclusively, or even excessively, on extrinsic motivation. Why this must be so is now explained.

Justifications of Behavior

One of the reasons that change in behavior (first level of culture) does not *necessarily* produce change in culture (third level of culture) is because of the intervening process of justification of behavior (the second level of culture in Chapter 1, and process 2 in Figure 12–1). This is what happened in the case of Joe Harrow as described in the Introduction to Part 4. His managers were behaving as called for by the new formal systems, but they continued to share the old beliefs and values in common and explained their new behavior to themselves by noting the external justifications for it.[5] For example, "We are doing it because it is required of us," and "We are doing it because of the incentives."[6] There was behavior compliance, not culture commitment. In a very real sense, these people were behaving the way they were because they felt they had no real choice, not because they fundamentally believed in or valued the change.

Thus one reason culture tends to perpetuate itself is that, even if behavior is changed (process 1, Figure 12–1), people tend to rationalize it in terms of external justifications (process 2) and continue to adhere to the prevailing pattern of beliefs and values. Managers attempting to change culture must remain alert to this danger and try to counteract it by using two basic approaches, one corresponding to process 1, the other involving process 2.

Intervention in Process 1: Intrinsic Motivation for Behavior Change   The first recommendation, which may appear counterintuitive, is to minimize the opportunity for external justification by inducing the appropriate behavior change with a minimal use of rewards, punishments, and other extrinsic forms of motivation.[7] This doesn't seem right at first for many of us who have become used to offering incentives to get what we want. However, others are likely to be going along just for the incentives rather than because they fundamentally believe in what they are asked to do. This is exactly what happened in the case of Joe Harrow. In contrast, Jim Henderson at Cummins offered no financial incentives and relied minimally on other extrinsic motivators (principally some unannounced plant visits to draw attention to the inventory problem) in order to produce the desired behavior. This exposed him to personal risk and criticism from his superiors, Irwin Miller and Don Tull, for not acting more forcefully to solve the growing inventory crisis. Henderson understood that the recommended strong measures would indeed solve the short-term inventory problem but would not help bring about the new culture he was seeking to create—a culture in which managers would take more personal responsibility for the problem (rather than waiting for directives from the top) and buy into and use the systems required to prevent its periodic recurrence.

To the extent possible, the necessary behavior change must be induced by using intrinsic forms of motivation. Essentially, this means that one must get people to see the inherent worth of what it is they are being asked to do. As Edgar H. Schein has explained, one way to do this is to persuade people to unlearn or question their current pattern of beliefs and values by helping them to see that their assumptions are not confirmed by reality testing, or are actually disconfirmed.[8] This lack of confirmation, or disconfirmation, which is typically accompanied by pain, guilt, anxiety, and lack of self-confidence, provide the necessary intrinsic motivation to learn the new behavior. Joe Harrow did very little in this area. In contrast, the weekly inventory meetings that Jim Henderson instituted at Cummins provided a forum for joint exploration that led people to see the value of the new approach he was advocating.

Since disconfirmation may be hard to generate (e.g., people may try to avoid the unpleasant outcomes by denying the validity of the disconfirmation), environmental threats, crises, and other major events that disrupt the normal equilibrium in the organization must be viewed as opportunities for creating such intrinsic motivation needed for culture change. Chapter 11 explained how such events help to generate intrinsic motivation. Culture itself affects the way in which such events are perceived by the people in the organization, but the leaders of change can also affect organizational perception by how they articulate these happenings and draw attention to them. Appropriate use of cultural language and symbols can help here.

For events that can be anticipated (an economic downturn, an expected strike, etc.), it pays to orchestrate the timing of the change so as to take advantage of these events to the extent possible. Unexpected happenings (for example, a piece of bad publicity or loss of a valued customer or employee) may also provide opportunities for building such intrinsic motivation. The key is to look upon these periods when the regular organizational routines are not observed as occasions that may make it possible to demonstrate the need to change existing assumptions or to adopt new ones.

Some use of extrinsic motivators may be unavoidable in orchestrating change. A second basic approach, corresponding to process 2, must therefore be used by managers seeking to create culture change.

Intervention in Process 2: Nullify Inappropriate Justifications A somewhat drastic technique for doing this is to give people a way out. Those who do not accept the new pattern of beliefs and values may be given the option to leave or transfer to a different organization. If it is perceived as a feasible and a real option, giving people the opportunity to leave can be a powerful tool in producing culture change because it weeds out those who are unlikely to take on the new pattern of beliefs and values (process 5). The choice will also make it hard for those left behind to come up with inappropriate rationalizations and justifications, since the perception of choice helps build commitment.[9] This technique is somewhat risky in that some valued people may choose to leave before one has had a chance to convert them. However, such people tend to be marketable and may leave anyway if they feel coerced.

Another technique is to attempt to directly nullify inappropriate justifications. Joe Harrow made no attempt to do so. In contrast, Jim Henderson helped remove the inappropriate rationalizations used by his subordinates at Cummins: "Why change? Those above will tell us what to do," and "The guy at the top will act sooner or later to get us out of this crisis." He removed them by demonstrating that he was going to operate differently from the way Don Tull had managed Cummins and such crises over the past 30 years. Henderson was not going to issue orders in the old way to get a quick fix, even if this meant that the inventory problem would worsen and thereby expose him to personal risk and criticism from above for not acting decisively according to the proven methodology.

Managers engaged in culture change must also communicate the new pattern of beliefs and values and get people to adopt them.

Cultural Communications

Cultural communications, which correspond to the second level of culture described in Chapter 1, take place in both explicit and implicit forms (process 3, Figure 12–1). The former include announcements, pronouncements, memos, and other explicit communications. The latter include rituals, ceremonies, stories, metaphors, heroes, logos, decor, dress, and other symbolic forms of communication. Both explicit and implicit communications must be relied on to persuade people to adopt the new cultural beliefs and values.

If the new pattern of beliefs and values in question are more intrinsically appealing to the people in the organization than is the prevailing pattern, the main problem in getting their adoption is the credibility of the communication. This is the case in much political campaign rhetoric: "I like what I am hearing, but is this what the communicator really believes?" However, suppose the new pattern of beliefs and values being communicated is *less* intrinsically appealing to the audience than is the prevailing pattern, as was the case for both Joe Harrow and Jim Henderson. If this is so, credible communications about the new pattern of beliefs and values results in their being perceived to be true intentions rather than mere corporate propaganda, but this perception doesn't mean people will adopt the new pattern. The audience may remain aware of the new pattern of beliefs and values, espouse them, and even comply with them, without internalizing them.

This is why culture change is far more difficult and problematic than it is sometimes made out to be in the business press and in the popular literature. First, more than just effective cultural communications are needed to effect culture change (see Figure 12–1). Second, communications must be credible to be effective, but this will not help in influencing culture change where the new pattern of beliefs and values is less intrinsically appealing. Third, slogans, banners, philosophy statements, and similar cultural paraphernalia that some people equate with culture change may not even succeed in generating credible communications, let alone culture change. Let us explore these topics in greater depth.

Intervention in Process 3: Credible Communication of the New Pattern of Beliefs and Values   As indicated earlier, moving too quickly with too clear a model of the intended change may cause rejection because the people feel no ownership for the change. On the other hand, waiting too long and allowing too much ambiguity concerning the new model could generate excessive confusion and frustration in the organization. Once the matter of timing is settled, managers interested in producing culture change must begin the process of crystallizing whatever consensus has been achieved and effectively communicating the new pattern of beliefs and values to the rest of the organization. This is a difficult task because explicit communications by managers of the new beliefs and values they hope the people in their organization will adopt, such as, "We believe people are our most important asset," may fall on deaf ears or be seen as mere corporate propaganda.[10] How can communications be made more credible?

First, *backing up words with deeds* gains credibility, especially for individuals who in the past have consistently lived by what they said. A leader who has lost the reputation for credibility cannot reestablish it immediately. A considerable period of demonstrated consistency between the communicator's espoused beliefs and actual behavior must elapse before explicit communications are accepted as true intentions rather than mere fluff. In some cases the change agent may have lost so much credibility that it is irretrievable. For instance, Bob Kirkland had been for several years a highly effective manager, known for his authoritarian approach, who worked under another manager who believed in the same approach. Changes at the top led to the departure of Bob's boss and his replacement by a good friend of Bob's, Gerald Ross, who wanted Bob to create a more participative culture in his organization. Bob, who had adopted the authoritarian style because of the former boss, was happy to go along with Gerald. When Bob preached the new value to his organization, however, the people were not convinced. Bob was not credible because he was seen as either to have lied to them before under the authoritarian boss or to be lying to them now under the participative boss. In such cases, a new face may be needed before the organization will believe the new communication because the old face has become so inextricably associated with the old values.

Second, communications tend to be accepted with less skepticism when they are *not apparently espousing something that is in the communicator's self-interest*.[11] Explicit communications about new beliefs and values are more credible if their advocates apparently stand to lose in some meaningful way if the organization adopts these beliefs and values or when they entail significant personal sacrifice for the proponents. It is not a bad idea, then, for a manager to think about how he or she will *suffer* as a result of the proposed changes and to communicate this to the organization. To be effective, the personal loss and sacrifice must seem significant and real, not phony.

Given these difficulties and limitations of explicit communication, two indirect means exist to get across a new pattern of beliefs and values so that they seem credible. One is to *spread the word by more informal means* of communication, including reliance on neutral intermediaries, especially those who formerly had been cynical. This is because people receive communications less skeptically when they don't think the communicators are *trying* to persuade them.[12] Second, implicit rather than explicit means of communications serve the purpose. Use of *appropriate cultural language and symbols* (Chapter 10) can be useful here. Research shows that communications are not only more memorable but also more believable when implicit forms, such as *telling stories and anecdotes from company history or individual experience*, are used to communicate intended beliefs and values.[13]

For example, when Thomas J. Watson, Jr., took over the leadership of IBM from his father, he tried to instill in the organization the virtues of constructive rebellion.[14] One way in which he tried to do this was directly stating it as an important value in his speeches to company employees: "I just wish somebody would stick his head in my office and say (to me) 'you're wrong.' I would really like to hear that. I don't want yes men around me." Reportedly, such pronouncements were met with skepticism, and as mere corporate propaganda, by many employees: "[Watson, Jr.] says to us to stick our heads into his office and say 'you are wrong'; you should see the collection of heads that he has."[15]

Much more credible were Watson's attempts to communicate this value by telling a variety of stories, including this one:

> Early in 1961, in talking to our sales force, I attempted to size up the then-new Kennedy Administration as I saw it. It was not a political talk. I urged no views on them. It was an optimistic assessment, nothing more. But at the close of the meeting, a number of salesmen came up front. They would listen to what I had to say about business, they said, but they didn't want to hear about the new Administration in a company meeting.
>
> On my return to New York, I found a few letters in the same vein. Lay off, they seemed to say, you're stepping on our toes in something that's none of your business.
>
> At first I was a bit annoyed at having been misunderstood. But when I thought about it, I was pleased, for they had made it quite clear they wore no man's collar, and they weren't at all hesitant to tell me so. From what I have read of organization men, that is not the way they are supposed to act.[16]

Why are stories more credible? Essentially, it is their concreteness, as well as the fact that the moral of the story is not explicitly stated. The listener draws his or her own conclusions and is more likely to believe them. The problem with such communications is that a different moral may be inferred from the one intended. For instance, another of Watson's stories on the virtues of constructive rebellion was this:

> The moral is drawn from a story by the Danish philosopher, Sören Kierkegaard. He told of a man on the coast of Zeeland who liked to watch the wild ducks fly south in great flocks each fall. Out of charity, he took to putting feed for them in a nearby pond. After awhile some of the ducks no longer bothered to fly south; they wintered in Denmark on what he fed them.
>
> In time they flew less and less. When the wild ducks returned, the others would circle up to greet them but then head back to their feeding grounds on the pond. After three or four years they grew so lazy and fat that they found difficulty in flying at all.
>
> Kierkegaard drew his point—you can make wild ducks tame, but can never make tame ducks wild again. One might also add that the duck who is tamed will never go anywhere anymore.
>
> We are convinced that any business needs its wild ducks. And in IBM we try not to tame them.[17]

Reportedly, this metaphorical story failed to convince many employees, and one skeptical recipient put his reaction this way: "Even wild ducks fly in formation."[18] In cases like this, stories can actually boomerang when they are used by listeners to undermine or ridicule the beliefs and values one is attempting to communicate and to draw an opposite interpretation from the one intended.[19]

Thus anyone faces a dilemma who relies on more implicit forms, such as storytelling, to communicate credibly the intended cultural beliefs and values. On the one hand, such communications are more believable because the listener draws his or her own conclusions about the moral of the story. On the other hand, the conclusions drawn may be contrary to those that were intended. One way to guard against this dilemma is to pick stories that minimize the potential for misinterpretation and for boomerang. Ultimately, however, the way to increase the credibility of communications is to ensure that they are backed by consistent action that is in keeping with the intended beliefs and values. Both Joe Harrow and Jim Henderson did a good job in this area.

Intervention in Process 3: Internalization of the New Pattern of Beliefs and Values   If they are credibly communicated, a new pattern of beliefs and values that is more intrinsically appealing than the present pattern will be accepted and eventually internalized. However, to the extent that the new pattern of beliefs and values is *less* intrinsically appealing—that is, perceived as alien by the people in question—communications about them must be not only emphatic and credible, but persuasive as well. Such "culture persuasion" cannot generally rely on statistics and other facts alone, for alien beliefs and values are not necessarily accepted and internalized on the basis of hard evidence.[20] The following documented account of what happened to a group of doomsday prophets is a somewhat unusual but provocative illustration of this:

> The passing of the doomsday was clear-cut evidence that their prophecy was wrong. However, rationalization and self-justification allowed the doomsdayers to emerge not only unshaken, but even more convinced about the truth of their beliefs.[21]

It is easy to dismiss this as one more example of what nuts are capable of doing, but both research and common observation indicate that it is no easy matter to get people to adopt new beliefs and values, particularly alien ones. This was the challenge that both Joe Harrow and Jim Henderson faced. There are two basic approaches to getting people to accept and eventually internalize new beliefs and values, especially alien ones: (1) identification and (2) "Try it, you'll like it."

Identification   The first approach relies on the audience's identification with one or more persons who credibly communicate their attachment or conversion to the pattern of beliefs and values in question.[22] Such a person could be the manager directing the culture change, or it could be anyone else the audience believes and identifies with. Here is one example:

In a company with a long tradition of authoritarian management, a new CEO with a strong belief in participative management was having a great deal of difficulty getting managers to do more than go through the motions. One of the senior executives from the old school, who was widely respected and admired as a company folk hero who would never say or do anything he didn't really believe in, then began to come around. As word of his "conversion" spread informally, others slowly began to change their beliefs. It got to the point that this idol's department became a model of the intended culture. The belief in participative management began to seep to the rest of the company and gradually became more widely shared.

There was no indication that this mechanism was at work in the case of either Joe Harrow or Jim Henderson.

Try It, You'll Like It   The following account of how this folk hero came to change his belief in participatory management in the first place indicates the second approach to the acceptance and eventual internalization of new beliefs and values, especially alien ones:

> He began to try the approach being advocated because he was a company loyalist who had an even stronger value: "I owe the new boss a fair shake." He was skeptical at first, but then came a few fairly dramatic changes having to do with the improved morale of certain valued but difficult employees, changes that he attributed to the "new philosophy." Gradually, he changed his mind about participative management. Advocacy followed, and eventually he became a "culture champion."

This case may appear to contradict the case previously cited concerning Bob Kirkland, who had a hard time convincing his organization of his conversion to participative management, but there are two key differences. First, the folk hero didn't appear to convert overnight, as Bob did, and the *reasons* for his conversion were as compelling and well known as the fact of his conversion—the dramatic improvement in the morale of certain valued but otherwise difficult employees. Second, people loved the folk hero and identified with him; Bob Kirkland was no folk hero to his people.[23]

If people can be persuaded to give it a fair chance and they like the experience that they attribute to it, the new pattern of beliefs and values may become accepted and eventually internalized. This is the approach Jim Henderson used successfully at Cummins. Persuasion to try the new behavior must not rely too heavily on financial and other extrinsic forms of motivation, otherwise the incentives may serve as external justification for the new behavior and may produce no changes in the prevailing beliefs and values.[24] This is especially important when the beliefs and values in question are alien. Where the intrinsic appeal of the beliefs and values in question is greater, one can rely more on extrinsic motivators to induce the new behavior without increasing the risk of inappropriate rationalizations. It also helps if it can be shown that people stand to benefit rather quickly if they try the new behavior. Further, both appeals and challenges can be effective tools in getting people to try a behavior without heavy reliance on extrinsic motivations and their attendant risk of external justification.

In the case just cited, the value of participative management was not intrinsically appealing, but the folk hero decided to try it because the appeal was to his higher value: "I owe the new boss a fair shake." A more general form of this appeal is one that asks people to give something a try in more tentative, exploratory, and relatively nonthreatening ways, like education and training programs.[25] The problem here is how to ensure that people will try the new behavior back *on the job*.

Another general form of appeal that can be used when the beliefs and values in question are part of the group heritage but not part of their current tradition is to keep *referring to that heritage*. If people can be shown that proposed changes are really nothing new, resistance is likely to weaken. For instance, this is one of the things AT&T management is currently doing to try to create a more marketing-driven organization. The appeal to engage in the new way of doing things is based on references to the company's heritage. If they can be activated, dormant beliefs and values can gently induce people and give them the confidence to try.[26]

Another way to get people to try the new behavior without relying heavily on incentives is to *challenge them* to do so. Here is how one general manager offered the challenge:

> In this division, people would consistently "explain" their poor performance by noting that their business was in an especially disadvantageous position for a number of reasons and that they therefore deserved special consideration in meeting stiff corporate performance standards. This general manager was not convinced. He began to point to higher-performing companies in the same industry that were generally believed to be comparable and ask: "Are you telling me *they* are better than *we* are?"
>
> Although plenty of explanations were offered to account for the differences in performance, this general manager would offer reasonable counterexplanations. Over time, this theme became accepted and helped raise the sights of the people in the division by getting them to see their situation in a new light.

Those approaches for dealing with resistance (Figure 11–1 in Chapter 11) that do not rely much on extrinsic motivation may also be used to induce the desired behavior without risking external justifications.

Intervention in Processes 4 and 5: Hiring and Socializing Newcomers and Removing Deviants   Finally, culture change may be influenced by (1) hiring and socialization of newcomers to fit into the intended culture and (2) weeding out and removing existing members who do not fit (processes 4 and 5, Figure 12–1). Neither of these processes were relied on to any great extent in the cases of George Coulter, Joe Harrow, and Jim Henderson. A summary of these three cases in terms of the cultural resistance, the approaches for creating culture change, and the outcomes, is provided in Figure 12–2. This summary should be reviewed in conjunction with the corresponding summary for behavior change (Figure 11–2) in Chapter 11.

Changes in the *content* of culture as to the number of important shared beliefs and values and the way they are ordered requires appropriate changes in administrative philosophy. Changes must occur in human resource management policies and practices that alter the "breed" of people hired and socialized into the organization, as well as those who are removed from it.

It is difficult to effectively assimilate a large number of new people in a short period, and this limits how rapidly culture can be changed by adding, socializing, and removing people from the organization. In addition, a large influx of people can lead to political infighting, ploys, and counterploys in the organization as people jockey for position, especially where large numbers of new people are brought in at higher levels.

Strength of culture is increased by adhering to a *consistent* philosophy to guide human resource management policies and practices over time. Keeping down the *rate* at which people are brought in and turned over also strengthens the culture. With a more stable work force, there is more opportunity for the beliefs and values to become more clearly ordered and widely shared.

Relevance of Part 2

Although the discussion in Part 2 was developed from the standpoint of the person entering or leaving the organization, an understanding of the forces at work also enables those interested in culture change to manage these processes appropriately. Two central points of this discussion bear repeating.

First, a "perfect" culture/person fit is not usually possible or even desirable. However, it is important to avoid irreconcilable mismatches between the person being hired and the intended culture. Both the individual and the organization bear responsibility for ensuring this.

Second, careful attention must be paid to the socialization process and how new members learn the important corporate realities, including culture. It may be added that informal socialization may have a greater impact on the recruit than formal socialization programs because the spontaneity with which the former takes place may bestow on it somewhat greater credibility.[27] Where the culture is weak, or where it is strong but has inappropriate content, formal orientation and training programs must be strong and internally consistent in order to make up for the lack

Figure 12–2
Summary of Three Illustrative Cases: George Coulter, Joe Harrow, and Jim Henderson (See Figures IV–1 and 11–2)

Case (see Figures IV–1 and 11–2)	Resistance to Culture Change			Approaches for Creating Culture Change (Corresponding to the Processes in Figure 12–1)					Outcomes (see Figures IV–1 and 11–2 also)
	Magnitude of Change in Culture's Content	Strength of the Prevailing Culture	Overall Resistance to Change	(1) Intrinsic Motivation for Behavior Change	(2) Nullify Inappropriate Justifications	(3) Credible and Persuasive Cultural Communications	(4) Hiring and Socialization	(5) Removal of Deviants	
George Coulter (300 partners) 1980–1984	Moderate to radical (alteration of three assumptions toward more "alien" beliefs and values)	Moderately strong	High	Largely intrinsic, some extrinsic	Compelling evidence from the environment, and success of "star partners"	Credible and persuasive because of compelling evidence from the environment	Some attempt to change qualifications for partnership to "star partner" profile	Some partners left	Moderate culture change was accompanied by limited change in the corresponding behavior four years after the change process began.
Joe Harrow (1,000 managers) 1976–1982	Radical (reversal and reordering of three central assumptions)	Very strong	Extremely high	Mostly extrinsic	Not done	Credible but not persuasive	A few people were brought in from the outside	A few people left	Limited to moderate behavior change was accompanied by little or no culture change six years after the change process began.
Jim Henderson (200 managers) 1974–1979	Moderate (modification of two assumptions toward more "alien" beliefs and values)	Strong	High	Mostly intrinsic	Plant visits, weekly problem solving, holding course in the face of growing pressure to fix the problem in the old way	Credible, and slowly became persuasive after "try it, you'll like it" led to success	None other than via normal hiring and socialization	None other than normal attrition	Moderate behavior change followed by corresponding culture change led to moderate permanent change five years after the change process began.

of appropriate informal socialization, or to overcome inappropriate socialization.

Socialization of newcomers continues past the liability of newness and the settling in period as these typically younger employees learn deeper corporate realities from more established, older employees. Slowly, the new employees become more aware of the full scope of the culture and feel progressively more committed to it.

Drawing on the literature on adult development, Donaldson and Lorsch have commented on the processes by which the belief systems of the top corporate managers of the companies they studied may have been transmitted from one generation of senior management to the next.[28] They suggest that this transmission may occur by the process of *mentoring*. The term *mentor* in this context connotes a broader meaning than usual to include the role of host, guide, and exemplar in addition to that of teacher or sponsor. Protégés may not only learn from their mentors, but also identify with them and seek to emulate them because of their virtues and accomplishments.[29] Since a manager may have several mentors during a career, this transmission and learning of deeper realities may continue as he or she advances in the organization. Identifying with these mentors may enhance attachment to the organization and lead the managers to internalize more completely the prevailing beliefs and values.[30]

Those responsible for creating culture change must take cognizance of these processes of socialization and mentoring and attempt to mold them in the appropriate manner. It must be recognized, however, that informal socialization and mentoring are emergent phenomena that are hard to anticipate and predict, so there are limits to how far they can be relied on to influence the needed changes.

Two Special Cases of Culture Change
Culture Acquisition and Divestiture   Divestiture of part of the organization's operations may be seen as the removal of a whole bunch of people (including deviants) that could affect the surviving culture (process 5). Analogously, acquisitions and mergers are potential mechanisms for effecting culture change because they represent the hiring of a large number of newcomers all at once (process 4).

Beyond the commonly considered fiscal, technological, and market criteria, managers interested in maintaining or enhancing their culture should pay careful attention to whether or not a prospective acquisition meets important cultural criteria. One company that has had great success in its acquisitions because of careful consideration of cultural fit is Dana Corporation, based in Toledo, Ohio. Mr. Borge Reimer, an executive vice president of Dana who has had responsibility for several of these company acquisitions, describes his approach in Reading 4–1.

Essentially, Mr. Reimer's approach is to walk away from a potential acquisition candidate if it is not a good cultural fit with Dana. Further, Dana does not directly assault the culture of the acquired company in an attempt to make needed cultural revisions, as Peter Strassman (Case 4–1) unsuccessfully tried to do with a small acquired company that had a very strong culture. Rather, Dana honors the culture and heritage of the acquired company and gradually gets it to buy into the notion of dual identity—keeping its old name and legacy and *adding* a new home, Dana. (See Reading 4–1.)

Culture Creation   Founders put their "imprint" on the culture by bringing in people (process 4) who share certain beliefs and values with the founder and will eventually share others as they identify increasingly with the founder and the enterprise. Changes in content and strength of nascent cultures depend on how fast the business grows, the turnover of personnel and, most important, whether or not the founder succeeds in institutionalizing the culture before departing from the scene. Reading 1–1, by Edgar H. Schein, considers this topic in greater depth. Toward the end of this reading, Schein has suggested that *hybrids* (those who maintain key old assumptions but incorporate new ones) represent an important mechanism by which cultures bearing the founder's assumptions evolve to incorporate other assumptions, including those of more professional management. Hybrids appear to be important vehicles for understanding and managing other types of culture change as well.

How to Know Whether or Not Culture Change Is Occurring

It is relatively easy to determine whether or not the attempted change in the organization's behavior patterns is being realized. However, since culture is shared in the *minds* of organizational members, how can one be sure that the attempted culture change is in fact occurring? If the prevailing culture is fairly open and confrontive, as it was in the cases of both Joe Harrow and Jim Henderson, the people involved will let it be known whether or not they are buying into the new beliefs and values. Unfortunately, however, the prevailing culture is often such that people will behave as they think they must, making the detection of culture change extremely tricky. Consider the following situation:

> Over a period of three years, Winn Hughes, an innovative division general manager responsible for 2000 people and $200 million in annual revenues, attempted to create an "entrepreneurial division culture." Several new ventures were launched by the division during this period, and one was highly successful. When Winn was promoted to a different part of the company, he belived he had left behind several promising ventures in the pipeline and,

more important, many *product champions*. Within one year of his departure, however, he learned that all these ventures had "died in the tracks" or had been killed.

It *wasn't* the case that Winn's replacement had ordered these actions, nor even that his successor was antientrepreneurial. Instead, the new head, who called himself a "balanced asset and growth" manager, said he would fund deserving projects and starve others—it was up to the people who believed in their projects to put their necks on the line for them. No one had come forward.

"Where are my product champions?" Winn asked himself with great disappointment when he heard about this. "They have disappeared into the woodwork!" he thought.

The real answer was that there never were any genuine product champions in that division, which had witnessed three general managers in five years. Under Winn's predecessor, a cost-cutting "hatchet man," these managers played the cost and efficiency game. During Winn's tenure, they played the entrepreneurial game. Then under Winn's successor, the "balanced" DGM whom they perceived to be an asset manager deep down, they played the this year's return on investment game. In short, these managers believed in playing the game that happened to be in town. That was their principal shared value, along with security consciousness and risk aversion. These were the underlying constants that explained these people's actions under three different general managers. Winn had been fooled because he mistook compliance for commitment. Turnover in management jobs in some companies tends to be so high (movement every two to three years), that a manager may discover that no culture change has taken place only after he or she has moved on, as in this case.

Behavior change does not necessarily indicate a corresponding culture change because the organization's leadership and systems (structures, measurements, controls, incentives, etc.) can effect behavior change without any culture change (see Model A, Figure 3–1), as they did in the case of Joe Harrow. It is also what happened in Winn's case. Culture change can be positively inferred only if the new behavior can be attributed to neither the organization's leadership nor to its systems. A good test of culture change is whether or not the new behavior persists after departure of the leadership that helped create the culture change or after the organizational systems used to create the culture change are further altered.

Although this is a good test of culture change, it is of little use to current leadership that wants to know whether or not the culture change they are attempting to create is in fact taking hold. That is what Winn Hughes should have asked himself and, in retrospect, says he would like to have known. The following three tests are not foolproof, but they may be used to make some reasoned judgments about whether culture change is occurring:

1. Is There Evidence of Intrinsically Motivated Behavior?

Would the new behavior persist if extrinsic motivations administered by the organization's leadership and systems were somewhat diminished? Winn could have eased off a bit on the bonuses and the public recognition he was giving for product championing to see how many were really committed to the concept. If this is deemed too risky a test, ("let's not mess with what is working"), one can look for opportunities that impose greater demands on the organization to see if the people respond appropriately *without* a corresponding increase in the extrinsic motivators. In the case cited, the deadlines on two key projects had to be advanced a bit for competitive reasons. The managers involved argued that the new deadlines could not be met without additional resources, which were not forthcoming because of a budget crunch. They said they would do their best, but there were no indications that they were stretching themselves to try. No one was putting in longer hours, for example. Both the projects failed to meet the slightly advanced deadlines.

2. Is There Evidence of Automatic-Pilot Behavior?

If a crisis on a novel situation is encountered, do the people involved automatically do what seems to be appropriate in light of the desired culture without waiting for directions from the organization's leadership or prodding from the organization's systems? In Winn's case, one of the new ventures was an outdoor product that encountered unexpected breakage on the customers' equipment on one particularly cold winter night during its first year on the market. Rather than acting immediately to offer free replacements, the managers involved took 48 hours to "investigate the problem" and reach a decision after consulting with Winn (who was on an overseas field trip and was difficult to reach) while irate customers waited. Winn was upset that his managers had waited to consult with him on this relatively straightforward issue, but he didn't probe further for the significance of this critical incident. Had they been product champions, these managers would have taken the modest personal risk of acting without the boss' input to do what had to be done.

3. Is There Evidence of Countermandated Behavior?

Do people behave in ways that run counter to established cultural values and/or organizational directives but that make sense in light of the desired culture? There was no evidence of such behavior in Winn's division. For example, the managers involved might have bootlegged resources from other parts of the company (which would have been counter to the company culture) or ignored certain policy directives (e.g., 20 percent of engineering time must be devoted to research projects rather than development projects) in an attempt to meet the advanced project deadlines mentioned earlier.

It may be infeasible or inadvisable to conduct these tests as planned experiments to determine the occurrence of culture change. However, one can look for occasions and situations that offer the opportunity to learn from "natural experiments," such as those illustrated, that provide telltale signs of culture change or lack thereof. Thus, with detective work and opportunistic testing, a manager can make reasoned judgments about whether or not culture change is occurring.

But what about those situations in which the new behavior cannot as yet be produced because of a skill or competence problem, as in the case of George Coulter? (see Figure IV–1). In these cases one must look for signs that people are *really trying* to engage in the required new behavior, that is, taking the appropriate steps and initiatives. Thus the three tests above can be generalized to all situations by replacing the word *behavior* in the questions posed with the words *behavior or initiatives*.

When to Attempt Culture Change

Culture change may involve a change in (1) the context and/or (2) the strength of the existing organizational culture.

When to Change Culture's Content

Change in a culture's content may be called for when the prevailing culture promotes behavior (Chapter 2) basically misaligned with the behavior required to achieve the desired level of organizational effectiveness and satisfaction (Model A, Figure 3–1). Culture's content may have to be changed in this case because it determines in what *direction* culture influences behavior, as explained in Chapter 1.

However, as Model A also indicates, it is possible to create the necessary change in actual organizational behavior patterns without any change in the corresponding beliefs and values. Since changes in beliefs and values are generally difficult and time-consuming, why bother to create such change? Why not rely on the organization's leadership and systems to create the necessary changes in organizational behavior patterns instead?

The answer is that, under certain conditions, creating behavior change without a corresponding culture change may not work at all or may work but at very high costs to the organization, and with unacceptable inefficiencies. The reason for this is that creating culture change in the organization is analogous to gaining the commitment of the individual. Just as it is possible to secure an individual's compliance without gaining his or her commitment, so also is it possible to secure behavior change without culture change, and with essentially the same three kinds of costs and risks.

Inefficiency   The costs of monitoring behavior to secure compliance and the costs of rewards and punishments administered via the organization's leadership and systems that are required to sustain compliance rise sharply as the organization gets larger and geographically more dispersed, because monitoring and rewarding/punishing appropriate behavior becomes increasingly difficult. In contrast, these costs are much smaller when behavior change is accompanied by appropriate culture change because the behavior is self-monitored and because the rewards and punishments driving the behavior are at least partly self-administered.

For instance, geographical dispersion was a factor in the case of George Coulter at Professionals because the firm's partners were spread out in local offices all across the country. The managers at Cummins were dispersed in several plants and facilities, unlike the old days when they were all based in Columbus. The Chemex managers were mostly located in one place, but there were many more managers involved in this case (about 1,000) than at Professionals (about 300 partners) or at Cummins (about 200 managers). Overall then, inefficiency was a moderately important consideration in the case of Chemex and Cummins and considerably more important in the case of Professionals.

Insufficiency   Compliance is often characterized by people doing just enough to get by. Committed people, on the other hand, will put in the energy, time, and effort to do what needs to be done, not just what they are minimally required to do. Compliance can be a problem also because the organization's leadership and systems can never fully anticipate every contingency that can arise. When something novel or unforeseen happens, the organization is at the mercy of the individual to do what is appropriate, which may be different from or even contrary to the specified behavior. Thus, where energy and commitment are critical and where novel or unplanned responses are frequently called for, behavior change without a corresponding culture change may be inadequate.

This was an important consideration in all three of the illustrative cases because the people in question were in managerial jobs with considerable discretion where initiative and commitment were necessary ingredients for success.

Irrelevancy   Finally, there are some considerations for which behavior change is irrelevant. Mental processes, such as perception and thinking, are only affected by culture change and not by behavior change.[31] The need to change mental processes was perhaps the most critical consideration of all for the three illustrative cases. As is true of many changes involving people in managerial jobs, the changes in question involved perceptual and mental processes that would not be addressed by behavior change (see the column for model M2 in Figure 11–2). In sum, these tests of inefficiency, insufficiency, and irrelevancy indicate that behavior change alone was not sufficient in these three cases because of the nature of the changes involved and the managerial level of the people in question. Under a different set of conditions, culture change may be less critical.

Given these shortcomings of simple behavior change, the next question is how to decide that an organization needs to undergo a major change in culture's content. There may be no alternative but to invest the time and resources necessary to secure such a change when the rules of the game are so significantly and permanently altered that basic changes in the organization's thinking and behavior are called for:

1. Persistent organizational performance and/or morale problems because the actual behavior is fundamentally misaligned with the required behavior (Model A, Figure 3–1) and other approaches haven't worked (George Coulter's story, for example).
2. A fundamental change in the organization's mission. (Joe Harrow)
3. Deregulation and fierce international competition.
4. Major technological change.
5. Major market changes (George Coulter).
6. Major changes in the social environment.
7. Acquisitions and mergers.
8. Organizational growth (Jim Henderson).
9. Family business going to professional management.
10. Domestic organization expanding overseas.

When to Change Culture's Strength

Such changes may be called for when even though the prevailing culture promotes behavior consistent with the behavior that is required to be successful (Model A, Figure 3–1), the results are not being achieved at the desired levels. The problem in this case is not the direction in which the prevailing culture promotes behavior (i.e., culture's content) but rather the *magnitude* of culture's influence on behavior (i.e., culture's strength). Such strength depends on how *widely* shared and *clearly* ordered the relevant beliefs and values are. If the prevailing culture has the appropriate content but is deemed to be too weak, it needs to be strengthened by clarifying the existing pattern of the cultural beliefs and values and getting more people to buy into them.

It should be recognized that a weak culture may be appropriate. One example is a conglomerate whose company culture may have only one or two important shared assumptions, for example, concerning financial performance only. The strength here may not be in the strong *company* culture but rather in the strong company *sub*cultures in the subsidiaries and acquired companies whose cultures the parent wishes to retain intact. A weak culture may also be appropriate where the business environment is highly unstable and requires frequent and abrupt changes in the organization's behavior patterns.

A culture that is too strong has other disadvantages. For one thing, it is very difficult to radically alter the content of a strong culture. For another, too strong a culture can blind people to its weaknesses. This is why the need for culture change often goes unrecognized until it is too late. It typically takes new leadership to see the extent to which culture has become a liability and the need to change it.

One way in which enlightened managers can avoid being blindsided by culture is to accommodate a certain degree of nonconformity in their organizations, especially in the case of individuals whose exceptional talents make them invaluable. People who believe and behave differently are difficult to deal with and retain, but they help keep others honest by demonstrating alternate ways of thinking and acting. Although including mavericks and rebels means a weaker culture and loss of some cultural efficiency, it is an insurance against culture's becoming so firmly entrenched that people can no longer see its blind spots.

Such nonconformists also represent potential cultural "seed crystals" around whom a different cultural pattern could be molded if needed in the future. Therefore organizational leaders must ask: What does the distribution of our membership look like on the culture map (Figure 4–1)? Is it what it should be in light of our situation? How many people do we have close to the good soldier, adapter, maverick, and rebel corners? Are we losing capable and talented people who are close to one or more of these corners? Why? Another way in which managers can help prevent a dysfunctional culture from perpetuating itself unheeded is to constructively deviate from it themselves when necessary.

Alternatives to Major Culture Change

Given the difficulties of producing cultural change, especially a radical change in the content of a strong culture, it makes sense to ask whether the desired results can be achieved in other ways. Indeed, this is one of the creative aspects of management. It is recommended that the following questions be seriously considered before planning a major onslaught on the prevailing culture, especially a strong one:

1. Can the Desired Results Be Obtained by Behavior Change without Culture Change? Using behavior change alone is a particularly attractive option where only temporary changes in behavior are required to deal with a transient situation. It may also be a better alternative where the culture must remain weak because the business environment is unstable and requires abrupt changes in the organization's behavior patterns.

There are also times when the necessary behavior changes must be effected quickly and when culture change is less critical. At Citibank in the early 1970s, for instance, John Reed converted the operating group from a service-oriented back office to a "factory" in order to cope with the rising tide of paper (Chapter 10). Reed had little time to spare and to effect the change relied on (1) a core group of managers with expertise in production management (many of them recruited from the Ford Motor Company), (2) heavy use of threats and punishments as extrinsic motivators, and (3) the attrition or removal of several people. Culture change did not follow, but that it was not essential is evident from applying the three critical tests just mentioned. Ineffciency was not great because having all people located on two floors in one building made behavior compliance relatively easy to monitor. Insufficiency was not a big problem because the changes were toward a predictable, routine technology that left little room for novelty or possibility of having to deal with the unexpected, once the operations were debugged and running. Finally, irrelevancy was not a major consideration because the important changes involved people's skills and behavior rather than their perceptions and other mental processes.

2.   Can the Desired Results Be Obtained by Creatively Utilizing the Existing Potential of the Prevailing Culture?   Rather than viewing culture as something to be changed, one can look upon it with the frame of mind that says: "Culture is my friend. How can I rely on it to accomplish the desired ends?" For example, in a professional consulting group with a Lone Ranger culture in which members worked on their own, several attempts to transform the group's culture into a more collaborative one failed. Finally, the business strategy and organization were reconceptualized as several independent entrepreneurs, each with a fiefdom, in lieu of the failed attempts to get them to collaborate and dominate a preferred market segment. Results improved dramatically and were sustained for a longer period of time than ever before.

3.   Can the Desired Results Be Obtained by Utilizing the Latent Potential of the Prevailing Culture?   Rather than looking upon culture as something to be changed, one can ask: "What hidden part of this culture can I awaken to achieve the intended results?" If appropriate dormant values can be detected and activated (constituting an incremental, rather than a radical, change in culture's content as explained earlier), the desired results may be more easily achieved. For example, the newly appointed head of a demoralized unit decided to challenge the group on what he correctly perceived to be their two hidden "hot buttons": self-confidence and pride in the group. The group responded tentatively at first, but these values were strengthened and reinstilled in the group as the new leader repeatedly showed the group how performance improved when these dormant values were adhered to.

4.   Can the Desired Results Be Achieved via a Culture Change toward More Intrinsically Appealing Beliefs and Values Rather than toward More Alien Ones?   A highly successful U.S. family business that had built a strong corporate culture around the central value of family spirit had considerable difficulty getting new offices in southeast Asia to buy into this value. When the head of international operations, a son of the founder, took it upon himself to build a stronger "international culture" by preaching this value in his visits to the new offices, he met with reactions ranging from apathy to hostility. He learned that most of his host country employees viewed the term *family* as an almost sacred symbol of kinship ties and resented its use in the context of their employment with a foreign company. There was greater receptivity to the notion that the employees were invited guests of the U.S. company, and eventually these people bought into the values of concern and caring for the U.S. "host," which helped to generate the spirit the company was seeking.

5.   What Evidence Is There That a Major Culture Change Can Be Successfully Carried Out in a Reasonable Period?   In the interest of constructive debate, consider the evidence for two rather different sets of somewhat arbitrary conditions.

Possibility of major culture changes being made in small- and medium-size organizations within a reasonable period (less than 5,000 people in less than five years) where there is high resistance. There is evidence available that such culture change is possible under these boundary conditions. The cases of George Coulter and Jim Henderson discussed here are two examples. Both conversion of existing organizational members (processes 1, 2, and 3 in Figure 12–1) and removal, addition, and socialization of new members (processes 4 and 5) are viable options in attempts to create such change.

Possibility of major culture change being made in large organizations in a reasonable period (more than 5,000 people in less than five years) where there is high resistance. Maybe the current attention to corporate culture change (see Reading 4–2) will yield some positive results in due course, but at this time I am unaware of any evidence to suggest that such a culture change is possible under these boundary conditions.

If this is true, readers of the best seller *In Search of Excellence* by Peters and Waterman are mistaken if they assume that a large corporation can readily transform its culture to become more like its "excellent" cousins.[32] Quite apart from the conceptual and methodological questions that have been raised about this work, as far as I can tell none of the excellent companies got to their present state via a major culture change in postadolescent years (i.e., once they got beyond 5,000 employees, with a change in less than five years).[33] The one possible exception, and it is frequently mentioned in the popular press as an example of successful culture change, is Dana Corporation (see Reading 4–1). However, this transformation began in the late 1950s under the leadership of Rene McPherson when Dana was a much smaller organization; my understanding is that even then it took more than five years for the new culture to form.

Indications are that the cultures of excellent companies were formed early in their history when they were small or medium size and were developed by succeeding generations of management that adhered to the cultural values and maintained these cultures by careful and consistent attention to human resource management over a long period of time, often spanning two decades or more (e.g., IBM, Procter & Gamble, 3M). (Reading 4–3, "Fitting New Employees into Company Culture" by Richard Pascale, describes the consistency and care with which some of these companies select and socialize their employees.)

If this is a valid analysis, there are serious implications for leaders of large organizations. They may need to recalibrate their expectations about how soon major culture change can be accomplished, and perhaps reconceptualize their strategies around the possibilities for more modest culture change within a reasonable period. Or they may need to contemplate and undertake more massive removal and addition of people (processes 4 and 5) than they might prefer to have to do, but there are limits to how quickly culture can be changed by utilizing these processes, as already discussed.

In sum, an understanding of these approaches and methods can help managers decide how best to utilize the prevailing culture to the extent possible, and how to transform it to the extent necessary, to most effectively achieve the desired results.

CASE 4–1
Peter Strassman

Roger Schwarz
Vijay Sathe

In May 1978, Peter Strassman was assessing his progress as general manager of Electechs, one of LEM Corporation's divisions. Since 1974 he had undertaken the task of creating a single divisional identity from the seven companies that LEM had acquired during the period 1972–78. Prime Motors was proving the hardest to fold into the division, although others were posing similar challenges. In addition to getting each acquired company to think in Electechs terms of planning and control, Strassman sought to ensure that the companies worked well together to offer better products and services to end users.

When you acquire a company, you have to provide directions. It's like a lieutenant who is always out in front of his troops. "Why are you always out in front?" someone asked him. "Because you can't push a toy with a string," he answered. Each acquisition is a community unto itself, and they are very resistant to change. They are small, entrepreneurial, and used to flexibility. They built their business on enthusiasm and pride around their name. . . .

Copyright © 1984 by the President and Fellows of Harvard College
Harvard Business School case 9–482–097.

Prime Motors has been the most difficult of all the acquisitions because of a couple of people at the top of the business. Their concept of how to run a business is dramatically opposed to mine. I could have let them run on their own, but that's not what I think we should do. I am trying to build an integrated business in motors and switches by using a unified strategy. I want to create crosspollination internally, and project this Electechs image outside.

By crosspollination, Strassman meant that each operation would work with the others toward meeting the customers' needs. For example, Strassman expected Prime Motors to tell customers about the other companies in the Electech Division. If a customer needed a product that none of the Electech companies produced, Strassman expected that two or more of them would work together to design a product that met the customer's needs.

Strassman had some simple ways to judge whether and to what extent the Electechs identity was being created. One was whether the switchboard operators answered calls with "Electechs-Prime Motors" or just "Prime Motors." Another indication was whether the acquired company used business cards that carried the Electechs name and logo. Strassman had found that most of the operation's cards did not carry the Electechs name. He solved the problem by having the Pittsburgh headquarters print business cards. Name recognition surveys also gave Strassman an indication of Electechs' identity as it affected competitors' and customers' perception.

Electechs had acquired three companies prior to 1974. Prime Motors, acquired in 1975, had been Strassman's first acquisition as division manager. Three more companies were acquired between 1975 and 1978. Strassman believed that each acquired company had its own methods of control, market strategies, and attitudes toward its workers. One couldn't shove changes in these areas "down the throats" of managers. Change was a slow process that involved building loyalty and demonstrating that the changes benefited the acquired company. Strassman felt that once the managers of an acquired company saw the benefits of the suggested changes, resistance would diminish.

Strassman was aware that the managers of the acquired companies tended to see him as constraining their autonomy and, at times,

exerting too much influence. Strassman realized that their view of him was not unlike his view of corporate LEM.

Career and Background

Peter Strassman began as project engineer with Aqua Motors in 1958. In 1963, he was named operations manager of Aqua. By 1970, when Aqua Motors was acquired by the LEM Corporation, he was senior vice president for marketing and engineering. His biographical sketch appears in Exhibit 1.

When Strassman took over as division general manager in 1974, the Electechs business was not very large—$22 million in sales. His operations managers were "pretty green" and Strassman spent considerable time developing them. This fit well with his active hands-on personal style. Strassman felt that his boss, Ted Landek, "nodded a lot" and took an essentially laissez-faire stance toward Strass-

Exhibit 1
Strassman's Background

Education	College—Rutgers University, B.S. Engineering 1962. Harvard Business School, Summer AMP program 1975–76.
Military Service	U.S. Air Force, June 1941–August 1944.
Professional Career	1945–1958: Employed by Atlantic Motors Corporation starting as technician and advancing to project engineer. 1958–1970: Joined Aqua Motors, Inc. Held positions of chief engineer, manager of manufacturing, marketing and sales manager during this period. Became senior vice president responsible for both marketing and engineering in 1966 and served as member of the Board of Directors. 1970–present: Became LEM Corporation employee in 1970 through the acquisition of Aqua Motors by LEM Corporation. Retained the position of senior vice president of Aqua Motors through 1972. Appointed Electechs' division general manager in 1974.

man and Electechs. As long as Strassman kept Landek informed, Landek made few requests, unless the president or chairman wanted something done.

Strassman believed that his major accomplishments as general manager of Electechs had been to develop business through diversification and internal product development and to provide efficient solutions to customer problems. His subordinates and those outside the division viewed him as an entrepreneur who often felt constrained by corporate policy but who recognized the need for corporate control. Strassman earned his reputation, in part, by jointly developing proprietary products with other corporations and by purchasing new technologies for making products. Strassman's actions were noticed at the upper levels. At one board meeting, the chairman stated that LEM needed more entrepreneurs and cited Strassman and another general manager as examples.

Prime Motors

In 1975, Electechs was looking to acquire a motor business that was compatible with and complementary to its other operations. Strassman wanted to develop the motor and switch business so that Electechs could sell motor systems rather than isolated components. A corporate acquisition group brought Prime to Strassman's attention.

When Strassman first visited Prime's operations near Los An-geles, California, he had mixed reactions. Prime had been in business for 35 years. It was started by three principals who had a proprietary technology—motors that were very reliable under extreme conditions. To Strassman, the high-performance plant looked like a glorified machine shop, but to the Prime employees, it was a sophisticated organization. They told Strassman they were always looking for products that would sell in large quantities, but Strassman got the impression they were really a specialty house.

All those who were in authority at Prime had grown up in the organization. That wasn't necessarily bad in Strassman's view, but he felt that many of the managers were not capable of developing new ideas or providing direction. Prime management believed in participative management. When Strassman asked to see an organization chart, they didn't have one. The president drew one up on a piece of paper; he drew a number of boxes: one each for the chairman, president, two vice presidents, and the remainder represented committees.

From talking with Prime president Scott Morgan, Strassman realized that the whole organization was built on conflict rather than cooperation. Each function distrusted the other functions, and each had individuals assigned to handle complaints from the others. Morgan said he wanted this type of conflict. He saw it as a way of auditing functional operations, a way for each function to keep the others honest. In addition, functions second-guessed each other: When a customer inquired whether Prime could make a certain product, marketing would forward the inquiry to engineering without any discussion. After engineering drew up a design it believed met the customer's needs, manufacturing costed out the product. When marketing received the plans and costs, it decided the price was too high. It sent the plans to the potential customer but cut the cost, believing that manufacturing could make the product for less than it had quoted. Once the customer placed the order and engineering drew up detailed plans, manufacturing found it could not make the product at the price marketing had quoted.

When Prime made decisions on larger issues, such as capital investments, a committee was set up to consider the issues. Sometimes the committee reached a decision only to find that Prime's chairman, Dan Steadman, had independently arrived at another. Once a committee that Steadman had appointed to decide whether and how much the machine shop should be expanded recommended that Prime invest several hundred thousand dollars; at that point Steadman told the committee he was willing to spend only $100,000 and suggested the specific pieces of machinery to be purchased. Strassman believed that Steadman, who started the business, could have made these decisions alone; the committees seemed to be a form of pseudoparticipation.

Strassman learned that Steadman, who owned 45 percent of Prime, was a conservative but paternalistic individual. For instance, the top 15 to 20 people at Prime were given an annual bonus, and all of the 400 employees were invited to visit and stay at Steadman's ranch in Arizona and his lakeside property in northern California during most of the weeks of the year when Steadman was not using them. There was no charge; even meals and drinks were on the house when employees took advantage of the standing offer from Steadman. This paternalism extended to job security—there never had been a layoff at Prime, even during the occasional offyear. As one old timer recalled: "Prime doesn't pay well, but we like the place and have a dedication to getting the job done. We bitch and moan about the low pay, but no one is leaving because we have a lot of fun here."

Prime Motors appeared to be an attractive acquisition because its extreme-condition, high-performance motor was the Cadillac of the industry. Strassman knew the company had a good reputation from his earlier years as a rocket propulsion engineer. Also, corporate LEM's analysis of the company revealed that it had good manufacturing facilities, a good location, and good growth potential. More important, the growth had been limited by the owner's desire to avoid debt. With corporate's approval, Electechs acquired Prime Motors for $18 million in the spring of 1975.

At that time Electechs bought out Prime Motors' president and chairman and offered them one-year consulting contracts. Scott Morgan, the president, was the marketing expert, and Dan Steadman, the chairman, had been responsible for the technical area. Steadman considered John Howell, the vice president of marketing, to be the heir apparent. Strassman learned that Steadman always looked after Howell, an engineering graduate from Stanford and that he had appointed Howell president just before selling Prime.

Strassman spent a day with Howell before the acquisition and was very impressed with his knowledge of the operation and the level of detail with which he spoke about it. A charismatic individual, who apparently had a strong following at Prime, Howell talked at length about manufacturing and spoke only briefly about marketing and engineering.

Management Differences

The first sign of differences between Strassman and Howell became evident when Electechs attempted to install its control system at Prime, as it did in all acquired companies. The control system required forecasts of sales and gross margins for the upcoming 30 and 60 days. Ideally, marketing and manufacturing worked with the controller to develop the forecasts. In acquisitions where marketing and manufacturing had not worked closely with the controller,

the burden of preparing the forecasts usually fell on the controller. One and a half years before the acquisition, Prime's controller had left and had not been replaced, so Strassman placed Harvey Burke, an LEM controller, in Prime to install the new system and to remain as controller. But Howell had his own "push-through" method of control, which he continued to use and from which he questioned the numbers that Burke worked up.

The push-through method of control dispensed with a perpetual physical inventory. Instead, Howell would decide how much profit he wanted to make in a given period and adjust the value of the inventory accordingly by declaring certain inventoried products obsolete and "recomputing" the cost of goods sold. Strassman pressed Howell to drop the push-through method and adopt the Electechs system, but Howell would either not respond or would agree half-heartedly and fail to follow up. He continued to use the push-through method and continually questioned the validity of the numbers Burke generated using the LEM control system.

From the beginning, Howell felt he should be allowed to run Prime as an autonomous operation. Whenever Strassman or other Electechs managers gave him advice, Howell would say that he had his own ideas on the topics or would try to appease them by agreeing, but would never implement their ideas. In personnel matters, he emphasized that California was different and that LEM didn't understand the needs of his employees.

Howell never told Strassman how their needs differed from those of other employees, but Strassman did concede there were some differences in attitudes and behavior. Prime employees were reluctant to work on weekends and sometimes refused to do so even when tight deadlines had to be met. This was usually not a problem for Electechs' operations outside California. Howell wanted to hire Californians to fill key positions at Prime, ostensibly because it took a Californian to understand and work with Californians.

Although Strassman thought Howell was technically well qualified, he became concerned that Howell was focusing too much on details. Howell did not seem to have enough understanding of the total business or to think about growth. While Howell believed the company would continue to grow, Strassman tried to convince him that Prime could grow even faster by melding with other Electechs operations, and through central distribution and advertising. Strassman's conception was that the combined products and efforts of the Electechs operations could provide comprehensive, unified systems and solutions that addressed customers' problems.

In October 1975, six months after the acquisition, Prime's performance was discussed at the annual Electechs Planning Meeting, which Strassman conducted. Prime had achieved good performance in fiscal year ending October 1975, its first year as part of LEM Corporation, with pretax ROS of 18.5 percent (Exhibit 2). Strassman attributed this largely to the accumulation of customer orders from the previous year, which re-

Exhibit 2
Sales and Return on Sales (ROS) for Electechs and Prime Motors

Electechs

		FY 1975	FY 1976	FY 1977
Sales ($ millions)	Plan	34.6	51.3	66.7
	Actual	51.2	57.6	69.9
ROS (pretax percentage)	Plan	16.2	14.0	17.0
	Actual	5.4	13.5	17.0

Prime Motors

		FY 1975	FY 1976	FY 1977
Sales ($ millions)	Plan	14.5	17.5	19.1
	Actual	16.3	16.8	20.6
ROS (pretax percentage)	Plan	13.8	20.0	14.0
	Actual	18.5	13.5	16.5

mained unfilled while Prime's owners were busy negotiating Prime's sale. Strassman noted the delayed shipments had left plenty of Prime's customers unhappy, and their resentment would soon have to be addressed.

There were other areas in which Strassman believed Prime could substantially improve performance. He felt that Prime, like many small, owner-managed companies, had inefficient work methods and inadequate planning and control systems. Productivity would be dramatically increased by rearranging existing equipment, by automating certain production processes, and by reducing the work force. For instance, Prime's current approach to planning and budgeting was to project increases in all expense categories by the same percentage as the projected percentage increase in sales. Thus failure to seek gains in operating leverage would lead to an overburdened operating plan. Similarly, level loading of manufacturing facilities was not planned for—a disproportionately high percentage of monthly production shipments occurred in the last two weeks of the month. Direct labor was staffed at the level required for these peak periods, resulting in underutilizing labor during the first two weeks of each month. Based on his analyses of these factors, Strassman reasoned that Prime could easily effect a permanent 10 percent reduction in the 400-person work force through more efficient production planning and labor utilization.

Strassman also believed Prime was not realizing its full earnings potential—the earnings it could return given the value of its service to customers. Prime offered customized products to aerospace companies, as well as more standardized commodity products for industrial use. The aerospace business, involving made-to-order items, commanded 75 percent in gross margins; the industrial business yielded 30 percent gross margin with efficient distribution of these commodity products. By emphasizing selected segments of the aerospace business and by better managing distribution of the industrial products, Strassman believed Prime could achieve its earnings potential—45 percent gross margin and 20 percent pretax ROS.

The 20 percent figure was cast in concrete when Strassman sent it to corporate LEM as part of Electechs' financial forecast. When Strassman told Howell about the 20 percent ROS target, Howell said he could not do better than 9 percent based on his push-through calculations. Between October 1975 and June 1976, Strassman and Howell discussed whether Prime's earnings potential was 9 percent, 20 percent or something in between. Strassman could not get Howell to see that Prime's earnings potential should be 20 percent. To Strassman, Howell seemed unable to grasp the concept of earnings potential.

In early June 1976, Strassman flew out to California to review Prime's performance with Don Johnson, Electechs' manufacturing director. Johnson was Howell's other superior in the matrix (Exhibit 3). During the operations review, the issue of the company logo also arose. As part of his plan to build a division identity, Strassman insisted that each operation's letterhead and advertising carry LEM Electechs' logo with the operation's name underneath. Howell wanted to keep the Prime Motors' logo and told Strassman that Prime's customers would not recognize the product without the logo. He also told Strassman that after 35 years, all old timers and most of the rest of the employees were emotionally attached to the logo and proudly looked up to it as their symbol of quality. Strassman responded, "We're not going to take the logo away immediately. Put the logo on the product if you want."

Howell argued that the logo was a $480,000 asset, and they could not claim it if they did not use it. Strassman told Howell that if they were really concerned about the

Exhibit 3
Electechs Division Structure—Prior to the June 1976 Reorganization

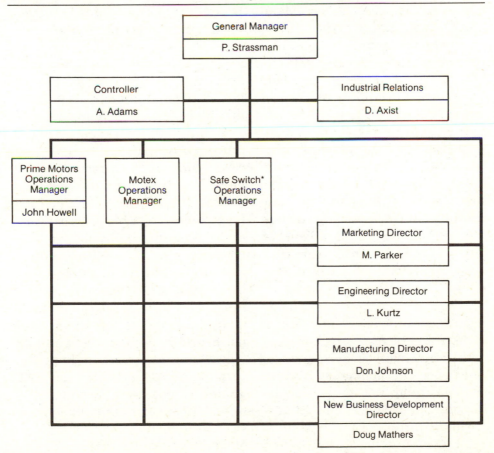

* Similar organizational reporting arrangement for Eastern Switch, Matel, Aqua Motors, and Allied Wire.

$480,000, he would find a way around it. In the end, Howell agreed to use the Electechs logo. Strassman realized why Howell was so adamant about the logo. His entire career had been with Prime: He had grown up with the logo and could not part with that symbol from his past.

When the subject turned to productivity, Strassman told Howell that Prime should be able to reach at least 14 percent pretax ROS in fiscal year 1976, instead of the 9 percent Howell had quoted last October. In the 14 months since Electechs had acquired Prime, Strassman had learned much about Prime's business. With more knowledge of Prime's costs and information about its competition, Strassman could better estimate Prime's earnings potential. He realized the 20 percent ROS was slightly high, although it was appropriate for fiscal year 1976 because of Prime's order backlog. Acknowledging that it would take some time for Prime to increase volume and cut costs, Strassman told Howell he would accept 14 percent ROS for fiscal year 1977 but insisted on an 18 percent ROS for fiscal year 1978 (Exhibit 2).

Strassman suggested reducing the number of Prime's 400 employees as a way of increasing productivity. Strassman believed that 20 could be cut immediately, but Howell would not entertain the thought. "I have never laid off anyone in the history of Prime Motors, and I am not going to start now." "It's not your decision to make," Strassman snapped, and added, "I

want a staff reduction plan on my desk by next Friday."

By the following Thursday, Strassman had not yet received the plan in Pittsburgh and called to see if it would be there the next day. Howell told Strassman he had not worked on the plan and was not going to. "Get on a plane Sunday night and be here first thing Monday morning," Strassman demanded.

When Howell arrived at Electechs' headquarters on Monday morning, he was indignant at having to fly out "under orders." Strassman and Howell met with Don Johnson and together developed a plan to lay off Prime's staff and increase productivity. Even after the plan had been developed, Strassman doubted that Howell was convinced, and Howell never said he would implement the plan.

A couple of weeks later, Howell called Strassman and asked for a raise. Surprised, Strassman told Howell he had not done anything to deserve one. Howell maintained he was due for a higher salary because similar positions in the industry paid more. Howell mentioned that under the LEM contract he had signed at the time of the acquisition, he was to receive "equitable salary increases." Strassman had not heard of this contract and told Howell this. Howell thought he was very employable and said he wanted to look elsewhere as well as to seek professional placement advice. Strassman encouraged him to do so, recognizing that it was important for Howell to "clear his conscience."

Strassman later called his boss, group vice president Ted Landek, and asked about the contract. Landek explained that Howell signed the standard LEM contract. The contract stated that, as an LEM employee, Howell was entitled to equitable salary increases, but it did not mention any specific timetable or amounts. As it turned out, Howell was earning more than anyone else in a comparable position in LEM.

Serious Doubts

By late June 1976, Strassman had serious doubts about Howell's ability to do the job in areas other than manufacturing. As Strassman saw it, he had three options. He could keep things as they were and expend what he felt was an inordinate amount of his time on Prime. He could replace Howell with Don Johnson, director of manufacturing and currently Howell's other immediate superior. Or he could effect a reorganization of the division to address the problem.

Leaving things as they were was intolerable to Strassman because of the 2,000 miles separating him from Howell. If Strassman were at Prime, he could give Howell objectives and control him more closely. Replacing Howell with Don Johnson was an attractive option. Strassman considered Johnson a supersound manager, a type Prime needed badly. Strassman believed Johnson, unlike Howell, was a generalist who worked through people and could bring the functions together. He was straightforward and loyal to those who worked for

him. If anyone from outside California could be accepted in Prime, Strassman believed it was Johnson. Johnson had been with LEM for 41 years and would have gone to California if Strassman had asked. However Johnson was planning to retire in two years, and Strassman thought it was unreasonable to ask him to move.

Strassman's third option was to reorganize the division, which is what he did. In late June 1976, Strassman dismantled the matrix and established the structure shown in Exhibit 4. The matrix structure had been set up in 1973 by John Hansen, then general manager of Electechs, upon his return from Harvard Business School's AMP program. Strassman, then senior vice president for operations, had each of the operations managers reporting to him, and he in turn reported directly to Hansen. The matrix structure had not been easy to work in. The managers who ran the operating groups had persistent difficulties with those heading the marketing, manufacturing, and engineering functions. For example, engineering director Larry Kurtz attempted to apply statistical quality control to the operations. His group wrote many reports and made recommendations, but none of the operations adopted the method (see Exhibit 3). The matrix was unwieldy, and Strassman felt he needed to establish clearer lines of authority. An even greater impetus for the reorganization was to help solve the problems at Prime. Strassman thought restructuring the division

Exhibit 4
Electechs Division, after the June 1976 Reorganization

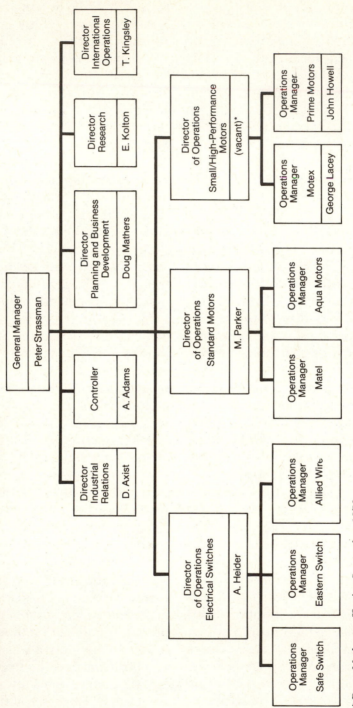

* Doug Mathers, effective September 1976.

would free up some of the time he was spending on Prime. Strassman grouped the seven operations into three areas: electrical switches under Arthur Heider; standard motors under Martin Parker; and small/high-performance motors, for which he was seeking an appropriate director (Exhibit 4).

Doug Mathers

In September 1976, Strassman made Doug Mathers director of the small/high-performance motor area. With the change, Howell reported directly to Mathers (see Exhibit 4). Mathers had sold his company, Motex, to Electechs in 1972 and through the sale became moderately wealthy. He served as Motex operations manager until May 1976, when Strassman gave him special aerospace projects to work on as director of Planning and Business Development.

Strassman described Mathers as a true entrepreneur, "the type that likes to work on the back of an envelope." As a business owner, Mathers had been a taskmaster. He had worked his employees long hours and often on holidays. He had been involved in the day-to-day workings of the company. When problems developed, he had been quick to get rid of the person responsible. Mathers had a solid grasp of engineering and marketing of aerospace products, which required working on a one-on-one basis with aerospace people.

Strassman knew Mathers' strong aerospace background could become his short suit as well. One of Prime's major problems, according to Strassman, was that it focused too much on the aerospace industry and not enough on industrial applications. Prime managers maintained that their strategy was to develop products for aerospace and then push them through the industry, a strategy that so far had succeeded with only one motor. Strassman believed the other push-through attempts failed because the motors were overdesigned and too expensive for industrial use. Since industrial sales accounted for 85 percent of Prime's volume, but only 55 percent of its earnings, Strassman wanted Prime to focus more on industry sales by raising prices slightly and by developing other products for industrial use. Strassman wondered whether Mathers would push the industrial side of the business, given his aerospace orientation, but decided to go ahead with his appointment as director of small/high-performance motors for lack of a better candidate.

The reorganization freed Strassman's time but absorbed Mathers'. Mathers was responsible for two operations but was spending literally 99 percent of his time on Prime, primarily on marketing and engineering. Mathers established basic marketing strategies and dealt directly with customers, something Howell had never done. He helped engineering develop new aerospace products.

Mathers became directly involved in these activities, rather than getting Howell to do them. As a result, he spent little time building the general small/high-performance motors area, his main responsibility as director. In addition, Strassman felt Mathers was beginning to side with Howell. On one trip back to Pittsburgh, Mathers told Strassman, "We have this problem with the logo, Peter." Strassman thought to himself, "He's starting to become one of them." Although not raised in California, Mathers' quick assimilation into the West Coast work style led Strassman to think of Mathers as having become "part of the granola bowl." Strassman believed Mathers' entrepreneurial instincts made him especially sensitive about being seen as a loser. He got defensive whenever Strassman pointed out problems or would rationalize that the problems were already present when he took over as director of small/high-performance motors.

Continuing Problems with Howell

Although Strassman continued to question Howell's attitude and ability, he was not ready to let him go. Howell was conscientious and personable, and Strassman had scored what he viewed as some victories with him. Howell had agreed to move advertising and promotion to the Electechs headquarters in Pittsburgh. Over the summer, Strassman had told Howell that he would not have complete autonomy in running Prime and would have to conform to Electechs' objectives, plans, and controls. Strassman thought Howell had understood and accepted this.

Strassman was also reluctant to let Howell go so soon after appointing Doug Mathers as director of small/high-performance motors because of the possible disruption this might create. Besides, Strassman felt he owed Mathers an opportunity to develop Howell. Mathers was confident that Howell would work out if he worked more closely with him and moved his office to Prime's operations in Los Angeles in order to work with Howell on a day-to-day basis. As an outsider to Prime, Mathers' strategy was to develop loyalty slowly, rather than to move quickly and possibly risk resistance. It was conceivable to Mathers that others at Prime would resist him if they saw that Howell did.

In December 1976, three months after Mathers' appointment as Howell's boss, Strassman had a conversation with Howell that left him in greater doubt about Howell's ability and judgment. Prime's marketing manager had just quit, and Strassman suggested that this would be a good opportunity for Howell to learn more about marketing; he wanted Howell to get a broader sense of the business. Howell admitted he did not know much about marketing, but showed no interest in Strassman's suggestion.

Other problems were also developing at Prime. Howell had decided to market a new motor (number 61) and had budgeted $500,000 of inventory. Howell built up $1 million in inventory instead, even though distributors showed little interest in the 61 motor. Prime was thus saddled with all the inventory. Essentially the same mistake had been made by Prime prior to the acquisition—distributors wanted to carry a full line of motors, rather than stand-alone items, such as the 61. Furthermore, Prime had bought specialized machinery to manufacture the 61, instead of the general-purpose machinery that Strassman had recommended. The specialized machinery was useless except to produce more 61 motors. At this point, Strassman's communication with Howell was principally through Mathers. He instructed Mathers to figure out a way to get rid of the 61 motor inventory. Mathers took on the responsibility himself, and soon Prime managers were bypassing Howell and going directly to Mathers instead.

About one year later, in December 1977, Strassman thought the attitudes at Prime had changed somewhat. Prime had accepted certain Electechs suggestions, and a few key managers were telling Strassman that his persistence was beginning to pay off. However, the personnel manager, Joanne Danbury, who had been secretary to Prime's chairman Dan Steadman, was creating more problems.

Joanne Danbury

Joanne Danbury was personnel manager when Electechs acquired Prime. Strassman dubbed her a "social worker type." Shortly before the acquisition, the union had attempted to organize Prime and had lost by one vote. Danbury believed that unions were necessary because management often did not give the workers what they deserved. Back in 1976, when Strassman was at Harvard Business School's Summer AMP program, Prime increased compensation for employees—something Strassman did not support. On a subsequent trip to Prime, Strassman had raised the subject with Danbury.

Danbury lectured Strassman on how workers at all levels were entitled to homes, food, and cars, and what was a minimum income to live on in California. Strassman said he understood, but that he didn't agree with her decision to raise compensation for Prime employees. Danbury then began to tell Strassman about Maslow's theory of hierarchy needs, and she started writing these on the board. Strassman interrupted, "Joanne, erase the board and stop right there. I'm not listening." Strassman thought, "She is trying to maintain the old ways. She is just like a union rep." The next day Strassman told Mathers to "get Danbury out of there."

As a first step, Strassman required that Danbury report directly to him, and he questioned her about everything. For example, she was not willing to place an engineer from outside Prime above an engineer who had been at Prime a long time. Strassman also placed Danbury on a corporate responsibility committee, "to give her a chance to broaden her perspective." She felt like an outcast there, realized she had no power to change things, and gave up.

Soon afterwards Danbury approached Mathers and expressed her frustration with Strassman. Mathers suggested that she probably would not be able to make the changes she wanted and that this was probably a good time for her to earn her doctorate in psychology that she had hoped to get. Three months after Strassman had told him to get rid of Danbury, Mathers had gotten her to leave. He had done it by patiently, periodically suggesting to Danbury that she would be better off if she left Prime.

Herb Gardner

With Danbury gone, Strassman told Mathers to find someone in LEM in industrial relations (IR) who was not from California. When Mathers suggested Herb Gardner, Howell resisted, feeling that only someone from California could be the IR person in California because California was different. When Strassman heard this, he told Mathers to "get them to accept Gardner." When Gardner was scheduled to fly out to Prime to meet Howell and other key managers, Strassman warned Howell, "If I get any indication that Herb was discouraged, I will be very upset."

Mathers and Gardner liked each other from the start. They were of the same religion, and Mathers helped Gardner find a home and a good school system for his children. The other key managers also liked Gardner. At first Gardner sometimes got ensnarled in policies Danbury had previously established. For example, Danbury had planned a job fair when Gardner took over. Danbury had placed an ad in the local paper which stated that engineering and other professional jobs were available and invited interested individuals to tour the plant. The purpose of the fair was to allow employees' families to see where Mom or Dad worked and also to attract potential new employees in an extremely tight hiring market (local unemployment was only 4 percent). When Strassman heard about this, he told Howell to cancel the job fair because he was concerned that Prime's competition would tour the plant and obtain useful information. With the ad in the paper, it was too late to cancel. The fair was held. A month later, ostensibly under pressure from Howell, Gardner held a second job fair. When Strassman found out a second fair had been held, he was furious.

After a while, Gardner was able to make changes that were accepted, such as changing the performance review system. In the past, supervisors had written narratives that focused on the subordinates' traits, rather than objectives the subordinates were to accomplish. The narratives were usually extremely complimentary, and it was difficult to distinguish among subordinates' performances.

The problem came to a head when Prime needed a new materials manager. Materials accounted for 40 percent of product cost, and it was important that Prime find a highly competent manager for this position. Within the last year, several people who had come up from the hourly ranks had filled the position; when one could not do the job, another replaced him or her. Gardner set up an MBO performance review system. Based on Strassman's instructions, Gardner had each superior rank order his or her subordinates. Strassman believed that ranking personnel would, among other things, prevent the "musical chairs" phenomenon that had plagued the position of materials manager.

Escalating the Battle with Howell

Howell continued to ignore Mathers' suggestions to drop the push-through accounting method. Harvey Burke, the LEM controller whom Strassman placed in Prime, had already quit in frustration. Before Burke had left, he told Strassman that he was quitting for five reasons and three of them were Howell. Strassman warned Howell, "If you don't get rid of your bookkeeping system, I will have to consider some serious changes."

Production problems also continued. Larger variances in the cost of production caused Prime to raise its prices, and Strassman thought Prime was close to pricing itself out of the market. Part of the problem stemmed from inefficient use of labor. The plant would plan on 20,000 earned labor hours for the year and get only 12,000.

When Strassman asked for specific costs, such as start-up costs, Howell would parry the question, stating he could dig up the information, but it would take a lot of time and probably would not be helpful.

Despite these problems, Prime's fiscal year 1977 ROS was 16.5 percent, better than the 14 percent goal Strassman had set. Later, Strassman found out that Prime reached the 16.5 percent figure by adjusting inventory profits. The unfavorable variance resulting from discrepancies between Prime's actual and standard costs had been capitalized and closed into finished inventory, effectively deferring the unfavorable flow-through to the income statement for the following year. This procedure, which was acceptable within the LEM accounting system, presumed fairly accurate standard costs, something Prime did not have.

Strassman, more and more frustrated with Howell, told Mathers to back off Howell. (Mathers had established Howell's previous set of objectives.) It was time for Howell to show he could set his own business objectives. Strassman added that if he had to tell Howell what the new opportunities were, then "someone is going to lose their situation." Mathers still had confidence in Howell, and Strassman respected Mathers' judgment. Yet Strassman wondered whether Mathers, after having sold his business to Electechs, had run out of gas in being demanding and just wanted to be a nice guy.

The Annual Planning Meeting

Strassman, those reporting directly to him, and each of the operations managers (Exhibit 4) met each year in March for the three-day Electechs Planning Meeting. The first two days were typically devoted to an informal but in-depth review of each of the divisions' businesses—objectives, strategies, products, markets, growth opportunities, critical issues, three-year plans, and annual budgets. From these preliminary discussions was to be synthesized a one-hour presentation on the third day for LEM's top brass. Those attending typically included Ted Landek, group vice president in charge of Electechs, Bob Delega, corporate vice president for planning, and Robert Schmidt, LEM's president. The three other divisions under Landek made similar presentations. Strassman traditionally elected to have his three directors of operations each make 20-minute presentations, limiting his own role to brief opening and closing remarks. Strassman participated much more actively in the informal but more critical give-and-take that typically followed the prepared presentations.

Strassman and other Electechs executives arrived in Palm Beach, Florida, for the annual planning meeting on Sunday, March 12, 1978. Since Doug Mathers was not going to attend because his wife was ill, Strassman suggested that either George Lacey or John Howell, the two operations managers reporting to Mathers (Exhibit 4), take on the additional responsibility of making the 20-minute presentation for small/high-performance motors before corporate senior management on Wednesday. It was decided that John Howell would undertake this task. Although Howell had been on a two-week vacation immediately preceding the planning meeting, he had attended the previous year's meeting and knew what was expected.

Strassman was disappointed with Howell's performance during the preliminary sessions on Monday and Tuesday, March 13 and 14. Howell did not appear to have done his homework and was unresponsive to questions from colleagues and superiors. Despite some reservations, Strassman decided he owed Howell the opportunity to make the 20-minute presentation to corporate senior management on Wednesday, March 15, as planned. Unfortunately, according to Strassman, Howell's presentation was long, poorly prepared, and overly detailed. Howell talked about the new machinery Prime had purchased and how well it operated. At one point, Howell began talking about how the new corporate bonus system was unfair, because it excluded several managers at Prime who were included in the previous corporate bonus system. Howell announced that, to rectify this inequity, he and Mathers would share their bonuses with these managers. Howell directed these last comments at Schmidt, the corporate president. Strassman thought Howell had made a fool of himself; he was embarrassed by Howell's performance.

When Doug Mathers reported to work, Strassman told him what had happened. "Doug, you have to come to grips with this. There is a problem in your organization, and John Howell is that problem." Strassman said he had spoken to some key managers at Prime and they were frustrated with the situation. Howell had begun to ask each of the key managers to develop reports; Strassman and the managers considered these reports unnecessary make-work projects. Strassman gave Mathers the option of either getting rid of Howell or quickly changing the situation.

Toward the end of April 1978, Strassman sent Electechs' controller Al Adams to Prime to assess what changes had been made since Strassman last spoke with Howell in March. While Adams was speaking with the Prime controller, the controller received a call from the shop foreman. The foreman wanted to know if 35 people, for whom he had no work, should be let go. Adams found it hard to believe that Howell had been resisting a layoff despite excess manpower.

During the week of May 8, 1978, Strassman planned to meet with Mathers at Prime to decide what to do about Howell. Howell was taking the remaining two weeks of his vacation. Mathers preferred that Strassman not come to the Prime plant because if he did, there would be some tough questions for Strassman that Mathers felt would be difficult to dodge. For example,

the managers were likely to ask Strassman if Howell would be replaced. Mathers said he did not want to put Strassman in the position where he would have to respond to that question. Instead, he suggested they meet for dinner in Los Angeles to decide what to do.

CASE 4–2
Jeff Bradley (A)

C. Paul Dredge
Vijay Sathe

Jeff Bradley looked back with considerable pride at the way he had thrived on the supposed adversity of his initiation into Heartland Heavy Industries, the company he had joined upon graduation from HBS in 1975. Jeff had survived difficult situations, and he felt he had built an enduring team spirit in an organization where none existed before. Jeff had been able to apply much of what he had learned at HBS, but he also knew that his own personal resources had been instrumental in his success.

Now, in early 1977, Jeff faced a new set of challenges as head of a problem Heartland plant. Three weeks into his new assignment as plant manager, a position in line management that he had coveted, Jeff had to deal with a boss who was constantly looking over his

This case was prepared by C. Paul Dredge (under the direction of Vijay Sathe).

shoulder, a "cowboy" work force whose indifference to danger had given the plant a poor safety record, and a machine called the "spinner" that both workers and supervisors believed could be tamed only by ritual and magic. Jeff knew his promising start at Heartland could come to a screeching halt if he could not bring these problems under control and turn the plant around.

Background

Jeff had grown up on a modest western Kansas farm, a life that he said had helped develop his ability to "sort the wheat from the chaff" quickly. After graduating as valedictorian in his engineering class at the University of Kansas, Jeff joined Rapid Air Lines in St. Louis, where he soon moved into a management track. The first few months of what was to become four years of experience in successively more responsible management positions at Rapid had confirmed Jeff's earlier suspicions that he would enjoy putting aside his drawing board and calculator for the satisfaction of managing and working effectively with other people. His next step in management would require additional training, and Jeff learned that Rapid would pay for at least part of his tuition for an MBA, with no obligation to return to Rapid, provided that he could get admitted to one of several top schools.

In his first year at HBS, Jeff studied hard and did well; his highly organized lifestyle gave him plenty of time for athletic activity, adequate rest, and correspondence with his fiancée, Carol, in Kansas City. During the summer after his first year, Jeff went to work for the Premium National Bank of Kansas, turning down an offer from Rapid in order to learn something in a new area of business and be with his fiancée. Jeff found that, for his own tastes, people at the bank were too interested in political games and the cut of their clothes and not enough in accomplishing something really concrete. As for Rapid Air Lines, Jeff felt that advancement in that large, rather bureaucratic organization would probably be safe and secure, but much too slow, and he was not looking for that kind of a career.

Job Luck

During his second year at HBS, Jeff started a systematic job search. His criteria limited his choices. One thing Jeff wanted to avoid was the East Coast. "No need to bang my head in New York with all the other MBAs, and Boston never interested me all that much." Jeff preferred to locate in the heartland, where he grew up, to be near his family and the family of his wife-to-be in Kansas City. More important than location, however, was his desire to find a position with a manufacturing company where he could use his engineering background. He also wanted to get a job that would guarantee line management experience within 18 months.

The beginning of April found

Jeff with offers to return to Rapid Air Lines and the Premium National Bank, and a certain feeling of desperation. Three or four weeks before he had to decide on these offers, he received a call at 11 one night from Harold Maxfield, a corporate VP at Heartland Heavy Industries in Omaha, Nebraska. Maxfield indicated that he had noted the engineering degree and the four and a half years' work experience on Jeff's resume in the HBS Engineers' Club resume book, which the club had sent to 500 companies. He asked if Jeff would be interested in talking to him when he visited Cambridge the following Saturday. "Yes, I'm interested," was Jeff's happy reply.

Jeff went to the Sonesta Hotel room expecting the standard interview procedure—"Nobody really saying what they think." Maxfield told him to take off his coat and tie, sit down wherever he pleased, and without any of the usual polite preliminaries, started firing questions about everything imaginable. Maxfield was wearing a turtleneck shirt and lying on the bed in his stocking feet. "Why do you want to work for Heartland? What can you do for us? Why is a Harvard MBA such hot stuff, anyway? What is r^2?" Jeff sensed that Maxfield didn't want "the usual interview stuff" and responded with tough-minded answers and some jibes of his own. "The guy who came out of there before I went in looked awful, and I figured that the most important thing was not to buckle." On the phone and now in the interview, what Maxfield said about Heartland was appealing, even though he himself was a bit abrasive.

Maxfield explained that Heartland executives had decided they would have to tighten their management style in order to prosper in an increasingly competitive environment. In the past, the corporation had been run as a loosely knit group of operations, and management was becoming concerned that it had not developed sufficient numbers of young managers. Their proposed method was to hire some high-potential people, familiarize them with the company through an intensive on-the-job training program, and then use their new employees' knowledge of more modern management techniques to improve Heartland's operations. When they parted, Maxfield indicated that there was a good chance of an offer, that he would be back in touch within a week, and that he would send additional information on the company to help Jeff make a decision. Jeff indicated that he had three or four weeks before he'd have to decide on another offer.

Jeff did receive a fair bit of information on the company as Maxfield had promised, but he didn't hear from Maxfield. Jeff found out that Heartland, a billion dollar corporation, had average performance within its industry. On a Monday, nine days after the interview, Jeff called Maxfield. He was very cordial, apologized for not calling back, and said: "You're on the short list." Maxfield indicated that he would be leaving the office until Thursday, but would call Jeff then with the final word. Jeff thanked him, but after hanging up he started to worry about the timing of the possible offer and his limited knowledge of Heartland. How could he make a decision for or against Heartland on the basis of a short interview with Harold Maxfield and the information in the reports he had received? Since Jeff was inclined to go to Kansas City anyway to visit Carol and do some on-site job hunting, he decided by Wednesday to call Heartland to see if he could arrange a visit to company headquarters in Omaha.

As expected, Maxfield wasn't there, but his secretary asked if Jeff would like to speak with Clark White, the president of the corporation. Jeff said that would be fine. When Clark White came to the phone, Jeff introduced himself, acknowledged that no firm offer of a job had been made, and then expressed his reservations about responding favorably to an offer that might come. Jeff said that although he had been impressed with the company, he was reluctant to make a decision on the basis of an hour's interview. If Heartland was still interested, Jeff wanted to know if it would be possible for him to visit company headquarters and talk to a few more people about the position. White indicated that he had talked with Maxfield about a possible offer, that they were indeed still interested, and that he fully understood Jeff's reservations. White then arranged for Jeff's visit for the next day.

Jeff spent Thursday at a Heart-

land plant in Pittsburgh and Friday at company headquarters in Omaha taking a closer look. He soon found, with some relief, that Maxfield's brusque manner was the exception among the company officers he met. On the other hand, he was impressed, as he had been with Maxfield, with the hard-driving, no-nonsense style of several of the managers. Jeff was particularly interested in the very lean staff at headquarters—it was obvious to him they had good people and did a lot of delegating to division-level managers.

At the end of the day on Friday, Jeff had another interview with Maxfield and was offered the job. When asked about salary, Jeff told Maxfield that he would be happy with at least as much as the $23,500 Rapid Air Lines was offering him. (The median starting salary for the Class of 1975 was $18,600). Maxwell offered Jeff a $24,500 starting salary and added: "If you are not making $35,000 with us in a couple of years, you are not the man we want." Jeff had one other stipulation: Assuming that he did well in his initial assignments, he wanted to be sure he could move into a line management position after 18 months. Maxfield indicated that the company's timetable already called for that.

Before the interview ended, Maxfield told Jeff about what they had in mind for his training in the company. Maxfield indicated that it was of the utmost importance that Heartland managers be able to get along with "the dirty hands people" in the plants. Jeff would start out with nitty-gritty experience as a foreman in a foundry, Maxwell said, but he wasn't sure just where Jeff would be placed for this initial assignment:

> Just six months in purgatory and the new training program will take you somewhere more hospitable. For now we want you to start out in the dirtiest, hottest, noisiest job we can find.

As he deliberated his offers, Jeff knew that he could go back to Rapid—a known, comfortable situation in the location he preferred —and retire after 35 years with a gold watch, a good pension, and an easy life. With Heartland he would take the risk of working in a new and unknown industry, but would have the job in manufacturing he was seeking and also live closer to where he wanted to live. He sensed that, more than the other two places from which he had received offers, at Heartland he could learn from old hands in the company and simultaneously apply and test what he had learned at HBS. Moreover, there was a noticeable lack of young management talent at Heartland, which boded well for the rapid advancement Jeff hoped to achieve.

The Fiery Furnace

On June 7, 1975, Jeff graduated from HBS, with his mother and new bride on hand to celebrate. In Kansas City on June 9, Jeff went to Sears to buy a black metal lunch box, steel-toed shoes, and some green work outfits. "Is this the kind of job you get after a Harvard MBA? You should have stayed at Rapid!" his father said. Even Carol asked why she should have to make sandwiches every day for this supposed "executive." But Jeff felt confident about his job decision.

Jeff went to work as a foreman in a Heartland iron pipe plant in Gary, Indiana. His responsibility was to supervise 18 men in what seemed to be the dirtiest, least interesting job in the place: cleaning off the newly cast, angled fittings (e.g., elbows, reducers or "cones") that were used to connect the standard lengths of pipe.

> Dickens never described anything worse than our section of the plant. Soot, boiling ladles of molten iron, the incessant din of pneumatic chipping hammers, welding, the wheelabrator machine, grinding, and banging. The steel toes saved my feet more than once.

Jeff knew that he was being tested and that his career with Heartland would not go well if he complained or faltered in the inferno. But the challenge was more than just enduring the environment. Headquarters had set Jeff the goal of a 30 percent increase in productivity for his department over the six months he was to be foreman.

For the first week or two, Jeff was like a detective, looking for clues to the problems in his fittings shop. Jeff learned that the foreman in the adjacent shop had for the past 10 months also supervised the group of workers Jeff was currently responsible for. The men in Jeff's shop were mostly emigrants from Italy, Portugal, and Greece. Jeff thought they were willing enough to work hard if he could give them some good reason to. He set about finding what was keeping production levels so low.

The first thing Jeff noticed was that the men were incessantly late, following the example of the foreman in the adjacent shop and of Mel Linton, Jeff's boss and the work floor supervisor who was near retirement. Jeff made sure he himself was on the floor 10 minutes early every morning, and he began to dock the pay of those who came in late.

Jeff's men spent a lot of time going to other parts of the plant in search of things like gloves, work aprons, and tools. Jeff had a large, new cabinet built and placed in his department, and he kept it well stocked with everything his men could possibly need. The men no longer had an excuse to wander.

The men in the cleaning shop were spending long periods of time with chisels, hammers, and pneumatic chipping tools, cleaning off by hand the imperfections that didn't get knocked off in the big wheelabrator machine that barraged the pipe castings with brass shot. Jeff ignored plant precedent and Linton's advice when, at the suggestion of one of the workers he had learned to respect (a fellow who in fact had complained that other foremen and supervisors never listened to any of the men's suggestions), he issued an order to triple the time spent for each fitting in the wheelabrator. The fittings came out much cleaner, and

the time necessary for hand chipping was drastically reduced. After this change, Jeff's men began to keep up occasionally with their production schedules; Jeff also sensed that they now felt he might be okay, after all.

Jeff's subordinates, peers, and even his boss, Mel Linton, didn't know that Jeff would be there for only six months. But Jeff felt they suspected he would stay for a short period of time, perhaps a year or two. Jeff didn't confine himself to his shop, but would periodically visit other parts of the plant to make new acquaintances and observe other comparable shops. One worker in an adjacent shop that he observed frequently, got to know, and came to respect, was an immigrant who kept hinting he had a secret formula ("The key is molasses") for the wash coating used in the casting molds. Following the usual method Jeff had developed for dealing with his boss, Jeff got "permission" to try the new wash coat:

Jeff:	Patrick, the Irishman, wants to use molasses in the wash.
Linton:	That so?
Jeff:	I think it's worth trying, so I'm willing to pay for the molasses out of my miscellaneous expense account.
Linton:	Mmmmm.
Jeff:	So we'll start working on it in the morning.
Linton:	Mmmmm.

Jeff knew Linton was not going to take a stand, and Jeff decided to go ahead on his own. Almost magically, the castings came out shiny clean with the new wash coat, even in the deep grooves where the fittings would be joined to the regular pipe. Jeff now had the wheelabrator time cut back by half, for the castings that came out from the new wash coat needed considerably less scouring.

Jeff tried for over a month to get division purchasing to procure for his department a renewed supply of short sledge-hammer handles. When his supply completely ran out, he finally gave up on them, got some petty cash, jumped into his car, and was back at the plant within an hour with a week's supply of handles (for $40) from a local hardware store. Jeff's plant manager, Howard McCall, got wind of the story on the handles and was soon on the phone asking division purchasing why his foreman could find in an hour what purchasing couldn't get in a month. George Kondopoulos, one of the Greek workers who used the hammers almost constantly, smiled and slapped Jeff on the back, holding his hammer in the air and pointing to the new handle.

After three months, Jeff's shop had increased production by 25 percent. It was then that Howard McCall announced a rush order to be shipped to Venezuela, something that would require the utmost efficiency in day-to-day operations if they were to meet the very tight shipping schedule. Jeff went to his men with enthusiasm and confidence, noting that they would have all the overtime they could

handle, and they responded by working even harder. Jeff designed a new reporting system that kept track of every fitting as it moved through casting and cleaning—he knew they couldn't afford to forget to recast even one fitting that got ruined the first time through. Previously, such lapses of memory and attention to detail had caused very costly and embarrassing delays in shipping out orders, but this time the fittings shop did not miss the boat.

After a full six months as foreman, Jeff was transferred out of the iron pipe plant. His department was operating with 40 percent higher productivity than when he began. There was also a backlog of worker applications to transfer into his fittings shop, which was formerly considered the "dog" of the plant.

Other Assignments

Jeff's next six-month assignment involved various products in different areas of the country. Commuting home on weekends at company expense, Jeff worked in Houston as an internal consultant in an oil rig repair operation that had been losing money since Heartland acquired it two and a half years previously. His final recommendation was to sell the operation off, even though acquiring it had been the brainchild of two Heartland corporate vice presidents. Jeff backed up his recommendation with a thorough quantitative analysis, which centered on the lack of competitive advantage for Heartland in the oil rig repair business. In the end, the vice presidents reluctantly sold their "baby" ($½ million sales) to a company ($2 million sales) that folded only four months later.

Jeff's next six-month assignment was as a heavy equipment salesman. He was surprised at how much he enjoyed sales, though he was also frustrated from time to time at not having enough control over the variables that affected the success of his sales. Jeff still felt more at home in manufacturing, where the people and decisions were largely internal to the organization, but he was glad for an opportunity to learn about another important aspect of Heartland's business.

Plant Manager

After 18 months with Heartland, Jeff was offered a line management position as a plant manager, right on schedule, as Harold Maxfield had promised. He had to choose between plants near Pittsburgh and Colorado Springs, Colorado. Carol's desire to continue her own professional development in the insurance industry happily coincided with Jeff's own preference for a move to Colorado.

Earlier in December 1976, a two-day visit to the Colorado Springs plant had given Jeff a feel for the task ahead. Jeff's new boss, Glen Morgan, the concrete pipe operations manager, and a new manager who was taking over a different plant under Morgan, had accompanied Jeff on this visit to learn

from Morgan and get initiated as well. Actually located in Widefield, a small town 20 miles from the center of Colorado Springs, the almost-new plant was unionized, was the largest single employer in town, and had defeated two previous managers in less than two years since it had begun operating. While the start-up management team had been very enthusiastic, they had been unable to deal effectively with the rather happy-go-lucky attitudes of many of the hourly workers. Work force problems, especially the high rate of accidents in the plant, combined with difficulties in some of the manufacturing processes—most notably the "spinner" machine—had helped to keep the operation in the red.

When he visited Colorado in December, Jeff inquired about his immediate predecessor, who had already left the company. Evidently Stu Little had felt that his boss, Glen Morgan, was too difficult to deal with. The foremen at the plant later told Jeff that Stu used to hide out in obscure corners of the plant to avoid Glen's phone calls, or even hide away somewhere during his frequent visits. Eventually, Stu quit.

Now, under the temporary management of the plant superintendent, a 17-year-veteran of Heartland named Dick Hill, the Widefield plant was struggling along with frequent accidents, production and shipping delays, labor unrest, and of course still no black ink. Glen Morgan, the concrete pipe operations manager, would spend days and weeks at the plant running the show. As with the previous manager, Glen was out of his Omaha office and onto a plane to Colorado the minute anything went wrong. He called once or twice a day to see if he was needed.

Jeff was impressed with the level of experience and dedication of the foremen and the supervisors, however, and felt that they and the hourly staff (about 120 people in all) could be built into a good team with the right approach.

Moving In

On January 4, 1977, Jeff moved into the corner office at the Widefield plant. The plant interior held a Spartan office area, with spaces for 10 people in small offices and a large space at one end where the foremen took breaks and ate their lunches. To the office Jeff brought his steel-toed boots (his were hiking style), which were required by safety regulations when he was on the plant floor. He had a white hard hat, too, with a piece of plastic name tape stuck on the front that spelled out "Jeff Bradley." Jeff liked the hat better than his silk tie, though he did keep the tie on at the plant.

Assigned Objectives

Jeff had been assigned six objectives to work toward in this new position, and safety had first priority. During 1976, Widefield had had the worst record of all Heartland's plants for accidents that caused lost production time; 24 such accidents had occurred in the plant during the year. The accident rate was important to labor relations, produc-

tivity, and to the pipe division generally because the company's contributions for insurance were tied directly to the accident rate. More accidents meant higher expenses for corporate. Jeff's assignment was to reduce accidents to *six or fewer* during 1977.

The other five objectives involved improvements in labor productivity, indirect and direct materials costs, task force ratings on safety, efficiency and housekeeping, improved communications between various levels and areas of plant operations and management, and a positive performance appraisal for Jeff at the end of the year. Bill Ashton, the division general manager, and Glen Morgan, Jeff's immediate boss, made sure Jeff understood that the overriding objective was to manage a profitable operation. The ratings on most of Jeff's specific objectives would be determined in biannual on-site inspections and reviews, carried out by a pipe division task force which visited each of the 21 Heartland plants to provide comparative assessments.

Making Pipe

The production of reinforced concrete pipe, in 24-foot lengths and widths varying from 14 inches to 54 inches in diameter, involved machine welding of rolled sheet steel into cylinders (known in the plant as "cans"), testing for and spot repairing of leaks in the welded seam, coating the inside of the can with up to a 2-inch layer of concrete, wrapping the outer steel surface with reinforcing wire (the more closely the strands were wrapped and the thicker the original sheet steel, the higher the "grade" of the pipe), and finally brush coating the outside of the pipe with a ¼- to ¾-inch layer of concrete. After both stages of adding concrete, the pipe was forklifted into large drying kilns for quick curing. Cans could become scrap anywhere along the assembly line, but it became progressively more expensive with added input of material and labor.

The operation that produced the most scrap was coating the inside of cans with concrete on the machine called the spinner. After loading onto the belts of the spinner, which was housed inside a steel mesh cage, cans were rotated at high speeds atop rolling belts while a long "spoon" full of concrete was hydraulically inserted into the center of the pipe. As the spoon slowly dumped its load of soupy concrete, the force of the gradually accelerated spinning motion distributed the concrete in an even layer inside the pipe.

A smaller space in the plant housed the quality control laboratory and the fittings shop. In the latter, all the odd-shaped and angled fittings, which attached to standard lengths of straight pipe, were made to order. Pipe orders were generated by a separate sales staff; the plant was solely a manufacturing concern.

Glen and Spinner Magic

Jeff soon learned that the spinner had an aura of mystery and intrigue and that it was dangerous and unpredictable, particularly when producing larger sizes of pipe. One hair-raising incident occurred during his first week at the plant with a relatively small 24-inch pipe on the spinner. The machine sent part of the can up through the roof into the tower where the concrete was mixed. The concrete-swathed can then plunged down the chute and crashed to the floor just a few feet from the man operating the wet concrete spoon. After that incident, Jeff supervised the rebuilding of the wire mesh cage, this time with two layers of a higher-strength mesh.

The mystique of the spinner stemmed from the fact that over 50 variables had to be set just right for the giant machine to function smoothly. Further, these settings had to be worked out separately for each size of the pipe by trial and error, because each machine was custom made. There was only one other spinner in another Heartland plant, and only six or seven other spinners with competitors in the United States.

Technicians and engineers who were calm and rational with other machines became masters of sorcery with regard to the spinner. Each of the five or six people involved in running the spinner had his own magical solution to getting it to work right. The complexity of the variables that affected how the spinning turned out made it very difficult to pinpoint just what the problem might be when a can flew off the spinner and was ruined.

Dick Hill, the plant superintendent, recalled for Jeff the famous "scrap of 48" incident, when Glen Morgan had established himself as the jinx of the spinner. It was in December 1976, a month before Jeff took over, and Dick had been supervising the running of an order of 48-inch pipe. The spinner threw one of the first cans, and Dick consulted with the operator, the foreman, and Guiermo Martinez, the quality control supervisor who had enjoyed some previous success at charming the spinner. Guiermo insisted that the problem was dry concrete. "You've gotta run soup," he said, so the mixture was watered down before loading the spoon, and they tried again. The can flew off and crumpled into a soupy concrete and steel pretzel.

"We forgot to adjust the height of the pulleys," said the operator, referring to one of the more logical steps needed to assure a good spin. The belts had to be tight enough that the can could sit on the belts alone, not on the pulleys that turned the belts. If the belts were *too* tight, the can could easily fly off. They adjusted the belts and pulleys, dumped the soup, and got another pretzel.

Guiermo made sure that water was poured on top of the belts. Putting water on the belts was one of the stranger rituals, one that had seemed to work the day Guiermo had first tried it a year earlier. Guiermo thought it kept the belts from overheating and thereby getting too loose. Since that first time they never neglected this step in the rites, but the machine operators really only added water to please Guiermo—they had other theories of their own. They sprinkled sand on the inside of the belts, their own part in what had become a canonized ritual sequence.

By now Glen Morgan had arrived and started calling the shots, and a number of the men had gathered around the spinner to see the spectacle of the white hats at work. As each can crumpled in turn, Glen barked more orders: "Slow it down!" "Adjust the torque!" "Speed it up!" "Lubricate the bearings!" During this episode, Glen was called to the front office to take a phone call. When he returned, the spinner was working, though no one, including Glen, knew why or how. From then on, whenever Glen was in the plant the men on the spinner tried to shut it down if they were ahead of schedule—they now knew that Glen was a jinx. "There are no demons in that machine," he would say, but the men had seen it all happen. In the following weeks, worker folklore around the lunch table often captured the spirit of the occasion in gleeful recollections of that day.

Getting Acquainted

Jeff's first, most obvious task was to dig out from under the paper work that had accumulated during the two months that Dick Hill had been both supervising production and managing the plant. Six feet tall, with a trim grey mustache and receding hairline, at 52 Dick Hill looked just right for his role as plant superintendent. Dick had first been an electrician, then maintenance foreman, and then plant superintendent for five years in one of Heartland's other concrete pipe facilities before coming to Widefield to help open the new plant. Jeff therefore felt Dick could be an invaluable member of his staff. But Dick knew little about calculating cost variances, indirect manufacturing expense (IME), or filling out other production reports; he was much more a floor man than an office man, and Jeff had lots of catching up to do.

Jeff learned that total plant manufacturing cost was about $30 million a year (roughly $120,000 in product cost per day), of which about $9 million a year (30 percent) were indirect manufacturing expenses. The modern, largely mechanized facility was highly capital-intensive, and direct labor accounted for only 6 percent of the product cost.

During his first week at the plant, Jeff had asked all 20 of the management and office staff employees to come in and visit with him, one at a time, so he could get to know them and find out what kind of support they needed. Dick Hill told Jeff that it was no problem to run the plant, but to do that *and* answer to Glen Morgan was very difficult. Jeff responded: "Don't worry about Glen—I'll do that and you just worry about running the plant operations." They agreed on a slight overlap in their working schedules so as to provide supervision over a longer period of the working day. Dick would be in the plant at 6:45 to start up and would leave between 3:30 and 4; Jeff would arrive at 7:45 and leave between 5 and 5:30.

Jeff underscored some of his basic management policies. One was that all his employees should be given authority commensurate with their responsibilities. This meant that Dick Hill would deal with the foremen and that Jeff would uphold Dick's authority. For instance, Jeff stood by Dick's decision one day to shut down the brush coat machine early for preventive maintenance, even though Jeff felt that by doing so they would fail to meet the week's production schedule. "I always tried my best to back Dick's decisions," Jeff said, "but instruct him on my own view when we disagreed. That week we missed our quota, but Dick learned I would back him even if I thought he was wrong— up to a point, of course."

One afternoon during the second week after Jeff took over, Dick had already left when the late shift foreman came to tell Jeff that one of the machines was down; it would take two hours to fix. Dick Hill's assignment to the late shift had been to produce 20 pipes—that now meant they would be in the plant until at least 11 P.M. Jeff decided to have the maintenance crew fix the machine immediately, but to send the other workers home. Before he left, Jeff wrote a detailed note to Dick, explaining what he had done and why. "That way, when Dick came the next morning and saw only three pipes finished, he didn't have to call around and find out what happened from someone else." It was important to Jeff that Dick, and the entire management team, be protected from looking bad or uninformed. He felt that his own policy of open, quick communication would encourage people to cooperate and share information rather than just cover for themselves.

Jeff discovered that the 100 unionized plant workers could be divided into two somewhat distinct groups. About 70 percent of the workers seemed interested in stable jobs, whereas the other 30 percent appeared transient and less committed to either the town or their jobs. The former group, whom Jeff referred to as the "regular guys," were mostly married and over 25 years of age. The latter group, "the cowboys," were mostly single and under 25 years of age. About one third of the members of each group were relatively highly skilled. These workers, about 30 in all, held the following jobs, which were highly specialized and specific to concrete pipe manufacturing: welders (10), spinner machine operators (5), and lift truck operators (15). These workers were especially difficult to replace, but even the 70 others who held relatively unskilled jobs were hard to replace because of a tight local labor hiring market.

Accidents and Safety

During his first three weeks as plant manager, while Jeff was digging out from under the paperwork and getting acquainted with his staff, there were four lost-time accidents in the plant. Luckily, they involved only minor injuries—a cut hand, a bruised foot, a smashed finger, a sprained wrist. But they were enough to put a significant crimp in Jeff's production schedule and use up two thirds of his annual accident quota.

Jeff had noted that workers in the plant, especially the cowboys, routinely neglected to wear their safety glasses, and often their blue hard hats as well. Many of the regular guys, and even the foremen, also failed to adhere to the safety regulations. Jeff found, moreover, that the cowboys were fatalistic about accidents; like some World War II flyers, they figured they would only get hurt when their number was up. They expressed a certain thrill in living "close to the edge," and the plant seemed to be one arena for their lifestyle of brinksmanship. Jeff's impression was that most of these self-professed cowboys found their deepest contentment in a case of beer and a full tank of gas. Though Heartland needed them, their macho, devil-may-care ideal was less than ideal for profits.

Many of Jeff's transient cowboys in Colorado were, as Jeff said, "short-sighted sons of fairly well-to-do ranchers and businessmen." They didn't seem to have any commitment to careers and knew they could get other jobs easily in what had been a booming economy. They were physically robust, outdoor types—most of them cultivated a Marlboro man image that interfered with taking orders willingly or being particularly cooperative. Working at the plant was a way of financing their *real* lives— fast pickup trucks, motorcycles, a horseback ride on the range, wild game hunting, and a boom town night life. Many of these cowboys considered working five days a week to be "the pits" and usually managed to skip work (with loss of pay) for a day or two every other week or so in order to have a good time outside the plant. Still, Jeff hoped to get most of them to take the plant a little more seriously. Poor attendance and safety hurt productivity badly, especially because the plant had a lean staff to begin with. If a worker was unavailable to do his or her job, worker assignments had to be shuffled to get the necessary work done, which was disruptive and frequently resulted in a less-than-optimal allocation of worker skills. Despite his concerns about his cowboys, Jeff knew that when they wanted to work hard, they were as good as *any* group of workers, *anywhere*.

Glen Morgan

As expected, Glen Morgan did not sit quietly by. From Jeff's first day on the job, he called daily in the morning and again in the afternoon. Jeff wasn't much concerned about Glen as a spinner jinx, but he badly wanted to find a way to make him quit calling so he could get his own work done. Glen sometimes called to talk about interesting and somewhat useful details, such as the prices of sheet steel out of Gary and Pittsburgh, but he usually relayed items that were low on Jeff's

list of priorities. At other times, Glen wanted to come down to the plant to do things that Jeff felt he should be free to handle in his own way. The accident problem was a case in point. Glen wanted to fly out and give the men a lecture on safety procedures.

On checking around discreetly, Jeff found out more about Glen Morgan. Like many other senior company managers, Glen had an engineering degree. He had been plant manager of a Heartland facility similar to the one at Widefield for 12 years before being promoted to his current job as concrete pipe operations manager six years earlier, in early 1971. Glen understood the pipe operations inside and out and continued to be a hands-on manager after his promotion. Jeff also learned that the wisdom of building a new plant at Widefield had been debated by senior Heartland management for several years and that Glen Morgan had been its chief proponent. About $18 million had been invested in the new facility, but the projected level of sales used to justify this investment had never materialized. As a result, the new Widefield plant had acquired the reputation of a "big white elephant," and Morgan had trouble finding a seasoned replacement for the manager who started up the Widefield plant, and later for the startup manager's successor, Stu Little, when he also failed. Experienced Heartland managers seemed unwilling to be associated with the Widefield plant, and Morgan had finally asked Dick Hill to take over on a temporary basis prior to Jeff's arrival. Jeff wondered how best to deal with his boss, the mystique of spinner magic, the safety issue, and the other problems at the plant.

CASE 4–3
Jeff Bradley (B)

C. Paul Dredge
Vijay Sathe

Jeff's rule of thumb for dealing with most problems was to stay calm and present not only the facts, but also a reasonable approach to solving whatever problem was being considered. He soon had a plan for dealing with plant safety. Jeff reasoned that since people were currently ignoring the detailed safety regulations already in effect, making more decrees would probably be a waste of time. He called Dick Hill in, and they arranged a meeting with the foremen to discuss safety. Jeff listened and asked questions.

Foreman: My guys on the forklifts don't need helmets, they're protected by the enclosed cab.

Jeff: Do they ever get out and forget to put on a helmet?

Foreman: My guys in welding can't fit helmets over their welding masks. How can they worry

about head protection while they're welding?

Jeff: Does falling steel say to itself: "I'll wait until he gets his mask off and his helmet on before I fall on his head?" Can't we find a helmet with a hinged mask on the front?

With Jeff asking his questions, his plant superintendent and foremen devised a new set of safety rules they thought were practical and enforceable. Paul Emmer, the union steward, was told about the new rules and, impressed that on the safety issue Jeff might well have the employees' interests at heart, he did his best to get his union's support for the revised rules. The bottom line was foot, eye, and head protection for everyone at all times. (The previous company regulations also boiled down to that, not surprisingly.) With the new safety rules, welders were required to wear hard hats. Dick Hill got on the phone and found three firms that sold special welders' helmets hinged attachments for welding masks. The mask could be lifted up from the face with the helmet still on. Dick got samples and let the men try out the various models. The welders, the craftsmen of the shop, were least unhappy with one model, so 10 were ordered at $45 each.

The Trial

The new safety regulations went into effect on January 26, 1977. After a week or so, the welders be-

This case was prepared by C. Paul Dredge (under the direction of Vijay Sathe).

gan complaining of headaches, dizzy spells, and stiff necks, attributing their ills to the new "Darth Vader masks," as they called them. Jeff instructed the foremen to let the welders know that only a letter from a doctor would give them an excuse not to play Darth Vader ("I figured the doctors would be on *my* side, and I wasn't convinced that these complaints were legitimate"). On a Thursday afternoon in February, Dick Hill dropped by Jeff's office. He had heard a rumor that the welders in the fittings shop were going to stage a sickout on Monday to protest the Darth Vader helmets. What to do?

Jeff was convinced that this was *the* test and that he would have to nip the movement in the bud to preserve his safety program. He had an idea for a useful ally in the safety battle. He called Hal Symons, the OSHA (Occupational Safety and Health Administration) officer for the region and asked him to come in on Friday and speak to the welders and union reps on the necessity of observing government and company safety policies. Hal had never been *invited* to do this anywhere and was happy, even if a bit bewildered, to oblige. By Friday afternoon, Hal Symons had given the men the word and had posted an official OSHA notice on the bulletin board requiring the welders and everyone else to observe the new safety policy.

Behind the scene, Jeff talked to the two foremen who supervised the welding operations. He showed them a helmet-mask combination

he had found with a webbed interior, one that had a ratchet-style adjustment mechanism just like the webbing of a standard welding mask. A sample was issued to one of the welders on Monday morning (none were out sick), and the foreman mentioned, as instructed, that it was "a special helmet for the specialists." All the guys gave it a try, and to a man they swore it was noticeably lighter and more comfortable. Another $450 was a small price to pay for the happiness of these wizards of the plant. A few days later Jeff took one each of the new and old helmets to the scales in the quality control department, pausing as usual to first put on his white helmet, his safety glasses, and his safety boots. ("What's good for the goose is good for the gander.") Jeff grinned when he read on the scale that the two different masked helmets were *exactly* the same weight.

Bingo

The safety program had a good stick in the combination of Hal and the foremen who had outlined the rules, but Jeff did not neglect the carrot. In Houston he had heard of a safety bingo game at a Heartland plant in Portland, and he had obtained a copy of the rules from the plant manager. When, on January 26, *all* the men began wearing helmets and glasses (the boots had never been a problem), the safety bingo game began too. There was a $50 prize for regular straight-line bingo, $100 for four corners, $150 for figure X on the card, and $200 for a full card (each game there-fore cost the company $500). The game would be canceled when a lost-time accident occurred, and the next day's new game would be closed to the person who had the accident. Otherwise, each game would go on as long as it took to fill someone's card completely (typi-cally a little over three months). Absentees were not eligible for the numbers drawn on the day(s) they were absent unless they presented a doctor's certificate of illness. The numbers, drawn daily in the hourly workers' lunchroom, all had safety slogans associated with them. (When posted on the bulletin board, the slogan was readily legi-ble from a distance; the number, in small print, was not). Members of both the union and the manage-ment (including Jeff Bradley), par-ticipated in the Bingo game, in or-der to foster the feeling of "We are in this together." However, to allay any suspicion that the game was be-ing rigged by management, the game rules specified that whenever a member of management won, the game would be continued until a member of the union also won.

Accidents that smashed fingers and wrenched ankles had previ-ously given the victim a day or two off *without* pay, something to break out of the five-day monotony. (In-juries had to be more serious to qualify for pay and workers' com-pensation.) Now, almost overnight, workers were willing to tape up the finger, bind the ankle, and find something productive to do at the plant for a day or two while the natural healing process mended

minor injuries. Every Joe was on the lookout for a careless fellow who might end the game just when Joe had only one number left to win the prize. For Jeff it was more important that the men were read-ing the slogans and thinking about the other guy's helmet. He was also glad that the fun of the lot-tery might make the difference to someone who was debating whether or not to get up and go to work. There occurred only one more lost-time accident in all of 1977, and the attendance record improved markedly. That meant that most machines, most days, were operated by experienced peo-ple, that time was not wasted in re-organizing the work team each morning, that plant operations functioned smoothly.

Dick Hill

Unlike some people Jeff had run into, Dick turned out not to feel any resentment at working under the direction of a younger man. For his part, Jeff came to respect Dick's technical knowhow, wide ex-perience in floor operations, and native intelligence. Jeff found that he and Dick could trade jokes on an equal footing, though both were careful to keep a certain respectful distance.

While it was clear from the be-ginning that Dick knew little about the deskwork, Jeff sensed that the only major things Dick lacked for the job of plant manager were more self-confidence and a more aggressive approach to problem solving. Dick came to appreciate

Jeff's interest in his opinions. He made a habit of reporting in at Jeff's office during midmorning for a quick rundown of what was happening on the floor and then again just before the workday ended with a summary of the day's production.

Managing the Boss

In early March, Dick Hill came into Jeff's office one morning with a question about the lifting capacity of one of the lift trucks. Jeff called Glen to find out if he might have the information. Glen called back after an hour or so and said that he couldn't find it just then. They didn't hear from him again for *four days*. When he did call back, he had the information. "I hate to be wrong about things (they *knew* that was true), so I double-checked this. Sorry to have taken so long to get back to you, but other things have gotten in the way, and I wanted to make sure I gave you the correct information."

Ah so! From then on Dick and Jeff began to turn over all their obscure, difficult, but not crucial, problems to Glen whenever they felt he was bugging them needlessly. "He didn't like to call us if we could ask him about something he hadn't finished yet. He always hated to have to say he didn't know or hadn't gotten to it. If we called him on something we really needed, he gave us the answer quickly and then hurried to get off the phone so we wouldn't ask him about the other thing." On one or two occasions Jeff and Dick had

even discovered the answer on their own, but delayed calling Glen while they enjoyed the infrequency of his calls. More generally, however, Jeff and Dick learned to manage Glen by keeping him *fully* informed via frequent and comprehensive updates.

Performance Appraisal

Heartland's policy was that plant managers should conduct a year-end performance appraisal with all their supervisory personnel. Jeff felt that once a year wasn't enough and that to wait until the end of the year to do a thorough appraisal might leave too much unsaid for too long. "There isn't any time for people to make adjustments in their performance if you only do appraisals at the end." Therefore, Jeff held meetings in June with all his foremen, supervisors, and office personnel.

In his performance appraisal with Dick Hill, Jeff was forthright in pointing to both the numerous good things Dick was doing and the areas where he thought there should be improvement. "Ninety percent of what I had to say to Dick was a bouquet, but the remaining 10 percent was a challenge to improve in some specific areas." One of the suggestions was that Dick should work on sticking by his own ideas and suggestions having to do with large-scale operational decisions. Jeff saw this as especially important in the light of his own decision-making style. Jeff thought it was a good idea to think of as many alternatives as possible before making a decision. Hence Jeff always posed several countersuggestions for the sake of providing a good range of choices. He felt that Dick took some of that too seriously and tended to back off in favor of Jeff's suggestions. Jeff also encouraged Dick to delegate more tasks to his foremen, especially the electronics and maintenance work that Dick often did himself because of his extensive experience in those areas. Dick needed to worry less about maintenance on a particular machine and develop a wider view of plant operations as a whole, Jeff told him.

Separating the Wheat from the Chaff

Though the safety program and the bingo game had changed their outward behavior, Jeff sensed that many of his cowboys were still saloon birds at heart. He also knew that he probably couldn't change them much as individuals, so he relied initially on outside motivators and peer pressure for much of his team-building program. As the next step, Jeff concluded that the hard-core bad apples among both the cowboys and the regular guys had to be ousted or tamed.

Jeff decided that the best way to do this was to design formal procedures for dealing with absenteeism, lateness, and poor job performance. He reasoned that those who could be saved would respond positively to more rigid expectations, while those who repeatedly ignored rules would get progressively more serious discipline.

Those who wouldn't conform could be given the gate without a lot of flack from the union about unfairness and favoritism. The new version of the absentee and lateness policy was pounded out in the same way the safety guidelines had been. Paul Emmer was glad to see something on paper for his men, for in the past they had been at the mercy of individual foremen who had made their own policies. Jeff felt that most of his foremen were either too easygoing or uneven and prejudiced in their disciplinary actions. He was satisfied that both he and the union could agree on a more impartial policy.

Steve Wilson, the 22-year-old personnel officer at the plant, was less than enthusiastic about making changes that would involve a lot of paperwork. He was quite satisfied to get the payroll out, take care of the accounting on employee benefits, and keep watch over his own territory. Jeff had not been happy with what he regarded as Steve's rather sloppy, nonserious approach to the job. He almost always found mistakes in Steve's reports. Some quite serious personal problems seemed to Jeff to provide additional explanations as to why Steve wasn't doing a very good job. Jeff had not made any move to fire him, partly because other matters had been more urgent, and partly because he thought that for Steve's rather small salary ($13,000/year) he was "just barely okay."

Perhaps in anticipation of added work under the proposed new policies on lateness and absenteeism, Steve came to Jeff and said he had been offered a job with another company for more money and would leave if Heartland couldn't match it. Jeff promised to talk to Glen, but when he did he recommended no raise. He also mentioned that if Steve left he would like to expand the job to include keeping track of disciplinary actions and personnel files and to offer at least an $18,000 salary to attract someone with experience and good ideas. Steve did quit, and Jeff hired Katherine Ellmore. Jeff had to twist Glen's arm rather hard, but he got a salary of $20,000 for Katherine, which proved to be a good investment.

The new progressive discipline policy, implemented in June 1977, called for strict records of absences and lateness to be kept by the foremen, with an official procedure for administering discipline. Two informal warnings would be given by the foreman, followed at the next infraction by a formal verbal warning to be written up and filed in the employee's record. The next step was to call the worker into the plant supervisor's office for a formal reprimand, accompanied by a written letter itemizing his infractions along with a notation that further infractions would bring more serious consequences. ("We didn't spell it out, since we wanted the option of firing someone anytime for a really serious dereliction of duty.") The next step was the three-day suspension, and then the gate.

Jeff's goal was to develop competent people: "We're in business to make pipe, and we hire and de-

velop capable people to help make it, not just to get them to conform to the rules." But no matter how skilled the person, Jeff was determined to get rid of anyone who proved, after ample opportunity, to be unwilling to play with the team. This attitude reflected Heartland policy, but it also made sense in terms of Jeff's relations with the local union. He could now fall back on a formally negotiated policy to justify personnel actions. The union had a stake in the procedures, too, since they also protected union members from the whims and prejudices of certain foremen.

Among those who soon ran afoul of the disciplinary policy was Jake Morris. "I sensed he was a bad apple from the beginning," recalled Jeff, "and in fact his foreman, Dave Kendall, was more than happy to use the new guidelines to try to get rid of him." Jake Morris was 5-feet-10-inches tall, a burly 210 pounds, and moody and antagonistic. He was an expert at riding the thin edge between discipline and dismissal: How little can I do to get by? How can I stretch this job into overtime? He would often work so as to generate a couple of hours of overtime each evening from Monday through Thursday and then, with his weekly pay assured, call in sick on Friday. Jake, a welder, was constantly in an argument with someone, and looked to the union to back him.

Jeff characterized his work force as a kind of bell-curved population, with 70 percent of the men located in the average pool; Morris was among the "bad 15 percent" fringe. Morris, a member of the cowboy group, was not only absent or late frequently, he had also on occasion left the plant during the day without punching out. People noticed that antifreeze was often missing from the maintenance shop after Morris had been on the night shift. When anyone confronted him about his behavior, Morris became surly and threatening. Dave Kendall had been afraid of him and reluctant to tackle the union, which had often taken a militant stance. But given the active support of the front office and the new formal procedure, Dave braved the storm and applied the disciplinary proceedings through two verbal warnings.

Morris's response to the pressure was sabotage. Scheduled to work the late shift one day, he was instructed to move a pulley on the critical spinning machine six inches to the right. He welded it 6 inches to the left instead, though the foreman had taken the time to show him the specific spot for the weld. The next day the first of the spinning cans flew off the machine at high speed, crashing against the safety wire of the cage that enclosed the machine. The plant was down for three hours while the pulley was relocated, the machine tested, and the mess cleaned up. Because of the danger that Morris's behavior posed to others in the plant, Dave recommended firing him on the spot. Jeff was happy to back him up. Morris stormed off the work floor, vowing to fight the decision.

The next day, Jake Morris appealed to the union, and a grievance proceeding was begun. Jeff challenged the union to show good cause why Morris should stay on. Paul Emmer, the union rep, decided to circulate a petition showing the men's support for Morris's reinstatement, but only three workers would sign it. Still the union initiated procedures for labor arbitration. The union contract stipulated that the cost of a labor arbitrator would be split between management and the union, but when the western regional representative of the union came in from Portland to examine the case, he persuaded the local to drop it. Jeff wasn't surprised.

Sensing a new level of both resolve and support from the plant manager, other foremen put pressure on their marginal cases. The behavior of several workers changed noticeably; some quit, a few were fired. Replacements were carefully screened by the personnel manager. Despite a relatively tight labor hiring market, no one was hired unless he or she passed appropriate tests of physical fitness, skill, and other job and attitude criteria. The turnover rate of hourly employees, which had been as high as 12 percent per *month* in June 1977, began a steady decline at a rate of about 1 percent per *month* for the rest of 1977.

Jerry Jones, a lift truck operator, was typical of the worst of the "regular guys." He had remarkable driving skills, but Jerry also had a serious drinking problem. When he was in the plant, he was fine, but he was almost always late and often didn't show up at all. He had been warned before, but when the new procedures went into effect it didn't take long for Jerry to get suspended. Some of the foremen had been worried that the three-day suspension might be just a way for the guys to get three days off, but when Jeff held the line and insisted that Jerry had to be fired, they saw at last that this was serious business. The union could make no protest when they were shown Jerry's documented record of discipline.

Hank, another heavy-drinking lift truck operator, posed a similar case to Jerry's that had a different resolution. A tall, slender, single man, he spent his evenings in the saloon and had the same kinds of troubles getting up in the morning as Jerry had failed to overcome. Jerry's foreman told Dick Hill that he thought Hank was probably just drowning his loneliness. Dick saw him one morning as Hank was staggering home from the bar and wasn't surprised later when he got a call from Hank saying he would miss work. Dick tried to encourage him to be more reliable; he was worried that Hank would get himself fired. Hank knew he was on the verge of losing his job—especially when he talked to Jerry, his friend and former co-worker, who visited the plant from time to time, miserable, to ask for his old job. When an opening came up in the afternoon shift, Dick got the idea that Hank might be able to avoid his evening loneliness by working from 3:30 to 11:30. Hank decided to give it a try and soon found that

he was too tired even to stop at the bar at midnight. Over time, Hank became a model employee.

In another case, a foreman's adherence to the rules pointed up some disadvantages of total reliance on a formal set of procedures. Jim Black, one of the cowboys, came to work late on a rainy Wednesday in September of 1977. Jim had been slapped with a three-day suspension during the previous week for repeated tardiness and excessive absenteeism. Now, after two good days on Monday and Tuesday, Jim showed up at 8 A.M., one hour late, and knew he was in trouble.

He walked onto the floor and went over to his foreman:

Jim: Well, I guess I'm fired; is my pay ready?

(They both knew the rule about infractions after a suspension, the most serious disciplinary action before a worker lost his or her job.)

Foreman: It will be by noon today.

Jim and Pablo, the foreman, then proceeded by separate paths to the union representative on the work floor to report the dismissal, and as soon as Jim Black had left the plant, Paul Emmer and Pablo were both in Jeff's office, with two different versions of the story.

Paul Emmer complained that many people with worse records of attendance were working out on the floor, and the problem lay with the inconsistency of the various department foremen in implementing the negotiated policy. Jeff couldn't argue too hard with that, since he knew that some of his foremen continued to be less than diligent in following up on the rules. Pablo, the foreman, argued that Jim had been given more than an even chance, and the time had now come to get rid of him.

At noon, Jim Black arrived to collect his pay. Waiting for him were Pablo, the foreman; Paul Emmer, the union rep; Katherine Elmore, payroll and personnel supervisor; Dick Hill, the plant superintendent, and Jeff Bradley. Invited to tell his side of the story, Jim recounted:

Jim: I went out about 6:45 to get on my motorcycle, but it wouldn't start, I guess because of the rain. I spent half an hour trying to get it started. Our house is too far from the nearest line to get a phone, so I decided that all I could do was walk to work. It took me 45 minutes in the rain to get here, but I knew that I was late and that I could be fired this time. I was so disgusted, I just said, "Well, I guess I'm fired," and then Pablo said that 'Yes, I was.'"

Jeff: "Pablo?"

Pablo: Well, I noticed he was wet, but I figured from what he said that if he didn't want his job badly enough to explain, we didn't need him.

Jeff Bradley sighed and leaned back in his chair, contemplating the issues and consequences. If he reinstated Jim Black, he knew there would be gleeful backslapping in certain quarters over a union victory that in itself didn't bother him, but he'd worked hard to smooth relations and develop a cooperative spirit between labor and management at the plant. Emmer was a reasonable union steward, someone Jeff felt good about working with, and he knew that a badly handled case could damage their smooth working relationship. There were, in fact, other good reasons to go with the union side, but Jeff also worried about a loss of face and perhaps effective authority for his foreman. Moreover, he couldn't help worrying about the continued legitimacy of rules of attendance if exceptions were made—the rules and procedures had already made a big, positive difference in plant productivity.

Jeff also had to consider the fact that Jim Black was a good, skilled worker on the job and that he had lately shown signs of developing something beyond what Jeff saw as the immature attitude of so many of the men toward their work. Perhaps the three-day suspension had made Jim realize how important his job really was. More significantly, Jeff perceived that though Jim had a pretty bad record, this particular incident, given the apparent extenuating circumstances, might not be the right situation in which to reemphasize the absentee/tardiness policy. Indeed, such an action might badly damage the credibility of plant management with the workers just when the hourly staff had begun to catch the vision of a smooth-running, productive, mutually profitable operation. He thought also of the difficulty of defending the dismissal if the case went to labor arbitration, something Emmer was threatening to do.

Jeff adjourned the meeting without announcing his decision but called Pablo in the next day and asked him to rehire Jim Black. Jim was back on the job Friday.

> I decided that the foreman had definitely been wrong. There's no quicker way to destroy a good labor-management relationship than for management to hold the line on an obviously bad decision.

Paydays

In another aspect of the labor issue, Jeff noticed from attendance reports that worker absence was noticeably higher on alternate Fridays—the usual level on those days was about 15 percent of the work force. It wasn't difficult to identify the cause of this seemingly strange pattern. Payday was every other Thursday. With their payday scheduled so that they would be able to cash their checks on Friday, many of the hourly workers were in fact rushing out during lunch break to go to the bank on Thursday. Thursday night was party night for a substantial number of the men. Unfortunately, Thursday paydays were written into the union contract, which would not expire until March 1978. Changing the payday schedule became one of the top items on Jeff's list of changes to work toward in the labor contract. Other items included decreasing the importance given to

seniority in rehiring after a layoff, tightening up on funds spent for company-supplied boots and glasses, and a refinement of the formal labor grievance procedure.

Teach the People Correct Principles

One morning late in September, Dick Hill came into Jeff's office to report that the automatic monitor on the winding machine was not working.

Dick: We can't make pipe today—and this part is going to take several days to get fixed.

Jeff: Couldn't you make lower-class pipe?

Dick: Maybe we could; I'll go see.

Dick returned a few minutes later to say that they were running one pipe through the winding machine to see what would happen.

Dick: I don't know whether we can do it or not.

Jeff: Please keep trying and keep me posted.

After a half hour, Dick was back.

Dick: We're making pipe.

Jeff: Good. I guess we'll have to delay the order on the high class, eh?

Dick: No, the machine's working even though the monitor isn't, so we're making high-class pipe as planned, spot checking by hand with a micrometer.

Jeff recalled: "One of the biggest problems I encountered when I took over as plant manager was the attitude of the personnel regarding plant problems. When a problem came up, their initial reaction was to throw up their hands and quit. I don't think like that, and I tried to get them to see that even if *everything* can't be done, *something* can. If you can't make pipe, what *can* you do?"

In October, Wentz Horsley, the new storage yard and pipe repair and finishing crew foreman, was out in the yard where the finished pipe was stored, looking for 2 of his 12 men. Wentz had been hired recently to replace Phil Benson, whom Jeff and Dick had finally decided to let go because of his apparent inability, even with plenty of chances to improve, to supervise his men properly. Repairs to finished pipe were often made outside in the storage yard, but Wentz found his guys not making the repairs but sitting inside a 48-inch pipe eating doughnuts and listening to the radio. With Jeff's instructions and vow of support still ringing in his ears, Wentz told the two that they were fired and that they had better pack up and get out. The men knew that gradual disciplinary procedures couldn't protect them in this situation; they had lost their jobs.

Jeff was not necessarily happy to see them go, but he did take some satisfaction in thinking of the contrast between how they must have bragged to friends at the bar about eating doughnuts on company time and the way they'd now be required to eat crow. The finishing crew had dwindled from 17, when

Jeff came to manage the plant, to the current 12, largely because fewer and fewer pipes needed special repairs after coming off the line. Jeff talked with Wentz, and they decided not to replace the two men.

Demystifying the Spinner

Production runs of the big 48-inch pipe at the plant were scarce and had historically been scheduled only when an actual order came in. There was seldom very much advance notice when orders came in, and the monthly production plan almost always had to be revised to make room for a run of the large pipe. Without any appreciable time to prepare or think the problems through, it had always seemed easier to just try to get through the runs on 48-inch pipe as well as possible, hoping for good luck. Jeff had been made aware of the problem with spinning large pipe from the beginning, but his mind had been on more general problems, and he had stood by as an observer in April, watching too large a proportion of 48-inch cans fly off the spinner. Jeff had not yet gotten to really tackling the challenge of the large 48-inch pipe when Glen told him in October 1977 to plan on a run of 48-inch in December. When Jeff told Dick Hill about the plan for a 48-inch run, Dick realized that in this instance there was enough time to get ready to try an idea that had been on his mind for a long time.

Dick had wanted to try wider belts for the spinner way back

when he was maintenance foreman at the Pittsburgh plant and had gone so far as to find a supplier and get prices. The wider belts were even cheaper; only $2,500 per set instead of $4,000. However, Glen Morgan had been afraid to try new belts and had squelched the idea. Glen's feeling was that the belts were the key to the spinning operation, and as such they were sacred. The narrow belts had worked well in the only other Heartland plant which had a spinner, where Glen had been plant manager for 12 years prior to his promotion to his current position. In fact, Glen regarded spinner belts the same way baseball players regard a special pair of socks or underwear during a winning streak: Don't change them and you'll keep winning. To Glen, and to many others, breaking in a new set of belts (one could never change just one belt) was a touchy process, fraught with the unknown, and the *last* thing to try when having trouble with the spinner. Dick's idea had therefore fallen on deaf ears. After almost a year of working with Jeff, Dick now felt that he could count on Jeff's being able to deal with Glen, even if his idea failed; and this time he had ample time to order and install the belts before the production of the big pipe.

Dick: Jeff, I think we could try using wider belts; that might give the big cans more stability and could prevent all the trouble.

Jeff: That might work, but what if we simply put on a new set of belts. The old ones are stretched and cut pretty badly.

Dick: Okay, let's do that.

Jeff: But I think we might be better off trying your idea first. Do you have a source for the belts?

Dick: There's a fellow in Denver who can get the belts I have in mind.

Jeff: Put them on, then; let's give it a try.

When the time came for December's run of 48-inch pipe, Dick had received the new, wider belts and had just barely had time to get the spinner rigged to go with them for the first time. The first couple of cans were failures, so Jeff had Dick call the operator, the foreman, and Guiermo in for coffee at the foremen's lunch table. They all discussed the various possibilities and listed each of the potential problems. Jeff was careful to elicit from his people every conceivable possibility for trouble with the spinner, for he felt the time had finally come to kill this spinner demon. His only contribution to the list was that pouring water on the belts might be causing a loss of traction. Guiermo couldn't imagine that being the case. Dick Hill evidently felt that putting new belts on was heretical enough; he had nothing to say, except that he'd just watch.

When they went back out on the floor they tested each theory, one by one, trying their best to control for everything but the variable to be tested. In testing out about 15 key variables from the 50 or so variables, they lost two more cans. When they put the third can on, they left the water off the belts. It spun smoothly. Jeff thought he might be able to administer the coup de grace. "Let's try it without sand, too." Another success. After two hours and no more ruined cans, Guiermo was still insisting on adding water to the belts. At Jeff's request, Dick Hill called the distributor, who said, "Don't worry about putting water on the belts for cooling. You can't heat those belts up high enough to damage them. The hotter they get the better they work. Water will only foul you up." From that day, only an occasional can flew off or buckled, apparently due to its own structural weakness. Jeff started talking with Glen Morgan about the possibility of 60-inch pipe.

From Sergeant to Lieutenant

On December 15th, Jeff was at a division meeting in Omaha when he got a call from Dick Hill at the plant.

Dick: The motor on the prestress machine is burnt out.

Jeff: Oh, no.

Dick: Anyway, here's what I've done: I phoned the regular supplier, and he didn't have stock. I phoned the other company, and they found one in Omaha. Cost is $7,500, shipped, and it can be here by air freight tomorrow and running in two days. We can get the original one fixed here and have it going in four days, for $3,500. I figure we save more by buying the new motor; if we don't, we can't make pipe for two more days, and we have to pay the men anyway. The Omaha place is waiting for your call, and you could even bring it back with you.

Jeff: I'll talk it over with Glen and let you know immediately.

Jeff talked to Glen Morgan, as was standard procedure for purchases at this level of expense. They agreed that it was best to buy the new motor, and it was shipped to Widefield that same day. The men at the plant busied themselves with housekeeping until the maintenance shop got the motor mounted and the machine back on line. Jeff noted in recalling the incident that "it was the first time on a major decision Dick didn't just wait for instructions or back down on his suggestion in favor of mine. Since then he has always come prepared to defend his choice of options."

Working with a Workaholic

Glen phoned Jeff at home on Saturday, December 20, 1977 at 6 P.M. He knew Jeff was planning to be away from the plant for a couple of weeks and wanted Jeff to bring in, on his way through Omaha, a written report on the objectives that had been set for the plant's operations between July and December. Jeff was surprised, since he had thought Glen would prefer to get the report when it included December information, and he was also a bit put off by the timing—he was planning to leave the very next evening for his long-awaited vacation. Carol was already in Omaha; they had planned to spend two days with her parents who were with her and then leave to visit a brother in St. Louis. When Jeff expressed doubts about getting the report out, Glen proposed that he go right then to the plant to get the information, do the report on the plane Sunday afternoon, and send the finished report to Glen by taxi from the Omaha airport. Jeff said that his wife and her parents were picking him up at the airport, and they could all drive over with the report.

Sunday evening Jeff and his in-laws arrived at Glen's doorstep. Jeff rang the bell and Glen invited him in, offering him a chair at the kitchen table. Jeff declined the chair and hung back in the hallway, as Glen started asking questions about what was in the report. Their standup discussion had run about 20 minutes, with Glen asking "just one more question," when Glen's wife saved Jeff by offering them a sandwich, thereby providing a break through which Jeff escaped. "Glen is at work every waking moment. He honestly had no idea he was causing me any trouble. He certainly wouldn't have thought twice about leaving his own family waiting while he talked business."

CASE 4–4 Metaphor Computer Systems

Robert Mueller, Jr.
Vijay Sathe

In the spring of 1983, Don Massaro, the 39-year-old president of Metaphor Computer Systems, stood at the window of his unfinished office in the 45,000-square-foot building that Metaphor had recently leased in Mountain View, California. Tanned and relaxed, he looked down at his red Ferrari Daytona in the lot below and said, "It's like the first day of spring! We've only been open four months, and so far, with no product, there are no problems—no sales quotas, no production schedules, no dissatisfied customers, no staff morale problems, no cost accounting problems. . . . All we have to do is figure out what our market is and what we're going to sell."

In fact, Don Massaro and his business partner, David Liddle, had founded Metaphor specifically to develop a computer system of hardware, software, and end-user support that would benefit busi-

This case was prepared by Robert Mueller, Jr. (under the direction of Vijay Sathe).

Copyright © 1984 by the President and Fellows of Harvard College
Harvard Business School case 0–484–106.

ness professionals in *Fortune* 500 companies. They had raised $5 million to finance 12 months of research and development, and a six-month marketing study was under way on the basis of which Metaphor's executive steering committee would soon be making its strategic choices.

In late June of 1983, the results of this study were ready for presentation to Metaphor's principals and staff at a two-day marketing meeting. As Katherine (K. C.) Branscombe, marketing director, told Metaphor's assembled executives and staff at the end of the first day, June 29, the meeting's goal would be to "reach a clear agreement on what our market is and who our competitors are." Reaching this agreement soon would be important, because Metaphor was currently "burning" available funds at the rate of $280,000 per month. Massaro and Liddle had estimated that the burn rate would grow by about $1 million a month to a total of $15 million before a product made it out the door in late 1984.

By March in 1984, Metaphor's computer startup was well along. Massaro was supervising its second round of financing. The organization had been restructured to some extent, with Don Massaro as CEO and chairman, and David Liddle as chief operating officer and president. Fellow executives who had joined them in their new venture had been working long hours to meet the autumn deadlines, as had most of the staff who had been hired away from neighboring high-tech companies. The year had been devoted to intensive planning and close scrutiny of the market. So far, they had achieved their goals in each stage of development, but every Metaphor employee knew that the major test lay ahead: the performance of their new product in a marketplace dominated by the giant competitor, IBM.

Xerox Projects and Trials

Massaro and Liddle were convinced that for their product to succeed they would have to "bring something really new to the party"—and that it should be "vital," not merely convenient. As president of Xerox's Office Products Division, Don Massaro had had primary responsibility for the development and marketing of that corporation's office of the future, including the Memorywriter typewriter, the 860 word processor, the 820 personal computer, and through David Liddle's efforts, the 8000 series Star and Ethernet. As competition began to reduce the profitability of Xerox's reprographics business in the early 1980s, questions were raised about continuing to invest in advanced office products and systems. When the combined sales of the two divisions in these areas failed to break even in 1981, criticism of Don Massaro's OPD strategy had grown at Xerox headquarters in Stamford, Connecticut. Massaro thought that the ability of OPD sales reps to sell at a higher level in customer accounts than copier salespeople could aim at had led to a fear that the power balance within Xerox might begin to shift to OPD. The longer the problems with OPD sales continued, the louder the criticism became.

Massaro had maintained since early 1980 that the major task facing Xerox was to reorient the OPD sales force from selling "boxes" (like copiers and word processors) to selling systems; he had been strongly supported in this outspoken position by David Liddle of the System Development Department (SDD) and by Bob Ruebel, OPD vice president for marketing. But many senior executives in Reprographics sharply disputed this view.

When Xerox president David Kearns told Don in April 1982 that he had decided to integrate the OPD sales force with the Reprographics sales organization, Don responded that he couldn't live with that and asked for another year to get his division in the black and show the importance of a concentrated systems sales force.

This request was denied, and although Kearns urged Don to continue, with P&L responsibility for the OPD business units, Don replied that without sales the position would mean nothing to him. He told Kearns he would be leaving Xerox to return to California. Kearns suggested several other positions, including manager of U.S. sales, but Don was still not interested.

In June 1982, David Liddle also decided to leave after talking with Don and turning over in his mind what his job at Xerox would be like for the next few years. Shortly after this, David Kearns asked Don to consider alternative ways in which he and David Liddle might continue to work together in the office automation area while preserving the idea of presenting a single face to the Xerox customer. Liddle had been considering how Xerox might move further into the data processing marketplace, rather than sticking to its traditional document-oriented strategic thrust. Now he and Don proposed the idea to Kearns of exploring the possibility of a new company to attack this market, with Xerox in an essentially venture capital role, for which it would receive 50 percent ownership. Xerox was interested and asked Don and David to draw up a proposal, which they submitted in August for evaluation.

But in late September Xerox announced its $1.6 billion acquisition of the Crum and Forster insurance company, and Don and David were told that their proposal would not be strategically relevant to Xerox. Within a week they had a commitment from the investment banking firm of Hambrecht & Quist to take the lead position in a similar proposal. Metaphor was about to appear in the high-tech firmament.

The New Venture

In September 1982, when Don was making contacts with venture capital groups, David spoke with development and applications people at Xerox about joining in the start-up. He was specifically interested in Charles Irby, Ralph Kimball, and Yogen Dalal. All three had previously turned down opportunities to join start-up companies, but had asked David to give them an opportunity to join him if he ever started a new company. David said their names were household words in Silicon Valley and had celebrity status in the technical community. They would attract people who would want to work and study under them. Like David, all three had Ph.D.s in engineering or physics and years of development experience at Xerox's Palo Alto Research Center (PARC) or Systems Development Department. Ralph Kimball and Charles Irby had developed Star's user interface, which employed graphic representations of computer functions and a "mouse" to give computer commands. Yogen Dalal had designed the communications architecture for the 8000 Series at Xerox, which defined the way the various work stations, computers, and printers would interact. These three first hires were brought on as principals in the new company, along with Katherine Branscomb, who came in as director of marketing in December. K. C. held an MBA from Stanford, had been a marketing manager for Tandem Computer and, before that, a corporate strategy consultant for The Boston Consulting Group. Others from the professional staff were considered as principals, but the

new steering committee (two partners and four principals) decided against them. The steering committee thereby became the arena for discussion of major company decisions, with consensus being their unwritten goal. Through the second round of hiring, no one was hired without the full agreement of the group.

The principals were attracted to the Metaphor start-up for both monetary and career reasons. The salaries were competitive, and attractive equity incentives were included. One engineer said the rewards were standard in Silicon Valley, but that they alone were not sufficient incentives. Several principals who had worked at PARC spoke of the mixed blessings of working in gilded cages where they could make important technical contributions without ever participating in the results. At Metaphor they saw the opportunity to be creative by designing a computer system that met the actual needs of end users. Whereas their achievements at Xerox had been relevant both to product and engineering, they now hoped to produce a product that was *consequent* in its larger impact upon the marketplace.

The second round of hiring brought in more technical and marketing professionals, as well as support staff, who also were attracted by the prospect of sharing in the entrepreneurial side of Silicon Valley. Some were young and eager to make money, and others with more experience could bring stability to the task. Young engineers knew of Don's reputation for succeeding at whatever he attempted, and the network buzz that Metaphor was the hot start-up of the year was an exciting inducement.

Money

Don's first venture capital commitment in October 1982 was from Bill Hambrecht at Hambrecht & Quist. They had worked together when Don was president of Shugart, and now Hambrecht expressed interest in taking the lead position. Don's proposal to raise $500,000 to hire key people and write a business plan did not appeal to him; Hambrecht said he didn't know how to raise that little, and he did not require a detailed business plan. He proposed the alternative of raising $2–$3 million, for which the investors could get 50 percent of the company. Under this plan, Hambrecht & Quist would take a million shares at $1 per share and leave about $1 million for other investors. The deal was closed, and Don and David went sailing for a week on Don's boat, *Chance.*

When they returned a new problem awaited them—$4 million had been raised for the $1 million opening left by Hambrecht & Quist. They raised the entry price to $1.50 per share to enlarge the venture stake to $5 million, but the flow of investment did not stop. The next time they looked, there was $8 million on the table. Don believed it would be a bad move to take in that much at the beginning,

and they set a cut-off point in December at $5 million.

The equity configuration at the start-up was 3.2 million shares for David and Don and an equal amount for the venture capital group, including Hambrecht & Quist and Sutter Hill on the West Coast and Oak Investment Partners and Dillon Read on the East Coast. An additional 660,000 shares were held out for the principals and as a stock option plan. By March 1983, only 250,000 shares in this pool were not committed. For future stock options, Don and David agreed to turn over some of their shares, with the board issuing a matching block, to avoid losing control of the company (as Don once had at Shugart Associates). With money in hand, the partners set about building a company that would have a business plan by June 1983 and a product shipped by late 1984.

Market Driven

From the outset the steering committee was convinced that Metaphor must be truly market driven. As one nonmarketing principal put it, "We will only get one look out the window, and if we are not sure of what we see—we are out of business." Another oft-repeated Metaphor saying was, "Once we start putting stakes in the ground, we are committed to a position."

The marketing research tactic in the first phase was to send teams into the field to meet with professionals in Fortune 500 companies. The marketing teams were made up of people with marketing or technical ability, or both. They were to select the professionals, determine their data analysis needs, and calculate the potential size of the market.

In the first phase (January–March), the marketing teams visited professionals in 30 companies with Don himself going to 13. The information gathered was collated into market segments to be evaluated by the steering committee when it decided which segments to pursue. Eight segments were identified: product marketing, retail buying, investment analysis and management, corporate financial analysis and control, manufacturing production, manufacturing materials purchasing, insurance product planning, and document indexing and retrieval. Narrowing this number to two or three would be one of the first major stakes for the steering committee to drive into the ground.

Metaphor's market orientation was bounded by several guiding assumptions which had sparked the creation of the company. These included the understanding that Metaphor would be an end-user company and not an original equipment manufacturer (OEM) and a belief that the professional information worker was inadequately served by either mainframe data processing systems or the personal computer. Mainframe systems did not allow for unstructured, ad hoc queries, and personal computers could not handle large data bases or connect to multiple

data sources and were a nuisance to learn how to use. Don said they were for computer enthusiasts only. One result, in the Metaphor view, was that senior managers rarely used computers and were reduced to analyzing DP printouts with hand-held calculators.

The Metaphor solution was built around a hardware and software package comprising user-friendly (icon and mouse) work stations, an ability to integrate multiple data sources, and connections to a network of shared resources; the software (70 percent of Metaphor development costs) would be designed specifically for one market segment. All this would be delivered to the end user and supported by a professional staff. The cost per work station should amount to $5,000–$6,000 in a complete system. If the market analysis of these professionals was accurate, and the system configuration was capable of solving real problems, then Metaphor would succeed.

Don and David: Electrons and Protons

As founders, partners, and managers of Metaphor's two primary functional areas, Don and David were bound to have a major impact on the style and direction of Metaphor (Exhibit 1). David was responsible for product development (hardware and software), system development (system architecture), applications (applying system to user need), and marketing. He referred to this group as "my peo-

Exhibit 1

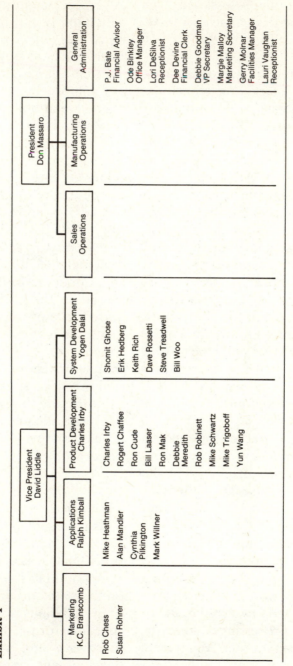

President
Don Massaro

Vice President
David Liddle

Marketing
K.C. Branscomb

Rob Chess
Susan Rohrer

Applications
Ralph Kimball

Mike Heathman
Alan Mandler
Cynthia Pilkington
Mark Willner

Product Development
Charles Irby

Charles Irby
Rogert Chaffee
Ron Cude
Bill Laaser
Ron Mak
Debbie Meredith
Rob Robinett
Mike Schwartz
Mike Trigoboff
Yun Wang

System Development
Yogen Dalal

Shomit Ghose
Erik Hedberg
Keith Rich
Dave Rossetti
Steve Treadwell
Bill Woo

Sales Operations

Manufacturing Operations

General Administration

P.J. Bate
Financial Advisor

Ode Binkley
Office Manager

Lori DeSilva
Receptionist

Dee Devine
Financial Clerk

Debbie Goodman
VP Secretary

Margie Malloy
Marketing Secretary

Gerry Molnar
Facilities Manager

Lauri Vaughan
Receptionist

ple," who were more in his image than Don's. David's philosophy was that "life is a science fair, and we have to win the fair." He was animated and affable, but a probing questioner. David said that depending on who you talked to, Metaphor was either Don's or his. As most of the start-up tasks to be accomplished by staff were within David's purview, he thought his management responsibilities were more extensive and more interesting than Don's. The technical people who were attracted to Metaphor were better acquainted with David than Don, who was known to them mainly as a flamboyant success story.

Don, as CEO, had general responsibility for the entire company and specific responsibility for sales, production, and general administration (including finance). As many of these areas were still dormant, most of Don's work in the early phase was strategic.

The differences in style between David and Don were mirrored in two types of people at Metaphor. David described them as "electrons and protons" (another principal described them as "balloons and ballast"). David saw himself, Yogen Dalal, and Charles Irby as the protons who supplied a compact, rotating center to Metaphor. The electrons, among whom David counted Don, Ralph, and K. C., provided a freer, whirling force that pulled and stretched the company beyond itself. According to David, companies that were either all protons or all electrons failed.

Success came when both worked together.

Environment

When Metaphor opened in December 1982, an early, major decision members of the steering committee had to make was the kind of environment they wanted from the viewpoint of effect on employees, ability to give technical support to the staff, and their own market image. After a temporary period in rented space in Santa Clara, they decided on a two-story, L-shaped building yet to be completed in an office park in Mountain View. The space was 20 percent more expensive than other sites they considered, but it was close to Stanford, and was surrounded by other new computer companies. Don's cynical comment was, "They can't all survive, but those that do can expand into the vacated space." There was time to plan how they would use their space. Metaphor moved into its new location in March 1983 when the first floor, which would house production and sales, was still unfinished except for the large bathrooms lined in earth-tone ceramic tiles with showers for after running and saunas for relaxing. Half of the second floor held the staff, a lunch room, and a computer room. In the occupied L, two long, parallel, 10-foot-wide halls were flanked by private offices. Don had advocated open, flexible work space, but David felt that the engineers would need quiet and privacy, so the compromise was for private offices with glass walls along the hall. The carpets were a subdued fawn and slate blue pattern, with furniture in complementary colors. Star work stations, at $15,000 apiece, were located in a number of the offices. It looked very much like the office of the future, with hardly any paper around.

The lunchroom next to the kitchen area accommodated 40 people at 10 tables. Don hoped the lunchroom would build a team feeling and encourage open communication.

The mainframe computer, a VAX 11/750, was not at the equipment level the Xerox employees were used to. The technical principals had picked it because they believed the VAX provided an adequate computing environment for the development people. If the choice was wrong, however, it would affect the product.

Learned at Xerox

Star's failure to take off at Xerox had been generally explained in one of two ways. Some there felt that their PARC scientists conducted research for its own sake, with little regard for applicability or cost. PARC scientists, on the other hand, felt that Xerox lacked the nerve to market and sell their products aggressively. One principal noted that, like missiles, new products, however powerful, were useless without an effective delivery system.

The same principal also believed that Metaphor had learned from both perspectives at Xerox. The

problem seemed to be to avoid the second generation syndrome. In the first generation, new technology tends to be simple and the goal is to see if a theory works. The second generation often gives way to creeping elegance and *mize wells*. As the developers become reluctant to give up a project until it is able to do everything they want, they reason that they "mize well" put as much into a system as they can to make the product elegant. The Star was elegant, but did more than anyone needed it to do. The goal at Metaphor was to take marketing seriously and design what the end users asked for.

Market Choice

On March 30 and 31, 1983, two meetings were held to "put important stakes in the ground." Don, David, and K. C. Branscomb attended the meeting on the 30th; the one the next day was attended by the partners, the principals, and two members of K. C.'s marketing staff—Rob Chess and Susan Rohrer. Their purpose was to narrow the market sectors to two or three and reach consensus around the choices.

At the first meeting in Don's office, K. C. went through the market segments explaining the needs and potential for each—without indicating her preferences. Questions arose as to whether they should be trying to find commonality or greater differentiation between market sectors, and whether the computer configuration would have to be known before the markets could be chosen, or vice versa. David's probing line of questioning prevailed through most of the meeting, with Don occasionally asking jovially, "Can I talk now?"

Toward the end of the meeting Don asked K. C. which markets she would choose if she had to choose only two. K. C. thought that it was too early to choose, but she did reveal her preferences, and Don and David both said, "Me too!" With the air thus cleared, K. C. asked David if the marketing information had changed or otherwise affected his decision, and David answered, "No." "Then why are we bothering with all this market research?" K. C. asked. David responded, "The information is extremely valuable, but it confirms rather than changes my original position." "I'm the only one who has changed his position," Don added.

On the following day the planned two-hour presentation to the steering committee, following a similar pattern, laster four hours. David and Ralph Kimball (applications) asked most of the questions, with the developers responding only to technical questions for which others needed information. Don's probes often came from outside the line of questioning, as when he suggested keeping their distance from investment analysts, whose imagination about Metaphor products would surely be better than the reality. He preferred not to let them know too much about Metaphor too early.

This March meeting ended with everyone feeling that in leading to a general market consensus, it had been their most productive meeting.

Pinpointing the Market: June 1983

Two months later, at meetings scheduled for June 29 and 30, 1983, Metaphor's marketing studies were ready to be discussed, and the steering committee would have to make decisions on market and final product. "Dave and I will have to make a business decision?" Don Massaro asked with mock concern. David Liddle, always facile with metaphors, added, "Now we're lined up at the window, and we'll have to decide which horse to put our money on." Charles Irby commented more gravely that he had often warned new staff members that "Metaphor would be either a dramatic success or a dramatic failure—because we're taking risks."

Massaro, Liddle, Kirby, and Branscomb had undertaken to clarify these risks by investing in Metaphor's intensive six-month marketing study. As K. C. now presented them, the strategic choices before the steering committee were: (1) whether the computer systems should be sold through end users, data processing, MIS managers, or a combination of all three; (2) whether the configuration should be a low-end system, and at what price level; (3) what the makeup of the sales/support team should be; and (4) which market sectors (functional areas) and market segments (job positions) should be pursued. All the principals frequently noted that Metaphor could not afford to guess wrong.

Second-Quarter Environment

During Metaphor's third three-month period (March–June 1983), improvements continued to appear in the work environment: a flashing neon sign at the ground-floor entrance directing guests to the second-floor reception area; framed composite photographs in the reception area of all Metaphor employees; stenciled names on the glass walls of the private offices. Staff had increased slightly to 40 people, all housed so far in one quarter of the building. Large, abstract paintings adorned the previously barren walls, many on loan from an area gallery. Above the copying machine, cutouts from Minolta copier ads showed business people exclaiming, "I left Xerox," "We left Xerox," or "We all left Xerox."

Work Fever

As a technical principal, Yogen Dalal felt encouraged by the sense of excitement among the 22 technical staff who had been hand picked in a ratio of seven applicants to each job offer. People hired from other companies seemed satisfied with the transition they had made from an ambience of Hewlett-Packard security to a Metaphor risk. Prospective staff members often commented favorably to Dalal on "seeing workers who show the same excitement that you do."

Dalal compared the feeling at Metaphor to that of a symphony orchestra. At Metaphor, he said, you saw "bright eyes everywhere trying to work their best because the concert will take place in a year."

Dalal, Irby, and Liddle (see Exhibit 1) felt they had a fairly clear agreement on what the market was like. As technical people, they were willing to listen to the marketing staff, since they generally agreed on market assumptions. One principal said he had no idea what would have happened if the marketing staff had recommended something like artificial intelligence computers.

Pearls before Swine

The major questions facing senior staff were what to sell, and to whom. Although Metaphor's original marketing strategy had been to tailor the product to the needs of the end user, it became evident in the course of the study that end users did not grasp the range of technical problems involved in interacting with central data processing facilities. They seemed to be unable or unwilling to assume responsibility for data base administration. The development staff thought that selling such a sophisticated system to end users would be throwing pearls before swine. Furthermore, data processing personnel in a potential customer's company might resist having these systems sold to end users because of their own overall responsibility for corporate data processing. Metaphor's senior executives now had to decide where to cast their pearls, and they wanted to be rational and methodical about the decision. Principals and partners alike conceded, however, that a start-up required certain choices to be made without all the information they might feel was necessary.

Open Meeting

The marketing meeting on June 29 started with an air of success. Don Massaro said K. C. and her team had done "an incredible job" and accomplished much original work. Charles Irby, who had spent the previous evening reading a written version of the presentation, came in exclaiming that the report was exactly what he had hoped from the study. David Liddle observed it was "as good as this stuff gets."

The conference room where the report was to be discussed was separated from the reception area by a glass wall, and its solid wood doors and wall blinds were open much of the time. In a sense, all 14 participants, partners, principals, and marketing staff were on stage. The group was young and casual. Don eschewed the seat at the head of the table, saying the meeting was K. C.'s. David entered later and took it, by then the only empty seat. Don set an upbeat opening tone with teasing comments to the staff and a market prediction that "there's $310 million in specific business out there."

Taking and Holding Beachheads

The Metaphor mission had been to provide senior managers with a system capable of sophisticated data queries without requiring so-phisticated computing skills. Now, Metaphor wanted to find "beach-heads" that could be taken as a tactical maneuver and held as part of a campaign to capture those desk tops.

Susan Roher of K. C.'s marketing staff presented the report aimed at resolving this sales strategy issue. David expected that Susan would be able to act as a pilot fish for Metaphor, because of her past experience with IBM. Susan provided several analytic frameworks for a final decision, noting that there were five different constituencies within a market segment: unsophisticated end users, sophisticated end users, end-user managers, data processing senior managers, and MIS-supported end users. These were subdivided according to their levels of MIS sophistication: no formal system, early MIS experience, and mature ability. Through a process of query and answer that Susan handled confidently, the mega point was made that end users were unsophisticated in corporate data processing. DP types seemed to know better what they wanted for corporate operations, but did not have much insight into end user applications.

During the discussion it became apparent that the end users would almost need a turnkey system. The presale time would be extensive, and the DP people, it was feared, could easily derail a sale. One marketing staffer noted that Metaphor could not be reactive toward MIS people but would have to go after them from the very beginning.

The implications of this largely uncontested assumption were that Metaphor would be selling high and would need a different type of sales force than had been anticipated. A by-product of this strategy would be that systems could easily be sold to the DP shop, thus serving what Don called Blue Bird accounts. Don underlined the quality of Susan's presentation with his reaction, "We know more about this business than almost anyone!"

Sector/Segment

At 11:45 on the first meeting day, Rob Chess took the spotlight and presented his description of possible specific market choices. Rob's trademark golf shirt was emblazoned with a Mickey Mouse emblem, a symbol those around the table had no trouble interpreting. Like the entire marketing staff, Rob had spent long days and nights working on his presentation. In the rush to finish, some of the printed materials ended up with a series of typos, and as a further characteristic noted by David Liddle, "Like all Harvard Business graduates, Rob gave his conclusions before presenting the data."

Rob's task was to define the market and help the group come to a common understanding of it. He used the term *market sector* to refer to organizational functional areas (financial analysis, product marketing, retail marketing, etc.) and *market segment* to refer to specific jobs within these areas (controller, product marketing manager, retail buyer, etc.). These terms had become familiar over the preceding months, but for many at the table their definition continued to remain elusive.

Rob displayed several comparative tables to help the group understand the pros and cons of various market considerations. Critical variables included: the potential long- and short-term growth of sales, profit, the amount Metaphor would need to invest, risk, revenue, sales fit, leverage to follow-on accounts, and steepness of the selling ramp (showing how fast sales in that account would grow). The analysis led to three market scenarios. The prime scenario comprised a sector/segment of product marketers, controllers, and retail buyers, with the initial selling effort on a sales pyramid, entering through the MIS-supported end users. The advantages to this strategy appeared to be $216 million in business, a fast ramp, long-term growth, high profit, and functional areas that provided each other with leverage. The disadvantage was that it would spread Metaphor resources thin. Everyone at the table supported this description.

At the close of the presentation, most people told Rob he had done a great job. One even called it "an incredible window which allows us to get into the market's psyches."

Applications and Configurations

From 2:45 until the meeting ended after 6 P.M., the presentations were led by Mark Willner and Ralph Kimball (Exhibit 1). The tone shifted from good-natured banter to unemotional queries and answers spoken in acronyms and numbers. A great deal of energy went into clarifying issues and technical solutions.

Don's concern was how to determine which product configuration and software applications would add true value for the customer rather than merely "getting around their objections." To this problem K. C. added that there were things the users only thought they needed. More mundane issues—such as whether to have laser printers, color graphics, whether managers would buy systems if they looked like secretaries' work stations, and whether the system competed effectively with an IBM PC—also got into the discussion. The problem was to sort out what the customer needed, wanted, and would purchase. By the end of the day, the consensus seemed to be for leading with a big system, with the MIS-supported end-user manager as a good entry point, though DP would play a major role in the sale.

Steering Committee

The next day, June 30, 1983, when the steering committee met, the doors were closed, and the wall window blinds were lowered and drawn. The on-stage feeling of the day before was replaced by Star Chamber secrecy. In the previous day's meeting, Massaro had acted as a light-hearted audience, but now he took a more challenging position, directly questioning a number of K. C.'s points and offering alternatives designed to startle her. Liddle's tone became more demanding, occasionally punctuating a point with an emotional appeal. The three technical principals lim-

ited their queries and comments to factual concerns as they watched this drama.

Beachhead

The tentative decision to sell to MIS-supported end users using a low-cost entry system left some concerned that with this strategy the selling ramp would be too slow. As K. C. put it, there would not be "a big sales bang in the first three months." Don suggested the possibility of Metaphor's selling as an OEM to *Fortune* 500 companies with Ethernet systems, thus "providing Blue Birds right up front." He saw the problem not as one of sales, but of producing fast enough to satisfy demand. David interjected more graphically that "this insulin rush would make a good initial sales slope."

The discussion shifted to K. C.'s concern with the need to be able to sell to "DP types." David and Don were apprehensive about Metaphor's looking like a minicomputer company; they didn't want a beachhead that would be impossible to hold. K. C. said the DP people could block sales to end users, so Metaphor had to have their support. The technical staff agreed and thought this would give Metaphor credibility. On this basis, the decision was made to use DP staff as an entry tactic toward the goal of capturing the MIS-supported end users.

Credible and Cheap

The low-end configuration discussion starting at 10 A.M. centered around whether Metaphor could provide the system it was claiming at a competitive price. Specifically, could the company provide a four- to five-work station system for under $50,000 and make money? In K. C.'s words, "The system has to be credible and cheap."

Don's concern was that the most expensive part of the system was being bought from another manufacturer. He wanted to know if Metaphor could produce it for half the price or buy a "dirt ball" version of it. Yogen Dalal said that producing it in-house would put delivery back at least a year. The company they were buying from was developing a cheaper version, but he pointed out that cheaper versions could not be the "Swiss army knife" that everyone wanted. Once assured that equipment prices would fall within two years, Don agreed to take the "margin hit" now and sell the low-end configuration of five work stations at $40,000.

Sales Support Strategy

After 45 minutes, the topic turned to the type of sales team necessary to sell to end users through the data processing staff—which proved to be the most difficult discussion of the day. K. C. emphasized that she needed a sales team led by an account manager with DP expertise. Don was upset by the emphasis on data processing; he said he wanted to "work with the DP guys, not make love to them," and DP was not a beachhead he could hold. He wanted the sales force to focus on the end user. Neither Don nor K. C. felt that both could be courted effectively.

The other steering committee members were not convinced.

The question of applications pointed up the importance of this discussion. Don felt that applications were reduced "from entrée to appetizer" when the sales focus moved to DP. He was fighting what he seemed to feel was a shift of the center of his company. The compromise was finally reached that the account manager could be trained to sell to the DP types. K. C. assented with some reluctance.

Bells and Whistles

In a general discussion after lunch on sales strategy, Don opposed "dividing the world by application," but favored "trying to impregnate as many places as possible with a generic product." David and K. C. disagreed: "Once we're over the DP hurdle, we can run like hell," they said, "but we're not ready to sell out of the box." This profitability/share argument was settled on the basis of salespeople's perceived inclination to follow repetitive yearly sales rather than to prospect for new accounts.

At 2 P.M., a one-and-a-half-hour discussion got going about what bells and whistles to place on the Metaphor computer. Wearing his sales hat, Don said that if he was to sell generically, the computer must have a wider variety of nonessential capabilities. To help him sell the product, Don wanted the work station to have automatic dialing, a voice box, electronic mail, a calendar, and a tickler file.

David objected that the voice box wouldn't sell it. Don countered rhetorically, "Are we an office automation company or not?" "Not if we have to put in every crazy idea!" Charles Irby threw in. K. C. said they should stick to substance. Charles offered a compromise to include the voice box as an option that could be connected at the buyer's request. Emphasizing his point strongly, Don said "I don't want to be eliminated from the big sales just because we don't have such things" and agreed to the compromise.

Battling the PCs

Don's final battle about product design and sales strategy centered around the problem of how to compete with personal computers (PC). He stated that Metaphor's margin would be in the sale of work stations; he did not want people buying IBM PC's and putting them on the Metaphor interconnect. "I have these new applications going," Don said, "and I want to sell them generically, but the IBM bigot will say, 'Why buy your 10 software packages when IBM has thousands of writers?'" Don asked rhetorically "What do I say?" His own answer was that he wanted the Metaphor system to emulate the IBM PC, and to do this, the development staff would have to make the system capable of handling Micro Soft's DOS.

Don met with almost complete disagreement from the others at the table. Yogen said the issue was not that simple, that programs based on MS/DOS would have to be completely recompiled to make it run. But Don reiterated, "If great software appears, the work station ought to be able to run it."

The entire group resisted this, saying that the value of the Metaphor system lay in its ability to get data on the manager's desk in a format that was easy to manipulate. David said they sounded like "the Bolsheviks not pushing ahead because it looked like rain." Don responded again that "this thing we are building is a PC. I don't want to be kicking myself later because this prevents me from selling generically. It could mean the difference between being a $100 million and a $200 million company."

Yogen's solution was to suggest that they not cross it off the list until they had talked with Micro Soft. David said, "Let's not mention it in our strategy—if it works out, great." It was agreed to explore the possibility, and the group compiled a list of what was required or only desired in the system.

Closure

Assignments were made to write operations plans for sales, marketing, and development, as well as a business plan. Don ended the meeting the way it had begun, with kudos for the work already accomplished. He told K. C., "I think your work is great; I don't know of anywhere where marketing this good is done; you have 20 stars in marketing and development." Charles Irby also reiterated what he had said the day before, "This is the best marketing department in the valley."

* * * * *

By early March 1984, Metaphor Computer Systems had decided on its market, built a computer prototype, completed its second round of financing, found its beta test sites and moved its launch date from November to September 1984. CEO Don Massaro still felt optimistic. "We're on an even keel, and slowly picking up speed," he said. People were working hard, but they found the work rewarding in contrast to most start-ups, which often resembled continuous fire drills. As Massaro put it, Metaphor didn't have the problem of "asses and elbows all over the place," but there were frequent marathon work sessions to keep on schedule.

Product

Metaphor now had an elegant looking computer system prototype, with most of the functions that the steering committee had envisioned one year earlier. One of its developers said it took three hours, working fast, just to demonstrate its capabilities. This system, which cost less than had been projected in June 1983, included work stations, a relational data base server, a communications server, and a print server. The work station resembled a more specialized and sophisticated MacIntosh, but its capabilities were more elaborate. The work station consisted of a screen that looked like a PC, and three detachable pieces, a keyboard, alpha/numeric pad, and function pad and mouse. The keyboard itself could be stored in the base of the terminal. All four detachables were cordless and used

an infrared signal. The keyboard's ability to be stowed away served to emphasize how much other work could be done at the station. The mouse and two other pads allowed the user to make sophisticated managerial queries simply through the use of icons on the screen. The cost of the system ranged from $50,000 for 5 stations to $100,000 for 15.

Money

During the third quarter of 1983 the steering committee had written a business plan, comprising marketing, sales, product development, manufacturing, and finance plans. This business plan was the basis for an investment memorandum they would use in October 1983 to raise $10 million to finance work in 1984. Since the original venture group was already committed to take half of this amount, new backers were needed for only $5 million.

The day before the memorandum was to be circulated, the venture capital group of Kleiner, Perkins, Caufield, and Byers was brought into Metaphor for a presentation (see Exhibit 2). (This group had passed on its original opportunity in 1982 to finance Metaphor, because Massaro and Liddle had had no business plan.) Massaro described the tone of their questions as "cold and firm," and toward the end of the day's session, Massaro and Liddle were asked to leave the room for a while. When members of the venture group called them back, they said they had made the mistake of not buy-

Exhibit 2
Betting Big on a Computer System for Managers*

Every now and then a company achieves star status even before it has shipped its first product. This is the enviable fate of Metaphor Computer Systems. Incorporated in October, 1982, it completed its business plan only six months ago and will not introduce its first machines until the third quarter. Nevertheless, the Mountain View (Calif.) computer maker has taken the venture capital world by storm, already attracting $15 million. In investment circles, Metaphor is seen as "a legend in the making," according to Brook H. Byers, a partner at Kleiner Perkins Caufield & Byers, a big Metaphor backer.

Metaphor's success with financiers has as much to do with its founders as it does with its strategy. Donald J. Massaro, Metaphor's chairman, and David E. Liddle, its president, are well-known former executives of Xerox Corp. "In this business, we basically back people," admits William R. Hambrecht, president of Hambrecht & Quist Inc., the investment bank that in 1982 helped raised Metaphor's first $5 million from a group of investors. It was the idea for the company, though, that closed the deal.

Metaphor plans to make work stations that are equipped with the sort of easy-to-use software that Xerox pioneered with its Star work station and that is now used by personal computers such as Apple Computer Inc.'s Lisa. The software is designed to extract information stored in mainframe computers made by International Business Machines Corp. But unlike IBM or even Xerox, which aim to blanket the office with general-purpose work stations, Metaphor plans to custom design the software in its systems for specific industries.

BACKLOG OF INVESTORS.   The founders claim they did not intend to start out on such a grand scale. When Liddle and Massaro left Xerox, they approached Hambrecht & Quist with a request for a mere $500,000 to do research and develop a business plan. But Hambrecht thought their idea was so good he offered them more money. "He said he had at least $5 million to $6 million worth of investors waiting to squeeze into the deal," says Liddle.

Hambrecht knew and admired Massaro from the days when he ran Shugart Associates Inc., a maker of disk storage devices for computers. A founder of Shugart, Massaro was named president in 1974, the year the company lost $2.5 million on revenues of about the same amount: "Don took over when he was just 29 years old and did a great job turning Shugart around," recalls Hambrecht, an investor in Shugart. The company was profitable one year later, and sales soared to about $100 million by 1978, when Massaro sold it to Xerox.

At Xerox, Massaro organized the thrust into office products. He soon acquired a reputation for being "brash, crazy, and bright—really very bright," according to Merrill E. Newman, a vicepresident at Convergent Technologies Inc., who was at Shugart with Massaro. Massaro "grew Xerox's office products division from roughly $100 million in size to about $500 million," says Sanford J. Garrett, an analyst with Paine, Webber, Mitchell, Hutchins Inc.

BEEP-BEEP.   But Xerox's office products division never turned a profit, and Massaro was constantly sparring with Xerox's conservative management. Once he handed out T-shirts with a picture of the Roadrunner cartoon character on them to inspire his office automation group and gave visitors from Xerox's Stamford (Conn.) headquarters T-shirts decorated with coyotes. "Don would say that the coyote never catches the roadrunner because coyotes are dumb—he really went out of his way to make everyone at Stamford mad," remembers Newman. Like most Xerox watchers, analyst Garrett agrees that "the culture within Xerox and the politics frustrated" Massaro.

The reputation of Metaphor's other founder, the fast-talking, witty, 39-year-old Liddle, rests almost entirely on his years at Xerox, which he joined right out of college as a researcher at the company's Palo Alto Research Center (PARC). Liddle was quick to appreciate the commercial potential for the work at PARC, in particular its easy-to-use work stations and the local area network, Ethernet. Before long, he persuaded his Xerox bosses to let him form a team to bring that research into the real world. Eventually that team numbered more than 300 and reported to Massaro.

The idea for Metaphor's work stations could have been part of that team's offerings. But Liddle and Massaro failed to convince senior management that the plan was viable. According to Massaro, Xerox's main objection was that their plan called for a specialized, direct-sales force, "whereas Xerox has been moving in the direction of having a single sales organization for everything." So Liddle and Massaro left Xerox to work on their pet project.

After they formed Metaphor and raised the $5 million, the partners set out to test the market. They conducted "hundreds of interviews" with potential customers in the 500 largest U.S. companies. Their data confirmed that no one was serving the needs of the key managers in large companies that are dependent on getting computer data quickly but who are ignorant of programming.

In theory, this type of manager is catered to by the corporate data processing department. But, in fact, the data processing department "has an average [work] backlog of 14 months," says Liddle. And to adapt personal computers to a specific industry requires more programming than most users can handle. Metaphor's plan is to provide these executives with systems equipped with software tailored to their needs that will allow them to swap data with IBM computers and will be priced competitively with top-of-the-line personal computers.

Exhibit 2   *(concluded)*

The key to Metaphor's success, however, will lie in its ability to identify the managers that need this equipment and sell directly to them. "We do not want to serve the 22 million white-collar professionals there are in the United States; there are just 113,500 users we'd like to serve," declares Liddle. To reach this group, Metaphor will use its own direct-sales force. "We know we are either going to make it or break it on our sales force's cost and productivity," says Massaro.

Metaphor is setting up sales offices in three U.S. cities, which it claims will let it reach 75 to 80 percent of the target users—"a potential market of $600 million," says Liddle. Initially, Metaphor plans to aim at only three industries—which it has not yet announced—and is currently completing the specialized software.

'BLIND LUCK'?   This direct-sales approach will give Metaphor relatively slow growth at first. The business plan has a revenue target of $100 million for 1987. (A recent computer startup, Compaq Computer Corp., reached $100 million in its first year of production.) Massaro concedes that "one of the problems of using an end-user sales force is that the first [few] years tend not to be very exciting, as you train and organize your sales force." But once it gets started, he adds, "you are looking at an average compound growth rate of about 40 percent."

For now, Metaphor has few rivals. One startup, Integrated Office Systems, however, is about to launch a similar product aimed at salespeople and marketing managers. And most large computer and office equipment suppliers are moving toward industry-specific product and marketing efforts. Metaphor's backers are counting on the company's experienced management, superior technology, and detailed research to keep it ahead. But as Massaro concedes, there are other factors at play: "A cornerstone of our strategy is that no amount of planning can replace blind luck."

* Reprinted from the March 26, 1984 issue of *Business Week* by special permission, © 1984 by McGraw-Hill, Inc.

ing it in the first round, but now they would like the remaining $5 million position. It was the largest venture investment Kleiner and Perkins had ever made. They got it.

A new stock configuration would be needed with this added investment, as well as a growing employee group. Massaro and Liddle anticipated they would need 1.6 million shares for stock option plans by 1985. In the first round of funding, the board had authorized 660,000 shares for this purpose. Massaro and Liddle now wanted a second similar issue totaling 940,000 shares (one half from the two partners, one half from the board). The net result would be that Massaro and Liddle would hold 2.7 million shares, employees would hold 1.6 million, and the investors would control 7 million. The 40% thus controlled by man-

agement was enough, Massaro felt, to control Metaphor's future.

Structure

By March 1984, Metaphor had begun to grow into the space that had looked cavernous just six months earlier. Outside, a lower-case, block-letter Metaphor sign stood out against the streetside anonymity of the building. At the ground floor entrance was a semicircular reception counter. Throughout the building, people were now dispersed in all wings on both floors, seemingly less crowded, even though the staff had grown to 80 since June 1983.

A new structure for Metaphor had been instituted primarily to clarify the responsibilities and reporting channels that would soon be necessary. The fundamental change in the organization was a reordering of Don Massaro's and

David Liddle's job responsibilities. Originally, Liddle had had responsibility for development and marketing, while Massaro's role was that of general manager for the company, with specific responsibility for sales, production, and administration. Members of the steering committee felt that this arrangement was too complicated. There were often decision overlaps that sometimes made it hard to determine where the buck stopped. It was also difficult for Massaro to switch back and forth between strategic and operations functions.

The result was that they redivided their work along a strategy/operations axis (see Exhibit 3), so that Massaro could work on large "galactic" issues (like business planning, financial strategy, and third-party relationships) as CEO and chairman, and Liddle could "run the railroad" as chief operations officer and president (see Exhibits 4 and 5). This added sales and manufacturing to Liddle's job description. Below them would be seven vice presidents, made up of the four original principals plus three more VPs: field operations (including sales), manufacturing, and finance (Exhibit 3). Massaro's focus was primarily external, while Liddle's was internal. In March 1984 one VP kept Massaro's and Liddle's job descriptions taped on the wall to keep them straight.

Environmental Protection Agency

Job descriptions notwithstanding, Massaro considered 50 percent of his job was to act as "Metaphor's Environmental Protection Agency." The environmental qualities he considered primary were strong leadership, open communications, and informality, coupled with high expectations for productivity. In the March 1984 issue of *Success*, Massaro wrote:

I want a building full of mutants. It's important to have a structural business. But to create the right environment for innovative workers, a risk-taking environment that produces results, you have to give those people some room. [While I have to stop them] from running off the cliff, I like to let 'em run wild.

In Massaro's opinion, leadership was not something that you achieve by straining for it. "If you've got it," Massaro said, "it comes across. . . . People get angry when management can't make up its mind." Without a sense of destiny, management could not impart a confidence that it knew where the organization was heading. He said, "A start-up is like an Outward Bound experience, and it's important to have Daniel Boone, not Woody Allen, leading the group." Massaro believed that confidence and a sense of destiny must be tempered by awareness that anyone can make mistakes. The leader must be confident enough to know his limits.

One VP noted that Massaro scheduled a lot of free time just so he could walk around and talk with people about their work. In meetings he displayed a willingness to admit errors and ability to learn,

Exhibit 3

```
                          D.J. Massaro
                        Chairman and CEO
                                │
                                │────────────────── Finance/Administration
                                │                    Glenn Jones
                          D.E. Liddle                Vice President and CFO
                        President and COO
                                │
    ┌───────────┬───────────┬───┴───────┬───────────┬───────────┐
Product      System        Marketing   Applications  Field       Manufacturing
Development  Development    K.C.        Ralph Kimball Operations   Arnaldo Hernandez
Charles Irby Yogen Dalal    Branscomb   Vice President Joe Binder  Vice President
Vice         Vice President Vice President            Vice President
President
```

Exhibit 4
Major 1984 Activities: CEO

Major Account Sales Program:
    Executive Selling
    Market Feedback
    Customer Satisfaction
Business Planning:
    Financial Model
    Long-Range Plan
    New Market Sector Selection
Order Administration System
Field Logistics Performance
Financial Strategy:
    Control Systems
    Investor Relations
    Financing
Corporate Positioning:
    Positioning Statement
    Strategic Advertising and PR
International Partnerships
Third-Party Relationships:
    Application Development
    Reference Selling
    OEM and Systems Vendors
IBM Relationship
MIS Strategy
Manufacturing Strategy
    Capacity
    Sourcing
    Automation
    Cost Reduction
    Document Control System
Product Acquisition Alternatives
Management Guide
Organizational Development

Exhibit 5
Major 1984 Activities: COO

Operating Plan Achievement:
    Expense
    Shipments
    Revenue
Program Management:
    Alpha Test
    Beta Test
    Announcement
    Launch
Development Priorities:
    Product Release Definition
    Design Standards
    Corrective Actions
Manufacturing Performance:
    Schedule
    Cost
    Quality
    Inventory
Marketing Support:
    Sales Collateral
    Product Documentation
    Sales Training
Application Development
System Readiness Board
Field Service and Support Strategy
Customer Feedback System:
    Product
    Applications
    Support
Pricing and Contract Administration
Field Operations Model and Performance
    Measurement
Forecasting and Supply/Demand

even while he hammered away at his own points. At monthly company meetings, held in the lunchroom at the end of the day, Massaro and Liddle gave state-of-the-company talks, including financials. A question-and-answer period followed, with refreshments. Staff members considered these invaluable.

To encourage informality, Metaphor sponsored several parties and outings during the year. At Christmas time, in addition to office festivities, each employee was given 200 shares of Metaphor stock as stocking stuffers.

On the work side of this environment, people were expected to get their work done and, at a minimum, meet expectations. Output was the measure. "You don't get graded on effort," Liddle said. Massaro did not want people sacrificing their families for their work, but he said that people liked hard work when it gave them a sense of accomplishment. Massaro consistently recognized these accomplishments.

What the New People Saw

Staff members hired after June 1983 came to fill a definite set of positions: development, applications, marketing, sales, production, training, finance, and so on. Their motives included money, achievement, and friendship, but most mentioned Metaphor's focus on people and its high expectations as reasons for joining the company. Some had been in companies that were business failures, while others had worked for successful companies that cared little about their employees. They thought they would find both success and consideration at Metaphor.

One new employee, who had made the double adjustment of moving to a Silicon Valley start-up company from the East, said that Metaphor was more like a club than a company. When he was negotiating for a job, Massaro and Liddle had topped the salary range he had proposed by $2,500. The medical coverage he wanted to keep cost $2,000 more per year than the one Metaphor offered, but they said, "It's no sweat, we'll pay it." When he first started working, Liddle had stopped by his desk and asked him to let him know after a couple of weeks how he was doing. "Gestures of this kind," the new employee said, "build a tremendous sense of loyalty."

This employee was impressed with what was going on at Metaphor. Employees seemed to be of high caliber and very professional. Of top management, he said, "You trust that these guys know where they are going. They think big—

they think in terms of where we'll be in a couple of years, because we're following the plan." Like others, he talked about the openness of meetings and how VPs explained to subordinates what was going on at higher levels. He said it was not uncommon to walk by a meeting room and hear hoots, cheers, and applause, "and you know they're saying 'Keep it up, don't slow down.'"

Various clerical staff members struck similar notes. An administrative assistant who had worked previously for Massaro at Shugart said, "He is the reason I came. He's up front about what he expects, and he makes working fun." She said that Massaro was employee oriented; "He demands a lot," she said, "but not too much, and he doesn't come down on you if you blow it."

One of the new vice presidents spoke of the importance of trust and planning at Metaphor. He described Massaro and Liddle, with their big overview, as intelligent and productive in sharing a tremendous amount of useful information. Careful planning had put the structure and bureaucracy in place in plenty of time. "When the bride comes to the alter on September 5," he said, "we have to make sure the groom is there." He noted that this had been accomplished through the use of dependency tables, "which were immense." (Dependency tables cross-referenced all the jobs to be completed by others before one's own work could be accomplished.) This VP said that he thought of trust in a new way since coming to Metaphor. More than honesty, it now seemed to mean being able to accept that another person may have responsibility for something you need, and you can trust that person to get it done." One new staffer said, "If there is a problem, we regroup and look for a positive solution."

Two senior managers in manufacturing and sales, 20-year veterans from other high-tech companies, could have made higher salaries elsewhere, but they said they preferred the professional, positive, planned Metaphor environment. The manufacturing staff member (who designed the testing equipment for Metaphor's soon-to-be-delivered automated assembly line), was excited that Metaphor would be responsible for its total product. As a result of building and selling hardware, software, user support, and applications, it would not be at the mercy of other firms. He said it was "easier to satisfy customers when you do it all."

The vice president of sales said, "This company *will* be successful. Direct sales and end-user support will be the basis of the company—not hardware." He was also attracted by the opportunity to build his own sales organization that would operate at a high gross margin. Success would come, he said, through the sale of applications.

What Are We?

Most employees felt that Metaphor was different from other places they had worked—"like a family," or "no, not a family," but "a team." As long as one could play on the team, there seemed to be room for self-interest.

Massaro himself saw his company as a person who was bright, aggressive, neat, but also a cut-up who knew his own strengths and weaknesses. Most staff members visualized Metaphor in personal terms as one who believed he or she will succeed.

Stakes in the Ground

On March 2, 1984, the development staff met its deadline beyond which no new functions could be added to the system. The weeks leading up to this date had been filled with some 20-hour days, hard work, tension, and occasional flare-ups. When the deadline was met, people exclaimed about what an accomplishment it was. The technical staff now had to work the bugs out of the system during the tests known as alpha (an in-house run-through of the system) and beta (conducted with a line client). During the same period, manufacturing had to get application packages completed, a sales force had to be hired, and customers had to be lined up by the stepped-up September launch and shipping date. The work remaining was hands-on rather than strategic work. In the Metaphor language, all the stakes were now in the ground.

Stack Ranking

In the middle of this development year, an extensive evaluation was made of each employee to determine salary increases. This "handicapped" each position by ranking everyone on a scale of 1 to 58 (the number of staff at the time) in comparison to everyone else in the company. Each employee's supervisor conducted the evaluation, which included what had been accomplished during the year, strengths and weaknesses, and how well one did one's job. The vice presidents reviewed the evaluations and determined each employee's final ranking. During 1983, only two people came out below expectations, and both were able to improve their performance through the evaluation. Only one person had left since the start of Metaphor—because of marriage and relocation.

Market Position

The steering committee, consisting of Massaro, Liddle, and seven vice presidents, had decided by early 1984 on the market niche where it would attempt to set its roots. The industry was expected to spend $750 million on advertising personal computers in 1984, and Apple had shown them that there was room for others in the PC market. They observed that personal computers, however, had a number of shortcomings: data base access, data security, networking, software applications, training, and support. Metaphor would be bringing relevant business solutions to the end user with an easy-to-implement product from a single manufacturer (for end-user data access, inquiry, and analysis application). The user would be able to sit at a "very friendly" terminal and make sophisticated queries of large data bases, using icons and mouse.

IBM

A fledgling Metaphor would be in danger if IBM saw Metaphor as another PC manufacturer. Conversely, Massaro said, they couldn't ignore the personal computer. The Metaphor system was an alternative to the PC, but he feared that the distinction might be lost on customers. "People don't live by reality," he said. "They live by what they perceive reality to be." If people perceived Metaphor's product as a PC, they would have to compete in a market they had not chosen. Metaphor's solution was to sell its system as a *better* alternative, one which could use IBM terminals and display IBM software on its own terminals. Thus, objections of IBM fans could be overcome, without making Metaphor just another PC company. The viability of this strategy had yet to be tested.

The Future

Massaro and his cohorts felt the marketing study they had done was the most complete ever conducted by a computer company. Compared to other Silicon Valley companies, Don was confident they had done a A+ job. (Compared to product marketing companies, he conceded that they might have done a B− job.) But Metaphor had not yet had to compete in a marketplace that included IBM. They still had to climb up and plant seeds in what they believed to be a fertile niche. And not having had any major problems, the staff lacked the experience of having been knocked down and recouping from a major error. Don Massaro wanted his staff to know that when problems came, they could roll with the punches.

COMPRE-HENSIVE CASE Bill Hudson

C. Paul Dredge
Vijay Sathe

Sitting in his simple, but tastefully furnished, office at ABC Electronics, Bill Hudson had to grin when he recalled what the staff psychologist at his first company had said to him on that day in 1959. "The results of the battery of tests you took make it clear," said the psychologist from personnel, "that you don't have the aptitude to get beyond the junior supervisor level at XYZ Electric Corp." Bill had replied: "That may be the way I am today, given my inexperience and immaturity and all, but what could be my ability to change?" "Well, in our experience we find that people basically just can't change those aptitudes, so you're

just going to have to face up to it and be satisfied as a section head or something at about that level—that's as good as you're going to be."

In 1981, after 18 years with his second employer, Bill was a division general manager at ABC, directing an operating division that employed 300 people and generated $50 million in annual revenues. Bill knew that he *had* changed and grown during his 22-year career and that a large part of his success had been due to his willingness to joust with the conventional wisdom—the wisdom on himself, on new ideas, on new methods—and prove them wrong.

Bill Hudson didn't look much like a system bucker. Mid-40s, 5 feet, 9 inches tall, he always dressed, as one observer put it, "like an IBM manager: dark suits, white shirts, conservative ties." Bill's automobiles—a red Jaguar roadster and, later, a black Olds Toronado with all the extras—were clues, however, to his more flamboyant side. Hudson not only saw himself as having changed considerably during his 18 years at ABC, but he felt he had been instrumental in helping ABC to change, too.

Bill received his electrical engineering degree from Cornell, served a stint at sea with the U.S. Navy as an ROTC-trained officer, and then in 1959 took a job with a big company, XYZ Electric in New York, where he began a two-year general management training program. It was after some months in the training program that he had

This case was prepared by C. Paul Dredge (under the direction of Vijay Sathe).

Copyright © 1984 by the President and Fellows of Harvard College
Harvard Business School case 0–484–061.

been given the battery of tests that indicated his apparent inability to make it to upper-level management. The results were to be permanently on record in his file. Bill was sure that the tests and the psychologist were wrong, and he had enrolled in an evening MBA program to prepare himself to move to a company with a more flexible attitude.

Finding a New Company

In mid-1963, after four years at XYZ, Bill began looking for another job. His Cornell connection immediately started generating offers. One invitation for an interview came from ABC Electronics in Utica, New York. Bill didn't take them seriously at first. Walter Hedstrom, recently appointed head of marketing research in ABC's corporate research department, had received a copy of Bill's resume. Hedstrom's department was a kind of internal consulting group for ABC's top management, and Hedstrom had been hired to shape up the marketing side of it—marketing had developed a reputation for being slipshod and unbusinesslike. When Hedstrom called, Bill said he might be interested in dropping by ABC sometime; then Bill forgot about it. Hedstrom and Norm Nielson from the planning department kept calling Bill over the summer, however, and they sent him annual reports, financial analyses, and trade journal articles on ABC. They said that ABC was trying to move from electric to electronic (and eventually microelectronic) products and that Bill's experience in electronics systems development would be invaluable. Nielson mentioned that Bill's MBA, now completed, was also a plus.

In November, Bill relented, arranging to meet Hedstrom and Nielson for dinner on a Thursday night in Utica, on his way home from a day trip on XYZ business. When they got down to serious talk, Bill was startled: "These guys were talking from first-hand knowledge of all the details of running the company. They referred to all the company's officers by first names, and were even in the obvious habit of addressing ABC's founder and chairman by his nickname, Fin (from Finlayson). They had enthusiasm and affection for the company and they knew what made it tick. They had all the numbers on the tips of their tongues: growth, sales, profitability, projections on market development." And they painted a picture of a pragmatic organization that would do what was needed to get the job done. The job they wanted to get Bill involved in was ABC's search for an orderly path through the chaos of the fast-developing electronics business. The conversation lasted until 2 in the morning.

The following Monday, Walt Hedstrom called and said that the officers of the corporation wanted to meet Bill. Bill talked to his wife about the possibility of moving back to Utica—it was, ironically, the town where she had grown up. She was less than thrilled at the prospect, however, but was willing to be there for three to five years (which was about what Bill thought he would spend). Bill took that Friday off and went to Utica, where he was interviewed by the company president, several other corporate officers, and by a number of people in Hedstrom's market research section. Walt Hedstrom evidently talked to each of the interviewers as Bill moved on to the next. At 4 P.M. Bill had a written offer in his hand.

Diagnosis and Decision

Bill considered the fast-growth history of the company, founded in 1941 by "Fin" Finlayson and a few friends to make "crimp attached," fork-shaped wire-end terminals for easy electrical connections. This basic product made it possible to make electrical connections quickly and easily without having to twist or bend bare wire. With a defense contract in hand, Fin & Co. had constructed a large plant in upstate New York, a location picked for the social and physical environment and the availability of nonunion labor. The plant had burned to the ground only six months after opening. The U.S. government underwrote reconstruction of the plant in order to get the aircraft electrical parts when they were needed, but this time Finlayson made sure it was three smaller plants that were built. The small plant policy was established because of the original fire and a wish to avoid unionization, and it had persisted since those early years. In

1963, no ABC plant employed more than about 150 people, and the company had no unions.

Bill had noted that ABC draftsmen wore no ties, the engineers wore ties but no jackets, and the managers all wore ties and jackets; hourly workers wore blue-collar clothing. Other manifestations of formal structure seemed minimal at ABC, however; Bill sensed that ABC was in the midrange "between paper company loggers in plaid shirts and AT&T rank and file with dark suits" in terms of organizational formality. Given ABC's history of success in generating new products, he regarded the company as one with enough flexibility to allow a creative person to do something new. During his day of interviews, Bill had met ABC's inventor of the dip switch, a man who typified the old guard of designers and engineers without degrees who knew how to think and tinker. ABC had been a bit too naive at the time to get the dip switch under patent control, but their more recent record had been better in that regard. Bill had also met Bill Naylor, the only *electronics* person in the company at the time, who quizzed him on "flip-flops and gates and all that."

With regard to the company's finances, Bill learned that Finlayson had gambled early on the idea that reliability would be more important than price. He had consistently been able to finance growth and production with relatively high prices and the sale of stock (though he refused for the first 20 years, until 1961, to provide a stock option plan—"employees are always at risk for their jobs; they shouldn't be encouraged to be at risk for their savings." Even after Finlayson decided to offer stock options, they were available only to a very limited number of management level employees). Stock market analysts became believers in this high-quality, high-price strategy after Finlayson doubled the price of one previously unprofitable component, and it actually held its large share of the market. In 1963, ABC revenues were $100 million and the company was in good financial condition.

Bill thought about his wife's ambivalence concerning the move back to Utica. But he also thought about the positive, progressive atmosphere at ABC and of the potential of the company that was positioned to grow quickly in the industry. Bill sensed that ABC's products would have a much wider potential than the primarily military applications they had been used for up to that time. ABC clearly wanted Bill, even though their salary offer was only in the midrange of what other companies had offered. Their enthusiasm was both flattering and challenging. Bill's perception of a solid career opportunity and his knowledge of the relatively lower cost of living in the Utica area made him less inclined to treat salary as a major consideration. Accepting a raise of $400, Bill Hudson started work as a market researcher in Walt Hedstrom's corporate research department in December of 1963, at a salary of $10,400.

First Assignments

Bill Hudson's first major assignment for Walt Hedstrom was to do a study of the future development of the electronic components industry, with a focus on the interconnector market. Bill's department was small: Hedstrom, Maurice Mendel, a graduate in business management, Bill, two liberal arts college students, and two secretaries. Walt expected Maury and Bill to make their own periodic reports to the corporate planning board; that meant that Bill had the opportunity for close contact with a number of corporate VPs and other officers.

Bill did a lot of field work, attending conventions and trade shows, meeting people from Motorola, IBM, DEC, and other big firms. Bill estimated there was a $250 million market in standard connectors, of which ABC already had a $59 million share. Beyond this "measured market" however, he found what he thought was a "creatable market" to be developed through innovation.

Bill asked the planning board why ABC should deal only with the "End of the Wire"—why not consider the wire itself? Why not some of the items the wire would connect? On the basis of his research, Bill saw a $1.5 billion market in interconnection. The people who really listened to what he said were not the members of the planning board, but the various development managers in ABC's divisions. Gradually, Bill developed these and other connections within the company and began to spark ideas in others based on his own research.

Corporate Double Agent

Bill also took on two specific trouble-shooting assignments, acting as an in-house consultant with instructions to report his recommendations back to the corporate planning committee. The first assignment was with the Data Communications Division (Datacom), headed by Charlie Green. Bill's other consulting junket was more delicate. Sent to Duritron Division, Bill was there ostensibly to learn about their high-voltage interconnection system as part of a corporate study on the power supply market. Bill's actual assignment was to take a close look at the management of the division. Duritron had been created as the result of a successful breakthrough in making a mica substitute for use in radar. The product was so unusual for ABC that it couldn't be marketed through regular channels, so corporate marketing took on the direction of the product and eventually even the Duritron Division manager reported to the corporate VP of marketing rather than to operations, as in the other divisions.

Bill discovered a management feud between David Frank, the division manager, and Morris Fenner, Duritron's marketing and sales director, centering on decisions about the high-voltage connector. Frank was adamant that in order to protect ABC's patent the connector had to be sold only as part of a larger product, such as

the radar modulators or post connectors made by Duritron. Fenner could see that the product had wider applications as a component and would sell well as a separate item. He felt that the patent was strong enough to protect ABC's interests, no matter how the product was marketed. Fenner, as a marketing man, had the ear of Al Stethem, VP of corporate marketing, the very person to whom Frank was reporting. People at Duritron, located in Cedarville, New York, were frustrated at the conflict, and they were happy to talk to someone like Bill from Utica, to whom they could express their feelings.

Bill returned to Utica with three recommendations: (1) Reorganize reporting so that Duritron's division manager no longer reported through marketing, but through operations, as in other divisions; (2) split up Frank and Fenner, and take a hard look at Frank's long-term management potential; and (3) get someone assigned to Duritron who would be able to redirect the division's product strategy. Bill's recommendations sparked a management shakeup. Ted Rigby, under Dave MacNeil in Interface Products, was brought in as division manager, and Frank was assigned to be his assistant (Frank took rather a long time to catch the hint before he resigned and left ABC.) Fenner was transferred into industrial sales. The high-voltage connector was eventually put on the component market where it was a big commercial success.

From what Bill knew, something

like Frank's demotion was quite an unusual event at ABC. Bill realized that his situation as a newcomer had made it easier for him to recommend changes, and corporate had been able to use his recommendations as an excuse to do what they didn't want to, but knew they probably had to do.

In June of 1964 Charlie Green, head of Datacom Division, asked Bill to come to work for him as new product planning manager. Corporate research had been a good testing, networking, and placement vehicle for Bill, but he and Walt Hedstrom agreed that he should make the move.

New Products in a New Place

Jack Packman had worked with Bill at XYZ Corporation and had kidded Bill a lot about being in a staff position rather than in line at ABC. Jack evidently felt surprised and threatened when Bill came on at Datacom as a manager, in a position only a small step below Packman's own level. Bill got a call from Charlie Green about a month after he had moved in at Datacom. Charlie said that Jack Packman had evidently been doing some after-hours engineering: He had consulted the company standards for office size and furnishing for various managerial levels and had found that the office constructed for Bill was 6 inches over standard. Packman had then lodged a complaint with Charlie, implying that *he* should get the office, since he was in a slightly higher position than Bill. Charlie apologized to Bill, but

said that in order to avoid everyone else griping about office size, he though he'd better move Bill. Charlie's twist was, however, to have Bill switch offices with an engineering manager of the same rank as Packman who had been housed in an undersized office. Bill said he didn't care what size office he had and would be happy to make the switch.

Bill had some new product ideas, among them a selective signaling system applied to radio telephones used in shipping and transportation. The largest users of marine signaling systems were in California, so Bill went there to explore the market possibilities, which he decided were very promising. Back in Utica, he soon persuaded Charlie Green to let him set up a group of engineers, a production facility, and begin hiring a work force of 30 people to service an anticipated $1.5 million contract.

Bill was pleased to have a position in line management. As a staff person, he had felt that he could only give advice, but now he had to sell his ideas, and himself, in order to accomplish what he wanted. During 1964, 1965, and 1966, Bill had to deal personally with not only division and corporate management, but in connection with the patents on the selective signaling device, he had to spend considerable time with the U.S. Patent Office and the FCC in Washington. The FCC's OK was not easy to get, but Bill patiently and persistently worked with them until they approved. It took two years to work through issues of public utility commissions and experimental tariffs and to demonstrate the workability and marketability of the device. Later, Bill would recall that it was at this stage of his career that he began to move away from an "introverted engineer personality" to one that would motivate people.

Trouble with the Contract

As the time drew near to sign the contract on the selective signaling system, the customer, a radio telephone common carrier, kept after Bill for little concessions here and there. The new plant had produced 2,000 units by January 1967, when Bill went to California with what he felt would be the final version of the contract. Right there, in the office of his client who was about to put his pen to the contract, Bill got a call from Charlie Green. Charlie said that ABC's president and the board had decided to cancel the business and get out of signaling systems altogether.

On returning to Utica, Bill made an appointment to see Dick Carson, then corporate vice president of operations. They talked for an hour or so about the cancellation of Bill's product and Carson was conciliatory: "I know it's hard for you to understand, but we feel that in the current downturn in the economy, we can't risk it. To make your product for this $1.5 million contract we'd have to build an addition onto the plant—something we can't afford just now. Furthermore, we're not a systems company, but a component company— we have to keep track of what we are. Your efforts on selective sig-

naling have been outstanding, but we just can't go forward with a program like that now, one that is outside the mainstream of ABC's business."

During the following week, Bill made what he later regarded as the dutiful mistake of sitting with his personnel representative as 38 people who had been hired on to develop and produce his product were terminated. "When I got through with that, together with two-and-a-half years of work on a cancelled product, I wasn't worth much." Bill began to wonder whether management was really for him and whether ABC was his kind of place. He got his resume ready.

ABC had reorganized its management structure in 1965, instituting a new level of group management between the divisions and corporate. Dave MacNeil, former division manager for connector products and one of Bill's early contacts through corporate research, had been made group vice president over four divisions, including Datacom. In the spring of 1967, a couple of months after the contract cancellation, Dave MacNeil asked Bill to drop by his office for coffee. He mentioned that he had heard rumors to the effect that Bill was looking to leave. "I'd probably be ready to resign, too, if I were you, but there are some important reasons why you should stay." Chief among those that he mentioned was the need he saw at ABC for someone like Bill who had a long-range, analytical perspective on the business and a proven ability to be creative. MacNeil was very complimentary concerning other aspects of Bill's work for the company, and when he suggested that Bill talk to the other division managers in the group about a possible place for himself, Bill took the names and made the appointments. Two of them had no idea what to do with Bill—it was clear that they were doing the interviews because MacNeil had asked them to. But Ted Rigby, the new Duritron Division manager (the one who replaced Frank, the manager who had been demoted and resigned), had some notion of who and what Bill was.

Rigby was interested in what Bill might be able to do in the development of new products for Duritron Division and presented Bill with the challenge. "I'll make you new products manager, and you can build what you need to do the job. You've got two years to make it work." Ted Rigby had been more than frank. He was desperate to get someone into the division to work on new products. He thought Bill could do it.

Bill already knew about Duritron. He had been instrumental in getting his friend Bill Cooper, a marketing associate from Bill's first months with corporate research, appointed there as division marketing manager. The operations versus marketing feud that had crippled the division under Frank and Fenner was a thing of the past. However, Duritron had a reputation as a substandard part of the company. Located south of Utica in Cedarville, its 90 people were housed in one big building, with production on the ground floor, engineering and management on the second, and a vacant third floor, waiting for some reason to be renovated and used. The offices at Duritron were significantly smaller than company standards; the engineers' desks were arranged side to side and end to end; people shared phones and the intercom paging system which, according to evident custom, was used less than the stand-up-at-your-desk-and-yell-across-the-big-room-to-the-guy-you-want method. Billings for the division were $3 to $4 million per year, and there was no profit.

It seemed to Bill that his career was headed downhill, that if he went to this backwater of the company after the disaster at Datacom, he might be cutting his throat for good. Bill thought it might be better to cut his losses instead and leave ABC.

Bill's wife was not so hasty. She had settled in and had been surprised with how happy she was back in her home town. She asked some hard questions over the following couple of weeks: "Would you leave ABC just for pride? Haven't the people at corporate been telling you you're doing well? Do you fundamentally disagree with the decision to cancel selective signaling?" To the latter Bill had to answer that he did understand why the decision was made, in the context of the economy at the time, and would probably have made the same decision himself. "Then what's wrong?" she asked. "I'm going off to a second-rate division to lose visibility—my career could be in bad shape," Bill replied. His wife responded with a challenge: "Why don't you just go down and show them you can do the job?"

Duritron in Cedarville

Bill moved into his office in the middle of the second floor of the Duritron building in mid-June of 1967. His office had been converted from an existing restroom, and one wheel of his chair kept getting stuck in the depression where the drain was still located. The drain had another feature—it conducted the sound of break-time gossip from the workers' women's room on the first floor.

Bill Hudson, the man who had evidently been responsible for the recent management shake-up in the division, was now to be its savior. People were skeptical and stand-offish regarding this new guy. The saying at Duritron was that corporate people were like seagulls: "They swoop in, eat all your food, and then shit on you when they fly away." Bill was from corporate; was he another one of those who would leave a cursory recommendation and go back thinking he was an instant hero?

The workers and lower-level management at Duritron were not proponents of fast change. They enjoyed what ABC tried to maintain as a family kind of atmosphere in the plant, with picnics, bus trips, birthday parties at work, lunching on homemade food, and a peaceful atmosphere. Such efforts by management were rewarded by a total lack of interest on the part of the workers in organizing or joining a union. The workers provided loyalty, hard work, honesty, and a tough skin for the outsider/newcomer to crack.

A few of the engineers who thought they understood what Bill was up to came to him with ideas for custom-built products, but his concept was one of developing not specialty, limited-market items, but products that could provide long-term benefits for the company and the division. He felt that he had to almost preach to them; certainly he had to sell. The drafting and modeling department would give him no support. "Do you have a customer for this thing? We have to give priority to work for which a customer is waiting." The marketing people, except for Bill Cooper, were not particularly helpful either—they thought Bill Hudson should be the one to answer the question of the possible demand for his product ideas. Cooper hadn't been there long enough to flex his muscles and make them do what Hudson wanted. They didn't really trust an engineer to represent the company to the customers, so while they were not willing to do it for him, they were afraid of Bill Hudson doing his own direct market research. Their solution to this dilemma was to try to forget about Bill.

Ted Rigby's continual comment was "do it on the cheap." Bill's office was a case in point. Bill protested that such a noisy location was hardly conducive to the peace and quiet he felt was necessary to foster creativity in product development. Ted just said it was the best he could afford. For an initial staff, Ted spared Bill three "brilliant" engineers, all of whom had spent several years with Duritron. It soon became apparent to Bill that two of the three were virtually useless. Ted had evidently based his opinion about them on the fact that they didn't do too well on released products and must therefore be of the unorthodox, creative type. Bill felt that Ted knew deep down that these were not good people, but wanted someone else to have to fire them. Bill obliged, though he took several months to make sure he was right.

On the basis of his own field marketing research, Bill developed three product ideas he thought might work well for Duritron. The first was a solid state relay device for radar applications. The second was a solid state magnetic radar modulator, and the third was a laminar power distribution system. In January of 1968, Bill talked Ted into letting him hire a new engineer and a designer for his projects. He then argued with Ted for several months about the noisy atmosphere in the middle of the second floor and finally got permission in June of 1968 to take his shop to an available space in the business section of Cedarville. Bill soon had a "corporate standard size" set of offices established in a former drug store, and he subleased the front window space to local merchants. Bill began "green carding" in surplus equipment from both division and corporate to furnish a model shop on the second floor of the old store—*green carding* meant that the equipment came from existing surplus corporate supplies and didn't cost Ted a dime on his expense sheet.

In that first year, Bill learned a great deal about the division and its people. ABC had a good reputation in the area and attracted loyal workers. By contrast with other local plants, ABC's Duritron facility was air conditioned and clean. The company paid UAW scale wages on an hourly (rather than piece rate) basis and was known to be less anxious than others to lay people off in a business cycle downturn. Corporate policy had created employee participation circles aimed not only at product quality but at job enrichment, cleanliness in the workplace, productivity, and fair compensation. As part of ABC corporate policy, Duritron gave awards only to teams and whole production units. The reasoning was that individuals have to have support from a good team to accomplish anything really good. Bonuses were based on a sliding scale related to annual earnings per share, with managers being rewarded not strictly for financial performance but on the overall performance and growth of the division. Suggestions, cost improvements, and patents were rewarded with appreciation, but no bonus payments. Bill saw these policies as promoting teamwork, practical rather than showy innovations, and the abilities of quiet, hard-working people who might have even more to offer than what he called the "extroverted, salesman types." Bill gently inserted himself into certain areas of the division where he needed help. His designer worked on others' projects in return for modeling shop help. He took some of the marketing people out to lunch and stayed in close contact with his old friend, Bill Cooper.

Bill Hudson and Ted Rigby developed a relationship in which confrontation was frequent but not destructive. Ted was a hard man to convince. The solid state relay device and the magnetic radar modulator never got very far because of Ted's conservative views on their financial futures and his unwillingness to pay for enough development engineering to get them working well. The first product died after only a year, the second took two more years to get axed. Bill felt that at least the laminar power distribution system should have made it, but Ted's "do it on the cheap" philosophy made it impossible to get enough development money to take the product to the point where it would meet minimal financial goals in production. At the end of three years, Bill had no new products. He did have, however, a lot of experience in the division. He had a small but congenial and hardworking staff, having added a technician and two engineers to his team after letting the "brilliant" ones go. He also had Ted's general support, such as it was, even though Ted's two-year deadline had passed. And in July of 1970, Bill had an idea to market a new product developed at corporate research.

The Ceramic Filter

The new product was an integrated filter circuit built into a ceramic frame. The idea was that signals could be sent through the filter to purify them of random impurities they picked up in transmission. The "three Bills"—Hudson, Cooper, and Naylor (the flip-flop man still at corporate research who had actually perfected this new integrated filter circuit) teamed together to spend two months testing demand for the product with defense and aerospace contractors. Bill Hudson had asked Ted for permission to experiment with the new product and had been turned down. This time Bill decided that he would ignore Ted's refusal of permission and instead confront him with accomplishments. That way he could work around Ted's Catch-22 of having to prove the workability of an idea which couldn't be tested without resources, resources that could only be devoted to the project if it had been proven workable.

Bill set what he regarded as a good example for his staff by using more than his share of what the division was paying for in corporate research. The first item corporate helped him on was a tunnel kiln for firing the ceramic casing for the filter. The kiln already available at Duritron yielded an uneven glaze, which then failed in tests because of spot weaknesses created in the firing. A tunnel kiln would even out the heat in the firing chamber, but was a $30,000 investment. Bill got a friend at corporate research to talk to the head of his department about getting one for *their* shop. When it was approved, Bill Naylor ran the production testing at corporate. A month later, he arranged to have the equipment transferred to Bill Hudson's shop in Cedarville and to transfer the charge to Ted Rigby's division. By the time Ted noticed the equipment charge and called Bill in to be bellowed at, Bill was able to produce productivity gains and statistical test results to justify the expenditure. Ted still couldn't resist a lecture on doing experiments which he had prohibited. Bill, sure of his success in developing a good product this time, replied that he'd rather ignore instructions than do something to hurt the company. "You either have to let us run the show you've given us or not—you have to either trust us or not trust us."

Another item Bill needed was an estimated $50,000 combination of machines to measure insertion loss, the degree of signal strength that would be lost in running a signal through the filter. Bill knew of no one machine to do the job, but he had a concept of how one should be built, and he knew how to get the components to assemble one. Bill talked Ted into going with him to see Dave MacNeil, the group vice president. MacNeil listened carefully to Bill's arguments on why it couldn't be done on the cheap this time and then offered his support. It came in the form of

MacNeil himself lobbying the corporate executive committee (MacNeil was a member) and his group controller spending many hours with Bill making sure that the capital equipment request (CER) was persuasive and clear enough so that corporate would approve it. Those to be convinced included not only the corporate controller's office and the executive committee, but also the corporate test lab— they didn't think that one of the divisions should have a piece of testing equipment better than what they themselves had. The others were wary of big expenditures for equipment that didn't produce anything. As Bill later recalled: "It was one thing to order another stamping press or bolting machine—they were things people knew about. But an insertion-loss measurement device for $50,000 made them uneasy: 'Is this a playtoy for engineers?' We really had to sell it, and I couldn't have done it without MacNeil, Naylor, and the others." The test lab never did agree, but they were overpowered by the opposition. Bill's new machine could measure things that no one else in the industry could measure. "I could play specsmanship against the competition because I could test for and finally produce a less noisy piece of gear."

Bill began to gather a staff for producing the filters and to set up a production facility on the vacant third floor of division headquarters. Within six weeks, there was a production line set up and running for the new product. Ted challenged Bill to find a commercial market for the ceramic filter—something to augment the defense and aerospace industry sales. Bill found an application for his filter in a machine made by Teletype Corporation in Chicago; he showed them how ABC's $1.33 filter could economically replace a 15-cent condenser that kept blowing out. His solution was so convincing that Teletype ended up designing seven other ABC products into their machines (this process of "designing in" the company's products once a relationship had been established had historically worked well for ABC with other customers, too).

During the first year of production, Duritron sold $10,000 worth of ceramic filters, during the second, it was $375,000 and in the third year, $700,000. The third floor of the facility, fallow for 15 years, was opened up to produce the filter, and Duritron had a new product. Fifty people were eventually employed on the third floor, though Bill's demand for excellence brought several new faces among them to replace those who couldn't perform up to his standards.

Assimilation

Bill recalled that during his first year with Duritron, people at Cedarville smiled at him, and the second year they were willing to have a conversation with him. Now, with the development of an actual new product, they were more willing to really communicate with him. Bill himself helped promote workers' cooperation with him in the way he approached his job. He was not afraid to get out on the production floor and see things for himself.

One Saturday morning, Bill went in to see if he could help speed up part of the production process for the filter, a process using a new heated mold. The workers were still in the stage of getting used to doing a new operation and were having trouble figuring out how it could best be done. Bill got on the line for a couple of hours and succeeded in methodizing the various motions necessary in the manufacturing and assembly process involved. The woman next to whom he was working started crying in frustration at how fast Bill was and how slow she was herself. ("I have very dextrous hands," Bill recalled.) Bill was quick to say that he wasn't trying to show anyone up or make it hard on anyone—just helping them all get the hang of a new process. "Just keep at it, it will come to you," he said. The woman was put in charge of her line two months later, having mastered the process thoroughly.

> The fact that I was in there working beside them treating them as regular people yielded more dividends than I imagined. I had just been there to try to get the rate up so that we could meet the demand of a customer.

Bill learned of a personal concern the Duritron workers had for the company when he observed one of the manufacturing managers on the first floor order an increase in the rate of operation on a die-casting machine. The machine operators were running it at 650 strokes/minute, hoping to avoid "crashing the die"—the shattering of both the plunger and the mold in a $40–$50 thousand engineering investment. Over the operator's protests, the managers ordered a speed of 1,000, noting that the machine was designed for as much as 1,200. It wasn't long before the die crashed, causing very costly delays and repairs. "Our ABC Yankees had good instincts—management just had to pay attention to them. Just by themselves, the operators would have gradually cranked the machine up, but they'd have known when to quit cranking."

Ted's Tirade

Ted Rigby was not an engineer, but he was a very conscientious manager. Bill regarded him as a bit of a workaholic, for he knew that Ted went in to the office every Sunday and read all the memos generated in the division that week. He noticed that on Mondays Ted would swoop down on people with suggestions and orders based on his Sunday review. One day he swooped down on Bill, demanding that the "too time-consuming" trinary binder process, which bonded the circuitry to the ceramic base of the filter, be cut from 28 to 15 days. Bill said it couldn't be done, period, and made an appointment to go to the plant the next Sunday to show Ted why. After the demonstration, Ted stood up on his own office chair and gave an angry speech about at least making an attempt to follow instructions ("You guys aren't listening to me!"), hurling his glasses to the floor as a final flourish. Bill laughed, applauded, and said: "Ted, you oughta patent that act." Bill recalled that it was a turning point in their relationship. "Ted began laughing, too, and we've been friends ever since."

It was after that incident that Ted began asking Bill questions that made it possible for Bill to teach him a few things about delegation and team building. Bill's philosophy was that the personnel selection process was the critical stage. "You have to get good people, then let them know that you expect more than they think they're capable of, support them to the hilt, and let them do it themselves." Bill's criteria for good people were straightforward: "I look for people who aren't afraid to be themselves and who will tell me if they think I'm wrong. I like to find people with self-confidence and above-average intelligence, who are endowed with enough humility to empathize with people who have problems. I like people who have had a wide range of experience, who have patience, maturity, and don't lose their tempers. I'll take the quiet, creative, humble person over the flashy fellow with a gift of gab."

Getting good people had become much easier for Ted as the new products coming out of Bill's department had made Duritron a more attractive organization. In 1973, Ted Rigby arranged for Bill to get a share of the managers' stock option plan. Ted also mentioned that Bill was on the list for promotion to division manager and that ABC appreciated what Bill was doing. Bill appreciated the pat on the back and felt that he had been more than equal to the challenge that his wife had given him. He was ready for something new.

Learning and Teaching

By late 1975, after 8½ years at Duritron, Bill had learned a great deal about the company and what made it tick. (ABC had grown from $100 million in annual revenues in 1963, when Bill had joined the firm, to $300 million in 1975. It had become the industry leader and was highly profitable.) Bill learned that ABC had become a respected firm because it was perceived as being good at understanding the needs of customers and at innovating new products in the field. ABC's products were seen to save customers money, not because they were cheap, but because they were well designed and of reliable quality. ABC also provided application support: If a customer needed a part but didn't know how to go about attaching it to the rest of what the customer was making, ABC sent in application engineers and designed machines to make the attachments (which they also produced and sold to the customer). ABC salespeople called on customers, and talked with them about product ideas and future needs. ABC field engineers serviced the application machines, and ABC managers made it a practice to get to know their customers well. ABC could also make the quick fix: Kodak had a terminal-

splicing problem with a photo filter made in the Duritron Division at Cedarville. They had to have an *immediate* solution, so Ted flew a field engineer to Rochester. The engineer discovered that it was a design problem that had arisen because of miscommunication between the design and production engineers. The machine was redesigned and set back on the line right on the spot.

Bill realized how much he had changed one day when he overheard a group of engineers grousing about the incredible "rape" of the customers presumably taking place with a 1,000 percent markup on one ABC product. Bill had heard it all before, not only from engineers but from field salespeople and representatives as well. On the spur of the moment, he called the group into a conference room and gave them a two-hour "basic course in financial management." Bill was tired of hearing about profit as an evil thing: He walked them through the various costs of capital, manufacturing expenses, and investors' return on equity. It all added up, as he knew it would, to a need for a 10x markup on the product to give investors a 9 percent return. The group was receptive; they even seemed to have a good time.

A Lateral Move

Late in 1975, Ted got the word from Dave MacNeil, group vice president, that Bill was to interview with Tom O'Brien, division manager, for the position of development manager at Alpha Communications division (Alphacom). Bill did the interview with some reservations—O'Brien had a reputation for what Bill called the "reward" mentality. From what Bill could gather, O'Brien saw his recent promotion to division manager as a reward for faithful service. He was rumored to be more a custodian than an action man, and some of his staff thought O'Brien was evolving into a bureaucratic nit picker. After the interview, Bill asked for an appointment with Dave MacNeil, for he felt that he should get something better than a lateral move after 8½ years in the outback.

MacNeil acknowledged that he had kept Bill at Duritron for about four years too long, but that the filter program was such a complex technical and manufacturing process that he needed Bill there until one of the younger people had learned enough to take over. McNeil dealt with the advisability of a lateral move by saying that Bill had been away from the headquarters at Utica too long and wasn't known well there anymore. (Bill reflected on the irony that he had spent four years up there before spending eight years commuting south to Cedarville to get some experience outside of Utica.) "Take a couple of years to get your connections at headquarters firmly reestablished," MacNeil advised. Bill decide to give it his best.

Rumors around town brought Bill an offer to leave ABC and go to work for ITT, but Bill was convinced that his career with ABC would now begin a takeoff. Besides, Bill didn't fancy himself as the type who would quit and go over to the competition. He settled into a new office in Utica, ready for the fresh challenge.

Advanced Development Manager

As advanced development manager in Alphacom, Bill inherited a department of four designers, three project managers, and four engineers. Bill talked to one of the basic product managers (BPMs) he met the first week, who told him that the people on the road—salespeople, BPMs, applications engineers—were coming up with a lot more new stuff than the development department ever had. Bill learned through the grapevine that the man he replaced had been so concerned about divulging trade secrets that many good product ideas and proposals were still sitting in the closet, now obsolete.

ABC's divisions were organized like small companies, with a full complement of functions: operations, marketing, finance and accounting, and development. A unique feature at ABC was the position of basic product manager. A BPM was responsible for seeing specific products through the final development, production, and application stages. BPMs had the power to set prices, sign contracts, and commit the divisions to delivery deadlines, and they had freedom to travel. They had no subordinates—no one reported to a BPM but his/her secretary. They had to be a miniversion of the division manager, and they spent a good deal of time on the road talking to customers about product possibilities and needs. Alphacom had three BPMs, and Bill made it a point to start getting to know them, even to the extent that he spent whole days on the road with them, visiting customers and talking about new products.

A few months after Bill joined Alphacom, Tom O'Brien was transferred, and Bill's old friend from corporate research, Maurice Mendel, was appointed division manager. Bill was pleased with the change, for he had great confidence in Maury and in their ability to work together. At the same time, group vice president Dave MacNeil was promoted to corporate vice president of operations, and Dick Carson moved up to president.

Bill's efforts to get the BPMs and others involved in helping him develop new products and markets for new products were aided by a new emphasis from Maury Mendel. As division manager, Maury instituted the first strategic planning process ever undertaken at Alphacom. Bill and many of his contacts participated in the planning. They gradually became as aware of their interdependence as Bill already was. Bill's encouragement for them to "while you're traveling, present mine too," began to make sense to them. Bill recalled that the people from the division all got so well acquainted with the products of departments other than their own that "on trips, instead of sending three or four people, we could send one out, and he

or she could present for everybody—we could get a lot more exposure around the country that way." Their teamwork in the planning program generated mutual confidence, to the point that people made decisions in the field that would have major implications for other managers in the division, all based on trusting each other and knowing what could be expected.

A New Opportunity

Early one Sunday in July of 1977, a year and a half into his current assignment, a senior manager in corporate operations called Bill at his place on Pennsylvania lake. "Jim McGuire (VP of the general products group) will be calling you today, to offer you the Radio Communications Products Division (Radcom). I wouldn't call like this, but two others have turned it down recently, and we want to make sure that doesn't happen again. We're not going to beg people to be division managers. We were going to save you for something a little more exciting, but the timing is right for us all now. Jack Butcher, previously the division manager of Radcom, has taken over Wiring Products because Mel Manning had to resign. Butcher has done a good financial job with Radcom— we think you can do them some good in other areas." Bill expressed his thanks and said he'd be waiting for McGuire's call.

Bill caught himself reviewing all the negative things he'd heard about Radcom. Started as a throwoff from the General Products Division, Radcom had begun its corporate childhood in 1959. Marketing managers had received preference over engineers for the post of division manager throughout the history of the division until Jack Butcher, a very astute operations man with an excellent knowledge of finance, had taken over in 1974. Before that, the division had been run as a marketing and sales support organization, neglecting operations and product development. Bill perceived that one of the division's problems was too much inbreeding. He felt that this had led to too few new ideas and too little shaking up for real growth to take place. Group and corporate were perhaps waking up to the inbreeding problem in the face of two people turning down what should have been a great promotion. The division had been doing very well financially in recent years because of the connectors they made for CB radios, a hot item. Bill and everyone else knew, however, that the CB craze was almost over. The two people who had turned down the division manager post must have been thinking about how hard it was going to be to come up with a new set of products to keep the division profitable.

Bill saw the job of division manager not as a reward, but as a challenge. He had seen many contemporaries move into higher positions where they were able to administer departments and divisions based on what they had already learned and experienced. Bill felt, however, that administration was not management, a word he reserved for putting one's stamp on an organization, for changing the way people thought about and did things. In his 14 years with ABC, Bill's confidence had grown as he met new challenges and became better acquainted with the organization and where he fit in it.

When group vice president Jim McGuire called later in the day, he introduced himself and got right to the point. "We need a new division manager at Radcom, and corporate has told us that you're the man. I've never worked with you, but you come with good credentials and high recommendations. I hope you'll consider the position seriously." Bill thanked McGuire for the offer, and the very next day, on Monday, he called McGuire and said he would take the job.

Division Manager

When Bill got a good look at the Radcom Division books, he saw that there was little time to spare. July orders for CB connectors had dropped drastically from the month before. By August, there were widespread cancellations on orders already received, plus a further drop in new orders over previous months. As he toured the various facilities and talked to the management team in place, Bill sensed that the people were at least competent and that his manufacturing manager, his basic product managers, his accounting manager, and the quality control people were all excellent. He asked each one of them to show him their business plans, and each one in turn indicated that there was no business plan. Bill gathered that the division had thoroughly milked old products by turning inward to hone manufacturing processes and cut costs. New products came by chance and were similarly exploited. Radcom was providing a very solid profit, and its profit was underwriting expansion of other divisions in the group. That could not last much longer, Bill felt, unless planning and product development got under way or, by remote chance, a new product just fell into the division's lap.

During his first month on the job, two of Bill's managers came to him and said that they just wanted him to know that they would support him, even though they thought they were qualified for his job and had been disappointed in not getting the offer themselves. Bill didn't argue but tried to get as much information from them as they were willing to give him about their perceptions of the division.

Bill soon had a strategy in mind for revitalizing his division. He rescheduled the division staff and management meetings to be held on a monthly rather than a quarterly basis. At the first meeting, he set his people a challenge: to come up with a well-conceived business plan. "What's our charter? What business are we in? (Bill remembered selective signalling for radio telephones once again, wryly). What's the total market? How much is our share? What are the sectors? Who are our competitors? Which sectors can we compete in best?"—these were the questions that Bill asked them. And he as-

signed them to bring forth a strategy for building market share and to then develop an itemized, step-by-step plan for executing the strategy. Staff members protested that they would have a difficult time getting accurate information and would be afraid to make decisions based on that kind of uncertainty. Bill's response was that it was more important to put things down on paper so that other people with other ideas and perspectives could critique them and help shape the plan than it was to be right the first time. He also told them he thought they might find new interest in the trade journals that were lying around on everyone's desks, mostly unread.

While the business plan was being developed, Bill addressed himself to some basic organizational problems he had found. The product development department had two managers and two engineers—there were "four chiefs and no Indians." They all seemed busy doing their own thing and patting each other on the back. Bill found that the entire product engineering department had only one drafter—that meant that the engineers were doing all their own drafting. Bill noticed that the engineers were constantly consulting the books of master drawings on the shelf at the end of the large, divided room where they all worked, ignoring the microfiche readers stationed around the department. Many hours were spent in waiting for the books to be used and passed on by other engineers ("those fiche are so hard to read"). There were no product designers in the division at all. Bill asked about the lack of such personnel, and his people told him that Group had consistently turned them down on personnel requests, saying that the division was providing a crucial gross margin, the loss of which could be very detrimental (i.e., "you guys keep costs down, keep putting out products, and let the other divisions do the growing"). Bill knew that he would have to do some arm twisting at Group to get what he needed, so he waited for the business plan to take shape—it would serve as documentation for his demands. In the meantime, he moved all the master drawing books to a lower level of the building. Bill also procured microfiche readers for *all* the engineers. At first, many of them kept walking downstairs to consult the drawings, but one by one they relented and dialed the drawings up on microfiche at their own desks.

Within six weeks, Bill got a completed business plan from his department and accounting managers. The plan indicated that in the next year, revenues in the division could increase 60 percent if the recommendations in the plan were implemented. Bill made two comments on the plan: "You'd better reflect a little more carefully on what your competition is likely to do in response to your strategy. Furthermore, you have to be more realistic about the need for people to support the engineering—you'll need more people than you have now to pull this off, so you should request more." The team saw that Bill was right about the competi-

tion, but they didn't know what to do about the additional people. They insisted that every time they had asked for additional manpower from Group, they had been turned down. Bill said that he would try to take care of that, and he thought to himself that their previous lack of success on support had probably been a result not only of Group's tight fistedness, but also of them not really knowing what they wanted—something which had undoubtedy led to weak presentations and weak results.

Bill added a few of his own ideas and took the plan to Jim McGuire, the Group VP. He asked McGuire for 5 percent of the division's gross margin to invest in the new strategy. Bill noted that the division had only about 5–6 percent of the market and could do better—specifically, the division could start producing soldered and crimp connectors for the markets they could develop, not avoid them as another division's territory. McGuire protested mildly that the gross margin from Radcom was keeping Group in the black while other new products were being developed. Bill insisted that Group had relied on Radcom long enough and that unless some of the division's profits were plowed back in, there would be no more gross margin to feed on. McGuire was persuaded to go along by the figures on CB connectors and the detail of the business plan. He also gave approval for Bill to go to Dave MacNeil, who was now senior vice president of operations, to ask for the rights within ABC to develop fiber optics. Another division was working on it, but Bill sensed that the division to be hurt most by innovation in this area would be Radcom and argued that Radcom should therefore be allowed to replace itself over the long run. He also argued that ABC could no longer afford two or three divisions in competition to market the same product—something that had been a hallmark of ABC's strategy up to that time. He would get exclusive corporate support or he would not pursue fiber optics, Bill argued.

After Bill went to see MacNeil, he had his 5 percent, the full support of Jim McGuire, and a refined business plan. MacNeil read the plan and was impressed: "That's the first time I've ever seen it laid out that clearly. You are, as you say, in the business of making connectors that handle high-complexity signals—that means fiber optics is in your part of the ball park. I'll talk it over and let you know." Bill got fiber optics.

New Name and New Blood

With the money to hire support staff and a new product line assured, Bill wrote a position paper to Group and corporate in which he proposed that the name of the division be changed. He reasoned that the old name implied that the division made only radio connectors, when they actually produced digital, analog, and now optical connector products. The "Radio Communications" aspect of the current name was also misleading, since radio signals were not the only kind carried by Radcom prod-

ucts. Bill felt that the division and its products had a not-entirely-undeserved "F Troop" image, something new products and a new name could help change. He provided six alternative names in his paper, and soon he had approval for a name change to Signal Components Division (Sigcom). Bill sensed that taking an important product away from another division and expanding the conception of what the division was about—symbolized in the name change—had breathed new life into his staff, a staff which had, for the most part, never won any battle with Group or corporate, much less the rights to a new product.

Bill was able to start recruiting new people for Sigcom. He found some he had not known before, and some old faces, all from within ABC. Fred Baker, from Interface Products Division, was brought in as product engineering manager. Baker's mandate was to inject some hierarchy into the department so that the engineers had time to do their own work. "You know already how a large department has to be organized; please structure this one accordingly." Baker did very well in the reorganization, as expected. "I always made sure I brought the best possible people in from outside the division so that when someone came in, the standard of the job moved up," Bill later recalled.

Bill put in place a detailed human resource development program to keep track of the progress of the people in his division. He also tried to encourage a feeling of teamwork in his division. He enjoyed walking around himself and rolling up his sleeves with a group of engineers and designers on an informal basis—in this way, he got to know his people.

Bill's deepening understanding of his people led him to the identification of three who were known to their associates as "the gripers." These men, all assigned as product engineers with desks close together on the same floor as Bill's office, usually ate lunch together, and their conversations evidently centered on the airing of their gripes against ABC. Bill examined their records. He found that Mark O'Toole, a former Navy chief petty officer, had only a couple of years to retirement. Bill was content to take the ribbing he always got from O'Toole for being a former naval officer and at the same time to keep some pressure on to make sure O'Toole was pulling his weight.

Rick Levier, a senior product engineer, had a very strong record early on as an innovator. Though he had no engineering degree, Levier was clearly a leader in his department. Bill made it a point to get to know him when he noticed all the engineers in the department beat a path to Rick's office whenever they had a problem. Finally, Bill sat down with Rick and asked him what was wrong. It came out that Rick had developed several new designs and refinements which the former division manager had taken credit for. "He got all the photos and smiles for work that

I did. I didn't want a banquet, just an acknowledgment would have been fine," Rick said. Bill sensed that the third griper, Jim Powell, was an ambitious young man who had been bottled up—someone who needed to be trusted with a supervisory role. Bill decided to use both of the younger gripers in his reorganization of the product development department, where he put them in as supervisors of new products.

The next move in reorganizing new products was to get the needed staff for a program in transmission cable connectors, something Bill had worked on at Duritron and which he had been successful in getting transferred to his new division. Part of the deal for the transfer was for the Duritron Division manager to give Bill three people who were working on the project already, people the Duriton manager regarded as "dead wood." Bill had hired one of the people when he was in Cedarville, a quiet young product designer. He knew that Duritron didn't know what they had in the designer. All three turned out to be golden. After a few weeks, Rick Levier mentioned how pleased he was with the designer. "My God, what have we been doing without these people before?" Bill took the gripers and the rejects and built a new product development department. They were soon keeping Bill busy reviewing their suggestions.

About that time, the two who had coveted Bill's job both came around and apologized. "If I had realized what the job took, I'm pretty sure I'd have known better than to think I was ready," said one. Bill's response was modest and encouraging, and he took the opportunity to reemphasize his idea that a manager should expand the definition of his own job and create a new and better organization to work with. "Managers make changes, while administrators are just caretakers," Bill noted—with tact.

In 1978, his first full year at Radcom/Sigcom, Bill's team put forth a much bolder business plan—their numbers were put down with much more informed confidence, and the competitive analysis was much deeper. The competition had ABC in a cozy niche as a military supplier of known character. Rick Levier and others in product development redesigned some of the division's sophisticated connectors that were being used in military applications. The price on one dropped from $1.22 to 92 cents for what would be a domestic/commercial product, resulting in a big contract from IBM. When the competition tried to impugn the product's quality and reliability, Sigcom had documented test results to show its customers. The business got so good that a new plant had to be built to accommodate the demand for the product. It was a plant designed to fit the division's new image of itself—one in which the entire operation was streamlined and structured for high efficiency and productivity. The division's gross margin, which

had been respectable already, improved by 27 percent that year.

John Laudie

Jim McGuire, group vice president, called Bill in the fall of that year (1978) and asked him for a favor. Tom Clark, in the Public Power Division, had an engineer, John Laudie, who had been with the company for 23 years and who was not pulling his weight. Tom felt that the company had not been totally fair with Laudie, that he could have had more support and better direction, and had given him a "very good" rating in the annual review. McGuire thought Laudie should either improve or be fired, but Tom felt that if McGuire wanted to fire Laudie, it was up to him to do it, and it was up to McGuire to transfer him too, if that was to be the approach. McGuire told Bill that no other division manager in the group could give the guy as fair a chance as Bill could—he was sending Laudie to Bill for a last chance. Bill was not thrilled, but he agreed. ("What can a green division manager say to his superior?") When Bill got John Laudie's personnel record, he noted again the "very good" rating. Bill went to Tom and asked him what that meant, since the memo from McGuire had said the personnel record had the guy overrated "Well, I didn't want the change in his rating to take place in my division," said Tom—someone Bill described as a "very humanistic guy." "Dang, Tom, that puts me in an awkward spot," was Bill's reply.

In Bill's division, John Laudie was assigned as a product engineer, a definite demotion from his former position. Laudie immediately complained, said the job was beneath him, and indicated that on the basis of a "very good" rating, he should have something better. Bill's response was to indicate that if Laudie proved himself, he would get a promotion.

Bill had recently begun a program to formalize performance standards for each job in the division. Each department manager met with his people and together they hammered out what they felt were reasonable standards. After some refinement, all the employees signed off on the description, indicating that they were aware of the standards for their jobs and that they would be evaluated on the basis of those standards. John Laudie refused to sign, and his manager came in to see Bill. Bill called Laudie in for a chat.

> I don't like the philosophy—I don't like the idea of people judging me.
>
> But you can set *objective* standards for your performance—you can take the subjectivity out.
>
> I don't like the format.
>
> Well, the standards will hold anyway, whether you sign or not, since others in your position are being judged by them too.

In fact, John Laudie was not keeping up with the standards. His designs were getting behind—he couldn't seem to make engineering decisions. When a young supervisor was put in charge of Laudie's department, Laudie slowed down even more. In a written assessment of John Laudie's job performance, the new supervisor criticized Laudie's lack of commitment to his work, his eagerness to complain to anyone who would listen, his insubordination. Without talking to anyone else about it, Laudie took the evaluation to the corporate personnel department, with his own detailed critique of all the comments.

A manager from corporate personnel got back to Bill, expressing his concern about the situation. At ABC, the corporate personnel department was as close to a neutral body as possible, representing management to employees and employees to management with a serious attempt at equal commitment and concern for both sides. ABC's founder had felt that such a system would promote the continuation of the kind of reasonable labor situation that had led him to the Utica area in the first place (where he could compete with the boys in the big city without the big city headaches). Though the personnel manager had tried to review the case as Laudie's advocate, he told Bill that he had a feeling that perhaps John Laudie should be fired. Bill felt that they should go a few steps further to ensure that they weren't doing him an injustice and volunteered to interview all the people who had employed Laudie over the past 23 years, if they could be found. Bill was able to contact and talk to 15 people— all but three of Laudie' previous supervisors.

It turned out that in his first 12 years with ABC, Laudie had never been rated at all, but had been transferred quite often from department to department and from division to division. When people started giving him ratings, they had shied away from downgrading what was always an acceptable previous record and had never confronted Laudie with an honest assessment of his work. Bill's conclusion was that John Laudie had been taking advantage of ABC for 23 years, hiding behind benevolent personnel policies while doing just enough work to get by. Bill knew that ABC had helped make John Laudie what he was, but he doubted that what had been done could be changed.

Bill had decided to fire John Laudie on a Friday, a day on which Laudie seemed to sense he shouldn't show up. When he did come in on Monday, Bill told him to clear out his desk and be gone in an hour. The collective sigh of relief among Sigcom employees that seemed to follow him out the door seemed a confirmation to Bill of his judgment in a tough case. McGuire expressed appreciation of Bill's efforts with the dirty work.

Feedback

Early one day in 1979, after about a year and a half at Sigcom, Bill attended a meeting where Jim McGuire announced his own appointment as corporate VP of operations and that of Alan Harrington, someone Bill had only heard of, to replace McGuire as the new group vice president. Bill was

concerned, since he had worked for McGuire for over a year without any performance feedback from McGuire. He had also never gotten a raise, or any other indication of whether he was doing a good job or not.

Bill called McGuire's secretary the next day and asked for a two-hour appointment with Jim McGuire. That afternoon he went to see Jim:

Well, I understand you want to talk to me.

Yes, I do.

I have anticipated what you might want to tell me.

Let me explain it anyway. I've worked with you for over a year now, and I've never really figured out whether I was doing a good job or not, at least in your opinion. I thought I'd come and ask before I got a new boss. And, you know, I haven't had any salary increase either, so I figure that you must not think I've done that great a job.

No. No. As I said, I anticipated what you might ask about, and here's your new salary (a hefty increase). To tell the truth, if you hadn't been doing a good job as division manager, you and I would have spent a lot of time together. Ed Palais (the group controller) and I have talked a lot about your performance. You walked in there like you'd had the job for 10 years. You had the financial perceptions and everything. Frankly, I couldn't teach you a dang thing, so I said to myself I'd best leave well enough alone. You're doing more than I thought a division manager could do. I've told

Harrington that too, and I just want to encourage you to keep it up. You've made that division something it never was—I was afraid to mess around with it.

Well, it's nice to know.

ABC's Apples

In the fall of 1980, the division's basic product managers (BPMs) and accountants converged on Bill's office with a request for the division to purchase a microcomputer. They showed him what it could do, and Bill, no stranger to computers, was enthusiastic. Bill knew, however, that stagflation was making corporate hypersensitive in approving new equipment requests, and he feared that by the time he could make a strong case for the positive cost/benefit of a microcomputer, the most intense part of the planning process where the computers could be most helpful would be over. Bill also thought about how difficult it was to prove the productivity of proposed new equipment when the company seemed to discourage experimentation by being tight fisted.

Bill went to corporate anyway, and got a cold shoulder. They said they were working on several such proposals and had decided to do some research on what kind of microcomputer the corporation as a whole should buy. The one they had come to favor was, Bill knew, not the best choice—at least not for his people. He also had the impression that some people at corporate were afraid of microcomputers— what they might have to relearn

and the changes the smaller computers might bring with them.

Bill Hudson thought that in spite of corporate's stance and the group controller's tight fist, he should go ahead with the Apple. In his years at ABC, there had often been situations in which he had been forced to "do it on the cheap" and some occasions when he had felt it necessary to finesse the corporate bureaucracy. This time his office requisitioned a printer. After a few days, another requisition went in for the Apple computer unit. A week later, the form was sent to purchasing for a video monitor, and shortly after that he requisitioned two disk drives. These components, each priced within the maximum for purchases which required neither a capital equipment request nor its approval at the Group level, were assembled in a formerly empty office. This soon became a center to which the more creative and adventuresome of Bill's engineers congregated for experimentation and discussion. Bill kept track of what they accomplished with the machine and wrote it all down for future reference. After just a week, there was no question about the improved speed and accuracy the microcomputer brought to the planning efforts of Bill's staff.

On January 20, 1981, Bill got a memo from corporate which stated that divisions of the company were not to invest in small computers until corporate had finished research on the subject. They said they were concerned about security. A few days later, Bill ran into the group controller, Fred Casey, at lunch. Casey was rather subdued, failed to look him square in the eye, and left Bill feeling uncomfortable. Their next encounter also lacked the mutual cordiality that had always characterized their relationship. In mid-February, Bill decided to go see Casey. "What's wrong?" Fred Casey hedged a bit and then responded with, "You've gone against the rules on microcomputers and I don't like it—I'm frankly surprised." Bill pointed out that the rules on computer purchases hadn't come until January 20, but Casey insisted that the "purchase order assembly of capital equipment components" was definitely against corporate policy. Bill conceded that point, but insisted that the results had been worth it. "Will you come and see what we can do with this thing?" Casey reluctantly agreed.

Bill asked his BPMs and other computer enthusiasts to organize a presentation for Casey on microcomputer applications. Bill decided to invite the other division managers from Group as well. After the very enthusiastic presentation, the manager of one division said: "My God, every division oughtta have one of these dang things." Casey was sold too, in spite of himself, and over the following weeks was successful in getting corporate procedures modified to permit the purchase of two more Apples for Sigcom.

Bill was ready for corporate now and offered to make a presentation at the April 1981 meeting of the corporate officers. The corporate Systems director was also invited to the meeting to see Bill's guys show off their talents and machines. The man from Systems liked what he saw, but expressed concern at the potential loss of control over database security. Bill pointed out that having little chunks of data spread out here and there was an advantage—any security leak would be relatively minor; printing data from *all* the small machines would be very difficult. He also emphasized once again the hard numbers he had on the productivity advantages of the microcomputers in his division. The corporate officers were won over by the improvements in his business plan that Bill could point to, and by the end of 1981 all of the divisions in the General Products Group had at least one microcomputer in use—the particular brand was up to them. Sigcom had 10; Bill parcelled them out to those who were willing to back up their request for one with well-documented cases for productivity benefits. ("That way they'll have their own incentives to use the computer well—it's not just another executive toy.")

Bill recalled that once the advantages and the ease of operation of the small computers had been demonstrated, previous skeptics climbed aboard the bandwagon. The human resource files, kept in each division to monitor career development and eligibility for raises and promotions, were now all kept on microcomputer discs. Even corporate Systems bought three Apples and put them on casters for use in any part of the department; and the director became one of the active members of the ABC Apple Users' Club that began meeting weekly in mid-1981.

Reflecting on the Apple incident Bill said:

> In some corporations directives have such power that people don't dare move because some auditor will say, "You've broken regulation #1–5–3–2, and that becomes a mark on your record." There are people like myself who have never read the company systems and procedures manuals from cover to cover. I don't know where they are—there's a whole shelf full of the dang things. How do I learn the company systems and procedures? When I run afoul of them!

The Signal Protection Mob

Another critical episode was one in which Sigcom's basic product managers (BPMs) confronted the problem of highly technical products being sold by a sales staff which had insufficient technical training. The practice in the division was to have periodic meetings in which engineers and product managers would make presentations to the corporate sales staff. ABC's Sales Division took care of product lines from all the divisions. Unfortunately, whenever the technical people got into the details they thought were important for the salespeople to understand in selling the products, the salespeople got bored and, as often as not,

fell asleep. The more complicated the product, the sleepier the meeting.

In November of 1981, a new line of products from Bill's division, developed to protect signals carried on ABC's connectors from outside radiation (and subsequent signal distortion), was ready to present to the sales force. Bill and his team sat down to try to figure out what they could do to liven up the presentation. One BPM started with a question he had learned to respect: "What are we making here?" Another BPM said, "Signal protection." Said a third, "We'll be the Protection Mob." From there, it was all a party. The group, designated as the Signal Protection Mob, adopted aliases, had mug shots taken, with Bill listed at 7 foot 2 inches! The mug shots were made up as slides to be flashed on a screen, with other photos of the mob surrounding Bill's Jaguar, extorting payment for protection from the customers, illustrating their devious but effective methods. In the actual presentation, the mob hid behind the projection screen while music from "Peter Gunn" played as the surprised salespeople entered the conference room. The mob pictures flashed on the screen, and then each mobster stepped forward and silhouetted while the mug shot was projected. Speakers dressed in mob attire held toy machine guns equipped with flashlights in the barrels for pointing to features of the products on the screen. All the products were relabeled with sinister names, e.g., a crimping tool was designated a "terminating tool." Salespeople caught sleeping were shot with toy tommy guns, and a loud whistle was blown to signal coffee breaks.

Bill later recalled that the salespeople told him the almost three-hour show was the most lively and informative presentation they had ever seen. Results in sales were also gratifying.

READING 4–1
Corporate Identity of Dana Corporation: Implications for Acquisitions

Borge Reimer
Executive Vice President of
Dana Corporation

One of the greatest challenges for any large corporation is to forge a single organizational identity. The task is difficult enough when dealing with individual personalities located in individual divisions; but it is especially complex when two organizations, each with its own corporate identities, combine through acquisition or merger. An acquisition must not only make sense in terms of finances, strategy, and markets—

there must also be a high degree of compatibility in the value systems of the companies that are joining forces. That is the key to making a truly viable acquisition.

For this reason, we at Dana, approach a potential acquisition candidate in a unique way. At the beginning of the negotiation, we invite the company's top management to visit our world headquarters in Toledo, where they can observe what we call "the Dana Style" in action. If a visit is not possible or if there is an interest in exploring the subject in further detail—which is most often the case—we also have several slide presentations available.

The purpose of explaining the Dana Style to potential acquisition candidates is to make sure they understand and are comfortable with our style.

The Dana Style has its mainspring in our basic business philosophy. That business philosophy has eight fundamental elements that define what we stand for as a company:

- Our *purpose* is to earn money for our shareholders and to increase the value of their investment.
- Our *business* in the engineered-components sector of Dana is the worldwide design, manufacture, and marketing of components and systems for the transmission and control of power.
- We believe that our *people* are our most important asset and should be involved in setting their own goals and judging their own performance. The people who know

best how the job should be done are the ones doing it.

- To earn an acceptable return for our shareholders, our *goals* are to reach a 20 percent return on investment and a 10.5 percent return on assets.
- Dana's business *objective* is for our divisions worldwide to implement the market strategies for growth in our six key target markets.
- The Dana *organization* key word is decentralization. Our division managers worldwide are entrepreneurs who report directly to a regional operating committee. The division managers have great latitude in operating within the "Market Strategies." Their respective operating committees will only intervene in case of non-performance.
- Within this decentralized organization, our *management style* depends on commitment and trust. Divisions develop their own one- and five-year business plans annually, make the commitment to implement them, and are trusted to do so with a minimum of corporate interference.
- *Identity* with Dana is the most important element of our business philosophy. Identity means that the people of Dana feel it is a good place to work because they know their needs are considered in business decisions.

Listing the elements of a business philosophy is one thing. Seeing that philosophy put into action is quite another. One way to visualize the process is to view business philosophy as the starting point of two paths. Each path leads to the same performance objective but emphasizes different elements to reach that objective. We'll label these two paths "pragmatic" and "people," and explore the three necessary steps of each one (Exhibit 1).

The first step of the pragmatic path is to have a *strategy* for philosophy implementation. We give our strategy an extra boost, emphasizing our *proprietary products* and *services,* to reach one goal—market leadership. That leadership is measured by *market share*. Dana is committed in all our markets to being or becoming number one or number two, sometimes number three, but never number four. If we have acceptable market share, we then have the potential for reaching our desired final step: *performance*. At Dana, performance means achieving our purposes of earning money for our shareholders and increasing the value of their investment.

But there is a second path to implement business philosophy. We'll call it the "people path" because it concentrates on the people aspect of the business. Each of the three steps here deals with identity, participation, and commitment.

The first step in this process is a matter of policy—another word for the personality, value system, or culture of a company. Every firm has a value system; at some it is only dimly perceived, at others it is well conceptualized and explicitly stated. Dana has a very carefully thought-out set of values, which we have condensed into a

Exhibit 1
Model of Business Policy Implementation Used by Dana Corporation

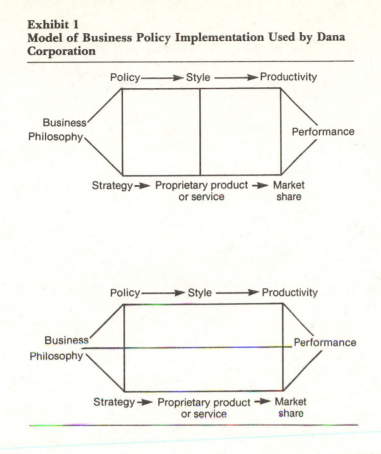

single-page Policy Sheet (Exhibit 2). This is the only operating guide that Dana managers are given. It states, briefly and clearly, our policies toward earnings, growth, people, planning, organization, customers, communication, and "citizenship" or social responsibility. An indication of where our emphasis lies is that over 80 percent of the Policy Sheet deals with the concerns and needs of people.

Policy and values mean nothing unless they are transplanted into style. Style is simply the way in which beliefs are brought to life and put into practice. The Dana Style builds identity among our people and with Dana. A little white booklet, "The Dana Style," a companion piece to "The Philosophy & Policy" of Dana, shows various examples of how to put our beliefs into practice—by working the Dana Way. We have summarized the booklet in a sheet of "40 Thoughts to Put into Practice." Examples include: "make all Dana people shareholders" (70 percent of Dana people own Dana stock), "promote from within" (moving people across functional lines), and "break organizational barriers." Such activities help build a people network, a collective "corporate" memory that encourages people to work with each other throughout the corporation to solve opera-

Exhibit 2
Policies

Earnings

The purpose of the Dana Corporation is to earn money for its shareholders and to increase the value of their investment. We believe the best way to do this is to earn an acceptable return by properly utilizing our assets and controlling our cash.

Growth

We believe in steady growth to protect our assets against inflation.

We will grow in our selected markets by implementing our market strategies.

People

We are dedicated to the belief that our people are our most important asset. Wherever possible, we encourage all Dana people within the entire world organization to become shareholders, or by some other means, own a part of their company.

We believe people respond to recognition, freedom to participate, and the opportunity to develop.

We believe that people should be involved in setting their own goals and judging their own performance. The people who know best how the job should be done are the ones doing it.

We endorse productivity plans which allow people to share in the rewards of productivity gains.

We believe in stability of employment. We believe that all Dana people should identify with the company. This identity should carry on after they have left active employment.

We believe that wages and benefits are the concern and responsibility of managers. The Management Resource Program is a worldwide matter—it is a privilege of all career Dana people. We endorse and encourage income protection, health programs, and education.

We believe that on-the-job training is an effective method of learning. A Dana manager must prove proficiency in at least one line of our company's work—marketing, engineering, manufacturing, financial services, etc. Additionally, these people must prove their ability as supervisors and be able to get work done through other people. We recognize the importance of gaining experience both internationally and domestically.

We believe our people should move across product, discipline, and organizational lines. These moves should not conflict with operating efficiency.

We believe in promoting from within. Career people interested in other positions are encouraged to discuss job opportunities with their supervisor.

Managers are responsible for the selection, education, and training of all people.

All Dana career people should have their job performance reviewed at least once a year by their supervisors.

We believe in providing programs to support the Dana Style. We encourage professional and personal development of all Dana people.

Planning

We believe in planning at all levels.

The Policy Committee is responsible for developing the corporate strategic plan.

Each operating unit within its regional organization is responsible for a detailed five-year business plan. These business plans must support the corporate strategic plan and market strategies. These plans are reviewed annually with the Policy Committee.

Commitment is a key element of the Dana Management Style. This commitment and performance will be reviewed on a monthly basis by the appropriate regional operating committee and on a semi-annual basis during Mid-Year Reviews.

Organization

We discourage conformity, uniformity and centralization.

We believe in a minimum number of management levels. Responsibility should be pushed as far into the organization as possible.

Organizational structure must not conflict with doing what is best for all of Dana.

We believe in small, highly effective, support groups to service specialized needs of the Policy Committee and the world organization at large as requested. We believe in task forces rather than permanent staff functions.

We do not believe in company-wide procedures. If an organization requires procedures, it is the responsibility of the manager to create them.

This organizational environment stimulates initiative and innovation. It develops the entrepreneurial expertise that is the cornerstone of our success.

Customers

Dana is a market-oriented company. We supply products and services to fulfill the needs of our selected markets.

Exhibit 2   *(concluded)*

We are dedicated to the belief that we have a responsibility to be leaders in our selected markets.

We believe it is absolutely necessary to anticipate our customers' needs for products and services of the highest quality. Once a commitment is made to a customer, every effort must be made to fulfill that obligation.

It is highly desirable to maintain a balance between in-house activity and outsourcing. This balance protects the stability of employment for our people. It also protects our assets and assures performance to our customers.

The Policy Committee is responsible to know our customers and their needs.

Communication

We will communicate regularly with shareholders, customers, Dana people, general public, and financial communities.

It is the job of all managers to keep Dana people informed. Each manager must decide on the best method of communication. We believe direct communication with all of our people eliminates the need for a third part involvement. All managers shall periodically inform their people about the performance and plans of their operation.

Citizenship

The Dana Corporation will be a good citizen worldwide. We will do business in a professional and ethical manner.

Laws and regulations have become increasingly complex. The laws of propriety always govern. The General Counsel and each General Manager can give guidance when in doubt about appropriate conduct. It is expected that no one would willfully violate the law and subject themselves to disciplinary action.

We encourage active participation of all of our people in community action.

We will contribute to worthwhile community causes consistent with their importance to the good of the community.

The Policy Committee
Dana Corporation

Approved by The Board of Directors
Dana Corporation

10/28/69   Rev. 9/20/83

---

tional problems on their own. Such networking inevitably leads to *participation* and *productivity*.

Respect for the people is another element of the Dana Style as manifested by the fact that many of our plants do not have bells or time clocks. Many of our facilities have participatory bonus programs, such as the Scanlon Plan, in which people are encouraged to improve their work efficiency and share the resulting rewards. Dana people participate in our own Dana University, which is dedicated to teaching and encouraging the Dana Style. Increased participation such as this leads to increased productivity. That shows in one simple statistic: Over the past 10 years, Dana people in the North American components sector have increased their inflation-adjusted sales dollars per person by nearly 40 percent. Productivity is the Dana way of life. That kind of productivity growth is a big step toward realizing our *performance* goal—which is to earn money for our shareholders.

Our model of business policy implementation is now complete and allows us to make a couple of interesting analyses (Exhibit 1). The model can be dissected vertically into three individual elements:

1. An input section (business philosophy, strategy, and policy). These are all abstracts expressed in terms of concepts, views, philosophies, etc.
2. An implementation section (style, proprietary products and services). This describes the dynamics of our business—the reason why our customers do business with us—the reason why our people want to contribute to the success and growth of Dana.
3. The output section (market share, productivity, and performance), all pragmatic and inert numbers, measured in dollars and percentages.

The implementation section is the driving force of Dana: "Style" and "Proprietary Products and Services."

The model can also be dissected laterally, dividing it into two elements: (1) a "pragmatic" element (strategy, proprietary products/services, and market share), and (2) a "people" element (policy, style, and productivity). Many companies expend their main energy in the "pragmatic" section and then wonder why they don't get productivity. At Dana, we try to strike a balance by allocating appropriate energies to both sections, to combine excellence in engineering, quality, manufacturing, and market penetration with productivity gains for a combined improvement in performance.

The people and pragmatic paths are not separate routes to policy implementation. Effective communication is the glue that binds them together. Dana stresses communication in every possible work setting: large groups in a plant meeting, small groups holding a department meeting, one-on-one interaction between people on the job. Because our knowledge package is the sum total of the knowledge of all our people, communication about what we know is a must. How well Dana people communicate determines how well we develop our knowledge package—how well we build identity—and thus succeed as a company.

The common denominator in this communication process is the corporate value system. That system shapes the degree to which each individual can, and is willing to, contribute his or her knowledge to the total knowledge package—and thus to the overall success of Dana. Going back to our original premise, it should now be obvious why we stress value system compatibility when making an acquisition. The compatibility of value systems, more than anything else, determines whether an acquisition will work.

Philosophy, Policy, and Style: Management Meeting—December 15, 1982

We are dedicated to the belief that our people are our most important asset. We believe people respond to recognition, freedom to participate, and the opportunity to develop. We believe that people should be involved in setting their own goals and judging their own performance. These are some of our policies that have established us as a people-oriented company in our industry and in our communities. We are both proud and sincere when we state: "Business is 90 percent people and 10 percent money." When the economy is expanding, when things are looking up, when business is prospering, these statements are easy to relate to. The period we are going through right now, however, is not this kind of scenario. On the contrary, over the last three years we have experienced the worst turmoil and slump in business since the depression in the 1930s. The severity of the downturn has caused major and permanent dislocations in our markets. In order for us to survive and remain viable, we have had to face plant closings, massive layoffs, cost containments, and cost restructuring measures.

When our people today view the policies in front of us on the bleak and unsettling background I have just outlined, it is quite understandable that these policies to some may be seen as less significant than before or of doubtful value. It was for that reason we included the subject "philosophy, policy, and style" in the program to reaffirm that there are no changes in our policies, that we view them to be as important today as when they were first created nearly 20 years ago, that there is no change in belief, intent, or commitment.

Let's try for a moment to examine the issue a little closer. The Pol-

icy Committee is responsible for our philosophy, policy, and style. Philosophy is our basic thinking of how we view the world in which we operate, our fundamental values of how we interact with our people, our customers, and our communities where we live and work. From this philosophical view flows a set of values and beliefs—our policies:

We believe people are our most important asset.

We believe people respond to recognition.

We believe in on-the-job training.

We believe in planning on all levels.

We believe in being a good citizen.

WE BELIEVE.

These are our policies. They can also be thought of as a value system, a set of beliefs, the Dana way of doing things—they can be expressed in many different terms. We have elected to refer to them as our policies. The term is irrelevant so long as we all understand what is intended.

The definition of style then is simple. It's the way we put our beliefs into practice. It is also the Policy Committee's responsibility to formulate and communicate this style—to explain how we perceive our beliefs should be put into practice. The little white style book is intended to do just that, to explain how we approach productivity—the Dana way.

The Divisions are responsible for the implementation of the Dana

Style—for putting the stated beliefs into practice. Not by distributing the Policy Sheet and the Styles Book—but by example—by working the Dana way. In this respect, then people in our organization are looking to the divisions and not to the corporation for their day-to-day work-life relationships—recognition, participation, opportunity, compensation, fringes, stability of employment, etc.

But wait a minute—isn't this statement contradictory to the statement made on several occasions, "Products are Divisional—People are Dana"? Not at all—what we are looking at is a dual relationship, one which exists on two different levels. One level relates to identity, which is an intangible yet very powerful concept. Identity stamps us as an organization with a unique personality and, in so doing, motivates all of us as Dana people to think and act in such a way as to "do what's best for Dana."

The second level relates to our day-to-day activities, satisfying our needs, opportunity for personal and professional growth, stability of employment, etc. We're looking at two distinct levels of relationships—a corporate and a divisional—an yet, the two of them are locked together inseparably.

Dual relationships are not uncommon. A good analogy would be that of a U.S. citizenship. The United States is made up of many different subcultures, ethnic, cultural, religious, race, and so on, distributed over 50 different states. A great diversity and yet the common bond that binds us together is

one of identity—being and above anything else, a U.S. citizen. This concept is what has made the United States the wealthiest and most successful country in the world.

Corporate identity is a similar concept. Dana is made up of many different subcultures, product divisions, marketing divisions, mechanical products, hydraulic products, and so on, distributed over hundreds and hundreds of locations. A great diversity and yet the common bond that binds us all together is one of identity, being over and above anything else, a Dana Person. This concept is what has made Dana one of the most successful companies in our industry.

Patriotism and Identity carry similar values. The United States is a melting pot, but in the process of integration, each subculture retains its proud heritage and traditions while at the same time establishing a common identity . . . most often expressed in terms of Patriotism. Similarly, Dana is also a melting pot, and when a new company joins the Dana Family, it retains its proud heritage and traditions without losing its deep-rooted, time-tested relationships with its people, while at the same time establishing a common identity with its sister divisions within Dana by sharing a common set of beliefs and, consequently, establishing a common identity—most often expressed by the term, "Identity with Dana."

A company with a strong identity like Dana is akin to a country with patriotism, like the United States, successful, growing and full of opportunity. Opportunity for all our people. Opportunity for personal and professional growth. Opportunity to be a member of a successful team—one of the leaders. That is what we meant by the statement: "PEOPLE ARE DANA."

READING 4–2
The Corporate Culture Vultures

Bro Uttal

U.S. business is in the throes of a cultural revolution. Even some of the hardest-nosed managers have started worrying about the appropriateness of their corporate cultures. Consultants have begun to offer high-priced advice on how to mesh a company's culture with its strategy. The problem is, it isn't clear that most corporations can consciously create a new culture for themselves. Or even that they should try.

The revolutionary concern for the soft, bewilderingly human underpinnings of business has several hard roots. Within the last three years a quartet of hot-selling management books—*Theory Z, The Art of Japanese Management, Corporate*

Fortune, October 17, 1983, pp. 66–72. Reprinted by permission of FORTUNE and Bro Uttal; © 1983 Time Inc. All rights reserved.

Cultures, and *In Search of Excellence,* now at a million copies in print and still rising—have hammered home the idea that companies with a record of outstanding financial performance often have powerful corporate cultures. The books also helped clarify what culture is: a system of shared values (what is important) and beliefs (how things work) that interact with a company's people, organizational structures, and control systems to produce behavioral norms (the way we do things around here). For example, at IBM customer service is a dominant value that keeps everyone, from the chairman to the factory worker, pulling in the same direction.

These aren't new notions, but recently they've become riveting. What thinking manager can ignore the connections increasingly drawn between, say, Toyota's success and the image of its workers intoning the company song? Or between Hewlett-Packard's long-term growth rate—an average of 25 percent a year in revenues—and its beliefs, which seem to lead almost everyone at the company to behave like an entrepreneur? The word is out: A survey of 305 chief executives published last month by William M. Mercer Inc., a New York City firm that designs compensation systems, showed that all but a handful think strong corporate values are important to their companies' success. Asked how much their companies had "addressed the issue of corporate values," two fifths of the group checked off "a great deal."

The idea that culture matters happened along at the right time, just as many managers were learning that corporate strategy alone, no matter how well formulated, can't produce winning results (see "Corporate Strategists Under Fire," FORTUNE, December 27, 1982). At best, big-league management consultants observe, only one company in 10 can successfully carry out a complex new strategy, say, to bring down production costs systematically, cut price, and gain share of market. But the need for devising and executing better strategies has, if anything, grown of late. Recession, deregulation, technological upheavals, foreign competition, and markets that seem to emerge and vanish by the month have cranked up the pressure on companies to adapt.

The fashionable view holds that the biggest stumbling block on the path to adaptation is often an inappropriate corporate culture. A widely cited example is AT&T, which has labored for years to behave like a marketing company, but with scant success. Efforts to serve different market segments in different ways have run afoul of the strong values, beliefs, and norms Bell managers have imbibed since the turn of the century— that it's important to furnish telephone service to everybody, that you do that by not discriminating too much among different kinds of customers. The solution seems obvious: Change the culture. As AT&T's dilemma shows, that's not easy.

A number of consultants, however, have sensed and abetted the shift in focus to the soft—they're eager to help the culturally distressed. Most of them have specialized for years in human resource problems such as organizational design. "The pendulum is swinging away from the strategists and toward the social architects," exults Paul V. Croke, vice president of Boston's Forum Corp., which focuses on training salesmen and managers.

The most ambitious of this crew is the Management Analysis Center, or MAC, of Cambridge, Massachusetts. Over the last few years, MAC has encroached on the turf of specialists in corporate strategy such as the Boston Consulting Group by arguing that you can't change strategies without taking heed of culture. Now the firm, with about 120 professionals in eight offices worldwide, sees a "window of opportunity" through which it hopes to squeeze by selling a new product—the "CEO's Change Agenda," a list of six steps for implementing strategy by massaging the softer side of management. MAC expects revenues—around $20 million in 1982—to grow by more than 25 percent this year.

The Management Analysis Center began delving into culture six years ago to help Willard C. Butcher, then heir apparent to Chief Executive David Rockefeller at Chase Manhattan Bank. Butcher wanted to execute a plan for regaining industry leadership and avoiding disasters like Chase's $61 million loss in real estate investment trusts in 1976. At his urging, Stanley M. Davis, a research professor at Boston University, and Howard M. Schwartz, a MAC consultant, interviewed Chase's top two dozen managers to collect anecdotes about the way the company worked. The two observed meetings and pored over logs of how executives spent their time.

The objective was to flush out the actual rules of behavior at the bank rather than the ones people professed. The consultants homed in on unwritten laws that governed relations among people when handling six general management tasks: innovating, decision-making, communicating, organizing, monitoring, and appraising and rewarding. Then they laid these norms— for example, "be a gentleman" and "avoid confrontations"—against the elements of Chase's plan for strategic redirection.

The result, naturally enough for consultants, was a matrix—a chart that plots some variable against two yardsticks—in this instance one that described the risk of making organizational changes. Each planned change was arrayed along a horizontal axis running from high to medium to low compatibility with Chase's patterns of behavior, and along a vertical axis indicating high, medium, and low importance to Butcher's strategy. Any change that showed up in this three-by-three matrix as being higher in strategic importance than in cultural compatibility was deemed an unacceptable risk. In those cases MAC advised the bank to find less dangerous tactics, rethink its strategy, or, as a last resort, try to change its culture.

Ultimately, the project flopped, as Chase's subsequent record suggests—the bank still is prone to unforeseen disasters, such as the collapse of Drysdale Securities last year. Neither party will discuss the grisly details, but it seems MAC's first report on Chase's unspoken norms was so scathing that it nearly wiped out any audience for the 100 pages of recommendations submitted later on.

The debacle did not, however, prevent Chase and other banks from pursuing cultural change, or keep consultants from going after their business (see Exhibit 1). It also helped spur MAC to come up this year with the CEO's Change Agenda, a less inflammatory recipe for yoking strategy and culture. The first three steps focus on planning. Honchos are advised to start by having senior managers reexamine the company's history, culture, and skills, as well as the traits of the business they're in. The process is aimed at culling bad strategies and uncovering good ones that the received corporate wisdom has masked. Next, the chief executive is to forge a vision of the new strategy and the shared values needed to make it work, then spread this gospel himself— in speeches, memos, and more informal contacts—and check up regularly on the number of converts.

Ideally, these steps work up

Exhibit 1
Cultural Therapy for Anxious Bankers

If trying to get a grip on your corporate culture can be compared to undergoing psychotherapy—and it can without much distortion—U.S. banks have good reason to put themselves on the couch. As they look out over the new, deregulated landscape, many are finding that they're not sufficiently adaptive, to use the therapist's favorite encomium, to chart a winning course. Brokers, insurance companies, and foreign institutions are trespassing on their turf, and yesterday's genteel behavior won't stand up to the new competitive pressure.

Not surprisingly, the appointment books of management-consulting firms that help companies work on their cultures are full of bank names. "When the definition of an industry changes, not only do strategies have to be reexamined, but also the fundamental beliefs and principles on which the strategies are premised," says Stanley Davis, 43, an independent consultant and self-described "organizational clinician," whose clients have included a number of money-center banks.

Among them is First Chicago, where personnel turnover was so hectic before and after his arrival that Chairman Barry Sullivan found himself a stranger among strangers. The bank's culture seemed to have been ousted along with its former chairman, A. Robert Abboud. "We needed to develop a standard of shared values, of how to behave to customers and to each other," explains Chief Financial Officer William McDonough, who guided the bank through eight months of soul-searching with Davis and the Management Analysis Center (MAC) of Cambridge, Massachusetts.

In evaluating staff behavior throughout the bank, McDonough and his crew identified one troubling predisposition—an aversion to risk—that was likely to hamper Sullivan's efforts to push First Chicago into the ranks of the nation's top five performers by 1985. "Serious credit losses in the late 1970s had made people gun-shy," McDonough says. "We had to make everyone realize that risk is part of this business." First Chicago has attempted to foster aggressiveness in the staff by implementing incentive plans geared to successful risk-taking. The new spirit seems to be taking hold, though not without risk—nonperforming assets are on the rise.

Bank of America recently engaged Davis and MAC to help it get back to the basics that rapid growth had obscured. "Our course over the last decade was to focus on profits. The customer didn't always come first," concedes Robert Beck, 43, an executive vice president of the bank. The formula began to fail B of A in the mid-1970s, when market share dropped. Return on assets fell soon after.

Still at an early stage, B of A's battle plan is to reacquaint the bank with the values of its founder, A. P. Giannini. On the then novel conviction that every man deserved a teller, Giannini turned the unassuming Bank of Italy in San Francisco's North Beach area into one of the world's largest commercial banks. Most companies don't have a home-grown hero around whom to rally, and both Davis and MAC agreed Bank of America should capitalize on its past to woo customers. Today this means a commitment to a more aggressive approach to marketing and more widespread use of automatic teller machines. Every man still deserves a teller—even an electronic one.

Too much too fast was also what drove Toronto-Dominion Bank to take a long, slow look at itself. Since 1970, assets at Canada's fifth-largest bank have ballooned eightfold, and branches have grown to 1,000. Qualified personnel to handle the challenge were in short supply and union rules made it nearly impossible to fire people. The prescription from Forum Corp. of Boston: Have subordinates evaluate their managers to isolate trouble spots. Forum then uses this feedback from the subordinates to train the managers in goal setting, coaching, teamwork, and accountability as needed. "Forum helps us keep our work force current, able, and competitive," says President Robert Korthals, 50. So far, the bank has appraised 375 managers and replaced their cost-of-living raises with bonuses based on individual performance. In phase two, bank customers will critique branch personnel.

While most executives are stuck with managing around an existing corporate culture, David Banks, 40, had the luxury of creating his own when he set up the Global Specialized Industries group at Chase Manhattan Bank. In 1979 Chase summoned the McKinsey & Co. consulting firm to help reorganize international lending. In the process, Banks unabashedly adopted and attempted to instill in his 200 officers the eight "excellent-company qualities" later celebrated in the book *In Search of Excellence*.

Among the book's more cryptic tenets is that "simultaneous loose-tight properties" are important in handling the troops. Banks's down-to-earth translation of the principle: "I give my managers enough latitude to achieve objectives in their own personal way. If someone closes a good deal, I give him a bottle of champagne. But I crack heads when the objectives aren't being met." Also heartily endorsed: "Stay close to the customer." Banks has cut back-office staff and increased the number of lending officers because he believes bankers in the field are better equipped to design the kind of financial deals that his clients are looking for.

Though it's still too early to tell if excellent qualities ensure excellent results, the global industries group appears healthy. Since 1980 its loans outstanding have grown some 30 percent a year, to about a quarter of the bank's corporate loan portfolio. The Drysdale fiasco originated elsewhere in the bank. So did Chase's Penn Square loans—after Banks had enough excellent instincts to turn them down.

Jaclyn Fierman

enough momentum to whirl a company through the trickiest part of the process—confronting mismatches between present behavior patterns and those the future requires. This may entail designing new organizational arrangements and control systems to encourage different behavior. Getting into cultural issues late in the game presumably makes them easier to face. "You can't change culture by working on it directly," Howard Schwartz says today. "You must have some strategic ground to stand on, then build a vision of what a company wants to be before rubbing their noses in what they are."

The last three items on the list specify methods of creating change. Chief executives are told to promulgate and reinforce the new values in everything they do, from the kinds of people they spend most of their time with to the incidents they choose to magnify to subordinates. They must reshuffle power to elevate exemplars of the new ways, including outsiders hired mainly for their values. The leader should use such levers of change as the budgeting process and internal public relations, constantly varying the pressure to keep people moving toward the right behavior.

MAC's approach is a lot for most companies to buy. Following it can cost up to $1 million a year in fees alone and take several years. But the agenda has appealed to some companies that face radical shakeups in their circumstances, especially deregulation. Theodore J. Saenger, president of Pacific Telephone, has coped with AT&T's reorganization by redefining his business according to the market segments that his company serves. He thinks MAC helped achieve behavioral changes to further that move: "We get much faster decisions about our lines of business, and I sense a willingness to get on with market positioning as well as clear agreement among middle managers and old hands on the need for a market orientation." Saenger tries to get people to think strategically by his own example: He used to spend 25 percent of his time on strategy and the rest on operations, but has now reversed that allocation. Pacific has also hatched plans to tie more of its top managers' compensation to corporate performance.

Still, the company has conceded much to a strong, old culture rather than risk changing it radically. Despite talk of marketing, Pacific retains a functional structure—one executive in charge of network operations, another responsible for engineering—and has no managers specifically accountable for attacking particular market segments. Saenger remains the only executive who must answer for profits and losses.

Consultants other than MAC treat culture less globally. They rely on questionnaires to measure organizational climate—how much a company should and actually does encourage individual responsibility, clear standards of behavior, appropriate rewards, and so forth—and on conventional tools for modifying behavior. These include feedback sessions (subordinates tell their supervisor how he's *really* doing) and team-building (getting them to work together).

Forum, for instance, with over 150 professionals in 13 offices, has started stressing the execution of strategy. The firm uses a method generally like MAC's—including the three-by-three matrix of cultural risk—though the names of the steps it recommends and their order differ. Forum concentrates on training people to change their patterns of behavior to fit the kind of culture a strategy implies. Often the company follows on the heels of strategy consultants with a climate survey, then helps managers to develop an ideal of new practices, to find out from subordinates how much current management practices fit the ideal, and to make plans for closing the gap. Smaller firms, such as McBer & Co. of Boston, as well as a horde of individual consultants, offer minor variations on the basic trilogy of survey, feedback, and plan for change. Their emphases differ according to whether their traditional specialities are compensation, motivation, or organizational design and development.

Larger, broader-based consulting firms have reservations about the upsurge of concern with culture. Booz Allen & Hamilton, for example, insists that culture is but one aspect of organization. "To assume that the tail wags the dog is inane," says Francis N. Bonsignore, a partner charged with developing organizational concepts for clients. To the extent that Booz Allen has embraced cultural change, he adds, "We're making hay of an issue that's topical."

Paradoxically, McKinsey & Co., the colosus of consulting, is the most reluctant to endorse the new wisdom, even though two McKinseyites, Thomas J. Peters and Robert H. Waterman Jr., wrote *In Search of Excellence* and another, Allan A. Kennedy, was the coauthor of *Corporate Cultures*. Peters and Kennedy subsequently left the firm; Waterman heads up what McKinsey calls the organizational effectiveness group, but it's just a handful of people with a minuscule budget.

The big consulting firms may be right to be skeptical. A review of the evidence suggests that anybody who tries to unearth a corporation's culture, much less change it, is in for a rough time. The values and beliefs people espouse frequently have little to do with the ones they really hold; these tend to be half-hidden and elusive. Diagnosing culture calls for unusual, time-consuming techniques: auditing the content of decision-making, using an anthropologist to code the content of popular company anecdotes, holding open-ended interviews with people ranging from the man working on the loading dock to the executive in the corner office.

Having grown out of a company's history, values are strengthened daily in a myriad of subtle ways, from observation of how people get ahead in the organization to the words employees choose to describe their companies. Moreover, people cling tightly, even irrationally, to their values and beliefs—a popular example among consultants and academics is the religious group that predicted the end of the world, and when the prophecy failed, advanced the date of doomsday, refusing any longer to specify it.

It may be easier to change the people instead. In the long term, according to many human-resource specialists, the key to culture is whom you hire and promote. People often get jobs and move up more for the degree to which they fit prevailing norms than for any objective reason. George G. Gordon, a partner at Hay Associates, which specializes in designing compensation schemes, says, "AT&T at one time had people in personnel who had been there for years hire the new marketing types. Is it any wonder the new hires turned out to be a lot like the old guard?" This is not to say that judging people solely on performance—"making the numbers"—is a good way to build a vibrant culture. "Hiring and promoting build culture and weed out incompatibles," notes Richard E. Boyatzis of McBer. "The companies that do the worst job of it have the sink or swim philosophy, and I predict they'll die when their main products do." A corollary, notes Vijay Sathe, who teaches a course on corporate culture at the Harvard Business School, is the importance companies like Minnesota Mining & Manufacturing, IBM, and Proter & Gamble attach to indoctrinating new hires. "The early stages are crucial," he thinks. "It's your greatest chance to make real changes in people's values."

In extreme cases, companies pressed to transform themselves just fire the recalcitrants who harbor fusty, intractable values and norms. As William T. Ylvisaker, chairman of Gould, went on a business-buying-and-selling spree to transform that auto parts and battery company into a power in electronics, he sold off longtime executives along with their operations. Two thirds of Gould's current senior managers came from acquired businesses or from somewhere else outside. Directors of Burroughs and Prime Computer concluded the best way to change those companies was to bring in a chief executive from elsewhere; in both cases, the new leaders have replaced many of the old guard with recruits from IBM (see "The Blumenthal Revival at Burroughs," FORTUNE, October 5, 1981). Such dramatic measures—in effect, cultural transplants—were deemed necessary to achieve desired financial results.

The Clarion message of the culture books is that high-performing corporations foster values beyond simple concern for the numbers. The IBM field engineer doesn't hesitate to use his own money for traveling to soothe a grumpy customer; his devotion to the value of service makes him do it, and the company's devotion to the same value ensures that he'll be reimbursed. Boeing and other "excellent" companies find it easier to assemble and disperse teams that cross organizational lines because shared values are more compelling than the boxes on an organization chart or a department's subculture. When Hewlett-Packard is forced to eliminate jobs and put the displaced workers through sometimes difficult retraining, managers reinterpret the H-P value of secure employment, building a new belief that workers are obliged to keep themselves well trained. Employees still regard H-P as a secure place to work.

If you long to instill such values in your company, can you do it? *Should* you? Most students of culture would answer "Probably not" to both questions. Notes Allan Kennedy: "There are only five reasons to justify large-scale cultural change: if your company has strong values that don't fit a changing environment; if the industry is very competitive and moves with lightning speed; if your company is mediocre or worse; if the company is about to join the ranks of the very largest companies; or if it's smaller but growing rapidly. Otherwise, don't do it." Kennedy's analysis of 10 cases of attempted cultural change shows that it will cost you between 5 and 10 percent of what you already spend on the people whose behavior is supposed to change, and even then you're likely to get only half the improvement you want. He warns, "It costs

a fortune and takes forever." Executives who have succeeded in fundamentally transforming a culture put a more precise estimate on how long the process requires: 6 to 15 years.

It's important to make sure you're not just caught up in a fad. "Corporate culture could be the Hula-Hoop of the 1980s," cracks one consultant. The prospect of a strong culture can seem a panacea for all your problems, much as getting the right corporate strategy did in the 1970s. "The fantasy is of some magic force, some secret ingredient, or some mystical glue that brings together all the people in an organization in a sense of shared purpose, commitment, and direction," notes David A. Nadler, founder of Organizational Research & Consultation Inc., a New York City firm. It's all too easy to pin your company's problems on an amorphous culture, forgetting the closely related, harder aspects of organization—control systems, planning meetings, divisional structures, and so forth—that both shape and express culture.

If you still covet the mystical glue, consider the obvious, low-cost adhesives. A tactic fairly standard by now is to develop a statement of corporate purpose, an awesome list of what the company believes in, and then remind everyone of it constantly. To be consistent, tailor your formal systems, structures, and personnel policies to reflect those declarations. You should reinforce the message by giving special awards for behavior in accordance with key values—inventiveness, say, or customer service—taking care to publicly shower "attaboys" on the folks with the right stuff. You can work your company's informal structures and processes, holding picnics for the elect and spreading stories about what Joe, the star salesman, did to get the big order. Some poetic license will help. Like McDonald's, Apple, and others, you could set up an internal "university" to indoctrinate employees.

These fixes may well change behavior, but they won't do much by themselves to instill the compelling culture you seek. As attentive readers of *In Search of Excellence* recall, the book posits that the great majority of outstanding companies trace their cultures back to an influential founder or other top manager who personified the value system. These revered characters—Robert Wood Johnson, Harley Procter, Thomas J. Watson Sr.—relentlessly hammered at a few basics that became the cultural core of their companies. Subsequent managements perpetuated the legacy. The despair of many corporations is that they can't point to such seeming superhumans in their past.

The lament for the extraordinary man doesn't cut much ice with the culturalists. Many of the stories that grow up around a Watson, they point out, are just legends born of the human tendency to attribute all values to an omnipotent, omniscient, preferably dead person. Legendary leaders, they insist, aren't uniquely charismatic, just savvy. They are smart enough to know what kind of culture is best for the business, persistent enough to harp on values in word and deed for decades, and dedicated enough to tailor all their actions to the value system. The top managers of Walt Disney Productions, for example, are known to instinctively pick up any gum wrappers and cigarette butts they spot defiling Walt's vision of Disneyland. They have followed the advice of IBM's Watson to put the business into their hearts.

Leaders driven by values are, above all, tuned in to symbolism. "They're showmen," says Tom Peters. Rene McPherson, one of the few executives Peters will credit with having transformed a culture, dramatized new values at Dana Corp. by tossing the auto parts company's multivolume policy manuals into a wastebasket during a staff meeting and replacing them with a one-page statement of beliefs. Renn Zaphiropoulos, the flamboyant cofounder and president of Versatec, a Xerox subsidiary that makes graphics plotters for computers, places a high value on loyalty—understandably, since Versatec sits in the middle of California's high-turnover Silicon Valley. Whenever a Versatec employee reaches his 5th or 10th anniversary with the company, he's invited to lunch with the president, who carries off the feted individual in one of his Rolls-Royces. The main features of Versatec's lobby are two plaques listing the names of 5- and 10-year veterans. It comes as no great surprise that as a young man Zaphiropoulos was a three-time winner on Ted Mack's *Original Amateur Hour.*

By the standards of most companies, managers given to such symbolic behavior would be considered near-fanatics who indulge themselves in grandstanding, corny stories, and other sundry foolishness. Indeed, Peters calls them "maniacs who overkill." The corporations they inspire are intolerant, at least when it comes to central values. A chief executive who wants to beef up his culture may well have to hire an extremely forceful, close-to-obsessive new leader or, if he doesn't want to replace himself, become a true believer. It's quite an unlikely transformation, suggests one student of corporate culture, because the real constituency of most top managers is not their organization at large, but their peers and immediate subordinates. The other fellows at the country club may not be amused.

The importance of management by symbolic behavior makes life awkward for consultants. Since most chief executives lack the theatrical skills to trumpet values powerfully, the hired gun must play drama coach. MAC, for instance, usually meets monthly with clients' chief executives to help them manage their daily behavior and review the kinds of signals they give out at company meetings. But few senior managers are likely to welcome tinkering with their personal styles, and few consultants are likely to be good at doing it. "To help out with

cultural change," says Bob Waterman of McKinsey, "you have to be a concerned analyst, a role model, a coach, a counselor, and a catalyst who will help the client's internal teams make their own decisions. Those activities undermine our traditional value—special knowledge—and haven't fallen within the skill sets of most MBAs and consultants." Waterman says that McKinsey can do such cultural consulting, but that his firm and others have good reason to approach the subject gingerly, at least for now.

If they listen to the academics, consultants may never enter the culture biz at all. Theoretically, charismatic founders of companies are ideally situated to shape culture. But according to Joanne Martin, an associate professor of organizational behavior at the Stanford Graduate School of Business Administration, who is studying several nascent Silicon Valley companies, fewer than half of a new company's values are those of the founder and chief executive. The rest develop because of the business environment and employees' need to attach meaning to their work. Says Martin, "Culture may simply exist."

In established firms, conclude experts who don't have a consulting ax to grind, the possibilities for influencing culture may be even slimmer. Says William P. Nilsson, who runs management development for Hewlett-Packard, "I don't think [President] John Young could fundamentally change our values if he wanted to." In sum, says Vijay Sathe of Harvard, it is exceedingly difficult to transform a culture. Waterman and Peters, he suggests, should have ended *In Search of Excellence* with a boldface warning: Caution—this may be impossible to duplicate.

For all the hype, corporate culture is real and powerful. It's also hard to change, and you won't find much support for doing so inside or outside your company. If you run up against the culture when trying to redirect strategy, attempt to dodge; if you must meddle with culture directly, tread carefully and with modest expectations.

READING 4–3 Fitting New Employees into the Company Culture

Richard Pascale

Many of the best-managed companies in America are particularly skillful at getting recruits to adopt the corporate collection of shared values, beliefs, and practices as their own. Here's how they do it, and why indoctrination need not mean brainwashing.

What corporate strategy was in the 1970s, corporate culture is be-

Fortune, May 28, 1984, pp. 28–40. Reprinted by permission of FORTUNE and Richard Pascale; © 1984 Time Inc. All rights reserved.

coming in the 1980s. Companies worry about whether theirs is right for them, consultants hawk advice on the subject, executives wonder if there's anything in it that can help them manage better. A strong culture—a set of shared values, norms, and beliefs that get everybody heading in the same direction—is common to all the companies held up as paragons in the best seller *In Search of Excellence*.

There is, however, one aspect of culture that nobody seems to want to talk about. This is the process by which newly hired employees are made part of a company's culture. It may be called learning the ropes, being taught "the way we do things here at XYZ Corp.," or simply training. Almost no one calls it by its precise social-science name—socialization.

To American ears, attuned by Constitution and conviction to the full expression of individuality, socialization tends to sound alien and vaguely sinister. Some equate it with the propagation of socialism—which it isn't—but even when it is correctly understood as the development of social conformity, the prospect makes most of us cringe. How many companies caught up in the corporate culture fad will be quite as enthusiastic when they finally grasp that "creating a strong culture" is a nice way of saying that employees have to be more comprehensively socialized?

The tradition at most American corporations is to err in the other direction, to be culturally permissive, to let employees do their own thing to a remarkable degree. We are guided by a philosophy, initially articulated by John Locke, Thomas Hobbes, and Adam Smith, that says that individuals free to choose make the most efficient decisions. The independence of the parts makes for a greater sum. Trendy campaigns to build a strong corporate culture run into trouble when employees are asked to give up some of their individuality for the common good.

The crux of the dilemma is this: We are opposed to the manipulation of individuals for organizational purposes. At the same time we increasingly realize that a degree of social uniformity enables organizations to work better. One need not look to Japan to see the benefits of it. Many of the great American companies that thrive from one generation to the next—IBM, Procter & Gamble, Morgan Guaranty Trust—are organizations that have perfected their processes of socialization. Virtually none talk explicitly about socialization; they may not even be conscious of precisely what they are doing. Moreover, when one examines any particular aspect of their policy toward people—how they recruit or train or compensate—little stands out as unusual. But when the pieces are assembled, what emerges is an awesome internal consistency that powerfully shapes behavior.

It's time to take socialization out of the closet. If some degree of it is necessary for organizations to be effective, then the challenge for managers is to reconcile this necessity with traditional American independence.

Probably the best guide available on how to socialize people properly is what the IBMs and the P&Gs actually do. Looking at the winners company by company, one finds that, with slight variations, they all put new employees through what might be called the seven steps of socialization:

Step One
The company subjects candidates for employment to a selection process so rigorous that it often seems designed to discourage individuals rather than encourage them to take the job. By grilling the applicant, telling him or her the bad side as well as the good, and making sure not to oversell, strong-culture companies prod the job applicant to take himself out of contention if he, who presumably knows more about himself than any recruiter, thinks the organization won't fit his style and values.

Consider the way Procter & Gamble hires people for entry-level positions in brand management. The first person who interviews the applicant is drawn not from the human resources department, but from an elite cadre of line managers who have been trained with lectures, videotapes, films, practice interviews, and role playing. These interviewers use what they've learned to probe each applicant for such qualities as the ability to "turn out high volumes of excellent work," to "identify and understand problems," and to "reach thoroughly substantiated and well-reasoned conclusions that lead to action." Initially, each candidate undergoes at least two interviews and takes a test of his general knowledge. If he passes, he's flown to P&G headquarters in Cincinnati, where he goes through a day of one-on-one interviews and a group interview over lunch.

The New York investment banking house of Morgan Stanley encourages people it is thinking of hiring to discuss the demands of the job with their spouses, girlfriends, or boyfriends—new recruits sometimes work 100 hours a week. The firm's managing directors and their wives take promising candidates and their spouses or companions out to dinner to bring home to them what they will face. The point is to get a person who will not be happy within Morgan's culture because of the way his family feels to eliminate himself from consideration for a job there.

This kind of rigorous screening might seem an invitation to hire only people who fit the mold of present employees. In fact, it often *is* harder for companies with strong cultures to accept individuals different from the prevailing type.

Step Two

The company subjects the newly hired individual to experiences calculated to induce humility and to make him question his prior behavior, beliefs, and values. By lessening the recruit's comfort with himself, the company hopes to promote openness toward its own norms and values.

This may sound like brainwashing or boot camp, but it usually just takes the form of pouring on more work than the newcomer can possibly do. IBM and Morgan Guaranty socialize with training programs in which, to quote one participant, "You work every night until 2 A.M. on your own material, and then help others." Procter & Gamble achieves the same result with what might be called upending experiences—requiring a recent college graduate to color in a map of sales territories, for example. The message is clear: While you may be accomplished in many respects, you are in kindergarten as far as what you know about this organization.

Humility isn't the only feeling brought on by long hours of intense work that carry the individual close to his or her limit. When everybody's vulnerability runs high, one also tends to become close to one's colleagues. Companies sometimes intensify this cohesiveness by not letting trainees out of the pressure cooker for very long—everyone has so much work to do that he doesn't have time to see people outside the company or reestablish a more normal social distance from his co-workers.

Morgan Stanley, for instance, expects newly hired associates to work 12- to 14-hour days and most weekends. Their lunches are not the Lucullan repasts that MBAs fantasize about, but are typically confined to 30 minutes in the unprepossessing cafeteria. One can observe similar patterns—long hours, exhausting travel schedules, and almost total immersion in casework—at law firms and consulting outfits. Do recruits chafe under such discipline? Not that much, apparently. Socialization is a bit like exercise—it's probably easier to reconcile yourself to it while you're young.

Step Three

Companies send the newly humble recruits into the trenches, pushing them to master one of the disciplines at the core of the company's business. The newcomer's promotions are tied to how he does in that discipline.

In the course of the individual's first few months with the company, his universe of experience has increasingly narrowed down to the organization's culture. The company, having got him to open his mind to its way of doing business, now cements that orientation by putting him in the field and giving him lots of carefully monitored experience. It rewards his progress with promotions at predictable intervals.

While IBM hires some MBAs and a few older professionals with prior work experience, almost all of them start at the same level as recruits from college and go through the same training programs. It takes about 15 years, for example, to become a financial controller. At Morgan Stanley and consulting firms like McKinsey, new associates must similarly work their way up through the ranks. There is almost never a quick way to jump a few rungs on the ladder.

The gains from this approach are cumulative. For starters, when all trainees understand there is just one step-by-step career path, it reduces politicking. Since they are being evaluated on how they do over the long haul, they are less tempted to cut corners or go for short-term victories. By the time they reach senior positions they understand the business not as a financial abstraction, but as a reality of people they know and skills they've learned. They can communicate with people in the lowest ranks in the shorthand of shared experience.

Step Four

At every stage of the new manager's career, the company measures the operating results he has achieved and rewards him accordingly. It does this with systems that are comprehensive and consistent. These systems focus particularly on those aspects of the business that make for competitive success and for the perpetuation of the corporation's values.

Procter & Gamble, for instance, measures managers on three factors it deems critical to a brand's success: building volume, building profit, and conducting planned change—altering a product to make it more effective or more satisfying to the customer in some other way. Information from the outside world—market-share figures, say—is used in the measuring along with financial data. Performance appraisals focus on these criteria as well as on general managerial skill.

IBM uses similar interlocking systems to track adherence to one of its major values, respect for the dignity of the individual. The company monitors this with surveys of employee morale; "Speak Up," a confidential suggestion box; a widely proclaimed policy of having the boss's door open to any subordinates who want to talk; so-called skip-level interviews, in which a subordinate can skip over a couple of organizational levels to discuss a grievance with senior management; and informal social contacts between senior managers and lower-level employees. Management moves quickly when any of these systems turns up a problem.

The IBM culture includes a mechanism for disciplining someone who has violated one of the corporate norms—handling his subordinates too harshly, say, or being overzealous against the competition. The malefactor will be assigned to what is called the penalty box—typically, a fairly meaningless job at the same level, sometimes in a less desirable location. A branch manager in Chicago might be moved to a nebulous staff position at headquarters. To the outsider, penalty box assignments look like just another job rotation, but insiders know that the benched manager is out of the game temporarily.

The penalty box provides a place to hold a manager while the mistakes he's made and the hard feelings they've engendered are gradually forgotten. The mechanism lends substance to the belief, widespread among IBM employees, that the company won't fire anybody capriciously. The penalty box's existence says, in effect, that in the career of strong, effective managers there are times when one steps on toes. The penalty box lets someone who has stepped too

hard contemplate his error and return to play another day.

Step Five

All along the way, the company promotes adherence to its transcendent values, those overarching purposes that rise way above the day-to-day imperative to make a buck. At the AT&T of yore, for example, the transcendent value was guaranteeing phone service to customers through any emergency. Identification with such a value enables the employee to accept the personal sacrifices the company asks of him.

Placing oneself at the service of an organization entails real costs. There are long hours of work, weekends apart from one's family, bosses one has to endure, criticism that seems unfair, job assignments that are inconvenient or undesirable. The countervailing force making for commitment to the company in these circumstances is the organization's set of transcendent values that connect its purpose to human values of a higher order than just those of the marketplace—values such as serving mankind, providing a first-class product for society, or helping people learn and grow.

Someone going to work for Delta Air Lines will be told again and again about the "Delta family feeling." Everything that's said makes the point that Delta's values sometimes require sacrifices—management takes pay cuts during lean times, senior flight attendants and pilots voluntarily work fewer hours per week so the company won't have to lay off more-junior employees. Candidates who accept employment with Delta tend to buy into this quid pro quo, agreeing in effect that keeping the Delta family healthy justifies the sacrifices that the family exacts.

Step Six

The company constantly harps on watershed events in the organization's history that reaffirm the importance of the firm's culture. Folklore reinforces a code of conduct—how we do things around here.

All companies have their stories, but at corporations that socialize well the morals of these stories all tend to point in the same direction. In the old Bell System, story after story extolled Bell employees who made heroic sacrifices to keep the phones working. The Bell folklore was so powerful that when natural disaster struck, all elements of a one-million-member organization were able to pull together, cut corners, violate normal procedures, even do things that would not look good when measured by usual job performance criteria—all in the interest of restoring phone service. Folklore, when well understood, can legitimize special channels for moving an organization in a hurry.

Step Seven

The company supplies promising individuals with role models. These models are consistent—each exemplary manager displays the same traits.

Nothing communicates more powerfully to younger professionals within an organization than the example of peers or superiors who are recognized as winners and who also share common qualities. The protégé watches the role model make presentations, handle conflict, and write memos, then tries to duplicate the traits that seem to work most effectively.

Strong-culture firms regard role models as constituting the most powerful long-term training program available. Because other elements of the culture are consistent, the people who emerge as role models are consistent. P&G's brand managers, for example, exhibit extraordinary consistency in several traits—they're almost all analytical, energetic, and adept at motivating others. Unfortunately most firms leave the emergence of role models to chance. Some on the fast track seem to be whizzes at analysis, others are skilled at leading people, others seem astute at politics: The result for those below is confusion as to what it *really* takes to succeed. For example, the companies that formerly made up the Bell System have a strong need to become more market oriented and aggressive. Yet the Bell culture continues to discriminate against potential fast-trackers who, judged by the values of the older monopoly culture, are too aggressive.

Many companies can point to certain organizational practices that look like one or two of the seven steps, but rarely are all seven managed in a well-coordinated effort. It is *consistency* across all seven steps of the socialization process that results in a strongly cohesive culture that endures.

When one understands the seven steps, one can better appreciate the case for socialization. All organizations require a degree of order and consistency. They can achieve this through explicit procedures and formal controls or through implicit social controls. American companies, on the whole, tend to rely more on formal controls. The result is that management often appears rigid, bureaucratic, and given to oversteering. A United Technologies executive laments, "I came from the Bell system. Compared with AT&T, this is a weak culture and there is little socialization. But of course there is still need for controls. So they put handcuffs on you, shackle you to every nickel, track every item of inventory, monitor every movement in production and head count. They control you by the balance sheet."

At most American companies, an inordinate amount of energy gets used up in fighting "the system." But when an organization can come up with a strong, consistent set of implicit understandings, it has effectively established for itself a body of common law to supplement its formal rules. This enables it to use formal systems as they are supposed to be used—as tools rather than straitjackets. An IBM manager, conversant with the concept of socialization, puts it this way: "Socialization acts as a fine-tuning device; it helps us make sense out of the procedures and quantitative measures. Any num-ber of times I've been faced with a situation where the right thing for the measurement system was X and the right thing for IBM was Y. I've always been counseled to tilt toward what was right for IBM in the long term and what was right for our people. They pay us a lot to do that. Formal controls, without coherent values and culture, are too crude a compass to steer by."

Organizations that socialize effectively use their cultures to manage ambiguity, ever present in such tricky matters as business politics and personal relationships. This tends to free up time and energy. More goes toward getting the job done and focusing on external considerations like the competition and the customer. "At IBM you spend 50 percent of your time managing the internal context," states a former IBMer, now at ITT. "At most companies it's more like 75 percent." A marketing manager who worked at Atari before it got new management recalls: "You can't imagine how much time and energy around here went into politics. You had to determine who was on first base this month in order to figure out how to obtain what you needed to get the job done. There were no rules. There were no clear values. Two of the men at the top stood for diametrically opposite things. Your bosses were constantly changing. All this meant that you never had time to develop a routine way for getting things done at the interface between your job and the next guy's. Without rules for working with one another, a lot of people got hurt, got burned out, and were never taught the 'Atari way' of doing things because there wasn't an Atari way."

The absence of cultural guidelines makes organizational life capricious. This is so because success as a manager requires managing not only the substance of the business but also, increasingly, managing one's role and relationships. When social roles are unclear, no one is speaking the same language; communication and trust break down. A person's power to get things done in a company seldom depends on his title and formal authority alone. In great measure it rests on his track record, reputation, knowledge, and network of relationships. In effect, the power to implement change and execute business strategies depends heavily on what might be called one's social currency—as in money—something a person accumulates over time. Strong-culture firms empower employees, helping them build this currency by supplying continuity and clarity.

Continuity and clarity also help reduce the anxiety people feel about their careers. Mixed signals about rewards, promotions, career paths, criteria for being on the "fast track" or a candidate for termination inevitably generate a lot of gossip, game playing, and unproductive expenditure of energy. Only the naive think that these matters can be entirely resolved by provisions in a policy manual. The reality is that many criteria of success for middle- and senior-level positions can't be articulated in writing. The rules tend to be com-

municated and enforced via relatively subtle cues. When the socialization process is weak, the cues tend to be poorly or inconsistently communicated.

Look carefully at career patterns in most companies. Ambitious professionals strive to learn the ropes, but there are as many "ropes" as there are individuals who have made their way to the top. So the aspirant picks an approach, and if it happens to coincide with how his superiors do things, he's on the fast track. Commonly, though, the approach that works with one superior is offensive to another. "As a younger manager, I was always taught to touch bases and solicit input before moving ahead," a manager at a Santa Clara, California, electronics firm says, "and it always worked. But at a higher level, with a different boss, my base-touching was equated with being political. The organization doesn't forewarn you when it changes signals. A lot of good people leave owing to misunderstandings of this kind." The human cost of the failure to socialize tends to go largely unrecognized.

What about the cost of conformity? A senior vice president of IBM asserts: "Conformity among IBM employees has often been described as stultifying in terms of dress, behavior, and lifestyle. There is, in fact, strong pressure to adhere to certain norms of superficial behavior, and much more intensely to the three tenets of the company philosophy—respect for the dignity of the individual, first-rate customer service, and excellence. These are the benchmarks. Between them there is wide latitude for divergence in opinions and behavior."

A P&G executive echoes this thought: "There is a great deal of consistency around here in how certain things are done, and these are rather critical to our sustained success. Beyond that, there are very few hard and fast rules. People on the outside might portray our culture as imposing lock-step uniformity. It doesn't feel rigid when you're inside. It feels like it accommodates you. And best of all, you know the game you're in—you know whether you're playing soccer or football; you can find out very clearly what it takes to succeed and you can bank your career on that."

It is useful to distinguish here between norms that are central to the business's success and social conventions that signal commitment and belonging. The former are essential in that they ensure consistency in executing the company's strategy. The latter are the organizational equivalent of shaking hands. They are social conventions that make it easier for people to be comfortable with one another. One need not observe all of them, but one wants to reassure the organization that one is on the team. An important aspect of this second set of social values is that, like a handshake, they are usually not experienced as oppressive. Partly this is because adherence doesn't require much thought or deliberation, just as most people don't worry much about their individuality being compromised by the custom of shaking hands.

The aim of socialization is to establish a base of shared attitudes, habits, and values that foster cooperation, integrity, and communication. But without the natural rough-and-tumble friction between competing co-workers, some might argue, there will be little innovation. The record does not bear this out. Consider 3M or Bell Labs. Both are highly innovative institutions—and both remain so by fostering social rules that reward innovation. Socialization does not necessarily discourage competition between employees. Employees compete hard at IBM, P&G, major consulting firms, law firms, and outstanding financial institutions like Morgan Guaranty and Morgan Stanley.

There is, of course, the danger of strong-culture firms becoming incestuous and myopic—what came to be known in the early days of the Japanese auto invasion as the General Motors syndrome. Most opponents of socialization rally around this argument. But what one learns from observing the likes of IBM and P&G is that their cultures keep them constantly facing outward. Most companies like this tend to guard against the danger of complacency by having as one element of their culture an *obsession* with some facet of their performance in the marketplace. For example, McDonald's has an obsessive concern for quality control, IBM for customer service, 3M for innovation. These obsessions make for a lot of fire drills. But they also

serve as the organizational equivalent of calisthenics, keeping people
fit for the day when the emergency
is real. When, on the other hand,
the central cultural concern points
inward rather than outward—as
seems to be the case, say, with Delta
Air Lines' focus on "family feeling"—the strong-culture company
may be riding for a fall.

Revolutions begin with an assault
on awareness. It is time to be more
candid and clear-minded about socialization. Between our espoused
individualism and the reality of
most companies lies a zone where
organizational and individual interests overlap. If we can manage
our ambivalence about socialization, we can make our organizations more effective. Equally important, we can reduce the human
costs that arise today as individuals
stumble along in careers with companies that fail to articulate ends
and means coherently and understandably for all employees.

Synopses of recommended supplementary readings

Part 1

The first two recommended supplementary readings, one building on the other, present four *ideal types* of cultures, which are described in Chapter 4 in the text (see Figure 4–3). Additional notes are included below.

1. Roger Harrison, "Understanding Your Organization's Character," *Harvard Business Review,* May–June 1972, pp. 119–28.

Harrison points out that an organization's ideology has a powerful impact on organizational effectiveness—it affects how decisions are made, human resources are used, and the external environment is approached. Using his typology, Harrison then illustrates how each ideology has certain consequences, both for individuals within the organization and for the organization as a whole. Individual and organizational interests are frequently at odds, Harrison argues, leading to ideological tension and struggle in organizations. Constructively resolving such ideological conflicts is one of the key tasks of management.

2. Charles Handy, *Gods of Management* (London: Souvenir Press, 1978), pp. 25–42 and 82–88.

Handy uses Roger Harrison's typology but prefers the term *culture* to *ideology*. (See Appendix 1–1 in Chapter 1 for my view of how the two may be usefully distinguished and related.) Handy adds value to Harrison's original typology in two ways. First, he attempts to categorize certain industries according to the typology (see Figure 4–3). Second, Handy provides a culture questionnaire (pp. 82–88 of his book) based on an instrument originally developed by Roger Harrison. Although somewhat transparent and plagued with the difficulties of validity and reliability, the particular items in the questionnaire constitute a useful checklist of the kinds of topics and specific questions one ought to be thinking about when describing and deciphering culture. More is said about this in Chapter 4.

3. Alan L. Wilkins, "The Culture Audit: A Tool for Understanding Organizations," *Organizational Dynamics*, Autumn 1983, pp. 24–38.

Wilkins discusses how to facilitate the discovery of shared assumptions by focusing on two relevant areas (implied work assumptions and implied reward or punishment assumptions) and two particular periods when the culture may be more apparent (during employee role changes and subculture clashes), as well as on top-management behavior.

4. Geert Hofstede, "Motivation, Leadership, and Organization: Do American Theories Apply Abroad?" *Organizational Dynamics*, Summer 1980, pp. 42–63.

Hofstede presents an empirically derived analytical framework for studying national cultural differences. Four cultural dimensions on which each national culture may be placed are: (1) power distance, (2) uncertainty avoidance, (3) individualism-collectivism, and (4) masculinity. A set of cultural maps of the world derived from his data are presented. Hofstede also discusses how national culture could influence development of theory and the implications of this for transporting behavioral theories developed in one national culture into a different one. Also included is a discussion of how national culture affects company culture.

Part 2

5. Harry Levinson, *Organizational Diagnosis* (Cambridge, Mass.: Harvard University Press, 1972) pp. 519–43.

As already indicated, several of the questions to think about in diagnosing an organization (Chapter 4, Appendix 4–1), were adapted from Appendix A of Levinson's work (pp. 520–26). Other questions, a structured interview outline, and a questionnaire for conducting an organizational diagnosis are contained in this selection from Levinson's book.

It should be noted, however, that these questions have been framed for use by *consultants* undertaking an organizational diagnosis. Because the skill, perspective, and relationship of a consultant with an organization are different from those of a person contemplating joining the organization, the latter cannot always ask questions in the same way as the former. Levinson's list, therefore, should not be used directly by prospective employees for interviewing during recruiting without taking this underlying difference into account.

6. Roy J. Lewicki, "Organizational Seduction: Building Commitment to Organizations," *Organizational Dynamics*, Autumn 1981, pp. 5–21.

As discussed in the section on "Subtle Traps" in Chapter 5, Lewicki coined the term *organizational seduction* but did not explicitly denote intent on the part of the organization to withhold potentially damaging information from the recruit. The position taken in this book is that, without such explicit intent, the term *organizational seduction* does not take on the tone of impropriety that usefully distinguishes it from the other more common forms of enticement, such as those mentioned in the text. Merely following the steps in Lewicki's seduction model cannot be viewed as improper if the organization is honest and aboveboard in its endeavor to attract a valued recruit. But if the intent is to mislead the recruit by causing him or her to suspend critical reasoning, the term *organizational seduction* seems appropriate.

Lewicki's discussion is engaging and well illustrated. The last section of the article (beginning with "The Final Step—Localistic Cooperation," p. 15) may be omitted without loss of the central message.

7. Irving Janis and Dan Wheeler, "Thinking Clearly about Career Choices," *Psychology Today*, May 1978.

Janis and Wheeler recommend two techniques—balance sheet procedure and outcome psychodrama—to help the individual avoid the subtle traps discussed in Chapter 5. This article describes these techniques in some detail and illustrates their use.

Part 3

8. John Gabarro, "Socialization at the Top—How CEOs and Subordinates Evolve Interpersonal Contracts," *Organizational Dynamics*, Winter 1979, pp. 3–23.

The section in Chapter 8 of this book on the development of credibility in general, and new working relationships in particular, drew on Gabarro's work. The summary of the characteristics, major tasks, issues, and questions in the development of new working relationships in Figure 8–2 is based on this article.

Gabarro has cautioned that the discussion is based on a study of *superior-subordinate* relationships and may or may not generalize directly to other types of working relationships, such as peer relationships. Despite the caveat, this article is recommended because it is the only systematic study of the evolution of such working relationships within the corporate context that I am aware of, and it provides much food for thought and application.

The article is written from the perspective of a fairly senior new executive attempting to build subordinate relationships, rather than from the perspective of the subordinate trying to build working relationships with new superiors and others in the organization (which is the point of view adopted in Part 3). However, the basic ideas seem to be more generally applicable.

9. Rosabeth Moss Kanter, *Men and Women of the Corporation* (New York: Basic Books, 1977), pp. 47–54 and 206–42.

The first excerpt from Kanter's book (pp. 47–54) is a vivid accounting of why there is a natural tendency for homosocial reproduction, why managers tend to reproduce themselves in their own image. This tendency was mentioned as a subtle trap in the discussion of recruiting realities in Chapter 5 of the text.

The second excerpt (pp. 206–42) is Chapter 8 of Kanter's book (Numbers: Minorities and Majorities) on how numerical proportions affect social experience. The discussion on the dynamics of tokenism in Chapter 8 of this text is based on Kanter's work. A reading of Kanter's Chapter 8 is highly recommended for those who wish to pursue this topic in greater depth.

10.　Robert W. Allen, Dan L. Madison, Lyman W. Porter, Patricia A. Renwick, and Bronston T. Mayes, "Organizational Politics: Tactics and Characteristics of Its Actors," *California Management Review*, Fall 1979, pp. 77–83.

This brief report, based on interviews with 87 managers, provides insight into how a sample of managers viewed politics in the organizational context, and the characteristics and tactics of its actors—the organizational politicians. The authors asked the subjects to provide their own definition of the term *organizational politics*, and many appear to have used it in a pejorative sense. As a result, the article provides a brief but illustrative account of various political strategies and tactics that may be used by those opposing responsible managerial action.

11.　Rory O'Day, "Intimidation Rituals: Reactions to Reform," *Journal of Applied Behavioral Science* 10, no. 3 (1974), pp. 373–86.

Although the organizational context is not made clear, this article appears to describe the dynamics set in motion by the initiatives of a "reformer" (an innovator) within a bureaucratic culture characterized by heavy emphasis on formal authority, rules, and procedures. Nonetheless, the insights offered seem to apply to situations in which managerial action threatens those with power. The article illustrates the strategies and tactics that such opponents may use in trying to eliminate the proponents.

12.　James P. Ware, "Bargaining Strategies: Collaborative versus Competitive Approaches," HBS Note 9–480–055 (Rev. 4/80).

A mix of collaborative and competitive approaches to bargaining and conflict resolution may be necessary in some circumstances. This note elaborates on how these circumstances may be analyzed and how to fashion an approach that is best suited to them.

The note is rather long, and those looking for a quick overview of the highlights may refer to Figures 1, 2, and 3 (on pages 8, 14, and 15 in the note) for a general orientation to the subject.

13.　Richard E. Walton, *Interpersonal Peacemaking: Confrontation and Third-Party Consultation* (Reading, Mass.: Addison-Wesley Publishing, 1969), Chapter 9, "Summary and Conclusions."

One approach to dealing with resistance (Chapter 10) under the general strategy of "Reason and Appeal" is third-party intervention—the third party being an appropriate organizational member or inside or outside professional. This brief excerpt from Walton's book summarizes the attributes of the third party and other situational factors.

14. Philip G. Zimbardo, Ebbe B. Ebbesen, and Christina Maslach, "On Becoming a Social Change Agent," in *Influencing Attitudes and Changing Behavior*, 2d ed. (Reading, Mass.: Addison-Wesley Publishing, 1977), Appendix C, pp. 221–33.

This book is based primarily on the literature of experimental social psychology. The appendix excerpted is a distillation of prescriptions for individuals attempting to change the attitudes and behavior of others in the society-at-large rather than in an organization. Here the interdependencies are usually greater, and thus the recommendations not necessarily directly applicable. Despite these caveats, this brief excerpt nicely summarizes some central ideas that may be applied to the question of attitude and behavior change.

Specifically, there is food for thought here for those attempting to change others by reason and appeal (Chapter 10). The techniques described that are covert raise difficult ethical questions; nevertheless, it seems wise to be aware of the research findings and their applicability. Regardless of whether the reader chooses to follow these prescriptions, others could be using these techniques against him or her.

15. James Brian Quinn, "Managing Strategic Change," *Sloan Management Review*, Summer 1980, pp. 3–20.

Whereas the reading from Zimbardo et al. appears most applicable when one is dealing with relatively few opponents, the Quinn article offers suggestions about how to proceed when the opposition is more numerous. The "strategic changes" discussed may or may not involve the kind of changes in organizational behavior patterns described in Part 4 of this book, but they do require dealing with the kind of political resistance and the "incrementalism" approach discussed under the general strategy of reason and appeal in Chapter 10. Again, to the extent that conscious withholding of important known information and covert techniques are involved, difficult ethical questions are raised.

16. Joanne Martin and Caren Siehl, "Organizational Culture and Counterculture: An Uneasy Symbiosis," *Organizational Dynamics*, Autumn 1983, pp. 52–64.

This is the case of John Z. DeLorean mentioned in the text under the discussion of counterculture clout. According to the authors, four core values at GM during DeLorean's tenure were: respect for authority, "fitting in," loyalty, and teamwork. The authors show how DeLorean was able to go against the grain of this culture and create a counterculture by articulating opposing values, translating them into concrete policy, and facilitating their implementation by personally role modeling the counterculture behavior.

17. Manuel Velasquez, Dennis J. Moberg, and Gerald F. Cavanagh, "Organizational Statesmanship and Dirty Politics: Ethical Guidelines for the Organizational Politician," *Organizational Dynamics*, Autumn 1983, pp. 65–80.

These authors provide a framework for systematically considering the ethical issues involved in organizational politics. As such, the article provides a set of guidelines for addressing the ethical dilemmas posed in the text under the section of "Going against Those Personally Threatened."

Part 4

18. Rosabeth Moss Kanter, "Change Masters and the Intricate Architecture of Corporate Culture Change," *Management Review,* October 1983, pp. 18–28, based on her book, *The Change Masters* (New York: Simon & Schuster, 1983).

In this excerpt from her book, Kanter shows the importance of understanding the history preceding any change—not just accounts as they are told, but events as they actually happened. Without a solid understanding of why things work as they do, one may be frozen into inaction, particularly when the organization is not in trouble, for fear that changing anything might upset everything. Armed with a theory of why things work as they do and an understanding of the forces that lead to change, managers are more likely to become agents of productive change.

19. Thomas J. Peters, "Symbols, Patterns, and Settings: An Optimistic Case for Getting Things Done," *Organizational Dynamics,* Autumn 1978.

As mentioned in the text, the article is an excellent exposé of the symbolic means by which leaders can both communicate expectations ("M2") and administer rewards and punishments ("M1") by paying attention to their actual behavior and its symbolic significance. Those seeking a more detailed discussion of Peters' "mundane tools" will also find the reading worthwhile. In general (to use the terminology we have developed), the article addresses behavior change rather than culture change.

20. John P. Kotter and Leonard A. Schlesinger, "Choosing Strategies for Change," *Harvard Business Review,* March–April 1979.

This is a succinct, well-illustrated discussion of resistance to change and approaches to dealing with it. Those seeking an elaboration of Figure 11–1 in our text and the section on methods of change ("M3") in Chapter 11, will find a reading of this article worthwhile.

Notes

Notes for Introduction to Part 1

1. For examples from the business press, see the "Corporate Cultures" section in *Fortune:*

"The Odyssey of Levi Strauss," March 22, 1982, pp. 110–24; "Managing by Mystique at Tandem Computers," June 28, 1982, pp. 84–91; "In Search of Style at the 'New Marine'," July 26, 1982, pp. 40–45.

Business Week carried a cover story on the subject "Corporate Culture: The Hard-to-Change Values that Spell Success or Failure," October 27, 1980, pp. 148–60. More recent examples are Readings 4–2 and 4–3 in the book.

2. There are two videotapes accompanying the case Cummins Engine Company: Jim Henderson and the Phantom Plant (Case 1–1 in the book): (a) "Managerial Philosophy, Personal Style, and Corporate Culture" (Videotape 9–880–001, 28 minutes); (b) "The Phantom Plant" (Videotape 9–880–002, 14 minutes). Both videotapes are available from Case Services, Harvard Business School, Boston, Mass. 02163.

Notes for Chapter 1

1. The word *culture* goes back to the classical Latin with the meaning of cultivation, as it still persists in such terms as *horticulture, bee culture, bacteria culture*. E. B. Taylor, *Primitive Culture* (London: J. Murray, 1871) is believed to have offered the first formal definition of culture in the context of anthropology. "Culture . . . is that complex whole which includes knowledge, belief, art, law, morals, custom, and any other capabilities and habits acquired by man as a member of society" (p. 1). Since that time, the concept of culture has taken on a wide variety of meanings. A. L. Kroeber and Clyde Kluckhohn—*Culture: A Critical Review of Concepts and Definitions* (New York: Vintage Books, 1952)—cite 164 definitions of culture.

2. The ideational school views culture as a system of shared ideas, knowledge, and meanings. The rival school, the cultural adaptationists, views culture as a system of socially transmitted behavior patterns that serve to relate human communities to their ecological settings. See Roger M. Keesing, "Theories of Culture," *Annual Review of Anthropology*, Volume 3, 1974, pp. 73–79.

3. This three-level model of culture was first proposed by Edgar H. Schein in "SMR Forum: Does Japanese Management Style Have a Message for American Managers?" *Sloan Management Review,* Fall 1981, pp. 64–67. Schein further elaborated on it in "Organizational Culture: A Dynamic Model," Working Paper Number 1412–83, Massachusetts Institute of Technology, February 1983.

The three-level conceptualization of culture used in the book is based on Schein's model, but two clarifications are in order. First, Schein uses the term *values* to denote espoused values, whereas the terms *beliefs* and *values* are used here to denote those assumptions that people actually hold—that is, the ones they have internalized. (See notes 7 and 8 for this chapter.) Second, Schein focuses on preconscious and unconscious assumptions because these are powerful, and people may not even become aware of them until they are violated or challenged. Such assumptions are hard to discover and debate because they are taken for granted. (Schein, "Organizational Culture," pp. 3–4). Conscious assumptions have also been included in the definition of *culture* used here because, although these may be easier to detect and debate, they too have a strong influence on behavior and are hard to change. People do not easily give up internalized beliefs and values, whether consciously or unconsciously held, as opposed to beliefs and values that they merely espouse or comply with, as explained in Chapter 4 of this book.

4. Within the ideational school, the definition adopted belongs to the functionalist perspective represented by cultural anthropologists, such as Ward Goodenough, who view cultures as systems of knowledge. The functionalists assume that an organization is composed of many interrelated elements, each of which serves a function for the organization. Culture, in this view, is a variable that an organization *has*. This contrasts with another view within the ideational school, the interpretative perspective, represented by such scholars as Clifford Geertz, who view cultures as systems of meaning. Culture, in this tradition, is viewed as a guiding metaphor or epistemological device to help frame and guide the study of organizations. From this point of view, culture is something an organization *is*. See Linda Smircich, "Concepts of Culture and Organizational Analysis," *Administrative Science Quarterly* 28, no. 3 (1983), pp. 339–58.

5. Clifford Geertz, *The Interpretation of Cultures* (New York: Basic Books, 1973), suggests that broad, all-encompassing definitions of culture, such as E. B. Taylor's, obscure a good deal more than they reveal. Geertz argues that a narrower, more specialized definition has more value for theory, a view shared by many others in modern cultural anthropology. Other analytical benefits gained by separating culture from behavior are cogently articulated by Marc Swartz and David Jordan, *Culture: An Anthropological Perspective* (New York: John Wiley & Sons, 1980), pp. 61–63.

6. These definitions follow Milton Rokeach, *Beliefs, Attitudes, and Values* (San Francisco: Jossey-Bass, 1968); and Daryl J. Bem, *Beliefs, Attitudes, and Human Affairs* (Monterey, Calif.: Brooks/Cole Publishing, 1970).

7. As Rokeach *(Beliefs, Attitudes and Values)* points out, there may be compelling personal or social reasons, conscious and unconscious, why a person will not or cannot report accurately what he or she truly believes: ". . . beliefs—like motives, genes, and neutrons—cannot be directly observed but must be inferred as best one can, with whatever psychological devices are available, from all the things the believer says or does" (p. 2).

8. Using the terms *values* and *assumptions* somewhat differently than in this book, Schein ("Organizational Culture," p. 3) makes a distinction between (1) ultimate, nondebatable, taken-for-granted values, which he calls "assumptions" and (2) debatable, overt, espoused values, which he calls "values." Schein argues persuasively that as a "value" leads to behavior, and as the behavior solves the problems that motivated it, the value gradually becomes transformed into an assumption about how things really are and, as it is increasingly taken for granted, drops out of awareness. Using our terminology, this explains why people may be unaware of *some* of their beliefs and values.

   It is useful to note the difference between conscious and unconscious beliefs and values because the latter are particularly hard to discover, debate, or confront. As Schein points out, a good signal that an unconscious organizational assumption is being encountered is that people in the organization refuse to discuss something, or that they consider the enquirer "insane" or "ignorant" for bringing something up. Conscious basic assumptions may be easier to discover and debate, but they too have a strong influence on behavior and are also hard to change. That is why it is important to include both conscious and unconscious assumptions in the concept of culture, as is being done in this book, but it is also important to be aware that people may be unaware of some of their basic beliefs and values.

9. These distinctions follow H. C. Kelman, "Compliance, Identification and Internalization: Three Processes of Attitude Change," *Conflict Resolution*, 1958, pp. 51–60. Kelman describes three underlying processes that individuals engage in when they adopt new responses: (1) *Compliance*—acceptance of new demands because the individual stands to gain valued rewards and avoid certain punishments. (2) *Identification*—acceptance of the demands because of the desire to remain associated with the other person or group. (3) *Internalization*—acceptance of the demands because they are intrinsically rewarding, the equivalent of the individual's own demands.

   Since our interest is in the individual's beliefs and values in the *organizational context*, it is both difficult and unnecessary to separate compliance from identification. In both cases the individual engages in the behavior because of the fear of punishment or to derive rewards that are external to the behavior, rather than because of personal satisfaction that the person derives from *engaging in the behavior itself*.

10. Rokeach (*Beliefs, Attitudes, and Values,* pp. 157–59) has provided an insightful commentary on the importance of distinguishing between attitudes and values:

> Several considerations lead me to place the value concept in nomination ahead of the attitude concept. First, value seems to be a more dynamic concept since it has a strong motivational component as well as cognitive, affective, and behavioral components. Second, while attitude and value are both widely assumed to be determinants of social behavior, value is a determinant of attitude as well as of behavior. Third, if we further assume that a person possesses considerably fewer values than attitudes, then the value concept provides us with a more economical analytic tool for describing and explaining similarities and differences between persons, groups, nations, and cultures

* * * * *

> It may seem somewhat paradoxical, in view of the more central theoretical status generally accorded the value concept, that we should have witnessed over the years a more rapid theoretical advance in the study of attitude rather than of value. One reason for this, I suspect, was the more rapid development of methods for measuring attitudes, due to the efforts of such men as Bogardus, Thurstone, Likert, and Guttman. A second reason, perhaps, was the existence of a better consensus on the meaning of attitude than of value. A third possible reason is that attitudes were believed to be more amenable to experimental manipulation than values. . . .

* * * * *

> Bypassing the problem of values and their relation to attitudes, we settled perhaps a bit too hastily for studies that I shall call problems of persuasion to the neglect of what I shall call problems of education and reeducation. We emphasized the persuasive effects of group pressure, prestige, order of communication, role playing, and forced compliance on attitudes, but we neglected the more difficult study of the more enduring effects of socialization, educational innovation, psychotherapy, and cultural change on values.

11. An individual's beliefs and values will be derived more or less from the cultures of each of these communities, depending on their relative influence on the individual's experience and development. Those communities the individual joined at a younger age, and in which the individual has spent a longer period of time, may be expected to have had a greater influence.

12. As Schein points out ("Organizational Culture"), to an extent this resistance to change is functional because it provides a measure of stability to organizational members who seek it as a defense against anxiety that comes from uncertainty and change.

13. More research is needed to better understand how various factors influence strength of culture and its specific properties—thickness, extent of sharing, and clarity of ordering. A beginning is being made by researchers: Meryl Louis, "Organizations as Culture-Bearing Milieux," in *Organizational Symbolism,* ed. Louis Pondy, Peter Frost, Gareth Morgan, and Thomas Dandridge (Greenwich, Conn.: JAI Press, 1983).

14. See note 7 for this Chapter, Rokeach, *Beliefs, Attitudes, and Values,* p. 2.

15. See Gareth Morgan, Peter J. Frost, and Louis R. Pondy, "Organizational Symbolism" in *Organizational Symbolism,* ed. Pondy et al.

16. *Time,* "The Talk of the Money World," April 16, 1984, pp. 44–45.

17. "Stanford Investigates Plagiarism Charges," *Science,* April 6, 1984, p. 35.

18. The process of deciphering culture can be aided by thinking about incidents that *could* offend the people in the community, but one must recognize that one is now moving from evidence to speculation. However, thinking about this issue may help generate questions that could be used to aid in the process of *joint* inquiry proposed by Schein (see note 8 and note 20).

19. See Meryl Reis Louis, "Surprise and Sense Making: What Newcomers Experience in Entering Unfamiliar Organizational Settings," *Administrative Science Quarterly,* June 1980, pp. 226–51.

20. See Schein, "Organizational Culture," p. 18.

21. These three types have been defined by Joanne Martin and Caren Siehl, "Organizational Culture and Counterculture: An Uneasy Symbiosis," *Organizational Dynamics,* Autumn 1983, p. 53.

22. Geert Hofstede, "Motivation, Leadership, and Organization: Do American Theories Apply Abroad?" *Organizational Dynamics,* Summer 1980, pp. 42–63, provides an analytical framework for studying differences in national cultures and comments on how these differences affect corporate culture.

23. G. H. Litwin and R. A. Stringer, Jr., *Motivation and Organizational Climate* (Boston: Division of Research, Harvard Business School, 1968).

24. This definition follows Renato Tagiuri, "Managing Corporate Identity: The Role of Top Management," HBS Working Paper 82–68, March 1982.

25. See George C. Lodge, *The New American Ideology* (New York: Alfred A. Knopf, 1980), especially pp. 7–9.

26. See Tagiuri, "Managing Corporate Identity."

Notes for Chapter 2

1. Calvin Pava, *Towards a Concept of Normative Incrementalism* (Ph.D. diss., The University of Pennsylvania, 1980) provides a good review of the literature on logical types and concludes that either cooperation or competition can be the *primary* social relationship in an organization, which constrains and qualifies the other. In so-called primitive societies, such as the Dobu culture studied by B. Malinovski (*Agronauts of the Western Pacific,* New York: E. P. Dutton, 1922), there is an overall cooperative relation to which all competition is subordinate. This is *qualitatively* different—a different logical type—from many industrial societies, where competition is the primary mediating relationship that constrains and qualifies cooperation. This distinction is important and has crucial consequences for modern industrial organization; the point is also emphasized by Elton Mayo in *Social Problems of an Industrial Civilization* (Cambridge, Mass.: Harvard University Press, 1947). Culture influences this logical typing; that is, whether cooperation or competition is the primary mediating relationship in the organization, thus exerting a powerful influence on organizational behavior.

2. William G. Ouchi, "Markets, Bureaucracies, and Clans," *Administrative Science Quarterly,* 1980, pp. 129–41.

3. Chester Barnard, in *The Functions of the Executive* (Cambridge, Mass.: Harvard University Press, 1938), postulated the concept of *zone of indifference* as one in which an individual will submit to authority without consciously questioning it (p. 167).

4. Richard T. Pascale and Anthony G. Athos, *The Art of Japanese Management* (New York: Simon & Schuster, 1981), p. 178.

5. Carl R. Rogers and F. J. Roethlisberger, "Barriers and Gateways to Communication," *Harvard Business Review,* July–August 1952, pp. 28–34, is a classic treatment of the problems of interpersonal communication.

6. Alvin Zander, *Groups at Work* (San Francisco: Jossey-Bass, 1979) discusses the phenomenon of secrecy within organizations. (See Chapter 2.)

7. Peter L. Beger and Thomas Luckmann, *The Social Construction of Reality* (Garden City, N.Y.: Doubleday Publishing, 1966); Jeffrey Pfeffer, *Power in Organizations* (Marshfield, Mass.: Pitman, 1981), pp. 298–303.

8. Alice M. Sapienza, *Believing Is Seeing: The Effects of Beliefs on Top Managers' Perception and Response* (Ph.D. diss., Harvard Business School, 1984).

9. Elliot Aronson, in *The Social Animal* (San Francisco: W. H. Freeman, 1976), has noted that people are not so much rational animals as rational*izing* animals. They are motivated not so much to *be* right, as to *believe* they are right. Citing the existential philosopher Albert Camus, Aronson states: "Man is a creature who spends his entire life in an attempt to convince himself that his existence is not absurd" (p. 88).

10. Self-justification and rationalization can be maladaptive, since they can prevent people from learning important facts or from finding real solutions to their problems. Thus, although rationalizing behavior may be psychologically functional in that it allows people to maintain a positive self-image, it can become irrational behavior that is ultimately dysfunctional. See Aronson, *The Social Animal.*

11. Daryl J. Bem, *Beliefs, Attitudes, and Human Affairs* (Monterey, Calif.: Brooks/Cole Publishing, 1970), Chapter 6.

Notes for Chapter 3

1. As can be seen from Figure 3–1, Models A and B are quite similar. Both are based on a tradition that conceptualizes human situations in terms of interrelationships among major factors in dynamic equilibrium, rather than as simple cause-and-effect relationships between two variables. If there is a change in any factor in the model, the ripple effect of that affects other factors until the old equilibrium is restored or a new equilibrium is established. See F. J. Roethlisberger and W. J. Dickson, *Management and the Worker* (Cambridge, Mass.: Harvard University Press, 1939), for an early exposition of the idea of an organization or individual as a dynamic system in equilibrium. (p. 326). More recent works based on the same perspective are: J. W. Lorsch and P. R. Lawrence, eds., *Studies in Organization Design* (Homewood, Ill.: Richard D. Irwin, 1970); and J. P. Kotter, L. A. Schlesinger, and V. Sathe, *Organization* (Homewood, Ill.: Richard D. Irwin, 1979), p. 2. For an understanding of organizational dynamics that distinguishes between short-run, moderate-run, and long-run dynamics, see J. P. Kotter, *Organizational Dynamics* (Reading, Mass.: Addison-Wesley Publishing, 1978).

The intent here is to show how analysis of salient features and their interrelationships makes the reality easier to understand. The test of a useful model is its ability to explain, predict, and provide useful insights. See Sergio Koreisha and Robert Stobaugh, "Modeling: Selective Attention Institutionalized," *Technology Review*, February–March 1981, pp. 64–66.

2. See Paul R. Lawrence and Jay W. Lorsch, *Organization and Environment* (Boston, Mass.: Harvard Graduate School of Business Administration, 1967); Fred E. Fiedler, *A Theory of Leadership Effectiveness* (New York: McGraw-Hill, 1967); J. W. Lorsch and John J. Morse, *Organizations and Their Members* (New York: Harper & Row, 1974).

3. See Chris Argyris, *Integrating the Individual and the Organization* (New York: John Wiley & Sons, 1964); Michael Beer, *Organization Change and Development* (Santa Monica, Calif.: Goodyear Publishing, 1980).

4. It is *not* presumed that these models can or should be used to guide every action, big and small. Managerial life is too busy and patterned to make that feasible or worthwhile. Ellen J. Langer, "Rethinking the Role of Thought in Social Interaction," in *New Directions in Attribution Research*, Vol.2, ed. Harvey, Ickes, and Kidd (Hillsdale, N.J.: Lawrence Erlbaum Associates, 1978) reports recent research indicating that much day-to-day behavior occurs with minimal information processing, and is guided by well-learned general "scripts." For instance, in the "restaurant script" used in everyday life, the individual expects the following sequence of events to occur—enter restaurant, seat yourself or wait to be seated (depending on the cue), look at menu, order food, eat it, pay the bill, and leave. Each individual carries in his or her head a multitude of such scripts, one for each predictable sequence of required behaviors. They serve a valuable function by freeing the mind of the need to consciously process information and act on it, an expensive and time-consuming activity that the mind seeks to conserve.

Such "mindless behavior" is not possible until it is repeated often enough that its script becomes part of the person's repertoire. Until then, the individual must think about the behavior to be executed, something the mind prefers not to have to do. Surprising as it may seem at first, we prefer behavior that no longer requires thoughtful deliberation, and resist that which does.

Models A and B in Figure 3–1 provide a basis for thoughtful and deliberate action, as well as a means for periodically testing whether taken-for-granted mindless behavior is really adaptive and functional. If it is not, appropriate changes and new scripts are called for.

5. Joan Woodward, *Management and Technology* (London: Her Majesty's Printing Office, 1958), demonstrated how system of production—batch, mass or process—affects organization. James D. Thompson, *Organizations in Action* (New York: McGraw-Hill, 1967), incorporated nonmanufacturing technologies into this relationship by indicating that technology affects organization by affecting the kind of *interdependence* it poses for the organization, i.e., pooled, sequential, or reciprocal.

6. A long line of research shows how and why environmental uncertainty has implications for organization design. See Tom Burns and G. M. Stalker, *The Management of Innovation* (London: Tavistock, 1961); Paul R. Lawrence and Jay W. Lorsch, *Organization and Environment* (Boston: Division of Research, Graduate School of Business Administration, Harvard University, 1967); Jay R. Galbraith, *Designing Complex Organizations* (Reading, Mass.: Addison-Wesley Publishing, 1973); Paul R. Lawrence and David Dyer, *Renewing American Industry* (New York: Free Press, 1983).

7. Another long line of research demonstrates the important impact of environment resource scarcity on organizations. See James G. March and Herbert A. Simon, *Organizations* (New York: John Wiley & Sons, 1958); James D. Thompson, *Organizations in Action* (New York: McGraw-Hill, 1967); Jeffrey Pfeffer and Gerald R. Salancik, *The External Control of Organizations* (New York: Harper & Row, 1978); Paul R. Lawrence and David Dyer, *Renewing American Industry* (New York: Free Press, 1983).

8. See K. R. Andrews, *The Concept of Corporate Strategy* (Homewood, Ill.: Dow Jones-Irwin, 1971); C. R. Christensen, K. R. Andrews, and J. L. Bower, *Business Policy: Text and Cases* (Homewood,

Ill.: Richard D. Irwin, 1977); Michael E. Porter, *Competitive Strategy: Techniques for Analyzing Industries and Competitors* (New York: Free Press, 1980).

9. Jay W. Lorsch and John J. Morse, *Organizations and Their Members* (New York: Harper & Row, 1974), demonstrate the validity and importance of this three-way fit. See also Kotter, Schlesinger, and Sathe, *Organization*.

10. See Burns and Stalker, *The Management of Innovation* (London: Tavistock, 1961), Chapter 7.

11. Karl Weick, *The Social Psychology of Organizing*, 2d ed. (Reading, Mass.: Addison-Wesley Publishing, 1979), p. 135; Robin Hogarth, *Judgment and Choice* (New York, John Wiley & Sons, 1980), p. 6.

12. Burns and Stalker, *The Management of Innovation*, found that firms were unable to adapt a more flexible organization needed to cope with increasing rates of environmental change because of resistance from the firm's political and social systems (see Chapter 7). Eric Tist and K. W. Bamforth, "Some Social and Psychological Consequences of the Long Wall Method of Coal-Getting," *Human Relations*, 4 (1951), pp. 3–38, was an early demonstration of how changes in the task can inadvertently disrupt the social system, causing serious difficulties. This work led to the notion of a sociotechnical system, calling for the joint assessment of the task/technical and the social system when undertaking organizational changes. Left out was explicit consideration of the effects of the political system, which the later work by Burns and Stalker took into account.

13. The problems created by this lack of a complete merging of individual and organizational interest in industrial societies was highlighted by Elton Mayo, *The Social Problems of an Industrial Civilization* (Cambridge, Mass.: Harvard University Press, 1947). Mayo advocated the development of small, cohesive work groups within organizations to address this problem, arguing that a complete merging of individual organizational interests was impossible. Chris Argyris, *Integrating the Individual and the Organization* (New York: John Wiley & Sons, 1964), makes the case for viewing the management of this tension as a challenge, one that could lead to both individual and organizational development.

14. See Robert H. Hayes and William J. Abernathy, "Managing Our Way to Economic Decline," *Harvard Business Review*, July–August 1980.

15. This is one of the reasons we have conceptualized important shared assumptions as culture and separated them from actual organizational behavior patterns, as pointed out in Chapter 1. Also illustrated is the advantage of separating culture from systems. These two organizational characteristics can affect each other but can also independently affect actual behavior patterns. This distinction between culture and systems is equivalent to the distinction between culture and social structure in anthropology. See Marc J. Swartz and David K. Jordan, *Culture: The Anthropological Perspective* (New York: John Wiley & Sons, 1980), Chapters 2 and 3.

16. The concept of an individual's agenda, i.e., personal plans for what one is trying to achieve on the job, was developed by John Kotter and Paul Lawrence, *Mayors in Action* (New York: John Wiley & Sons, 1974). The concept of the organization's agenda being suggested here is a mirror image of an individual's own agenda—it is the agenda that *others* in the organization have in mind for the individual.

17. The psychological contract is an implicit contract between an individual and the organization that specifies what each expects to give and receive from the other in the relationship (see John Kotter, "The Psychological Contract: Managing the Joining-Up Process," *California Management Review*, 1973, pp. 91–99). Organizational and personal agendas are more encompassing in that they include the *unspeakables* (issues that are awkward, inappropriate, or illegal to raise, such as "Can this individual be trusted?" or "Is he or she loyal to the organization?"), the *unknowables* (issues that cannot be resolved in advance, such as "Will this person fit into our culture over time?"), as well as *subconscious* expectations, which only become apparent when the individual does not behave or perform in a manner that was expected of him or her by others without their being consciously aware of it. See note 18 below.

18. In their study, *Mayors in Action*, Kotter and Lawrence found that few mayors had an explicit or proactive agenda—that is, a clear view of what they wanted to achieve in their job and career and the strategy and tactics to use in achieving these aims. Building on this work, Rosemary Stewart ("Managerial Agendas—Reactive or Proactive," *Organizational Dynamics*, Autumn 1979, pp. 34–47) also found that few managers seemed to have explicit, proactive agendas. However, Stewart discovered that when queried by a small group of other managers, individuals were able to come up with much more explicit agenda statements than they could come up with alone. It is apparently easier to discover the agenda of another individual than to recognize one's own agenda, a finding that *strongly suggests that agendas may be partly or largely subconsciously held* (see note 17). Both the Kotter and Lawrence study and the Stewart study demonstrate that individuals in similar jobs may have very different personal agendas. The concept of an organization's agenda is the mirror image of one's personal agenda—it refers to the conscious and subconscious expectations that relevant others (especially organizational leaders) have of the individual.

19. The idea that dissatisfaction is *necessary* for personal and organizational change is well articulated by Michael Beer, *Organization Change and Development* (Santa Monica, Calif.: Goodyear Publishing, 1980). See, especially, the model of change presented on p. 46. The notion that a *moderate* level of stress is conducive to individual change, in particular creativity, is developed by Michael B. McCaskey, *The Executive Challenge* (Marshfield, Mass.: Pitman, 1982).

Notes for Chapter 4

1. These reasons correspond to the twin needs for internal integration and external adaptation discussed by Edgar H. Schein in "Role of the Founder in Creating Organizational Culture" (Reading 1–1 in this book). See also F. J. Roethlisberger and William J. Dickson, *Management and the Worker* (Cambridge, Mass.: Harvard University Press, 1939), p. 523. Robert F. Bales, *Interaction Process Analysis* (Chicago: University of Chicago Press, 1950) has argued that the organization tends to swing back and forth between two theoretical poles: optimum adaptation to the outer situation at the cost of internal malintegration or optimum internal integration at the cost of maladaptation to the external situation (p. 157).

2. This is so because the advocacy of alternate beliefs and values threaten the common human "need to be correct" about one's behavior and opinions. See Charles A. Kiesler and Sara B. Kiesler, *Conformity* (Reading, Mass.: Addison-Wesley Publishing, 1969), p. 44.

3. The basic argument derives from an understanding of an individual's inducements and contributions to the organization, see Chester I. Barnard, *The Functions of the Executive* (Cambridge, Mass.: Harvard University Press, 1938); Herbert A. Simon, *Administrative Behavior* (New York: Free Press, 1976), Chapter 6; and the literature on the psychological contract, Edgar H. Schein, *Career Dynamics: Matching the Individual and the Organization* (Reading: Mass.: Addison-Wesley Publishing, 1978), Chapter 9.

4. See Edgar H. Schein, "Organizational Socialization and the Profession of Management," *Industrial Management Review,* Winter 1968, pp. 3–10. One approach is for the individual to accept only the most central organizational beliefs and values. Such "creative individualism," as Schein calls it, may ultimately be in the best interest of the individual and the organization. This option and others available for managing one's misfit with the organization are further discussed in Chapters 7 and 8.

5. There is always the danger that one is simply rationalizing past actions, a possibility that must be discounted for and guarded against, as discussed in Chapter 5.

6. John Kotter, Victor Faux, and Charles McArthur, *Self-Assessment and Career Development* (Englewood Cliffs, N.J.: Prentice-Hall, 1978). Other sources are R. N. Bolles, *What Color Is Your Parachute?* (Berkeley, Calif.: Ten Speed Press, 1972); G. A. Ford and G. L. Lippitt, *A Life Planning Workbook* (Fairfax, Va.: NTL Learning Resources, 1972); and H. A. Shepard and J. A. Hawley, *Life Planning: Personal and Organizational* (Washington, D.C.: National Training and Development Service, 1974).

7. This typology is based on the work of Milton Rokeach, *Beliefs, Attitudes, and Values* (San Francisco: Jossey-Bass, 1968). See, especially, Chapter 1 and Appendix 1–1 of his book. Rokeach's Type A and Type B beliefs have been collapsed into one category—*sensory beliefs;* the Type C beliefs (concerning which authorities to trust) and Type D beliefs (derived from authorities one believes in) have been combined under the category *authority beliefs.* Type E in Rokeach's scheme (unconsequential beliefs) is not included here, to keep the discussion focused on the important beliefs. The classification adopted here closely parallels that proposed by Daryl Bem, *Beliefs, Attitudes, and Human Affairs* (Monterey, Calif.: Brooks/Cole Publishing, 1970), who also draws on Rokeach's work. Bem's two principal primitive beliefs correspond to the sensory and authority beliefs mentioned here, and his higher-order beliefs are what are here referred to as derived beliefs.

8. Rokeach, *Beliefs, Attitudes, and Values,* see especially pp. 5–12.

9. Ibid., p. 182; Bem, *Beliefs, Attitudes, and Human Affairs,* refers to such consistency as "psycho-logic" (p. 13).

10. The classic study of a group of doomsday prophets by Leon Festinger, H. W. Riecken, and S. Schacter, *When Prophecy Fails* (Minneapolis: The University of Minnesota Press, 1956) is a somewhat unusual but provocative illustration of this phenomenon. The passing of the doomsday was clear-cut evidence for the doomsdayers that their prophecy was wrong, but rationalization and

self-justification allowed them to emerge not only unshaken, but even more convinced about the truth of their beliefs.

11. See Rokeach, *Beliefs, Attitudes, and Values,* Chapter 7; and Bem, *Beliefs, Attitudes, and Human Affairs,* pp. 6–7.

12. Clyde Kluckhohn, "Values and Value Orientations in the Theory of Action," in *Toward a General Theory of Action,* ed. T. Parsons and E. A. Shils (Cambridge, Mass.: Harvard University Press, 1951).

13. Rokeach, *Beliefs, Attitudes, and Values,* p. 161.

14. Robert N. McMurry, "Conflicts in Human Values," *Harvard Business Review,* May–June 1963, pp. 131–32.

15. Charles L. Hughes and Vincent S. Flowers, *Value System Analysis Theory and Management Application* (Dallas, Tex.: Center for Value Research, 1978) is one such test covering the following values for working: existential, sociocentric, manipulative, conformist, egocentric, and tribalistic. Charles Handy, in *Gods of Management* (London: Souvenir, 1978, pp. 83–88), offers another test based on a typology of cultures developed by Roger Harrison, "Understanding Your Organization's Character," *Harvard Business Review,* May–June 1972, pp. 119–28. The Harrison/Handy classification is: club/power orientation, role orientation, task orientation, and person/existential orientation. See the recommended supplementary reading (numbers 1 and 2) at the back of the book.

16. Eduard Spranger, *Types of Men,* trans. P. Pigors (Halle, Germany: Niemeyer, 1928). Spranger does *not* imply that a person belongs exclusively to one or another of the six basic types. Rather, his descriptions are entirely in terms of ideal types. The test developed to measure the *relative* strength of these values for an individual is G. W. Allport, P. E. Vernon, and G. Lindzey, *Manual for the Study of Values* (Boston: Houghten Mifflin, 1970). The test was originally developed by Allport and Vernon in 1931, and the revised version was first published by Allport, Vernon, and Lindzey in 1951. William D. Guth and Renato Tagiuri, "Personal Values and Corporate Strategies," *Harvard Business Review,* September–October 1965, report results obtained for senior executives on the Spranger value classification scheme using the Allport, Vernon, Lindzey test. The article also contains an excellent discussion of the importance of values for managers.

17. In addition to technical problems having to do with reliability (does the test produce consistent results?) and validity (does the test measure what it is supposed to measure?), is the more basic problem that such tests only reveal what one *thinks* one believes, values, does, or would do. What one *espouses* about these and other matters may or may not be closely related to one's *actual* position as revealed by the choices one in fact makes and the way in which one actually behaves. Further, one may not even be conscious of such discrepancies between espoused and actual values, a point made by Chris Argyris and Donald Schon, *Theory in Practice* (San Francisco: Jossey-Bass, 1974).

18. John Kotter, Victor Faux, and Charles McArthur, *Self-Assessment and Career Development* (Englewood Cliffs, N.J.: Prentice-Hall, 1978), and other sources listed in note 6.

19. John Wanous, *Organizational Entry* (Reading, Mass.: Addison-Wesley Publishing, 1980) provides a summary discussion of the assessment center approach and its limitations (pp. 143–59).

20. Rosemary Stewart, "Managerial Agendas: Proactive or Reactive," *Organizational Dynamics,* Autumn 1979, p. 35.

21. Julian B. Rotter, "Generalized expectances for internal versus external control of reinforcements," *Psychological Monographs* 80, no. 1 (1966); Richard de Charms, *Personal Causation* (New York: Academic Press, 1968); Richard de Charms, "Origins, Pawns, and Educational Practice," in *Psychology and the Educational Process,* ed. G. S. Lesson (Glenview, Ill.: Scott, Foresman, 1969).

22. Constructive introspection is particularly difficult in connection with experiences that are personally threatening or painful because one's defense mechanisms are geared to deal with these situations realistically and rationally only to the extent possible, and illogically and irrationally to the extent necessary (see Rokeach, *Beliefs, Attitudes, and Values,* pp. 9, 164, and 182). Pain, like body fever, should be viewed as a symptom that indicates something is wrong and that additional investigation is needed. With the frame of mind that says, "Pain is my friend, pain is invitation to learning," constructive introspection becomes possible. Abraham Zaleznik, "Management of Disappointment," *Harvard Business Review,* November–December 1967, argues that with such introspection it is possible for one's disappointments to become occasions for accelerated personal growth and mark the commencement of truly outstanding performance.

23. Harry Levinson, *Organizational Diagnosis* (Cambridge, Mass.: Harvard University Press, 1972). Appendix A of Levinson's book (pp. 520–26) contains a comprehensive list of questions for use by consultants undertaking an organizational diagnosis and is a recommended supplementary

reading (number 5). Because the skill, perspective, and relationship of a consultant with an organization are different than those of a person contemplating joining the organization, the latter cannot always ask questions like the former can. Levinson's list, therefore, should not be used by prospective employees for interviewing during recruiting without taking this underlying difference into account. The list does provide good food for thought, however.

24. This question looks at where *attention* is focused in the organization. As argued by Herbert Simon, "Applying Information Processing Technology to Organization Design," *Public Administration Review* 33 (1973), pp. 268–78, modern information processing systems feed today's organizations with an increasingly rich soup of information; in this environment, it is not information per se but *attention* that is the scarce resource. Much can be learned about the functioning of an organization by understanding how this critical resource is allocated.

25. The discussion of homosocial reproduction in the next chapter elaborates on this phenomenon.

26. Jeffrey Pfeffer, *Power in Organizations* (Marshfield, Mass.: Pitman, 1981), p. 50, and Chapter 5 of Pfeffer's book contain a good discussion of why power is used "unobtrusively."

27. John P. Kotter, *Power in Management* (New York: AMACOM, 1979); Pfeffer, *Power in Organizations;* Jeffrey Pfeffer and Gerald R. Salancik, *The External Control of Organizations* (New York: Harper & Row, 1978).

28. Florence R. Kluckholm and Fred L. Strodtbeck, *Variations in Value Orientations* (Evanston, Ill.: Row, Peterson, 1961) indicate that all human groups have to make basic assumptions about each of the following: human nature, "man"-nature relationships, time, activity, and "man-man" relationships (p. 11). Edgar H. Schein, "SMR Forum: Does Japanese Management Style Have a Message for American Managers?" *Sloan Management Review,* Fall 1981, proposes three interconnected levels of culture with such basic, taken-for-granted, typically unconscious assumptions composing the core of culture (pp. 64–67). Schein further elaborates on this model in "Organizational Culture: A Dynamic Model," Working Paper No. 1412–83, Massachusetts Institute of Technology, February 1983, which was adapted for use in Chapter 1.

29. Louis R. Pondy, Peter J. Frost, Gareth Morgan, and Thomas C. Dandridge, eds., *Organizational Symbolism* (Greenwich, Conn.: JAI Press, 1982) contains several papers, particularly in Chapter 3, that explain how culture is propagated and transmitted via language, stories, folklore, sagas, myths, ceremonies, rituals, slogans, and other symbolic means.

30. L. W. Porter and R. M. Steers, "Organizational, Work, and Personal Factors in Employee Turnover and Absenteeism," *Psychological Bulletin* 80 (1973), pp. 157–76.

31. John J. Gabarro and John P. Kotter, "Managing Your Boss," *Harvard Business Review,* January–February 1980, present thoughtful suggestions for better managing this key relationship.

32. John J. Gabarro, "Socialization at the Top—How CEOs and Subordinates Evolve Interpersonal Contracts," *Organizational Dynamics,* Winter 1979, describes the process by which expectations, influence, and trust develop in new boss-subordinate relationships. One's *first* boss in an organization is especially crucial because one's experiences during the *first* year in the organization have a significant impact on later performance. See D. W. Bray, R. J. Campbell, and D. L. Grant, *Formative Years in Business* (New York: John Wiley & Sons, 1974).

33. John P. Kotter, "Power, Dependence, and Effective Management," *Harvard Business Review,* July–August 1977, provides a discussion of power dynamics and influence tactics.

34. A discussion of the dynamics of stereotyping is included in Chapter 8.

35. If one has a frame of mind built on the assumption that one will invariably be stereotyped, one can always find the "facts" to support this, partly by behaving in a way that produces the facts one is looking for. Those who have experienced the trauma of severe stereotyping are understandably prone to do this, but that does not diminish its self-destructive potential.

Notes for Chapter 5

1. For a discussion of observation techniques, and the drawing of inferences from them, see James P. Spradley, *Participant Observation* (New York: Holt, Rinehart and Winston, 1980); and Michael B. McCaskey, "The Hidden Messages Managers Send," *Harvard Business Review,* November–December 1979. An excellent discussion relevant to the reading of people's use of time, space, things, body language, and words is contained in the first three chapters of Anthony G. Athos and John J. Gabarro, *Interpersonal Behavior* (Englewood Cliffs, N.J.: Prentice-Hall, 1978).

2. Several authors have advocated *realistic recruitment* and *realistic job previews* for their salutary effects on employee turnover, satisfaction, and effectiveness. The former attempts to provide the recruit with all pertinent information without distortion, the latter attempts to set employee

expectations closer to reality, thereby "vaccinating" the individual against later disappointment and disillusionment. Much of the earlier work looks at the problem primarily from the organization's perspective. See J. Weitz, "Job Expectancy and Survival," *Journal of Applied Psychology* 40 (1957), pp. 346–61; W. J. McGuire, "Inducing Resistance to Penetration," in *Advances in Experimental Social Psychology*, Vol. 3, ed. L. Berkowitz (New York: Academic Press, 1974). More recent work includes the individual's perspective as well. See Edgar H. Schein, *Career Dynamics* (Reading, Mass.: Addison-Wesley Publishing, 1978); and John Wanous, *Organizational Entry* (Reading, Mass.: Addison-Wesley Publishing, 1980.)

3. Schein, *Career Dynamics*, contains an excellent elaboration of these dynamics and dilemmas of the period prior to entry (see Chapter 7 of his book).

4. Roy J. Lewicki, "Organizational Seduction: Building Commitment to Organizations," *Organizational Dynamics*, Autumn 1981. Lewicki does not explicitly emphasize the organization's intent to conceal damaging information from the individual while attempting to attract him or her as the test of seduction. The position taken here is that, without such an explicit test, the term *organizational seduction* does not take on the tone of impropriety that usefully distinguishes it from other more common forms of enticement, such as those mentioned in the text under "Organizational Oversell."

5. See Gerald R. Salancik, "Commitment Is Too Easy," *Organizational Dynamics*, Summer 1977, pp. 62–80.

6. I am indebted to Jeffrey Pfeffer of Stanford University for suggesting this label, in lieu of "Homosexual Reproduction," which is the original phrase coined by Wilbert Moore, *The Conduct of the Corporation* (New York: Random House, 1962); see Rosabeth Moss Kanter, *Men and Women of the Corporation* (New York: Basic Books, 1977), p. 48.

7. Wanous, *Organizational Entry*, reports research that indicates judgments of interviewers may be affected by the degree of similarity between interviewer and job candidate (p. 142). Evidence has been found of "inbreeding": Vijay Sathe, *Controller Involvement in Management* (Englewood Cliffs, N.J.: Prentice-Hall, 1982). Companies whose CEO had a financial background had a significantly higher proportion of top executives also with financial backgrounds than did other companies. The work of D. D. Bowen, "An Evaluation of Motivational Similarity in Work Groups" (Ph.D. diss. Yale University, 1971) indicates the presence of a personality type in most organizations.

8. See Kanter, *Men and Women of the Corporation*, pp. 48–54.

9. Limitations in human information processing capacity, and the need to conserve mental effort account for this. See Robin Hogarth, *Judgment and Choice* (New York: John Wiley & Sons, 1980), p. 4.

10. B. M. Springbelt, "Factors Affecting the Final Decision in the Employment Interview," *Canadian Journal of Psychology* 12 (1958), pp. 13–22.

11. Edward E. Lawler III and John Grant Rhode, *Information and Control in Organizations* (Santa Monica, Calif.: Goodyear Publishing, 1976), particularly p. 1 and Chapter 6 contain good illustrations and a discussion of misuse of measurement systems.

12. Schein, *Career Dynamics*, p. 85.

13. Peer O. Soelberg, "Unprogrammed Decision Making," *Industrial Management Review* 8 (1967), pp. 19–29.

14. Cognitive dissonance theory predicts that an individual will gather information *after* the decision is made in order to justify it, to reduce postdecision "dissonance." See Leon Festinger, *A Theory of Cognitive Dissonance*, (Evanston, Ill.: Row, Peterson, 1957).

15. See Charles A. O'Reilly III and David F. Caldwell, "The Commitment and Job Tenure of New Employees: Some Evidence of Postdecisional Justification," *Administrative Science Quarterly* 26, no. 4 (1981) pp. 597–616.

16. I. L. Janis and L. Mann, *Decision Making: A Psychological Analysis of Conflict, Choice, and Commitment* (New York: Free Press, 1977); I. L. Janis and D. Wheeler, "Thinking Clearly about Career Choices," *Psychology Today*, May 1978.

Notes for Chapter 6

1. A comprehensive review of these studies is provided by John Van Maanen, "Breaking In: Socialization to Work," in *Handbook of Work, Organization and Society*, ed. Robert Dubin (Skokie, Ill.: Rand McNally, 1976), pp. 78–80 and 117.

2. Van Maanen, "Breaking In," p. 78.

3. L. M. Lyman and M. B. Scott, *A Sociology of the Absurd* (New York: Meredith, 1970). From this perspective, socialization may be understood as equivalent to the coping strategies developed by stage neophytes, such as rehearsals when they follow the lines strictly.

4. The concept of socialization, which holds a prominent place in cultural anthropology and sociology, refers to the process by which an individual learns the beliefs, values, attitudes, skills, and behaviors needed to become an accepted member of a particular society. The concept of *organizational* socialization is used to refer to the analogous process in organizations. For a general discussion of socialization, see I. Child, "Socialization," in *Handbook of Social Psychology*, ed. G. Lindzey (Reading, Mass.: Addison-Wesley Publishing, 1954); and Van Maanen, "Breaking In." The importance of socialization, to both the individual and the organization, cannot be underestimated. Edgar H. Schein has put it succinctly:

> [T]he process is so ubiquitous and we go through it so often during our total career that it is all too easy to overlook it. Yet it is a process which can make or break a career, and which can make or break organizational systems of manpower planning. The speed and effectiveness of socialization determine employee loyalty, commitment, productivity and turnover. The basic stability and effectiveness of organizations therefore depends upon their ability to socialize new members.

"Organizational Socialization and the Profession of Management," *Industrial Management Review* 9, no. 2 (1968), p. 2.

5. Robert A. LeVine, *Culture, Behavior, and Personality* (Hawthorne, N.Y.: Aldine Publishing, 1973) points out that the term *enculturation* has at times been used interchangeably with the term *socialization* (p. 62). It may be used to refer to the process of learning the culture. Socialization is a broader concept that includes, in addition to enculturation, the process of learning the appropriate behaviors and skills needed to become an accepted member of the community. This conceptualization is consistent with the view of socialization as composed of three distinct aspects—(1) learning appropriate role behaviors, (2) work skills and abilities, and (3) norms and values—as proposed by Daniel Feldman, "The Multiple Socialization of Organization Members," *The Academy of Management Review* 6, no. 2 (1981), p. 309.

6. Although the phases or stages overlap and cannot be sharply delineated, several authors have concluded there are these three more or less distinct socialization periods. John Wanous, *Organizational Entry* (Reading, Mass.: Addison-Wesley Publishing, 1980) presents a good summary of this work in Chapter 6 of his book.

7. Meryl Louis, "Surprise and Sense Making: What Newcomers Experience in Entering Unfamiliar Organizational Settings," *Administrative Science Quarterly*, June 1980, pp. 226–51.

8. This staged conceptualization of the process of acquiring cultural knowledge is proposed by Caren Siehl and Joanne Martin, "Learning Organizational Culture," Working Paper, Stanford Graduate School of Business, September 1981.

9. This observation is based on the cases in this book, and other cases developed by the author.

10. E. C. Hughes, *Men and Their Work* (New York: Free Press, 1958).

11. "Total institutions" have close to absolute control over their members; see Erving Goffman, *Asylums* (Garden City, N.Y.: Doubleday Publishing, 1961). In such institutions (e.g., mental hospitals, prisons, religious cults) newcomers are typically socialized by harsh methods and experience more intense shocks during the process. See A. Shiloh, "Sanctuary or Prison—Responses to Life in a Mental Hospital," in *Total Institutions*, ed. S. E. Wallace (Hawthorne, N.Y.: Aldine Publishing, 1971); and S. Dornbush, "The Military Academy as an Assimilating Institution," *Social Forces* 33 (1955), pp. 316–21.

12. Louis, "Surprise and Sense Making," pp. 226–51.

13. Abraham Korman, "Task Success, Task Popularity and Self-Esteem as Influences on Task Liking," *Journal of Applied Psychology* 52 (1968), pp. 61–73.

14. John P. Kotter, *The General Managers* (New York: Free Press, 1982), p. 47.

15. Research indicates that meaningful and challenging first assignments are generally a very effective method of breaking in the newcomer. Such meaningful early testing can also pave the way for accelerated individual development and contribution to the organization. See Edgar H. Schein, *Career Dynamics* (Reading, Mass.: Addison-Wesley Publishing, 1978).

16. Schein, *Career Dynamics*, p. 106.

17. Ibid., p. 95.

18. Cases in this book bear this out.

19. Decisions should not be made on the basis of "sunk costs," of course, but rather on the basis of future streams of costs and benefits associated with various courses of action. The newcomer is at an advantage because one's *organization-specific* knowledge, skill, and status, which generally rise the longer one stays in an organization, would not be fully transportable if one were to leave.

Notes for Chapter 7

1. When the expectations and aspirations of the groups in question are in conflict, they are brought into fuller awareness because one is forced to select or reconcile them. In other cases, the consequence may be a nonconscious ideology—a set of attitudes, beliefs, and values that one accepts implicitly but that remain outside one's awareness. Such ideology has a subtle but powerful influence on the individual because it is difficult to challenge, and it remains unrecognized. See Sandra L. Bem and Daryl J. Bem, "Case Study of a Nonconscious Ideology: Training the Woman to Know Her Place," in *Beliefs, Attitudes, and Human Affairs,* Daryl J. Bem (Monterey, Calif.: Brooks/Cole Publishing, 1970), pp. 89–99.

2. A. Strauss, "Some Neglected Properties of Status Passage," in *Institutions and the Person,* ed. H. S. Becker, G. Geer, D. Reisman, and R. S. Weiss (Hawthorne, N.Y.: Aldine Publishing, 1968).

3. Research indicates that substantive individual change can occur in organizations within the context of "affective" relationships, i.e., those characterized by personal rapport and positive feelings. Ibid.

4. Edgar H. Schein, *Career Dynamics* (Reading, Mass.: Addison-Wesley Publishing, 1978), Chapter 9.

5. John Van Maanen, "Breaking In: Socialization to Work," in *Handbook of Work, Organization, and Society,* ed. Robert Dubin (Skokie, Ill.: Rand McNally, 1976), p. 111.

6. Robert Dubin, "Deviant Behavior and Social Structure: Continuities in Social Theory," *American Sociological Review* 24 (1959), pp. 332–44.

7. Edgar H. Schein, "Organizational Socialization and the Profession of Management," *Industrial Management Review* 9, no. 2 (1968), p. 11; Lyman W. Porter, Edward E. Lawler, and J. Richard Hackman, *Behavior in Organizations* (New York: McGraw-Hill, 1975), use the term *individualization* (called *personalization* by others) to refer to the process by which the individual attempts to put his or her distinctive stamp on the organization. Without this, it is argued, the organization is likely to get into a rut and be unable to renew itself. Overconformity has been referred to as "regrettable socialization" by William H. White, Jr., *The Organization Man* (New York: Simon & Schuster, 1956).

8. Edgar H. Schein, "Personnel Change through Interpersonal Relationships," in *Interpersonal Relationships,* ed. W. G. Bennis, D. E. Berlew, E. H. Schein, and F. L. Steele (Homewood, Ill.: Dorsey Press, 1973).

9. As Meryl Louis points out, the research on organizational socialization has focused on the "joining up" process and virtually ignored the "leave taking" process. There are indications from related literature that the latter may significantly influence the former. See Meryl Reis Louis, "Surprise and Sense Making: What Newcomers Experience in Entering Unfamiliar Organizational Settings," *Administrative Science Quarterly,* June 1980, p. 231.

10. Schein, *Career Dynamics,* Chapter 9.

Notes for Chapter 8

1. The literature on social structure is sociology and anthropology uses the concept of status to denote a social category and all the expectations assigned to those in that category; husband and wife are each a status in the social organization of the family. See Robert K. Merton *Social Theory and Social Structure,* 1968 Enlarged ed. (New York: Free Press, 1968); Marc J. Swartz and David K. Jordan, *Culture: The Anthropological Perspective* (New York: John Wiley & Sons, 1980). The definition adopted here is from the tradition in social psychology that views status as a reflection of an individual's importance and contribution to the group. See Michael A. Olmstead and A. Paul Hare, *The Small Group,* 2d ed. (New York: Random House, 1978); Robert F. Bales, *Interaction Process Analyses* (Chicago: University of Chicago Press, 1950).

2. This representation of status is consistent with the work of Robert F. Bales, *Interaction Process Analysis:* "Every individual . . . who is concerned with the reaching of goals will be impelled to

evaluate other persons in terms of how they relate to the achievement of these goals and in terms of whether their activity tends to maintain or destroy the norms upon which emotional safety depends . . . . If and when a basic consensus as to the proper status order of persons is established in the group, the group may be said to be stratified" (p. 77). Relating to the concepts used here, status depends on the person's: *(a)* achievement of goals (credibility) and *(b)* whether his or her activities maintain or destroy norms (acceptance). This representation of status is also consistent with the work of E. P. Hollander, "Conformity, Status, and Idiosyncracy Credit," *Psychological Review* 65, no. 2 (1958), pp. 117–27: "[S]tatus has special value as a kind of middle ground in relating the individual's to the group. It exists in the first place as a result of someone's perceptual field, for without reference to a perceiver, status has no intrinsic value or meaning in itself . . . [it] represents an accumulation of positively disposed impressions residing in the perceptions of relevant others; it is defined operationally in terms of the degree to which an individual may deviate from the common expectancies of the group" (p. 120). Relating to the concepts used here, both credibility and acceptance: *(a)* rest on perceptions of relevant others, *(b)* capture "positively disposed impressions," and *(c)* together affect one's capacity to deviate from the culture.

3. This section on understanding working relationships and the next one on the development of new working relationships draw heavily on the work of John J. Gabarro. See his two articles: "The Development of Trust, Influence, and Expectations," in *Interpersonal Behavior* by Anthony G. Athos and John J. Gabarro (Englewood Cliffs, N.J.: Prentice-Hall, 1978), pp. 290–303; and "Socialization at the Top—How CEOs and Subordinates Evolve Interpersonal Contacts," *Organizational Dynamics,* Winter 1979, pp. 3–23.

4. John Gabarro uses the term *influence* rather than *power.* The two terms are closely interrelated, but the following terminology will be adopted here. Power is the capacity or potential to affect the behavior and thinking of others. Influence is the process of using power to alter the behavior and thinking of others. More will be said about power and influence in Chapter 9 under the section on political pressures.

5. M. Deutsch, "Cooperation and Trust: Some Theoretical Notes," in *Nebraska Symposium on Motivation,* ed. R. Jones (Lincoln, Neb.: University of Nebraska Press, 1962), pp. 275–319.

6. Gabarro, "The Development of Trust," pp. 295–98. Following Gabarro's other article on the subject, the basis of trust called judgment has been dropped as a separate item because, as he points out, "judgment transcends the other bases of trust" (p. 297). The bases of trust that rest on competence are also bases of power (expertise, broadly defined), but they are included here because Gabarro's research indicates that, in the business setting at least, managers think of both bases of character *and* competence when they speak of trust.

7. The list is based on the works of Gabarro ("Socialization at the Top" and "The Development of Trust") as well as John P. Kotter, "Power, Dependence, and Effective Management," *Harvard Business Review,* July–August, 1977, pp. 125–36.

8. This simplified representation has been derived from Gabbaro, "The Development of Trust"; and Richard E. Walton, *Social and Psychological Aspects of Verification, Inspection, and International Assurance* (West Lafayette, Ind.: Purdue University Press, 1968). As Gabarro's research discovered, the concept of *credibility* as used by managers is broader and more holistic than *expertise,* which is a personal base of power. Credibility also encompasses trustworthiness (see Gabarro's footnote 12 on page 300). Walton's review and synthesis of the literature indicates that assurance, a concept in the analysis of international relations that is analogous to the concept of credibility in the context of interpersonal relationships, is a multiplicative function of trust and power: High power or high trust alone is insufficient to produce high credibility, and at least a moderate level of the other must also be present.

9. Gabarro, "The Development of Trust."

10. This observation is based on cases in this book, and other cases developed by the author.

11. Ibid. *Successive* gains in credibility appear to take place more slowly than *successive* losses. For instance, five points may be lost the first time a critical incident is poorly managed by the newcomer, 15 points may be lost in the next one, 50 in the third, and so on.

12. T. Caplow, *Principles of Organization* (New York: Harcourt Brace Jovanovich, 1964).

13. Edgar H. Schein, "Personal Change through Interpersonal Relationships," in *Interpersonal Relationships,* ed. W. G. Bennis, D. E. Berlow, E. H. Schein, and F. L. Steele (Homewood, Ill.: Dorsey Press, 1973).

14. See Renato Tagiuri, "Person Perception," in *Handbook of Social Psychology,* ed. G. Lindzey (Reading, Mass.: Addison-Wesley Publishing, 1969).

15. See ibid. and Renato Tagiuri, "Movement as a Cue in Person Perception," in *Perspectives in Personality Research,* ed. H. P. David and J. C. Brengelman (New York: Springer Publishing, 1960).

16. Rosabeth Moss Kanter, *Men and Women of the Corporation* (New York: Basic Books, 1977). See Chapter 8 of her book, "Numbers: Minorities and Majorities," which is included as a recommended supplementary reading (number 9). See also *A Tale of O: On Being Different,* available on videotape or slidetape from Goodmeasure, Inc., Cambridge, Massachusetts.

17. Kanter uses the term *assimilation* to describe the stereotyping tendency; ibid., pp. 210–11. I have opted for *stereotyping* instead, which seems to be a better descriptor.

18. This response is not mentioned by Kanter; it is based on a token strategy that was observed in the cases in this book.

19. See Elliot Aronson, *The Social Animal,* 2d ed. (San Francisco: W. H. Freeman, 1976), p. 175.

20. Some prejudice may be a reflection of the individual's own insecurities. The highly prejudiced individual may deny or repress his or her own weaknesses by projecting them onto the objects of the prejudice. See Daryl J. Bem, *Beliefs, Attitudes, and Human Affairs* (Monterey, Calif.: Brooks/Cole Publishing, 1970), Chapter 3.

Notes for Chapter 9

1. This view of authority and the concept of the zone of indifference were proposed by Chester I. Barnard, *The Functions of the Executive* (Cambridge, Mass.: Harvard University Press, 1938), p. 167. See also Herbert A. Simon, *Administrative Behavior,* New York: Free Press, 1976. Although controversial and subject to the limitations of laboratory methods, the classic Milgram experiments suggested just how wide the zone of indifference can be: Stanley Milgram, "Behavioral Study of Obedience," *Journal of Abnormal and Social Psychology* 67 (1963), pp. 371–78; and "Some Conditions of Obedience and Disobedience to Authority," *Human Relations* 18 (1965), pp. 57–76.

2. Reinhard Bendix, *Work and Authority in Industry* (New York: John Wiley & Sons, 1956) explores how managerial ideology determines the bases for the exercise of authority in the industrial work setting.

3. Much of the line-staff conflict stems from the fact that the staff must work through the line to get ideas and suggestions implemented. The differences in backgrounds and orientations between those in line and staff positions also contribute to the problem. As organizations have grown larger and more complex, the number of staff positions has increased to cope with the increased demand for specialist knowledge and expertise, thus intensifying the difficulties.

  To ease these difficulties, several writers on organization have suggested that the staff be given formal authority in their areas of expertise. Such staff or functional authority permits the staff to issue instructions and directives but does not carry the right to discipline. Compliance must still be sought by going through the line, thus preserving the unity of command. See Vijay Sathe, *Controller Involvement in Management* (Englewood Cliffs, N.J.: Prentice-Hall, 1982), p. 14.

4. Some argue that the line-staff distinction is obsolete. Those taking this position have in mind the traditional definition of line roles as those responsible for the primary objectives of an enterprise and staff roles being those supporting the primary ones. The problem with such a definition is that it leads to futile debates over which roles are to be considered primary.

  The position taken here is: Both operating and staff roles are important, or they would not exist; and distinctions based on degree of importance serve no useful purpose. Both operating and staff roles have authority in their areas of activity. The distinction here is based on the kind of behavior demanded of those performing these roles. Operating roles are concerned with the development, production, and sale of the business unit's products and services. Staff roles are concerned with assisting and/or monitoring the performance of these activities. So defined, staff roles can hardly be considered obsolete. A company of any size has several of them; in a large corporation there are literally hundreds of such positions. See Sathe, *Controller Involvement in Management,* pp. 151–52.

5. Research indicates that mechanistic organizations are more effective in a stable environment, and organic ones are more suitable for rapidly changing environment. Tom Burns and G. M. Stalker, *The Management of Innovation* (London: Tavistock, 1961).

6. It has been argued that managers in an organization must be insured against "bad luck" if risk taking is to be encouraged. But this creates a "moral hazard": It is so difficult to distinguish between bad decisions and bad luck that the insurance may unintentionally cover bad decisions too. See Kenneth J. Arrow, *Essays in the Theory of Risk-Bearing* (Chicago: Markham, 1971).

7. The philosopher and psychologist George Herbert Mead has cogently articulated the profound sense in which men and women are social creatures, taking not merely their surface characteristics but the very essence of their psyche from the social environment in which they live and grow. See Mead, *Mind, Self, and Society* (Chicago: University of Chicago Press, 1934).

8. The classic exposé on this theme is F. J. Roethlisberger and William J. Dickson, *Management and the Worker* (Cambridge: Harvard University Press, 1939). See, especially, Chapters 22 and 24.

9. Charles A. Kiesler and Sara B. Kiesler, *Conformity* (Reading, Mass.: Addison-Wesley Publishing, 1969), p. 42; Robert F. Bales, *Interaction Process Analysis* (Chicago: University of Chicago Press, 1950), p. 157.

10. The classic "autokinetic effect" experiments vividly demonstrated this phenomenon. M. Sherif. *The Social Psychology of Social Norms* (New York: Harper & Row, 1936).

11. See Kiesler and Kiesler, *Conformity,* pp. 29 and 44.

12. David McClelland, *The Achieving Society* (Princeton, N.J.: Van Nostrand Reinhold, 1961).

13. D. Byrne, "Interpersonal Attraction and Attitude Similarity," *Journal of Abnormal and Social Psychology* 62, pp. 713–15.

14. Experimental research has shown that people attempting to ingratiate themselves with others will voice opinions similar to those held by others and will agree with them (though not completely, lest it be too obvious). In general, persons with lower status attempting to get those of higher status to like them will agree on important issues and disagree on unimportant ones. When "ingratiating down," a higher-status person will agree with the lower status person on unimportant issues but not on the important ones (which would entail a threat of loss of status). Thus two people of different status each trying to get the other to like them will soon agree on most, if not all, issues. See E. E. Jones, *Ingratiation* (New York: Appleton-Century-Crofts, 1964).

15. Experimental research indicates that at first a deviant receives increased attention as the group attempts to persuade him or her to fall in line. If these attempts fail, the group begins to ignore the deviant. See Stanley Schacter, "Deviation, Rejection, and Communication," *Journal of Abnormal and Social Psychology* 46 (1951), pp. 190–207.

16. John P. Kotter, *Power in Management* (New York: AMACOM, 1979).

17. Jeffrey Pfeffer, *Power in Organizations* (Marshfield, Mass.: Pitman, 1981), p. 7.

18. It is primarily because of the *dependence* inherent in managerial jobs that power is necessarily an important facet of managerial life, as pointed out by John Kotter, "Power, Dependence, and Effective Management," *Harvard Business Review,* July–August 1979. Others who have argued the beneficial aspects of power and politics include Rollo May, *Power and Innocence* (New York: Dell, 1972); David C. McClelland, "The Two Faces of Power," *Journal of International Affairs* 24 (1970), pp. 29–47; Rosabeth Moss Kanter, "Power Failure in Management Circuits," *Harvard Business Review,* July–August 1979; and Pfeffer, *Power in Organizations.*

19. John P. Kotter, *Beyond Naivete and Cynicism,* draft manuscript, Harvard Business School, October 1982.

20. Kotter, "Power, Dependence, and Effective Management," p. 133.

21. Thomas V. Bonoma and Gerald Zaltman, *Psychology for Management* (Boston: Kent, 1981), p. 171.

22. Richard E. Walton and R. B. McKersie, *A Behavioral Theory of Labor Negotiations* (New York: McGraw-Hill, 1965), describe two basic forms of bargaining situations: (1) *distributive,* in which the situation is more or less zero sum and calls for a distribution of some scarce resource that generally requires a more competitive negotiation, and (2) *integrative,* which has significant nonzero-sum elements and calls for joint problem solving requiring more collaborative negotiations. The use of power in distributive bargaining may or may not be dysfunctional, but there is evidence that the use of raw power or force does not facilitate creative problem solving as needed in the integrative situation. For instance, Paul R. Lawrence and Jay W. Lorsch, *Organization and Environment* (Boston: Division of Research, Harvard Business School, 1967) found that problem solving was facilitated by the use of confrontation ("By digging and digging the truth is discovered") rather than force ("Might overcomes right").

23. Samuel Bacharach and Edward J. Lawler, *Power and Politics in Organizations* (San Francisco: Jossey-Bass, 1980), have argued that use of threat when the other side has roughly equal power leads to a conflict spiral. Threats are more effective when the other side doesn't have the capacity to retaliate. Compliance is now possible without loss of face, since the weaker side can justify its actions in light of the hopeless situation (see their Chapter 8: Coercion in Interorganizational Bargaining).

24. Bonoma and Zaltman, *Psychology for Management,* p. 172.

Notes for Chapter 10

1. See Louis R. Pondy, et al., *Organizational Symbolism,* (Greenwich, Conn.: JAI Press, 1983).

2. John A. Seeger, Jay W. Lorsch, and Cyrus F. Gibson, *First National City Bank Operating Group (A) and (B),* Cases 9–474–165 and 9–474–166, 1975, Case Services, Harvard Business School, Boston, Mass. 02163.

3. See Daryl J. Bem, *Beliefs, Attitudes, and Human Affairs* (Monterey, Calif.: Brooks/Cole Publishing, 1970), Chapter 5.

4. The idea that deviating from the prevailing culture drains one's credibility (i.e., uses up one's existing credit) has been well developed by E. P. Hollander, "Conformity, Status, and Idiosyncrasy Credit," *Psychological Review* 65, no. 2 (1958), pp. 117–27.

5. This is because deviance by conformists is more readily tolerated than the same nonconformity would be in others. See ibid., p. 125; Robert B. Edgerton, "The Study of Deviance—Marginal Man or Everyman?" in *The Making of Psychological Anthropology,* ed. George D. Spindler (Berkeley: University of California Press, 1978), pp. 444–76; Robert Dubin, "Deviant Behavior and Social Structure: Continuities in Social Theory," *American Sociological Review,* April 1959, pp. 147–64.

6. Joanne Martin and Caren Siehl, "Organizational Culture and Counterculture: An Uneasy Symbiosis," *Organizational Dynamics,* Autumn 1983, pp. 52–64.

7. Based on Ruth Leeds, "The Absorption of Protest: A Working Paper," in William W. Cooper, Harold J. Leavitt, and Maynard W. Shelly II, *New Perspectives in Organizational Research* (New York: John Wiley & Sons, 1964), pp. 115–33. Leed's study is based on "normative" organizations, such as religious groups and the military, where symbolic and other intrinsic rewards are important motivators. This is analogous to the case of a business organization with a strong culture that people join for its symbolic and intrinsic rewards as much as for extrinsic rewards, such as pay and monetary benefits. The last part of the process described by Leeds (which is not described in the text) concerns the counterculture's "routinization" and forces that cause the cycle to repeat.

8. Several studies have highlighted the importance of constructive airing and resolution of conflict to enhance organizational effectiveness. See Paul R. Lawrence and Jay W. Lorsch, *Organization and Environment* (Boston: Division of Research, Harvard Business School, 1967); and Irving L. Janis, *Victims of Groupthink* (Boston: Houghton Mifflin, 1972).

9. Lawrence and Lorsch, *Organization and Environment.*

10. R. E. Walton and R. B. McKersie, *A Behavioral Theory of Labor Negotiations* (New York: McGraw-Hill, 1965).

Notes for Introduction to Part 4

1. Chris Argyris, *Reasoning, Learning and Action* (San Francisco: Jossey-Bass, 1982), describes in some detail the difficulties managers had in behaving in accordance with what Argyris calls "Model II" organizational values—use of valid information, free and informed choice, and internal commitment to the choice—they had bought into. See also Chris Argyris, "Double-Loop Learning in Organizations," *Harvard Business Review,* September–October 1977: "[A]s the presidents [Argyris studied] found out, understanding and believing in Model II did not ensure that they would be able to produce Model II behavior" (p. 123).

2. Some would argue that in this case people are not behaving in accordance with new beliefs and values because they haven't really bought into them. Similarly, it can also be argued that people who continue smoking don't really believe that smoking is bad for them, else they would give it up. These critics have in mind what we have here referred to as the permanent change that occurs when both one's behavior and one's corresponding beliefs and values are transformed and brought into alignment with each other (Figure IV–1). As the new beliefs and values continue to be reinforced by the new behavior, they become taken-for-granted and drop out of awareness, thus becoming new preconscious or unconscious assumptions. See Edgar H. Schein, "Organizational Culture: A Dynamic Model," Working Paper, Massachusetts Institute of Technology, February 1983, for more on the process by which taken-for-granted assumptions form.

   The position taken in this book is that people have "really" bought into certain beliefs and values *if they are really trying* to acquire the necessary skills and perform the required behavior, whether or not such intentions and efforts have borne fruit as yet, as opposed to merely paying lip service or going through the motions to espouse or appear to comply with certain beliefs and values because of external pressure rather than internal commitment. See notes 3, 7, 8, and 9 in Chapter 1 for more of this.

3. The word *skill* as used here denotes the technical, social, interpersonal, and other competences required to become effective in a particular social context. See F. J. Roethlisberger, *The Elusive Phenomenon* (Cambridge, Mass.: Harvard University Press, 1976).

Notes for Chapter 11

1. Michael Beer, *Organizational Change and Development* (Santa Monica, Calif.: Goodyear Publishing, 1980), p. 46, traces the origin of this formula to Dr. Alan Burnes, a former associate of his at Corning Glass Works, and indicates that a similar representation is proposed by Richard Beckhard and Reuben T. Harris, *Organizational Transitions: Managing Complex Change* (Reading, Mass.: Addison-Wesley Publishing, 1977), who attribute it to David Gleicher. Thus there appears to be considerable support for the general nature of the formulation. I have chosen to use terms different from those employed by Beer because they seem to me to better suit the distinction between behavior change and culture change being made here. For instance, Beer uses *dissatisfaction* where I have used *motivation*. The former term catches the attention of managers by highlighting the conditions that must prevail (dissatisfaction with the status quo) to produce the internal motivation that can energize and sustain change. People may also change their behavior simply because they feel compelled to do so, as in compliance—they may be motivated by the promise of rewards and the threat of punishment, rather than dissatisfaction with the status quo. The term *motivation* is broad enough to capture such extrinsic incentives for changing one's behavior.

2. See Ellen Langer, "Rethinking the Role of Thought in Social Interaction," in *New Directions in Attribution Research* ed. Harvey, Ickes, and Kidd, Vol. 2 (Hillsdale, N.J.: Lawrence Erlbaum Associates, 1978).

3. R. Shank and R. Abelson, *Scripts, Plans, and Knowledge* (Hillsdale, N.J.: Lawrence Erlbaum Associates, 1978).

4. F. J. Roethlisberger and William J. Dickson, *Management and the Worker* (Cambridge, Mass.: Harvard University Press, 1939). As Paul R. Lawrence, "How to Deal with Resistance to Change," *Harvard Business Review*, May–June 1954 (*HBR* classic, January–February 1979), has pointed out, what employees frequently resist is not technical change so much as changes in human relationships that accompany such change.

5. Tom Burns and G. M. Stalker, *The Management of Innovation* (London: Tavistock, 1961) found that the social and political systems were among the principal barriers that prevented the organization from adapting to the needs of its environment (see Chapter 7 of their book, "Working Organization, Political System, and Status Structure within the Concern").

6. As Edgar H. Schein, *Organizational Psychology*, 3d ed. (Englewood Cliffs, N.J.: Prentice-Hall, 1980) points out, the complexity of organizational change derives from the need to *orchestrate* change in various individuals to produce the desired organizational outcome (p. 247).

7. See Paul R. Lawrence, "The Uses of Crises: Dynamics of Ghetto Organization Development," in *Social Interaction in the City*, ed. Richard S. Rosenbloom and Robin Morris (Cambridge, Mass.: Harvard University Press, 1969).

8. Abraham Korman, "Task Success, Task Popularity and Self-Esteem as Influences on Task Liking," *Journal of Applied Psychology* 52 (1968), pp. 61–73.

9. Thomas J. Peters, "Symbols, Patterns, and Settings: An Optimistic Case for Getting Things Done," *Organizational Dynamics*, Autumn 1978, contains an excellent list of various symbolic rewards that leaders can offer to induce desired behavior.

10. Ibid. Some of these "mundane tools" do more than communicate the desired behavior—they actually reward or reinforce it, as mentioned in the earlier section of this chapter on "Extrinsic Motivation."

11. John P. Kotter and Leonard A. Schlesinger, "Choosing Strategies for Change," *Harvard Business Review*, March–April 1979.

12. This possibility is not discussed by Kotter and Schlesinger (note 11).

Notes for Chapter 12

1. Some have argued that this is one of the most critical responsibilities of organizational leaders. Philip Selznick, *Leadership in Administration* (New York: Harper & Row, 1957) indicates that one of the critical functions of leadership is to infuse the organization with values beyond the

technical requirements of the task at hand. Jeffrey Pfeffer, *Power in Organizations* (Marshfield, Mass.: Pitman, 1981) states that one of the principal challenges for administrators is the development of "shared paradigms" (p. 124) or shared assumptions within the organization (p. 180).

2. Gordon Donaldson and Jay W. Lorsch, *Decision Making at the Top* (New York: Basic Books, 1983), make the basic distinction between incremental versus fundamental change when referring to changes in the belief systems of the top managements of a dozen large industrial corporations they studied. The specific conceptualization of the degree of change in culture's content developed here was not proposed by them, however.

3. George David Smith and Lawrence E. Steadman, "Present Value of Corporate History," *Harvard Business Review,* November–December 1981, p. 168, make the useful distinction between *heritage* (the entire discoverable history) and *tradition* (selective transmission of heritage). Dormant values may thus be viewed as those that are part of the heritage but not part of the tradition.

4. Daryl J. Bem, *Beliefs, Attitudes, and Human Affairs* (Monterey, Calif. Brooks/Cole Publishing, 1970), Chapter 6.

5. See ibid.; Eliott Aronson, *The Social Animal* (San Francisco: W. H. Freeman, 1976); and note 9 in chapter 2.

6. In this case, people are behaving the way they are because it is a means to a higher end—such as for money, to fullfill a requirement, the benefits that come as a result, and the penalties for not doing so. The behavior is being guided *not* by the person's beliefs and values concerning the *behavior in question* but rather by the person's higher beliefs and values: the importance of money, doing what is required, or the importance of the associated benefits and penalities. When the person's highest values are challenged and such rationalizations are not possible, the person will either not engage in the behavior or will realign his or her value system to rationalize the behavior adequately. An extreme but graphic illustration of the former is the case of Sir Thomas Moore—who refused to bow to the wishes of the King of England because his value system would not permit it and was executed as a result.

7. Aronson, *The Social Animal,* Chapter 4, see especially pp. 109–117.

8. See Edgar H. Schein, "Personal Change through Interpersonal Relationships," in *Interpersonal Dynamics,* ed. W. G. Bennis, D. E. Berlew, E. H. Schein, and F. L. Steele (Homewood, Ill.: Dorsey Press, 1973), pp. 237–67. Schein elaborates on a three-stage model of change: labeled *unfreezing, changing,* and *refreezing*—terms he attributes to Kurt Lewin. This is presented as a model of individual change, but the concepts appear to be generally applicable to the kind of fairly *deep* or *central* changes (to use Schein's terms) involved in what we have defined as culture change—that is, changes in internalized beliefs and values. Schein presents three "unfreezing" mechanisms: *(a)* lack of confirmation or actual disconfirmation of present attitudes and behavior, *(b)* guilt or anxiety to motivate change, and *(c)* creation of psychological safety so the person feels secure to "let go" of the old attitudes and behavior.

9. See Gerald R. Salancik, "Commitment Is Too Easy," *Organizational Dynamics,* Summer 1977, pp. 62–80.

10. Both *propaganda* and *education* seek to influence changes in beliefs and values. However, in the case of the former, there is a clear intention to bias opinions, judgments, beliefs, and values in a particular way, often by covert means. The latter relies on more overt methods and on valid information, logical reasoning, and free and informed choice. See Philip G. Zimbardo, Ebbe B. Ebbesen, and Christina Maslach, *Influencing Attitudes and Changing Behavior,* 2d ed. (Reading, Mass.: Addison-Wesley Publishing, 1977), p. 156. In practice, people tend to view communications as education when they are consistent with their own basic values and as propaganda when they are not. See Aronson, *The Social Animal,* p. 54. This is one reason explicit communications about new beliefs and values may be received with emotion, skepticism, and even cynicism.

11. Aronson, *The Social Animal,* p. 62.

12. This research finding is well captured by the line in E. F. Hutton commercials: "When E. F. Hutton talks, people listen." People who are overhearing the stockbrokers' advice *intended for someone else* are more likely to believe in its validity. Of course, what E. F. Hutton wants to communicate to the television audience is different: that their credibility draws attention. Research also indicates an exception to the general rule that communications are received with skepticism when they are seen as intended to influence the receiver. *If* the receiver identifies with or likes the communicator, the receiver may be persuaded to change his or her opinions, at least on issues that are of marginal rather than central importance to him or her. See ibid., Chapter 3.

13. Joanne Martin, "Stories and Scripts in Organizational Settings," in *Cognitive Social Psychology,* ed. A. Hastorf and A. Isen (New York: Elsevier—North Holland Publishing, 1982).

14. The "IBM Stories" that follow (Notes 15 through 19) and their general analysis are from Joanne

Martin and Melanie E. Powers, "Truth on Corporate Propaganda: The Value of a Good War Story," in *Organizational Symbolism*, ed. L. Pondy, P. Frost, G. Morgan, and T. Dandridge (Greenwich, Conn.: JAI Press, 1983).

15. R. Malik, *And Tomorrow . . . the World? Inside IBM* (London: Mullington HD, 1975), p. 210.

16. T. J. Watson, Jr., *A Business and Its Beliefs: The Ideas that Helped build IBM* (New York: McGraw-Hill, 1963), p. 26.

17. Ibid., pp. 27–28.

18. Malik, *And Tomorrow . . . the World?* p. 210.

19. This concept is proposed by Joanne Martin and Caren Siehl, "Organizational Culture and Counterculture," *Organizational Dynamics*, Autumn 1983, pp. 52–64. The authors show how DeLorean was able to make several GM stories boomerang by arguing that they actually reinforced values directly opposite to those espoused by the dominant GM culture.

20. Because of their nature, one of the *least* effective ways of attempting to change beliefs and values is by attacking them directly. See Jeffrey Pfeffer, *Power in Organizations*, p. 325; Robert N. McMurry, "Conflicts in Human Values," *Harvard Business Review*, May–June 1963, especially pp. 139–40.

21. Leon Festinger, H. W. Riecken, and S. Shacter, *When Prophecy Fails* (Minneapolis: The University of Minnesota Press, 1956).

22. Schein, "Personal Change," also includes "defensive identification" as a change mechanism in settings the person has entered involuntarily and from which he or she cannot escape—e.g., prisons, POW camps. At first glance this mechanism doesn't appear to be relevant in the corporate context, but there is the interesting question of whether it is applicable in those cases where the individual feels similar "confinement" because of extreme dependence on the organization in which he or she works.

23. See the last two sentences of note 12.

24. As Elliot Aronson, *The Social Animal*, points out, the same mechanism that makes a person cling to existing beliefs and values can induce him or her to change them, i.e., cognitive dissonance reduction. What happens depends on whether it is easier to reduce the discrepancy between behavior and belief by "explaining away" the behavior with external justifications or whether it is easier to change the existing belief, e.g., when external justification is not possible (p. 104). In the case of the so-called insufficient justification condition, research shows that the changes induced are relatively enduring. They are confirmed not just on the basis of what people *say* but also by what they *do*, under conditions *different* from those that induced the belief change (pp. 129–31). See also, Pfeffer, *Power in Organizations*, p. 169.

25. A number of Organizational Development techniques are available in this connection. See Warren Bennis, *Organizational Development: Its Nature, Origins and Prospects* (Reading, Mass.: Addison-Wesley Publishing, 1969); Edgar Schein, *Process Consultation: Its Role in Organization Development* (Reading, Mass.: Addison-Wesley Publishing, 1969); and Michael Beer, *Organization Change and Development* (Santa Monica, Calif.: Goodyear Publishing, 1980).

26. This is consistent with analogous methods that may be used in activating dormant values in the individual's personal history. See McMurry, "Conflicts in Human Values," p. 141.

27. Meryl Louis, "Surprise and Sense Making: What Newcomers Experience in Entering Unfamiliar Organizational Settings," *Administrative Science Quarterly* 25 (1980), pp. 226–51.

28. Gordon Donaldson and Jay W. Lorsch, *Decision Making at the Top* (New York: Basic Books, 1983), Chapter 5, "Stability and Flexibility in Belief Systems."

29. Daniel J. Levinson, Charlotte N. Darrow, Edward B. Klein, Maria H. Levenson, and Braxton McKee, *The Seasons of a Man's Life* (New York: Ballantine Books, 1978), pp. 97–101.

30. Donaldson and Lorsch, *Decision Making at the Top*, Chapter V, point out that this may be one important reason managers become so emotionally attached to the prevailing belief systems.

31. Alice M. Sapienza, *Believing Is Seeing: The Effects of Beliefs on Top Managers' Perception and Response* (Ph.D. diss., Harvard Business School, 1984). Sapienza found that the top managers of two comparable hospitals perceived and conceptualized a major environmental event very differently, and these differences were directly related to basic differences in the belief systems of these two management teams.

32. Thomas J. Peters and Robert H. Waterman, *In Search of Excellence* (New York: Harper & Row, 1982).

33. Daniel T. Carroll, "A Disappointing Search for Excellence," *Harvard Business Review*, November–December 1983.

Bibliography

Allen, Robert F., and Saul Pilnick. "Confronting the Shadow Organization: How to Detect and Defeat Negative Norms." *Organizational Dynamics,* Spring 1973.

Allen, Robert W.; Dan L. Madison; Lyman W. Porter; Patricia A. Renwick; and Bronston T. Mayes. "Organizational Politics: Tactics and Characteristics of Its Actors." *California Management Review,* Fall 1979, pp. 77–8.

Allport, G. W.; P. E. Vernon; and G. Lindzey. *Manual for the Study of Values.* Boston: Houghton Mifflin, 1970.

Andrews, K. R. *The Concept of Corporate Strategy.* Homewood, Ill. Dow Jones-Irwin, 1971.

Argyris, Chris. *Executive Leadership.* New York: Harper & Row, 1953.

————. *Personality and Organization.* New York: Harper & Row, 1957.

————. *Integrating the Individual and the Organization.* New York: John Wiley & Sons, 1964.

————. "Personality and Organization Theory Revisited." *Administrative Science Quarterly,* June 1973, pp. 141–67.

————. "Double Loop Learning in Organizations." *Harvard Business Review,* September–October 1977.

————. *Reasoning, Learning, and Action.* San Francisco: Jossey-Bass, 1982.

Argyris, Chris and Donald A. Schon. *Theory in Practice.* San Francisco: Jossey-Bass, 1974.

Aronson, Elliot. *The Social Animal.* 2d ed. San Francisco: W. H. Freeman, 1976.

Arrow, Kenneth J. *Essays in the Theory of Risk-Bearing.* Chicago: Markham, 1971.

Athos, Anthony G., and John J. Gabarro. *Interpersonal Behavior.* Englewood Cliffs, N.J.: Prentice-Hall, 1978.

Avery, R. W. "Enculturation in Industrial Research." In *Organizational Careers: A Source Book for Theory,* ed. B. G. Glaser. Hawthorne, N.Y.: Aldine Publishing, 1968.

Bachrach, Peter, and Morton S. Baratz. "The Two Faces of Power." *American Political Science Review,* 1962, pp. 147–952.

Bacharach, Samuel, and Edward J. Lawler. *Power and Politics in Organizations.* San Francisco: Jossey-Bass, 1980.

Baker, Edwin L. "Managing Organizational Culture." *Management Review,* July 1980, pp. 8–13.

Barnard, Chester I. *The Functions of the Executive.* Cambridge, Mass.: Harvard University Press, 1938, pp. 167.

Bales, Robert F. *Interaction Process Analyses.* Chicago: University of Chicago Press, 1950.

Becker, Howard. *The Efficient Organization.*

_____. *Outsiders: Studies in the Sociology of Deviance.* New York: Free Press, 1963.

Beckhard, Richard, and Reuben T. Harris. *Organizational Transitions: Managing Complex Change.* Reading, Mass.: Addison-Wesley Publishing, 1977.

Beer, Michael. *Organization Change and Development.* Santa Monica, Calif.: Goodyear Publishing, 1980.

Bendix, Reinhard. *Work and Authority in Industry.* New York: John Wiley & Sons, 1956.

Bennis, Warren. *Organizational Development: Its Nature, Origins and Prospects.* Reading, Mass.: Addison-Wesley Publishing, 1969.

Berger, Peter L., and Thomas Luckmann. *The Social Construction of Reality.* Garden City, N.Y.: Doubleday Publishing, 1966.

Bem, Daryl J. *Beliefs, Attitudes, and Human Affairs.* Monterey, Calif.: Brooks/Cole Publishing, 1970.

Blake, Robert R., and Jane S. Mouton. *Building a Dynamic Corporation through Grid Organization Development.* Reading, Mass.: Addison-Wesley Publishing, 1969.

Bolles, R. N. *What Color Is Your Parachute?* Berkeley, Calif.: Ten Speed Press, 1972.

Bonoma, Thomas V., and Gerald Zaltman. *Psychology for Management.* Boston, Mass.: Kent, 1981.

Bower, Joseph L. *Managing the Resource Allocation Process.* Homewood, Ill.: Richard D. Irwin, 1972.

Bray, D. W.; R. J. Campbell; and D. L. Grant. *Formative Years in Business.* New York: John Wiley & Sons, 1974.

Burns, Tom, and G. M. Stalker. *The Management of Innovation.* London: Tavistock, 1961.

Byrne, D. "Interpersonal Attraction and Attitude Similarity." *Journal of Abnormal and Social Psychology* 62, pp. 713–15.

Caplow, T. *Principles of Organization.* New York: Harcourt Brace Jovanovich, 1964.

Carroll, Daniel T. "A Disappointing Search for Excellence." *Harvard Business Review,* November–December, 1983.

Child, I. "Socialization." In *Handbook of Social Psychology,* ed. G. Lindzey. Reading, Mass.: Addison-Wesley Publishing, 1954.

Child, John. *Organization.* New York: Harper & Row, 1977.

"Corporate Culture." *Business Week,* October 27, 1980, pp. 148–60.

Cyert, Richard M., and James G. March. *A Behavioral Theory of the Firm.* Englewood Cliffs, N.J.: Prentice-Hall, 1963.

Davis, Tim R. W., and Fred Luthans. "Managers in Action: A New Look at Their Behavior and Operating Modes." *Organizational Dynamics,* Summer 1980, pp. 64–80.

de Charms, Richard. *Personal Causation.* New York: Academic Press, 1968.

_____. "Origins, Pawns, and Educational Practice." In *Psychology and the Educational Process,* ed. G. S. Lesson. Glenview, Ill.: Scott, Foresman, 1969.

Deal, Terrance E., and Allan A. Kennedy. *Corporate Cultures: The Rites and Rituals of Corporate Life.* Reading, Mass.: Addison-Wesley Publishing, 1982.

Deutsch, M. "Cooperation and Trust: Some Theoretical Notes." In *Nebraska Symposium on Motivation,* ed. R. Jones. Lincoln: University of Nebraska Press, 1962, pp. 275–319.

Donaldson, Gordon, and Jay W. Lorsch. *Decision Making at the Top.* New York: Basic Books, 1983.

Dornbush, S. "The Military Academy as an Assimilating Institution." *Social Forces* 33, 1955, pp. 316–21.

Dubin, Robert. "Deviant Behavior and Social Structure: Continuities in Social Theory." *American Sociological Review* 24, 1959, pp. 332–44.

Dyer, David, and Alan M. Kantrow. "The Manager as Anthropologist" Working Paper, Harvard Business School, 1980.

Edgerton, Robert B. "The Study of Deviance—Marginal Man or Everyman?" In *The Making of Psychological Anthropology,* ed. George D. Spindler. Berkeley: The University of California Press, 1978, pp. 444–76.

Faux, Victor A. "Unobtrusive Controls in Organizations: An Action Approach to Change." Ph.D. dissertation, Harvard University, Graduate School of Business Administration, 1982.

Feldman, Daniel. "The Multiple Socialization of Organization Members." *The Academy of Management Review* 6, no. 2, 1981.

Festinger, Leon. *A Theory of Cognitive Dissonance.* Evanston, Ill.: Row, Peterson, 1957.

Festinger, Leon; H. W. Riecken; and S. Shacter. *When Prophecy Fails.* Minneapolis: The University of Minnesota Press, 1956.

Ford, G. A., and G. L. Lippitt. *A Life Planning Workbook.* Fairfax, Va.: NTL Learning Resources, 1972.

Freedman, Jonathan L., and Anthony N. Doob. *Deviancy: The Psychology of Being Different.* New York: Academic Press, 1968.

Friedrich, Carl J. *Constitutional Government and Democracy.* New York: Harper & Row, 1937.

Gabarro, John J. "The Development of Trust, Influence, and Expectations." In *Interpersonal Behavior,* ed. John J. Gabarro and Anthony G. Athos. Englewood Cliffs, N.J.: Prentice-Hall, 1978.

————. "Socialization at the Top—How CEOs and Subordinates Evolve Interpersonal Contacts." *Organizational Dynamics,* Winter 1979, pp. 3–23.

Gabarro, John J., and John P. Kotter. "Managing Your Boss." *Harvard Business Review,* January–February 1980.

Galbraith, Jay R. *Designing Complex Organizations.* Reading, Mass.: Addison-Wesley Publishing, 1973.

Geertz, Clifford. *The Interpretation of Cultures.* New York: Basic Books, 1973.

Goffman, Erving. *Asylums.* Garden City, N.Y.: Doubleday Publishing, 1961.

Greiner, Larry. "Patterns of Organizational Change." *Harvard Business Review,* May–June 1967.

Guth, William D., and Renato Tagiuri. "Personal Values and Corporate Strategies." *Harvard Business Review,* September–October 1965.

Hall, D. T., and R. Mansfield. "Organizational and Individual Response to External Stress." *Administrative Science Quarterly,* 1971, pp. 553–47.

Handy, Charles. "Gods of Management." London: *Souvenir Press,* 1978.

Hare, A. Paul. *The Small Group.* 2d ed. New York: Random House, 1978.

Harrison, Roger. "Understanding Your Organization's Character." *Harvard Business Review,* May–June 1972.

Hayes, Robert H., and William J. Abernathy. "Managing Our Way to Economic Decline." *Harvard Business Review,* July–August 1980.

Hellriegel, Don, and John W. Slocum, Jr. *Management: Contingency Approaches.* 2d ed. Reading, Mass.: Addison-Wesley Publishing, 1978.

Hofstede, Geert. "Motivation, Leadership and Organization: Do American Theories Apply Abroad?" *Organizational Dynamics,* Summer 1980, pp. 42–63.

Hogarth, Robin. *Judgment and Choice.* New York: John Wiley & Sons, 1980.

Hollander, E. P. "Conformity, Status, and Idiosyncracy Credit." *Psychological Review* 65, no. 2, 1958, pp. 117–27.

Homans, George. *The Nature of Social Science.* New York: Harcourt Brace Jovanovich, 1967.

————. *The Human Group.* New York: Harcourt Brace Jovanovich, 1950.

Hughes, Charles L., and Vincent S. Flowers. *Value System Analysis Theory and Management Application.* Dallas, Tex.: Center for Value Research, 1978.

Hughes, E. C. *Men and Their Work.* New York: Free Press, 1958.

Janis, Irving L. *Victims of Groupthink.* Boston: Houghton Mifflin, 1972.

Janis, Irving L., and Dan Wheeler. "Thinking Clearly about Career Choice." *Psychology Today,* May 1978.

Jones E. E. *Ingratiation.* New York: Appleton-Century-Crofts, 1964.

Kanter, Rosabeth Moss. *Men and Women of the Corporation.* New York: Basic Books, 1977.

————. "Power Failure in Management Circuits." *Harvard Business Review,* July–August, 1979.

————. *The Change Masters.* New York: Basic Books, 1983.

Keesing, Roger M. "Theories of Culture." *Annual Review of Anthropology.* Vol. 3, 1974, pp. 73–79.

Kelman, H. C. "Compliance, Identification, and Internalization: Three Processes of Attitude Change." *Conflict Resolution* 2, 1958, pp. 51–60.

Kiesler, Charles A., and Sara B. Kiesler. *Conformity.* Reading, Mass.: Addison-Wesley Publishing, 1969.

Kluckhohn, Clyde. "Values and Value Orientations in the Theory of Action." In *Toward a General*

Theory of Action, ed. T. Parsons and E. A. Shils. Cambridge, Mass.: Harvard University Press, 1951.

Kluckhohn, Florence R., and Fred L. Stadtbeck. *Variations in Value Orientations*. Evanston, Ill.: Row, Peterson, 1961.

Koreisha, Sergio, and Robert Stobaugh. "Modeling: Selective Attention Institutionalized." *Sloan Management Review*, February–March 1981, pp. 64–66.

Korman, Abraham. "Task Success, Task Popularity and Self-Esteem as Influences on Task Liking." *Journal of Applied Psychology* 52, 1968, pp. 61–73.

Kotter, John P. "The Psychological Contract: Managing the Joining-Up Process," *California Management Review*, 1973, pp. 91–99.

——————. "Power, Dependence, and Effective Management." *Harvard Business Review*, July–August 1977, pp. 125–36.

——————. *Organizational Dynamics: Diagnosis and Intervention*. Reading, Mass.: Addison-Wesley Publishing, 1978.

——————. *Power in Management*. New York: AMACOM, 1979.

——————. *The General Manager*. New York: Free Press, 1982.

Kotter, John P., Victor Faux, and Charles McArthur. *Self-Assessment and Career Development*. Englewood Cliffs, N.J.: Prentice-Hall, 1978.

Kotter, John P., and Paul Lawrence. *Mayors in Action*. New York: John Wiley & Sons, 1974.

Kotter, John P., and Leonard A. Schlesinger. "Choosing Strategies for Change." *Harvard Business Review*, March–April 1979.

Kotter, John P.; Leonard A. Schlesinger; and Vijay Sathe. *Organization*. Homewood, Ill.: Richard D. Irwin, 1979.

Kroeber, A. K., and Clyde Kluckhohn. *Culture: A Critical Review of Concepts and Definitions*. New York: Vintage Books, 1952.

Langer, Ellen. "Rethinking the Role of Thought in Social Interaction." In *New Directions in Attribution Research*, Vol. 2, ed. Harvey, Ickes, and Kidd. Hillsdale, N.J.: Lawrence Erlbaum Associates, 1978.

Lawler, Edward E. III, and John Grant Rhode. *Information and Control in Organizations*. Santa Monica, Calif.: Goodyear Publishing, 1976.

Lawrence, Paul R. "How to Deal with Resistance to Change." *Harvard Business Review*, May–June 1954 (HBR Classic, January–February 1979).

——————. "The Uses of Crises: Dynamics of Ghetto Organization Development." In *Social Interaction in the City* by Richard S. Rosenbloom and Robin Morris. Cambridge, Mass.: Harvard University Press, 1969.

Lawrence, Paul R., and Davis Dyer. *Renewing American Industry*. New York: Free Press, 1983.

Lawrence, Paul R., and Jay W. Lorsch. *Organization and Environment: Managing Differentiation and Integration*. Boston: Division of Research, Harvard Business School, 1967.

Leeds, Ruth. "The Absorption of Protest: A Working Paper." In *New Perspectives in Organizational Research*, ed. William W. Cooper, Harold J. Leavitt, Maynard W. Shelly II. New York: John Wiley & Sons, 1964, pp. 115–33.

Levine, Murray. "Investigative Reporting as a Research Method." *American Psychologist* 35, no. 7, pp. 626–38.

LeVine, Robert A. *Culture, Behavior, and Personality*. Hawthorne, N.Y.: Aldine Publishing, 1973.

Levinson, Daniel J., et al. *The Seasons of a Man's Life*. New York: Ballantine Books, 1978.

Levinson, Harry. *Organizational Diagnosis*. Cambridge, Mass.: Harvard University Press, 1972.

Lewicki, Roy J. "Organizational Seduction: Building Commitment to Organizations." *Organizational Dynamics*, Autumn 1981.

Lorsch, Jay W., and P. R. Lawrence, eds. *Studies in Organization Design*, Homewood, Ill.: Richard D. Irwin, 1970.

Lorsch, Jay W., and John J. Morse. *Organizations and Their Members*. New York: Harper & Row, 1974.

Louis, Meryl. "Surprise and Sense Making: What Newcomers Experience in Entering Unfamiliar Organizational Settings." *Administrative Science Quarterly*, June 1980, pp. 226–51.

——————. "Organizations as Culture-Bearing Milieux." In *Organizational Symbolism*, ed. L. Pondy, P. Frost, G. Morgan, and T. Dandridge. Greenwich, Conn.: JAI Press, 1982.

Lyman, L. M., and M. B. Scott. *A Sociology of the Absurd.* New York: Meredith, 1970.

Malik, R. *And Tomorrow . . . the World, Inside IBM.* London: Mullington, HD, 1975.

March, James G., and Herbert A. Simon. *Organizations.* New York: John Wiley & Sons, 1958.

Margulies, Walter P. "Make the Most of Your Corporate Identity." *Harvard Business Review,* July–August 1977.

Martin, Joanne. "Stories and Scripts in Organizational Settings," In *Cognitive Social Psychology,* ed. A. Hastorf and A. Isen. Elsevier-North Holland Publishing, 1982.

Martin, Joanne, and Melanie E. Powers. "Truth on Corporate Propaganda: The Value of a Good War Story." In *Organizational Symbolism,* ed. L. Pondy, P. Frost, G. Morgan, and T. Dandridge. Greenwich, Conn.: JAI Press, 1983.

Martin, Joanne, and Caren Siehl. "Organizational Culture and Counterculture: An Uneasy Symbiosis," *Organizational Dynamics,* Autumn 1983, pp. 52–64.

May, Rollo. *Power and Innocence.* New York: Dell, 1972.

Mayo, Elton. *The Social Problems of an Industrial Civilization.* Cambridge, Mass.: Harvard University Press, 1947.

McCaskey, Michael B. "The Hidden Messages Managers Send." *Harvard Business Review,* November–December 1979.

————. *The Executive Challenge.* Marshfield, Mass.: Pitman, 1982.

McClelland, David. *The Achieving Society.* Princeton, N.J.: Van Nostrand Reinhold, 1961.

————. "The Two Faces of Power." *Journal of International Affairs,* 1970, pp. 29–47.

McMurry, Robert N. "Conflicts in Human Values." *Harvard Business Review,* May–June 1963, pp. 131–32.

McGuire, W. J. "Inducing Resistance to Penetration," In *Advances in Experimental Social Psychology,* Vol. 3, ed. L. Berkowitz. New York: Academic Press, 1974.

Mead, George Herbert. *Mind, Self, and Society.* Chicago: University of Chicago Press, 1934.

Merton, Robert K. *Social Theory and Social Structure.* Enlarged ed. New York: Free Press, 1968.

Milgram, Stanley. "Behavioral Study of Obedience." *Journal of Abnormal and Social Psychology.* 1963, pp. 371–78.

————. "Some Conditions of Obedience and Disobedience to Authority." *Human Relations* 18, 1965, pp. 57–66.

Moore, Wilbert. *The Conduct of the Corporation.* New York: Random House, 1962.

O'Day, Rory. "Intimidation Rituals: Reactions to Reform." *Journal of Applied Behavioral Science* 10, no. 3, 1974, pp. 373–86.

Ogburn, William Fielding. "Social Change with Respect to Culture and Original Nature," Part I, New 1950 ed. New York: Viking Press, 1952.

O'Reilly, Charles A. III, and David F. Caldwell. "The Commitment and Job Tenure of New Employees: Some Evidence of Postdecisional Justification." *Administrative Science Quarterly.* 1981, pp. 597–616.

Ouchi, William G. "Markets, Bureaucracies, and Clans." *Administrative Science Quarterly* 25, 1980, pp. 129–41.

Ouchi, William G., and Raymond L. Price. "Hierarchies, Clans, and Theory Z: A New Perspective on Organization Development." *Organizational Dynamics,* Autumn 1978.

————. *Theory Z: How American Companies Can Meet the Japanese Challenge.* Reading, Mass.: Addison-Wesley Publishing, 1981.

Pascale, Richard T. "Fitting New Employees into Company Culture." *Fortune,* May 28, 1984, pp. 28–40.

Pascale, Richard T., and Anthony G. Athos. *The Art of Japanese Management.* New York: Simon & Schuster, 1981.

Pava, Calvin. "Getting a Handle on Company Culture." Working Paper, Harvard Business School, 1982.

————. "Towards a Concept of Normative Incrementalism: One Prospect for Purposeful Non-Synoptic Change in Highly Fragmented Social Systems." A dissertation in Social Systems Science, University of Pennsylvania, Philadelphia, 1980.

Peters, Thomas J. "Symbols, Patterns, and Settings: An Optimistic Case for Getting Things Done." *Organizational Dynamics,* Autumn 1978.

————. "Management Systems: The Language of Organizational Character and Competence." *Organizational Dynamics,* Summer 1980, pp. 3–26.

————. "Putting Excellence into Management." *Business Week,* 1980.

Peters, Thomas J., and Robert H. Waterman. *In Search of Excellence.* New York: Harper & Row, 1982.

Pettigrew, Andrew. "On Studying Organizational Cultures." *Administrative Science Quarterly,* December 1979.

Pfeffer, Jeffrey. *Power in Organizations.* Marshfield, Mass.: Pitman, 1981.

Pfeffer, Jeffrey, and Gerald R. Salancik. *The External Control of Organizations.* New York: Harper & Row, 1978.

Pondy, Louis R. "Leadership is a Language Game." In *Leadership: Where Else Can We Go?* ed. Morgan W. McCall, Jr., and Michael M. Lombardo. Durham, N.C.: Duke University Press, 1978, pp. 87–99.

Pondy, Louis; Peter J. Frost; Gareth Morgan; and Thomas C. Dandridge; eds. *Organizational Symbolism.* Greenwich, Conn.: JAI Press, 1983.

Porter, Lyman W., Edward E. Lawler, and J. Richard Hackman. *Behavior in Organizations.* New York: McGraw-Hill, 1975.

Porter, Lyman W., and R. M. Steers. "Organizational, Work, and Personal Factors in Employee Turnover and Absenteeism." *Psychological Bulletin* 80, 1973, pp. 157–76.

Porter, Michael E. *Competitive Strategy: Techniques for Analyzing Industries and Competitors.* New York: Free Press, 1982.

Roethlisberger, F. J., and William J. Dickson. *Management and the Worker.* Cambridge, Mass.: Harvard University Press, 1939.

Rokeach, Milton. *Beliefs, Attitudes, and Values.* San Francisco: Jossey-Bass, 1968.

Rosnow, Ralph L., and Edward J. Robinson, eds. *Experiments in Persuasion.* New York: Academic Press, 1967.

Rotter, Julian B. "Generalized Expectancies for Internal Versus External Locus of Control of Reinforcements." *Psychological Monographs* 80, no. 1, 1966.

Salancik, Gerald R. "Commitment Is Too Easy." *Organizational Dynamics,* Summer 1977, pp. 62–80.

Sathe, Vijay. *Controller Involvement in Management.* Englewood Cliffs, N.J.: Prentice-Hall, 1982.

Sayles, Leonard. *Managerial Behavior.* New York: McGraw-Hill, 1964.

Schacter, Stanley. "Deviation, Rejection, and Communication." *Journal of Abnormal and Social Psychology* 46, 1951, pp. 190–207.

Schein, Edgar H. "The Mechanics of Change." In *Interpersonal Dynamics,* ed. W. G. Bennis, E. H. Schein, F. Steele, and D. C. Berlew. Homewood, Ill.: Dorsey Press, 1964.

————. *Organizational Psychology.* 3d ed. Englewood Cliffs, N.J.: Prentice-Hall, 1980.

————. "Organizational Socialization and the Profession of Management." *Industrial Management Review,* Winter 1968, pp. 3–10.

————. *Process Consultation: Its Role in Organization Development.* Reading, Mass.: Addison-Wesley Publishing, 1969.

————. "Personal Change through Interpersonal Relationships," In *Interpersonal Dynamics,* ed. W. G. Bennis, D. E. Berlew, E. H. Schein, and F. L. Steele. Homewood, Ill.: Dorsey Press, 1973.

————. *Career Dynamics.* Reading, Mass.: Addison-Wesley Publishing, 1978.

————. "SMR Forum: Does Japanese Management Style Have a Message for American Managers?" *Sloan Management Review,* Fall 1981, pp. 64–67.

————. "Organizational Culture: A Dynamic Model." Working Paper number 1412–83, Massachusetts Institute of Technology, February 1983.

————. "The Role of the Founder in Creating Organizational Culture." *Organizational Dynamics,* Summer 1983, pp. 13–28.

Schwartz, Howard, and Stanley M. Davis. "Matching Corporate Culture and Business Strategy." *Organizational Dynamics,* Summer 1981.

Selznick, Philip. *Leadership in Administration.* New York: Harper & Row, 1957.

Shank, R., and R. Abelson. *Scripts, Plans, and Knowledge.* Hillsdale, N.J.: Lawrence Erlbaum Associates, 1977.

Shepard, H. A., and J. A. Hawley. *Life Planning: Personal and Organizational.* Washington, D.C.: National Training and Development Service, 1974.

Sherif, M. *The Social Psychology of Social Norms.* New York: Harper & Row, 1936.

Siehl, Caren, and Joanne Martin. "Learning Organizational Culture." Stanford Graduate School of Business, September 1981, working paper.

Silverzweig, Stan, and Robert F. Allen. "Changing the Corporate Culture." *Sloan Management Review* 17, 1976, pp. 33–49.

Simon, Herbert A. *Administrative Behavior.* 3d ed. New York: Free Press, 1976.

————. "Applying Information Processing Technology to Organization Design." *Public Administration Review* 33, 1973, pp. 268–78.

Smircich, Linda. "Concepts of Culture and Organizational Analysis." *Administrative Science Quarterly* 28, no. 3, 1983, pp. 339–58.

Smircich, Linda, and Gareth Morgan. "Leadership: The Management of Meaning." *Journal of Applied Behavioral Science,* September 1982.

Smith, George David, and Lawrence E. Steadman. "Present Value of Corporate History." *Harvard Business Review,* November–December 1981.

Soelberg, Peer O. "Unprogrammed Decision Making." *Industrial Management Review* 8, 1967, pp. 19–29.

Spindler, George D., ed. *The Making of Psychological Anthropology.* Berkeley: University of California Press, 1978.

Spradley, James P. *Participant Observation.* New York: Holt, Rinehart & Winston, 1980.

Spranger, Eduard. *Types of Men.* Translated by P. Pigors. Halle, Germany: Niemeyer, 1928.

Springbelt, B. M. "Factors Affecting the Final Decision in the Employment Interview." *Canadian Journal of Psychology* 12, 1958, pp. 13–22.

Stewart, Rosemary. "Managerial Agendas: Reactive or Proactive." *Organizational Dynamics,* Autumn 1979.

————. *Choices for the Manager.* Englewood Cliffs, N.J.: Prentice-Hall, 1982.

Strauss, A. "Some Neglected Properties of Status Passage." In *Institutions and the Person,* ed. H. S. Becker, G. Geer, D. Reisman, R. S. Weiss. Hawthorne, N.Y.: Aldine Publishing, 1968.

Strauss, George. "Organizational Development: Credits and Debits." *Organizational Dynamics,* Winter 1973.

Swartz, Marc, and David Jordan. *Culture: An Anthropological Perspective.* New York: John Wiley & Sons, 1980.

Tagiuri, Renato. "Managing Corporate Identity: The Role of Top Management." Working Paper, Harvard Business School, 1982.

Tagiuri, Renato, and G. H. Litwin, eds. *Organizational Climate: Exploration of a Concept.* Boston: Division of Research, Graduate School of Business Administration, Harvard University, 1968.

Taylor, E. B. *Primitive Culture.* London: J. Murray, 1871.

Tedeschi, James T.; Barry R. Schlenker; and Thomas V. Bonoma. *Conflict, Power and Games: The Experimental Study of Interpersonal Relations.* Hawthorne, N.Y.: Aldine Publishing, 1973.

Thompson, James D. *Organizations in Action.* New York: McGraw-Hill, 1967.

Tichy, Noel M., and Joanne Martin. "The Key to Corporate Culture: Strategic Management." October 15, 1981, Working paper.

Trust, Eric, and K. W. Bamforth. "Some Social and Psychological Consequences of the Long Wall Method of Coal-Gilting." *Human Relations* 4, 1951, pp. 3–38.

Thompson, Victor A. "Dramaturgy." *Modern Organization.* New York: Alfred A. Knopf, 1961, pp. 139–51.

van Gennep, Arnold. *The Rites of Passage.* Chicago: The University of Chicago Press, 1960.

Van Maanen, John. "Breaking In: Socialization to Work." In *Handbook of Work, Organization, and Society,* ed. Robert Dubin. Skokie, Ill.: Rand McNally, 1976.

————. "People Processing: Strategies of Organizational Socialization." *Organizational Dynamics,* Summer 1978, pp. 19–36.

Vancil, Richard F. *Decentralization: Managerial Ambiguity by Design.* Homewood, Ill.: Dow Jones-Irwin, 1978.

Wallace, S. E., ed. *Total Institutions.* Hawthorne, N.Y.: Aldine Publishing, 1971.

Walton, Richard E. *Interpersonal Peacemaking: Confrontations and Third Party Consultation*, Reading, Mass.: Addison-Wesley Publishing, 1969.

—————. *Social and Psychological Aspects of Verification, Inspection, and International Assurance*. West Lafayette, Ind.: Purdue University Press, 1968.

Walton, Richard E., and R. B. McKersie, *A Behavioral Theory of Labor Negotiations*. New York: McGraw-Hill, 1965.

Wanous, John. *Organizational Entry*. Reading, Mass.: Addison-Wesley Publishing, 1980.

Watson, T. J., Jr. *A Business and Its Beliefs: The Ideas that Helped Build IBM*. New York: McGraw-Hill, 1963.

Weick, Karl. *The Social Psychology of Organizing*. 2d ed. Reading, Mass.: Addison-Wesley Publishing, 1979.

Weitz, J. "Job Expectancy and Survival." *Journal of Applied Psychology* 40, 1957, pp. 346–61.

White, William H., Jr. *The Organization Man*. New York: Simon & Schuster, 1956.

Wilkins, Alan L. "The Culture Audit: A Tool for Understanding Organizations." *Organizational Dynamics*, Autumn 1983, pp. 24–38.

Woodward, Joan. *Management and Technology*. London: Her Majesty's Printing Office, 1958.

Zaleznik, Abraham. "Management of Disappointment." *Harvard Business Review*, November–December 1967.

Zimbardo, Philp G., Ebbe B. Ebbesen, and Christina Maslach. *Influencing Attitudes and Changing Behavior*. 2d ed. Reading, Mass.: Addison-Wesley Publishing, 1977.

Name index

Simon, Herbert, A., 543 n,
  545 n, 547 n, 552 n
Smircich, Linda, 540 n
Smith, George David, 556 n
Soelberg, Peer O., 548 n
Spradley, James P., 547 n
Spranger, Eduard, 95,
  546 n
Springbelt, B. M., 548 n
Stalker, G. M., 543 n, 544 n,
  552 n, 555 n
Steadman, Lawrence, 556 n
Steele, Fritz, 283–84
Steers, R. M., 547 n
Stewart, Rosemary, 544 n,
  546 n
Stobaugh, Robert, 542 n
Strauss, A., 549 n
Stringer, R. A., 542 n
Strodtbeck, Fred L., 547 n

Swartz, Marc J., 540 n,
  544 n, 550 n

T

Tagiuri, Renato, 542 n,
  546 n, 551–52 n
Taylor, E. B., 540 n
Thompson, James D., 543 n
Tist, Eric, 544 n

V–W

Van Maanen, John, 125–26,
  128, 243–44, 548 n,
  549 n, 550 n
Velasquez, Manuel, 537–38
Vernon, P. E., 546 n
Walton, Richard E., 290,
  293, 536–37, 551 n,
  553 n, 554 n

Wanous, John, 546 n, 548 n
Ware, James P., 290, 536
Waterman, Robert H. 406,
  518, 521–22, 557 n
Watson, T. J., 557 n
Weick, Karl, 544 n
Weitz, J., 548 n
Wheeler, Dan, 535, 548 n
Wheeler, Stanton, 244
White, William H., Jr., 550 n
Wilkins, Alan L., 543
Woodward, Joan, 543 n

Y–Z

Ylvisaker, William T., 519
Zaleznick, Abraham, 546 n
Zaltman, Gerald, 553 n
Zander, Alvin, 542 n
Zimbardo, Philip G., 537,
  556 n

Subject index

Hay Associates, 519
Hewlett-Packard, 513, 520, 522
"Hidden Messages Managers Send, The," 547 n
Homosocial reproduction, 114–15, 535–36
Honeymoon, 128, 135, 240
"How to Deal with Resistance to Change," 555 n
Humility, in newcomer, 525–26
Hybridization, founder, 79–80

I

IBM; *see* International Business Machines
Ideational theory of culture, 9–10
Identity
  defined, 24
  socialization and, 140–42
Ideology
  defined, 24
  typology of, 533
Image, 24
Indifference, zone of, 27, 271–72
Individual
  acceptance and, 252, 261–69
  credibility of, 252–70
  ideal types, 95–96
  organization and, 112–18, 533
  relationship with others, 255–61
Individual behavior
  actual versus required, 42–46
  ideal, 44
  satisfaction and, 44–45
  stress and, 44–45
Individual dynamics, 32, 42–46
Individual effectiveness, 45
Individual socialization, 229–31
Individual status, organizational fit and, 104–6
"Inducing Resistance to Penetration," 548 n
Influence
  covert, 278
  culture and 275–79
  defined, 275

Influence—*Cont.*
  techniques of, 276–79
  working relationships and, 257–58
Influencing Attitudes and Changing Behavior, 556 n
Informal socialization, 227–29
Information and Control in Organizations, 548 n
Information sources, newcomers and, 129
Ingratiation, 552 n
Initiation rites, 139, 241
Innovation, founder and, 78–79
In Search of Excellence, 406–7, 513, 518, 521, 523, 557 n
"In Search of Style in the 'New Marine,'" 539 n
Integrating the Individual and the Organization, 543 n, 544 n
Interaction Process Analyses, 545 n, 550 n
Internalized beliefs, 12–13
Internalized values, 12–13
International Business Machines (IBM), 14, 15–16, 244, 390–91, 407, 513, 519–20, 521, 524, 527, 529, 530–31
"Interpersonal Attraction and Attitude Similarity," 553 n
Interpersonal Behavior, 547 n
Interpersonal contract, 259
Interpersonal Peacemaking: Confrontation and Third-Party Consultation, 536–37 n
Interpretation of Culture, The, 540 n
Interviewer, motives of, 115–16
Interviewing, 109–16, 534
Intimidation, 536
"Intimidation Rituals: Reactions to Reform," 536 n
Investitute socialization, 240–42

J

"'Job Expectancy and Survival," 548 n

Job selection, 109–22, 535
Job training
  fixed socialization and, 233–35
  formal socialization and, 227–29
  individual/collective socialization and, 229–31
  investiture/divestiture socialization and 240–42
  sequential socialization and, 231–33
  serial/disjunctive socialization and, 238–40
  as step in socialization, 525–26
  tournament/contest socialization and, 235–38
Job transition
  anxiety and, 224
  individual identity and, 225
Judgment and Choice, 544 n, 548 n
Justifications of behavior
  cultural levels and, 10
  external, 118
  shared assumptions and, 30

K–L

Knowledge
  behavior and, 32, 44
  of organization, 99–108
Lack of focus, 117
Language, 282–83
Leadership
  behavior patterns and, 39–40
  corporate culture and, 14, 66–76, 521–22
  organizational fit and, 104
Leadership in Administration, 555–56
Learning
  by newcomer, 126–30
  socialization and, 223–44
"Learning Organizational Culture," 549
Learning to Work, 244
Life Planning: Personal and Organizational, 545
Life Planning Workbook, A, 545
Locus of control, 98

This book has been set Linotron 202 in 11 and 10 point Baskerville, leaded 3 points. Part numbers are 24 point Baskerville Bold and part titles are 27 point Baskerville Bold. Chapter numbers are 18 point Baskerville Bold and chapter titles are 24 point Baskerville Bold. The size of the type page is 30 by 51 picas.